economics for business

Economics for Business

Third edition

David Begg
Damian Ward

McGraw-Hill
Higher Education

London   Boston   Burr Ridge, IL   Dubuque, IA   Madison, WI   New York   San Francisco
St. Louis   Bangkok   Bogotá   Caracas   Kuala Lumpur   Lisbon   Madrid   Mexico City
Milan   Montreal   New Delhi   Santiago   Seoul   Singapore   Sydney   Taipei   Toronto

Economics for Business
Third edition
David Begg and Damian Ward
ISBN-13 978-0-07-712473-1
ISBN-10 0-07-712473-1

McGraw-Hill
Higher Education

Published by McGraw-Hill Education
Shoppenhangers Road
Maidenhead
Berkshire
SL6 2QL
Telephone: 44 (0) 1628 502 500
Fax: 44 (0) 1628 770 224
Website: www.mcgraw-hill.co.uk

British Library Cataloguing in Publication Data
A catalogue record for this book is available from the British Library

Library of Congress Cataloging in Publication Data
The Library of Congress data for this book has been applied for from the Library of Congress

Acquisitions Editor: Natalie Jacobs
Development Editor: Tom Hill
Marketing Manager: Vanessa Boddington
Head of Production: Beverley Shields

Text Design by Hard Lines
Cover design by Adam Renvoize
Printed and bound in Italy by Rotolito Lombarda

ISBN-13 978-0-07-712473-1
ISBN-10 0-07-712473-1

Dedication

To my ever fabulous and loving wife Mel
and my vibrant, energetic
and gorgeous children Lucy,
Emily and Oscar – Damian Ward

For my beloved Jen – David Begg

Brief Table of Contents

Detailed Table of Contents

This book is for students interested in business. It is not an economics book with some business applications. Instead, we highlight problems faced by real businesses and show how economics can help solve these decision problems.

Our approach

This approach is new, and focuses on what as a business student you really need. It is issue driven, utilizing theories and evidence only after a problem has been identified. Business decisions are the focus on the screen, and economic reasoning is merely the help button to be accessed when necessary. Of course, good help buttons are invaluable. . . .

Our coverage

Our book offers a complete course for business students wanting to appreciate why economics is so often the backup that you require. After a brief introduction, we help you to understand how markets function and how businesses compete, then we train you to evaluate problems posed by the wider economic environment, both nationally and globally.

As a business student, you do not need to know, nor should you want to master, the whole of economics. Your time is scarce and you need to learn how to manage it effectively. *Economics for Business* gets you off to a flying start by focusing only on the essentials.

Cases and examples

Business does not stand still and neither should you. You need a course embracing topical examples from the real world as it evolves. Whether we are discussing the pricing of Madonna's concert tickets, the location of Google's server farms, or the collapse of the global banking system, we aim to bring you the business issues of the day and challenge you to think about how you would respond to them.

Strategic learning

Business students want an instant picture of where they are, what the problem is, and how an intelligent response might be devised. Each chapter begins with the executive summary 'What you need to know at a glance' and concludes with a summary and learning checklist, providing an informative link in the flow of ideas.

You are thus encouraged to become a 'strategic learner', accessing resources that support your particular lifestyle and learning pattern. You can follow the order that we propose, but you can also browse and move from one topic to another, as you might on the Internet. Active learning both engages your interest and helps you remember things.

Online of course

Our online supplements include both an Instructor Centre and a Student Centre. The Instructor Centre provides key teaching aids to help your lecturers impress you. The Student Centre offers readers a testbank for self assessment, a glossary of terms you may wish to check, a moving update of Economics in the News, and links to other interactive economics tools. With this edition students and lecturers also get access to Connect, which is McGraw-Hill's new web-based assignment and assessment platform.

Summing up

We were prompted to write this book because fewer and fewer students are studying economics for its own sake. More and more students are switching to courses that study business as a whole.

This creates a market opportunity. Instead of trying to convert books designed for economics courses into books that will suffice for business students, we aimed to write a book that asks what business students want and that meets your needs directly.

Identifying market opportunities, and deciding how to respond, is of course a large part of what *Economics for Business* is about. We hope you get as much fun out of reading it as we had in writing it.

David Begg
Damian Ward

August 2009

About the Authors

David Begg is Principal of Imperial College Business School. He has been a Research Fellow of the Centre for Economic Policy Research since its inception in 1984 and an adviser to the Bank of England, the Treasury, the IMF, and the European Commission.

Damian Ward is Senior Lecturer in Economics at Bradford University School of Management. He has experience of teaching undergraduate and MBA students, including senior managers from the BBC and Emirates Airlines. His research interests focus on the application of economic theory to the workings of the financial services industry. He regularly appears on TV and radio providing economic commentary and has acted as an advisor to the UK Financial Services Authority.

Acknowledgements

Our thanks go to the following reviewers for their comments at various stages in the text's development:

Stephen Allan	University of Kent
Giovanni Caggiano	University of Padua
Roger Fitzer	University of Surrey
Michael Funke	University of Hamburg
Tim Goydke	Hochschule Bremen
Rob Hayward	University of Brighton
Philip Jones	University of Bath
John Old	Durham University
Alex de Ruyter	University of Birmingham
Bibhas Saha	University of East Anglia
Jonathan Seaton	Loughborough University
Abhijit Sharma	Bradford University
Steven Telford	University of London, Queen Mary
Michael Wood	London South Bank University

Thanks to Tom Hill, Natalie Jacobs and Hannah Cooper from the editorial team at McGraw-Hill. Also thanks to the copy editor, proof reader and everyone who has spent time producing this book.

Every effort has been made to trace and acknowledge ownership of copyright and to clear permission for material reproduced in this book. The publishers will be pleased to make suitable arrangements to clear permission with any copyright holders whom it has not been possible to contact.

Technology to enhance learning and teaching

Visit www.mcgraw-hill.co.uk/textbooks/begg today!

Online Learning Centre (OLC)

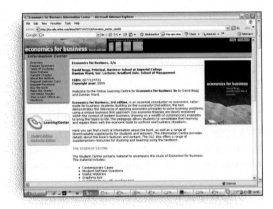

After completing each chapter, log on to the supporting Online Learning Centre website. Take advantage of the study tools offered to reinforce the material you have read in the text, and to develop your knowledge of economics in a fun and effective way.

Resources for students include:

- MP3 Revision notes
- Glossary
- Weblinks
- Case studies
- News articles
- Graphing tool with questions
- Graded multiple-choice questions

Also available for lecturers:

- PowerPoint presentations
- Artwork from the book
- Technical worksheets and answers
- Topical worksheets and answers
- Case studies and answers
- Guide answers/teaching notes

Test Bank available in McGraw-Hill EZ Test Online

A test bank of over 1000 questions is available to lecturers adopting this book for their module. A range of questions is provided for each chapter, including multiple-choice, true or false, and short-answer or essay questions. The questions are identified by type, difficulty and topic to help you to select questions that best suit your needs and are accessible through an easy-to-use online testing tool, **McGraw-Hill EZ Test Online**.

McGraw-Hill EZ Test Online is accessible to busy academics virtually anywhere – in their office, at home or while travelling – and eliminates the need for software installation. Lecturers can choose from question banks associated with their adopted textbook or easily create their own questions. They also have access to hundreds of banks and thousands of questions created for other McGraw-Hill titles. Multiple versions of tests can be saved for delivery on paper or online through WebCT, Blackboard and other course management systems. When created and delivered though EZ Test Online, students' tests can be immediately marked, saving lecturers time and providing prompt results to students.

To register for this FREE resource, visit www.eztestonline.com

Students can connect to knowledge, connect to learning, connect to their futures.

McGraw-Hill Connect Economics™ is a web-based assignment and assessment platform that gives you the power to create assignments, tests and quizzes online, while saving you time!

Connect Economics provides the problems directly from the end-of-chapter material in your McGraw-Hill textbook, so you can easily create assignments and tests and deliver them to your students. Connect Economics grades assignments automatically, provides instant feedback to students, and securely stores all student results. Detailed results let you see at a glance how each student performs, and easily track the progress of every student in your course.

Create Assignments

With 4 essay steps, set up assignments using end-of-chapter questions from your McGraw-Hill textbook and deliver it to your students . . . all online

Students Take Assignments & Receive Instant Feedback

Connect Economics helps close the feedback loop on students' homework and reduce the time you spend grading. Once an assignment is completed, students can see immediately how they've performed and receive feedback on each question.

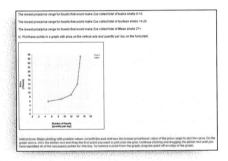

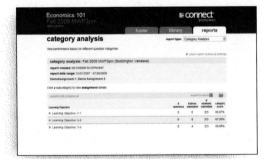

View Grades & Reports

Track each student's progress in your Connect Economics Grade Reports Student results on each assignment automatically feed to the grade reports so you can track student or class progress on any concept. Learning objective tags help you track course outcomes and aid in Assurance of Learning.

Contact your local McGraw-Hill representative to learn more about Connect Economics.
http://connectdemo.mcgraw-hill.com

Custom Publishing Solutions: Let us help make our content your solution

At McGraw-Hill Education our aim is to help lecturers to find the most suitable content for their needs, delivered to their students in the most appropriate way. Our **Custom Publishing Solutions** offer the ideal combination of content delivered in the way which best suits lecturer and students.

Our custom publishing programme offers lecturers the opportunity to select just the chapters or sections of material they wish to deliver to their students from a database called Primis at www.primisonline.com

Primis contains over two million pages of content from:

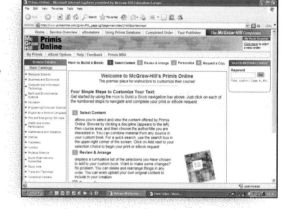

- textbooks
- professional books
- case books – Harvard articles, Insead, Ivey, Darden, Thunderbird and BusinessWeek
- Taking Sides – debate materials

Across the following imprints:

- McGraw-Hill Education
- Open University Press
- Harvard Business School Press
- US and European material

There is also the option to include additional material authored by lecturers in the custom product – this does not necessarily have to be in English.

We will take care of everything from start to finish in the process of developing and delivering a custom product to ensure that lecturers and students receive exactly the material needed in the most suitable way.

With a Custom Publishing Solution, students enjoy the best selection of material deemed to be the most suitable for learning everything they need for their courses – something of real value to support their learning. Teachers are able to use exactly the material they want, in the way they want, to support their teaching on the course.

Please contact your local McGraw-Hill representative with any questions or alternatively contact Warren Eels **e:** warren_eels@mcgraw-hill.com.

Guided tour

Learning outcomes

Each chapter opens with a set of learning outcomes, summarizing what you will take away from each chapter.

'At a glance' boxes

At the start of each chapter the 'At a glance' box provides a snapshot of the chapter and what's to come.

Key terms

These are highlighted throughout the chapter, so you can clarify key terms as you work through the topics.

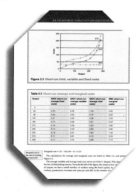

Figures and tables

Each chapter provides a number of figures and tables, which will help you to visualize key economic models, and illustrate and summarize important concepts.

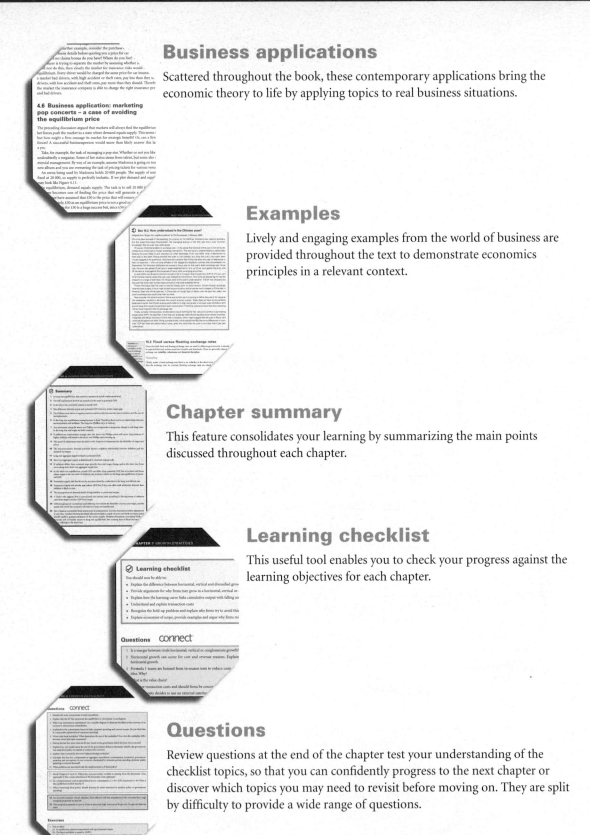

Business applications

Scattered throughout the book, these contemporary applications bring the economic theory to life by applying topics to real business situations.

Examples

Lively and engaging examples from the world of business are provided throughout the text to demonstrate economics principles in a relevant context.

Chapter summary

This feature consolidates your learning by summarizing the main points discussed throughout each chapter.

Learning checklist

This useful tool enables you to check your progress against the learning objectives for each chapter.

Questions

Review questions at the end of the chapter test your understanding of the checklist topics, so that you can confidently progress to the next chapter or discover which topics you may need to revisit before moving on. They are split by difficulty to provide a wide range of questions.

Section I
Introduction

Section contents

Chapter 1
Economics for business

Chapter contents

 Learning outcomes

By the end of this chapter you should understand:

Economic Theory

LO1   Economics is the study of how society resolves the problem of scarcity

LO2   The concept of opportunity cost

LO3   The difference between microeconomics and macroeconomics

LO4   The difference between market and planned economies

Business Application

LO5   How firms operate within microeconomic and macroeconomic environments

Economics for business at a glance

The issue

What is economics and how does economics relate to business?

The understanding

Economics seeks to understand the functioning of marketplaces. Microeconomics examines consumers, firms and workers within markets, seeking to understand why prices change for particular products, what influences the costs of firms and in particular what will influence a firm's level of profitability. Macroeconomics examines the whole economy as one very large market. Macroeconomics seeks to address how the government might manage the entire economy to deliver stable economic growth. Through the development of the production possibility frontier and an initial discussion of markets the basic economic concepts will be introduced to you.

The usefulness

Firms operate within an economic environment. The revenue they receive from selling a product is determined within a market. Furthermore, the costs that the firm has to pay for its labour, raw materials and equipment are also priced within markets. Microeconomics addresses the various market influences that impact upon a firm's revenues and costs. Macroeconomics addresses the economy-level issues which similarly affect a firm's revenues and costs. Understanding, reacting to, and possibly even controlling micro- and macroeconomic influences on the firm are crucial business skills.

1.1 What is economics?

Think about everything you would like to own, or consume. Table 1.1 contains a list of material items as examples, but it could equally contain items such as a healthy life and peace in the world.

Now list the resources that might contribute to paying for these desirable items; Table 1.2 shows ours.

You will be quick to note that the wish list is significantly longer than the resources list and there will be a significant gap between the expense required by the wish list and the likely yield of the resources list.

Table 1.1 Wish list

Big house	Luxury restaurant meals
Luxury car	Designer clothes
Top of the range mobile phone	Membership of a fitness club
Holiday in an exotic location	A case (or two) of fine wine
Designer shoes	Large flat-screen TV
Swiss watch	Games console
HD camcorder	Tickets to the Monaco Grand Prix

Table 1.2 Resources list

Salary	Royalties from book
Consulting fees	Generous friends

Infinite wants are the limitless desires to consume goods and services.

Finite resources are the limited amount of resources that enable the production and purchase of goods and services.

So we have a problem: we have a wish list that is very long and a resources list that is very short. What will we spend our resources on and what will we decide to leave in the shops? This problem is economics, one which recognizes the difference between **infinite wants** and **finite resources.**

We as individuals would all like to consume more of everything; bigger houses, bigger cars. But we only have finite resources with which to meet all our wants.[1] Firms also have infinite wants. They would like to be operating in more countries, selling larger product ranges. But firms are limited by their access to shareholders' funds and good labour. Governments too have infinite wants, providing more healthcare and better education, but are limited by their access to tax receipts.

Factors of production

Factors of production are resources needed to make goods and services: land, labour, capital and enterprise.

Economists start their analysis by focusing on the entire economy and noting that there are a variety of wants from individuals, firms and governments, and only a limited number of resources, or **factors of production**, which economists group into four categories: land, labour, capital and enterprise.

Land is where raw materials come from: oil, gas, base metals and other minerals. Some economies have enormous access to such resources and build entire economies around resource extraction. These would include Saudi Arabia and oil; Australia and iron, copper and coal; and Qatar and gas, see Box 1.1.

 Box 1.1 Qatari GDP will grow 8.5 per cent on gas output

Adapted from an article in the Gulf Times, *9 February 2009*

Qatar's economy will grow faster than any other in the Gulf as gas production increases by 80 per cent in the next two years, Standard Chartered has said. The country's real gross domestic product will expand by 8.5 per cent this year, down from 11 per cent last year.

Qatar has the world's third-largest natural gas reserves after Russia and Iran. Already the world's biggest producer of liquefied natural gas, the Qatari government has said it plans to more than double output to 77 million tons a year by 2012 for export to Europe, Asia and the US.

The International Monetary Fund (IMF) has an even more optimistic outlook for the Qatari economy. The Fund said last week that the economy will grow by 29 per cent this year, the fastest rate in more than a decade. The economy of Qatar expanded by an estimated 16.4 per cent last year, and is expected to 'perform at least as strongly in 2009,' according to the IMF.

Labour is the ability of individuals to work. Populous economies such as India and China have workforces that run into hundreds of millions. This provides these economies with the huge potential to generate enormous amounts of economic activity and wealth. In modern developed economies in Europe, labour forces are much smaller, but they are more highly educated and skilled. This enables many high valued goods and services, such as aeronautics and banking, to be produced. Whereas India and China create value through the volume of workers, Europe achieves wealth creation through the quality of workers.

Capital is production machinery, computers, office space or retail shops. Again, in many modern economies access to productive capital is good. Many banking and retail companies have good access to IT infrastructure. In economies like Dubai there has been a massive expansion of commercial and residential construction, providing much needed offices and homes. In China, the government is spending huge sums of money improving and expanding road, rail and energy infrastructure.

Enterprise is the final factor of production that brings land, labour and capital together and organizes them into business units that produce goods and services with the objective of making a profit. Shareholders are perhaps the simplest form of enterprise. Shareholders provide companies with financial backing that enables risk taking and the pursuit of profits.

In spotting new market opportunities entrepreneurs are often innovators and risk-takers, committing resources to commercial projects that may flourish or, alternatively, perish. Proven entrepreneurs might include Richard Branson of Virgin, Bill Gates of Microsoft and, in Box 1.2,

 Box 1.2 Can Apple fill the void?

Adapted from an article by Brad Stone in the New York Times, *15 January 2009*

Founder of Apple, Steve Jobs, has left the company. How important to Apple was Jobs?

By all accounts, Mr Jobs's perfectionism, autocratic managerial style and disregard for conventional wisdom are at the heart of Apple's remarkable streak of success. Since he returned to Apple in 1996, the company has set a new standard for design in personal computers, built a chain of sleek and always-crowded stores, jump-started the sale of digital music and turned the mobile phone into a fun, flexible computer.

The stories about Mr Jobs are well known, such as his insistence that even the insides of the Macintosh computer, which hardly anyone ever sees, should look good. His obsession with detail permeates everything Apple does.

But there are other aspects of his role that do not get as much attention and may be more difficult to replace. At many technology companies, various divisions often work at cross purposes, competing with one another to develop related products. This can lead to devices and software that are sometimes incompatible, frustrating customers.

'Steve is terrific at attracting and retaining people, creating an agenda and getting people to stick to it,' said Stephen G. Perlman, a Silicon Valley entrepreneur who was a principal scientist at Apple in the 1980s. 'It's very hard to find somebody who is so credible, and who has such a strong following that he is able to cut through corporate politics.'

Mr Jobs has also been Apple's chief deal-maker. After introducing the iTunes store in 2003, he persuaded entertainment companies to sell digital versions of their products when they were largely bivouacked, hiding in fear of piracy. In large part because of Mr Jobs's efforts, those barriers have fallen, though other challenges remain, such as getting the Hollywood studios to relax their restrictions on renting or downloading movies over the Internet.

Still, there are those who worry that Mr Jobs's absence from Apple will have an impact even beyond Apple:

'The whole world is concerned about Apple. I'm concerned about Silicon Valley,' said Mr Perlman, the entrepreneur. 'I need Apple to be harrying Microsoft. We need someone stirring the pot. God forbid that there is no one stirring the pot any more. We'll become Detroit.'

Steve Jobs of Apple. Perhaps an important feature of very successful entrepreneurs is their drive, motivation and ability to stamp their own personality on a company. Entrepreneurs can bring far more to a company than simply risk-bearing capacity. They can bring management skill, vision and purpose and strategic direction. When they retreat from running companies, as with Apple, then question marks over the future success of the company can be raised.

Production possibility frontier

The **production possibility frontier** is an important illustrative tool because it can be used to highlight crucial economic concepts. These are:

The **production possibility frontier** shows the maximum number of products that can be produced by an economy with a given amount of resources.

◆ Finite resources
◆ Opportunity costs
◆ Macro- and microeconomics
◆ Planned, market and mixed economies

We will discuss each in turn.

Finite resources

Figure 1.1 shows the production possibility frontier for an imaginary economy that only produces two goods, pizza and beer, and highlights the constraint created by access to only a finite amount of resources. With a fixed quantity of resources an infinite amount of beer, or pizzas, cannot be produced. If all resources were allocated to the production of beer, then we would be at point A on the diagram, with a maximum amount of beer being produced and no pizzas. But if all resources were allocated to pizzas, then we would be at point B, with a maximum number of pizzas being produced and no beer. The curve between points A and B indicates all

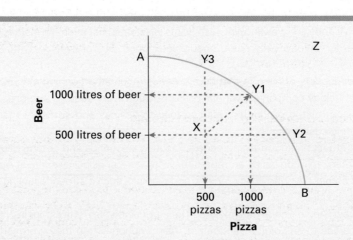

Figure 1.1 Production possibility frontier

The production possibility frontier shows the maximum amounts of beer and pizza that can be produced with a fixed amount of resources. At Y1, 1000 litres of beer and 1000 pizzas can be produced. At Y3, more beer can be produced but some pizza production has to be sacrificed, while at Y2, beer can be sacrificed in order to produce more pizzas. Z cannot be achieved with current resource levels and X represents unemployment, with production of beer and pizzas below the optimal levels attainable on the frontier, such as Y1, Y2 and Y3.

the maximum combinations of beer and pizza that can be produced. The frontier shows what it is possible to produce with a limited amount of resources.

Operating on the frontier is optimal; all finite resources are employed. Operating at a point such as Z is currently impossible. The economy does not have the resources to produce at Z. Operating at X is inefficient, because some resources must be unemployed. More output could be produced by employing all factors of production and moving towards the frontier.

Opportunity costs

> **Opportunity costs** are the benefits forgone from the next best alternative.

If pizza production is reduced in order to make more beer, then the **opportunity cost** consists of the benefits that could have been received from the pizzas that have not been made. Opportunity costs give the production possibility frontier a negative slope; simply, more pizzas must mean less beer. Reading this book now has an opportunity cost. You could be watching TV. Recalling that the economic problem is one of infinite wants and finite resources, ideally you will try to make your opportunity cost as low as possible. With your limited resources you will try to maximize your gains from consumption. This way you are sacrificing the least amount of benefit.

 Box 1.3 Maximizing gains

If the benefit of reading this book to you can be estimated at £1 per hour and the benefit of watching TV can be estimated at £0.50 per hour, then the opportunity cost of reading this book, rather than watching TV, is £0.50, the benefit you have given up. In contrast, if you watched TV, then the opportunity cost would be £1 – the benefit forgone from not reading this book. Given the ratio of these benefits, you can minimize your opportunity cost by reading this book. If we add in an option to reflect the true student lifestyle, a night out with your friends might be worth £5 per hour to you. Staying in and reading this book would then represent an opportunity cost of £5 per hour, while going out and not reading the book would only represent an opportunity cost of £1 per hour, the benefits forgone by not reading this book. In terms of opportunity cost, it is cheaper to go out with your friends than to stay in and read this book. If you fail this module, at least you can understand why.

Macroeconomics and microeconomics

> **Macroeconomics** is the study of how the entire economy works.
>
> **Microeconomics** is the study of how individuals make economic decisions within an economy.

By focusing on points X, Y and Z in Figure 1.1, we can draw your attention to two important distinctions in economics: (i) the study of **macroeconomics** and (ii) the study of **microeconomics**.

Points X and Z represent mainly macroeconomic problems. At point X, the economy is not operating at its optimal level; we said point X was likely to be associated with unemployment. This occurs during a recession. Part of macroeconomics is understanding what creates a recession and how to remedy a recession. Governments and the central bank adjust interest rates, taxation and government spending to try to move the economy from point X towards point Y. Point Z is also a macroeconomic issue. The economy cannot achieve point Z now, but in the future the economy could grow and eventually attain point Z. How do we develop policies to move the economy over the long term to point Z? This question has been the recent focus of economic policy-makers, with the focus placed upon the issue of 'sustainable economic growth'.

Microeconomics places the focus of analysis on the behaviour of individuals, firms or consumers. Rather than looking at the economy as a whole, it attempts to understand why consumers prefer particular products. How will changes in income or prices influence consumption patterns? In relation to firms, microeconomists are interested in the motives for supplying products. Do firms wish to maximize sales, profits or market share? What factors influence costs and how can firms manage costs? What determines the level of competition in a market and how can firms compete against each other?

By focusing on individual consumers, firms and the interaction between the two, the economist is particularly interested in the functioning of markets. This particular aspect of economics can be highlighted by examining movements along the production possibility frontier. Point Y1 on the frontier has been described as being efficient. But points Y2 and Y3 are also on the frontier and are, therefore, equally efficient. At Y1, the economy produces a balanced mix of pizza and beer. At Y2, the economy specializes more in pizza and, at Y3, the economy specializes more in beer production. How will the economy decide among operating at Y1, Y2 and Y3? The answer lies in understanding resource allocation mechanisms.

Planned, market and mixed economies

In a pure **planned economy**, the government decides how resources are allocated to the production of particular products.

In a **planned economy**, the government plans whether the economy should operate at point Y1 or another point. Historically, these systems were common in the former Soviet Bloc and China, and are still in use in Cuba.

In a planned economy, the government sets an economic plan, typically for the next five years. Within the economic plan are decisions about which industries to support and how much output each industry should produce. This could include a plan for car production, house building and the expansion of travel infrastructure, including rail, roads and air. The economic plan may also go so far as to set prices for goods, services and wages.

In planned economies, the government is the major owner of the factors of production, and in the case of Cuba around 76 per cent of the entire workforce is employed by the government.

In a pure **market economy**, the government plays no role in allocating resources. Instead, markets allocate resources to the production of various products.

In a **market economy**, private individuals own the majority of economic factors of production. Market economies have two important groups: consumers that buy products and firms that sell products. Consumers buy products because they seek the benefits associated with the consumption of the products. For example, you eat food because it stops you feeling hungry; you drive a car because it helps you to travel between various locations. Similarly, firms sell products in order to make a profit.

In the marketplace information is exchanged between consumers and firms. This information relates to the prices at which consumers are willing to buy products and, similarly, the prices at which firms are willing to sell. For any particular product you will have a maximum price at which you are willing to buy. The more desirable you find the product, the greater will be your maximum price. In contrast, firms will have a minimum price at which they are willing to sell. The easier, or cheaper, it is to make the good, the lower this minimum price will be. If the minimum price at which firms are willing to sell is less than consumers' maximum willingness to pay, then the potential for a market in the good exists. Firms can make the product in the clear expectation of making a profit.

Firms are likely to move their productive resources – land, labour, capital and enterprise – to the markets that present the greatest opportunities for profit. Given our discussion above, profits will vary with the willingness of consumers to pay and the costs incurred by firms. If consumers are willing to pay higher prices, or production costs fall, then profits will increase. Increasing profits will lead firms to move resources into the market. In contrast, as consumers reduce their willingness to buy a product, or if firms' costs increase, profits will fall and firms will look to reallocate their resources into more profitable markets.

Box 1.4 Pizza and beer

In our pizza and beer example, let us consider the following: we are at point Y1 on Figure 1.1 and suddenly scientists show that beer is very good for your health. Following this news, we would expect consumers to buy more beer. As beer increases in popularity, beer producers are able to sell for a higher price and make greater profits. As consumers allocate more of their income to beer, pizza producers begin to lose sales and profits. Over time, pizza makers would recognize that consumers have reduced their consumption of pizzas. In response, pizza producers would begin to close down their operations and move their resources into the popular beer market. The economy moves from Y1 to Y3 in the figure.

Comparing command and market economies

Market economies rely on a very quick and efficient communication of information that occurs through prices. Firms ordinarily set a price that indicates their willingness to sell. Consumers communicate their willingness to buy by purchasing the product at the given price. The problem of what should be produced and what should not be produced is solved by the price system.

The command (or planned) economy, in setting production levels for various goods and services, requires similar market-based information regarding the costs of production and the consumption requirements of consumers. But how would you go about setting food, clothing, drink, transport and education output levels for an economy? You might conduct a questionnaire survey asking consumers to rank the different products by level of importance. But this has a number of problems. It is costly, the respondents might not represent the views of all consumers and it might not be timely with the questionnaire only being carried out every couple of years. The collection of information required for effective planning is very complicated and costly within a command economy, especially when compared with the simple and efficient exchange of information in the market economy through the pricing system. It is of little surprise that, in recent years, planned economies have become less popular.

In reality, many economies function as an amalgam of planned and market economies – a **mixed economy**.

For example, within many modern economies the sale of groceries is a purely market solution, with private firms deciding what they will offer to consumers within their own supermarkets. The provision of public healthcare is an example of the government deciding what healthcare treatments will be offered to the population.

A means of measuring the planned side of the economy is to examine the size of government expenditure as a percentage of gross domestic product, **GDP**. Government expenditure can include spending on infrastructure such as roads, healthcare, education, defence and social contributions such as unemployment benefits.

Figure 1.2 illustrates the size of the planned or public sector for a number of European economies. For most economies, the size of the planned economy is large. Even in Latvia, with the smallest government sector, it still represents almost 38 per cent of GDP.

In summary, economics studies how individuals, firms, governments and economies deal with the problem of infinite wants and finite resources. Microeconomics examines the economic issues faced by individuals and firms, while macroeconomics studies the workings and performance of the entire economy. We will now indicate why an understanding of economics can provide an essential understanding for business.

In a **mixed economy**, the government and the private sector jointly solve economic problems.

GDP is gross domestic product and is a measure of overall economic activity within an economy. See Chapters 9 and 10 for more details.

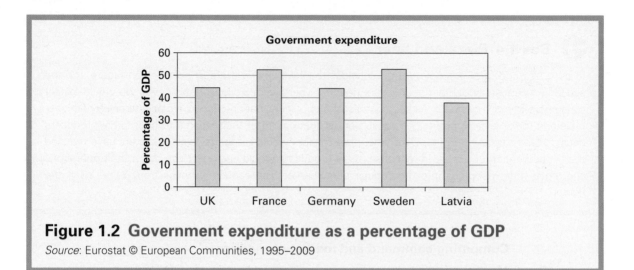

Figure 1.2 **Government expenditure as a percentage of GDP**
Source: Eurostat © European Communities, 1995–2009

1.2 Why study economics for business?

Business and management draw upon a number of different disciplines, including, but not limited to, accounting and finance, human resource management, operations management, marketing, law, statistics and economics. Each discipline has a particular focus and set of issues that it specializes in understanding.

The economist's analysis of business begins with a simple assumption: firms are in business to make profits for their owners. Moreover, firms are in business to maximize profits, or make the highest amount of profit possible.

The assumption that firms are profit-maximizers is clearly a simplification. Firms represent a collection of workers, managers, shareholders, consumers and perhaps individuals living within the locality of the firm's operations. Each of these groups may have a different interest within the firm. For example, shareholders may seek greater profit, but workers and managers may seek increased wages. These conflicts generate complexity within the organizational environment of firms. Economists try to simplify the complex nature of reality. Therefore, rather than attempt an understanding of all the complex interrelationships within a firm, economists simply assume that the firm is in business to maximize profits.

Economists are not arguing that the complex interrelationships between the various interest groups within a firm are not important. However, economists are assuming that, without profits, firms would find it difficult to survive financially. Therefore, while subjects such as human resource management, organization theory and corporate social responsibility focus upon how the firm might manage the conflicting relationships between the competing interest groups of shareholders, workers and wider society, business economists have focused upon an understanding of firms' profits.

Firms, as profit-making organizations, can be viewed as a combination of revenue-based cash flows going in, and cost-based cash flows going out. Within this view of firms, economics for business can be simplified to an analysis of the economic influences that enhance revenues and reduce costs, thereby increasing firm-level financial performance or, more directly, profit.

In Figure 1.3, the firm is positioned between its revenue and its costs. In placing the firm in the middle of the diagram, it is also recognized that the firm operates within micro- and

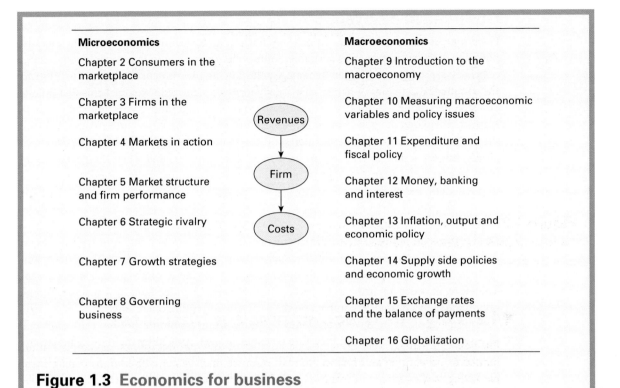

Figure 1.3 Economics for business

macroeconomic environments. The micro and macro environments are covered in detail by the various chapters within this book but, importantly, and perhaps simplistically, each chapter adds to an understanding of how the firm can improve its revenue and/or cost position. Broad areas of interest and importance are now discussed.

Markets and competition

The particular focus of economics is on the functioning of markets. Markets are important for firms in a number of ways. First, a marketplace is where a firm will sell its product and, therefore, generate revenue. Second, a firm's inputs – land, labour, capital and enterprise – are all purchased through markets and, therefore, markets influence a firm's level of costs. The level of competition varies across markets: some are highly competitive; others are not. Throughout life, if you wish to be a winner, it is easier to achieve success when the competition is weak; and business is no different. In highly competitive business environments prices will fall, while in low competitive environments price competition will be less severe. If interested in enhancing revenues, it is important to understand how to recognize issues likely to promote competition and influences that will enable competition to be managed and controlled. It is also important to understand how a firm can change its mode of operations in order to improve its competitive advantage. Growth by acquisition of a rival clearly reduces competition, but growth by the purchase of a raw material supplier into the industry also places your rivals at a disadvantage, because you then own what your rivals need. Good businesspeople understand how to manage and exploit competitive opportunities.

Government intervention

Governments can also intervene in markets. Society, or government, does not view excessive pollution of the environment as desirable. Some pollution may be an unavoidable consequence of beneficial production. In order to manage pollution the government can attempt to influence the commercial activities of firms. This usually involves increased taxes for firms that pollute, and subsidies, or grants, for firms that attempt to operate in a more environmentally friendly manner. Therefore, the government can seek to influence firms' costs and revenues, boosting them when the firm operates in the interest of society, and reducing profits when the firm operates against the public interest. Firms need to be able to understand when their activities are likely to attract the attention of government, or pressure groups, and what policies could be imposed upon them.

Globalization

Finally, firms do not operate within singular markets; rather, they function within massive macroeconomic systems. Traditionally, such systems have been the national economy but, more recently, firms have begun to operate within an increasingly global environment. Therefore, in order for firms to be successful they need to understand how macroeconomic events and global change will impact on their current and future operations.

National economies have a tendency to move from economic booms into economic recessions. If a firm's sales, and therefore revenues, are determined by the state of the macro-economy, then it is important for the firm to understand why an economy might move from a position of economic prosperity to one of economic recession. Similarly, during a recession firms struggle to sell all of their output. Price discounts can make products and inputs – such as labour, raw materials and capital equipment – cheaper, thereby reducing a firm's costs.

While understanding the state of the macroeconomy is important, it is also beneficial to have an understanding of how the government might try to manage the economy. How will changes in taxation affect consumers, firms and the health of the economy? How will interest rate changes influence inflation and the state of the economy? These are common governmental policy decisions with important implications for business.

Moreover, within the global economy matters of international trade, exchange rates, European monetary union and the increasing globalization of business all impact upon the operations and competitive position of business. Operating internationally may enable a firm to source cheaper production or access new market and revenue streams. However, equally, international firms can access UK markets, leading to an increase in competition for UK domestic producers. Successful companies will not only recognize these issues but, more importantly, they will also understand how these issues relate to themselves and business generally. From this, strategies will be developed and firms will attempt to manage their competitive environment.

In order to develop your understanding of these issues, this book is separated into a number of parts that build on each other. In Section II you will be introduced to the workings of marketplaces. Section III will develop an understanding of competition in markets, followed by an overview of firm governance by shareholders and government. This will conclude the microeconomic section of the book. Macroeconomics is split into two obvious parts: macroeconomics in the domestic economy and macroeconomics in the global economy. At the domestic level, you will be introduced to how the macroeconomy works, the factors leading to the level of economic activity and the options available to a government trying to control the economy. At the global level, you will be provided with an understanding of international trade and the workings of exchange rates. This will lead to the important issue of European monetary union. Finally, an assessment of globalization and the implications for business will be provided.

In order to highlight the relevance of economics to business, each chapter begins with a business problem. Theory relevant to an understanding of the problem is then developed. Each chapter closes with two applications of the theory to further highlight the relevance of the theory to business and management. In this way, economic theory is clearly sandwiched between real-world business issues and practices, highlighting for you that economics, where appropriate, is a subject to be applied in the understanding of business problems.

1.3 Appendix: the economist's approach

Economics as a subject has a number of characteristics associated with it and, to aid your learning, it is worth pointing them out to you.

Language

The economist makes use of terms and phrases that are particular and peculiar to economics. For example, from the above discussion economics is the study of why you cannot have everything. But the economist talks about infinite wants, finite resources, opportunity costs and production possibility frontiers. Using the economic terminology will help you. Economists use particular terminology because it helps them to understand each other when communicating ideas. Succinct terms, such as opportunity cost, once understood, convey complex ideas quickly to anyone else who understands the phrase.

Abstract models

> **Models** or **theories** are frameworks for organizing how we think about an economic problem.

Economists think about the world in terms of **models** or **theories**.

Economists recognize that the world is extremely complicated and, therefore, prefer to make models using simplifying assumptions. The complexity of the real world is stripped out in favour of a simple analysis of the central, or essential, issues. As an example, consider Box 1.5, where we discuss how an economist might approach how David Beckham bends free kicks.

Normative and positive economics

> **Positive economics** studies objective or scientific explanations of how the economy works.
>
> **Normative economics** offers recommendations based on personal value judgements.

A **positive economics** question and a **normative economics** statement will help to clarify the differences:

Positive question: What level of production will maximize the firm's profits?
Normative statement: Firms should maximize profits.

The positive question seeks to address a technical point – can economics identify the output level where firms will make the largest profit? The normative statement, in contrast, seeks to assert the opinion that profit maximization is best – it is making a value judgement. In the case of the positive question, economists can make a response with theory consisting of a set of accepted rational arguments that provide a technical answer to the question. However, in respect of the normative statement, economists can only reply with similar, or alternative, value statements: for example, firms should not focus entirely on profit maximization; I believe they should also consider the needs of wider stakeholders such as workers, the environment, suppliers and customers.

This is an important distinction. Positive economics is the technical and objective pursuit of economic understanding. As a subject it seeks to provide answers to questions and propose solutions to problems. Normative economics is different in that it does not seek to answer questions; rather, it seeks to assert and represent particular beliefs – which are difficult, if not impossible, to provide positive answers to.

Box 1.5 Bend it like Beckham

In modelling David Beckham's ability to bend free kicks, economists would strip out the complex issues, such as natural talent, good practice and high-pressure championship experience, and take the simplifying assumption that David Beckham behaves like a world-class physicist. David Beckham must behave like a highly accomplished physicist because he can clearly calculate all the angles and force needed to bend a free kick and score a goal.

In reality, David Beckham probably has no more understanding of physics than many of us. So, to say that David Beckham behaves like a physicist seems peculiar. However, the important point is that the theory *predicts*; it need not *explain*. The theory does not *explain* why David Beckham can bend free kicks and score goals with such accuracy. But it does *predict* that David Beckham will score spectacular goals if he behaves like a world-class physicist. This is because a leading physicist, indeed any physicist, could use the Newtonian laws of motion to work out the perfect angle and trajectory for the football to travel in a spectacular arc into the back of the net. But why should economists wish to develop strange abstract assumptions about reality, leading to theories that predict, as opposed to theories that can explain?

The answer to this question is that economists try to keep things simple and extract only the important points for analysis. The world is very complex, so what we try to do as economists is to simplify things to the important points. David Beckham is probably a football player because of some natural talent, a good deal of practice, championship experience and perhaps some poorer opponents. All these would explain why David Beckham can score great goals. But to keep things simple we will assume he behaves like a leading physicist. If theoretically true, then David Beckham will also be an amazing free-kick specialist. Therefore, the predictive approach is a theoretical short cut that enables economists to simplify the complex nature of reality. So, whenever you come across a theory in this book that is not a true reflection of reality, do not worry. We economists are happy in our little fantasy world where people like David Beckham double up as Einstein.

Economics is not peculiar in exhibiting a tension between objective and subjective approaches to reason. In art, the positive approach may centre on a technical understanding of various media. But the use of these media, the choice of images to create and how to interpret them are all normative, value laden and subjective; as highlighted by judges' views of Turner-winning artist Mark Leckey described in Box 1.6.

 Box 1.6 Leckey scoop Turner

Adapted from an article on BBC News Online, 1 December 2008

Artist Mark Leckey has won this year's Turner Prize. The artist's work combines sculpture, film, sound and performance.

Leckey told the audience it was 'great to do something that has some kind of effect on British culture'. His winning works include the film *Cinema in the Round*, which shows him lecturing about his love of animation.

The key motifs of Leckey's work, footage based on contemporary culture, are desire and transformation. According to judges, he uses his 'own state of being' – an artist in London who grew up in northern England in the 1980s – to explore those motifs. 'He celebrates the imagination of the individual and our potential to inhabit, reclaim or animate an idea, a space, or an object,' they added.

© bbc.co.uk/news

Diagrams

A **positive relationship** exists between two variables if the values for both variables increase and decrease together.

Quickly flick through all the pages of this book. How many diagrams did you see? Economists like diagrams. For the economist, diagrams are an effective way of communicating complex ideas. In order to develop your understanding of economics, you will need to develop your competence in this area, as it is almost impossible to manage without them – which is disappointing for any of you who detest them with a passion.

As a brief reminder, diagrams, at least as we will be using them, provide a visual indication of the relationship between two variables. For example, consider a fridge and an oven. Neither are currently switched on. When we do switch them on we are interested in seeing how the temperature inside the oven and the fridge changes the longer each appliance is on. This is not rocket science: the fridge will get colder and the oven hotter. A maths teacher would say that there is a **positive relationship** between time and temperature in the cooker.

A **negative relationship** exists between two variables if the values for one variable increase (decrease) as the value of the other variable decreases (increases).

In our example of the oven, as time increases – one minute, two minutes, etc. – the temperature of the oven also increases. Our two variables, time and temperature, increase together.

In contrast, the maths teacher would say that there is a **negative relationship** between time and temperature in the fridge.

In our example of the fridge, as time increases, the temperature of the fridge decreases. Figure 1.4 is a diagram showing the positive relationship between time and temperature within the oven, while Figure 1.5 is a diagram of the negative relationship between time and the temperature inside the fridge.

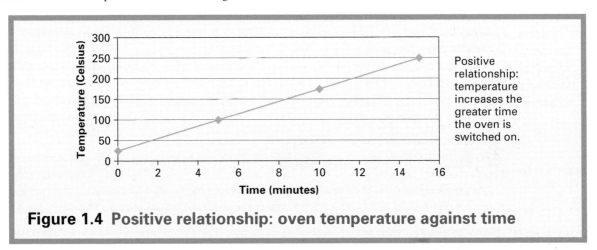

Positive relationship: temperature increases the greater time the oven is switched on.

Figure 1.4 Positive relationship: oven temperature against time

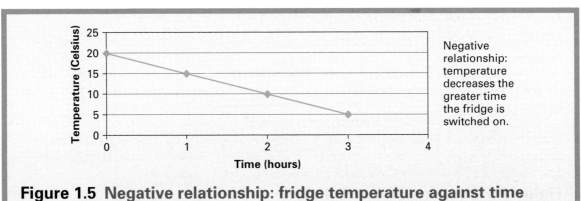

Negative relationship: temperature decreases the greater time the fridge is switched on.

Figure 1.5 Negative relationship: fridge temperature against time

We will be doing nothing more complicated than this. We might reasonably argue that, as prices increase, consumers will buy less; we therefore expect to see a negative relationship between the price of a product and the amount of the product purchased by consumers. Similarly, in the case of a positive relationship we might argue that consumer expenditure increases as income levels rise. Essentially the diagrams are a simple visual illustration of the relationship between two variables. The more you try to understand them and gain confidence in using them, the easier economics becomes.

Equations of lines

> **Equation of a straight line** is $Y = a + bX$.

We can also describe relationships between variables using equations. If there is a linear relationship between two variables, then we can use the general **equation of a straight line** to describe the relationship. The general linear relationship states that $Y = a + bX$, where 'a' is the intercept and 'b' is the gradient of the line. The intercept is the value of Y when X is zero. The gradient is the steepness of the line.

In Figure 1.6, the two axes are Y and X and the equation of the straight line describing the relationship between Y and X is $Y = 2 + 1X$; that is, a = 2 and b = 1. So, when X is zero, Y = 2; and for every one-unit increase in X, then Y also increases by 1. So if X is 4, Y must be 2 + 4 = 6.

In Figure 1.7, we have altered the equation to make the gradient twice as steep. The relationship between Y and X is now $Y2 = 2 + 2X$. So, when X = 4, then Y = 2 + (2 × 4) = 10. If we changed the intercept to, say, 4, then the line for Y2 would move up the Y axis and start from Y = 4, and not Y = 2.

If we require a negative relationship, then we simply change the sign of the gradient to minus. So $Y = 10 - 2X$. This is illustrated in Figure 1.8. When X = 0, then Y = 10. When X = 3, then Y = 10 - (3 × 2) = 4.

> A **quadratic** is generally specified as $Y = a + bX + cX^2$.

We may also need to consider a non-linear relationship, such as a **quadratic**. A quadratic is generally specified as $Y = a + bX + cX^2$. In Figure 1.9, we have plotted two quadratic relationships, one of the form $Y = 20 - 6X + X^2$, which creates a U-shaped relationship. Then, by simply changing the signs on b and c, we can create $Y = 25 + 6X - X^2$, which creates an n-shaped relationship. (We changed a, the intercept, to generate vertical distance between the two lines.)

Gradients and turning points

> The **gradient** is a measure of the slope of a line.

The **gradient** measures the slope or steepness of a line. One method of measuring the gradient of a line is to calculate the ratio $\Delta Y/\Delta X$, where the symbol Δ means change. The values for ΔY

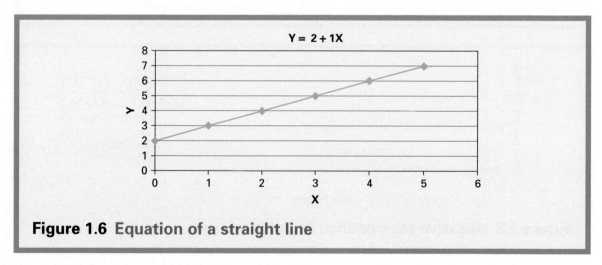

Figure 1.6 Equation of a straight line

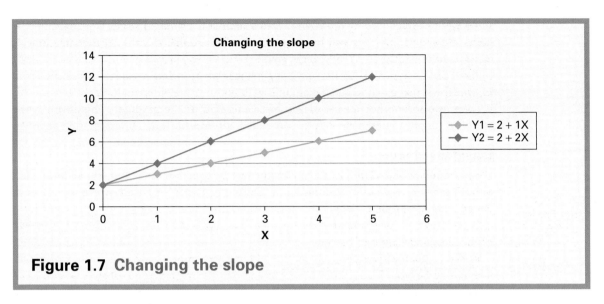

Figure 1.7 Changing the slope

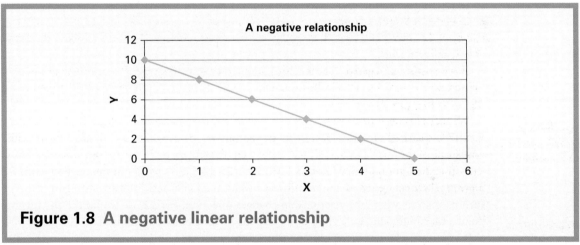

Figure 1.8 A negative linear relationship

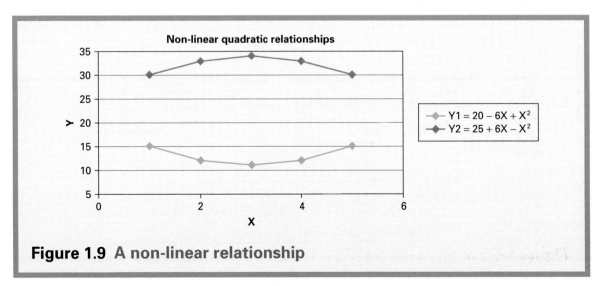

Figure 1.9 A non-linear relationship

and ΔX can be calculated by drawing a triangle against the slope of a line. If we examine the slopes in Figure 1.7, for Y2 over the range $X = 3$ to $X = 4$, then $\Delta X = 1$. At the same time, Y increases from 8 to 10, so $\Delta Y = 2$. So the gradient $= 2/1 = 2$.

Recall that the general equation of a straight line is $Y = a + bX$, where b is the gradient. From Y2, we can see that $b = 2$, which corresponds with our measure based on Figure 1.7.

There is also another means of gaining a measure of the gradient. This involves the use of a simple mathematical function called **differentiation**. Differentiation involves a very simple rule: the differential of X^n is nX^{n-1} (and all constants become zeros); so the differential of X^3 is $3X^2$.

> **Differentiation**
> is a means of
> understanding
> the gradient.

Importantly, if you differentiate any mathematical equation, then you will always be left with the gradient. For example, consider the linear equation $Y2 = 2 + 2X$, which is laid out in Table 1.3 and then differentiated.

Table 1.3 An example of differentiation

Equation	Differentiate	Differential
Y2 =		
25	is a constant and so becomes →	0
+	+	+
2X	can be written $2X^1$. So this becomes $1*2X^0$ →	2

So differentiating equation Y2 results in the answer of 2, which we already know is the gradient.

Differentiation is an important tool because it enables us to work out the turning point for a given relationship. Recall the non-linear u- and n-shaped relationships in Figure 1.9. The turning point is where the relationship changes direction. For Y2, we would call the turning point a maximum and, for Y1, we would call the turning point a minimum.

If we want to know where a relationship is maximized (or minimized), we simply need to recognize that at the turning point the gradient is flat and therefore equal to zero. So if we have an expression for the gradient, then we have to equate it with zero and solve. Consider $Y2 = 25 + 6X - X^2$, which is laid out in Table 1.4.

Table 1.4 Differentiating an equation

Equation	Differentiate	Differential
Y2 =		
2	is a constant and so becomes →	0
+	+	+
6X	can be written $6X^1$. So this becomes $1*6X^0$ →	6
$-X^2$	So this becomes $-2X^1$ →	$-2X$

So the differential and therefore the gradient for Y2 is 6 − 2X. At the turning point, the gradient is equal to zero. So, at the turning point 0 = 6 − 2X, therefore X = 3. Check this answer by looking back at Figure 1.9.

Mathematical equations and differentiation can be powerful tools for economists and business analysts. If we wish to know the price that maximizes revenues, then we need to find a mathematical equation which describes the relationship between prices and revenues. We then simply differentiate, set to zero and solve to find the best price to maximize revenues. Equally, if we want to discover the level of production that leads to minimum costs per unit, then we need a mathematical equation which links production and costs, differentiate, set to zero and solve to find the ideal level of production.

Economic data

Time series data are the measurements of one variable at different points in time.

Cross-sectional data are the measurements of one variable at the same point in time across different individuals.

Economists make use of data to examine relationships between variables. Data can be categorized into **time series data** and **cross-sectional data**.

For example, the price of a cinema ticket recorded for each year between 1990 and 2010 is an example of one variable measured at various points in time. The time period between each observation is usually fixed. So, in the case of cinema tickets, the variable, price, is measured once every year. However, time series can be measured in a variety of periods – yearly, monthly, daily, hourly or by the minute. The price of shares on the London stock market is measured in all of these formats.

The profits of individual companies in the supermarket industry in 2010 would be an example of cross-sectional data, with profits of different companies being measured at the same point in time.

Panel data combines cross-sectional and time series data.

Rather than measure the profits of individual supermarkets in 2008, we could also measure individual companies' profits in 2009, 2010, 2011 and so on. This way, we are combining cross-sections and time, thus providing us with **panel data**.

Using data

In using data economists employ a number of simple mathematical techniques, including calculations of percentages and the use of index numbers. Both are simple to understand, but a refresher may help your understanding.

In order to measure the change in a variable, we can use **percentages**.

We can use Table 1.5 to understand how big a particular percentage change is.

A percentage measures the change in a variable as a fraction of 100.

Since a percentage measures the rate of change in a variable, we need both the variable's original and new value.

We calculate the percentage as the absolute change divided by the original number, then multiplied by 100:

$$\frac{(\text{New value} - \text{Original value})}{\text{Original value}} \times 100$$

For example, the share price of Company A was £2.00 in 2010 and £3.00 in 2011. The percentage change is therefore:

$$\frac{(£3.00 - £2.00)}{£2.00} \times 100 = 50\%$$

Table 1.5 Percentage changes

Percentage	Size of change	
10	10% = 10/100 = 1/10	The variable has increased by one-tenth of its original value
25	25% = 25/100 = 1/4	The variable has increased by one-quarter of its original value
50	50% = 50/100 = 1/2	The variable has increased by one-half of its original value
100	100% = 100/100 = 1	The variable has increased by the same amount as its original value; it has doubled in size
200	200% = 200/100 = 2	The variable has increased by twice its original value; it has tripled in size
500	500% = 500/100 = 5	The variable has increased by five times its original size

Index numbers

Index numbers
are used to
transform a data
series into a series
with a base value
of 100.

As an example of the use of **index numbers**, take the data series in Table 1.6, which measures the price of a pint of beer.

The price of beer is in pounds sterling. To convert this data series into a unitless series with a base value of 100, we first need to select the base year. In Table 1.6, we have selected 2009 as the base year. In order to generate the index, we simply take the price of beer in any year, divide by the base year value and times by 100. So, in 2009, we have (£2.40/£2.40 × 100 = 100. In 2010, we have (£2.60/£2.40) × 100 = 108.

A sensible question to ask is why do we use index numbers? There are a number of reasons. The first is to recognize that, since we have a base value of 100, it is very easy to calculate the percentage change in the variable over time. From Table 1.6 we can readily see that between 2009 and 2012 beer increases in price by 25 per cent.

The second reason is that index numbers facilitate averaging. Assume we are interested in how prices across the economy are rising. If an index was created not only for beer prices but also for car prices, cigarettes and in fact all products that are commonly sold, then an average of all the indices would enable an assessment of average price rises in the UK.

The Retail Price Index does exactly this. It is an average of many individual product price indices. The average is weighted by the importance of the product within the average household's consumption. For example, since housing costs represent a major element of household consumption, the house price index receives a higher weight in the Retail Price Index than the price index for sweets and confectionery. The FTSE 100 is another example of an index and combines as an average the prices of all shares in the FTSE 100. The value of the index increases (decreases) if, on average, shares in the FTSE 100 increase (decrease).

In summary, index numbers are used to create data series that are unitless. They have a base year of 100 and can be used to calculate percentage changes from the base year with ease. By virtue of having a common base year value of 100, index numbers can also be used to create averages from many different indices, such as price level indices or stock market indices.

Table 1.6 Index numbers

Year	Price of beer	Index
2009	£2.40	100
2010	£2.60	108
2011	£2.90	121
2012	£3.00	125

Methods of averaging in economics

Economists tend to use two different types of averages: the arithmetic and geometric means. The arithmetic mean is the more familiar one and simply adds up all the observed values for a variable and then divides by n, the number of observations. The geometric average calculates the product of all the observations and then calculates the nth root. See Table 1.7 for examples.

In the first example, we have two observations, both of which are equal to two. So the arithmetic mean is 2. The geometric mean is also 2. We have used this simple example so that both means can be worked out easily and without the aid of a calculator. However, you should not be fooled into thinking that the two means will always be the same. In the second example, we use three observations, all of which are different. This time, the arithmetic mean is larger than the geometric mean.

An important question to ask is, why use two different ways to calculate the mean? The answer is because economists are often interested in rates of growth. How fast is the economy growing? How slowly have prices increased? What rate of return is an investment generating? When measuring growth, the use of arithmetic means would create a compounding problem. For example, if the value of a share was £100 and then increased by 5 per cent in year one and 15 per cent in year two, then the arithmetic average rate of return would be 10 per cent. This would suggest that the value of the share at the end of year two is £100 × 1.1 = £110; and then £110 × 1.1 = £1.21. But if we use the actual growth rates, 5 and 15 per cent, we get £100 × 1.05 = £105; and then £105 × 1.15 = £120.75. The arithmetic mean therefore generates an error. This is simple to understand because we are dealing in percentages. Five per cent of £100 and 15 per cent of £105 are not comparable, because the base values (£100 and £105) are not the same. The geometric mean solves this problem.

Table 1.7 Arithmetic and geometric means

Observations	Arithmetic mean	Geometric mean
2, 2	$(2 + 2)/2 = 2$	$(2 \times 2)^{1/2} = 2$
2, 3, 4	$(2 + 3 + 4)/3 = 3$	$(2 \times 3 \times 4)^{1/3} = 2.88$

Summary

1   Economics assumes that everybody would like to consume more of everything, but we only have a limited amount of resources with which to facilitate such consumption.

2   Economic factor resources are split into four categories: land, labour, capital and enterprise.

3   The production possibility frontier is used by economists to provide an illustration of finite resources. The production possibility frontier shows the maximum total output that can be produced using the limited amount of factor inputs. As more of one good is produced, less of the remaining good can be produced.

4   Opportunity cost is measured as the benefits forgone from the next best alternative.

5   Operating on the frontier represents full employment and is defined as productively efficient. Operating inside the frontier is inefficient as the output of both goods can be increased by making an efficient utilization of the underemployed factor resources. Operating outside the frontier is currently impossible. However, over time the economy may become more productively efficient, producing more output for a given level of input; or the economy may gain access to additional factor inputs, also enabling output to increase.

6   Macroeconomics is an examination of the economy as a whole and, therefore, considers issues such as the level of economic activity, the level of prices, unemployment, economic growth, and international trade and exchange rates.

7   Microeconomics focuses upon the economic decision making of individuals and firms. Micro-economics examines how individual markets function and how firms compete with one another.

8   Where on the frontier an economy operates, producing more beer than pizza, or vice versa, depends upon the resource allocation mechanism. In command economies, the government plans how much of each good to produce. In market economies, the interaction of consumers and firms through the pricing system of the market directs resources away from non-profitable markets and towards profitable ones.

9   Economics has a language and terminology; this aids communication of ideas and should be mastered.

10 Economics uses abstract models. In reality, the world is very complex. In economics, simplifying assumptions are deployed in order to make the world simple. As a consequence, an explanation of reality is often sacrificed for prediction.

11 Positive economics seeks to address objective questions with theory. Normative economics seeks to assert value judgements on what is preferable economic behaviour.

12 Economists place an emphasis on diagrams when explaining ideas and theories. A positive relationship exists between two variables if both variables increase together. A negative relationship between two variables exists when, as one variable increases, the other decreases.

13 Economic data can be time series, cross-sectional or a combination of the two (panel data). Time series data are the measurements of one variable at various points in time. Cross-sectional data are the measurements of one variable at the same point in time, but across a number of firms or individuals.

14 A percentage measures the change in a variable as a fraction of 100. You can calculate a percentage change as (New value − Original value)/Original value × 100.

15 An index converts a variable into a unitless data series with a base year of 100. This is achieved by dividing each value by the base year value and then multiplying by 100.

16 Index numbers can be combined to create averages. Common examples are the retail price index and the FTSE 100. Changes in the individual price indices then lead to changes in the average indices.

Learning checklist

You should now be able to:

♦ Explain the economic problem of scarcity

♦ Understand the concept of opportunity cost

♦ Explain the difference between microeconomics and macroeconomics

♦ Highlight the differences between market and planned economies

♦ Explain why an understanding of economics is important for business

Questions connect™

1 Explain the concept of opportunity cost.

2 List goods, or services, that compete for your income. Similarly, list activities that compete for your time. In deciding what you will spend your income on and how you will allocate your time, do you minimize your opportunity costs?

3 Consider whether it is ever possible to solve the problem of scarcity.

4 An economy produces two goods, Ferraris and Ray-Ban sunglasses. Using a production possibility frontier, assess what must happen to the production of Ferraris if the production of Ray-Ban sunglasses decreases.

5 The same Ferrari and Ray-Ban economy receives an influx of migrant workers. What do you think will happen to the production possibility frontier for this economy?

6 How does the production possibility frontier illustrate the concept of opportunity cost?

7 Why does the law of diminishing returns require the production possibility frontier to be curved rather than a straight line?

8 Explain the resource allocation mechanism within a market economy and also a planned economy.

9 Using examples, highlight why your own economy is probably best described as a mixed economy.

10 State whether the following relate to macro- or to microeconomics. (a) During the last 12 months average car prices have fallen; (b) inflation for the past 12 months has been 3.5 per cent; (c) strong sales in the housing market have prevented the Bank of England from reducing interest rates.

11 Is the labour market a micro- or macroeconomic topic?

12 Why does business need to understand the functioning of markets?

13 Why does business need to understand the functioning of the economy?

Questions 14 and 15 relate to material within the appendix

14 Which of the following is positive and which is normative? (a) It is in the long-term interest of the UK to be a member of the euro. (b) Will entry into the euro reduce UK inflation?

▶

▶ 15 Using the data listed below, plot house prices on the Y axis and time on the X axis. Is there a positive or a negative relationship between time and house prices? Convert the data series on house prices into an index using 2005 as the base year.

Calculate the percentage increase in house prices for each year.

Year	Average price of a house
2005	£100 000
2006	£120 000
2007	£155 000
2008	£190 000
2009	£170 000
2010	£150 000

Exercises

1 True or false?
 (a) Economics is about human behaviour and so cannot be a science.
 (b) An expansion of the economy's productive capacity would be reflected in an outward movement of the production possibility frontier.
 (c) China is an example of a command economy in which private markets play no part.
 (d) When you make a choice there will always be an opportunity cost.
 (e) 'Firms should operate in the interests of their wider stakeholders' is an example of a normative economic statement.
 (f) Economists assume that business operates in a purely economic environment.

2 In Figure 1.10:

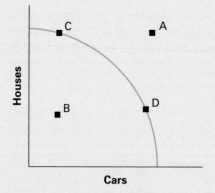

Figure 1.10

(a) Which combination of goods can be produced, with surplus resources being unemployed?
(b) Which combination of goods would represent full employment, with resources mainly allocated to the production of houses?
(c) Which combination of goods cannot currently be achieved?
(d) Which combination of goods represents full employment, with resources mainly allocated to the production of cars?
(e) How might the level of output identified in (c) be achieved in the future?
(f) Can you envisage circumstances under which the production possibility frontier could move to the left?

Note

1   This is true at least at one point in time. In the future, capital could be expanded by firms investing in additional capital.

Section II
Understanding markets

Section contents

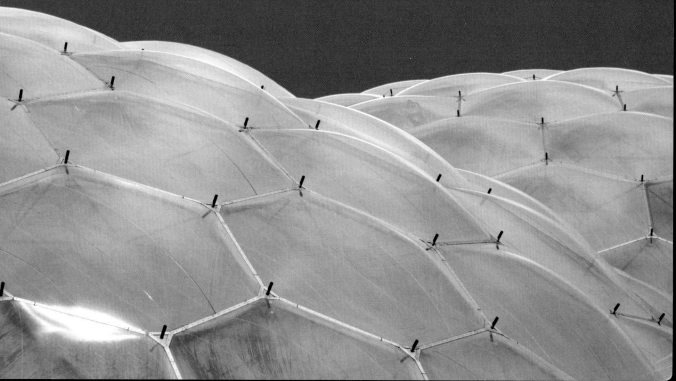

Chapter 2
Consumers in the marketplace

Chapter contents

 Learning outcomes

By the end of this chapter you should understand:

Economic Theory

LO1   Demand curves

LO2   Factors leading to a change in demand

LO3   The price elasticity of demand

LO4   Cross-price and income elasticity

Business Application

LO5   How measures of elasticity can lead to improved management of total revenue

LO6   How an appreciation of consumer surplus can lead to enhanced pricing strategies

Demand theory at a glance

The issue

Setting the price for a product is crucial for the product's and a company's success. But what is the best price for a particular product?

The understanding

As a product becomes more expensive, consumers will begin to demand less. In some markets, consumers will be very sensitive to a change in price. In others, they may not react at all. This reaction is measured using elasticity. An examination of demand theory and the concept of elasticity will develop these ideas more fully.

The usefulness

If the price of the product can be made to rise at a quicker rate than the decline in demand, then total revenue will rise. Therefore, by understanding how consumers respond to price changes we can optimize the price charged.

2.1 Business problem: what is the best price?

What is the best price? The best price is determined by the firm's objectives. The following provides a common list of objectives for a firm:

1 Maximize the amount of profit made by the firm
2 Maximize the market share for the firm's product
3 Maximize the firm's total revenues

These are all commercial objectives. Firms could also adopt non-commercial objectives, such as reducing environmental impact or being a socially responsible employer. But, for the purpose of this chapter, we will concentrate on the three objectives listed above. It is generally not possible for a firm to choose more than one of these objectives. For example, in order to maximize market share, a firm might reasonably be expected to reduce its prices in order to attract more customers. But, by dropping its prices, the firm could be sacrificing profit. Therefore, we will assume that a firm seeks to maximize one of our three objectives[1] and the best price can be defined as the one that enables the firm to meet its preferred objective.

How are prices set? Take the case of supermarkets. When walking around a supermarket have you, as a consumer, ever set the price for a product? The answer is probably no. Now compare the case of supermarkets with buying a house, or a car. When we purchase a house or a car we might make an opening offer to the vendor as part of a negotiation over the price. At the supermarket, by contrast, we would never consider negotiating over a trolley full of shopping; nor would we negotiate in many other types of shop, such as a clothing retailer. Admittedly, we may have an indirect effect on prices by refusing to buy a product that we consider too expensive but in the main it appears that supermarkets, retailers and perhaps even the producers of the products are controlling the prices that we have to pay.

As business students, it is important to recognize the position of product suppliers. This is because control is essential when seeking to set the best price and achieve the firm's objectives.

But herein lies the business problem: what is the best price? To illustrate the problem, consider the following: very high sales can be generated with low prices, while very high prices will tend to generate low sales. But which option is preferable? As an example, we can show that these alternative scenarios can be similar. If a low price of £5 generates ten sales, then total revenue is £50; if a high price of £10 generates only five sales, then total revenue is also £50. Given that these options are identical, a businessperson would really like to know if there is a pricing option of around £8, selling to eight customers, making a total revenue of £64.

Whether £8 is the best price, or indeed whether £8.25 is even better, is a difficult question to address. When a national supermarket chain is selling beer, soap powder or even oven chips by the hundreds of thousands, a small change in the price can generate huge changes in total revenue. By the end of this chapter you will understand how you assist the supermarkets in finding the best price. Every time you pass through the till at the supermarket, scanner data are stored and matched with promotional offers such as 'buy one get one free'. This is then modelled and used to address strategic price changes.

It is clearly important to recognize that firms will price items relative to their cost structures. If a firm wishes to make a profit, then the price must be greater than costs. If the firm wishes to maximize market share, while not making a loss, then the price cannot fall below the cost of making the product. While recognizing the importance of costs, in this chapter we will simply focus on the interaction between pricing and consumers' willingness to buy a particular product. Through Chapters 3, 4 and 5 we will develop a fuller understanding of pricing decisions by recognizing both firms' cost structures and consumers' willingness to purchase. In this chapter, we begin this analysis by developing a clear understanding of demand theory.

2.2 Introducing demand curves

The **demand curve** illustrates the relationship between price and quantity demanded of a particular product.

In attempting to understand consumer behaviour, economists use a very simple construct known as the **demand curve**.

Figure 2.1 is an example of a demand curve, where the line Q_D represents quantity demanded. The slope of the demand curve Q_D is negative. This simply depicts the rather obvious argument that, as prices fall, more of a product will be demanded by consumers. Using our previous

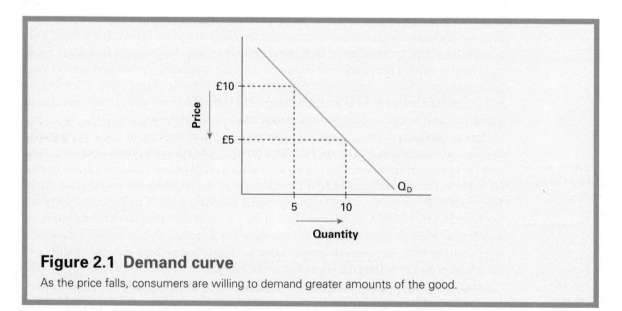

Figure 2.1 Demand curve

As the price falls, consumers are willing to demand greater amounts of the good.

example, at a price of £10 the demand curve indicates that consumers across the market are willing to demand five units in total. But if the company dropped the price to £5, then it might expect to sell ten units.

The negative relationship between price and quantity demanded is often exploited by businesses. For example, Figure 2.1 could be an example of a 'buy one get one free' offer. Firms use such offers because they are sometimes reluctant to reduce the price of their product. This is because overt price reductions could lead to a retaliatory price war from rivals. Lower prices may also provide a signal to the market that the product is of an inferior quality. A 'buy one get one free' offer allows the published price to stay the same, but the effective price for consumers is halved. Under such an offer, consumers are more willing to demand the product and, not surprisingly, companies use such promotions to boost sales and gain market share.

Furthermore, we all like end-of-season sales at our favourite clothing retailers. But sales simply represent an attempt by the retailer to shift stock that we, as consumers, would not buy at the higher price and are, therefore, another example of the demand curve in action.

In Box 2.1 we have a business example of price cutting to attract demand. In this particular case, the price reductions are attracting consumer interest, but are not generating sales. This is because of other factors which all affect demand, including income, the cost and availability of complementary products, and future price expectations. These will all be discussed in the next section.

 Box 2.1 Price cuts fail to put car sales on the fast track

Adapted from an article in the Economic Times, *India, 16 December 2008*

The recent cut in car prices is yet to trigger demand. December, a lacklustre month, saw all the major manufacturers, such as Maruti, Tata Motors, General Motors, Toyota and Ford, offering huge discounts to clear inventory. This was followed by a recent 4 per cent reduction in tax and excise payments.

While enquiries and footfalls have increased over the last week, they have yet to translate into sales. 'Consumers seem to be postponing purchases hoping for some more price reductions,' said a Mumbai-based car dealer.

Industry officials said demand is sluggish owing to lack of financing options, expectations of further price cuts and uncertain consumer sentiment.

2.3 Factors influencing demand

The demand curve shows a negative relationship between price and quantity demanded. But the willingness to buy a product is influenced by more factors than simply price. Therefore, in order to capture these alternative factors, economists make reference to four broad categories:

Substitutes are rival products; for example, a BMW car is a substitute for a Mercedes, or a bottle of wine from France is a substitute for a bottle from Australia.

1 Price of substitutes and complements
2 Consumer income
3 Tastes and preferences
4 Price expectations

Price of substitutes and complements

Substitutes are competing products in the same marketplace, seeking to gain customers from their rivals. So, if French wine producers decided to reduce the price of their wine, they would

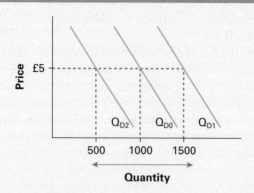

Figure 2.2 Movements in demand

Demand shifts to the left following: (i) a reduction/increase in the price of a substitute/complement product; (ii) a reduction/increase in income if the good is normal/inferior; (iii) a fall in consumers' preferences for the product.

Demand shifts to the right following: (i) an increase/reduction in the price of a substitute/complement product; (ii) an increase/reduction in income if the good is normal/inferior; (iii) an improvement in consumers' preferences for the product.

hope to gain some of the Australian wine producers' customers. As a result, the Australians sell less wine for the same price. This is depicted in Figure 2.2, with the demand curve for Australian wine moving in to the left to Q_{D2} and Australian wine consumption decreasing from 1000 to 500 units at a constant price of £5 per bottle. Clearly, the opposite will also be true. If the French increased their prices, then they might expect to lose customers to the Australians. This would be depicted as a rightward shift in the demand curve, from Q_{D0} to Q_{D1}.

Complements are products that are demanded together. For example, if you buy a car, then you will have to buy petrol. This, therefore, means that the demand for the two products is related. If cars become cheaper, then more cars will be demanded. As a consequence, more petrol will also be demanded. If Figure 2.2 represents demand for petrol, then a reduction in the price of cars will lead to increased demand for cars. This increased demand for cars will lead to a higher demand for petrol. The demand curve for petrol will shift to the right from Q_{D0} to Q_{D1}, with more petrol being demanded at the existing price of £5 per gallon.

> **Complements** are products that are purchased jointly. Beer and kebabs would be a youthful and modern example; another would be cars and petrol.

Consumer income

> **Normal goods** are demanded more when consumer income increases and less when income falls.
>
> **Inferior goods** are demanded more when income levels fall and demanded less when income levels rise.

In understanding the effect of income on demand, we need to distinguish between **normal** and **inferior goods**.

If we consider Australian wine to be a normal good, as income increases we buy more. Then, in terms of Figure 2.2, when income increases, the demand curve for Australian wine shifts right to Q_{D1} and more is demanded at every possible price. However, during a recession, when incomes are likely to fall, consumers will cut back on wine and the demand curve shifts left to Q_{D2}.

Inferior goods tend to be those characterized as cheaper brands – products that we stop purchasing once our income rises and we move to more normal types of goods. Inferior does not necessarily mean that the product has a lower quality than a normal good. Rather, we consume less when incomes fall and vice versa.

Think about the things you buy at the supermarket as a poor indebted student and the things your parents buy as significant income earners. You will tend to be buying inferior types of goods, such as supermarkets' own-label items. Your parents will be buying normal types of goods, such as branded lines in bread, alcohol and frozen foods. In terms of Figure 2.2, as income rises, the demand curve for an inferior good would shift left to Q_{D2}. When income falls, the demand curve for an inferior good would shift right to Q_{D1}. In brief, the behaviour of the demand curve for normal goods is opposite to that of inferior goods.

In Box 2.2 the effect of the global recession and the complementary effect of less credit are discussed in relation to the demand for private jets.

 ### Box 2.2 Business-jet makers to cut production

Adapted from an article in The Economist, *10 November 2008*

Weakening global economic growth is starting to hit production plans at leading business-jet makers as new order volumes shrink and corporate and private flyers reduce activity. Cessna is cutting its planned production by more than 10 per cent. Hawker Beechcraft is cutting 500 jobs.

'Due to the unprecendented worldwide economic decline . . . events have had a serious impact on the global business climate and represent a serious risk to general aviation. The decline in wealth and available credit directly affect our customers' ability to purchase new aircraft,' said Jim Schuster, head of Hawker Beechcraft.

© The Economist Newspaper Limited, London 2009

Tastes and preferences

Tastes and preferences reflect consumers' attitudes towards particular products. Over time, these tastes and preferences are likely to change. Fashion is an obvious example: what might be popular this year will be out of fashion next year. Technological development might be another. Mobile phones capable of sending images and connecting to the Internet are becoming increasingly popular. We can survive quite well without such technology but, through advertising, companies try to influence our tastes and preferences for such advanced capabilities.

In order to represent a positive improvement in tastes and preference for a product, in Figure 2.2 the demand curve would shift right to Q_{D1}, with more products being sold at any given price, while a reduction in consumer backing for a product would lead to a leftward shift in the demand curve, with less being sold at any given price. For example, in recent times flat-screen, high-definition televisions have begun to replace cathode-ray televisions, reflecting changed tastes and preferences for flat-screen technologies and, therefore, lower demand for cathode-ray televisions at all prices.

The role of advertising

Advertising can play at least one of two roles in demand theory. First, it provides consumers with information about products. Advertising informs consumers that new products have arrived on the market, that a product has new features, or that a product is being offered at a lower price. In this way, advertising plays a very valuable informational role for firms and for consumers. Demand for products increases simply because consumers are informed about the nature and availability of the product. Therefore, when advertising plays an informational role, the demand curve for the product shifts out to Q_{D1} as more consumers become informed about the existence of the product.

There is, however, another role for advertising. If adverts are simply about informing consumers about the existence of products, why are they played repeatedly over very long periods of time? Moreover, why do product suppliers hire well-known celebrities to appear in their adverts? How many adverts do you see on the television, or in the press, that provide information about the product's characteristics, price or availability? Advertising is also about trying to change consumers' tastes and preferences. We all know that mobile phones are capable of sending pictures and video, so why would we be interested in knowing that celebrities use such technology? We all know that a Swiss watch looks good and can keep reasonable time, so why would we be interested in knowing which celebrities wear such watches? One possible answer is that the product provider is not simply selling a product. Instead, they are selling you a desirable lifestyle. We do buy technologically advanced mobile phones because they are useful; but we also buy such phones because we believe that they say something positive about who we are. By emphasizing these less tangible aspects of a product, it is possible to build additional differentiation into the product. Two mobile phones might provide the same functions, but only one is used by a world-class footballer. Accordingly, advertising is not simply about informing consumers about what they *can* buy; it is also about informing them about what they *should* buy. Whether advertising is providing information, or developing consumers' tastes and preferences, the overriding aim is to shift the demand curve from Q_{D0} to Q_{D1}, while at the same time shifting the competitors' demand curves from Q_{D0} to Q_{D2}.

Price expectations

If you expect prices to fall in the future, then it may be wise to wait and delay your purchase. For example, recently launched computers, televisions and DVD systems are often sold in the market at premium prices. Within three to six months, newer models are brought out and the old versions are then sold at lower prices. If you do not have a taste or preference for cutting-edge technology, you can cut back on consumption today in the expectation that prices will fall in the future. In terms of our demand curves, if we expect prices to fall in the future, then demand today will be reduced, shifting back to Q_{D2}. But the demand curve for three to six months' time will shift right to Q_{D1}.

> **Price expectations** are beliefs about how prices in the future will differ from prices today.

Opposite **price expectations** can also be true. It is possible to believe that in the future prices will rise. Property may be more expensive in the future, share prices might increase or oil will be more expensive in six months' time. Therefore, if you expect prices to rise in the future, you are likely to bring your consumption forward and purchase now. In terms of our demand curves, your demand for now shifts out to Q_{D1}, but your demand in the future shifts back to Q_{D2}.

We now understand that the demand for a product is influenced by (i) its own price, (ii) the price of substitutes and complements, (iii) the level of consumer income, (iv) consumers' tastes and preferences, and (v) price expectations. We are now in a position to introduce the **law of demand**.

> The **law of demand** states that, *ceteris paribus*, as the price of a product falls, more will be demanded.
>
> *Ceteris paribus* means all other things being equal.

Accordingly, as long as (ii) the price of substitutes and complements, (iii) the level of consumer income, (iv) consumers' tastes and preferences, and (v) price expectations remain constant, there must be a negative relationship between price and quantity demanded.

Do higher prices attract higher demand?

The negative relationship between price and quantity demanded can cause students and business managers problems. For example, designer clothes and perfumes would not be purchased if they were cheap. So, does a positive relationship exist between price and willingness to demand luxury items? While it remains an appealing idea, the answer to this question is still no, since all products have a negative demand curve. This is because even when you are very rich you still have a budget constraint.

Assume you are fortunate to have an annual expense account of £500 000. Your designer clothes cost £300 000 per year, champagne is another £100 000 and the private jet another

£100 000. If your favourite designer suddenly increases their prices by £50 000, you are faced with a choice. If you continue to buy the same quantity of clothes, they will now cost £350 000, and you will have to cut back on the champagne and the jet. Alternatively, you could cut back on your clothes and maintain the same amount of champagne and the private jet. However, most probably you will reduce some of your demand for designer clothes, perhaps buying fewer clothes at the higher price of £325 000, as opposed to the £350 000 it would cost to buy the same quantity as last year. The extra £25 000 might come from reducing your flights and the amount of champagne that you drink.

It is important to understand, from the example above, that higher prices for one product limit how much money you can spend on *all* goods and services that you like to consume. The demand curve for designer clothes should have a negative slope, because you will decrease the quantity of clothes purchased in order to retain consumption of the champagne and jet travel.

Therefore, for luxury items, how do we explain the positive relationship between price and quantity demanded? Some consumers prefer products that have an element of exclusivity. A high price not only ensures exclusivity, but also signals that the product is special. A low price would not create the same image. Therefore, the high price attracts particular consumers into the market. This leads to the demand curve shifting out to the right in Figure 2.2 and means that the positive relationship between price and quantity is associated with a change in tastes and preferences. As such, the positive relationship of price and demand is best described as a shift of the demand curve, rather than a movement along the curve.

These points are picked up in Figure 2.3, with product providers such as Louis Vuitton keen to avoid their product being sold at discount prices. The high price of the product and the

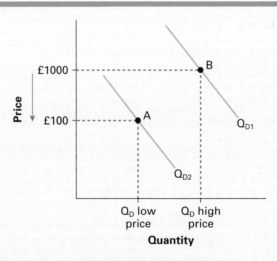

Figure 2.3 Demand for Louis Vuitton

Q_{D1} and Q_{D2} are the demand curves for Louis Vuitton bags. Under Q_{D1}, stores are not allowed to sell Louis Vuitton bags at discount prices, while under Q_{D2}, they are able to sell them at discounted prices. Consumers with a taste and preference for expensive and exclusive bags are willing to buy bags at £1000. But once discounting by stores makes Louis Vuitton bags become cheap and not exclusive, consumers are less willing to buy bags. Demand shifts from Q_{D1} to Q_{D2} and fewer bags are purchased. The reason we sometimes think there is a positive relationship between price and willingness to demand is because we only focus on points A and B. If we joined up these two points, we would see a positive relationship between price and quantity demanded. But this is a mistake, as we really need to focus on the shifts in the demand curves reflecting a change in tastes and preferences.

distribution of the product through licensed clothing retailers is deliberately managed in a way to promote the product's high-quality image. Consumers' tastes and preferences have been developed by Louis Vuitton to the extent that consumers expect Louis Vuitton bags to be expensive and more exclusive than cheaper alternatives. Louis Vuitton will be concerned to protect the high-price image of its product, fearful that a low price would have a detrimental effect on consumers' tastes and preferences. The demand curve for Louis Vuitton will shift to the left, reducing the number of bags sold.

In Figure 2.3, Q_{D1} represents the demand for Louis Vuitton handbags among consumers who have a strong taste and preference for expensive and exclusive bags. At a price of £1000, demand is Q_D. Q_{D2} is the demand for Louis Vuitton among consumers who do not have a strong taste and preference for expensive and exclusive bags. We can see that, at a price of £1000, none of these consumers will buy – the line from £1000 does not touch Q_{D2}. However, at a discounted price of £100, consumers represented by Q_{D2} are willing to buy Louis Vuitton. The demand curves Q_{D1} and Q_{D2} both have a negative slope. However, if we were to focus mistakenly on points A and B, and draw a line connecting the two points, then we might be led to believe that increases in price lead to increases in demand. This would be a mistake, because it is the differing tastes and preferences for cheap and exclusive brands that lead to the shift between the two points A and B.

2.4 **Measuring the responsiveness of demand**

You have been introduced to the demand curve and the factors that cause demand to shift. However, for the businessperson it is not enough to know that the demand for a product is determined by (i) its own price, (ii) the price of substitutes and complements, (iii) the level of consumer income, (iv) consumers' tastes and preferences, and (v) expectations regarding future prices. As a person in the marketplace making real pricing decisions, the businessperson needs to know the impact of price changes on the quantity demanded.

> **Elasticity** is a measure of the responsiveness of demand to a change in price.

Figure 2.4 provides an illustration of **elasticity**. In Figure 2.4a, a small change in the price leads to a much bigger change in the quantity demanded. But in Figure 2.4b, a very large change in the price leads to a small change in the quantity demanded. So, we might say that in

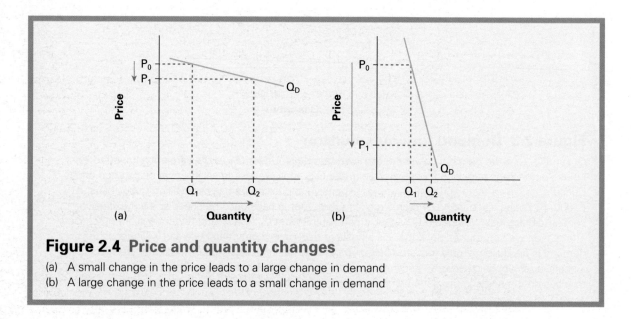

Figure 2.4 **Price and quantity changes**

(a) A small change in the price leads to a large change in demand
(b) A large change in the price leads to a small change in demand

Figure 2.4a demand is responsive to a change in price, while in Figure 2.4b demand is not very responsive to a change in price.

Businesses use elasticity ideas to formulate and perhaps even fund price wars. See Box 2.3.

 Box 2.3 Supermarkets' PR-driven food price wars

Adapted from an article by Richard Fletcher in The Daily Telegraph, *11 July 2008*

According to the hype, we are on the verge of 'an all-out supermarket price war'. Despite all the noise in recent years, the recent Competition Commission report into the grocery sector reported that operating margins for both supermarkets and suppliers have remained remarkably stable over the last seven years.

So what is going on? Okay, supermarkets and suppliers can offset the cost of some of the price cuts with savings, but if they really have slashed the hundreds of millions of pounds off prices that they claim to, surely we would have seen some hit on margins?

According to the anecdotes, there are numerous tricks of the trade. Take, for example, a price-cutting campaign launched by one supermarket of £30 million worth of cuts. But data passed to me at the time by a rival suggested that, although the supermarket had slashed the prices of low-volume goods, it had increased the prices of best-sellers. For example, the price of its four-pack own-brand baked beans rose from 69p to 78p. Selling more than 13 million packs a year, this price rise alone saved the company more than £1 million. In the same week, the supermarket cut the price of L'Oreal ginger hair colouring by 2p – a move that could have cost it as little as £200.

The net effect – claimed the rival – was that rather than cutting prices by £30 million, the supermarket had in fact profited to the tune of several million pounds.

© Telegraph Media Group Limited 2008

Determinants of elasticity

The elasticity of a product is determined by a number of factors:

1 Number of substitutes
2 Time
3 Definition of the market

Substitutes

As the number of substitutes increases, the more elastic will be demand. For example, if a product has no substitutes and the supplier decides to increase its prices, then consumers cannot switch to a cheaper alternative. Therefore, when the price increases for this product, demand will only fall by a small amount. In contrast, when a product has a very large number of substitutes, its price elasticity will be very high. If the price of the product increases, consumers will very quickly switch to the cheaper alternatives. Cigarettes – and, more importantly, nicotine as an addictive drug – have few, if any, substitutes. Therefore, if the price of cigarettes increases, then few smokers will quit cigarettes. Alternatively, in the market for mobile tele-communications, with many competing suppliers, if one provider reduces its prices, then there will be a rapid change in demand, with consumers switching to the cheapest provider.

Time

Time is also important, as it is likely to influence the development and introduction of sub-stitutes. Initially, new products or markets will only have a small number of substitutes. Only if these products are successful will new entrants come into the market and begin to compete.

Therefore, in the early periods of a new market, demand is likely to be inelastic, but in the long term, as more products enter the market, demand is likely to become more elastic. For example, the launch of alcoholic drinks for the youth market, mixing alcoholic drinks with soft drinks, started with a small number of product offerings. As sales in the market have grown, the number of competing products has also increased.

Market definition

Market definitions are also important when measuring elasticity. The demand for beer is relatively unresponsive to a change in price. As the price of beer increases, consumers still continue to buy beer, because they perhaps view wine as a poor alternative. In contrast, the demand for a particular brand of beer is likely to be price responsive. This is because all the separate beer brands are competitive substitutes. So, if one brand becomes more expensive, it is likely that drinkers will switch to the cheaper alternatives.

Measuring elasticity

Mathematically, economists can measure elasticity, or the responsiveness of demand to a change in price, using the following formulae.

Formulae for elasticity

$$1 \quad \varepsilon = \frac{\text{Percentage change in quantity demanded}}{\text{Percentage change in price}}$$

$$2 \quad \frac{\text{Change in quantity demanded}}{\text{Change in price}} \times \frac{\text{Price}}{\text{Quantity demanded}}$$

The value of ε for elasticity will lie between zero and infinity $(0 < \varepsilon < \infty)$.[2] This is a very large number range, so economists break the range down into regions that they can describe and utilize. Using the first formula, each of these regions is described in Table 2.1.

We will begin with an easy example. If the price of cigarettes increased by 10 per cent, how many smokers would cut back on the number of cigarettes smoked? Many smokers would

Table 2.1 Important elasticity measures

	Percentage change in price	Percentage change in demand	Numerical calculations	Elasticity value	Description
1	10	0	$\frac{0}{10} = 0$	$\varepsilon = 0$	Perfectly inelastic
2	10	5	$\frac{5}{10} = \frac{1}{2}$	$\varepsilon < 1$	Inelastic demand
3	10	10	$\frac{10}{10} = 1$	$\varepsilon = 1$	Unit elasticity
4	10	20	$\frac{20}{10} = 2$	$\varepsilon > 1$	Elastic demand
5	10	Infinitely large		$\varepsilon = \infty$	Perfectly elastic

Where elasticity ε < 1, demand is described as **inelastic**, or a change in the price will lead to a proportionately smaller change in the quantity demanded. When ε = 1, demand has **unit elasticity**, or demand is equally responsive to a change in price. Where ε > 1, demand is described as **elastic**, or demand is responsive to a change in price. **Perfectly elastic demand** exists when ε = ∞. In other words, demand is very responsive to a change in price.

continue smoking. In an extreme situation, a 10 per cent change in the price of cigarettes could lead to no change in the quantity demanded. (In reality this would not happen, but the example provides a reasonable description of a theoretical extreme.)

In economic terms, demand is said to be perfectly inelastic when ε = 0; that is, demand does not respond to a change in price. This is detailed in the first row of Table 2.1.

Clearly, *perfectly inelastic demand* is an extreme situation. So, in the second row of Table 2.1, we consider the situation where a 10 per cent change in the price leads to a 5 per cent change in demand.

The demand for Coca-Cola may well be **inelastic**. If Coke increased its prices by 10 per cent we might expect it to lose a small, rather than large, number of customers. So, demand is not very responsive to a change in price.

In row 3, we have the situation where a 10 per cent change in the price leads to a 10 per cent change in the quantity demanded – **unit elasticity**.

In row 4, we consider the situation where a 10 per cent change in the price leads to a much bigger change in quantity demanded, in this case 20 per cent, resulting in **elastic demand**.

Consider the price of mobile phone contracts; nearly all competing networks offer very similar menus and prices. One of the reasons for this is because demand is reasonably elastic. If one company raised its prices, then over time many of its subscribers would switch to another network. Therefore, similar prices are offered because each network recognizes that demand is responsive to price differences.

Finally, in row 5, we consider **perfectly elastic demand**. In this case, the change in price is 10 per cent and, in response, demand changes by a very large amount. The London financial markets come close to a situation of perfectly elastic demand. If the market price of shares in Shell is £10, then you can sell all of your holdings at £10. But if you offered to sell at £10.01, you would not sell a single share, as potential buyers would move to the many other sellers offering to sell at £10.

Elasticity and the slope of the demand curve

We mentioned above that the slope of the demand curve is only an indication of how elastic demand is. In fact, we can now show that the elasticity of demand changes all the way along a particular demand curve. We will do this by using the second formula for elasticity (see Figure 2.5).

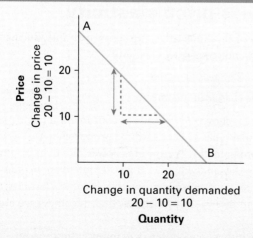

(2) Elasticity = (Change in demand/Change in price) × (Price/Quantity)

The change in price equals 10 and the change in quantity demanded also equals 10

At A the price is so high, quantity demanded is zero, so:

elasticity at A = (10/10) × (P/0) = ∞

At B the price is 0, and the quantity demanded is very high, so:

elasticity at B = (10/10) × (0/Q) = 0

Figure 2.5 Elasticity changes along the demand curve

During a basic maths course you will have been told that, to measure the slope of a line, you need to draw a triangle next to the line. The slope, or gradient, of the line is then the change in the vertical distance divided by the change in the horizontal distance. In our case, the gradient is the change in price (the vertical) divided by the change in quantity demanded (the horizontal). For our second formula we need the 'inverse' of the slope; that is, we need the change in quantity demanded (horizontal) divided by the change in price (vertical). But what we can say is that the slope of the line is constant, so the inverse of the slope is also constant. We have measured the slope and the inverse in the middle of the line and it is equal to 10/10 = 1. In fact, in our example, because the slope is constant, it does not matter where we measure the slope – it is always 10/10 = 1.

We can now calculate the elasticity of demand at two special points, A and B. At A, the demand line just touches the vertical axis. The price is so high that demand is zero. At B, the demand line just touches the horizontal axis. The price is zero and demand is very high.

Using our second formula for elasticity, at A the elasticity is:

$(10/10) \times (\text{price}/0) = \text{infinity} = \infty$

Because at A the demand is zero, the elasticity of demand must be infinite. We know that this means that demand is perfectly elastic.

The elasticity at B is:

$(10/10) \times (\text{quantity demanded}/0) = 0$

Because at B the price is zero, the elasticity of demand must be zero. We know that this means that demand is perfectly inelastic.

Therefore, all the way along the demand curve the elasticity changes from being perfectly elastic to perfectly inelastic, even though the slope has remained constant. This is because the elasticity of demand is influenced by the slope of the demand line *and* by the ratio of price and quantity demanded. When the price is very high, a small reduction in the price will generate a proportionately bigger change in demand. But when the price is very low, a small change will not generate a proportionately bigger change in demand.

In simple terms, consumers react to price reductions when a product is very expensive. But they are less motivated by price reductions when a product is already very cheap. Therefore, demand is more elastic at higher prices than at lower ones.

2.5 Income and cross-price elasticity

Income elasticity measures the responsiveness of demand to a change in income.

Cross-price elasticity measures the responsiveness of demand to a change in the price of a substitute or complement.

Before considering the application of this knowledge, it is also worth introducing you to two related measures: **income elasticity** and **cross-price elasticity**.

$$\text{Income elasticity} = Y_\varepsilon = \frac{\text{Percentage change in demand}}{\text{Percentage change in income}}$$

For normal goods, income elasticity is above zero because as consumers' income rises, say during an economic boom, more normal types of goods will be produced. If $Y_\varepsilon < 1$, the product is described as income inelastic, or demand will grow at a slower rate than income; while, if $Y_\varepsilon > 1$, demand is income elastic, or demand will grow at a faster rate than income. The recent UK and US housing booms were a reflection of positive income elasticity, with consumers being more willing to spend money on property as their incomes increased within a prosperous economy.

For inferior goods, income elasticity lies between zero and minus infinity because, as incomes rise, consumers buy fewer inferior goods. This time demand is income inelastic if Y_ε lies between zero and −1, or is income elastic if Y_ε is smaller than −1, e.g. −5.

$$\text{Cross-price elasticity} = XY_\varepsilon = \frac{\text{Percentage change in demand of product X}}{\text{Percentage change in the price of product Y}}$$

If X and Y are substitutes or rivals, then, as the price of Y increases, the demand for X will increase, so XY_ε for substitutes lies between zero and plus infinity. If X and Y are complements, then, as the price of Y becomes more expensive, less X will also be purchased; XY_ε must lie between zero and minus infinity.

In Box 2.4 we have examples of price, cross-price and income elasticity for bus travel. With a price elasticity of demand equal to 0.1, demand is price inelastic. A drop in prices would not generate many more bus travellers. A cross-price elasticity of +0.3 indicates that buses and cars are substitutes and, since the value is less than 1, the relationship is inelastic. Therefore, even if cars became more expensive few drivers would opt for buses instead. The income elasticity of −2.4 suggests that bus travel is an inferior good and highly income elastic. Therefore, even a small rise in income will cause bus travellers to cut their demand for bus travel, and perhaps move to car travel.

 Box 2.4 Elasticity measures for bus travel

Price elasticity	(−) 0.1
Cross-price elasticity (with cars)	+0.3
Income elasticity	−2.4

2.6 Business application: Pricing Strategies I – exploiting elasticities

Finding the best price was this chapter's business problem. After introducing demand theory and the concept of elasticity, we are now able to return to this particular problem.

Cost-plus pricing

A rather simple approach to pricing is to simply take the costs of producing the product and add a mark-up, such as 30 per cent. This might cover some stray, unaccounted-for costs and also the required profit margin. The benefit of this approach lies in its computational simplicity, only requiring a basic idea of costs and a grasp of a desirable profit margin. It may also appear to be fair. Who would begrudge a firm asking for a 30 per cent mark-up? After all, they are taking a risk and they should be able to generate a decent financial return.

Unfortunately, while appealing, cost-plus pricing neglects almost everything we have introduced you to in this chapter. That is, it fails to take account of consumers' willingness to demand. There is no guarantee that consumers will be willing to buy your product when the mark-up is 30 per cent. Alternatively, 30 per cent may not be a sufficiently high mark-up. Consumers may exhibit a very keen preference for your product and a low elasticity of demand. While 30 per cent appears fair, you might be able to gain good sales volumes with a mark-up of 50–100 per cent. It therefore appears that we need also to consider demand theory when setting prices.

'Buy one get one free' – discounting or price experiment?

In simple terms, the need to find the best price stems from a broader need to generate revenues. At the beginning of this chapter, in the business problem example, it was suggested that, at a price of £5, we might sell ten units, making £50 of revenue. But, at a price of £8, we might sell eight units, making a total revenue of £64. This looks like a better option. But how can we be sure that moving from £5 to £8 is a good idea? We might have ended up selling only six units, making a total revenue of only £48 (see Table 2.2).

Price elasticity measures the response of demand to a change in price. We face two outcomes when changing the price: demand falls to eight or six units. Falling from ten to eight units is a small response to a change in price or, in our new terminology, demand is inelastic. But when demand falls to six units, the response is much bigger and demand can be described as elastic. But what happens to total revenues? When demand is inelastic, total revenues have increased to £64. But when demand is price elastic, total revenues have fallen to £48. We can expand upon these simple ideas using Figure 2.6.

In Figure 2.6a, we have a price elastic demand curve. So, at a price of P_0, we can expect to sell Q_0 units. Therefore, **total revenue** is represented by the rectangle defined by P_0 and Q_0.

> **Total revenue is price multiplied by number of units sold.**

If we drop the price to P_1, then sales increase to Q_1 and total revenue is now equal to the new rectangle defined by P_1 and Q_1.

The impact of a price reduction on total revenue is the difference in size between the two rectangles. By selling at a lower price, we lose some total revenue. For example, if we were selling at £10 and now we are only asking for £8, we are losing £2 per unit. But by reducing the price we will also gain some total revenue by selling to more customers – in this example, Q_1 as opposed to Q_0 customers. Hence, when demand is price elastic, selling at a lower price will boost total revenues. In contrast, if we examine the case of inelastic demand in Figure 2.6b, we see that reducing the price leads to a drop in total revenues.

We now have economic guidance for business. If demand is elastic, then dropping prices raises total revenues; but if demand is inelastic, prices should be increased in order to increase total revenues.

If we return to our business problem, the best price occurs when price elasticity equals 1, which is exactly in between the elastic and inelastic region. With unit elasticity, a 10 per cent increase in the price leads to a 10 per cent change in quantity demanded. Total revenue does not change; the maximum has been found.

Admittedly, firms may not always target a price elasticity equal to 1. They may not have revenue maximization as their objective. They may wish to maximize market share or profits. Changing the price involves the development of new pricing plans and the communication of price changes to retailers of the product. As a result, change can be costly and not offset by improvements in revenue. Change can also represent a risk. Competitors could react to your

Table 2.2 Total revenue

Price	Quantity	Total revenue
£5	10	£50
£8	8	£64
£8	6	£48

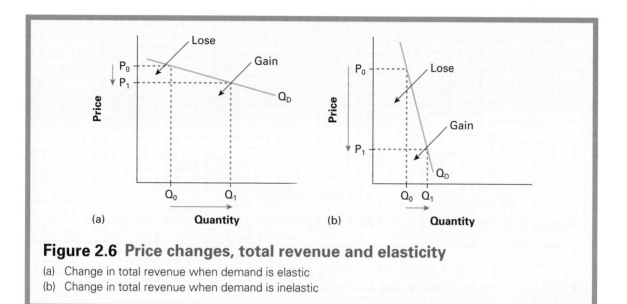

Figure 2.6 Price changes, total revenue and elasticity

(a)   Change in total revenue when demand is elastic
(b)   Change in total revenue when demand is inelastic

price changes. A reduction in your price could lead to a price war, which you may not find attractive. Furthermore, you may not fully understand the price elasticity of demand for your product. If you consider the demand for your product to be elastic, you should think about reducing your price. But if you have got it wrong and demand is inelastic, your revenues will fall, not rise. It is, therefore, important to understand how you might measure your elasticity of demand.

Elastic or inelastic?

Cigarettes were used as an example of inelastic demand and mobile phone networks as an example of elastic demand. Cigarettes have few substitutes: if all cigarettes become expensive, smokers will not switch to another type of vice, as there are few sources of nicotine. If one telephone network increases its prices, however, mobile phone users can switch to the cheaper networks. It is the level of competition for a product that influences its elasticity.

The level of competition provides an indication of how elastic demand is. However, if we wish to target unit elasticity we will need a measure of how far our current pricing is from this best price. To find the best price we need to gather data that will enable the demand curve for our product to be plotted, or mathematically modelled.

Once we have a demand curve, we can see the relationship between price and quantity and measure the elasticity of demand at various prices. Unfortunately the data required for a demand curve is difficult to find. Ideally, an experiment should occur where the price of a product is changed and the effect on demand noted, but product suppliers are not keen to change the price of the product to see what happens to the demand. Indeed, if they raise the price they are likely to lose customers to a rival brand. Recognizing this problem, market researchers can make use of promotional exercises. For example, a 'buy one get one free' offer is basically a 50 per cent discount in the market. A 'buy two get the third free' offer is a 33 per cent discount. When you buy a product at the supermarket, so-called 'scanner data' are created. Therefore, for any given period of time the supermarket knows how much soap powder was sold and what discounts were on offer. Market research companies make it their business to buy scanner data from a large selection of supermarkets across the country. They then use this

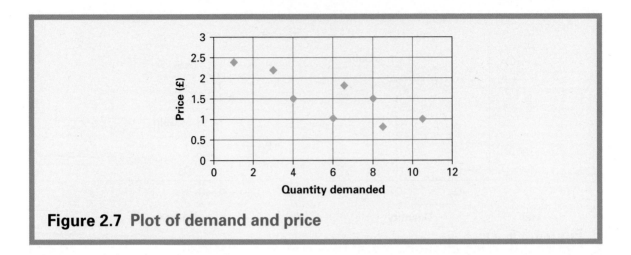

Figure 2.7 Plot of demand and price

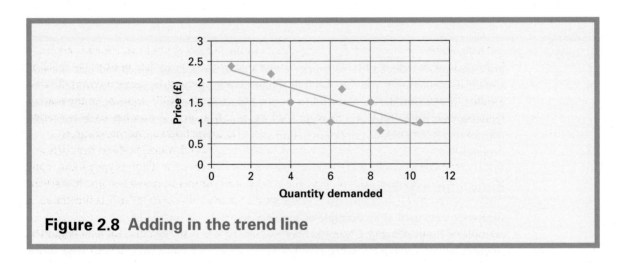

Figure 2.8 Adding in the trend line

to advise companies on pricing, because by using the data on sales and promotional discounts they can begin to estimate the elasticity of demand. For each price at which the product is sold, the market researchers also note down how many units of the product are sold at the tills. They then plot this as in Figure 2.7. The plot shows a negative relationship between price and quantity demanded. To smooth out this relationship the researchers then use a computer to calculate the trend line, as in Figure 2.8. The trend line is in fact the demand curve that we have been using throughout this chapter.

By using mathematical techniques known as econometrics, the trend line can be analysed and manipulated to provide an estimate of the price elasticity of demand. Knowing that unit elasticity is optimal, product managers can then make an informed decision about whether to raise or lower prices. In your working life you are unlikely ever to calculate the elasticity of demand for a product, but being able to understand the concept will be very important.

Product life cycle and pricing

The preceding discussion analysing elasticity and total revenue for the most part neglects the time-varying nature of competition and elasticity. When a new and innovative product emerges

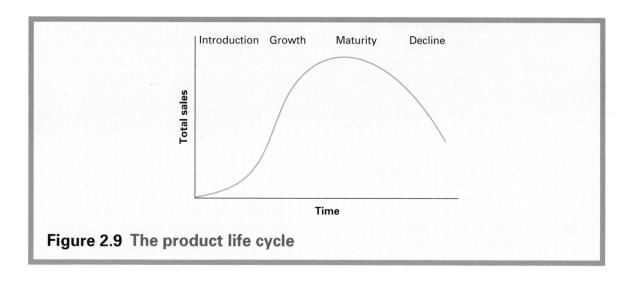

Figure 2.9 The product life cycle

onto the market, it faces very few competitors. In the technology industry, BlackBerry was a leader in bringing email, Internet and telecommunications to the mobile market. But this lead was quickly chased down by Apple and its iPhone. While, in the automobile industry, Renault was the first to convert a Mégane into a Scénic and create the MPV segment of the market. Citroën soon followed with a Picasso, Ford has a C Max and Toyota has its Verso range. Successful innovation spawns imitation and aggressive competition as the market grows.

Eventually consumers will become tired of old designs and concepts. Newer models and ideas will emerge and sales will track the latest fashion. Demand for iPhone-type products and MPVs will fall, competitors will leave the market and competition will become less severe. These arguments are captured in the concept of a product life cycle, which is illustrated in Figure 2.9.

Successful products go through four phases of the product life cycle: introduction, growth, maturity and decline. (Unsuccessful products never pass introduction.) At each stage of the product life cycle the number of competitors is different. This leads to differing substitutability and differing elasticities of demand for the products.

Pricing at launch

In the introduction stage, an innovative product is likely to be unique and face few, if any, competitors. For early adopters who wish to be seen with the latest technology, demand will be price inelastic. Firms could, therefore, seek to price high in order to capture the high demand from this set of consumers.

Pricing during growth

In the growth phase, companies who have witnessed the success of the innovative product also join the market. This increases competition and substitutability and increases the elasticity of demand. Recognizing the inverse relationship between price and consumers' willingness to demand, firms can seek to gain a dominant position by cutting prices in the hope of gaining market share. Under this strategy firms are trading a revenue-maximizing strategy for a sales-maximizing strategy. This could be temporary: maximizing sales and market coverage in the short run and winning the hearts and minds of customers, only to then exploit this commercial position in the long run with a strategy which maximizes revenues.

Pricing during maturity

The ferocity of competition is most acute during the mature phase of the cycle, sales are at a peak and the market can be supplied by the largest number of competitors. The potential for a high degree of price elasticity in the mature phase of the cycle provides a basic rationale for the sales-maximization strategy during the growth phase – gain market share, cut out competition or face the consequences of merciless price competition in the mature phase of the cycle. High price elasticity means little control over pricing, as competitive pressures force the price down to the lowest possible level.

Pricing during decline

In the decline phase of the market, consumers will begin to leave the market. In response some firms will also exit, seeking better commercial opportunities elsewhere. Competition will fall and the degree of price sensitivity among consumers will diminish. Firms remaining in the market will see the elasticity of demand begin to become more inelastic, and an element of price stability, and hopefully price rises might occur. Therefore, throughout the product life cycle the pricing strategy has to be reactive to the changing competitive nature of the market.

2.7 Business application: Pricing Strategies II – extracting consumer surplus

Consumer surplus – the island of lost profits

> **Consumer surplus** is the difference between the price you are charged for a product and the maximum price that you would have been willing to pay.

Here is a true but curious thought: when you buy a product you are nearly always willing to pay *more* for it. This is the concept of **consumer surplus**.

For example, you may have been willing to pay £750 for a flight to Australia, but you manage to find a flight for £500. Your consumer surplus is £250.

Figure 2.10 illustrates the idea of consumer surplus using the demand curve. You are charged £500, but you are willing to pay £750. Indeed, in the market there may be some consumers who would be willing to pay even more than you. The entire amount of consumer surplus in the market is the area under the demand line down to the price charged of £500. This area represents the amount each consumer would be willing to pay in excess of the price charged.

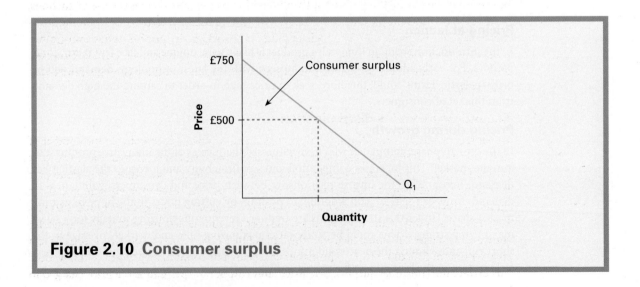

Figure 2.10 Consumer surplus

Consumer surplus represents a benefit for consumers, but clearly for a firm it represents missed profits, because you were willing to pay £750 and were only charged £500. This is not good. So, as a businessperson, how do you discover a consumer's true willingness to pay and charge them accordingly?

Price discrimination

In order for a firm to extract consumer surplus, it needs to undertake **price discrimination** – the act of charging different consumers different prices for the same good. For price discrimination to be successful, three conditions must exist. First, the firm must have some control over its prices: it therefore cannot face a perfectly elastic demand line. Economists refer to this as having some degree of market power in setting prices. Second, the firm must be capable of identifying different groups of consumers who are willing to pay different prices. Third, resale of the good or service must be prohibited. If it isn't, a consumer who buys at a low price can then sell to a consumer who is willing to buy at a high price. The profits from price discrimination then flow to the consumer, rather than the firm. Economists identify first-, second- and third-degree price discrimination.

> **Price discrimination** is the act of charging different prices to different consumers for an identical good or service.

First-degree price discrimination

Under first-degree price discrimination, each consumer is charged exactly what they are willing to pay for the good or service. This is unlikely to work in practice because it would involve each customer freely admitting to the top price that they would be willing to pay. For example, an airline might line up all of its passengers and ask them to write on a large card the price they would be willing to pay to fly on the aircraft. The passengers would then be admitted onto the aircraft in price order. Highest first, lowest last. Those who bid too low may not fly if the aircraft is full. However, passengers might not write a truthful price and why should they? In addition, the entire process is very costly in terms of time and administration to carry out.

First-degree price discrimination is therefore seen to be difficult to carry out in practice. Instead, a seller looks for cues or signals of a consumer's willingness to pay. For example, a builder, plumber or electrician might charge for work based on the type of car parked on the drive. Car sales people are trained to look at items worn by a potential buyer, such as the watch, coat, clothes and even areas where they live. These all provide reasonable, but imperfect, signals of someone's ability to pay and perhaps willingness to pay. Finally, there is the use of auctions, where each potential buyer is forced to bid for an item. In bidding, each buyer is communicating their willingness to pay. The highest bidder wins when the price is above every other bidder's willingness to pay – that is, every other bidder has no consumer surplus. However, auctions are costly to organize, only one sale at a time occurs and there is no guarantee that bidders will attend.

Second-degree price discrimination

Under second-degree price discrimination, consumers are charged according to the number of units they buy. For example, gas, electricity and telephones tend to be offered under two-part tariffs. The first part is a fixed element to cover the cost of the infrastructure. The second part covers the cost of using additional units of electricity gas, etc. If the fixed element is £10 per month and each unit costs £0.1, then a user of 100 units a month is charged £10 + (100 × £0.1) = £20. Taking account of the fixed element, the cost per unit is £20/100 = £0.2. Now consider someone who uses 200 units: their monthly bill is £10 + (200 × £0.1) = £30, which equates to a cost per unit of £30/200 = £0.15. The higher user gains a discount of 25 per cent. But how does this extract the consumer surplus? The listed unit cost of £0.1 per unit is the price charged to all consumers. The fixed price element is set to extract the consumer surplus. Because the consumer surplus is not constant across all consumers, the fixed element can also be varied across consumers through the provision of pricing menus. High users with a presumably high willingness to pay are offered a high fixed access price, but a low cost per unit. Low users with a presumably low willingness to pay select a low fixed access price but a high cost per unit. These pricing strategies are also used beyond the utility industry – for example, membership of gyms and golf clubs often includes a fixed and variable element.

Third-degree price discrimination

Finally, we have third-degree price discrimination where each consumer group is charged a different price. This tends to occur where firms can identify different market segments for a similar product or service. In the case of airlines, young students are fairly flexible when it comes to flying around the world. If the plane is full on Monday, they can fly on Tuesday. In fact, demand by young travellers is elastic, as different days of travel provide substitutes. A business traveller is more likely to have very specific needs. The overseas meeting will take place on a specific date and they will need to be back in the UK very quickly to attend more meetings. These travellers are less sensitive to price and so exhibit price-inelastic demand.

Therefore, rather than offering each traveller the same product at the same price, you can segment the market. Offer two different products at different prices: cheap economy tickets with no frills to the student; and expensive business-class tickets to the businessperson, with comfortable seats, good food and access to airport lounges.

Premium television channels use the same idea. Instead of paying one fee for all digital channels, consumers are offered a menu. The base price includes the standard assortment of channels. The sport and movie channels are additional extras. Consumers that value sport highly will pay the higher price.

This is known as de-bundling the product. If the product is composed of many different parts, in our case various television channels, the offering is not sold as one bundle; rather, it is sold as a number of separate bundles, each with an individual price.

This stripping-out of valued products from the standard range enables companies to deal with the problem of consumer surplus by targeting customers with the combination of products that they value the most.

Similar tactics are arguably employed by Apple when marketing iPhones, iTouches and iPods. Within the iPod range is a selection of devices – nano, classic, etc. – and each range is further differentiated by the amount of storage capacity. Rather than sell one version of iPod to all customers at one price, Apple instead sells a range of iPods at different prices. This is an attempt by Apple to extract some of the available consumer surplus. Customers who are willing to pay a high price are those who are most likely to place the highest value on features and storage space. To access these features, such customers have to buy the most expensive iPod. Customers who just want a portable music player are likely to buy the cheapest iPod.

Apple differentiates the market further by offering iPhones and iTouches. If you want an iPod and a mobile phone, then the iPhone is for you. If you want all the features of an iPhone, but without a phone, then the iTouch is an attractive option. By meeting a variety of demand needs at various prices, Apple has become a profitable company. More importantly, by targeting a variety of segments, Apple has achieved revenue growth through the extraction of consumer surplus. The alternative route to revenue growth involves cutting prices and driving volumes. This approach can be self-defeating, requiring ever cheaper versions of the product to continually drive volume growth. By pricing high and meeting consumer needs across many segments, Apple has successfully managed a premium price strategy. Of course, this may fail if a recession cuts demand for premium goods, such as Apple's.

Box 2.5 Apple goes Wal-Mart, just NOT at $99

Adapted from a blog by Jim Goldman of CNBC, 8 December 2008

The headlines screamed all weekend long: **The Apple iPhone was coming to Wal-Mart**, likely before Christmas, and at the family and recession friendly new price point of $99. Great story, if it were true.

The iPhone/Wal-Mart rumours have been circulating for months. Honestly, the move by Apple to reach the broader consumer is nothing new. But that $99 price point is a pipe dream. It would be seismic enough for Apple to get its products into the Wal-Mart eco-system, which up until this deep recession was the retail stop of choice for a decidedly un-Apple crowd. No more. Everyone shops at Wal-Mart. And that means the potential of a massive new audience for Apple's iPhones.

Apple's bid to reach a mass-market consumer while maintaining the Apple premium that it enjoys on its products has been the hallmark of its sales strategy, and the envy of just about every other gadget and gizmo company. Apple's move to sell iPhone at Wal-Mart should be lauded. If it can get away with selling the device at existing pricing, that should be lauded too.

© www.cnbc.com

 # Summary

1 A key characteristic of modern economic life is that companies set prices. With companies in such a powerful position, what is the optimal price to set for a product?

2 The demand curve shows consumers' willingness to demand a product at various prices. As the price increases, consumers are less willing to demand the product.

3 Demand is also seen to be influenced by the price of substitutes and complements.

4 Substitutes are rivals; complements are products that are purchased together. As a substitute becomes more expensive, demand for the rival product will increase. As the price of a complement rises, demand for the remaining product will fall.

5 Rising income will lead to an increase in demand for normal goods. But it will lead to a fall in demand for inferior goods.

6 The tastes and preferences of consumers change over time. As goods become popular, consumers move into the market. As products become unfashionable, consumers leave the market and demand falls.

7 Price elasticity, income elasticity and cross-price elasticity measure how much demand changes when price, income or the price of a substitute or complement changes.

8 If the percentage change in demand is greater than the percentage change in price, then demand is said to be elastic. If the percentage change in demand is less than the percentage change in price, demand is said to be inelastic.

9 Companies use the concept of elasticity when setting prices. If demand is elastic, reducing prices will lead to a rise in total revenue. When demand is inelastic, raising prices will lead to an increase in total revenue.

10 Companies measure the elasticity of demand by analysing mathematically what happens to sales when they offer promotional discounts in the market.

11 Consumer surplus is the difference between the price charged and how much a consumer would have been willing to pay. This difference represents lost profits.

12 It is possible to capture some consumer surplus by de-bundling product offerings. Consumers can be offered a base package but extras are offered at much higher prices.

Learning checklist

You should now be able to:

◆ Draw a demand curve for a good or service

◆ Understand how changes in income, the price of substitutes and complements, tastes and price expectations shift the demand curve left or right

◆ Explain the concept of price elasticity of demand and understand the distinction between elastic and inelastic demand

◆ Explain how total revenue can be improved by understanding how elastic demand is for a good or service

◆ Explain how firms can develop strategies to access consumer surplus

Questions   connect™

1 Draw a demand line which illustrates the effect of a price reduction on consumers' willingness to demand.

2 Identify the main factors which can lead to a shift in demand.

3 If a consumer's willingness to demand a product is sensitive to a change in the price, then their elasticity of demand is elastic, or inelastic?

4 The price of pasta at the supermarket falls. What do you think will happen to the demand for rice?

5 Explain the difference between an inferior and a normal good.

6 How would you expect your consumption of normal and inferior goods to change over your lifetime?

7 Provide examples of your own consumption activities where your consumer surplus is high and also where it is small.

8 A successful advertising campaign has a slogan which is adopted by teenagers across your economy. Illustrate what will happen to the demand line for the product being advertised.

9 How does consumer surplus vary with elasticity? How might firms use this to their advantage?

10 Products that have low price elasticity have low prices and high volumes. Products that have high elasticity have smaller volumes and higher profit margins. Do you consider these statements to be true?

---

11 Assess how easy it is for firms to measure the elasticity of demand for a given good or service.

12 List five products that you think are price elastic. List five products that you think are price inelastic.

13 Is consumer surplus greater under elastic or inelastic demand?

---

14 How would you advise a company to go about changing the elasticity of demand for one of its products?

15 Using ideas relating to income elasticity, how would you build a portfolio or collection of products that would perform well when the economy was growing during a boom and contracting during a recession?

Exercises

1 True or false?

(a) An increase in income will cause an increase in demand for all goods.

(b) Two goods are complements if an increase in the price of X results in an increase in demand for Y.

(c) Price elasticity measures the responsiveness of the quantity demanded to the change in the price.

(d) The price elasticity is constant along the length of a demand line.

(e) If a car costs £15 000 and a consumer is willing to pay up to £18 000, then the consumer surplus is £3000.

(f) If a product is price inelastic, revenues will rise following an increase in the price.

2 (a) Plot the following demand curve and associated total revenue curve.

Price £	10	8	6	4	2
Demand	1	2	3	4	5
Total revenue					
Elasticity					

- ◆ Calculate the elasticity at each price.
- ◆ What is the change in total revenue if the firm moves from a price of £8 to £4?
- ◆ Which price maximizes total revenue?
- ◆ What is the elasticity when revenue is maximized?

(b) As a result of rising income, demand increases at all prices by five units. Explain whether this good is normal or inferior.

Is the new demand line more or less elastic than the original? Why do you think this should be the case?

3 You have been hired by Louis Vuitton to advise the firm on its pricing strategy. Your brief is to cover each of the following:

(a) The benefit of raising its existing prices.

(b) The potential of broadening the brand's appeal through a gradual reduction in prices.

(c) The potential benefits of launching a new brand called 'Louis'. Who should this product be sold to and at what price level?

Notes

1 We will examine the objectives of a firm more fully in Chapters 5 and 7.

2 You will shortly understand that elasticity must lie between zero and minus infinity. This is because if we increase prices, then quantity demanded will decrease. So a negative change in demand will be divided by a positive change in the price. So the elasticity measure will always be negative. Economists ignore the negative sign and simply look at the numerical value for elasticity.

Chapter 3
Firms in the marketplace

Chapter contents

 Learning outcomes

By the end of this chapter you should understand:

Economic Theory

LO1   The difference between the short and the long run

LO2   The difference between variable, fixed and total costs

LO3   The concepts of marginal product and marginal costs

LO4   The law of diminishing returns

LO5   Economies of scale

LO6   The concept of minimum efficient scale

Business Applications

LO7   Why low pricing and high volume sales strategies, deployed by budget airlines, reflect high fixed costs

LO8   Why qualification for the Champions' League by leading football clubs is a strategy for dealing with the high cost of owning and employing footballers

LO9   When times get tough, when to decide to quit and when to hang on for a bit

Cost theory at a glance

The issue

World-class footballers cost in excess of €40 million, and the Superjumbo A380 costs $264 million. Neither are cheap. So how does a business make money when using such expensive assets?

The understanding

Such assets represent costs that do not vary with the level of output. The way to exploit such assets is to make them productive. The more games Ronaldo plays for Real Madrid, the cheaper per game he becomes. The more flights a plane flies, the cheaper per flight the plane becomes. Unfortunately, over short periods of time, volume may come up against a problem known as the 'law of diminishing returns', while in the long run firms can encounter an additional problem known as 'diseconomies of scale'. By the end of this chapter you will understand each of these problems and how costs can be managed in the short and the long run.

The usefulness

This chapter will enable you to understand why successful airlines sell their seats at low prices, why teams such as Manchester United are desperate to stay in the Champions' League and why R&D-intensive technology products need to conquer world markets.

3.1 Business problem: managing fixed and variable costs

Economists categorize costs as being fixed or variable.

Supermarket stores represent **fixed costs**. If the store attracts one shopper or 1000 shoppers per day, the cost of developing and maintaining the store is fixed. However, the number of checkout staff does change with the number of shoppers and, therefore, represents a **variable cost**. The cost of developing Apple's iPhone was a fixed cost. Development costs do not increase if more iPhones are sold. Rather, the cost of producing more iPhones increases. Universities are a vast collection of fixed costs. The cost of lecture theatres, lecturers, library resources, central administration units and computer facilities is not hugely influenced by the number of recruited students. For example, the cost of lecturing to 50 students is the same as lecturing to 250 students.

The nature of fixed and variable costs has enormous implications for business. As an example, consider the contrasting differences between employing burger flippers and professional footballers.

Burger flippers at fast-food restaurants are perhaps paid no more than £6 per hour. The majority of employed hours are on weekends, evenings or lunchtimes, periods when consumer demand is highest. This is because the employment of burger flippers is linked to the demand for burgers. More burger flippers are employed at lunchtimes and weekends when demand, and therefore the production of burgers, is highest. As a result, the cost of employing burger flippers is a predominantly variable cost. The wages paid rise and fall with the level of output. Ultimately, if demand for burgers drops dramatically, restaurants can generally terminate the employment of their burger flippers by giving one month's notice.

> **Fixed costs** are constant. They remain the same whatever the level of output.
>
> **Variable costs** change or vary with the amount of production.

Professional footballers can be paid £150 000 a week when they play a game. This may fall by a fraction if they are on the substitutes' bench or when they are injured. Similarly, the wage may increase with bonuses if goals are scored or after a specified number of first team appearances. It is important to remember that the bulk of a professional footballer's wages is not linked directly to the creation of output, namely football games. Playing games or sitting on the subs' bench only leads to relatively small changes up or down in the wages paid to the player. The cost of employing professional footballers is, therefore, a predominantly fixed cost. A club's wages bill is changed very little by the number of games played. Furthermore, because footballers' contracts are fixed for anything up to five years, if the club wishes to terminate the employment of the player two years into the contract, it would have to pay three years' worth of compensation. These employment differences between footballers and burger flippers are crucial.

The business problem associated with employing footballers, or fixed costs, is *not* that they cost huge sums of money, but that the *nature* of the cost *does not change* with *output* and *revenues*.

If the revenues received from fans and television rights drop, clubs still have to honour their contractual obligations with their players. In contrast, fast-food restaurants can change the number of burger flippers when demand falls. The transfer of football players between clubs is both the transfer of an asset and a liability. The buying club gains what it believes is a good player, but at the same time it also commits itself to an increase in its fixed costs.

It is important for businesses to recognize the various components of their cost structures and to differentiate between fixed and variable costs. By doing so, they can then develop business models that accommodate the financial commitment associated with fixed costs. Box 3.1 clearly highlights the importance of understanding fixed costs in the cruise sector. Ships are enormous fixed costs, as is the fuel used to move them around the world. By keeping an eye on sales, the cruise operator Carnival is trying to ensure that sufficient revenue is generated to cover these enormous fixed costs. By the end of this chapter you will understand how to manage such cost structures highlighted by our initial discussion. But in order to achieve this, you need to develop a broader understanding of cost theory.

 ## Box 3.1 Carnival's steady cruise could be about to hit choppy waters

Adapted from an article by Nick Hasell in The Times, *19 September 2008*

After two years of being clobbered by crude, oil prices are finally coming to the aid of Carnival. Shares in the world's largest cruise ship operator have rallied more than 40 per cent from their July low. Not that fuel bills are no longer a headache for Carnival. It still expects to spend $678 million more on fuel this year than it did in 2007.

More important, Carnival has left its near-term sales forecasts unchanged: advance bookings are running slightly below last year, but ticket prices have risen. Given the necessity for cruise operators to ensure that their ships sail full – because of their high fixed costs – the fact that Carnival has been able to resist cutting prices so far is a powerful sign of its confidence; especially given that the launch of five new vessels next year will increase capacity by nearly 9 per cent.

The insulation to date of its typical European customer from the credit crunch – older couples with grown-up children and low borrowings – provides hope that bookings remain firm. However, it seems churlish to assume that rising unemployment and the erosion of its customers' wealth from falling stock markets will leave it wholly unscathed.

© 2009 Times Newspapers Ltd.

3.2 The short and long run

We will begin by considering a firm that employs two factors of production: labour in the form of workers and capital in the form of computers and office space.

If a firm needs to increase its level of output in the **short run**, it is fairly easy to employ more workers. Agencies specializing in temporary employment are able to offer suitable candidates within a day, or even an hour. In contrast, it is not as easy to expand the amount of office space. It takes time to find additional buildings, arrange the finance to purchase the buildings, and then fit the buildings with suitable furniture and equipment. The problem also exists when trying to downsize. It is fairly easy to lay off workers, but it takes time to decommission a building and sell it to some other user. Therefore, only in the **long run** are all factors of production seen to be variable.

Given our business problem, we should not confine our thinking to capital as the only fixed factor of production. Clearly, the nature of employment can make labour fixed. Contracts signed by footballers, company chief executives and many academics are for a fixed period of time. Contracts for burger flippers and many other types of work are open-ended, with the employer and employee given the right to terminate the relationship with, typically, one month's notice. In the latter case, the employment of labour is reasonably variable, whereas for footballers labour is fixed.

A reasonable question is, how long is the long run? The answer is, it depends. For some companies it can be very long. Airlines place orders with aircraft suppliers up to five years in advance, while an Internet company might be able to buy an additional Internet server system within a week and double its output capacity.

However, an important issue is to understand how costs behave in the short and long run. In the next two sections we will see how in the short run costs are determined by the fixed amount of capital being exploited by more workers, while in the long run costs are influenced by varying the amount of capital.

3.3 The nature of productivity and costs in the short run

Productivity in the short run

If we are interested in knowing how the level of costs changes with the level of output, then we need to consider more than just the cost of employing labour and capital. We are also interested in understanding how the productivity of labour and capital changes. If labour becomes more productive, then output increases for any given amount of cost.

In assessing productivity, we need to distinguish between **total product** and **marginal product**.

Consider the following. An online supplier of electrical goods has two vans for deliveries, the fixed factor of production. The firm can also employ up to ten workers, the variable component. The total product and marginal product at each level of employment are detailed in Table 3.1. When the firm employs one worker, total product is 40 delivered items per day. This worker has to collate the orders, pick the items from the warehouse, package them for delivery, print off invoices, load the van, deliver the items and then deal with any enquiries and returned items. When the firm employs a second worker, total output increases. This second worker can utilize the additional van and may specialize in dealing with enquiries and returns. When the third worker is employed, they do not have access to a van, but they could help by specializing in collating orders, picking and packing. This again would help to raise output. The fourth

The **short run** is a period of time where one factor of production is fixed. We tend to assume that capital is fixed and labour is variable.

The **long run** is a period of time when all factors of production are variable.

Total product is the total output produced by a firm's workers.

Marginal product is the addition to total product after employing one more unit of factor input.

In economics, **marginal** always means 'one more'.

Table 3.1 Total and marginal product of labour with a fixed amount of capital

Labour input (workers)	Total product (number of deliveries)	Marginal product of labour (number of deliveries)
1	40	40
2	90	50
3	145	55
4	205	60
5	255	50
6	295	40
7	325	30
8	345	20
9	355	10
10	360	5

Task specialization occurs where the various activities of a production process are broken down into their separate components. Each worker then specializes in one particular task, becoming an expert in the task and raising overall productivity.

The law of diminishing returns states that, as more of a variable factor of production, usually labour, is added to a fixed factor of production, usually capital, then at some point the returns to the variable factor will diminish.

worker might load vans and print invoices. The fifth worker might then help the third by specializing in picking orders from the warehouse; and so on and so on. The important point is that task specialization helps to raise productivity, as evidenced by the increasing marginal product for workers two, three and four, but thereafter diminishes. There is only so much **task specialization** that can occur without leaving a worker without a full day's work. Workers five, six and seven and onwards will be filling the remainder of their working day by answering emails, checking their text messages, making coffee and collecting sandwiches for lunch – activities which do not raise the total product of the firm.

The productivity of all the workers in our example is constrained by the number of vans the firm uses. With only two vans, there is an upper limit to how many orders can be met per day, no matter how much task specialization occurs at the warehouse.

Most working environments are characterized by a mixture of workers and capital, in various forms: lecturers and lecture theatres, office staff and computers, burger flippers and burger grills. The relationship depicted in Figures 3.1 and 3.2 is therefore very important and economists know it as the **law of diminishing returns**.

The law of diminishing returns is highlighted by the marginal product of labour (see Figure 3.2). When we have a fixed factor of production, such as capital, and we add workers to the production process, these workers can exploit an underutilized resource. So, the marginal product rises. When we begin to over-resource the production process with too much labour, there is no more capital to utilize. As a result, the marginal product begins to fall. This is the point at which the law of diminishing returns occurs. In our particular example, additional workers are able to exploit the vans and become more productive. But once we begin to employ more workers, and there are not enough vans, the productivity of labour must begin to fall.

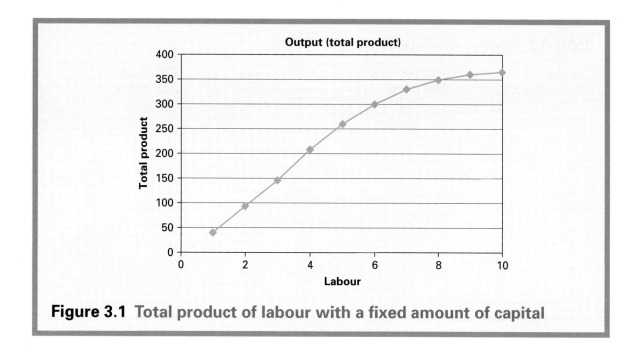

Figure 3.1 **Total product of labour with a fixed amount of capital**

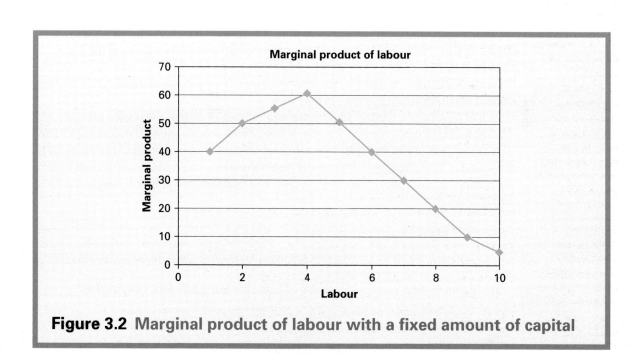

Figure 3.2 **Marginal product of labour with a fixed amount of capital**

Table 3.2 Short-run costs

Output	SFC (short-run fixed costs)	SVC (short-run variable costs)	STC (short-run total costs)
0	30	0	30
40	30	22	52
90	30	38	68
140	30	48	78
180	30	61	91
210	30	79	109
235	30	102	132
255	30	131	161
270	30	166	196
280	30	207	237

Variable costs are costs associated with the use of variable factors of production, such as labour.

Fixed costs are associated with the employment of fixed factors of production, such as capital.

Total costs are simply fixed costs plus variable costs.

Average total cost is calculated as total cost divided by the number of units produced.

Average variable cost is calculated as total variable cost divided by the number of units produced.

Average fixed cost is calculated as total fixed costs divided by the number of units produced.

Costs in the short run

Now that we have an understanding of how productivity changes, we need to begin to think about how costs behave. In the short run, we have three types of cost: **variable**, **fixed** and **total costs**.

Variable costs change with the level of output. This was picked up when we discussed the burger flippers. The higher the level of output, the more labour we employ and the higher the amount of variable cost.

Fixed costs do not change with the level of output. If we produce nothing, or a very large amount of output, fixed costs remain the same.

Each of these costs is listed in Table 3.2 for various levels of output, and plotted in Figure 3.3.

Fixed costs are represented as the purple line, which is horizontal. In this example, fixed costs are constant at £30. Variable costs rise, slowly; then, as output increases, they begin to rise more quickly. This simply reflects the law of diminishing returns. As additional workers become less productive, costs rise quicker than output. The total cost line in blue is simply fixed plus variable costs.

Average costs

The next step is to consider how the cost per unit changes with the level of output. We measure the cost per unit using **average cost**.

In addition to the average costs, we also examine the **marginal costs**, calculated as:

$$\frac{\text{Change in total cost}}{\text{Change in output}}$$

(Since the marginal cost is the cost of producing one more unit, the change in output should be 1.)

However, firms rarely increase output by one unit and in our example output initially increases from 0 to 40 units of output: therefore, by dividing the change in total cost by the change in output of 40, we can approximate the marginal cost, or the cost of making one more unit:

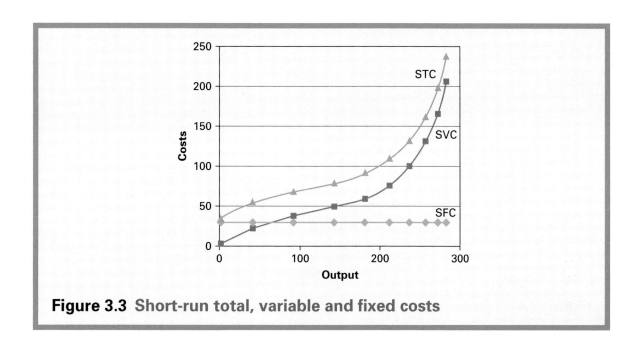

Figure 3.3 Short-run total, variable and fixed costs

Table 3.3 Short-run average and marginal costs

Output	SAFC (short-run average fixed costs)	SAVC (short-run average variable costs)	SATC (short-run average total costs)	SMC (short-run marginal costs)
0				
40	0.75	0.55	1.30	0.55
90	0.33	0.42	0.76	0.32
140	0.21	0.34	0.56	0.20
180	0.17	0.34	0.51	0.33
210	0.14	0.38	0.52	0.60
235	0.13	0.43	0.56	0.92
255	0.12	0.51	0.63	1.45
270	0.11	0.61	0.73	2.33
280	0.11	0.74	0.85	4.10

Marginal cost is the cost of creating one more unit.

Marginal cost = (52 − 30)/(40 − 0) = 0.55

The calculations for average and marginal costs are listed in Table 3.3, and plotted in Figure 3.4.

The average variable and average total cost curves are both U-shaped. This simply reflects the law of diminishing returns. Towards the left of the figure, the output is low. At this low level of output, we have a small number of workers using the fixed capital. As we employ more workers, productivity increases and costs per unit fall. As the number of workers continues to

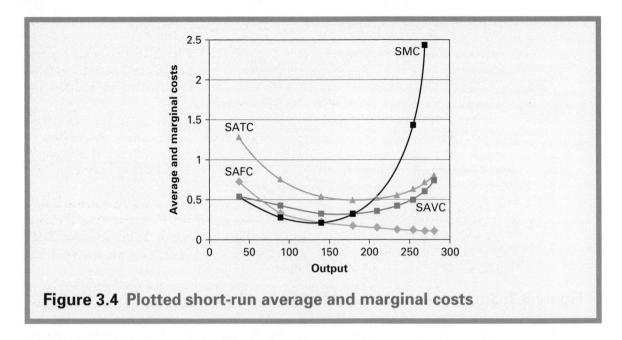

Figure 3.4 **Plotted short-run average and marginal costs**

increase, however, the law of diminishing returns predicts that productivity will fall. As a consequence, the cost per unit will increase. This point is also picked up in the marginal cost curve, which is the cost of producing one more unit. As labour becomes less productive, then costs of producing additional units must rise.

Relationship between the average and the marginal

It should also be noted that the marginal cost curve cuts through the minimum points of the average total and average variable cost curves. This is because of a simple mathematical relationship between the marginal and the average. Assume your average examination score is 50. Your next exam is your marginal exam. If you gain a score of 70, then your average will increase. But if you gain a score of 20, your average will come down. Therefore, whenever the marginal is lower than the average, the average will move down; and whenever the marginal is higher than the average, the average will rise. Therefore, the marginal cost curve has to cut through the average cost curves at their minimum point.

Average fixed costs

The average fixed cost curve is different. It is always falling as output increases. This reflects simple mathematics. If fixed costs are £100 and we produce ten units, the average fixed costs are £100/10 = £10. But if we increase output to 100 units, then average fixed costs become £100/100 = £1. Accountants refer to this as 'spreading the overhead'. As fixed costs are spread over a larger level of output, the fixed costs per unit will fall.

This relationship has important implications for managers. Consider the case of the Super Jumbo Airbus A380. Development costs have been estimated at €12 billion. If we assume Airbus finds two customers to buy the A380, the average fixed cost will be €12/2 billion = €6 billion. Therefore, in order for Airbus to break even, it will require its two customers to pay at least €6 billion; and then there is the cost of making the aircraft! Airbus has orders for just over 100 A380s, which helps to reduce the fixed cost per unit. But at a list price of €250 million, Airbus will have to sell many more A380s in order to recoup its variable costs of manufacturing and its fixed costs of development.

3.4 Output decisions in the short run

Now that we have an understanding of how costs behave in the short run, we can begin to examine the firm's output decisions. In Chapter 5 we will see how we can find the level of output that will maximize the firm's profits. However, at this point we merely wish to show you when the firm will produce and when it will close down.

If the output is being sold at the same price to all consumers for £1.50, then the average revenue is also £1.50. If we now re-examine the short-run average total costs, SATC in Table 3.3 and plotted in Figure 3.4, we can see that the maximum value for SATC is £1.30 at an output level of 40 units. As output grows, SATC drops to a minimum of £0.51. Clearly, therefore, at the current price of £1.50 the firm can make a profit at any output level.

Now consider two much lower prices, £0.45 and £0.30. At both prices the firm will make a loss as its minimum SATC is only £0.51, so its revenues will never be greater than its costs at either of these prices. But there is an important difference between the two scenarios. In the short run, the firm will operate and make a loss at prices of £0.45, but it will shut down and cease operating at prices of £0.30.

The understanding rests on whether or not the firm can make a positive contribution to its fixed costs. If the firm produces nothing, its fixed costs are £30 and its losses will also be £30. However, if the price is £0.45 there are output levels where the firm's average variable costs, SAVC, are less than £0.45. For example, at an output of 180 units, SAVC = £0.34. So, if the firm operates at 180 units of output, it can cover its variable cost per unit of £0.34 and have £0.45 − £0.34 = £0.11 per unit left over. Selling 180 units represents 180 × 0.11 =£19.80. The £19.80 can be used to make a contribution towards the fixed costs. So, by producing 180, the loss drops to £30 − £19.80 = £11.20, as opposed to a loss of £30 (the fixed costs) if it produced nothing.

However, when the price drops to £0.30 the firm cannot cover any of its variable costs. Therefore, if it did decide to operate, then, not being able to cover its entire wage bill, it would be adding to the losses generated by its fixed costs. Hence, the best the firm can do is to shut down and incur only the fixed-cost losses of £30.

We can now go one step further. The marginal cost is the cost of producing one more unit. If the firm can receive a price that is equal to or greater than the marginal cost, then it can break even or earn a profit on the last unit. If the firm maximizes profits, clearly it will supply an additional unit of output when the price is equal to or greater than marginal cost. If we couple this argument with the previous point, that firms will not operate below short-run average

Box 3.2 Theme parks

Theme parks offering thrilling rollercoaster rides often close down during the winter. We can now offer an economic explanation for why they close. The rides are capital and represent fixed costs. The staff who operate the rides and keep the theme park clean are the variable costs. During the summer months many people are willing to go to a theme park and pay the entrance fee. The revenues generated cover the theme park's fixed and variable costs. However, in the winter, when it is cold and wet, very few people are willing to go to the theme park. The revenues generated by the theme park would be unlikely to cover the wages it would have to pay to its staff to open the park. It is, therefore, best for the theme park to close and incur no variable costs during the winter; and simply incur its fixed costs. If the theme park decided to stay open during the winter, its losses would rise since the wage bill would not be covered by the small number of paying visitors to the park. Firms, therefore, are only willing to supply output if revenues are greater than variable costs.

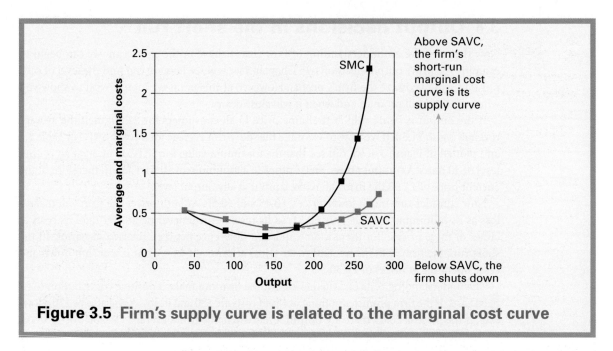

Figure 3.5 Firm's supply curve is related to the marginal cost curve

variable cost, we can show, as in Figure 3.5, that the firm's supply curve is in fact the firm's short-run marginal cost curve above short-run average variable costs.

3.5 Cost inefficiency

Our discussion so far has assumed that firms are operating on the cost curve. This is troublesome, since some firms are more cost-effective than their rivals; and in addition some firms are better at raising productivity over time. In Box 3.3, after suffering a huge financial loss, British Airways is seeking to get as near as possible to its cost curve in order to improve efficiency.

If firms have the same productive technology, they have the same knowledge and manufacturing know-how. As such, they are assumed to share the same cost curves. However, if one firm pays more for its workers, or uses them less effectively, then this firm will operate off its cost curve, as illustrated in Figure 3.6.

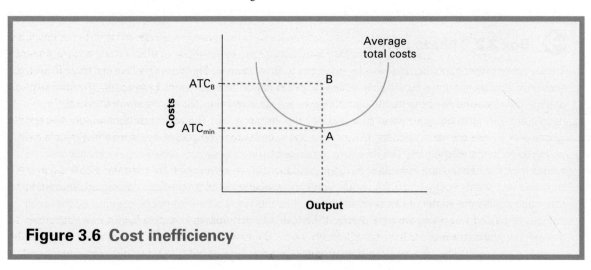

Figure 3.6 Cost inefficiency

Box 3.3 British Airways posts loss

Adapted from 'British Airways Posts Loss, Focuses on Exchange Rates' by Kaveri Niththyananthan in the Wall Street Journal, *9 February 2009*

British Airways posted a net loss of £127 million ($188 million) for the nine months ended December 31, compared with a year-earlier net profit of £642 million. The latest results were hit by a 48 per cent spike in fuel costs to £2.24 billion. The carrier didn't break out quarterly results.

'We have already taken several actions to offset the unprecedented economic conditions,' BA Chief Executive Willie Walsh said. 'We have increased our sales activity in markets with stronger foreign currencies to benefit from exchange rates and continue to offer competitive fares in both premium and nonpremium cabins.'

Mr Walsh said BA would continue to review its business to control costs while improving customer service. The airline has begun talks with trade unions about pay and productivity, a move BA said was necessary to improve financial performance. BA will use a voluntary-layoff plan similar to the one offered to managers, Mr Walsh said. About 450 managers took up BA's offer for severance last autumn.

He declined to comment on the number of job cuts the airline was targeting. All departments will be looked at to see how efficiency can be improved, a BA spokeswoman said. A 'consolidation of roles' is under consideration, she continued. An example could include making Heathrow Airport cabin crew work long- as well as short-haul routes, which is already the case at Gatwick Airport.

Firms A and B are both operating at the output level which is associated with the lowest short-run average total cost. However, only A is operating on the curve and achieving minimum average total cost ATC$_{min}$. B has much higher costs and this reflects a significant degree of cost inefficiency and, as such, A has a cost advantage over its rival. The reasons why this can occur are numerous, and in the case of British Airways relate to the employment of too many workers and an ineffective roster system. This means that British Airways is at point B and its more efficient rivals are at point A.

3.6 The nature of productivity and costs in the long run

In the long run, both capital and labour are variable. Firms can change the number of machines or the amount of office space that they use. Therefore, the law of diminishing returns does not determine the productivity of a firm in the long run. This is simply because there is no fixed capital in the long run to constrain productivity growth. So, in the long run, productivity and costs must be driven by something else. This something else is termed **returns to scale**.

Returns to scale simply measure the change in output for a given change in the inputs.

Increasing returns to scale exist when output grows at a faster rate than inputs. Decreasing returns exist when inputs grow at a faster rate than outputs. Constant returns to scale exist when inputs and outputs grow at the same rate.

This is not complicated. Look at Figure 3.7: in quadrant 1, we have the short-run average total cost curve, SATC, with which we are familiar. Now consider adding more capital and labour to the production process.

In so doing we have changed the scale of operation and we now have a new cost curve. In quadrant 2, we have the situation where the new cost curve SATC$_2$ moves down and to the right. The company can now produce the same level of output Q$_1$ for the lower average cost of

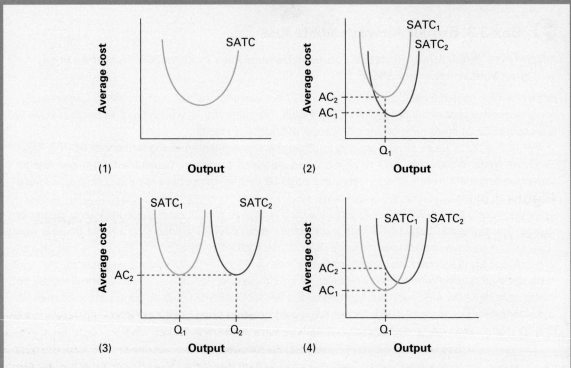

Figure 3.7 Changing the capital input and impact on short-run cost curves

When a firm changes its level of capital, e.g. machines, number of offices or shops, it moves to a new short-run cost curve. If the investment in capital makes the firm more efficient, then the cost curve will move down to the right, as in quadrant 2. If investment in capital leaves productivity unchanged, as in quadrant 3, then there is no change in average costs. If capital investment makes the firm less productive, then average costs will increase, as in quadrant 4.

AC_2. This is increasing returns to scale. As we increase inputs, outputs grow faster, so the cost per unit must fall. In quadrant 3, increasing the scale moves the cost curve $SATC_2$ to the right and leaves average costs constant, a case of constant returns to scale. In quadrant 4, increasing scale leads to the new cost curve $SATC_2$ shifting upwards and to the right, leading to an increase in costs, a case of decreasing returns to scale.

What economists tend to find in practice is that firms experience increasing, then constant and finally decreasing returns to scale: that is, firms move through quadrants 2, 3 and 4 in order. Therefore, the family of short-run cost curves can be put together and the long-run cost curve can be derived, as in Figure 3.8.

The long-run average total cost curve, LATC, is a frontier curve. It shows all the lowest long-run average costs at any given level of output and is really nothing more than a collection of short-run cost curves. What we can clearly see, however, is that as we increase the scale of operation, the long-run average cost initially falls and then begins to increase. So, the long-run cost curve is also U-shaped. However, the reason for the U-shape is not the law of diminishing returns; rather, in the long run economies of scale are the important issue.

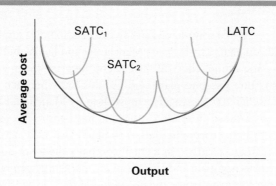

Figure 3.8 Long-run average costs

The long-run average cost curve is simply a collection of short-run average cost curves, illustrating how costs change as fixed inputs.

Economies of scale: production techniques

Through **economies of scale** long-run average costs fall as output increases.

Economies of scale exist for a number of reasons. Consider the production process associated with making Fords and Ferraris. At a Ford production facility, workers might be capable of making 1000 cars in a 24-hour shift. Ferrari workers may only make 1000 cars in a year. At massive levels of scale, Ford employs mass-production techniques; one person is responsible for fixing tyres, another for exhausts. This task specialization aids productivity and cuts costs. At Ferrari it is not possible to use mass-production techniques. The scale of operation is much lower. Therefore, as firms change their level of scale, they also change their production process and long-run costs fall.

The same consideration also applies to the generation of food miles, where it now appears that the economies of scale generated through global transportation of food result in lower CO_2 emissions than for food driven in small batches from local producers. See Box 3.4.

 Box 3.4 Why long-haul food may be greener than local food with low air-miles

Adapted from an article by Richard Woods in The Times, *3 February 2008*

If you buy a packet of Waitrose blueberries from Chile, it's a crime against humanity. If you nibble mange tout from Africa, you're practically murdering the planet. And if you eat apples from New Zealand, well, you're in league with the devil.

Why? Food miles, of course. It's obvious that if you buy food from thousands of miles away, the transport alone must consume vast amounts of energy, thus fuelling climate change and global meltdown. As any concerned citizen knows, think green, think local. Or think again. Researchers are finding that food miles are far from the whole story when assessing the environmental impact of what we eat.

Local production and a distribution system involving lots of vans and cars miss the environmental benefits of economies of scale. Just over a ton of goods moved six miles as part of a 22-ton lorry load generates about 14 oz of CO_2; moved in 50 cars, each carrying 40 lb, it generates about 22 lb of CO_2.

Indivisibilities

In order to operate as a commercial airline you have to buy a jumbo jet. Assume the jumbo has 400 seats and you plan to fly between Manchester and Dubai, but only manage to find 300 passengers a day. You cannot chop off the back of the plane to cut your costs! But if you increase your scale and buy a second plane and use this to fly between Dubai and Hong Kong, you might find another 100 passengers who wish to fly Manchester to Hong Kong, via Dubai. In essence, this is nothing more than spreading fixed costs. The same arguments can be made regarding professional corporate staff. A company may only need one accountant, one lawyer and one marketing executive. In a small company there are not many accounts to manage, many contracts to negotiate and sign, or many marketing campaigns to organize. However, as the scale of the company grows, the utilization of these expensive professional staff improves. The accountant manages more accounts and the lawyer oversees more contracts and, as a result, the cost per unit of output falls. Box 3.5 discusses the world's tallest building, Burj Dubai. The indivisibility is land space. Once this has been purchased it can be increasingly exploited by building more floors. Air space is free, land space is not. Therefore, while often being monuments to engineering ingenuity and visually appealing, skyscrapers rest on the economic foundations of economies of scale. This is very true in areas of high population density and where land prices are high: New York, Shanghai, Taipei and Dubai – all places where skyscrapers are popular.

 Box 3.5 Dubai claims record for world's tallest building

Adapted from an article in The Times, *1 September 2008*

Developers in Dubai have claimed a new record for the tallest building in the world, saying that the *Burj Dubai* skyscraper has now topped 688 metres (2257 feet). The slender, rocket-shaped tower is still under construction. Its final height remains a closely guarded secret, although it is expected to reach 800 metres.

Emaar Properties announced last summer that the skyscraper had surpassed Taiwan's Taipei 101, which – at 508 metres (1667 feet) – had been officially the world's tallest building since 2004. For the time being, Taipei 101 is still the world's tallest inhabited structure.

In a laconic statement issued today, the developer said that work on the exterior of Burj Dubai was now almost finished and construction would soon begin on the interior. So far the silvery steel-and-glass construction has soared more than 160 storeys into the air. The company gave no further details.

© 2009 Times Newspapers Ltd.

Geometric relationships

Have you ever noticed that bubbles are always round? Engineers and business managers have. Bubbles are round because they provide the biggest volume for the smallest surface area. More specifically, volume grows at a faster rate than the surface area. Volume is a measure of storage capacity. So, if we need to create a tank to brew beer, and we decide to double the volume of the tank, the material needed to cover the surface area, the sides and bottom, will not double in size. Instead, it will grow at a slower rate. Hence, it becomes proportionately cheaper to build larger tanks than it does to build smaller tanks. Look around your lecture theatre – we expect it will be big.

Diseconomies of scale

Long-run average costs will eventually begin to rise. The most obvious reason is that, as companies increase in size, they become more difficult to control and co-ordinate. More managerial input is required to run the business and managers themselves require additional management. So, as the scale of the company increases, the average cost also increases. Excessive bureaucracy now offsets any productivity gains.

Competitive issues

The **minimum efficient scale** (MES) is the output level at which long-run costs are at a minimum.

The issue of long-run costs has important insights for a competitive assessment of one firm against another. The lowest point on the long-run average total cost curve is defined as the **minimum efficient scale**. This is illustrated in Figure 3.9.

If a company operates at a level of scale significantly below the minimum efficient scale, then it is likely to be uncompetitive, with higher average costs.

The size of this cost disadvantage varies. In some industries, economies of scale are small and the long-run average cost curve is fairly flat across all output ranges. In other industries, economies of scale are significant and the long-run cost curve is markedly U-shaped. As a general rule, industries that are capital intensive generate higher fixed costs and lead to higher minimum efficient scale. Supermarkets, banking and car manufacturing all require large capital inputs and therefore exhibit high minimum efficient scale. In contrast, hairdressing, firms of solicitors and window cleaners do not require significant capital inputs. Minimum efficient scale in these industries is less of an issue.

In order to deal with an uncompetitive cost base, companies can try to do a number of things. First, they might merge with another company in the same line of business. Clearly, the new company will be bigger than the two separate parts and economies of scale can be realized.

Managers often propose mergers as a way of pursuing cost economies. But they could just as well be pursuing market power. A merger effectively reduces the amount of competition in the market. This lowers the price elasticity of demand for the merged company's product. The bigger company has one less competitor and, therefore, has more scope to raise its prices.

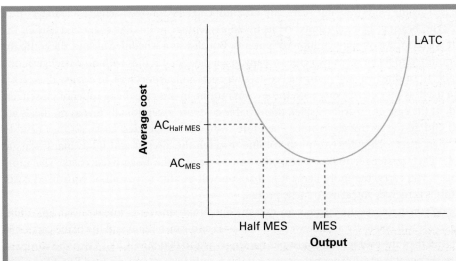

Figure 3.9 **Average costs and the minimum efficient scale**

The minimum efficient scale (MES) is the size of operation with the lowest average cost. Operating with a company size only half of the MES results in higher average costs.

3.7 Business application: linking pricing with cost structures

Fixed costs have been a dominant feature of this chapter. Professional footballers were shown in the business problem to be fixed costs. The development of the Airbus A380 was seen as a fixed cost; and the indivisibility of a skyscraper was also seen as a fixed cost.

In every example, the fixed cost is a major component of total costs. Because an Airbus A380 without fuel weighs around 280 tons, the cost of moving the plane between two airports massively outweighs the cost of moving you and your suitcase. In fact, most airlines would let you fly between London and Sydney for as little as £30 – the same amount as many cheap flights from the UK to some European destinations. This trivial amount is again the variable cost and this time is associated with the cost of issuing tickets, handling your luggage and feeding you en route. This is nothing more than the marginal cost of carrying you between two cities. Prices above £30 are a bonus. Using this cost-based knowledge, we can now explore the commercial decisions faced by the airlines that have ordered A380s.

More than any other commercial aircraft the A380 is a fixed cost for its operators, and moving the huge airframe between airports represents the bulk of the operators' costs. Interestingly, the aircraft is certified to carry 853 passengers, yet airlines appear to be ordering seating configurations between 480 and 580, presumably filling the free space with extra leg room, bars, gyms and other in-flight leisure facilities. However, we know that volume is crucial when fixed costs are high, because additional volume helps to spread the fixed cost over additional units of output. This lowers cost per unit sold, which ultimately lowers prices. With a simple piece of economic knowledge, it is easy to envisage airlines very quickly moving towards 850 seats on A380s in the pursuit of a cost advantage over their rivals. History also provides a precedent. When the Boeing 747 was first launched, no one knew what to place inside the front end 'bubble'. Ideas of gyms and bars were discussed, before operators decided on extra seating.

Discount airlines, while not yet flying A380s, gain competitive advantage by being cost efficient. They know how to keep variable costs down through no-frills service and they are extremely effective in dealing with their fixed costs. Load factor is reported by all discount carriers such as Ryanair and easyJet on a monthly basis. Load factor measures how good the airline is at selling all its available seats, and discount carriers can often achieve a load factor of 85 per cent, beating their scheduled rivals by 20 percentage points. As suggested earlier, the aircraft is a fixed cost of many millions of pounds. But also, as a scheduled airline, the company has committed to fly between two cities on any given day. So, if it flies with no passengers, or a full plane, the airline will still incur fuel costs, staff costs and airport fees. In a sense these costs are also fixed, as they do not vary with the level of output, in this case the number of passengers carried. In the case of no-frills easyJet, the variable costs are exceptionally low as no meals are offered and all tickets are electronic. Therefore, with such high fixed costs, airlines need to utilize their assets. They have to push volume through the aircraft and fill as many seats as possible. Each passenger makes a contribution to paying the huge fixed costs. The more passengers you carry, the more likely it is that you will be able to pay all of your fixed costs. Once this is achieved, you start to make profits.

How do you drive volume through an aircraft? The simple answer is volume itself. For example, if it costs £10 000 to fly a jet between Manchester and Amsterdam and the plane carries 50 passengers, then the average fixed cost per passenger is £10 000/50 = £200. Then the company needs to charge at least £200 per passenger and this is only for a one-way ticket! But if the plane carries 150 passengers, then the average fixed cost is £10 000/150 = £67.

From demand theory we know that we can generate higher demand at lower prices. So, we can drive volume by dropping the price. In part, easyJet tries to achieve this with a twist. If you want to book a flight three months in advance the price will be very cheap. This is because easyJet have lots of seats available and they have a higher need to drive volume. Once momentum picks up in the market and the flight date approaches, it raises the price and begins to extract profits from late bookers. But, crucially, what can be observed from a business perspective is that easyJet is using a fine-tuned pricing strategy to deal with a cost-based problem.

However, we should not be fooled into thinking that in ordering A380s with only 480 seats the likes of Singapore Airlines have got it all wrong. This is because Singapore Airline bums are worth more money; easyJet succeeds in driving the load factor forward by sacrificing revenue. Its heavy discounts in the marketplace are used to drive sales volumes. But driving volumes through price reduction damages revenue yields, and easyJet counters this revenue strategy by also minimizing its costs. It is a no-frills airline.

So, no meals, no reissue of the ticket if you miss the flight, plus the use of unpopular airports where the landing fees are lower. In contrast, Singapore Airlines uses popular airports. It undertakes extensive brand development. It provides meals and drinks onboard. It will assist passengers who have missed their flight. In summary, Singapore Airlines provides more than simply a means of transport between two points. It also provides extras such as late checking, drinks and meals during the flight and rerouting if you miss your flight. In addition, some of the earlier adopters of the A380 such as Singapore Airlines have an ability to offer a unique travel experience and can charge a premium price – see Box 3.6. With few other operators owning an A380, at least in the early years after launch, the demand for a flight on an A380 will be price inelastic. The added extras of gyms and bars are designed to exploit this demand. However, in ten years' time, when the world is awash with A380s, 850 seats is likely to be common; and do not be surprised if easyJet or Ryanair owns one, or two, for short hops into Europe.

 Box 3.6 The search for the best A380

Adapted from an article by Richard Green in The Times, *18 January 2009*

Yesterday, the first Qantas A380 Superjumbo took off from Heathrow, bound for Sydney. There are now three airlines flying these monster planes from London to Australia – Singapore Airlines, Emirates and Qantas – but each is flying different routes and each is offering completely different onboard amenities, services and fares.

The latest to enter the fray, Qantas, offers an A380 all the way from Heathrow to Sydney, with return fares from £699 (the same as to Melbourne on a 747). Its rivals, by contrast, are looking to cash in by charging considerably more for some of their A380 flights. With Emirates, an A380 return from Heathrow to Dubai starts at £530; its four daily non-A380 flights start at £305. And business class with Singapore is a whopping 60 per cent extra: from £3403 return to Changi, as opposed to £2127 on a 747.

3.8 Business application: footballers as sweaty assets

A common business term for making your fixed inputs work harder is 'to sweat the assets' and this is exactly what easyJet is trying to do by making its planes operate at maximum capacity. But how are Premiership football teams utilizing their very expensive football stars?

Few football clubs are looking at the huge expense of footballers as a problem that requires a pricing solution. Admittedly, pricing may play a role. Football fans are willing to pay a higher

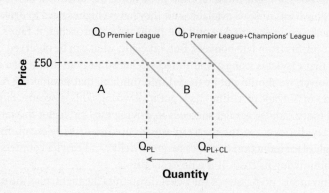

Figure 3.10 Demand for Premiership games and the Champions' League

Higher output resulting from more football games played yields more total revenue. This can go to paying the large fixed costs associated with employing top-class footballers.

price to watch a top Premiership side than, say, a Championship one. But the real and most obvious solution for Premiership sides is to increase the volume of games played.

In Figure 3.10, we have the demand for tickets at football games. Assuming the ticket price is £50, the demand curve for Premiership games indicates how many fans will buy at £50. Total revenue from Premiership games is illustrated by rectangle A. If the team qualify for the Champions' League, then more games are played and ticket demand rises. Assuming a similar ticket price of £50, rectangle B defines the additional total revenue. In the recent past, Manchester United have been very successful in using this strategy. By focusing on qualifying for the Champions' League and progressing within the competition they can literally sweat their assets, namely the players. (Admittedly, making sports stars work harder may diminish their average performance and make them injury prone, so there could also be a variable cost to playing more games.)

However, by selling TV rights to their games, replica team kits and other merchandizing products, Manchester United do not rely only on the revenue streams from the turnstiles. However, once they fail to progress within the Champions' League, then a financial hole appears in their business model. Players are utilized less, resulting in less TV revenue and gate receipts. Moreover, the value of the brand and the worth of merchandise decreases. Exposure and utilization of the players is a critical success factor for the business model underpinning the club.

Whether the problem is easyJet's or Manchester United's, it is the same problem: one of exploiting fixed costs. Economics provides you with an ability to identify this type of problem and suggests some possible solutions. Implementing and managing the strategic solution is perhaps a more challenging problem.

 Summary

1 In the short run one factor of production, usually capital, is assumed to be fixed.

2 Adding more variable factors of production, such as labour, to a fixed amount of capital will eventually lead to diminishing returns. This can be illustrated by plotting the marginal product of labour.

3   The impact of diminishing returns is a gradual decline in the productivity of labour. This lower productivity leads to a rise in average costs per unit.

4   The U-shaped nature of the average total and average variable cost curve is related to the change in productivity brought about by the diminishing returns.

5   Average fixed costs are always declining, as the fixed costs are divided by higher levels of outputs.

6   Marginal cost is the cost of producing one more unit. The marginal cost curve is, in effect, a reflection of the marginal product curve for labour. As marginal product declines due to the law of diminishing returns, the marginal cost increases.

7   In the long run all factors of production are variable. Costs are no longer determined by the law of diminishing returns. Instead, they are related to economies of scale.

8   Initially, as companies grow in size, they benefit from economies of scale and unit costs fall. But eventually they will grow too big and diseconomies of scale will cause average costs to rise.

9   High levels of fixed costs generally require high levels of volume.

 Learning checklist

You should now be able to:

◆   Explain the difference between the short and long run

◆   Calculate and explain the difference between variable, fixed and total costs

◆   Explain the concepts of marginal product and marginal costs

◆   Explain and provide examples of the law of diminishing returns

◆   Understand the concept of economies of scale and explain why economies of scale may exist

◆   Explain the concept of minimum efficient scale and understand the importance of operating at the minimum efficient scale

◆   Explain, using reference to fixed costs, why budget airlines sell at low prices

◆   Provide economic reasons relating to costs as to why Premiership clubs wish to be in the Champions' League

Questions   connect™

1   Explain the difference between the short and the long run.

2   Is it sensible to consider capital, rather than labour, as a fixed factor of production?

3   How does the law of diminishing returns explain the short-run productivity of a firm?

4   What is the difference between total fixed costs, total variable costs and total costs?

5   In the short run, why do average total costs initially fall and then increase?

6   Explain why average fixed costs are always declining. What commercial strategies can be supported by falling average fixed costs?

7 What are marginal product and marginal costs?

8 Marginal costs must go through the minimum point of which other cost curves: average total costs, average variable costs, or average fixed costs?

9 When should a firm shut down? Is it when prices go below average total costs, or average variable costs? Explain.

10 It is reported in the news that two firms have agreed to merge in the belief that they can generate cost savings. Which economic idea would support this belief?

11 Explain why airlines suspend some of their routes during the winter.

12 What are economies of scale and what are considered to be the main sources of economies of scale?

13 From a cost perspective, why do you think ice cream is on special offer in November, but not in July?

14 Is it ever sensible to operate at prices below average variable costs?

15 Do economies of scale offer a competitive advantage?

Exercises

1 True or false?
  (a) Specialization can lead to economies of scale.
  (b) Holding labour constant while increasing capital will lead to diminishing returns.
  (c) The long-run cost curve meets the bottom of each short-run cost curve.
  (d) Pursuit of minimum efficient scale can be a reason for merger.
  (e) A rising marginal cost is a result of diminishing returns.
  (f) Investing in brands represents a fixed cost.

2 A firm faces fixed costs of £45 and short-run variable costs (SAVC) as shown in Table 3.4.

Table 3.4 Short-run costs of production

Output	SAVC	SAFC	SATC	STC	SMC
1	17				
2	15				
3	14				
4	15				
5	19				
6	29				

  (a) Fill in the remainder of the table, where SAFC is the short-run average fixed cost; SATC is the short-run average total cost; STC is the short-run total cost; and SMC is the short-run marginal cost.
  (b) Plot SAVC, SAFC, SATC and SMC, checking that SMC goes through the minimum points of SAVC and SATC.
  (c) The firm finds that it is always receiving orders for six units per week. Advise the firm on how to minimize its costs in the long run. Now consider Table 3.5.

Table 3.5 Short- and long-run decisions

Price	Short-run decision			Long-run decision		
	Produce at a profit	Produce at a loss	Close down	Produce at a profit	Produce at a loss	Close down
18.00						
5.00						
7.00						
13.00						
11.50						

Cost conditions are such that LAC is £12; SATC is £17 (made up of SAVC £11 and SAFC £6). In Table 3.5, tick the appropriate short- and long-run decisions at each price.

3 Referring to Box 3.6, consider the following questions:
(a) What type of costs do aircraft represent to airlines?
(b) Explain and evaluate the different strategies used by airlines to deal with the cost of running A380s.

Chapter 4
Markets in action

Chapter contents

 Learning outcomes

By the end of this chapter you should understand:

Economic Theory

LO1 The concept of market equilibrium

LO2 How changes in demand and supply lead to changes in the market equilibrium

LO3 How price elasticity influences the size of changes in market price and output

LO4 Market shortages and surpluses as instances of market disequilibria

LO5 The difference between pooling and separating disequilibria

Business Application

LO6 How firms can try to manage a market shortage to boost sales – and product, or brand – awareness

LO7 The importance of being able to assess short- and long-run influences on demand, supply, market output and prices in the short and long run

Market theory at a glance

The issue

The price and the amount of goods and services traded change over time. But what causes these changes in particular product markets?

The understanding

Price changes in all markets, whether it is the price of beer, entrance to a nightclub or the price of a DVD, stem from changes in supply and demand. Sometimes the price may change simply because demand or supply has changed. In more complex cases, demand and supply could change together. Understanding how and why supply and demand change and the implications for market prices are important business skills.

The usefulness

Markets with upward price expectations will look more attractive than markets with downward price projections. If businesses can appreciate how competing factors will influence the price for their products or of key inputs, they can begin to develop successful strategies for the firm.

4.1 Business problem: picking a winner

How does a firm, or businessperson, know which product to promote and sell, and which to leave alone? Take Boxes 4.1 and 4.2, which contain two articles on shipping rates. The articles were published less than one month apart. The first describes a collapse in the price of hiring cargo ships. Many are lying idle and will take business for close to zero price. Within a month, the second article reports that shipping prices are rebounding.

Volatility in prices makes financial planning very difficult for ship owners. Ocean-going freighters and tankers cost many millions to build and are usually financed by mortgage-backed loans. The ship owner borrows from the bank over the expected lifetime of the ship. But what repayment is affordable? This question is difficult to answer if the market price for carrying cargo is so uncertain.

Perhaps the period under review in the articles is especially volatile and reflects the massive economic uncertainty brought to the global economy by the credit crisis. If you were a ship owner, then you might think about the long-term trend for shipping prices. If global trade continues to grow and China continues to suck in imports, then the trend for shipping prices may well be up. But of course the price also depends on the number of competitors offering ships for hire. How many old ships are out there? How many new ships can the shipyards of the world produce in a given year; and who, if anyone, is willing to offer finance to pay for these ships? Having an expert view of the factors that drive price in the shipping market makes it much easier to purchase and run a multi-million dollar cargo vessel.

The problem of predicting future prices and volumes is not just limited to shipping rates. Consider your own futures. Some of you may wish to supply yourselves as marketing executives, others as accountants and perhaps some as business economists. The wage or price at which you will be hired will depend upon how many other workers wish to supply themselves to your chosen occupation; and how many firms demand such types of workers. Greater supply will increase competition and the price or wage rate will fall, while higher demand by firms will

Box 4.1 Shipping rates hit zero as trade sinks

Adapted from an article by Ambrose Evans-Pritchard in The Daily Telegraph, *14 January 2009*

'They have already hit zero,' said Charles de Trenck, a broker at Transport Trackers in Hong Kong. 'We have seen trade activity fall off a cliff. Asia–Europe is an unmitigated disaster.'

Shipping journal *Lloyd's List* said brokers in Singapore are now waiving fees for containers travelling from South China, charging only for the minimal 'bunker' costs. Container fees from North Asia have dropped $200, taking them below operating cost.

Industry sources said they have never seen rates fall so low. 'This is a whole new ball game,' said one trader.

The Baltic Dry Index (BDI), which measures freight rates for bulk commodities such as iron ore and grains, crashed several months ago, falling 96 per cent.

A report by ING yesterday, said shipping activity at US ports has suddenly dived. Outbound traffic from Long Beach and Los Angeles, America's two top ports, has fallen by 18 per cent year-on-year, a far more serious decline than anything seen in recent recessions.

'This is no regular cycle slowdown, but a complete collapse in foreign demand,' said Lindsay Coburn, ING's trade consultant.

Idle ships are now stretched in rows outside Singapore's harbour, creating an eerie silhouette like a vast naval fleet at anchor. Shipping experts note that the number of vessels moving around seem unusually high in the water, indicating low cargoes.

© Telegraph Media Group Limited 2009

 Box 4.2 Rush for ships feeds hope of revival in commodities

Adapted from an article by Carl Mortished in The Times, *10 February 2008*

A surge in shipping rates for bulk carriers, used to transport cargoes of wheat, coal and iron ore, has created a frisson of excitement about signs of recovery in trade with China.

The Baltic Dry Index, a measure of freight rates for dry bulk vessels, gained 10 per cent in value yesterday after a 50 per cent increase last week as mining companies scrambled to hire ships to deliver iron ore to China.

The burst of upward momentum follows last year's collapse as Chinese mills and factories shut down. Many fleet owners faced bankruptcy as rates plunged below the economic cost of their vessels and the Dry Index fell 90 per cent over six months.

Rates for the largest Capesize vessels have doubled from $17 270 per day at the end of January to more than $34 000 per day and the cost of shipping coal from South Africa to Rotterdam has leapt from $7 per ton in January to $10 per ton.

Optimists see the renewed interest in vessel chartering as evidence that China's $600 billion infrastructure stimulus is beginning to generate demand from Chinese steel mills.

© 2009 Times Newspapers Ltd.

lead to higher wages. You, therefore, have to decide if the supply of workers into your chosen profession will rise or fall, and whether or not demand will rise or fall. Predicting correctly can potentially lead to higher income levels in the future.

The discussion in this chapter will present you with an economist's understanding of the marketplace, explicitly highlighting the link between demand and supply in marketplaces and illustrating how changes in demand and supply lead to changes in the market price of a product. By the end of the chapter you will have an understanding of how markets work and, more importantly, how business managers might try to make markets work for them.

4.2 Bringing demand and supply together

In Chapter 2, where we examined the price set in the market, we cheated by simply focusing on the willingness to demand. When considering markets and price setting, we also need to think about firms and their willingness to supply at various prices. In Chapter 3, when examining the short-run costs of firms, we argued that the firm's supply curve is its marginal cost curve at prices above short-run average variable cost. We are now at a point where we can explore the supply curve more fully.

In Figure 4.1, we have a **supply curve** for the firm and the industry. Unlike the demand curve, the supply curve has a positive slope. In Chapter 3, when discussing short-run costs, we showed in Section 3.4, Figure 3.7, that the supply curve is the firm's marginal cost curve, at prices above average variable cost. As a summary, if the firm wishes to maximize profits, then it will be willing to supply additional units of output if the price it receives is greater than, or equal to, the marginal cost. Since the marginal cost increases as output increases, higher prices are needed in order to induce additional supply. Therefore, the supply curve shows a positive relationship between price and output.

> A **supply curve** depicts a positive relationship between the price of a product and firms' willingness to supply the product.

At each price, firm B is willing to supply more output than firm A. This is because the marginal cost at each output level is lower for firm B. At a price of £5, B is willing to supply 1500 units; A is only willing to supply 1000 units. Therefore, at all prices B is more willing to supply than A. The industry's willingness to supply is equal to the sum of A and B's willingness to supply.

Therefore, at a price of £5, the industry willingness to supply is 1000 + 1500 = 2500.

The industry supply curve in Figure 4.1 is the sum of each firm's willingness to supply at each possible price.

Just as we discussed with the demand curve, we also need to think about the factors that will lead to a shift in supply:

- If more firms enter the market, then supply must shift out to the right with more industry output being offered for sale at any given price. Conversely, if firms close down and exit the market, then the supply curve must shift in to the left, with less industry output being sold at any given price.
- If the costs of labour, or other inputs, increase, profits must fall. As the potential to make profits decreases, then firms will be less willing to supply and so the supply curve will move in to the left. Conversely, if input prices fall, then the ability to make a profit increases and supply will shift out to the right.
- If a new technology is invented that enables firms to be more productive, then their costs will fall. This makes profits increase and firms are willing to supply more. The supply curve will then move out to the right.

> The **market equilibrium** occurs at the price where consumers' willingness to demand is exactly equal to firms' willingness to supply.

Market equilibrium

In order to understand the marketplace we now need to bring consumers and firms together. In Figure 4.2, we have the supply and demand curve together. Where demand and supply meet is known as the **market equilibrium**.

As a more realistic example, consider buying a second-hand car. Assume the seller (supplier) offers to sell the car for £5000. You examine the car and make an offer to buy at £4000. This is

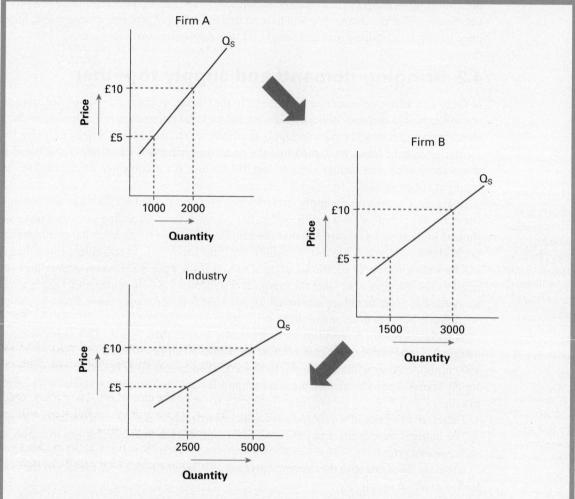

Figure 4.1 Individual firms and market supply

For firms A and B, as the price increases, willingness to supply also increases. At each price, firm B is more willing to supply than firm A. For example, at £5 A is willing to supply 1000 units and B is willing to supply 1500. The industry supply is simply the sum of A and B. So, at £5 the industry's willingness to supply is 1000 + 1500 = 2500. Clearly, as more firms enter the industry, the industry's willingness to supply will increase and the industry supply curve will shift to the right. Similarly, as firms leave the industry, the willingness to supply will reduce and the industry supply curve will shift to the right.

not equilibrium as you and the seller are willing to buy and sell at different prices. A trade will not occur because you cannot agree on the price. But assume the seller is now willing to reduce the asking price to £4500 and you accept. This is the equilibrium – you have both agreed a price at which you are willing to buy and the owner is willing to sell. As such, a trade will occur.

Before moving on it is worth making a few comments about the equilibrium. First, we assume that the equilibrium is unique. The demand and supply curve only intersect at one point. Given the condition of *ceteris paribus*, all other things being equal, the equilibrium is a stable position as there are no forces acting to move the price away from the equilibrium. In the

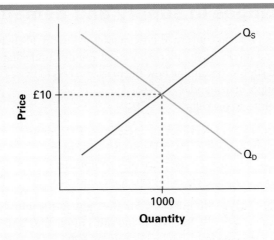

Figure 4.2 Market equilibrium

Market equilibrium occurs at the price where the willingness to demand by consumers meets the willingness to supply by firms. In this case, at a price of £10 consumers are willing to purchase 1000 units and firms are willing to sell 1000 units.

> In situations of **disequilibria**, at the current price the willingness to demand will differ from the willingness to supply.

case of our car, both the seller and the buyer are happy to trade at the agreed price of £4500. Second, any other combinations of price and quantity that are not the equilibrium values are described as market **disequilibria**.

Third, if the market is in disequilibrium, then, as with the case of our car traders, negotiations and resulting price changes will push the market towards its equilibrium position. We will explain these points as we develop your understanding of the market.

For those readers who are mathematically inclined, it is possible to think of the market equilibrium as the solution to a simultaneous equation problem. See Box 4.3 for further details.

➡ Box 4.3 Market equilibrium as simultaneous equations

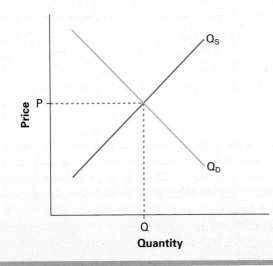

Since the demand and supply lines are linear, they can be expressed using the equation of a straight line.

$$Q_D = a_d - b_d P$$

where a_d is the intercept and $-b_d$ is the (negative) slope of the demand line

$$Q_S = a_s + b_s P$$

where a_s is the intercept and b_s is the (positive) slope of the supply line.

In equilibrium $Q_D = Q_S$; we can therefore solve the two equations above for P.

So,

$$a_d - b_d P = a_s + b_s P$$

$$b_s P + b_d P = a_d - a_s$$

$$P = (a_d - a_s)/(b_d + b_s)$$

4.3 Changes in supply and demand

The business problem concerned how market prices are likely to develop in the future. Now that we have a model of the market, we can use our understanding of the factors that shift demand and supply to examine how the market reacts to these changes. We will begin by considering changes in demand.

Demand shifts to the right:

♦ for a normal good when income increases, or for an inferior good when income falls
♦ following an increase in the price of the substitute
♦ following a reduction in the price of a complement
♦ when tastes and preferences for this good improve

Figure 4.3 illustrates a shift in demand to the right. At the initial equilibrium point, 1000 units are traded at a price of £10. But as demand shifts out to the right, a new equilibrium is achieved and now 2000 units are sold at a higher price of £20.

This can be used to explain property prices when the price of loans is cheap and income is growing steadily. Loans are a complement when buying a home. If you buy a house, you buy a loan. So, cheaper loans increase both the demand for loans and the demand for houses. As income increases, then as a normal good, demand increases for homes. So, for these two reasons the demand line shifts to the right and the equilibrium price and quantity increase.

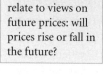

Price expectations relate to views on future prices: will prices rise or fall in the future?

We can also bring **price expectations** into the analysis. If you think prices are going to rise in the future, then you will bring forward your consumption. The demand curve for consumption now, as opposed to consumption in the future, shifts to the right.

We can now explore what happens when demand shifts to the left, as in Figure 4.4.

Demand shifts to the left:

♦ for a normal good when income falls, or for an inferior good when income rises
♦ following a decrease in the price of the substitute
♦ following an increase in the price of a complement
♦ when tastes and preferences for this good deteriorate

This time we have simply changed the diagram around. We start at an equilibrium price of £20 selling 2000 units and then demand shifts to the left. The equilibrium price falls to £10 selling only 1000 units. This has occurred in shipping, as described in Box 4.1. Fewer companies are

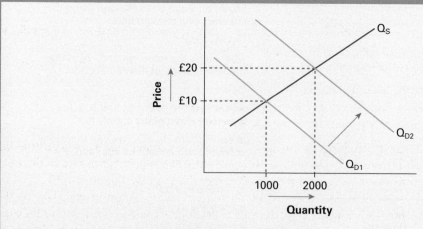

Figure 4.3 Shift in demand to the right

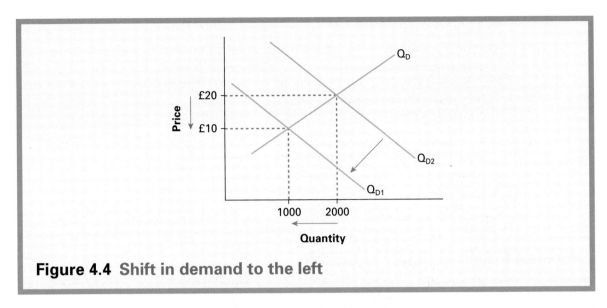

Figure 4.4 Shift in demand to the left

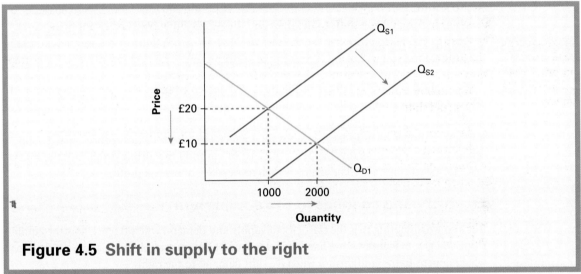

Figure 4.5 Shift in supply to the right

exporting goods around the world, so there is less demand for ships. The demand line shifts to the left and the equilibrium price and quantity fall.

Now let us consider supply. Supply shifts to the right:

◆ if more firms enter the market
◆ if the cost of inputs, such as labour, becomes cheaper
◆ if technological developments bring about productivity gains

In Figure 4.5, supply has shifted to the right. The equilibrium moves from a price of £20 selling 1000 units to £10 selling 2000 units. If we assume that the supply has moved to the right because more firms are competing in the market, then this outcome appears sensible.

Increased competition should lead to a drop in prices and more consumers taking up the product. The Internet is a significant technological development and it effectively cuts the costs of being a product provider. For example, rather than having to buy or lease many high-street shops, a new retailer can deal with its customers over the Internet. This significantly reduces its costs. Hence the market price, in major Internet areas such as travel, should fall. Lower prices

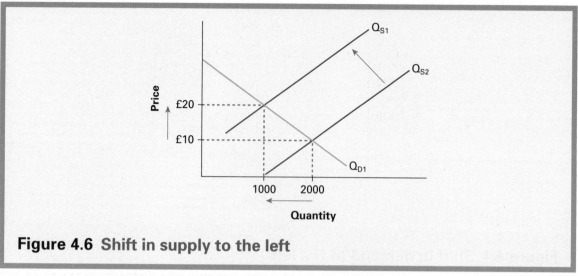

Figure 4.6 Shift in supply to the left

mean lower profits and therefore economists predicted the dot.com crash with ease. We will return to Internet-based business in the business applications at the end of the chapter.

Let us now examine a shift in supply to the left. Supply shifts to the left:

◆ if firms exit the market
◆ if the cost of inputs, such as labour, become expensive

If supply shifts to the left, as in Figure 4.6, then the equilibrium price moves from £10 selling 2000 units to £20 selling 1000 units. This might occur if one firm exited the market or took steps to reduce its capacity. Airlines sometime use this strategy. They take aircraft off unpopular routes, or swap large jumbos for smaller ones. Both tactics reduce capacity/supply on particular routes. As this happens, the cost of running the airline drops and the market price for tickets increases. The airline is then more likely to make a profit.

Elasticity and changes in the equilibrium

It is also worth noting that the elasticity of supply and demand will influence how the equilibrium changes. In Figure 4.7, we have an inelastic and an elastic supply curve and we can observe what happens to the equilibrium when we shift demand to the right.

Under inelastic supply we should expect that supply will not react strongly to a change in the price, and this is what we observe. The price rises from £10 to £30, but output only increases from 100 to 200 units. In the case of elastic supply, the increase in demand brings about a large change in output, 100 to 500 units, but only a small rise in the price, from £10 to £13.

In the real world there are lots of examples where successful businesspeople engineer supply to be inelastic, as opposed to elastic, as this leads to price rises, as opposed to output rises. Lawyers and accountants restrict supply into their professions through the need to pass professional exams in order to act as a lawyer or an accountant. Some people comment that lawyers and accountants have a licence to print money and, in part, you now know why.

Sport is also a successful industry. Formula 1 motor racing strictly controls the number of teams in the sport and the number of races in a season. It also controls television rights for the F1 season and it can thereby limit the means by which the races are supplied to the viewing public. This is all done with the objective of running a commercially profitable sporting event. Premiership football is the same. Television access to games is strictly controlled by the Football Association, which sells television rights to Sky. The alternative would be for each club to sell

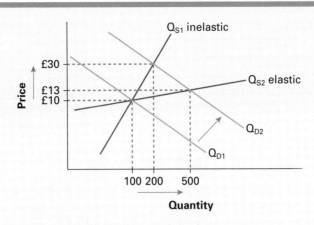

Figure 4.7 Impact of demand changes when supply is elastic or inelastic

Following a change in demand, price changes are greater if supply is inelastic, while output changes are greater if supply is elastic.

its games on an individual basis. For example, one week Manchester United might sell their game with Liverpool to the BBC, while the week after they could sell their game with Chelsea to ITV. Instead, Sky controls the supply of Premiership games and, out of 400 games a season, they only show around 60. So, by making the product scarce, or by engineering inelastic supply, the price in the market for Premiership games will rise.

In Figure 4.8, we consider how a change in supply affects the equilibrium when demand is elastic or inelastic. When demand is elastic, the increase in supply brings about a small change

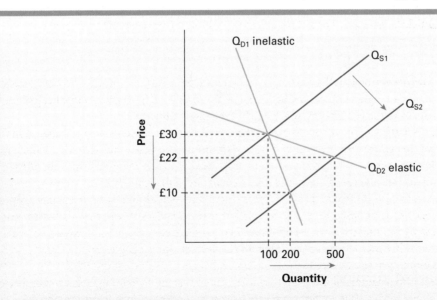

Figure 4.8 Supply changes under elastic and inelastic demand

Following a change in supply, the price change is greater if demand is inelastic. But the output change is greater if demand is elastic.

in the price, dropping from £30 to £22, with output increasing from 100 to 500 units. In the case of inelastic demand, the increase in supply generates a large drop in the price from £30 to £10, but only a small change in output from 100 to 200 units.

The clear lesson from this example is that, if faced with inelastic demand for your product, do not increase your production capacity and thereby increase supply, because the price will drop quicker than output increases and your total revenues will fall. However, if you are faced with elastic demand, do consider increasing your capacity and supplying more to the market, as output grows at a faster rate than the declining price and so total revenues will rise.

4.4 Disequilibrium analysis

So far we have only considered the market to be in equilibrium, where demand equals supply. In reality, markets may never be in equilibrium; they may instead always be moving between equilibrium positions. First, let us consider a situation in which the price is higher than the equilibrium.

In Figure 4.9, the current market price of £10 is higher than the equilibrium price of £8. At a price of £10 consumers are willing to demand 1000 units, but firms are willing to supply 2000 units. This is clearly not an equilibrium position. With supply exceeding demand by 2000 − 1000 = 1000 units, the market is said to be running a surplus. In effect, firms will be left with excess stock in their warehouses. We suggested earlier that natural forces would push the market towards the equilibrium, so how might this happen?

If the firm has too much stock, then, in accounting terms, its working capital is tied up. The firm has spent money making the product and it now needs to sell the product in order to free its cash for future production. The only way to sell the excess stock is to begin discounting the price until everything is sold. The more excess stock a firm has, the bigger the discount it has to offer. You will have noticed the trick used by clothing retailers: '50% off' is written large but 'on selected ranges' is written much smaller. The goods that are discounted by 50 per cent will almost certainly be those that few, if any, people wanted at the original price. The biggest

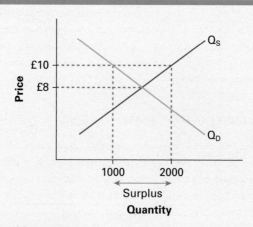

Figure 4.9 A market surplus

When the price is set above the equilibrium, firms are very willing to supply but consumers are not willing to demand. As a consequence, more is supplied than demanded. Firms are left with excess stock. In this case, at a market price of £10, firms supply 2000 units but consumers only demand 1000 units, leaving a surplus of 1000 units.

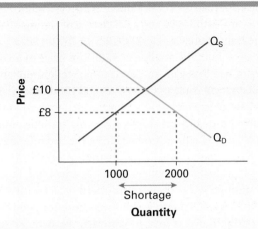

Figure 4.10 A market shortage

When the price is set below the equilibrium, firms are less willing to supply but consumers are very willing to demand. As a consequence, more is demanded than supplied. In this case, at a market price of £8, firms supply 1000 units but consumers demand 2000 units, leaving a shortage of 1000 units.

discounts are generally offered on the products where the retailer has observed the biggest difference between its willingness to supply and consumers' willingness to demand. Therefore, the biggest discounts are offered on the products where the retailer has the biggest level of unwanted stock.

Figure 4.10 illustrates the opposite situation, a market shortage. This time we have the market price of £8, which is below the market equilibrium price of £10. At £8, we can see that consumers are willing to demand 2000 units, but firms are only willing to supply 1000 units. We now have a shortage of 2000 − 1000 = 1000 units. Consumers would like to buy twice as much of the product as firms are willing to provide. Two responses are likely. Firms may recognize the high demand for their products and raise the price. Or consumers may begin to bid up the price in order to gain access to the product. If you really want to see the market in action, then watch the Internet auction sites for the most popular Christmas presents, such as the Xbox 360, the latest mobile phones or recent film releases on DVD.

4.5 Pooling and separating equilibria

> A **separating equilibrium** is where a market splits into two clearly identifiable sub-markets with separate supply and demand.

Consider the second-hand car market and assume good-quality cars cost £5000 and bad-quality cars cost £2500. Sellers of good and bad cars specialize in each type of car. So, if you want a good car, you go to a good car seller. Under these arrangements you would be willing to pay £5000 if you wanted a good car, or £2500 if you wanted a bad car. This is a **separating equilibrium**, as each type of product is sold in a separate market.

> A **pooling equilibrium** is a market where demand and supply for good and poor products pool into one demand and one supply.

Now consider a more realistic situation where good and bad cars are sold together. This is a **pooling equilibrium**, where the consumer finds it difficult to differentiate between good and bad products. So, unlike the separating equilibrium, both types of car are sold in the same market.

When you arrive at the dealership you are offered the following option. In a cloth bag are a number of car keys: 50 per cent open up good cars, 50 per cent open up bad cars. How much would you be willing to pay to put your hand in the bag and drive away with a car?

The statistical approach is to work out the expected value of the car. You have a 0.5 chance of gaining a good car worth £5000 and a 0.5 chance of ending up with a bad car worth £2500. The expected value is therefore $0.5 \times £5000 + 0.5 \times £2500 = £3750$.

So, all cars are sold at the pooling equilibrium price of £3750. If this permeates across the market, sellers of bad cars gain an extra £1250, while suppliers of good cars lose £1250. Over time more bad cars will come to the market and good cars will leave the market. This is known as **Gresham's Law**, where bad products drive out good products.

> **Gresham's Law** states that an increasing supply of bad products will drive out good products from the market.

Suppliers of good-quality cars under a pooling equilibrium are disadvantaged because they are unable to differentiate their products from the bad offerings. In order to solve this problem they need to find a way of creating a separating equilibrium. The way to achieve this is to do something that the bad suppliers would be unwilling to copy. Therefore, in the used car markets we can observe car dealerships offering cars with 100-point checks and 12-month warranties. Offering a 12-month warranty is cheap for good car sellers because the likelihood of the car breaking down is low. In contrast, the bad car suppliers are unwilling to offer warranties because the bad cars are likely to break down and, therefore, the cost of honouring the warranties would be very high.

In terms of a further example, consider the purchase of car insurance. The insurance company asks for many details before quoting you a price for car insurance. How old are you? How many years no claims bonus do you have? Where do you live? What type of car do you drive? The insurer is trying to separate the market by assessing whether you are a good or bad risk. If it did not do this, then clearly the market for insurance risks would move towards a pooling equilibrium. Every driver would be charged the same price for car insurance. However, in such a market bad drivers, with high accident or theft rates, pay less than they should, while good drivers, with low accident and theft rates, pay more than they should. Therefore, by separating the market the insurance company is able to charge the right insurance premiums for good and bad drivers.

4.6 Business application: marketing pop concerts – a case of avoiding the equilibrium price

The preceding discussion argued that markets will always find the equilibrium. So-called market forces push the market to a state where demand equals supply. This seems fairly reasonable, but how might a firm manage its market for strategic benefit? Or, can a firm control market forces? A successful businessperson would more than likely answer this last question with a yes.

Take, for example, the task of managing a pop star. Whether or not you like Madonna, she is undoubtedly a megastar. Some of her status stems from talent, but some also stems from commercial management. By way of an example, assume Madonna is going on tour to promote her new album and you are overseeing the task of pricing tickets for various venues.

An arena being used by Madonna holds 20 000 people. The supply of seats at this venue is fixed at 20 000, so supply is perfectly inelastic. If we plot demand and supply, then the result may look like Figure 4.11.

In equilibrium, demand equals supply. The task is to sell 20 000 tickets, so your business problem becomes one of finding the price that will generate a demand of 20 000. In this example, we have assumed that £50 is the price that will ensure a demand of exactly 20 000.

Unfortunately, £50 as an equilibrium price is not a good outcome for Madonna. Selling all of the 20 000 tickets for £50 is a huge success but, since £50 is the equilibrium price, the concert is

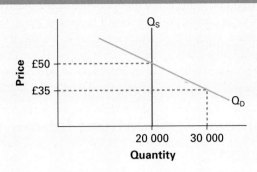

Figure 4.11 Managing the market

The equilibrium price of £50 clears the market with supply equalling demand. But at a discounted price of £35, a market shortage of tickets can be engineered, with demand outstripping supply. This helps to ensure an instant sell-out success for the concert.

only just a sell-out. Madonna is a megastar and, as such, the media and press expect her to sell out in a matter of hours. A price of £50 will *only just* ensure that she sells out.

However, if we set a ticket price of £35 we can engineer a ticket shortage in the market. At £35, 30 000 fans are willing to buy a ticket. With only 20 000 seats the concert will be a sell-out, with an additional 10 000 fans still trying to find a ticket on the black market. The importance of a sell-out concert will be evidenced by the positive media attention. Column inches in the celebrity pages of the press confirming Madonna's success will help to reinforce her image as a major celebrity. In this way, Madonna's management company is sacrificing ticket revenue, but it is gaining free advertisements in the press.

 Box 4.4 Sticky and sweet and hot, hot, hot: MADONNA summer shows sell out in minutes!

Adapted from a press release by Live Nation, 9 February 2009

Already the biggest grossing tour in history for a solo artist, Madonna's 'Sticky & Sweet Tour' is once again set to be the sweet success story of the summer. Ticket sales for the 2009 leg of Madonna's phenomenally successful tour went on sale this weekend and tour promoters Live Nation have already reported immediate sell-outs.

In London and Manchester, where tickets sold out in minutes on Friday, second shows have now been confirmed for 5 July in London and 8 July in Manchester, marking Madonna's final UK dates in 2009. On Saturday, having never previously performed in Belgium, over 70 000 tickets were sold for the Werchter Festivalpark concert, making it an incredible one-day sell-out event.

This morning, tickets in Oslo sold out as quickly as they could be processed and disappeared in under 30 minutes. In Helsinki, Madonna's Sticky & Sweet 6 August performance (76 000 tickets sold) will be the biggest show by one artist ever organized in Finland. Gothenburg's performance was also an immediate sell-out, with over 55 000 tickets sold in two hours.

In 2008, the 'Sticky & Sweet Tour' was seen by 2 350 285 fans in 58 cities, with record-breaking ticket sales everywhere, including 650 000 tickets sold in her series of South American dates, 72 000 tickets at Zurich's Dubendorf Airfield – the largest audience ever assembled for a show in Switzerland, 75 000 tickets in London and four sell-outs in New York's Madison Square Garden (60 364 tickets).

The price reduction in the marketplace also generates positive momentum in the market for Madonna's other products. As a successful recording artist, fans will be more willing to buy Madonna's album, calendars, T-shirts and DVDs. Furthermore, a sell-out concert this year ensures that Madonna can tour next year. However, if the tickets are mispriced and sales are slow, negative press will follow. This is only likely to slow demand for Madonna's products. Her megastar status will come under question and next year's tour will be in doubt.

4.7 Business application: labour markets

Input markets

> **Input markets** are where factor inputs, such as land, labour, capital or enterprise, are traded.

Firms not only sell into markets, they also buy inputs, such as labour and raw materials, from markets. It is therefore important to understand how these **input markets** will develop as rises in input prices will lead to increases in firms' costs.

For example, consider the market for professional staff, bankers, lawyers and accountants. In recent years the wages offered to these individuals were very high. These high wages reflected a booming economy, where the demand for services offered by professionals in lending, property transactions and financial management were high. The demand shifted to the right, as in Figure 4.12, and wage rates increased.

Two further influences then occurred. First, the high wage rates being paid to professional staff attracted workers into the banking, legal and accounting industries, graduates entered the sector and new student recruitment at university level moved towards professional services courses. The supply of capable workers shifted to the right and wage rates softened. Then the credit crunch recession led to many firms going bust and massive cutbacks in employment.

So, when thinking now about your future employment plans, it is essential to have a view on the future path of demand and supply in your chosen career area.

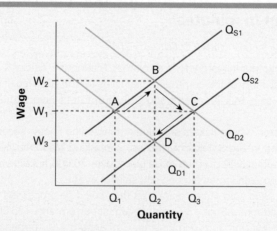

Figure 4.12 Input price changes over time

Beginning at A: demand for professional workers shifts to the right following a rise in demand for their services in a booming economy. The equilibrium moves to B and wage rates rise to W_2. Higher wages attract new additional workers into the market and supply shifts from Q_{S1} to Q_{S2}. The equilibrium is now at C and wages fall to W_1. Following the credit crunch recession, demand for professional staff shifts back to the left from Q_{D2} to Q_{D1}. The equilibrium is now at D and wages have fallen to W_3.

Box 4.5 Linklaters to shed almost 10% of partners and juniors

Adapted from an article by Alex Spence in The Times, *24 January 2009*

Linklaters, the world's second-largest law firm, will lose up to 50 partners in the biggest shake-up in the legal services market in decades. It is a second blow to the Magic Circle (London's group of leading law firms), coming two weeks after Clifford Chance, the world's largest law firm, revealed it had asked partners to inject more than £40 million in fresh capital.

Yesterday, Linklaters told *The Times* that the crisis in the financial markets and wider economy had forced the review. 'This is vital as part of the sound management of the firm,' Simon Davies, managing partner, said.

The overhaul could also see 10 per cent of the firm's junior salaried lawyers – as many as 200 worldwide – lose their jobs, the magazine reported.

Linklaters, one of the City's most powerful law firms, has grown rapidly in recent years, to 540 partners and about 2400 lawyers. It earned fee income of £1.29 billion last year, up 22 per cent, only narrowly behind Clifford Chance, which had revenue of £1.33 billion. Yet Linklaters' performance had been the subject of rumours in recent weeks despite securing a prize role on the administration of Lehman Brothers.

© 2009 Times Newspapers Ltd.

 Summary

1   The supply curve shows a positive relationship between the market price and the willingness to supply.

2   The industry supply curve is the sum of all the individual firms' supply curves.

3   The market equilibrium occurs where the willingness to supply equals the willingness to demand.

4   The equilibrium is changed whenever demand or supply changes. If demand increases, the price will rise and more will be traded. But if supply increases, the price will drop while more will be traded. A reduction in demand leads to a reduction in prices and the amount traded, while a reduction in supply leads to higher prices and less being traded.

5   If the current price is above the equilibrium, supply will exceed demand and the market will show a surplus. Suppliers are likely to discount the price to shift excess stock and eventually return to the equilibrium price.

6   When the current price is below the equilibrium, demand will exceed supply and the market will show a shortage. The price will rise in the market as consumers seek out scarce supply and eventually the market will return to its equilibrium.

7   If consumers cannot differentiate between quality differences among competing products, the market is said to exhibit a pooling equilibrium. Providers of good-quality products will strive to create a separating equilibrium by undertaking behaviour that poor-quality providers are unwilling to match.

8   Good businesses can attempt to control or influence the market. Setting a price below the market equilibrium can help to launch a product and gain valuable market share.

9   Understanding how the market will develop in the future requires an understanding of supply and demand. Such an understanding can be used to forecast changes in product prices and input prices, all of which are essential for strategic planning.

Learning checklist

You should now be able to:

♦ Explain the concept of market equilibrium and use a demand and supply diagram to show the equilibrium

♦ Use demand and supply diagrams to analyse changes to price and quantity following changes in demand and supply

♦ Explain how changes in the equilibrium price and quantity are influenced by the elasticity of demand and supply

♦ Explain the difference between a shortage and a surplus

♦ Explain the difference between a pooling and a separating equilibrium

♦ Explain how firms can benefit from pricing below the equilibrium price

♦ Explain how an understanding of future trends in demand, supply and prices is of use to business

Questions   connect™

1   At a price of £10, consumers are willing to demand 20 000 units and firms are willing to supply 20 000 units. Is this market in equilibrium?

2   Following an economic crisis, a number of banks collapse. What do you think happens to the supply of banking services and the price of banking services in general?

3   If income levels fall in an economy, what do you think will happen to the price of inferior goods and services?

4   As incomes in China rise, the global price of chicken and pork increases. Why?

5   An expansion of the world's shipping fleet threatens to depress the daily charter rates for ocean-going freighters. What must happen to demand in order to keep charter rates relatively constant?

6   Draw a diagram to illustrate a market surplus and a market shortage.

7   If there is a surplus amount of rental office space in a city, what do you expect to happen to rents? Use a diagram to explain your answer.

8   The elasticity of demand for electricity is relatively price inelastic. Will a change in supply have a large or a small impact on the equilibrium price and quantity?

9   What is the difference between a pooling and a separating equilibrium?

10   List three markets where pooling equilibria are a problem.

11   Why is the market for new staff characterized by the problem of adverse selection?

12   Celebrity status brings riches, but will the increase in the number of boy bands, docusoaps and reality TV programmes, such as *Big Brother*, change the market price of celebrities?

13   If incomes were falling in an economy would you wish to invest in a house-building company?

14 Is studying for a degree a strategy for creating a separating equilibrium in the labour market?

15 Healthcare in the UK is free. Draw a diagram illustrating how waiting lists for hospital treatment in the UK reflect a market shortage at zero price.

Exercises

1 True or false?
  (a) An increase in demand for coffee will lead to a higher price at Starbucks.
  (b) The merger of two firms can lead to higher prices.
  (c) The equilibrium price is always optimal for a firm.
  (d) Demand and supply are said to move separately under a separating equilibrium.
  (e) The adoption of clam phones by celebrities will raise the equilibrium price of clam phones.
  (f) Prices above the equilibrium will create a shortage.

2 Suppose that the data in Table 4.1 represent the market demand and supply for baked beans over a range of prices.

Table 4.1 Demand and supply

Price	Quantity demanded (million tins per year)	Quantity supplied (million tins per year)
8	70	10
16	60	30
24	50	50
32	40	70
40	30	90

  (a) Plot on a single diagram the demand and supply curve, remembering to label the axes appropriately.
  (b) What would be the excess demand or supply if the price was set at 8p?
  (c) What would be the excess demand or supply if the price was 32p?
  (d) Find the equilibrium price and quantity.
  (e) Suppose that, following an increase in consumers' incomes, demand for baked beans rises by 15 million tins per year at all prices. Find the new equilibrium price and quantity.

3 Consider Box 4.4:
  (a) Explain the difference between a market surplus and a market shortage.
  (b) Draw a demand and supply diagram which illustrates a surplus for Madonna's live performances.
  (c) Is the practice of minimizing the supply of concerts by leading artists one of risk minimization or sales maximization?

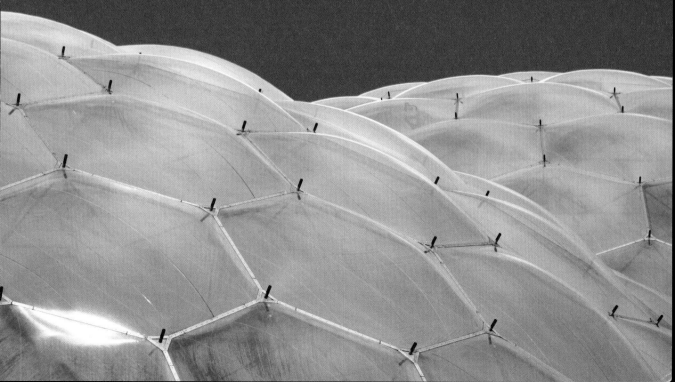

Section III
Competition and profitability

Section contents

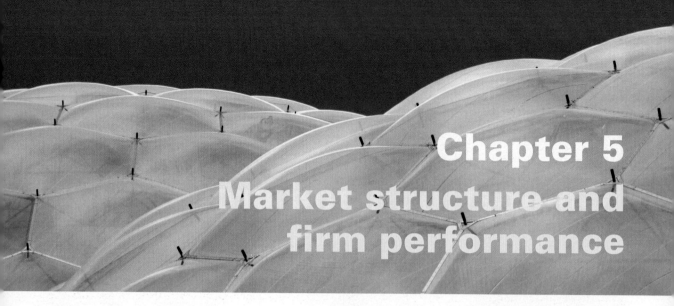

Chapter 5
Market structure and firm performance

Chapter contents

 Learning outcomes

By the end of this chapter you should understand:

Economic Theory

LO1 Why firms maximize profits by producing an output where marginal cost equals marginal revenue

LO2 Perfect competition

LO3 The difference between normal and super-normal profits

LO4 How profit and losses lead to entry and exit

LO5 Monopoly

LO6 How barriers to entry protect supernormal profits

LO7 The key differences in profit, output and prices between perfect competition and monopoly

Business Application

LO8 How a firm's behaviour is determined by its market conditions

LO9 To what extent a firm can change its market environment

Perfect competition and monopoly at a glance

The issue

An essential business skill is being able to understand why different market structures create differing levels of competition and, therefore, business performance, particularly in terms of profit. On this matter, economics offers some interesting insights.

The understanding

The understanding rests on how firms compete with each other. Firms can find themselves with any number of competitors. But instead of modelling every possible scenario, economists have concentrated on three: perfect competition, where there are many competitors; monopoly, where there are no competitors; and oligopoly, where there are only a very small number of competitors.

The usefulness

This chapter will provide you with an understanding of the important industrial characteristics which in part influence the level of competition and profitability that your business will generate.

5.1 Business problem: where can you make profits?

The simple answer is that you can make profits in any market where consumers are willing to pay a price that exceeds your costs. But an economist and a successful businessperson have a more valuable insight into this problem. They can identify markets that are more likely to make profits. They can do this because they understand the factors that determine whether the market price will be in excess of the firm's costs.

However, before we begin the theory, we will take a semi-empirical approach to this problem. Think about a business that you are familiar with and consider how profitable it is. We will take some common examples. Consider the pizza and kebab shops located near your university or accommodation. Are they profitable? We suspect that they make money. But you rarely see a local outlet growing and operating more than one or two outlets. The interiors of the shops are often basic and the decorations tend to be worn. Refurbishments occur only occasionally. So, given that the owners do not grow the business, or invest in new fixtures and fittings, it might be argued that profits are limited.

Now consider Google, a company so large and profitable that it is valued at $144 billion. The article in Box 5.1 suggests that Google is hoovering cash into its bank account. Its co-founders are billionaires and wherever it decides to spend its money, companies shake with fear.

So why is it that Google has risen to a value of $144 billion and kebab shops have not? It can be argued that Google has been successful in managing its market and principally its competition. By managing competition effectively, Google has grown into a successful company. In contrast, there are many kebab and pizza shops around your university. They are all competing with each other. Demand is elastic: if one shop drops its prices, students will flock to this shop. So price competition, or the threat of price competition, keeps prices low. Google currently faces little competition, its search engine performs better than all of its rivals. It attracts

Box 5.1 Is Google too powerful?

Adapted from an article in BusinessWeek, *9 April 2007*

It's the year 2014, and Googlezon, a fearsomely powerful combination of search engine Google Inc. and online store Amazon.com Inc. has crushed traditional media to bits. Taking its place is the computer-generated Evolving Personalized Information Construction – an online package of news, entertainment, blogs and services drawn from all the world's up-to-the-minute knowledge and customized to match your preferences. And it's all collected, packaged and controlled by Googlezon.

Google's accelerating lead in search and its moves into software and traditional advertising are sparking a backlash among rivals. Do you think Google is too powerful?

That simple little search box we all use every day? As the place at which nearly 400 million people each month start on the Internet, it's the No. 1 gateway to the Net's vast commercial potential. With more data on what people are searching for, Google can serve up the most targeted and relevant advertisements alongside the results – drawing more clicks, more cash. Consumers love Google's simplicity and results, which is why it draws 56 per cent of all searches. No wonder eager advertisers shoveled some $10.6 billion into Google's coffers last year, up an astonishing 73 per cent from 2005. If you can believe it, Google's $144 billion market value tops that of Time Warner, Viacom, CBS and the *New York Times* combined.

To the consternation of many of those companies and more, Google is now using that market cap, along with its $11 billion hoard of cash and investments, to storm a wide range of traditional markets. It's selling ads in newspapers, magazines, radio and, in a trial programme, television. In February it fired a torpedo at the software industry with a suite of online office software it is selling for a small fraction of the price of Microsoft Corp's Office. It's spooking the telecom industry with fledgling efforts to provide free wireless Internet access. Google's phenomenal ad machine, in short, has the potential to vaporize the profits of any industry that traffics in bits and bytes and to shift the economics to the advantage of Google, its users and its cadre of partners. 'It's Google's world,' shrugs Chris Tolles, vice-president of marketing at Topix Inc., which makes money from running Google ads on its news aggregation site. 'We just live in it.'

customers/searchers and advertisers at a better rate than any of its competitors. With limited substitutes, Google faces relatively inelastic demand.

In this chapter we will present the assumption that firms are in business to maximize profits. After explaining how firms should maximize profits, we will examine how the different market structures of perfect competition and monopoly influence the amount of profits earned by a firm in each type of market structure.

> **Average revenue** is the average price charged by the firm and is equal to total revenue/quantity demanded: (PQ)/Q.
>
> **Marginal revenue** is the change in revenue from selling one more unit.

5.2 Profit maximization

Economists assume that firms are in business to maximize profits. This seems reasonable. As an investor, you take a risk when investing in a company and so you expect a financial return. In Chapter 7, we will challenge the assumption of profit maximization, but for now it will suffice as a reasonable assumption for the firm.

The profits of a company are determined by the degree to which revenues are greater than profits. Therefore, in order to understand both (1) the output level at which profits are maximized and (2) the amount of profit generated at the maximum, we need to understand average and marginal revenue, plus average and marginal costs. We discussed average and marginal costs in detail during Chapter 3, but we need to develop your understanding of **marginal** and **average revenues**.

Average and marginal revenues

Consider the demand data in Table 5.1. In the first two columns we have data from a demand curve; as the price increases in column 1, the quantity demanded, listed in column 2, decreases. Total revenue = price × quantity; for example, at a price of £7 demand is six units, therefore total revenue = £7 × 6 = £42. The remaining total revenue values are provided in column 3. Average revenue = (price × quantity)/quantity. Therefore, at a price of £7 we have (£7 × 6)/6 = £7. The average revenue is the same as the price. You can see this clearly by noting that the column for price and the column for average revenue in Table 5.2 are identical. If you were asked to plot the demand curve (price against quantity demanded) and then also asked to plot the average revenue line (average revenue against quantity) on the same piece of graph paper, the two lines would lie on top of each other. If you are not convinced, take the data from Table 5.1 and use a spreadsheet package such as MS Excel to create an XY scatter plot of the demand and average revenue. You will only see one line on the screen, not two.

The demand line and the average revenue line are therefore the same thing.

In the final column, we have the values for marginal revenue. Marginal revenue is the revenue received by selling one more unit. Therefore, in moving from one unit to two units

Table 5.1 Demand and total, average and marginal revenue

Price (£)	Quantity demanded	Total revenue (PQ)	Average revenue (PQ/Q)	Marginal revenue
12	1	12	12	
11	2	22	11	10
10	3	30	10	8
9	4	36	9	6
8	5	40	8	4
7	6	42	7	2
6	7	42	6	0
5	8	40	5	−2
4	9	36	4	−4
3	10	30	3	−6
2	11	22	2	−8
1	12	12	1	−10

Table 5.2 Monopolistic average and total revenues

Price	Quantity	Total revenue (PQ)	Average revenue (PQ/Q)	Marginal revenue
12	4	48	12	
11	5	55	11	7
10	6	60	10	5

(selling one more unit), our revenues have increased from 12 to 22. Marginal revenue is therefore $22 - 12 = 10$. All the values for marginal revenue are plotted in Figure 5.1.

The marginal revenue line slopes down. This is because of two factors. First, marginal revenue is related to the demand curve. In order to sell one more unit, we know from Chapter 2 that we have to reduce the price of the product. Second, in reducing the price we are also reducing the price of all the previous units. Consider the following. We can sell seven units at a price of 6, or reduce the price to 5 and sell eight units. In comparing the two situations, we gain one more unit at a price of 5, but we are reducing the price from 6 to 5 on the other seven units. Therefore, the marginal revenue associated with selling one more unit is $+5 - (7 \times 1) = -2$. We can see that in order to sell one more unit we also have to accept a reduction in marginal revenue and not just the price.

Finally, in the bottom half of Figure 5.1, we have the plot of total revenue. You can see that maximum revenue occurs where marginal revenue equals zero in the top diagram. This is because a marginal revenue of 0 lies between positive and negative marginal revenue. When marginal revenue is positive, each unit adds a positive amount to total revenue. Once marginal revenue becomes negative, each additional unit reduces total revenue.

Profit maximization

We can now combine our understanding of revenue and costs to understand how firms maximize profits. Firms will maximize profits or, in other words, make the most amount

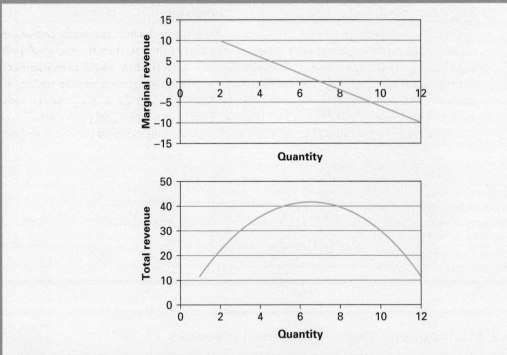

Figure 5.1 Marginal revenue and total revenue

The marginal revenue line slopes down, reflecting an increase in output which requires a reduction in the price and the impact of the price reduction on the price of previous units. Total revenue is greatest when marginal revenue is zero; this is because selling one more unit neither adds to nor subtracts from the total revenue.

of profit, when the marginal cost of the last unit of output equals the marginal revenue, or MC = MR.

It is important to note that MC = MR and profit maximization are not policy prescriptions for firms. Economists are not saying firms must behave in this way. Rather, economists have said profit maximization is a reasonable assumption to hold about the behaviour of firms; and if we do model firms as profit-maximizers, then output must be at the point where MC = MR. In Chapter 8 we will revisit the assumption of profit maximization and consider other assumptions, including growth maximizationa and revenue maximization.

> **Profit maximization** is the output level at which the firm generates the highest profit.

In understanding how the economist arrives at the **profit-maximization** rule of MC = MR, we need to make some assumptions. The firm does not decide to produce 10 or 20 units of output; rather, it decides if it wants to produce one unit of output. Then it decides if it wants to produce the second unit. At some point it will decide not to produce any more. So the economist is assuming that the firm is making stepped decisions.

In Table 5.3, we have added marginal cost data to the marginal revenue data discussed above. In the fourth column we have marginal revenue minus marginal cost.

> **Marginal profit** is the profit made on the last unit and is equal to the marginal revenue minus the marginal cost.

The firm maximizes profits when marginal cost equals marginal revenue, i.e. MC = MR. If MC = MR, then MR − MC = 0. The firm maximizes profits when the **marginal profit** = 0. This is similar to revenue maximization in Figure 5.1. When MR > MC, the firm is making a marginal profit – each additional unit generates a positive profit and adds to overall profits. However, once MR < MC the firm is making a marginal loss – each additional unit generates a loss and therefore diminishes total profits. We can, therefore, argue that the firm will increase production if marginal revenue is greater than marginal cost, i.e. MR > MC. But the firm will reduce output if it is incurring a marginal loss, i.e. MR < MC.

Using these insights we can take our stepped approach to discover the profit-maximizing output. From Table 5.3, if the firm produced one unit of output, then the marginal profit would be 6. Since this is positive, the firm will make one unit. The firm now decides whether or not to make the second unit. The additional or marginal profit associated with making the second unit is 8. Again, since this is positive the firm will make the second unit. Likewise, the firm will decide to make units three, four, five and six, as the marginal profits are all positive. The firm will not produce beyond the sixth unit because the marginal profits are negative.

Table 5.3 Marginal revenue and marginal cost

Quantity	MR	MC	MR – MC	Output decision	Profit
1	21	15	6	Raise	6
2	19	11	8	Raise	14
3	17	8	9	Raise	23
4	15	7	8	Raise	31
5	13	8	5	Raise	36
6	11	10	1		37
7	9	12	−3	Lower	34
8	7	14	−7	Lower	27
9	5	16	−11	Lower	16
10	3	18	−15	Lower	1

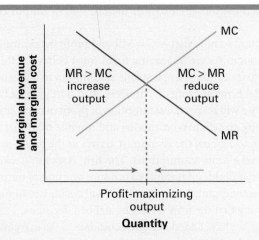

Figure 5.2 Marginal revenue, marginal cost and profit maximization

The firm maximizes profits where MC = MR. Alternatively, the firm will produce an additional unit of output if the MR is greater than the MC, because it then makes additional profit. But it will not produce any more output if the marginal revenue is less than the marginal cost because this will generate a loss on the last unit produced, leading to a reduction in overall profits.

For example, a loss of 3 is associated with making the seventh unit. Profits are, therefore, maximized at six units of output. This can be seen in the final column of Table 5.3, with profits peeking at 37 with an output of six.

Admittedly, we stated that the firm will maximize profits when MC = MR and in our example profits appear to peak at six units of output, where marginal revenue is one unit greater than marginal cost. From an examination of the data, we might argue that MC = MR somewhere between six and seven units, let us say 6.5. Some products are easy to divide into smaller units of output, for example oil, beer and milk. A firm could decide to produce 6.5 litres of milk. But it would not be sensible to produce 6.5 cars. We can, therefore, say that MC = MR is strictly and mathematically correct, but it is not always the most practical output level for a firm to maximize profits at. If the firm produces whole units, it will stop at the highest level of output with a positive marginal profit. This way, the firm chooses a level of output that is nearest to its profit-maximizing level of output.

Figure 5.2 provides a diagrammatic illustration of profit maximization where marginal cost equals marginal revenue. Firms will increase output if marginal revenue is greater than marginal cost; and they will reduce output if marginal cost is greater than marginal revenue.

Profit maximization and differences in demand

In Chapter 3, when considering costs, we saw that marginal cost always has a positive slope, that is, all firms face diminishing returns in the short run. However, firms in different markets face different demand conditions and this leads to different average revenue and therefore different marginal revenue lines. However, under the assumption of profit maximization the optimal output will still occur where MC = MR.

In Figure 5.3, we consider an important and special case where demand is perfectly elastic. We explained in Chapter 2 that a perfectly elastic demand line is horizontal. Firms can sell *any* amount of output at the current price, but if they price above the market price they sell nothing, because customers are extremely price sensitive.

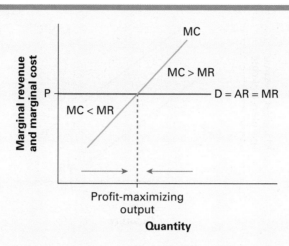

Figure 5.3 Profit maximization under perfectly elastic demand

The consequences of a perfectly elastic demand line are that average revenue and marginal revenue are also horizontal lines. Each unit of output is sold for the same price, so the average revenue is constant (and equal to the price); and the revenue from the last unit is equal to the revenue from the previous unit. Therefore, marginal revenue is also constant and equal to the price.

Figure 5.3 follows a similar reasoning to Figure 5.2. When marginal cost is below marginal revenue, the firm can expand output and raise profits. However, once marginal cost is greater than marginal revenue, the firm should reduce output and profits will rise. The important difference between Figures 5.2 and 5.3 is the relationship between marginal cost and price. In Figure 5.3, under profit maximization MC = MR = AR = P, or in shorthand MC = P. However, in Figure 5.2, MC = MR, but MR ≠ AR (also see the columns in Table 5.1 and Figure 5.1 to remind yourself of this fact). Therefore, MC ≠ P. As we explore perfect competition and monopoly later in this chapter, the importance of this distinction will become clearer.

Changes in costs and revenues

In Figures 5.4 and 5.5 we examine what happens if either marginal revenue or marginal cost changes. If demand increases for a product, then the marginal revenue curve will similarly shift to the right. This is because when the market price increases at all output levels, the firm will receive a higher price for each additional unit of output. In Figure 5.4, we illustrate this idea and see that marginal revenue now meets marginal cost at a much higher level of output. In response, the firm can maximize profits at a much higher level of output. Therefore, firms do not increase output because prices rise; rather, they increase output because the marginal revenue has risen above marginal cost. The motive for increasing output is, therefore, one of increased profits, not increased prices. In contrast, if demand for the product fell, then the marginal revenue curve would shift to the left. With lower marginal revenues, the profit-maximizing output would be reduced.

In Figure 5.5, we illustrate a reduction in marginal cost. We saw in Chapter 3 that marginal cost is influenced by the price of factor inputs such as labour and factor productivity. If labour became more productive it could produce more output and the marginal cost would fall. We see from Figure 5.5 that, if this did occur, then the marginal cost would fall below marginal revenue and the firm would increase output in order to maximize profits. Similarly, marginal

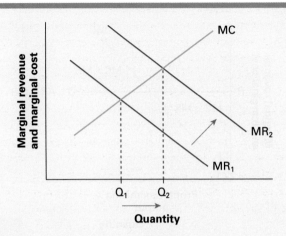

Figure 5.4 Increases in marginal revenue

If demand increases for the firm's product, then the marginal revenue curve will also move out to the right. Marginal revenue now equals marginal cost at a much higher level of output and the firm will therefore produce more output in order to maximize profits. We can now view increased output as a reflection of increasing profits rather than simply increasing prices.

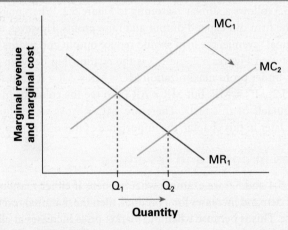

Figure 5.5 Falling marginal costs

If a firm experiences productivity growth, then its marginal costs may fall. With lower marginal costs at all levels of output the firm will be more able to maximize profits at a higher level of output. We can now view increased output as a reflection of increasing profits rather than simply decreasing costs.

cost could increase because labour wage rates increase. The marginal cost curve would then shift to the left. With higher marginal costs at all levels of output the profit-maximizing level of output would be reduced.

We have now brought together the understandings of demand and prices from Chapter 2 and cost theory from Chapter 3. Combining the two enables an understanding of how the firm will maximize its profits. Unlike in Chapter 2, where we discussed a firm's response to changes in the price of the final good or service, and in Chapter 3, where we analysed a firm's responses to cost changes, we can now see how the firm changes its output level based on an interaction of revenue and costs. In the economic sense, the firm is not concerned with prices or costs per se, but rather profit, which is a combination of the two.

Having highlighted profit as the major incentive for firms, we now need to consider how market structure will impact upon the marginal revenue and perhaps even marginal cost of a firm. By examining perfect competition and monopoly, we will see how the level of profits at the profit-maximizing output level is likely to be lower under perfect competition than under monopoly. However, before we embark upon the theory it is fairly straightforward to understand that profits will be lower in perfect competition. This can be seen from our definition that perfect competition is the market environment with the greatest amount of competition. With lots of competitors all chasing the same customers, profits have to be small. Now let us provide the theoretical, rather than commonsense, framework.

5.3 The spectrum of market structures

We can see in Figure 5.6 that **perfect competition** and **monopoly** are extreme and opposite forms of market structure. In reality, it is difficult to find true perfectly competitive markets or even monopolies. Financial markets trading shares in companies are highly competitive, as are commodity markets trading such goods as oil, copper and gold. But, as we will see below, while such markets are *highly* competitive, they are not necessarily *perfectly* competitive.

Perfectly competitive signifies that competition in the market is the greatest possible. No alternative market structure can be more competitive. Similarly, Microsoft is not a perfect example of a monopoly, as its products compete with a number of smaller suppliers, such as Linux. Likewise, the Beckhams have a monopoly on their lifestyle, image and personalities but, in the celebrity market, they still face competition from a range of married celebrity couples.

Other types of market structure are **imperfect competition** and **oligopoly**. Imperfect competition is very competitive, but differs from perfect competition by the recognition of product differentiation. Small service sector industries tend to have the characteristics of imperfect competition. The supermarket industry and the banking industry are oligopolistic. These are clearly more common modes of **market structure** and we will analyse imperfect competition and oligopoly in more detail in Chapter 6.

We will see when we examine the alternative market structures of perfect competition and monopoly that important competitive structures are: (1) the number of competitors; (2) the number of buyers; (3) the degree of product differentiation; and (4) the level of entry and exit barriers. Further explanation of these concepts will be provided when we discuss perfect competition in detail, where we will see very clearly how the structure, or characteristics, of a market determines the level of competition and, ultimately, profitability.

> Briefly, **perfect competition** is a highly competitive marketplace. **Monopoly** is a marketplace supplied by only one competitor, so no competition exists.
>
> **Imperfect competition** is a highly competitive market where firms may use product differentiation.
>
> **Oligopoly** is a market that consists of a small number of large players.
>
> **Market structure** is the economist's general title for the major competitive structures of a particular marketplace.

Figure 5.6 Range of possible market structures

5.4 Perfect competition

Perfect competition is the most competitive type of market structure. Economists assume that perfect competition is characterized by the following structure:

◆ Many buyers and sellers
◆ Firms have no market power
◆ Homogeneous products
◆ No barriers to exit or entry
◆ Perfect information

These elements are explored below:

◆ **Buyers, sellers and market values** – the first two assumptions are related. The market has many different buyers and sellers. Because of this, no firm, or indeed buyer, has any market power. Market power is the ability to set prices. By many buyers and sellers we do not mean ten, 50 or 100 – we mean *many*! Each buyer and seller is a very small part of the market. For example, the market for shares in any FTSE 100 company might be in excess of 10 million traded shares per day. But an individual shareholder may only hold 1000 shares, which is clearly small when compared to the entire market. The individual shareholder, therefore, has little power over the market price; they simply accept the current price on the stock exchange screens.

◆ **Homogeneous products** – if all products are homogeneous, all firms provide identical products. Milk is an example; milk from one supermarket is the same as milk from another. Cars are heterogeneous or differentiated.

◆ **No barriers to exit or entry** – in order to operate a 3G telecommunications network you require a licence from the government and a very large amount of investment. Both restrict entry into the market and, therefore, act as an **entry barrier**. Similarly, if a firm decides to leave the 3G market, then the cost associated with selling the accumulated assets, whether technical network infrastructure or brand name capital, will be costly and act as a restraint on exit. Alternatively, if you wished to start selling flowers from your garden, then you only need some seeds, sunshine and water. The entry barriers into the flower market are limited. Similarly, if you decided to stop producing flowers in your garden, then you would face little if any **exit barriers** or costs. You simply pull up the flowers and lay some additional turf.

> **Barriers to entry** make entry into a market by new competitors difficult. **Exit barriers** make exit from a market by existing competitors difficult.

No barriers to exit or entry means that a businessperson can move economic resources into a market in the pursuit of profit and can also move them out. This transfer of resources is assumed to be effortless and relatively inexpensive, if not free.

◆ **Perfect information** – if you have a secret ingredient for your kebabs, then any competitor will be able to discover what the ingredient is. They can send in a customer and then arrange for the kebab to be analysed by a scientist or master kebab chef. So any informational advantage will be short-lived. Similarly, if a firm decided to sell at a higher price than its competitors, everyone in the marketplace would know that the price was expensive. In the stock market, all offers to sell and buy are published on the brokers' screens, hence there is **perfect information** regarding prices.

> **Perfect information** assumes that every buyer and every seller knows everything.

Perfect competition and the firm's demand curve

We will now see how the assumptions of perfect competition drive the outcomes of a perfectly competitive market. For example, the assumption regarding a lack of market power is illustrated in Figure 5.7.

In the marketplace many buyers and sellers come together and the market price of £10 is set. This is illustrated in the right-hand side of Figure 5.7. As the firm has no market power it simply accepts the market price.

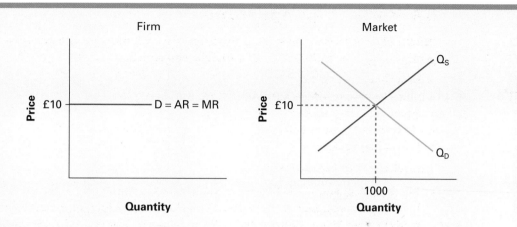

Figure 5.7 Perfect competition and the firm's average and marginal revenues

Buyers and sellers in the marketplace set the price of £10. Each firm, as a price taker, then accepts the market price and can sell any amount of output at the market price. Therefore, the firm's average revenue (AR) is £10, and so is marginal revenue.

If a firm accepts the market price, it is a **price taker**.

As a **price taker**, the demand curve for a perfectly competitive firm is perfectly elastic. The firm can sell whatever quantity it likes at £10. This is illustrated on the left-hand side of Figure 5.7. While a perfectly competitive firm can sell whatever quantity it likes at the market price, this does not mean that the firm produces everything the market can bear. Rather, all firms can reasonably expect to sell their profit-maximizing level of output at the market price.

Since the firm faces many competitors, its market share will be extremely small. When this competition is coupled with perfect information, if the firm raised its prices above the equilibrium level it would sell nothing, with customers quickly swapping to the cheaper suppliers. In contrast, because the firm can sell all that it likes at the current market price, there is no reason to sell below the market price. Taking these points together, the firm faces a perfectly elastic demand curve, because demand reacts instantly, fully and perfectly to an increase or decrease in the firm's price.

Average and marginal revenue

Marginal revenue is the revenue received by selling one more unit. In perfect competition, the firm faces a perfectly elastic, or horizontal, demand line. If it decides to sell one more unit, then it does not have to reduce its price. Therefore, if the market price is £10, the firm can sell one more unit and receive an additional £10. Unlike in our discussion of Table 5.1 and Figure 5.2, the perfectly competitive firm does not have to suffer a reduction in revenue on its previous units. Therefore, the marginal revenue line is also horizontal and equal to the average revenue line, but only in the special case of perfect competition.

Adding in costs

We can now take Figure 5.7 and add in the short-run average cost curves developed in Chapter 3 to produce Figure 5.8. In so doing, we will have average revenue and costs on the same figure as well as marginal revenue and marginal cost. We can then examine the profitability of the firm.

The diagram is fairly straightforward. Remember, we are assuming the firm is a profit-maximizer and we would simply like to know how much profit the firm would make. So:

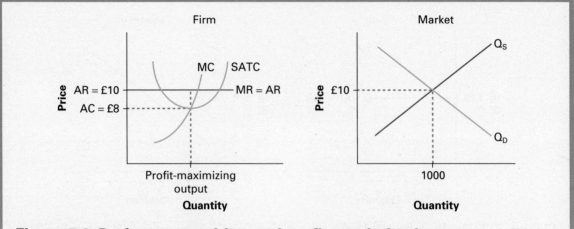

Figure 5.8 Perfect competition and profit maximization

Introducing costs into the analysis enables an examination of the firm's profits. The firm produces at the profit-maximizing output, where MC = p. The average cost of this output is AC = £8, while the average revenue is AR = £10. Total profit is (£10 − £8) × output.

♦ **Step 1**: The firm maximizes profits by producing the profit-maximizing level of output associated with MC = MR.
♦ **Step 2**: What does it cost to produce the profit-maximizing output? Simply draw the line up from the profit-maximizing output until it touches the short-run average total cost curve, SATC. So, in this case, £8 per unit.
♦ **Step 3**: What revenue will the firm earn by selling the profit-maximizing output? Simply draw the line up from the profit-maximizing output until it touches the average revenue line, AR. So, in this case, £10.
♦ **Step 4**: Profit per unit is AR minus AC, so £10−£8 or £2 per unit.
♦ **Step 5**: Total profit is profit per unit times the number of units produced. Or, in our figure, the rectangle defined by AR − AC and the profit-maximizing output.

So, we can see that this particular firm is making a profit. In economic terms, it is making a 'supernormal profit'. See the next section on normal and supernormal profits.

We can also consider the situation where a firm is making a loss, and this is depicted in Figure 5.9. In comparison to Figure 5.7, we have simply reduced the market price from £10 to £7, and therefore the AR and MR to £7. At this market price, the firm's average revenue is below even the lowest point on the firm's average cost curve, so the firm cannot make a profit at any output level. The firm will now seek to minimize its losses rather than maximize its profits. It will achieve this in the same way as it maximizes its profits – that is, by selecting the output level where MR = MC. The loss generated by the firm will be equal to (AR − AC) × loss-minimizing output.

> **Accounting profits** are revenues less raw material costs, wages and depreciation.

Normal and supernormal profits

Importantly, economists and accountants differ in their definition of profits. In Figure 5.10, we illustrate each of these views. An accountant calculates profits by taking total costs away from total revenues. The accountant would generally categorize raw materials, labour and depreciation as costs. Taking these costs from revenue leaves **accounting profits**.

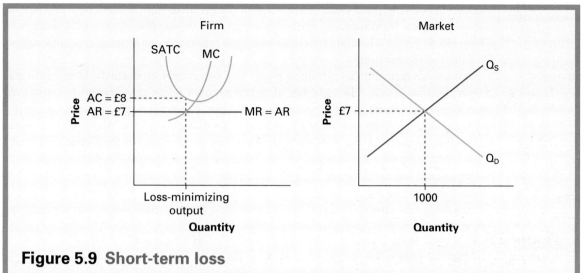

Figure 5.9 Short-term loss

With the average revenue of £7 less than the average cost of £8, the firm will seek to minimize its losses. It will do this by selecting the output level where MC = MR. The overall loss will therefore be (AR – AC) × loss-minimizing output, or (7 – 8) × loss-minimizing output.

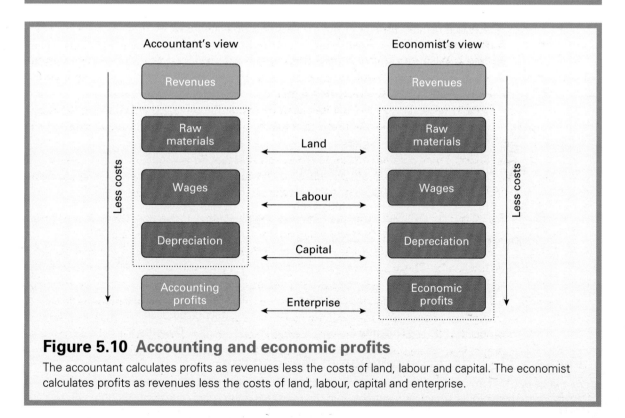

Figure 5.10 Accounting and economic profits

The accountant calculates profits as revenues less the costs of land, labour and capital. The economist calculates profits as revenues less the costs of land, labour, capital and enterprise.

The economist also takes costs away from revenues. But the economist thinks about the costs of using economic factors of production. These, from Chapter 1, are land, labour, capital and enterprise. The first three in this list map directly onto the accountant's cost categories. For example, the cost of labour is wages. But what is the cost of our fourth factor of production,

> **Economic profits** are revenues less the costs of all factors of production.
>
> **Normal economic profits** are equal to the average rate of return which can be gained in the economy.
>
> **Supernormal profits** are financial returns greater than normal profits.

namely that of enterprise? Recall that enterprise is individuals who are risk-takers and provide financial capital for companies. Entrepreneurs receive the benefits of taking financial risks. They receive profits. Therefore the economist views profits as a cost of using enterprise and we call these **economic profits**.

Economists further divide economic profits into two categories, **normal** and **supernormal**. Normal profits are the minimum rate of return required for an entrepreneur to retain their investment in a company. If the entrepreneur can gain 5 per cent by placing their money in a bank account, then this may act as a benchmark rate of normal return. We would then adjust this figure upwards for the degree of risk offered by the company. If the company was very risky, then we might say the normal rate of return for the company is 10 per cent. If the company was less risky, we might expect an entrepreneur to be seeking 7 per cent from their investment.

Anything above the normal rate of return is called **supernormal profits**; and anything less than normal profits is called a supernormal loss.

Long-run equilibrium

Having seen supernormal profits and losses in the short run, it is now time to recall the remaining assumptions regarding perfect competition. Perfect information implies that all businesspeople outside the industry are aware of the profits to be made inside this industry. No barriers to entry imply that entry into this market is easy. Therefore, businesses know about the profitable opportunities in this market and can enter the market with ease. The consequences of increased market entry for profits are illustrated in Figure 5.11.

If we begin in market equilibrium at QS_1 and QD, the market price is £15. This sets an average revenue AR_1, which is higher than firms' short-run average costs, SATC. Firms are

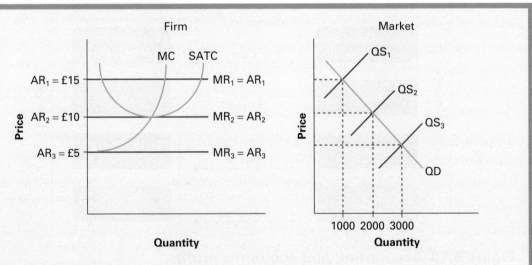

Figure 5.11 **Perfect competition in the long run**

At a price of £15, firms are making supernormal profits, with average revenues greater than average costs. These high profits attract new entrants into the market and the supply curve moves from QS_1 to QS_2. The price falls until it reaches £10. At this price the average revenue and average cost are equal, the firm earns normal profits, and firms are no longer attracted into the market. At a price of £5, firms are making losses, with average revenue below average costs. These losses force some firms out of the industry. Supply moves from QS_3 to QS_2. The price rises to £10 and firms earn normal profits.

making supernormal profits and this attracts new entrants into the industry. The supply curve moves to QS_2, the market price falls to £10 and firms are making normal profits. There is no longer any reason to enter the market as similar risk-adjusted profits can be earned by putting money in the bank.

We can also consider the situation where firms are making a loss. When market supply is at QS_3, the market price is £5 and this sets average revenue AR_3 less than short-run average cost, SATC. Firms are making losses and some exit the market. This leads to QS_3 moving towards QS_2. Once the market price returns to £10, the remaining firms in the industry are making normal profits and exit stops.

Clearly, entry and exit are not the only factors that will influence the market equilibrium. We can envisage a number of short-term scenarios leading to a long equilibrium. In Scenario 1, the good is a normal good. Income increases and, therefore, the market demand shifts to the right. The market price increases and the firm's marginal revenue and average revenue rise relative to costs. Increased profits then attract new entry into the market. The market supply curve shifts to the right and the market equilibrium price drops until average revenues equal average costs and only normal profits are earned. These points are highlighted in Figure 5.12.

In Scenario 2, following wage negotiations the cost of labour increases. The firms' marginal cost curves shift to the left and average costs rise upwards. Firms' profits decrease. Exit occurs and the market supply curve shifts to the left. As a result, the market equilibrium price increases

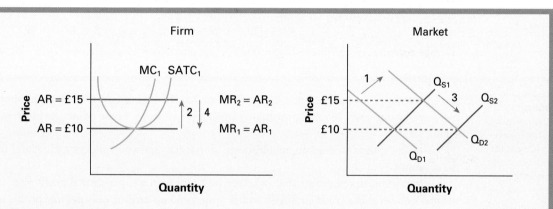

Figure 5.12 Changes in market demand and adjustments to long-run equilibrium

The market is in equilibrium where Q_{D1} equals Q_{S1}. The market price is £10. At this price the firm earns a normal profit, with average revenue equal to average cost at the profit-maximizing output, where $MR_1 = MC$. Then:

1 Income levels in the economy increase. The good is income normal and therefore the demand curve shifts to the right to QD_2 (consumers use the increased income to buy more of the good). The equilibrium price rises to £15.
2 The average revenue for the firm rises to £15, reflecting the increased market price. The marginal revenue also increases to £15 and the profit-maximizing output increases. Since average revenues exceed average cost, the firm is making a supernormal profit.
3 The supernormal profits attract new entrants into the market and supply shifts from Q_{S1} to Q_{S2} and the market equilibrium price falls to £10.
4 The average and marginal revenues fall to £10. The profit-maximizing output returns to its original level and the firm generates normal profits.

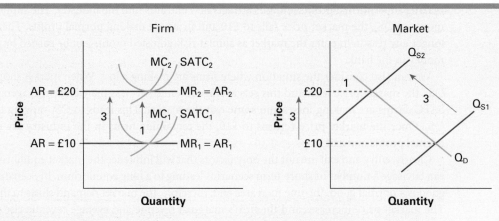

Figure 5.13 An increase in firms' costs and adjustment to long-run equilibrium

The market is in equilibrium where Q_D equals Q_{S1}. The market price is £10. At this price the firm earns a normal profit, with average revenue equal to average cost at the profit-maximizing output. Then:

1 Negotiations lead to a rise in the wages paid to the firms' labour forces. This leads to an increase in the individual firm's costs. The average and marginal costs rise to MC_2 and $SATC_2$.

2 The firms' costs are now greater than the average revenue of £10, leading to losses. Some firms exit the industry and the industry supply curve shifts to the left, to Q_{S2}.

3 The equilibrium market price rises to £20, also raising average revenue to £20. This is just enough to cover the increase in the firms' costs. Firms again generate normal profits at the profit-maximizing output.

Productive efficiency means that the firm is operating at the minimum point on its long-run average cost curve.

Moreover, in long-run equilibrium the firm is charging a price that is equal to the marginal cost. This means that the firm is also allocatively efficient. We highlighted this outcome in Section 5.2 and Figure 5.3.

Allocative efficiency occurs when price equals marginal cost, or $P = MC$.

until the average revenues earned by the firms match the higher cost level brought about by increased labour costs. Normal profits are earned and exit stops. These points are illustrated in Figure 5.13.

The review questions contain an additional scenario to test your understanding and use of the diagrams.

It is important to remember that, whether we begin with a supernormal profit or a supernormal loss, firms in perfect competition will always end up earning only normal profits in the long run. That is, firms in a perfectly competitive long-run equilibrium will be indifferent between being in business and placing their money in the bank.

In the long-run equilibrium, the perfectly competitive firm is operating at the minimum point of the average cost curve. This means that the firm is **productively efficient** as it is producing at least cost.

Recall that the cost of using scarce factor resources to produce one more unit of output is the marginal cost; and the price paid by consumers reflects the value placed on the final good. If the marginal cost of making a laptop computer is £300 and consumers are willing to pay no more than £250, then there is an inefficient use of society's scarce resources. The £300 of resources, including labour, capital and raw materials, which went into the laptop are not worth £300 to consumers. If the same resources could have been used to produce the latest hi-tech mobile phones and consumers were willing to pay £300 per phone, then society's scarce resources have been allocated efficiently. The value of the phones produced is exactly equal to the value of the resources used. In summary, **allocative efficiency** occurs when price = marginal cost. We will return to these points when we compare perfect competition with monopoly.

A quick consideration of kebab shops

Now let's consider kebab shops. There are many students. There are many kebab shops. A kebab is a fairly homogeneous product. Kebabs from different shops are fairly similar. Prices are listed on boards inside the shop and are usually visible from the street, so information regarding prices is near perfect. Barriers to entry are fairly limited. You need a shop, a food licence, some pitta bread and some cheap meat. All are easily available. The market is not perfectly competitive, but its characteristics are nearly so. Therefore, we now know or can predict that the kebab market is not a fantastic business proposition. Let us now consider monopoly.

5.5 Monopoly

In a strict sense, a monopoly is said to exist when only one firm supplies the market. In practice, the UK competition authorities define a monopoly to exist if one firm controls more than 25 per cent of the market. So, clearly, a monopoly exists if there is a dominant firm in the market with few rivals.

Monopolies tend to exist because of barriers to entry; where barriers to entry restrict the ability of potential rivals to enter the market.

Let us begin with some easy examples.

Licences

The National Lottery is a monopoly. Only one firm, currently Camelot, is licensed by the government to operate a national lottery in the UK. Licences also act as a barrier to entry on the railways. Only Virgin is allowed to operate high-speed trains between Leeds and London King's Cross.

Patents

When a pharmaceutical company develops a new drug it can apply for a patent. This provides it with up to 20 years of protection from its rivals. While everyone can discover the ingredients within Viagra, only the patent owner, Pfizer, is able to exploit this knowledge in the market. So patents also act as a barrier to entry.

Natural monopoly

Consider long-run average costs, introduced in Chapter 3. The minimum efficient scale, MES, is the size the firm has to attain in order to operate with minimum costs. If the MES is a plant capable of producing 1 million units per year and consumers demand around 10 million units per year, then the market can support about ten firms. However, if the MES is a plant producing around 10 million units, then the market can only support one firm – creating a **natural monopoly**.

> A **natural monopoly** exists if scale economies lead to only one firm in the market.

Natural monopolies were thought to exist in the utility markets, such as water, gas and telecommunications, where the infrastructure required to operate in these markets was so large that it restricted entry. For example, the scale needed to operate an effective telecommunications network in the UK was thought to be so large, because of all the cables, switches and exchanges that were required, that only one firm was capable of investing and generating a return. Two firms would double the amount of investment, but at best share the market and, therefore, the financial returns. However, when telecommunications began to move from copper wire to mobile communications, other firms could build networks much more cheaply. The barriers to entry fell and more firms now operate in the telecommunications market.

What does one firm and significant entry barriers mean for firm-level profitability?

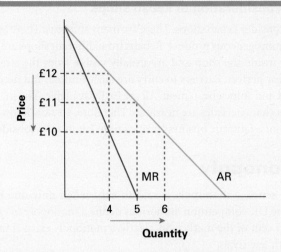

Figure 5.14 Monopoly's marginal and average revenue

When the price falls from £12 to £11, average revenue falls. But marginal revenue falls by more. One more unit is sold for £11, but the previous four units sold at £12 are now selling for £11, resulting in lost revenue of £4. Marginal revenue is therefore +£11 − £4 = £7.

Revenues and costs in monopoly

Just like perfect competition, we need to think about the revenues and costs generated by a monopoly. In perfect competition, MR and AR are the same. As a price-taker, if the firm sells more output it does not cause the market price to fall, so its MR and AR stay constant. In a monopoly, the situation is different. As the only supplier in the market, the monopoly faces the downward-sloping market demand curve. Therefore, if it sells more output, the price must fall. This has implications for the monopoly's AR and MR.

Consider Figure 5.14. The average revenue line, AR, is downward sloping and this follows from above. If the firm sells more output, then, under the law of demand, consumers will only demand more output at lower prices. So, as the price drops, the average price per unit must drop.

Marginal revenue is more difficult to understand. Again, consider Figure 5.14 and Table 5.2. Initially, we are selling four units at £12. Total revenue is £48 and average revenue is the price, £12. To sell one more unit, we need to drop the price to £11. This generates total revenue of £11 × 5 = £55, and the average revenue is now £11. But what has happened to marginal revenue? Two things have occurred. First, we are selling one more unit for £11 but, second, we are losing £1 per unit on the previous four units. So marginal revenue = +£11 − (4 × £1) = £7. So, MR = £7, while AR = £11. Now let us drop the price to sell one more unit. Selling six units at £10 generates a total revenue of £10 × 6 = £60. The marginal revenue from selling the sixth unit is £60 − £55. So, MR = £5, while AR = £10. Going from the fifth to sixth unit changed the price from £11 to £10; in effect, we reduced the average revenue by £1. However, the marginal revenue changed from £7 to £5, a change of £2. We can therefore see that, in selling more units, we have to accept a bigger reduction in marginal revenue than in average revenue. Reflecting this point, in monopoly, the marginal revenue line will always be steeper and below the average revenue line.

As with perfect competition, we now need to add in the firm's cost curves (see Figure 5.15).

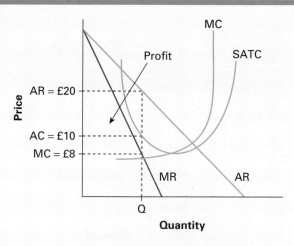

Figure 5.15 Monopoly and profit maximization

The monopoly's profits are maximized at Q, where MC = MR. The average cost of producing Q is £10; the average revenue from selling Q is £20. Total profit = (£20 – £10) × Q. Unlike perfect competition, the price of £20 charged by the monopoly is greater than the marginal cost of £8. This difference between the price and the cost of making the last unit is an indication of market power.

The monopoly will also maximize profits where MC = MR. This point defines the profit-maximizing output. If we then draw the line up from Q until it touches the short-run average total cost curve, SATC, then we see that the average cost equals £10. Drawing the line further until it touches the average revenue line, we see that the output can be sold for £20 per unit, making a profit per unit of £20 – £10 = £10. Total profit is £10 per unit multiplied by the profit-maximizing output Q. This is the short-term profit-maximizing position and, because of significant entry barriers, this profit will not be competed away in the long run. So, unlike perfect competition, monopolies can expect to earn supernormal profits in both the short and long run.

Perfect competition and monopoly compared

The long-term profit position of monopoly is not the only difference and so it is worth comparing perfect competition and monopoly in more detail. In order to do this, we will assume that we have a perfectly competitive industry, with 1000 firms supplying the market. Overnight, a businessperson buys out all the firms and begins to act as a monopoly.

As a consequence of this transfer of ownership from 1000 people to one person, the cost structure will not change; the monopoly will simply have a cost curve that is the sum of all the 1000 individual cost curves under perfect competition. The same will apply to the marginal cost curve and this is illustrated in Figure 5.16. The customers in the market have not changed, so the demand curves or AR lines faced by the perfectly competitive industry and the monopoly are identical. The marginal revenue lines are different. Remember, in perfect competition, marginal and average revenue are the same, but in monopoly they are different. We can now use Figure 5.16 to assess the differences between perfect competition and monopoly.

In order to maximize profit, the perfectly competitive industry will set $MC_{pc} = MR_{pc}$. Its profit-maximizing output is Q_{pc} and the price it sells for is PC. The monopoly sets $MC_{mp} = MR_{mp}$

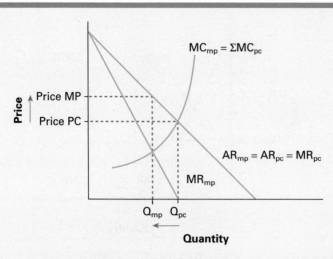

Figure 5.16 Comparing perfect competition and monopoly

To maximize profits, the perfectly competitive firm sets $MC_{pc} = MR_{pc}$, while the monopoly sets $MC_{mp} = MR_{mp}$. When compared with monopoly, perfect competition provides more output at lower prices.

and its profit-maximizing output is Q_{mp} and the price it sells this output for is MP. It is now clear to see that, in moving from perfect competition to monopoly, the industry output drops and the price increases. Furthermore, in perfect competition the price equals the industry's marginal cost, but in monopoly the price is higher than the industry's marginal cost.

This difference between price and marginal cost in monopoly is known as 'market power', which is the ability to price above the cost of the last unit made.

Monopoly and economies of scale

However, the arguments put forward are weak. The idea that a monopoly would have the same cost curves as a perfectly competitive industry neglects the points made in Chapter 3 relating to economies of scale. A monopoly may be capable of reducing costs. A single company is unlikely to operate 1000 separate plants. Instead, it is more likely to rationalize the 1000 plants into a smaller number of very large plants, which can exploit economies of scale. If this is true, then the cost reduction would lead to the monopoly's marginal cost curve moving out to the right. This is shown in Figure 5.17, with the marginal cost for the monopoly shifting to the right. At all output levels, the marginal cost of the monopoly is now lower than the marginal cost of the perfectly competitive industry. The monopoly is now more cost-efficient than perfect competition. The profit-maximizing output for the monopoly now occurs where marginal revenue intersects the new marginal cost curve under economies of scale. Output is higher than in perfect competition and the market price is lower than in perfect competition.

Of course it also needs to be recognized that a monopoly has no incentive to improve efficiency, as it has no competition. So why should it try to exploit economies of scale? Moreover, it is also possible that the monopoly may be too large and displays diseconomies of scale. Its costs would then be greater than the perfectly competitive industry, with the marginal cost curve shifting to the left. This would lead to even higher prices and a greater reduction in output under monopoly.

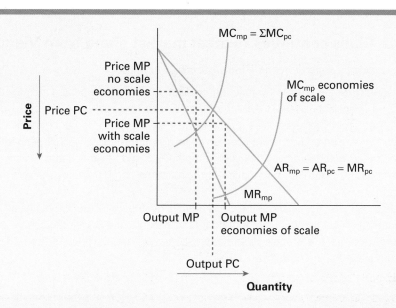

Figure 5.17 Monopoly and exploitation of economies of scale
By exploiting economies of scale, the monopoly's marginal cost curve shifts to the right. Therefore, at all output levels the marginal cost of the monopoly is lower than the marginal cost of the perfectly competitive industry, illustrating the improved cost efficiencies of the monopoly.
 The profit-maximizing output for the monopoly is now greater than the output of the perfectly competitive industry and the monopoly price is also lower.

Creative destruction

Creative destruction occurs when a new entrant out-competes incumbent companies by virtue of being innovative.

Rent-seeking behaviour is the pursuit of supernormal profits. An economic rent is a payment in excess of the minimum price at which a good or service will be supplied.

An alternative argument in favour of monopoly is that of **creative destruction**. Under this approach, monopolies are generally accepted as raising prices, restricting output and earning supernormal profits, which are potentially all bad. However, what should also be recognized is the benefits which stem from the supernormal profits, especially when they act as an incentive to innovate. Firms which are not monopolies can be motivated to be innovative and creative, developing new products for the market or new production techniques which provide them with a competitive advantage and destroy the entry barriers of the incumbent firms or monopoly. The innovating firm, through creative destruction, then becomes a monopoly. The firm benefits from higher profits; and society benefits from the supply of new innovative goods and services. One potential drawback with this approach is that firms have to undertake expensive **rent-seeking behaviour** and they may not always be successful. Some inventions work, others do not. So, for every monopoly brought about by innovation, there can be many failures which have used the scarce resources of the economy.

The power of creative destruction is to be found in the continued competition brought about by innovation. In Box 5.2, the case of Viagra is discussed. When Viagra was launched it completely changed the treatment of erectile dysfunction for men. Overnight, Viagra became a successful monopoly. Since then, alternative treatments have entered the market and through innovation Cialis is breaking down Viagra's dominant market position.

By way of a summary, Table 5.4 provides a concise comparison of the key aspects of perfect competition and monopoly.

Box 5.2 Cialis continues to steal market share from Viagra

Adapted from an article by Rupert Kircz on UKmedix.com, 28 July 2008

Eli Lilly, who manufacture the erectile dysfunction medication Cialis, have posted increased sales for the drug in the second financial quarter. At the same time, *Pfizer,* who make the erectile dysfunction drug Viagra, have reported slightly reduced sales for the world's number one impotence medication.

When Viagra first came on to the market over ten years ago, it obviously had 100 per cent market share as there were no rivals. With the arrival, however, of both Cialis and Levitra, Viagra has consistently been losing market share but nevertheless continues to maintain the largest market share in most countries around the world.

What is so fascinating, however, about the Cialis erectile dysfunction drug is that it is so different from Viagra in that, instead of working for just a four-hour time window, the Cialis drug can be effective for as long as 36 hours. Doctors and erectile dysfunction specialists say that this is the reason why it has consistently taken market share from Pfizer's Viagra.

© www.ukmedix.com

Table 5.4 Key comparisons of perfect competition and monopoly

	Perfect competition	**Monopoly**
Assumptions:		
Number of buyers	Many	Many
Number of suppliers	Many	One
Barriers to entry and exit	None	High
Product	Homogeneous	Not considered
Information	Perfect	Not considered
Outcomes:		
Costs	Productive efficiency – average total costs minimized	Productive inefficiency – average total costs not minimized
Average revenue and marginal revenue	Average revenue = marginal revenue	Average revenue > marginal revenue
Short-run losses and profits	Supernormal	Supernormal
Long-run profits	Normal	Supernormal
Price	Allocative efficiency: price = marginal cost	Allocative inefficiency: price > marginal cost
Level of prices	Monopoly price is higher than in perfect competition unless monopoly benefits from economies of scale	
Level of output	Monopoly output is lower than in perfect competition unless monopoly benefits from economies of scale	

5.6 Business application: understanding the forces of competition

From a business perspective, monopoly is preferable to perfect competition. In monopoly, there is no competition, the price is higher and barriers to entry ensure that supernormal profits are long term. So, a businessperson would clearly like to be in a monopoly or be capable of deriving a business strategy that takes them from a perfectly competitive market to a monopoly. We can now help business managers to understand the sources of competition. Importantly, the discussion within this chapter has been driven by the key assumptions and characteristics of perfectly competitive and monopoly industries. These ideas have been drawn together by Harvard Business School professor Michael Porter in a single and extremely usable framework, known as Porter's five forces model – Figure 5.18.

Around the outside of Figure 5.18 are four drivers of competition: the threat of entry, the threat from substitutes and the buying power of buyers and suppliers. These characterize an industry's initial competitive environment. The firms within the industry then have to decide how to react. The level of competition and rivalry could be high, or they may decide to collude with each other and lower competition. The intensity of each of these five competitive forces determines the overall level of competition within the industry, which ultimately determines profits.

Porter's five forces model is closely related to the assumptions of perfect competition. Many buyers and many sellers relates to the bargaining power of buyers and sellers. The threat of new entrants is linked to the assumption of no entry barriers. The threat from substitutes links to the assumption of homogeneous products, where the threat of substitutes is very high

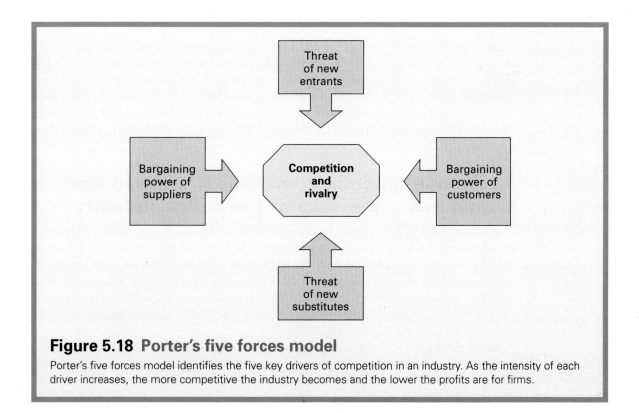

Figure 5.18 Porter's five forces model
Porter's five forces model identifies the five key drivers of competition in an industry. As the intensity of each driver increases, the more competitive the industry becomes and the lower the profits are for firms.

under perfect competition. In essence, Porter has taken the abstract assumptions of perfect competition and turned them into tangible concepts that business managers can understand and use to assess the degree of competition in their industry.

Porter's approach is very useful in enabling managers to scan and audit their business environment. The approach directs managers to assess sensible and measurable drivers of competition. So, for example, under each heading managers need to assess the following:

- Bargaining power of suppliers:
  - Number of suppliers
  - Differentiation of inputs
  - Ratio of input supply price to the output price
- Bargaining power of customers:
  - Number of buyers
  - Number of substitutes available to buyers
  - Price sensitivity of buyers
- Threat of entry:
  - Existence of entry barriers
  - Capital entry requirements
  - Access to distribution
  - Threat of retaliation
- Threat of substitutes:
  - Price of substitutes
  - Differentiation of substitutes
- Strategy and rivalry:
  - Number of firms
  - Exit barriers
  - Rate of industry growth

Armed with data on the types of information listed above, managers can then begin to think about which drivers of competition are favourable, which can be managed and which are just givens. The importance of economics is that, through the models of perfect competition and monopoly, it highlights to businesses the consequences for profit. If a company has a weak understanding, or lack of control over its competitive forces, then profits will plummet. In contrast, if the firm can understand and manage the forces of competition that it faces, then it has a better chance of becoming a monopoly.

5.7 Business application: 'Oops, we're in the wrong box' – the case of the airline industry

Financial performance is essential, or, in other words, profits count. The firm's revenues and costs determine profits. If we look closely at revenues and costs, we find they are both influenced by prices. A firm's revenues are determined by the price it sells its output for and a firm's costs are determined by the price it has to pay for its labour, capital and raw materials. Price is determined by market structure – it is higher in monopoly and lower in perfect competition. We can use this to think about business structures that are optimal for business by considering the input–output matrix in Figure 5.19.

Across the top, we have the market structure of the firm's output market, where it sells its product. Down the side, we have the market structure for the firm's input markets, where the firm purchases its labour, capital and raw materials. Box C could be the worst box to be in. The input markets are characterized by monopoly supply, so cost will be high, and the output

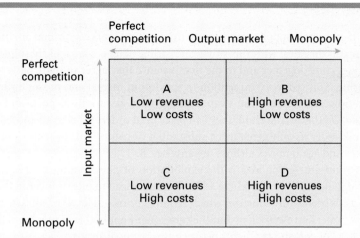

Figure 5.19 Optimal mix input and output markets

Output markets are where firms sell products. Input markets are where firms buy their labour, raw materials and capital inputs. When selling output the firm desires a high price, so monopoly is best. But when buying inputs the firm likes to keep its costs down, so perfectly competitive markets are preferable. Therefore, from a firm's perspective the best combination is associated with box B.

markets are perfectly competitive, so revenues will be low. Box B is the best box for business. Inputs come from a perfectly competitive market, so costs are low, while output is sold in a monopoly market, so revenues will be high. Box B is where there is the greatest chance to make a profit. Box A is probably preferable to box D. In A, both markets are perfectly competitive so supernormal profits are unlikely. But how do you think box D compares with box C? In C and D, both firms face a monopoly input supplier. But firms in C have a perfectly competitive output market. This could actually make it more attractive than D. With a perfectly competitive output market the firm will make only normal profits, so the monopoly input supplier cannot afford to squeeze the perfectly competitive firms. In fact, there are no profits to squeeze; but in D, the monopoly output will create profits that the monopoly supplier can try to expropriate for itself by charging higher input prices. So D may be less attractive than C.

Rarely will a firm find itself comfortably inside box B, but it might be expected to try to move towards box B over time. For example, in box D the obvious solution is to purchase the monopoly input supplier and make it part of your company. This is known as vertical integration, and it will be discussed at length in Chapter 7. While in box A, you would try to buy up your competitors or force them out of the market. This way, competition is reduced and the market moves towards monopoly.

But, for a more illuminating example, let us look at the airline industry. First, examine its key inputs: aircraft, landing rights at international airports, and pilots. There are only two major aircraft manufacturers in the world, Airbus and Boeing. The market is not perfectly competitive. Most major cities have one airport, a monopoly. Pilots are expensive and unionized. Unions are effectively a monopoly supplier of labour. So, on the input side, airlines are not in a good position. In terms of output, tickets for airlines are sold via travel agents or via the Internet. Most travellers say, 'I would like to go on this date between these two cities: who is offering the cheapest fare?' Ten options appear upon the screen and the cheapest option is generally selected. This would suggest that the market is highly competitive. This is clearly not good for the airline industry.

Solutions

With monopoly suppliers and competitive output markets, airlines are firmly located in box C. How can they deal with this situation? Airline alliances are a likely solution. In such alliances, airlines come together and in the first instance they agree to share passengers – so-called code sharing. This reduces competition in the output market and moves airlines towards box B. In addition, airlines may also swap landing rights at various airports and share the training of pilots. On the aircraft front, they can place joint orders for aircraft and, as with many products, a bulk order usually generates a substantial discount. This provides some control over input prices and again moves airlines towards box B.

A more intriguing idea is the exploitation of natural monopolies. As discussed earlier, a natural monopoly exists where scale economies lead to one supplier in the market. Often these are associated with industries which require enormous levels of infrastructure such as utilities – gas, water and electricity – but they are equally applicable in much smaller markets. Consider the level of demand for flights between two regional airports, say, Leeds in the UK and Nice in France. It is a two-hour flight and around 80 people a day wish to fly direct between the two airports. A small commercial jet might carry 120 passengers, so this route will only be supplied by one airline – a monopoly.

Now consider flying from Leeds to Singapore. Here are a couple of suggested routings: Leeds, Heathrow, and then either direct to Singapore or via Dubai, Bangkok or Kuala Lumpur; or Leeds, Amsterdam and then either direct, or via Dubai, Bangkok or Kuala Lumpur. There are many other options. Therefore, because international airlines utilize hub-and-spoke operations, the market for flights from Leeds to Singapore is a combination of many sub-markets. There is no natural monopoly on these routes. Airlines can fill planes with passengers who are travelling to multiple destinations.

What can we learn from this? Discount airlines tend to fly point-to-point between small regional airports. International carriers operate hub-and-spoke operations. Discount airlines make huge profits; international airlines do not. So are discount airlines natural monopolies? If they are, the very intriguing thought is that they could charge a lot less than they currently do.

 Summary

1 The profitability of a market is determined by the competitive structure of the market.

2 Perfect competition is highly competitive. It has no entry barriers, perfect information, homogeneous products and buyers and sellers.

3 In the short run, firms in perfect competition can earn supernormal profits. But in the long run, rivals will enter the market and compete away any excess profits.

4 Monopoly is a market supplied by only one firm.

5 Entry barriers such as licences, patents, economies of scale or switching costs make it difficult for competitors to enter the market.

6 Supernormal profits can exist in the short run and, because of high entry barriers, can also persist into the long run.

7 In monopoly, output is lower and prices are higher than in perfect competition.

8 Monopolies are seen as desirable by business but usually undesirable by government.

9 Many successful business ventures occur because managers are capable of steering a strategic path from competitive environments to low competitive environments.

Learning checklist

You should now be able to:

◆ Explain why firms maximize profits when marginal cost equals marginal revenue

◆ Recall the main assumptions behind perfect competition

◆ Explain why the demand curve faced by a perfectly competitive firm is perfectly elastic

◆ Explain the level of profits in the short and long run in a perfectly competitive industry

◆ List the potential barriers to entry used by a monopoly

◆ Explain why the marginal revenue line is steeper than the average revenue line in monopoly

◆ Draw a diagram to illustrate the amount of profit earned by a monopoly

◆ Explain the key differences between perfect competition and monopoly

◆ Explain when perfect competition and monopoly are good for a firm

◆ Provide examples of how firms have created monopolies

Questions connect

1 If a firm is a profit-maximizer, then marginal cost and marginal revenue must be .... (Fill in the blank)

2 A firm discovers that its marginal cost is less than its marginal revenue. Should it increase or decrease output?

3 Describe the key assumptions that characterize a perfectly competitive market.

4 In the short run, a firm in perfect competition finds that average revenues exceed average costs. Is this firm making a normal profit, a supernormal profit, a normal loss or a supernormal loss?

5 Taking the scenario described in Question 4, what do you think will happen to supply in the long run?

6 How would you establish a benchmark for normal profits in your own economy?

7 What barriers to entry are associated with monopolies?

8 Is equilibrium in monopoly associated with allocative efficiency?

9 List markets that you think are (a) perfectly competitive and (b) monopolies.

10 Does the concept of creative destruction paint monopolies as good or bad for an economy?

11 Explain the difference between accounting profits and economic profits.

12 Draw a diagram for a perfectly competitive industry with firms earning normal profits. All firms in the industry use oil as a key input. Using your diagram, illustrate a reduction in the price of oil. Will firm-level profits increase or decrease and will market supply increase or decrease?

13 Identify the key differences between perfect competition and monopoly.

14 Assess whether Porter's five forces model of competition has greater value to business managers than the models of perfect competition and monopoly.

15 Would the lack of competition in monopoly result in the company making losses?

Exercises

1 True or false?
  (a) Price is equal to marginal revenue for a firm under perfect competition.
  (b) A firm making normal profits is said to be breaking even by an accountant.
  (c) A monopoly makes supernormal profits because it is more efficient than a perfectly competitive firm.
  (d) A perfectly competitive firm will sell at a price equal to marginal cost. A monopoly may sell at a price above marginal cost.
  (e) A patent protects a monopoly by not enabling perfect information.
  (f) In perfect competition, if price is above short-run average cost, firms will exit the market.

2 Figure 5.20 shows the short-run cost curves for a perfectly competitive firm.

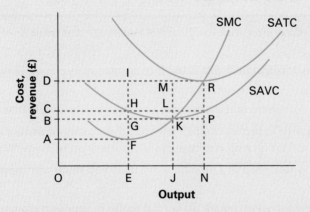

Figure 5.20 Short-run cost curves for a perfectly competitive firm

  (a) What is the shutdown price for the firm?
  (b) At what price would the firm just make normal profits?
  (c) What area would represent total fixed cost at this price?
  (d) Within what range of prices would the firm choose to operate at a loss in the short run?
  (e) Identify the firm's short-run supply curve.
  (f) Within what range of prices would the firm be able to make short-run supernormal profits?

A perfectly competitive industry is taken over by a monopolist who intends to run it as a multi-plant concern. Consequently, the long-run supply curve of the competitive industry (LRSS) becomes the monopolist's long-run marginal cost curve (LMC_m); in the short run, the SRSS curve becomes the monopolist's SMC_m. The position is shown in Figure 5.21.

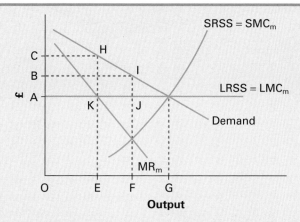

Figure 5.21 The monopolization of a perfectly competitive industry

(g) What was the equilibrium price and industry output under perfect competition?
(h) At what price and output would the monopolist choose to operate in the short run?
(i) At what price and output would the monopolist maximize profits in the long run?
(j) What would be the size of these long-run profits?

3 (a) List the key characteristics of a perfectly competitive market.
  (b) Which of the characteristics do not apply to Google and why?
  (c) Do you think Google has undertaken any rent-seeking behaviour?
  (d) Do you think Google will suffer creative destruction?

Chapter 6
Strategic rivalry

Chapter contents

 Learning outcomes

By the end of this chapter you should understand:

Economic Theory

LO1 Monopolistic competition

LO2 Natural and strategic entry barriers

LO3 Oligopoly and interdependence

LO4 The kinked demand curve model

LO5 Game theory and strategic behaviour

LO6 Auction theory

Business Application

LO7 Why it may be better for leading technology firms to co-operate on standards, rather than compete

LO8 Why supermarkets use blind auctions to prevent co-operation between suppliers

Strategic rivalry at a glance

The issue

Firms in perfect competition earn normal economic profits. But can firms avoid direct price competition, say by product differentiation; and, if so, what are the consequences for pricing and profits? In addition, in markets where there are only a small number of large players, should firms compete or try to co-operate with each other? Co-operation leads to increased profits; competition does not.

The understanding

Many firms in highly competitive markets, such as bars, restaurants and hairdressing, differentiate themselves by location, style and range of products or services. Prices then often vary across differentiated providers, but this may not necessarily lead to supernormal profits. We will address these issues using the model of monopolistic competition.

In terms of co-operation, or competition, we will examine the concept of strategic interdependence. For example, while co-operation is likely to lead to increased profits, it is not necessarily the correct option. If you decide to be friendly and your rival is aggressive, then they will win. So, given that your rival is aggressive, it is best if you are also aggressive. This is an essential part of the understanding; optimal strategies are developed from an understanding of what your rival is going to do, not from what you would like to do. This is known as strategic interdependence. The strategy of one firm is dependent upon the likely strategy of its rivals. We will explore these ideas more fully by examining game theory.

The usefulness

An understanding of monopolistic competition provides insights into the consequences for prices and profits resulting from product positioning and differentiation, especially in service sector markets characterized by numerous small-scale providers.

An understanding of strategic interaction from the perspective of game theory is extremely powerful. Government uses game theory when designing auctions for telecommunications licences. Sporting associations and team owners use game theory and auctions when selling television rights. Car dealerships use game theory when selling second-hand cars, and so should you. Finally, supermarkets use it to reduce the price that they have to pay for own-label products by applying game theory to auctions.

6.1 Business problem: will rivals always compete?

A good competitor can control their rivals. In sport, Formula 1 drivers try to achieve this from pole position and, in war, armed forces try to gain control through air supremacy. In fact any successful competitor, whether it be in sport, war, politics or business, will ordinarily have a good strategy.

An important recognition is that competition is expensive. War is hugely expensive, particularly in terms of lost lives. Ferrari's annual racing budget exceeds $200 million. Competition in business is also expensive. In monopoly, with no competition, profits are higher and more sustainable than in the highly competitive environment of perfect competition.

So, if competition is expensive, should rivals always compete? The answer depends on the expected response of your rival. Consider this old, but illuminating, true story. When the Spanish arrived in Central America in the seventeenth century they were greeted by fearsome-looking locals, sporting warpaint and shaking menacing spears in the air – a clear declaration that they were willing to compete with the Spanish invaders. In response, most of us would sensibly pull up the anchor and sail away. The Spanish burnt their boats and walked onto the beach. If a fight between the Spanish and the Incas started, the Spanish had to fight or die: no boats, no escape plan. The local Incas quickly understood the Spanish soldiers' need and desire to win and retreated inland. So, by committing to a fight, the Spanish influenced the behaviour of their rivals. This is a significant point for business.

In perfect competition, the behaviour of one firm will not influence its rivals. Each firm is a price-taker and it can sell any amount of output at the market price. If the market price is £10, there is no point starting a price war and selling at £5 because you can sell everything at £10. There is said to be no **strategic interdependence**. We will also assume that there is no strategic interdependence when we discuss monopolistic competition. However, under **oligopoly**, if one firm begins a competitive move, such as starting a price war, then this will have immediate implications for its rivals. The actions of one firm are linked to the actions of its rivals. Strategic interdependence exists.

In developing your understanding we will begin by introducing the model of monopolistic competition. While not directly addressing the issue of strategic interdependence, it does examine the profitability of many small firms under product differentiation. As such, it provides an insight into how firms in near-perfect competition try to deal with competitive rivalry. We then develop the analysis through an examination of the characteristics of an oligopolistic market. In discussing why oligopolies exist, we will consider both natural and strategic entry barriers. Finally, we will turn our discussion to strategic responses and in so doing develop your understanding of game theory. We will then utilize the insights from game theory to understand the operation and optimal design of auctions.

> **Strategic interdependence** exists when the actions of one firm will have implications for its rivals.
>
> **Oligopoly** is a marketplace with a small number of large players, such as banking, supermarkets and the media.

6.2 Monopolistic competition

> **Monopolistic competition** is a highly competitive market where firms may use product differentiation.

We begin with an examination of **monopolistic competition**, which for the most part is an industry much like perfect competition except for the existence of product differentiation. So, we are still assuming a large number of competitors, freedom of entry and exit, but not homogeneous products. Rather, firms produce similar goods or services which are differentiated in some way.

There are many examples of monopolistic competition and they all must relate to differentiation in some form or other. Bars can be differentiated by location, the beers or other drinks offered for sale, type of food served, or theme, such as a cocktail or sports bar. Shops can be differentiated by distance. Local shops sell newspapers and many people will not walk more than 300 yards for a paper. They will, however, drive a number of miles to access a supermarket. Even bread, a fairly standard product, is differentiated: brown, white, soft, with seeds, with fruit, and different varieties from around the world. Even your classes are differentiated by day of the week and time of day.

Importantly, because each supplier offers a similar but not identical product, each supplier does not face a perfectly elastic (horizontal) demand line, as they would in perfect competition. Instead, the element of differentiation lowers the degree of substitutability between rival offerings – and results in each firm facing a downward-sloping demand line.

The result of this differentiation is for each small firm to have a monopoly over the differentiated version of the product or service that it provides. We, therefore, have lots of small firms offering similar but slightly different competitive offerings to consumers with varied tastes and preferences. This combination of competition and monopoly gives rise to the term monopolistic competition.

Each monopolistic firm can influence its market share to some extent by changing its price relative to its rivals. By lowering drink prices a bar may attract some customers from its rivals, but it will not attract all the rivals' customers. Differentiation will lock in some customers to the more expensive provider; for example, if one bar provides beers while another specializes in fruit and alcoholic cocktails. Cheap prices in the beer bar will not attract drinkers who have a strong taste and preference for cocktails.

Monopolistic competition also requires an absence of economies of scale. Without the ability, or need, to exploit size and scale, a monopolistic industry will be characterized by a large number of small firms. We will see that, when we discuss oligopoly in the next section, the existence of economies of scale can lead to a small number of large players.

The demand curve for the firm depends upon the industry demand curve, the number of firms and the prices charged by these firms. A bigger industry demand, with a fixed number of firms, will result in a higher demand for each firm. An increase in the number of firms will lead to a reduced share of the market for each firm. While finally the price of a firm, relative to its rivals, will also determine its level of demand.

In Figure 6.1, we have drawn a diagram depicting a firm's supply decision under monopolistic competition. Initially, the firm faces an average revenue line of AR_1 and marginal revenue line MR of MR_1. Under profit maximization, the firm will produce Q_1 units and sell at a price of P_1. With an average cost per unit of AC_1, the firm will make $(P_1 - AC_1) \times Q_1$ profit. These supernormal profits will attract entry into the market. As more firms enter this market, the firm will lose market share and the demand curve for the firm will move back towards the origin. Entry stops when each firm is breaking even. This is when the new demand line, AR_2, just touches the average cost line at a tangent. The firm now makes Q_2 units at a price of P_2. Economic profits are now zero since $P_2 - AC_2 = 0$; and therefore entry into the industry stops.

> **Tangency equilibrium** occurs when the firm's average revenue line just touches the firm's average total cost line.

Excess capacity

The monopolistic long-run equilibrium has some important features. First, the **tangency equilibrium** results in average costs being above minimum average costs. In comparison with

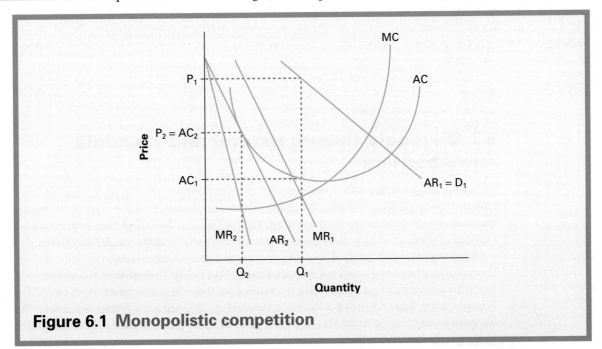

Figure 6.1 Monopolistic competition

perfect competition, long-run equilibrium in monopolistic competition does not result in firms operating at minimum average total costs. Therefore, monopolistic competition is not productively efficient. In fact, firms in monopolistic competition operate with excess capacity. They could increase output and reduce costs.

This productive inefficiency might suggest that the excess capacity in monopolistic competition is bad for society. It may be, but it is also important to recognize that monopolistic competition delivers greater choice for consumers that have varied tastes and preferences. So, in assessing whether monopolistic competition is good or bad for society, it is necessary to consider the gains from increased choice against the costs of excess capacity and inefficient production.

Market power

In long-run equilibrium, firms in monopolistic competition have some monopoly power because price exceeds marginal cost. In perfect competition, freedom of entry and exit ensures that in long-run equilibrium price, average cost and marginal cost are equal. There is no market power in perfect competition. Firms in perfect competition are indifferent between serving a new customer and turning them away. This is because the revenue from one extra sale is equal to the cost of the sale (P = MC). In monopolistic competition, the revenue from one more sale is always higher than the costs (P > MC). Firms in monopolistic competition will always be willing to sell to one more customer. This in part may explain why firms in monopolistic competition, such as food outlets, bars and hairdressers, are willing to engage in promotional activities such as advertising as a means of drawing in extra customers.

The characteristics of monopolistic competition – product differentiation, few opportunities for economies of scale, zero economic profits, but yet some power over pricing – are those we often associate with service sector businesses, such as, bars, restaurants, local grocery stores, hairdressers, estate agents and fast-food outlets. As such, the model of monopolistic competition has some merit in being able to explain the characteristics of many service sector industries. However, apart from a simple consideration of product differentiation, the model does not provide much of an insight into strategic interdependence. This is principally because monopolistic competition still assumes a large number of small players. As such, each firm is small relative to the market, and its competitive actions have only limited consequences for all of its rivals. This negligible impact results in strategic interdependence being almost entirely ignored. We will address this concern by considering oligopolies and, in particular, game theory.

6.3 Oligopoly theory: natural and strategic entry barriers

An oligopoly is a market with a small number of large players. Unlike in perfect competition, each firm has a significant share of the total market and therefore faces a downward-sloping demand curve for its product. Firms in oligopolies are price-setters as opposed to price-takers. Obvious examples of oligopolies include supermarkets, banks and the soft drinks market.

Oligopolies are often referred to as highly concentrated industries, implying that competition is concentrated in a small number of competitors. A simple measure of concentration is the **N-firm concentration ratio**, which is a measure of the total market share attributed to the N largest firms. Table 6.1 presents the market shares for the leading five UK supermarkets. The five-firm concentration ratio is 81 per cent. Table 6.2 lists the most and least concentrated industries for the UK economy.

The **N-firm concentration ratio**, CR, is a measure of the industry output controlled by the industry's N largest firms.

Table 6.1 Supermarket market shares

Supermarket	Percentage market share
Tesco	32
Asda	17
Sainsbury's	17
Morrisons	11
Somerfield	4

Source: TNS 2008

Table 6.2 Most and least concentrated UK industries

Most concentrated industries (5-firm CR > 80%)	Least concentrated industries (5-firm CR < 10%)
Sugar	Metal forging
Tobacco	Plastic pressing
Gas distribution	Furniture
Banking	Construction
Soft drinks	Structural metal products

Source: *ONS Economic Trends* 2004

A natural question to ask is why are some industries, such as soft drinks, highly concentrated and others, such as furniture, not? The key to the answer lies in recognizing the importance of entry barriers.

Entry barriers can exist for natural or strategic reasons.

Natural entry barriers

> **Entry barriers** represent an obstacle to a firm's ability to enter an industry.

The costs for a firm can be exogenously or endogenously determined. Our natural entry barriers are concerned with **exogenous costs**, so let us concentrate on them first.

> **Exogenous means** external, outside. The **exogenous costs** of the firm are outside its control.

The fact that exogenous costs are outside the firm's control does not mean that these costs are uncontrollable; rather, the firm does not influence the price of labour, machines, raw materials and the production technology used. For example, the price of labour is a market price determined outside the firm's control. The level of costs associated with a particular industry, as we saw with monopolies, can create an entry barrier.

In Figure 6.2, we have the long-run average cost curve LRAC and the minimum efficient scale. (We considered these in Chapter 3.) At the minimum efficient scale, MES, the average cost is £10. But with a much smaller plant, Q_1, the cost per unit rises to £20. In order to enter and compete in the industry it is essential to build a plant that is at least as big as the MES. In oligopolies, the MES is large when compared to the overall market. For example, if we have 50 million customers and the MES is 10 million units per year, then we might reasonably expect 50m/10m = 5 firms in the market.

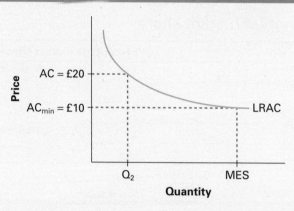

Figure 6.2 Economies of scale and natural entry barriers

The minimum efficient scale (MES) is the minimum scale of operation, or size of factory, that is needed in order to operate at lowest cost. If, however, the firm chooses a lower level of operation, then average costs will be higher. If the MES is very high, it can act as a barrier to entry.

If we consider supermarkets, it is easy to see why natural barriers to entry may exist. In the case of supermarkets, the big players have in excess of 500 stores each. So the MES must be around 500 stores. This level of scale is probably essential when trying to negotiate discount from product suppliers, optimizing marketing spend and building efficient distribution systems to move stock from suppliers to the stores. Given that the UK is a small island with around 60 million inhabitants, it is sensible that we should only see a small number of large supermarket chains. Four large players operating at 500-plus stores is all that the UK market is capable of supporting. So, it is the natural, or exogenous, cost characteristics, coupled with the market size that leads to a natural entry barrier and the creation of an oligopoly.

Strategic entry barriers

What happens if the MES is not very big when compared with the market size? Entry is easier and aids competition. Consider the case of soft drink manufacturers. If you wish to enter the soft drinks market, then you need to buy a bottling plant and a big steel factory to house it in and a warehouse; and a couple of trucks for deliveries will also help. The cost will not exceed £5 million. (Amazing what you can learn when taking summer jobs as a student.) For many businesses £5 million is not a huge sum of money. The MES is not big and, therefore, the entry barrier into the market is limited. So, as a firm inside the market, how do you prevent entry? Easy – you change the cost characteristics of the industry and make the MES bigger, or, as the economist would say, you **endogenize** the cost function.

Coca-Cola and Pepsi are clear examples of how to achieve this strategy. The core assets for these companies are not production facilities; rather, they are brand names. A successful brand may cost £100 million or more to buy, or develop through advertising. Therefore, the entry barrier is not a £5 million factory, it is instead a £100 million brand.

Figure 6.3 illustrates these points. $LRAC_{Production}$ is the cost curve that relates to production only. $LRAC_{Production+Advertising}$ is the cost curve when we consider production and advertising together. The MES for production is much smaller than the MES for production and advertising. Therefore, by strategically changing the cost nature of the soft drinks industry, from production based to managing brands, the dominant players can try to prevent entry.

> If costs are **endogenized**, then the firms inside the industry have strategically influenced the level and nature of costs.

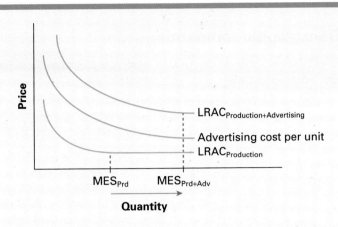

Figure 6.3 Strategic entry barriers

When the MES is naturally low, entry can be easy. Incumbents can change this by altering the cost characteristics of the industry. One suggestion is to move away from production and build in large investments in intangible assets such as brand names. This can substantially increase the MES and reduce entry.

A **sunk cost** is an expenditure that cannot be regained when exiting the market.

Perhaps more important, the £100 million brand development fee is a **sunk cost**. This means that if the entrant decided to exit the market after spending £100 million on brand development, it would be unlikely to sell the asset on. The asset has no value to any other business and so the cost is sunk. In contrast, the production facility could be sold on. A soft drinks manufacturer may not buy the plant, but some other food processing company could be interested in the facility. This asset can be sold on, so its costs are not sunk. As a consequence, the need for a brand simultaneously increases the size of entry into the market and it makes it more risky as the asset cannot be sold on. The investment is lost.

A **contestable market** is one where firms can enter and exit a market freely.

The existence of sunk costs is important because without them markets are **contestable**. With freedom to enter and exit, contestable markets proxy perfectly competitive markets. So, even if the market has only a small number of large players, the absence of sunk costs enables potential rivals to threaten future entry. The only way to prevent entry is to make it look unattractive, with low levels of profit. So, contestable markets, even with oligopolistic structures, only produce normal economic profits.

Examples of contestable markets

The airline industry is commonly used as an example of contestability. An aircraft does not represent a sunk cost. A jumbo jet can be used on a route between Heathrow and New York. It can equally be used on a route between Heathrow and Hong Kong. There are no costs in moving the asset (aircraft) between the two routes, or any other route. Therefore, the airline can quickly and easily move the aircraft to the most profitable route. This ability should keep profits low on all possible routes, as the threat of entry by rivals is very real, with no entry barriers. However, access to take-off and landing slots at international airports is very limited and this reduces the contestable nature of the airline industry. To alleviate this problem, the Open Skies policy has sought to promote free competition in air travel by enabling new entrants greater access to airports. Box 6.1 provides some background data on the degree of competition for slots at Heathrow airport.

Box 6.1 Transatlantic competition

Adapted from 'Sir Richard Branson: Why British Airways' monopoly game must be stopped',
in The Daily Telegraph, *5 September 2008*

A combined BA/AA would operate 79 per cent of all flights between Heathrow and Boston, 66 per cent between Heathrow and Chicago and 63 per cent between Heathrow and JFK. Heathrow airport, which accounts for nearly a quarter of all passengers travelling between Europe and the US, is full. The rare slot that does emerge is usually at a time of day that does not work for transatlantic carriers or is snapped up for huge sums of money. This situation makes it physically and financially impossible for any carrier to offer any meaningful level of competitive service, let alone attempt to replicate the network that BA/AA would have.

It's already impossible to get anywhere near the 42 per cent of slots that BA holds today; there is no free and unfettered access to Heathrow. The Open Skies accord, which was introduced in March, has barely opened up Heathrow at all. The accord certainly hasn't created major new competition to rival BA's dominance.

6.4 Oligopoly theory: competition among the big ones

Now that we have an understanding of why oligopolies exist, it is important to understand how competition occurs between rival firms within an oligopoly. A simple fact is that firms in an oligopoly are torn between a desire to compete and the benefits of colluding. The following discussion illustrates this point.

Optimally, all firms in an oligopoly should agree to co-operate and act as one monopolist, as this generates the highest level of profits. This is known as a cartel and is illustrated in Figure 6.4. For simplicity, assume all firms face identical constant marginal and average costs. These are shown as a horizontal line in Figure 6.4. The profit-maximizing output occurs where MR = MC. This output maximizes the joint profits of all the firms in the cartel, acting as a monopoly. However, each firm will quickly recognize that it can undercut the market price and raise its own profits at the expense of its rivals. Why?

The answer rests in an understanding that a profit-maximizing monopoly will only operate in the price-elastic region of its demand curve. Marginal cost has to be positive, because it is impossible to produce an additional unit of output without incurring additional costs. Therefore, if profits are maximized when MC = MR, then, because MC is positive, MR must also be positive. If marginal revenue is positive, reducing the price to sell one more unit has made a positive contribution to total revenue. We saw in Chapter 2 that cutting prices and raising total revenue only occurs when demand is price elastic.

Therefore, a single firm within the cartel illustrated in Figure 6.4 can see that its marginal and average costs are constant. However, reducing prices will generate greater revenues because demand is price elastic. The individual firm can, therefore, earn more profit by cheating on its cartel colleagues and expanding output. Unfortunately, any member of the cartel could recognize that, being on the elastic part of the demand curve, it could also drop its own prices and raise revenues. Therefore, all rivals would respond by dropping their prices, leaving the cartel and in effect competing with each other. This is strategic interdependence in action. Should firms in oligopoly co-operate with each other and act as a monopoly, or compete with each other and start a price war?

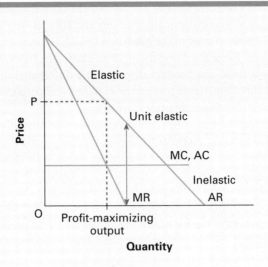

Figure 6.4 Collusion versus competition

Marginal cost has to be positive. It is not possible to produce one more unit of output for a negative amount of money. Resources such as labour will have to be paid for. Under profit maximization MR = MC, therefore if MC has to be positive, MR also has to be positive in order for the two to be equal. From the above, positive marginal revenue is only associated with output levels where demand is price elastic. With price-elastic demand, reducing the price and expanding output will lead to higher total revenues. Since costs are constant, revenues will grow more quickly than costs and profits will increase for the individual firm. With constant cost levels, the individual firm can expand output, raise revenues and therefore boost profits.

When a cartel might work

Some basic points at this stage help in understanding when a cartel can work and when competition will prevail. Collusion is likely to fail when there is:

♦ a large number of firms
♦ product differentiation
♦ instability in demand and costs

Collusion is much harder when there are many firms in the industry: co-ordination and enforcement is too complex and it is easy for firms to blame each other for cheating. If the product is not standardized, perhaps differentiated in some way, then collusion is unlikely to work. Differentiation is a means of reducing substitutability. Why agree on price fixing when your products are not near-substitutes? Finally, collusion benefits from stability in demand and costs. If the equilibrium is changing frequently, then the cartel has frequently to adjust its agreed prices. It is costly to co-ordinate and the variation in market conditions provides firms with the cover needed to cheat and not get caught.

Examples of price fixing include the Organization of Petroleum Exporting Countries (OPEC), which meets on a frequent basis to agree oil production levels for all member countries. By managing oil production, OPEC is seeking to influence oil supply in the world and ultimately set the world price for oil. Since this is an agreement between countries it is not illegal, although perhaps it is not desirable.

Commercial examples include the agreement between British Airways and Virgin to fix fuel surcharges on transatlantic flights. Sony and Hitachi were suspected of agreeing to fix the price for LCD screens used in the Nintendo DS, while German authorities investigated Nestlé, Mars, Kraft and Ritter for fixing the price of chocolate. In all these cases the number of large competitors is small, the product displays little differentiation; and, in the case of fuel surcharges and chocolate, stable cost increases in fuel and cocoa, respectively, provided a possible mechanism for co-ordinating price increases.

Price fixing can have economy-wide implications. In Australia, a cartel of cardboard suppliers was accused of harming every Australian who bought a good that was transported in cardboard. The chief prosecutor commented that, 'price fixing is theft, usually by well dressed thieves'. Cases of price fixing now tend to come to light because information is passed to the investigating authorities. So great is the policy concern regarding price fixing, that many governments now offer freedom from prosecution for being a so-called whistle-blower and informing on the other members of the cartel. The penalties for being found guilty of price fixing include financial penalties against the company and even imprisonment for the managers involved. See Box 6.2.

 Box 6.2 Well-dressed thieves

Adapted from The Economist, *21 March 2008*

There is a growing hard line against price fixing throughout the rich world. Cartels have long been prohibited, but conspiring to rig markets is now punishable by prison in Germany, France, Ireland, Japan and Canada, as well as America and Britain. Australia is about to join the club too. But why are executives being targeted?

For big and sophisticated firms, entering into an agreement to fix prices is a clear and knowing conspiracy against consumers. And because such pacts are secret and hard to uncover, harsher penalties are needed if the expected costs of price fixing are to exceed the likely benefits. In principle, a big fine might suffice. But in practice a fine large enough to work as a deterrent would financially cripple a company, further impairing competition and harming innocent bystanders, such as suppliers and workers.

Sanctions against culpable executives ought to be more effective. Fining managers, however, has some of the same problems as fining firms. Because there is only a small chance of being caught, a penalty big enough to put off a budding price fixer may be many times their wealth – and hence unpayable. Punishment by prison may, then, have the desired effect.

© The Economist Newspaper Limited, London 2009

6.5 Competition among rivals

We now understand that oligopolies are industries characterized by a small number of large firms and that entry barriers are a likely cause of them. We now need to develop a framework which will enable an understanding of how firms within an oligopoly will decide to compete or co-operate.

A kinked demand curve shows that price rises will not be matched by rivals, but price reductions will be.

Economists' earliest attempts to model oligopolies involved the **kinked demand curve**, shown in Figure 6.5. The idea behind the kinked demand curve is that price rises will not be matched by rivals, but price reductions will be matched. The kinked demand curve is therefore often used to explain the pricing behaviour of competing petrol stations. Since car drivers can

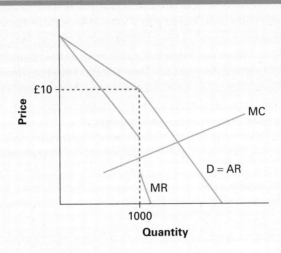

Figure 6.5 Kinked demand curves

Above the equilibrium price, demand is price elastic; competitors do not follow price increases. Below the equilibrium price, demand is inelastic; competitors match price cuts.

always drive on to the next filling station, each petrol station has a number of nearby competitors. If one station increases prices, then all others will hold prices and attract additional traffic. If a station cuts prices, then more traffic will flow to that station and competing outlets will counter the move by matching the price cut. It is only when the price of oil changes that all petrol stations move prices together.

At the price of £10, there is no point in a firm changing its prices. If it increases prices, all rivals will hold their prices; but if the firm drops prices, all rivals will also reduce their prices. Therefore, above the price of £10 demand is price elastic and below demand is inelastic, thus leading to the kinked demand curve.

The marginal revenue line is vertical at the profit-maximizing output. This is because the demand curve changes slope at this output level. The difference between the elastic and inelastic demand curves leads to a stepped change in the marginal revenue.

As a result, the demand curve has a different shape above and below the current market price:

1 If the firm raises its price, rivals will keep their prices constant. The firm will, therefore, lose customers when it raises prices. As a result, demand above the current market price is elastic.
2 In contrast, if the firm reduces its prices, all rivals will match the price reduction. The firm will not gain more demand by reducing prices. Demand below the current market price is therefore inelastic.

We will see below that economists question the theoretical merits of the kinked demand curve, but it provides a reasonable starting point for understanding some real-world examples. The pricing of petrol, or at least the reduction in petrol prices, can be explained using the kinked demand curve. See Box 6.3 for a common discussion of price changes at the pump. Once one firm announces a price reduction, all other firms respond with similar price reductions in order to protect their market share. We might therefore argue that demand is inelastic for price reductions. Similarly, no firm would increase prices without full knowledge that other firms would follow. This occurs in the petrol market because of the cost of oil. So price rises only occur when all firms face increased input costs and are therefore willing to increase prices together. But no firm would make a decision to be more expensive than its rivals. Furthermore, because of the vertical portion of the marginal revenue line, the change in the marginal cost of oil has to be quite large in order to deliver a change in the equilibrium price of petrol. Therefore, because of the kinked demand line, modest daily changes in oil prices are unlikely to feed into erratic daily price changes at the petrol pumps.

 Box 6.3 Pump wars

Adapted from an article on BBC News Online, 22 July 2008

Drivers are set to benefit after a number of petrol suppliers said they were cutting the price of fuel. Asda said it was cutting the price of unleaded petrol and diesel by 3 pence per litre, while Morrisons said it had cut both prices by 4p per litre. BP said petrol and diesel at the 310 stations where it controls prices had fallen by 2p a litre on average. Tesco said it would cut prices by up to 4p, but its prices are set locally. Sainsbury's said it would look to match the prices of competitors nearby.

Fuel prices have risen in recent months as the price of crude oil has increased. Oil prices hit record levels above $147 a barrel in early July. However, oil prices have dropped recently, to about $132 a barrel, resulting in a 6 per cent fall in the wholesale price of petrol since mid-July.

© bbc.co.uk/news

In contrast to the petrol market, Box 6.4 provides an example of how Nokia reacted to a price war in the mobile handset market. Rather than cut prices and match cheaper rivals, Nokia was willing to run the risk of losing market share. The difference between the pricing strategy of the petrol retailers and Nokia probably reflects the degree of substitutability. Petrol is very homogeneous and so the market demand is very elastic below the equilibrium price and so all suppliers follow price cuts. Nokia handsets are differentiated and therefore not perfect substitutes for those offered by cheaper rivals. Market demand is likely to be less elastic below the equilibrium price.

 Box 6.4 Nokia issues warning as price war hots up

Adapted from The Times, *5 September 2008*

Nokia, the world's biggest mobile phone maker, gave warning today that it would lose market share in the current quarter as it refused to join in a price war waged by its rivals. Shares in Nokia dived 14 per cent, the most since April 2004, and settled later at 114.05, 11 per cent down.

The company did not identify which competitors had cut prices. Motorola and Sony Ericsson, the third- and fifth-largest handset makers, lost share to Nokia in the second quarter. Samsung Electronics ranked second in market share last quarter, while LG Electronics was fourth. 'There is an undercutter in the market and Nokia doesn't want to sacrifice its margins,' Michael Schroder, an analyst at Glitnir Bank in Helsinki, said.

© 2009 Times Newspapers Ltd.

Problems with the kinked demand curve

The kinked demand model has a number of positive features. First, the demand curves for the firm are based on potential or expected responses from the firm's rivals. Hence, strategic interdependence is a feature of the model. Second, the model predicts stability in pricing. This occurs because of strategic interdependence; rivals will react to price changes in a way that makes them ineffective. Also, price stability occurs because, even when the firm's costs increase, as a result of the vertical portion of the firm's MR line the profit-maximizing output and price are unlikely to change. Only when costs change by a large amount will the intersection of marginal cost and marginal revenue move from the vertical portion of the marginal revenue line.

The major drawback associated with the kinked demand curve is that it does not explain how the stable price is arrived at in the first place. There must be a prior process that determines the price. The kinked demand curve merely explains the stability once the price is set. We therefore need an approach that understands strategic interdependence more fully.

6.6 Game theory

Game theory seeks to understand whether strategic interaction will lead to competition or co-operation between rivals.

In response to this challenge, economists have now turned to **game theory** as a means of understanding strategic interdependence. In economic jargon, a game has players who have different pay-offs associated with different strategic options. In the business sense, we could have two firms (players): they could start a price war and compete against each other or they could try to co-operate with each other (strategic options). Each combination has different profit outcomes (pay-offs) for the two firms.

The original version of game theory is known as the Prisoners' Dilemma, where two criminals have to decide to co-operate or compete with each other in order to win their freedom. The Prisoners' Dilemma is similar in style to the end game in the TV show *Golden Balls*, where opposing players have to decide to steal or share, in order to win the cash prize.

The Prisoners' Dilemma

Two criminals, Robin Banks and Nick Scars, are arrested by the police. There is little evidence against the criminals and they face a short spell in prison if convicted. The police decide to offer each prisoner a deal. If they provide evidence against their fellow criminal, then they will go free. The dilemma facing the prisoners is illustrated in Figure 6.6.

The matrix of sentences represents the possible pay-offs to each prisoner. If they both stay silent, then they will receive a short sentence. If Nick Scars stays silent and Robin Banks provides evidence, then Nick Scars receives a long sentence and Robin Banks goes free. Sitting in separate cells, with no ability to communicate, both prisoners are most likely to provide evidence and receive medium sentences. They will cheat, or compete with each other, when it would have been in their interests to co-operate and stay silent. Just as with the game *Golden Balls*, sharing is attractive, but it is possibly outweighed by the gains of stealing – but only if the other player does not steal as well.

Nash equilibrium occurs when each player does what is best for themselves, given what their rivals may do in response.

To understand why competing, rather than co-operating, with a rival is preferable we need to understand the importance of the Nash equilibrium.

The Nobel Laureate John Nash proved that the optimal solution for any game must result in each player making an optimal decision given the potential response of its rival. This is now known as the **Nash equilibrium**. The important point to note from the Nash equilibrium is that each firm considers what its rivals can do before deciding on its own strategy. A player does not simply decide what it wants to do. For example, Liverpool or Barcelona do not decide to run on the pitch and kick the ball in the back of the opposition's net. Clearly, this is what

		Robin Banks	
		Stays silent	Betrays
Nick Scar	Stays silent	Nick Scar: short sentence Robin Banks: short sentence	Nick Scar: long sentence Robin Banks: goes free
	Betrays	Nick Scar: goes free Robin Banks: long sentence	Nick Scar: medium sentence Robin Banks: medium sentence

Figure 6.6 The Prisoners' Dilemma

they want to do. Instead, they think about what their rivals will do, how they play, what formation they might use and who their opponent's key players are. Liverpool or Barcelona can then develop a football strategy based on what their rivals are going to do. The Nash equilibrium is just formalizing this obvious decision-making process by saying, 'Consider your rival's likely behaviour before you decide what you are going to do.'

Now let us examine a price war game in Figure 6.7, using Nash's argument. Firm A looks at firm B and sees that B can do one of two things: co-operate or start a price war. We can begin

		Firm A	
		Co-operate	Price war
Firm B	Co-operate	50:50	20:60
	Price war	60:20	30:30

Figure 6.7 Game theory, pay-off matrix

The numbers in each box are the pay-offs to each firm (firm B is always on the left and firm A on the right). The Nash equilibrium is where both firms choose to start a price war, earning £30m each. This is because when choosing its strategy A examines B's options: if B tries to co-operate, A's best response is to start a price war; and if B starts a price war, A's best response is again to start a price war. B will come to the same conclusion when examining its response to A.

by examining what happens if B decides to co-operate. If A then also co-operates, it will earn £50 million, but if A begins a price war, then it will earn £60 million. Firm A now thinks about B's other option, which is to start a price war. If A tries to co-operate, it will only earn £20 million, but if A also takes up the option of a price war, then it will earn £30 million. Firm A now knows that, whatever B does, it is always optimal for A to start a price war. Firm B will go through a similar decision-making process and come to the same conclusion – that whatever A does, B will start a price war. The Nash equilibrium has both firms embarking on a price war earning £30 million each.

In this example, each firm's optimal decision is independent of its rival's decision. A's optimal decision is to cheat, regardless of whether B cheats or co-operates. A is known as having a **dominant strategy** and, given that our example has symmetric pay-offs for B, then B also has a dominant strategy.

> A **dominant strategy** is a player's best response, whatever its rival decides.

When each player has a dominant strategy, the Nash equilibrium will be unique – only one cell in the pay-off matrix will provide an equilibrium solution. However, this unique equilibrium is not necessarily optimal. In the case of the Prisoners' Dilemma, both players would be better off if they co-operated.

Repeated games

Starting a price war or displaying 'non-cooperative' behaviour is a general response in a **single-period game**. Therefore, as a rule, whenever you play a game once, as our rivals did in Figure 6.6, or strategically interact with someone once, then cheat. For example, consider buying a second-hand car from the classified ads. You see a car and go to meet the owner. You will say the car is not perfect and the owner will tell you that the car is fantastic. It does not matter whether the car is good or not; you are both displaying non-cooperative behaviour. You both do this because you do not expect to meet again to buy or sell cars in the future. It is a one-period game, so you both cheat. You would like the price to fall; they would like the price to rise.

> In a **single-period game**, the game is only played once. In a repeated game, the game is played a number of rounds.

The way to move from a non-cooperative Nash equilibrium to a co-operative Nash equilibrium is to play the game repeatedly and use a strategy known as 'tit-for-tat'. Under tit-for-tat, you will co-operate with your rival in the next round if they co-operated with you in the last round. If they cheated on you in the last round, you will never co-operate with them again.

In the game above, if A and B co-operate they both receive £50 million. If, in the next round, A decides to cheat and start a price war, it will earn £60 million, or £10 million more than from co-operation. But in the next rounds B will always commit to a price war, so the most A can earn is £30 million. Firm A has the choice of gaining £10 million in the next round and then losing £50 million − £30 million = £20 million for every round afterwards. Therefore, short-term gains from cheating are outweighed by the long-term losses of a repeated game.

However, in order for tit-for-tat to work, the threat to always display non-cooperative behaviour, if your rival cheated in the last round, has to be a **credible commitment**.

> A **credible commitment** or threat has to be one that is optimal to carry out.

Recall the Spanish invaders who burnt their boats – their threat to fight the local Incas, rather than sail off to a safer shore, was very credible when they no longer had any boats!

For a business illustration, let us go back to the car example. This time consider buying a car from a dealer of one of the major manufacturers. With a second-hand car they usually provide a warranty. They do this because they value your repeat business. The dealer does not want to sell you a bad car. Instead, they would like you to feel secure in the fact that the car is good and they will fix any problems. They are not cheating; they are trying to co-operate. In fact, by offering warranties they are making a credible commitment to provide you with a trouble-free motor car. They are willing to do this because the potential revenue streams from your repeat business outweigh any gains from selling you a bad car at an expensive price.

Finally, we can consider the market for love. Marriage is a repeated game. If one partner cheats by seeing someone else, then divorce is a fairly robust method of never agreeing to co-operate with the cheating partner again. In the singles market, in contrast, seeking co-operation for fun with someone you find attractive could be a one-period game if you only expect to see them once. If they ask what you do, it is better to cheat. Claiming to be a catwalk model or a professional footballer are better options than admitting to being an indebted student.

In summary, strategic decisions require an understanding of the potential responses. If a firm, or individual, plays a game once, they should cheat. If they play repeatedly, then they should try to co-operate for as long as their rivals co-operate.

6.7 Game theory extensions: reaction functions

The Prisoners' Dilemma is a simplification and the existence of joint dominating strategies is not always assured. We therefore need to understand how interdependent firms should react to the expected behaviour of their rivals. We can achieve this by considering a market with two firms – known as a duopoly.

Assume two firms, A and B, face an industry demand D_1 and constant marginal costs MC. This situation is illustrated in Figure 6.8. Firm A must decide how much to produce based on what it expects firm B to produce. To begin the analysis, A assumes that B produces nothing. A, therefore, faces the entire industry demand D_1 and the associated MR_1. As a profit-maximizer, A selects the output Q_0, where MC is equal to MR_1. If A now assumes that B produces four units, then A faces the **residual demand** line D_4 and the associated marginal revenue line MR_4. The profit-maximizing output for A is now Q_4. We can continue allowing A to alter its assumption about B. So, if A assumes that B produces eight units, then A faces the residual demand D_8 and the marginal revenue MR_8. The profit-maximizing output for A is now Q_8.

> **Residual demand** is equal to the market demand less the amount produced by the firm's rivals.

The model depicted in Figure 6.8 is referred to as a **Cournot model**, after the French economist Augustin Cournot. Under a Cournot model, each firm treats its rival's output as a given. In our example, A assumed B's output was 0, 4 and then 8. If we continued the analysis by enabling A to consider each possible output by B, we would understand how A would react to

> In a **Cournot model** each firm treats its rival's output as a given.

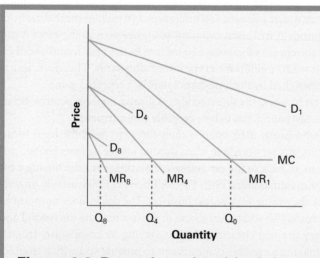

If firm A assumes that B produces zero output, then A will produce Q_0 output. If A assumes that B will produce 4 units of output, then A faces a residual demand of D_4 and will produce Q_4 output. Assuming that B produces 8 units of output, then A will produce Q_8.

Figure 6.8 Duopoly and residual demand

every possible output choice available to B. This would derive the **reaction function** for A. Similarly, the analysis can be repeated in order to derive the reaction function for B.

Figure 6.9 presents the reaction functions for A and B. R^A is the reaction function for A and R^B is the reaction function for B. Both reaction functions slope down, indicating the negative relationship between the output choices made by A and B. If B decreased its output, then A would react by increasing its output. Importantly, A would increase its output by less than B's reduction. This ensures that output falls overall and that the price increases in the market. Since A is not cutting its output, it now receives a higher revenue on all its previous units.

The equilibrium output occurs where both reaction functions intersect. This is a Nash equilibrium since each firm is making an optimal decision based on what its rival is expected to do. This equilibrium is also sub-optimal, just as in the case of the Prisoners' Dilemma. This is because each firm takes its rival's output as a given and then determines its own profit-maximizing output. There is no consideration of what effect this level of output will have on the rival's profits. As such, overall output is increased beyond the profit-maximizing output of a monopoly, which would maximize joint profits.

An alternative to the Cournot model is the Bertrand model. Under a Bertrand model, firms treat the prices of rivals as given. Again, it is possible to derive reaction functions. This time, firm A assumes a price level for B and then chooses a price level for itself which maximizes its own profits. It is simple to understand that the Nash equilibrium occurs where both firms set a price equal to marginal cost. This is because, if B is assumed to set a price above marginal cost, A can go slightly below and gain the entire market. In reaction, B will go slightly lower than A. So, in equilibrium, A and B will choose a price equal to marginal cost and earn normal profits. Since the Bertrand model predicts a perfectly competitive outcome for a duopoly, economists tend to prefer the output-based approach of the Cournot model.

Stackelberg models and first-mover advantage

Until now we have assumed that both players make simultaneous decisions. It is also interesting to consider the nature of the Nash equilibrium when one firm acts as the leader and other firms then act as followers. In such scenarios it is possible to identify a **first-mover advantage**.

> A **reaction function** shows that a firm's profit-maximizing output varies with the output decision of its rival.

> A **first-mover advantage** ensures that the firm which makes its strategic decision first gains a profitable advantage over its rivals.

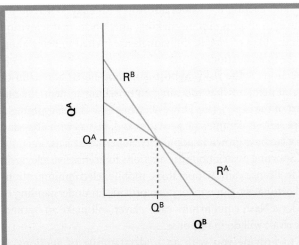

RA and RB represent the reaction functions for firms A and B. Each firm faces the same costs and same market, so the reaction functions are symmetric. The reaction functions show how each firm reacts to a change in output by its rival. In equilibrium, each firm's assumption about its rival is correct and each firm produces an identical level of output because the reaction functions are symmetric. Therefore $Q^A = Q^B$.

Figure 6.9 Reaction functions

A **Stackelberg model** is similar to the output approach of Cournot, but firms do not make strategic decisions simultaneously.

First-mover advantage can be examined using a **Stackelberg model**, which is similar to a Cournot model in its examination of output, but differs in enabling one firm to makes its decisions first, rather than simultaneously with its rival. Let us assume that firm A is the leader and firm B is the follower. A now has a considerable advantage over its rival. In full knowledge that B will react to A's decision, it is clear to A that the equilibrium must be located on B's reaction function. A must therefore choose an output which maximizes its own profits and is located on B's reaction function. If A goes higher than the Cournot equilibrium output, B must reduce output and this helps to support a higher price and greater profits for A.

Under a Stackelberg model, A's marginal revenue in Figure 6.8 will be higher than under Cournot. This is because A knows that B will support the market price by reducing its output Q^B in response to an increase in Q^A. A will therefore choose a higher level of profit-maximizing output. In the case of Figure 6.9, A's reaction function R^A becomes steeper and intersects R^B higher up and in equilibrium $Q^A > Q^B$, with A earning higher profits than under a Cournot equilibrium. Of course, this equilibrium is only feasible if A's output decision constitutes a sunk cost and is thereby a credible commitment to produce at Q^A. If B suspects that A has incurred no sunk costs, then it will be likely to increase output and A will follow with a cut in output. The equilibrium will then revert to the Nash–Cournot solution.

A business example may help to illustrate the complexities of the model. If a leader is planning to build a production facility, then the Stackelberg model would suggest that the leader can gain a first-mover advantage by building a bigger facility. The followers will then observe the leader's productive capacity and follow with a smaller facility. If additional profits do accrue from being first, then these can be reinvested in additional plant, R&D and new product lines. As such, first-mover advantages become persistent advantages. Of course, there are risks with first-mover advantages. Costs can be high, risks can be unknown and followers can learn from your mistakes.

6.8 Auction theory

Auctions have become a popular pastime. The online auction site eBay offers for sale everything from the mundane to the bizarre. If you are trying to find something, eBay is generally worth a search, even for those of us who are not addicted to bidding online. Amazingly, if all the transactions across the world on eBay were added together, this auction site would be the world's fourth largest economy; and auction fever does not stop with eBay. Where home makeover shows once dominated television programme-making, auction format television shows now lead the schedules. With the likes of *Flog It*, individuals are invited to bring along heirlooms and see what they can make in an auction.

While clearly an attraction of auctions is the risky, almost gambling-based adrenalin of seeing what you have to pay to gain an item, or what you can gain by selling an item, the uncertainty is also a very important part of the experience. However, while eBay and *Flog It* might be a bit of fun, for firms auctions are serious commercial activities and, just as with eBay and the like, auctions for commercial services have grown in popularity. Supermarkets use auctions to place orders for own-label items. Sporting associations use auctions to license live television rights, and governments use them to license railway operators, mobile telecommunications and even the right to run lotteries. Fortunately, game theory can provide an understanding of optimal behaviour in auctions. Under a Nash equilibrium, each player will make an optimal bid based on what they believe their rivals will do in response.

The purpose of this section is to provide you with an understanding of auctions. It will begin by explaining the four main types of auction format and introduce the important concepts of private versus common values. With these basic blocks of knowledge in place, the discussion assesses auctions from both a buyer's and a seller's perspective. Understanding optimal bidding strategies under each auction format will enable a seller to assess the auction format that will deliver the greatest revenue; while recognizing the problem of the winner's curse will provide a cautionary note to bidders.

Auction formats

There are seen to be four auction formats: the English auction, the Dutch auction, the first-price sealed-bid auction and the second-price sealed-bid auction.

In an English auction, bids begin low and are increased incrementally until no other bidder is willing to raise the bid. Bids can either be cried out by the auctioneer, with bidders nodding, or waving their papers in acceptance, or they can be input electronically, as is the case with eBay. In a Dutch auction, prices start high and are gradually reduced until a bidder accepts the price and wins the auction. This type of auction is commonly used in Holland to sell flowers and agricultural produce. Under the first-price sealed bid auction, bidders must submit a single bid, usually in writing. Bidders have little idea what anyone else has bid; and the highest bidder wins. The second-price sealed bid is a variation on the first-price auction. Again, bids are submitted in writing, but the highest bidder pays the price of the second-highest bid.

Common versus private values

Private values means each bidder has a private, subjective, value of an item's worth.

Auctions can also differ in the values held by bidders. With **private values** each bidder forms a private, probably subjective, view of the item for sale. This would be especially true with an item on eBay such as a watch, suit or an antique. Some individuals will like the item, but others will love it! Each bidder knows their own value of the item, but they do not know the value of the item to the other bidders. Furthermore, each bidder is unlikely to change their assessment of the item's value, even when they become informed of other bidders' valuations.

Under common values, an item is worth exactly the same to all bidders, but no bidder is sure what the item is truly worth. For example, as part of a game you might be shown a jar filled with coins. Along with your friends, you are asked to bid for the jar; the highest bid wins the jar. Clearly, in this example the jar is worth the same to each bidder, but no one is sure how much the jar is worth (without opening it and counting the coins). Real-life commercial auctions tend to be characterized by **common values** – the rights to an oil field, to show live football games or to run a national lottery. The commercial value of the rights is common to all bidders, but what they are truly worth is presently unknown. Significantly, under common values a bidder might be willing to change their bid once they know all the bids. For example, a comparison of bids will help to inform bidders about the accuracy of their own valuation of the item for sale. If other bidders are bidding high, then a bidder might be led to believe that they have undervalued the item.

Common values means the value of the item is identical for all bidders, but each bidder may form a different assessment of the item's worth.

With this basic understanding of auction formats, we can now consider which is the best auction format for a seller. If we assume that a seller wishes to maximize their revenue, we need to find the auction format which results in the highest bid. We will therefore analyse bidding behaviour in each auction format under which bidders have private values.

English auction with private values

A second-hand Swiss watch is offered for sale. You value the watch at £1000, a rival bidder values the watch at £900. What is your optimal bidding strategy? Under a Nash equilibrium, you should consider what your rival will do in response. So, if your rival bids £500, offer £501. Your rival may back out of the auction and you win at £501, saving yourself £499. Or your rival may top your bid and you are no worse off, since it cost you nothing to bid and you gained nothing. This strategy of raising the bid should continue until either your rival quits, or you reach your maximum willingness to pay. Significantly, in English auctions the winning bid will always be a fraction higher than the second-highest valuation. For this example, you will win the auction with a bid of £901.

Second-price sealed bid auction with private values

Under this auction format each bidder's dominant strategy is to submit a bid equal to their maximum willingness to pay. So, in the case of the Swiss watch, you will bid £1000 and your rival will bid £900. Since the highest bidder pays the second-highest price, you will win the auction for £900, which is almost identical to the outcome from the English auction.

To see why submitting a bid equal to your maximum willingness to pay is optimal, consider the following:

♦ **Lowering the bid.** If you lower your bid below your maximum willingness to pay, this will only alter the outcome if your new lower bid is less than your rival's. For example, a bid of £950 will still ensure you win the auction and pay £900. But a bid of £850 will result in you losing the auction (and your rival gaining the item for £50 less than they were willing to pay). So, in simple terms, you cannot win by lowering your bid, you can only lose.

♦ **Raising your bid.** If you bid £1050, this will not help you if your rival is going to bid less than £1000, your maximum willingness to pay. You will still win the auction and still pay the second price. If your rival is going to bid more than £1050, then again raising your bid has no impact. However, if your rival was to bid between £1000 and £1050, say £1030, you would now win the auction, but at a penalty. You would now have to pay £30 more than your maximum value. So, raising your bid above your maximum willingness to pay can only harm you.

So, you should not raise or lower your bid, simply submit your maximum willingness to pay.

First-price sealed bid auction with private values

Again, we are bidding for the Swiss watch and you value it at £1000. Should you submit a bid equal to your maximum willingness to pay as in the second-price sealed bid auction? To answer this question, consider Figure 6.10. The line S has a positive slope indicating that an increase in your bid raises the probability of winning the auction. If you bid your maximum willingness to pay, £1000, the expected payment on winning the auction will be equal to the areas A + B + C + D + E + F. If you lowered your bid to, say, £900, your expected payment upon winning the auction will be E + F.

The expected value (the benefit) from winning at £1000 will be A + B + C + D + E + F; exactly equal to the expected payment. The expected value (the benefit) of winning at £900 will be made up of the expected value of £900, plus the expected value of saving £100. So the expected value will be E + F + D.

In the case of bidding £1000, the expected value equals the expected cost, so you break even. But when reducing your bid to £900, the expected value exceeds your expected payment by the area D. It is therefore always optimal to bid below your maximum willingness to pay. You reduce your chances of winning, but you raise your potential gains.

The question now becomes by how much should you reduce your bid below your maximum willingness to pay. The answer rests on understanding the likely behaviour of your rival bidders and recognizing the interdependence of your bids. While beyond the scope of this discussion, it can be shown in Nash equilibrium that the optimal bid is (N − 1)/N multiplied by

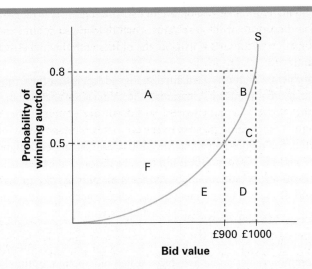

Figure 6.10 Optimal bidding under first-price sealed bid auction with private values

the bidder's maximum willingness to pay, where N is the number of bidders. So, with two bidders, the bid should be a half of your maximum willingness to pay. The winning bid will turn out to be the expected value of the second-highest willingness to pay.

Dutch auction with private values

Under this type of auction, prices are called out and you bid when they have fallen to a level which is optimal for you to make a bid. In the case of our Swiss watch, you will not bid when prices are above your valuation of £1000. You will also not bid when the watch reaches the price of £1000, because you would not save yourself anything. Rather, you will let the price fall and try to maximize the difference between the price you pay and the price at which you value the item. In essence, you would be trying to maximize area D in Figure 6.10. But how far should you allow the price to fall? The answer to this question is the same as for the first-price sealed bid auction. You would consider the likely bidding behaviour of your rivals and as long as your rival had not accepted a higher price, you would bid $(N - 1)/N$ multiplied by your maximum willingness to pay. In Nash equilibrium, the price received by the seller would again be the expected value of the second-highest willingness to pay.

The revenue equivalence theorem

The revenue equivalence theorem states that under private values each auction format will generate the same level of revenue for the seller.

This brings us to an important result. Under all auction formats, the bidder with the highest willingness to pay wins, but they always pay a price roughly equal to the second-highest valuation. So, since the auction format does not alter the amount of revenue received by the bidder, we observe **revenue equivalence** across competing auction formats.

Auctions and common values: the problem of the winner's curse

Let us return to our jar filled with coins. The auction will be a first-price sealed bid auction. No bidder is better or worse at estimating the value of the jar of coins. Some will overestimate, others will underestimate, but on average (if the auction was repeated) all bidders would form an unbiased estimate of the jar's value. Each bidder also submits a bid which is increasing in their estimation of the jar's worth. So, the bidder with the highest valuation submits the highest bid and wins.

The problem with this type of auction for bidders is that the winner must by definition have formed an overly-optimistic valuation of the jar of coins. They will therefore end up paying more for the jar than it is actually worth. So the **winner's curse** is that the winner actually loses. Knowing that the winner's curse exists will alter bidders' behaviour. If you think the jar is worth £100, you might then adjust your bid down to compensate for the risk of overestimating its worth and bid, say, £50. If all bidders are rational, they will all reduce their bids for this reason. In addition, bidders might reduce their bids further in order to maximize area D in Figure 6.10. Therefore, the problem for the seller in auctions with common values is that bidders will behave conservatively in order to avoid the winner's curse, leading to a lower sale price.

> The **winner's curse** is where a winning bid exceeds the true value of the sale item.

Unlike the case with private values and first-price auctions, where the optimal bid increases with the number of bidders, e.g. when $N = 2$, $(N - 1)/N = 1/2$; and when $N = 3$, $(N - 1)/N = 2/3$; under common values and a first-price sealed bid auction, optimal bids will decrease with an increase in the number of bidders. For example, if there are three bidders and you win, you have outbid only two other people. However, if there are 101 bidders, then you have outbid 100 other bidders and your estimate must have been very wrong. So, with an increase in the number of bidders, individual bidders will behave more conservatively and reduce their bids by more to avoid the winner's curse.

What can sellers do to avoid this problem? Simple, the winner's curse and conservative pricing occur because of a lack of information. If bidders had more information regarding other bidders' valuations, then they could more appropriately gauge the accuracy of their own willingness to pay. English auctions offer a solution. As bids are called out, each bidder can observe the valuation and willingness to pay by other bidders. If bids rise quickly, pessimistic bidders can revise their valuation of the item and enter the bidding. Therefore, within an English auction and common values, the incentive to be conservative is removed and the final price is higher. This perhaps helps explain why the English auction is the most commonly observed format.

6.9 Business application: compete, co-operate or gain a first-mover advantage?

If we return to our game theory illustration in Figure 6.7, the most desirable box for firm A is top right, where it earns 60. However, from our discussion we know that A will never find itself in this box. In a one-period game its rival will also compete and the two firms will earn 30 each, while in a repeated game both firms will try to co-operate and earn 50 each. Earning 60 in the top right is a situation where firm A competes and B decides to be friendly. A, therefore, dominates its rival B and in so doing controls the market. So, how do you convince your rival not to compete? We now know that the answer to this question rests on gaining a first-mover advantage.

This is a problem which has taxed Sony and Toshiba, who have been locked in a battle for supremacy in the emerging high definition DVD market. Sony developed and launched Blu-ray, while Toshiba led the HD DVD project. The competing approaches use different recording formats and are therefore incompatible with each other.

The race to win this market can be viewed as a game. If Toshiba and Sony agreed to co-operate and develop the same format, then movie-makers and consumers would be very happy. Movie-makers would feel assured that they could sell high-definition DVDs of their films; and consumers would be happy to purchase a high-definition DVD player and television to view the films. The market would grow and Sony and Toshiba would share a higher level of overall profits. This would be the top-left box of Figure 6.7.

In contrast, if Sony and Toshiba continue competing, then movie-makers do not know which format to support and consumers run the risk of buying a machine that can only play one format of discs. Worse still, their chosen format might be the less popular and their machines may become obsolete. The overall market shrinks and both firms earn reduced profits. This would be the bottom-right box of Figure 6.7.

Alternatively, one company could win enough support that it became commercially unattractive for the remaining competitor to continue. The winner would then be a monopoly and earn huge profits. Depending upon which firm wins, this would be the top-right or bottom-left box of Figure 6.7.

In order to try to win, Sony and Toshiba have sought out and gained the support of leading film studios. At times, some film studios have changed sides and the balance of power between Blu-ray and HD DVD has been finely balanced. Fortunately for Sony, it possessed a strategic option which offered the chance of first-mover advantage – Playstation 3 (ps3). By building Blu-ray into the ps3, Sony accelerated the adoption of its technology into many households around the world. In contrast, Toshiba's hopes of being adopted rested on the family decision to upgrade the trusted and reliable DVD player. By going first, or quickest, into households Sony has gained a commanding advantage. Film studios are beginning to recognize this and switch allegiance from Toshiba to Sony. The question now is whether Toshiba will withdraw and leave Sony to exploit its first-mover advantage.

 ### Box 6.5 Everything's gone Blu

Adapted from an article in The Economist, *10 January 2008*

On 4 January, Warner Bros said it would drop its support for HD DVD and only support Blu-ray from 1 June. This tips the balance decisively in favour of the Blu-ray camp. 'Game over,' said one analyst; HD DVD would now 'die a quick death', predicted another. Blu-ray's triumph seems almost inevitable.

Sony had two advantages: it now owns one of Hollywood's biggest studios, and it built a Blu-ray drive into its ps3 games console, thus seeding the market with millions of players. Despite HD DVD exclusives such as *Transformers* and *Shrek 3*, sales of Blu-ray discs outpaced those of HD DVDs by two to one in 2007.

Blu-ray's victory would be good news for the industry, allowing it to unite to promote a single next-generation format as sales of DVDs start to decline (they fell by nearly 5 per cent in America last year, the first ever year-on-year decline, and by around 3 per cent worldwide). For consumers, most of whom have chosen to steer clear of both formats until a winner emerges, it would also be good news – except, that is, for those who have already bought HD DVD players.

6.10 Business application: managing supply costs – anonymous auctions for supermarket contracts

We have seen that, in repeated games, firms are likely to behave co-operatively. This presents a substantial risk to supermarkets who repeatedly run auctions to provide them with products.

In particular, because supermarkets are retailers, they do not ordinarily manufacture their 'own-labelled' products. Instead, they ask competing manufacturers to bid for contracts. Today, it might be next month's lemonade contract; tomorrow, it might be fishfingers or soap powder. The firm that can produce the product most cheaply wins the contract. With supermarkets coming to the market repeatedly, it is in the interest of competing manufacturers to co-operate with each other. For example, rival manufacturers of fishfingers could agree to split the market. When bidding for supermarket X's contract, company A would never undercut company B. In return, when bidding for supermarket Y's contract, B would never undercut A.

For a supermarket, this is a serious problem. The way to stop it is to prevent co-operation. Supermarkets try to achieve this by organizing blind auctions over the Internet. The fishfinger contract opens for bidding at 2.00pm on Wednesday and companies make bids. The web page shows the amount of it, but it does not say who made it. The bidders now find it difficult to co-operate. In fact, it is now very easy to cheat because only the supermarket knows who you are. In this example, supermarkets can see the problem of co-operation and take steps to prevent its occurrence.

There is, however, a problem with the supermarket's strategy. In generating competition among its suppliers, it runs the risk of pushing some of them out of business. Therefore, in the long run the supermarkets could end up with monopoly suppliers in their key product markets rather than competitive industries, and we saw in Chapter 5 that such a situation could be dangerous.

Summary

1   Under monopolistic competition, there are a large number of small firms, freedom of entry and exit, few opportunities for economies of scale, and the use of product differentiation.

2   Long-run equilibrium in monopolistic competition is a tangency equilibrium, which results in zero economic profits, excess capacity, above-minimum average costs and price in excess of marginal costs.

3   Oligopolies are marketplaces with a small number of large firms, typically four or five. UK banking, supermarkets and even the media industry are good examples.

4   An important feature of oligopolistic markets is strategic interaction. If one firm makes a strategic change, all other firms react. When one UK supermarket decided to open on Sundays, all other supermarkets followed.

5   Two interesting questions occur when examining oligopolies: (i) Why do oligopolies exist? (ii) How will firms compete with each other?

6   Oligopolies can exist because of exogenous economies of scale. The natural cost structure of the industry results in only a small number of large firms meeting the minimum efficient scale.

7   Alternatively, natural scale economies might be limited and so, in order to create entry barriers, existing firms might manipulate the cost characteristics of the industry by perhaps making advertising a large component of operating costs. This creates high levels of endogenous costs and reduces entry.

8   Sunk costs cannot be recovered when exiting a market. If large costs are associated with brand development, then these will be sunk. This increases the risk of entry and so can also lead to the creation of entry barriers.

9   Without sunk costs, markets are contestable. Potential rivals can threaten to enter a market. In order to limit entry, firms within the market will reduce prices and profits to make entry less attractive. As a result, even with a small number of large firms, contestable markets will approximate to perfect competition.

10 Game theory can be used to understand strategic interaction. Games consist of players, pay-offs and decision rules.

11 A Nash equilibrium is where players make an optimal decision based on what their rivals might do. In single-period games, the Nash equilibrium requires each player to cheat or display non-cooperative behaviour. In a multi-period game with no known end, the optimal strategy is tit-for-tat, where if you co-operated last round, your rival should co-operate with you in the next round. If not, you should never co-operate with them again.

12 Reaction functions illustrate a firm's best response given the possible responses of its rival.

13 A Cournot game involves firms making decisions over output. A Bertrand game involves firms making decisions over prices.

14 The Nash equilibrium for a Bertrand game has both firms charging a price equal to marginal cost.

15 The Stackelberg model illustrates first-mover advantages.

16 There are four auction formats: English auction, first-price sealed bid auction, second-price sealed bid auction and Dutch auction.

17 Under private values, the value of an item differs across bidders. Under common values, the item has the same intrinsic value to each bidder, but bidders are unsure of the true value of the item.

18 Under private values, all four auction formats enable the bidder with the highest willingness to pay to win the auction. But they only pay the second-highest price. This is known as the 'revenue equivalence theorem'.

19 Under common values, bidders face the problem of the winner's curse, where the highest willingness to pay vastly exceeds the intrinsic value of the item.

20 To avoid conservative bidding under the winner's curse, an English auction format provides bidders with clearer information on the item's true value.

21 In the repeated environment of firms bidding for supermarkets' own-label contracts, it is likely that co-operation will occur, where rivals agree not to undercut each other on price. In order to prevent this and generate competition in the auction, supermarkets run blind auctions, where it becomes difficult for rivals to co-ordinate their bids. It even enables rivals to cheat on each other behind a cloak of secrecy.

Learning checklist

You should now be able to:

- Explain monopolistic competition
- Provide examples of oligopolies
- Explain the concept of strategic interdependence

- ◆ Identify natural and strategic entry barriers
- ◆ Understand the kinked demand curve model of oligopoly and provide a critical review
- ◆ Explain game theory, the concept of a Nash equilibrium and optimal strategies in single-period and repeated games
- ◆ Understand reaction functions
- ◆ Discuss the key differences between the Cournot, Bertrand and Stackelberg models
- ◆ Explain how game theory can be used to control the behaviour of rivals in auctions
- ◆ Identify the main types of auction and discuss the difference between common and private values
- ◆ Explain the revenue equivalence theorem and the winner's curse

Questions connect™

1. How do the assumptions of perfect competition and monopolistic competition differ?
2. List five industries which are likely examples of monopolistic competition.
3. How do the equilibrium conditions differ between perfect competition and monopolistic competition?
4. What are the main types of entry barrier that are likely to be associated with oligopoly?
5. Under a kinked demand line, is demand more or less elastic above and below the equilibrium price?
6. When is collusion likely to fail?
7. What is a Nash equilibrium?
8. In the single-period Prisoners' Dilemma, both prisoners confess. Is this optimal?
9. How might two strategically interdependent players be encouraged to co-operate with each other?
10. Is it possible and sensible to gain a first-mover advantage?

11. Monopolistic competition is sometimes criticized for displaying excess capacity. Explain why excess capacity exists in equilibirum and evaluate whether it is bad for society.
12. Do you consider it fair that whistle-blowers, who are the first to admit to being in a cartel, are immune from prosecution?
13. Assume your company is operating in a cartel, agreeing to raise prices and reduce output. If the cartel is ongoing, then the game is in effect repeated. Under what circumstances would your company cheat?

14. Electrical retailers promise to match each other's prices. Is this co-operation or competition?
15. A firm is considering whether it should be first to invest in a new market. Provide the company with your best economic advice.

Exercises

1 True or false?
   (a) A key aspect of an oligopolistic market is that firms cannot operate independently of each other.
   (b) Cartels may be workable if members enter into binding pre-commitments.
   (c) Under a kinked demand curve, demand is assumed to be price inelastic under a rise in prices.
   (d) In a one-period game, the strategy of tit-for-tat is optimal.
   (e) In a repeated game with no known end, it is always optimal to cheat.
   (f) With private values, an English auction format will raise the highest revenue for an item.

2 Suppose that there are two firms (X and Y) operating in a market, each of which can choose to produce either 'high' or 'low' output. Table 6.3 summarizes the range of possible outcomes of the firms' decisions in a single time period. Imagine that you are taking the decisions for firm X.
   (a) If firm Y produces 'low', what level of output would maximize your profit in this time period?
   (b) If you (X) produce 'high', what level of output would maximize profits for firm Y?
   (c) If firm Y produces 'high', what level of output would maximize your profit in this time period?
   (d) Under what circumstances would you decide to produce 'low'?
   (e) Suppose you enter into an agreement with firm Y that you both will produce 'low': what measures could you adopt to ensure that Y keeps to the agreement?
   (f) What measures could you adopt to convince Y that you will keep to the agreement?
   (g) Suppose that the profit combinations are the same as in Table 6.3, except that if both firms produce 'high' each firm makes a loss of 8. Does this affect the analysis?

Table 6.3 Firms' decisions

		Firm Y			
		Low output profits		High output profits	
	Profits:	**X**	**Y**	**X**	**Y**
Firm X	**Low output profits**	15	15	2	20
	High output profits	20	2	8	8

3 Consider the case of Sony in Box 6.5.

   In what ways can an understanding of game theory be used to understand the development of competition between Sony and Toshiba in the market for high-definition DVD players?

Chapter 7
Growth strategies

Chapter contents

 Learning outcomes

By the end of this chapter you should understand:

Economic Theory

LO1 The difference between horizontal, vertical and diversified growth

LO2 Learning curves

LO3 Transaction costs

LO4 The hold-up problem

LO5 Economies of scope

Business Application

LO6 Why a small company within an oligopoly wished to merge with a rival

LO7 Why the media company Sky has vertically integrated its entire value chain

LO8 Why Google is branching out beyond search technology

Growth strategies at a glance

The issue

If firms are profit-maximizers, then it seems reasonable to assume that, in the longer term, increasing profits will be associated with increased size. Admittedly, in the near term some profits may have to be sacrificed in order to grow the business. Managerial time might be diverted to finding and selecting growth opportunities, rather than concentrating on generating profits from the current operations. It therefore becomes important to understand how a firm can grow, benefit from and manage the problems associated with different modes of growth.

The understanding

A firm can grow in three main ways. First it can 'do more of the same'. A car maker might decide to make more cars. Second, a firm might reduce its trading relationships by providing its own inputs, or by organizing its own distribution and retailing. Third, a firm might begin to operate in a completely different market. These three options are, respectively, known as horizontal, vertical and diversified growth. The reasons behind each type of growth are varied, but essentially they relate to the ability to increase revenues and reduce costs. This chapter will provide an understanding of these issues.

The usefulness

An understanding of growth options is essential for understanding how a business can exploit profitable opportunities. Moreover, an understanding of growth options provides an insight into strategic behaviour and, therefore, how the firm can gain greater control over its markets and its competitors.

7.1 Business problem: how should companies grow?

Organic growth is an increase in sales from the same or comparable retail space.

Horizontal growth occurs when a company develops or grows activities at the same stage of the production process.

Box 7.1 highlights the different types of growth achieved by supermarkets. First, there is simple sales growth over time. Morrisons reports growth of 8.2 per cent; Tesco achieved 2.5 per cent. Like-for-like sales strip out the effect of opening new stores and so represent pure **organic growth**. A key question for business managers is how fast and how sustainable is organic growth. In a market with rapidly expanding demand, organic growth can be very sustainable. In mature markets, such as supermarkets, organic growth can be slow and limited to the rate of growth of consumer spending on food and other grocery items. Also, as the article notes, organic growth can be reduced by competition. Strong competition can cut prices and volumes. Prices across all supermarkets fall and customers may move to the cheapest competitor. So organic growth can be good, but it also has its problems.

Importantly, not all growth has to be organic. Companies can expand their existing capacity by acquiring or combining their current assets with those of another company and/or competitor. Such growth is categorized by economists into horizontal, vertical and diversification.

Merging two similar companies is referred to as **horizontal growth**. Previously, Morrisons mergered with Safeway and in the article the supermarket chain now plans to buy 38 stores from its rival the Co-operative group. While such growth brings in more sales, it may also enable a company to achieve economies of scale and bring down operating costs.

Box 7.1 Growth and competition among the supermarkets

Adapted from 'Wm Morrison beats rivals with strong Christmas showing' by Lucy Killgren in The Financial Times, *22 January 2009, and 'Tesco gets ready for "very tough" year' by Maggie Urry in* The Financial Times, *13 January 2009*

Morrisons confirmed its position as the UK's best performing supermarket group after reporting a like-for-like sales increase of 8.2 per cent over the Christmas period. The retailer claimed it had pulled in an additional 2.2 million customers as its promotional offers and fresh foods found favour with a broad range of consumers.

Marc Bolland said on Thursday: 'We are the only retailer which is growing in value and in premium [lines].' Despite stellar sales and Mr Bolland's assurances that margins had 'kept up', the retailer said expectations for full-year profits remained unchanged for 2008/09. The consensus forecast is £625 million.

On Thursday, Morrisons said it was still awaiting certain approvals to complete the acquisitions of the 38 stores it was buying from the Co-operative group. Morrisons announced it was buying the stores for £223 million plus costs of £98 million, in December. It will be the first big expansion of the chain since it acquired Safeway in 2004, in a deal which took longer than expected to integrate successfully.

But analysts were concerned that, in an increasingly competitive market, it would become harder for Morrisons to improve share. 'We . . . are likely to see greater discounting from Tesco trying to recapture market share.'

Tesco said it was expecting the next few weeks and months to be tough, as its performance over Christmas failed to live up to that of its rivals in what is proving to be one of the poorest festive seasons for retailers in a generation. Tesco delivered underlying sales up just 2.5 per cent in the seven weeks to 10 January.

Chief financial officer, Mr Higginson, was quick to defend Tesco's performance as 'strong', even though it fell behind its rivals. '[Group] sales are up 11.6 per cent. How many big retailers do you know growing at that rate?' he said. International sales, which account for about 28 per cent of overall sales, were up 32.7 per cent, he pointed out.

Mr Higginson said Tesco had been hit by the weakness in the non-food market as shoppers avoided non-essential items. But the retailer did manage to deliver like-for-like growth in non-food over the quarter by starting its sales in clothing about ten days before Christmas.

But there were worrying signs in Europe, where sales rose 24 per cent, against a 43 per cent uplift in Asia, as the economic slowdown hit the Republic of Ireland and Hungary.

The company also said that savers were flocking to open savings accounts at its finance arm, Tesco Personal Finance, which is offering 3.6 per cent on its Internet savings account.

© The Financial Times Ltd. 2009

When examining Tesco, the article also indicates how the supermarket has expanded into non-food areas such as banking, electronics and clothing. Tesco has also expanded operations into Europe, South East Asia and North America. This expansion of variety by product and geography would be considered diversification by an economist. **Diversification** is not a particularly easy category to define because it can include related and unrelated diversification. For example, Tesco operates in grocery, banking, electronics and food. These all appear to be unrelated, but could equally be related as different aspects of the retail market.

> **Diversification** is the growth of the business in a related or unrelated market.

A company may grow in a diversified way to offset risk. Non-food sales may grow more than food sales. Equally, sales in non-UK locations may grow at a faster rate, thus reducing Tesco's dependence on the UK economy for sales and profits.

Vertical chain of production encapsulates the various stages of production from the extraction of a raw material input, through the production of the product or service, to the final retailing of the product.

A company is said to be **vertically integrated** if it owns consecutive stages of the vertical chain.

There is also a third means of growth and this is known as vertical growth. Supermarkets are a collection of separate and sequential operations. Sourcing, producing, distributing and retailing constitute what economists refer to as separate aspects of the **vertical chain of production**.

The vertical chain is composed of all the separate commercial activities that add value to a product. Morrisons, for example, owns farms and produces much of its own meat and vegetables. Morrisons also owns many processing facilities which turn the farm produce into packaged items for its stores. In contrast, Tesco prefers to buy in produce from independent producers and packagers. Why have Morrisons and Tesco decided to take such different routes. One reason is that, by integrating all stages of production, Morrisons is seeking to gain greater control over its value chain and is described by economists as being **vertically integrated**. As a retailer of fresh produce, Morrisons derives greater security and quality in relation to its supplies by growing vertically.

In order to understand why a company might wish to grow horizontally, vertically or in a diversified manner, we need to understand the benefits and problems associated with horizontal, vertical and diversified expansion.

7.2 Reasons for growth

If we begin by accepting the general proposition that firms are in business to maximize profits, then it seems reasonable to suggest that firms grow in order to improve profitability. If this is true, then, examining Figure 7.1, a firm seeking horizontal, vertical or diversified growth must be expecting to gain from increases in total revenues and/or decreases in total costs. In this way, the two curves in Figure 7.1 will move further apart from each other. As the curves move apart, both the profit-maximizing level of output and the amount of profit-maximizing profit will increase.

We will examine horizontal, vertical and diversified growth in turn.

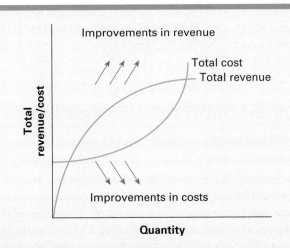

Figure 7.1 Total revenue and costs

If a firm is a profit-maximizer, then the pursuit of growth opportunities is arguably linked to either revenue or cost improvements. As revenue increases and costs are reduced, the profitability at each level of output is improved.

7.3 Horizontal growth

Horizontal growth, or expansion at a singular point on the vertical chain, can occur in a number of ways.

Organic growth is associated with firms growing through internal expansion.

For example, a manufacturer might build additional production facilities, such as assembly lines, or a new factory. A retailer, such as a supermarket, might build more outlets. An airline might buy more aircraft. Crucially, the firm is growing by investing in new assets, which add to its current stock of capital. As an alternative, a firm might consider growth by **acquisition** and **merger**.

In either case, the company grows by merging its activities with those of an existing operator. By going back through the theory established in previous chapters, we can now begin to analyse the benefits of horizontal growth.

Acquisition involves one firm purchasing another firm. This might occur by mutual consent or, in the case of a hostile takeover, the managers of the acquired firm might try to resist the takeover.

Merger generally involves two companies agreeing by mutual consent to merge their existing operations.

Horizontal growth and revenue

In Chapter 2 we examined the elasticity, or responsiveness, of demand to a change in price. The greater the number of substitutes, or rival products, the greater the price elasticity of demand. If demand is elastic, then a small change in the price results in a huge change in the quantity demanded. Therefore, in price-elastic markets, with lots of substitute products, we argued that there is a clear incentive for firms to engage in a price war. If one firm reduces its prices, it quickly attracts market share from its rivals. However, in response, rivals may also drop their prices and each firm will retain the same market share but be selling at a lower price. If demand is price inelastic, or not responsive to a change in price, then a price reduction will not have a significant impact on demand. Moreover, total revenues will decline. Therefore, the optimal response under price-inelastic demand is to raise prices in order to boost total revenues.

Reducing competition

If we now think about merger and acquisition, by definition the number of competitors in the market is reduced by one. Therefore, because merger and acquisition lead to a reduction in the number of substitutes, it is likely that the elasticity of demand is reduced. When competition is reduced, price wars are less likely and firms have more scope for increasing, rather than decreasing, prices. See Box 7.2 and the case of the UK's new superbank.

➡ Box 7.2 HBOS and Lloyds TSB superbank lists on Stock Exchange

Adapted from an article by Brian Donnelly in The Herald, *19 January 2009*

Consumers are braced for the era of the superbank, as HBOS and Lloyds TSB merge to become Lloyds Banking Group today. The newly enlarged group is by far the biggest bank in the UK.

The move will combine the UK's biggest mortgage lender and third-biggest lender into a single group. In the long term this could lead to a reduction in competition. There is also concern that the enlarged group will cherry-pick the best mortgage customers, making it harder for people with small deposits or bad credit histories to borrow. The Office of Fair Trading has also raised concerns that the takeover could reduce competition in the current account sector, mortgage market and lending to small businesses.

The extent of the services now under one umbrella is shown in HBOS's 40-plus individual brands, including Clerical Medical, esure and Sheilas' Wheels. Lloyds TSB also operates under the Cheltenham & Gloucester and Scottish Widows brands.

If we also think about perfect competition, oligopoly and monopoly, as discussed in Chapters 5 and 6, we can reinforce the arguments made above. Under perfect competition with a large number of competitors, prices and profits are lowest. Under monopoly, prices and profits will be highest. In the case of oligopoly, consolidation in the industry can lead to greater co-operation as opposed to increased competition. As discussed in Chapter 6, it is optimal for a cartel to act as a monopoly supplier and reduce output to the market. However, it is in each firm's interest to cheat and increase output. It is easier to monitor and enforce the tacit or explicit agreement made among the members of a small cartel than of a large one. In a small cartel you only need to gain agreement among, say, two or three companies. In a large cartel you need to gain agreement among a much larger number of companies, which is difficult. Therefore, mergers and acquisitions can lead to increased co-operation and the success of cartels.

Exploiting market growth

Aside from any changes in the price elasticity of demand, horizontal growth may be undertaken in order to exploit revenue growth. Growing demand could stimulate organic growth. As more customers move into a market, the firm can exploit increased revenue opportunities by investing in more productive assets. As more passengers have been willing to fly with low-cost airlines, easyJet and Ryanair have purchased more aircraft. In recent years, coffee bars have suddenly appeared on many high streets, seeking to meet and exploit the rapid increase in customers.

In summary, the incentives from revenue and horizontal growth emanate from two main sources: first, a reduction in the number of competitors and, therefore, a fall in the price elasticity of demand, making price rises easier and price wars less likely; second, to take advantage of customer growth opportunities in the market.

Horizontal growth and costs

The obvious reason for horizontal growth relates to costs. In Chapter 3, we discussed economies of scale at length. However, in summary, as a firm increases its scale of operation, by increasing its capital input, it generally experiences a reduction in long-run average costs. Therefore, we can argue that a firm will try to grow in order to exploit economies of scale. This is often used as a rationale for merger. When bringing two companies together, managers often talk up the potential for cost reductions by reducing and sharing managerial functions. Two companies need two chief executives; one company needs only one chief executive. Two companies need two finance, legal, marketing and HRM departments; one company needs only one of each. These single departments will generally be capable of operating at a size which is

> **Rationalization** is associated with cutbacks in excess resources in the pursuit of increased operational efficiencies.

less than the sum of the two separate departments, achieving this through greater staff utilization. This is often referred to as **rationalization**.

However, it is also possible that a firm can become too big. We saw in Chapter 3 that a very large firm can experience diseconomies of scale, where problems of control and co-ordination make the productivity of a large firm decrease, leading to a rise in long-run average costs. Therefore, it is sometimes the case that large firms decrease the scale of their operations in order to bring about cost improvements.

An alternative cost reason for horizontal expansion is the benefit to be had from the **learning curve**.

> The **learning curve** suggests that, as cumulative output increases, average costs fall.

This is depicted in Figure 7.2 and shows that, as the firm produces successive units, or adds to its cumulative output, average costs fall. Importantly, the firm is considered to be in long-run equilibrium. The fall in average costs is not driven by the law of diminishing returns. Instead, as a firm produces additional output, it learns how to improve productivity. The classic example is the production of a jumbo jet. This is a massive project and requires careful

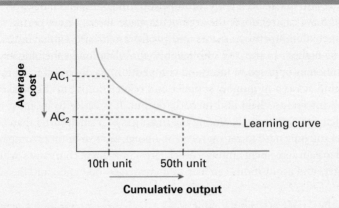

Figure 7.2 Learning curve

As the firm produces additional output, its cumulative output increases. By learning how to make the product more efficiently, the cost per unit falls. This is the so-called learning effect.

planning and learning. In what order should the plane be assembled? When are the wings attached, when is the wiring completed, when can the seats be added? If wings are added too early, then there is the risk of having to remove them at a later date in order to finish another task, such as adding the fuel tanks. However, once the mistake is made and learnt, it will not be made again. So, when the next plane is built, fewer assembly mistakes will occur. The plane will be built more quickly and at a lower cost. As more planes are built, the assembly teams will learn how to carry out each assembly task more quickly and develop new operating techniques. Eventually, at high levels of cumulative output, all learning opportunities are exploited and the reduction in costs diminishes to zero. At this point the learning curve becomes flat.

A firm producing 100 units a day learns faster than a firm producing ten units a day. In recognizing this point, a firm could grow organically in order to be in a position to exploit the learning effect sooner than its rivals. Alternatively, a competitor may have already produced many units and acquired the relevant cumulative experience through learning. An attractive strategy is to merge with or acquire the existing firm, in an attempt to gain the acquired experience. However, it is debatable how easy it is to transfer experience between organizations. The experience of one company is likely to be related to the systems, producers and cultures of that company. The learning effect stems from the experiences of a group of individuals with shared memories, values and understanding. Transferring such intangible understandings and benefits effectively to another organization is likely to be problematic.

7.4 Vertical growth

Cost reasons

When a firm grows vertically, either moving up or down its vertical chain, it is attempting to integrate additional value-adding activities into its existing activities. There can be a number of reasons for doing this.

Location benefits

Integrating consecutive activities from the vertical chain can reduce production costs. For example, steel smelting plants are often located next to steel rolling plants. This reduces transport and heating costs. Extremely high temperatures are needed to produce steel. Similarly, in order to roll the steel into usable sheets, the steel has to be hot. With the plants co-owned and located next to each other, the hot steel can be transferred easily to the rolling plant. If the two activities were separate, the new hot steel would have to be cooled, transferred by road to the rolling plant, re-heated and then rolled – resulting in much higher production costs.

The importance of co-location is also relevant in computing, the Internet and server farms. In Box 7.3, the same issue as in steel is at work. When you need energy, the best location is to be near the source of power.

 Box 7.3 Down on the server farm

Adapted from an article in The Economist, *22 May 2008*

Quincy, a small town in the centre of the state of Washington, is home to half a dozen huge warehouses that power the global 'computing clouds' run by Internet companies such as Yahoo! and Microsoft. The size of several football pitches, these data centres are filled with thousands of powerful computers and storage devices and are hooked up to the Internet via fast fibre-optic links.

Yet, even more intriguing than the buildings' size, is their location. Quincy is literally in the middle of nowhere, three hours' drive from the nearest big city, Seattle. But it turns out to be a perfect location for data centres.

Internet firms need ever larger amounts of computing power. Google is said to operate a global network of about three dozen data centres with, according to some estimates, more than 1 million servers. To catch up, Microsoft is investing billions of dollars and adding up to 20 000 servers a month.

As servers become more numerous, powerful and densely packed, more energy is needed to keep the data centres at room temperature. Often just as much power is needed for cooling as for computing. The largest data centres now rival aluminium smelters in the energy they consume. Microsoft's $500 million new facility near Chicago, for instance, will need three electrical substations with a total capacity of 198 megawatts. As a result, finding a site for a large data centre is now, above all, about securing a cheap and reliable source of power.

The availability of cheap power is mainly why there are so many data centres in Quincy. It is close to the Columbia River, with dams that produce plenty of cheap hydroelectric power. There is water for cooling, fast fibre-optic links, and the remoteness provides security. For similar reasons, Google chose to build a new data centre at The Dalles, a hamlet across the Columbia River in the state of Oregon.

© The Economist Newspaper Limited, London 2009

Economies of scale

In contrast, when economies of scale are important, vertical disintegration may also result in cost benefits. For example, the manufacture of a product may require a particular raw material input. If the manufacturer developed its own raw material division, then, without supplying other companies, the division is likely to be operating at a very small scale. However, if a raw material supplier is able to operate independently and supply many manufacturers, it is possible that it can exploit economies of scale. If economies of scale are important in a value-adding activity, it could be better for the manufacturer to abandon its raw material division and instead buy from a larger independent company.

Problems from monopoly

While economies of scale might be important cost considerations, it is also possible that raw materials might be supplied by a monopoly, in which case the price of the raw material could be higher than under a competitive market. A simple solution to this problem is to purchase the monopoly supplier and transfer the raw material between divisions of the same company. But what price will the production division pay the raw material division? The optimal price for transferring the raw material to the production division is the marginal cost of production in the raw material division. Under such a price, allocative efficiency would hold with the price being equal to marginal cost. As an explanation, the price paid and, therefore, the value of the last unit will be exactly equal to the cost of producing the last unit. This enables the combined profits of the raw material division and the production division to be maximized. More import- ant, if we return to an argument made in Chapter 5, the monopoly price is always greater than the marginal cost. Therefore, buying the raw material supplier and charging an internal price equal to the marginal cost has to be cheaper than the price charged by a monopoly supplier.

Transaction costs

In order to fully develop your understanding of the various cost reasons for vertical growth, we need to introduce a new cost concept. In Chapter 3, when examining costs, we only focused on production costs. These are the costs of the factor resources – land, labour, capital and enterprise – used by the firm in the production of the good or service. In addition to production costs, we also need to consider what are known as **transaction costs**.

> **Transaction costs** are the costs associated with organizing the transaction of goods or services.

When goods or services are traded, the costs of organizing the transaction can range from low to very high. At the most simplistic level, if a contract or agreement is entered into for the supply of goods or services, the time of managers negotiating the contract and the cost of lawyers hired to write the contract both represent transaction costs. Economists highlight a number of factors that are likely to lead to higher transaction costs. These factors are all related to the degree to which the contract or agreement can be declared 'complete'.

> Under a **complete contract**, all aspects of the contractual arrangement are fully specified.

For example, the nature of the product, including its characteristics, the materials used to make it and its size, will all be described within the contract terms. The price and time of delivery will also be covered by the contract. Finally, the contract will also set out how the performance of the product supplier will be measured and how the contract will be enforced through the legal system, should the terms of the contract be breached.

Clearly, given the conditions detailed above, no contract is ever complete. However, for some products it is much easier to write a nearly complete contract, while for others it is almost impossible. As examples, it is much easier to write a complete contract for a bag of sand than it is for lecturing services. Sand comes in standard bag sizes, a limited number of ranges, such as river sand or building sand, and if a company agreed to deliver a bag you would be able to verify its arrival. Now consider writing a contract for lecturing services. For a complete contract it would be necessary to define many things, including: during which hours the lectures would be given; what textbooks should be used; what topics should be covered each week; how the module should be examined; what topics and questions should be used during the tutorials; how difficult the examination should be; how marks should be awarded; how many students are expected to pass; how tutorial staff should be managed; and much more. It is clearly very difficult to define in full all the actions a lecturer should take during the running of a module. As a consequence, universities, like many employers, use incomplete contracts. Instead of defining all possible actions, contracts resort to simple statements such as 'a lecturer will be expected to communicate and expand knowledge'.

Rather than being complete, the contract is extremely vague. A sensible interpretation of the statement is that a lecturer is expected to communicate knowledge through teaching and expand knowledge through research. But of course there are many other interpretations. For example, answering the telephone and handling student enquiries is communicating and expanding knowledge. If the university expected the lecturer to teach and research, but the lecturer decided to simply answer telephone enquiries, then the university would experience substantial transaction costs. This is because the lecturer is choosing to undertake activities that the university did not intend. Aside from the ability to reinterpret the meaning of the contract, it is also very difficult for the university to measure the lecturer's performance. For example, let us assume many students fail the module. There could be many explanations, but let us concentrate on two. First, the lecturer did not perform well and the students did not benefit from the lectures. Second, even if this is true, the lecturer could blame the poor performance on the students' lack of effort during tutorials and revision. Because the effort of the lecturer and the students is not monitored by anyone from the university, it is difficult to support either argument. This therefore creates an environment within which the lecturer could act less than professionally. Lower performance by the lecturer represents a transaction cost.

We will shortly see how firms, and in our case universities, try to deal with these problems. But, first, it is useful to provide an understanding of the general factors which lead to greater transaction costs.

Complexity

Complexity is an obvious factor. Sand is an uncomplicated product; lecturing is a very complicated product. As the product or service becomes more complex (simple), the more incomplete (complete) the contract becomes. As the contract becomes more incomplete (complete), the higher (lower) are the costs of transacting.

Uncertainty

Uncertainty also affects the ability to write a complete contract. In the case of a bag of sand, uncertainty is less of an issue. You are not going to request a different bag of sand depending upon the nature of the weather. By contrast, in the case of lecturing services a university will expect the lecturer to be adaptable in the face of future changes. New theories may enter the subject, new ways of teaching might emerge, or the quality of the students each year could change. The university cannot write a contract detailing how the lecturer should deal with these changes, but a good lecturer will be expected to deal with these problems and opportunities using their professional discretion.

So, as uncertainty increases, the ability to write a complete contract diminishes and the cost of transacting increases.

Monitoring

While complexity and uncertainty are problems associated with writing a contract, monitoring and enforcement are problems associated with managing a contractual arrangement. The more simple and certain the environment, the easier it is to monitor a contract. Again, let us compare a bag of sand with the lecturer. It is very easy to monitor whether or not a bag of sand is delivered. You can see it, you can feel it and you can weigh it. But how do you know if a lecturer has communicated and expanded knowledge? How do you measure effective communication, or teaching? A high pass rate for the module could indicate good teaching. But it could equally indicate good students, or an easy examination.

In general when the good or service is more complex and the environment is more uncertain, the ability to monitor the incomplete contract is more difficult and costly.

Enforcement

When the contract is incomplete, the enforcement of the contract, by use of the legal process, is much more difficult.

If a company does not deliver your sand, it is fairly easy to prove breach of contract and ask a court to enforce delivery. However, if you cannot effectively define or measure the activities of a lecturer, then it is almost impossible to prove breach of contract. For example, if the university says that the lecturer has not communicated knowledge effectively, it will have to find a way of measuring the lecturer's level of effective communication. Since measuring communication is very difficult, it will be almost impossible to ask a judge to enforce the contract on a lecturer. The legal system cannot be used to enforce the contract. In knowledge of the fact that a university will find it difficult to measure and enforce performance, the lecturer can use the discretion provided within the contract to teach what they like, in a fashion that they prefer and examine the topics that they would like. Some do it well, others less well. The difference is transaction costs.

Make or buy?

In the case of production costs, we argued that firms are cost-efficient when they operate with minimum average costs at the lowest point on the average cost curve. It therefore also seems sensible to argue that firms will try to minimize transaction costs. In fact, the reduction or control of transaction costs is of fundamental importance for economists, because transaction costs are the very driving force behind firms. Without transaction costs, firms would not exist.

Transaction costs can be managed through competing systems. These are the market and the hierarchy, or managerial structure, of a firm. Theoretically, the system with the lowest transaction cost will be chosen.

The hierarchy, or managerial structure, of a firm is composed of the various managerial layers, beginning with directors, then moving down to senior managers, and eventually ordinary workers.

Transaction costs and markets

For market-based transactions to have a low transaction cost, the contract has to be as complete as possible. This requires low complexity and low uncertainty. In addition, monitoring must be easy and enforcement feasible. In such situations the ability to write a contract is easy and, therefore, low cost. Furthermore, the scope of the provider to perform below expectation in the delivery of the good or service is constrained by the easy monitoring and legal enforcement of the contract. The transaction costs of operating through the market are low.

In contrast, when the product is complex and uncertainty is high, it becomes more difficult and, therefore, more costly to write a contract. In addition, as the contract becomes more incomplete, greater discretion is handed to the provider of the good or service. Monitoring of the output becomes difficult, as the output is not clearly defined by the contract. As a result, enforcement becomes impossible. Recall the lecturer communicating and expanding knowledge. The output of the lecturer is not defined. It is left to the lecturer to use their discretion when designing the syllabus and delivery of the module. The potential for very high transaction costs by operating through the market becomes very high.

Transaction costs and hierarchies

The alternative is to organize the transaction within the firm and use the hierarchy or managerial structure to organize the transaction. The problem with incomplete contractual relationships is that they provide the producer of the good or service with too much discretion. To economize on writing a complete contract the university uses the phrase 'communicate and expand knowledge'. But by using the managerial structure of the university, it is possible to minimize the resulting transaction costs. For example, when a lecturer begins employment they will ordinarily be placed on probation for perhaps three years. Removal from probation and the confirmation of employment will only follow a set of successful lectures. Before a module begins the lecturer will not generally be allowed to choose any set of topics. Rather, they will be required to work to a module descriptor, which details the topics to be taught, the nature of the assessment and the key learning outcomes of the module for the students.

At the end of the module, students are asked to evaluate the module on various criteria. This is monitoring, and over a number of years and across a range of taught modules the university can develop an understanding of how well the lecturer performs. Through annual appraisals, annual training programmes and departmental discussions, the lecturer can begin to understand peer expectations regarding the acceptable level of lecturing performance and the nature of acceptable teaching styles. Management and colleagues have the potential to condition the lecturer's discretion, by advising on what is acceptable behaviour at work. Finally, with a shared understanding of acceptable performance the university can attempt to enforce acceptable delivery of lecturing services through pay awards and promotions. Lecturers who continually provide superior services, develop new teaching methods and lead research will generally be promoted. In contrast, over time, management will also be able to see who is not performing optimally and their cases for promotion might be declined.

Essentially, in the marketplace the legal process and competition among the various suppliers are used to enforce contractual commitments and keep transaction costs low. Within firms, contractual commitments are enforced through long-term monitoring by the managerial hierarchy and the periodic pay awards and promotion associated with good performance. In this way, transaction costs are reduced.

Firms therefore exist in order to reduce transaction costs. In fact, economists often refer to firms as a **nexus of contracts**.

Nexus of contracts is a collection of interrelated contractual relationships, where the firm represents a nexus or central point, at which all these interrelated contractual relationships are managed in the pursuit of profit.

Transaction costs and vertical growth

How can we use these insights in order to understand how and when a firm will grow or shrink along its vertical axis?

If we consider the vertical chain, the answer is simple. The firm as a nexus of contracts will grow up or down its vertical chain when it needs to reduce its transaction costs by making use of its hierarchy or managerial structure to control its transactions. Similarly, a firm will shrink, or reduce in size as a nexus of contracts, when it believes it is possible to use the market to control its transactions. Consider the following examples.

Hospitals produce healthcare, but we need to recognize that healthcare is a combination of various value-adding activities: medical treatment from doctors and nurses, plus catering and cleaning services. Traditionally, all three services were performed by employees of the hospital. More recently, catering and cleaning services have been subcontracted to independent private companies. In doing so, the hospital has not grown vertically; rather, it has reduced its vertical boundaries. This is illustrated in Figure 7.3. The dotted lines represent the boundaries of the hospital's activities. In the left half of Figure 7.3, cleaning, catering and medical treatment are all inside the dotted lines. This is how hospitals traditionally organized themselves. Staff of the hospital carried out all three activities. In the right half of Figure 7.3, we see that only medical treatment is within the dotted lines of the overall healthcare provided by a hospital. Catering and cleaning are within their own dotted lines. This signifies that private companies provide catering and cleaning. Cleaning and catering are now being provided, or transacted, through the market. Periodically, the hospital will hold a tendering process, where it in effect holds an auction for its catering or cleaning contracts. The firm willing to offer its services at the lowest cost may win the contract.

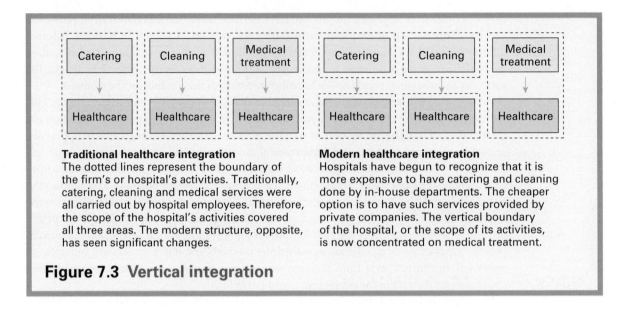

Traditional healthcare integration
The dotted lines represent the boundary of the firm's or hospital's activities. Traditionally, catering, cleaning and medical services were all carried out by hospital employees. Therefore, the scope of the hospital's activities covered all three areas. The modern structure, opposite, has seen significant changes.

Modern healthcare integration
Hospitals have begun to recognize that it is more expensive to have catering and cleaning done by in-house departments. The cheaper option is to have such services provided by private companies. The vertical boundary of the hospital, or the scope of its activities, is now concentrated on medical treatment.

Figure 7.3 Vertical integration

Why have cleaning and catering been moved into the market, while medical treatment has been retained inside the hospital? The answer is that, from a transactional perspective, it is cheaper to buy catering and cleaning services from the market, but it is cheaper to provide medical treatment in-house. Consider trying to write a contract for cleaning services. It is reasonably easy to write a near complete contract: each hospital ward must be cleaned twice a day, each waiting room once, and operating theatres after each operation. Now consider trying to write a complete contract for a heart surgeon. For each possible heart problem the contract would have to stipulate how the surgeon would treat the patient. This is very complex and, therefore, just as in the case of the university lecturer, it is better to leave treatment to the surgeon's discretion using an incomplete contract, where the contract might simply state that the 'surgeon will provide medical expertise in the cardiovascular department'. The hospital needs to measure the surgeon's performance against the contract. However, the performance of the surgeon can only be monitored over time by the hospital's management team. Good surgeons are promoted; poor ones are advised to move on. This long-term monitoring is best done inside the hospital's management systems, where other medical consultants can periodically provide a review of the surgeon's efforts and expertise. Such a process is very difficult if the hospital decided to contract surgeons on a short-term basis through the market.

Vertical growth: strategic considerations

The **hold-up problem** is the renegotiation of contracts and is linked to asset specificity.

An important transactional problem, not discussed above, is associated with asset specificity and the **hold-up problem**.

An aircraft can be used on a number of routes. Its use is more general than specific. A production line designed to make bumpers for a Ford Focus is a very **specific asset**, as it is very difficult to use the production line to make bumpers for any other car.

A **specific asset** has a specific use; a general asset has many uses.

Consider the vertical chain for airlines. A new aircraft is purchased and used to fly between cities A and B. Additional value-adding inputs are landing slots at each city's airport. If the route between A and B is highly profitable, one of the airports, say B, might try to gain some of the airline's profit by increasing its landing charges. However, since the aircraft is a general asset, the airline has the option of moving the aircraft to a route between A and C (assuming

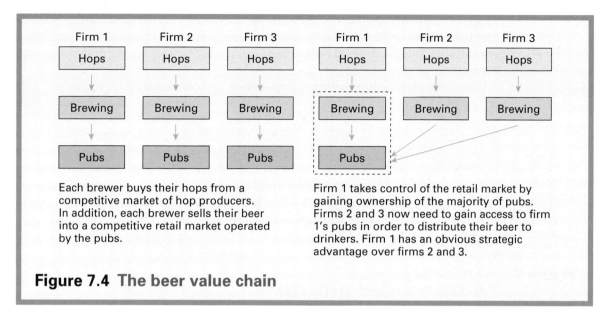

Firm 1 | Firm 2 | Firm 3 | Firm 1 | Firm 2 | Firm 3

Hops → Brewing → Pubs (×3)

Hops → Brewing → Pubs (×3)

Each brewer buys their hops from a competitive market of hop producers. In addition, each brewer sells their beer into a competitive retail market operated by the pubs.

Firm 1 takes control of the retail market by gaining ownership of the majority of pubs. Firms 2 and 3 now need to gain access to firm 1's pubs in order to distribute their beer to drinkers. Firm 1 has an obvious strategic advantage over firms 2 and 3.

Figure 7.4 The beer value chain

this route is also profitable). The airline can use the general nature of aircraft to discipline airport B and prevent an increase in landing charges.

Now consider the producer of bumpers for a particular car. Each car model is unique and the shape of the car's bumper will be very specific. The production plant will be dedicated to producing bumpers for this one type of car. The car manufacturer could approach the bumper manufacturer and ask for a new production facility to be built for its bumpers. In return, the car manufacturer agrees a price for each bumper. We might assume that the agreed price is £100 per bumper. This price per bumper will make the investment in the new plant profitable for the bumper manufacturer. However, once the plant is up and running, the car manufacturer has a substantial incentive to renegotiate a discount price for the bumpers. Why? Because, unlike the airline company, the bumper manufacturer has a specific asset; it only makes one type of bumper. The plant cannot be used to produce bumpers for another car manufacturer, so it is dependent upon the one car maker. This is the hold-up problem.

The car manufacturer can take advantage of the bumper producer's investment in a specific asset. In fact, so obvious is this type of hold-up problem that the bumper producer would not invest in the production facility. The car producer, therefore, has to build its own bumper-producing plant. The car manufacturer grows vertically and begins to produce one of its key inputs. For many car parts, this approach is very common. Take a look at a car and find the most obvious component on the car that has not been made by the car maker itself. It will probably be the tyres. This is because tyres are round and will fit on many different types of car. Tyres, or more correctly the plant making tyres, is a general asset. The production of tyres for Ford can easily be switched to the production of tyres for Toyota. A producer of tyres, therefore, does not face a hold-up problem, because it is not dependent upon one buying relationship. A bumper manufacturer would be.

The hold-up problem can also represent a strategic opportunity when one firm is able to gain a monopoly position in the vertical chain. Consider Figure 7.4. For simplicity, assume an industry has three firms, all manufacturing a similar product, beer. In the left half of Figure 7.4, each firm is a producer of beer, buying hops from farmers and selling the beer on to independent pubs. In the right half of Figure 7.4, firm 1 has gained ownership of the pubs. As a monopoly supplier of beer retailing, firm 1 can promote its own brands and negotiate cheap beer supplies from the remaining brewers. An equally effective growth strategy would have been to gain control of the hop supply and gain a monopoly position at the top of the vertical chain. It could then sell hops to itself cheaply, but charge brewing rivals a very high price.

In summary, firms will grow vertically up or down the vertical chain if the transaction costs of operating through the market are too high. By internalizing transactions, or making the value-adding product or service inside the company, the firm will attempt to control its transaction costs more effectively. Similarly, when the transaction costs of the market are very low, a firm will seek to reduce its vertical integration and begin to seek subcontractors for some of its inputs. Buying in, rather than making the product or service, has lower transaction costs. In addition to the costs of organizing the transaction, we also need to consider the transaction costs generated by the hold-up problem. The firm will grow vertically along the vertical chain whenever it can gain strategic advantage over its rivals and whenever the market refuses to supply products for fear of the hold-up problem. We will return to these issues in the business application of the BBC and BSkyB.

7.5 Diversified growth

Diversification involves a company expanding its operations into related or unrelated markets. This can occur for a variety of reasons, but a strong cost reason centres on the concept of **economies of scope**.

If two products, A and B, are being produced, then economies of scope are sometimes expressed as:

$$\text{Cost (A)} + \text{Cost (B)} > \text{Cost (A + B)}$$

This suggests that the costs of producing A on its own, Cost (A), plus the cost of making B on its own, Cost (B), is greater than making A and B together, Cost (A + B).

An obvious example can be found in the news-gathering services of the BBC. News on politics, business, world affairs and crime can be collected centrally. This is then drawn on by BBC News 24, BBC Evening News, Radio 1, 2, etc., and by BBC News Online. If each division operated separately, then the news would be collected many times. By centralizing news gathering, the BBC cuts down on duplication and exploits economies of scope. An alternative example can be found in the business activities of Virgin. The brand name of Virgin is very important, but just like the news gathering of the BBC, it can reduce duplication. As Virgin initially invested many millions developing its brand name for the music industry, the brand could then also be used to launch products in other markets. This has included airlines, mobile phones, financial services and much more. Admittedly, money has to be spent building the Virgin airlines brand, but the expense is arguably much less than starting with no brand and launching all these different commercial activities separately.

> **Economies of scope** are said to exist if the cost of producing two or more outputs jointly is less than the cost of producing the outputs separately.

Diversification and risk reduction

Diversification can reduce a company's exposure to risk. Consider a company operating in only one market. The company could be making good profits. However, there is a risk that in the future profits will change. Profits will fall if new competition enters the market, a recession occurs and sales fall, or a raw material becomes expensive. Equally, profits will rise if the level of competition falls, sales increase during a recession, or the cost of a raw material decreases.

Profits can, therefore, go up or down. But they can go up or down for any firm, or industry. More importantly, profits at any particular point in time might go up for one firm or industry, but come down for another. It is, therefore, possible to have multiple operations and reduce the variability in overall profits. By operating in more than one market, or industry, falling profits in one operation can hopefully be offset by rising profits in another part of the business.

Tesco, the leading UK supermarket chain, is a reasonable example. Operating across grocery, non-food items such as CDs, magazines and home electricals, and financial services, including insurance and banking, enables Tesco to reduce its operating risks. If grocery and non-food profits fall, it is possible that financial services profits could rise. In order for this to be true the various operations must form a **diversified portfolio** of business activities.

> A **diversified portfolio** of activities contains a mix of uncorrelated business operations.

If two business activities are correlated, then the profit levels of each activity will move together. As such, the combined profits will still show large swings over time. For a diversified portfolio, business activities must be uncorrelated. This means the level of profits from one business activity is not related to the level of profits from another activity. The combined profits from diversified activities will now be less variable; as one operation incurs losses, another is likely to rise into profitability.

While diversification can reduce the financial risks of a company, it does not add value to the company. The problem lies in the fact that variability in profits is the risk of shareholders. If an individual shareholder wishes to diversify their risks, then they can do so at low cost. They achieve this by simply buying small amounts of shares in various different uncorrelated companies. If a Tesco shareholder is worried about future losses in the grocery business, they can buy shares in any high street bank. They do not need Tesco to create its own bank. Furthermore, the investor may already have shares in a bank. As a result of Tesco moving into the personal financial services sector, the investor's risk or exposure to the financial services sector has increased, not diminished. Therefore, diversification by a company does not add value for shareholders. So, why do companies diversify?

As we will see in Chapter 8, we need to make a distinction between shareholders and managers. On a day-to-day basis it is managers who run and control companies. Managers have a great deal of asset tied up in the company they work for. The company pays their salary and funds their pension. If the company closed, due to substantial losses, how likely is it that the manager would gain employment elsewhere? Managers, therefore, face substantial non-diversified risk from employment. Diversification is arguably more in the interests of managers than shareholders.

7.6 Evidence on mergers

In examining how mergers of all types improve firm-level performance, economists have used a variety of techniques. These techniques have included stock market studies, financial ratio analysis and case studies.

Stock market studies investigate whether shareholders from the buying firm or the acquired target firm gain most. Evidence tends to suggest that most of the stock market gains from merger accrue to shareholders of target firms. The price of target firms rises rapidly prior to merger and the stock price for the buying firm stagnates or even falls post-merger.

Financial and accounting studies examine merger activity within similar industries; banking, brewing and automobiles would be examples. Using statistical techniques, economists look for increases in revenues, reductions in costs, increased market share and improvements in operating efficiencies. The evidence is at best mixed; some firms and some industries have a greater tendency to deliver post-merger benefits. But this is not a common pattern and many firms manage to destroy value post-merger.

Case studies examine specific mergers and look for firm-specific examples of merger benefits. Again, these studies confirm the message from the stock market and financial accounting-based studies: mergers are not always a good idea.

So, if mergers are at best risky strategies – some work, some do not – then why do firms continue to engage in merger activity? A possible answer is that mergers are very much in the interests of managers. The pay of managers tends to increase more with firm size than with financial performance of the firm. Merger increases firm size and therefore can boost managers' pay. Faced with such incentives, managers may seek to convince shareholders that a merger is a good idea.

The catastrophic consequences of a failed merger are exemplified by the Royal Bank of Scotland's decision to buy the Dutch bank ABN Amro; see Box 7.4.

 Box 7.4 Sir Fred's heady firsts

Adapted from an article by Peter Thal Larsen in The Financial Times, *4 October 2007*

Sir Fred Goodwin, head of Royal Bank of Scotland (RBS) is on the verge of completing the impossible. No European bank of any size had succumbed to a cross-border hostile bid. No large lender had ever been broken up into its component parts. No bidder had ever stumped up as much cash as the 166 billion (£46 billion) the consortium, which includes Santander and Fortis, promised to raise.

Many believed the consortium's members – and their shareholders – would lose their nerve. So Sir Fred and his team could be forgiven for feeling vindicated. However, victory has come at a cost.

RBS investors have seen the bank's shares lose more than 20 per cent of their value since they peaked in March. Even after a bounce in recent days, RBS is now worth about 175 billion, only a little more than the 170 billion valuation for ABN Amro implied by the consortium's offer.

Sir Fred and his consortium partners now must persuade investors the price they have paid, and the complexities of unravelling a large banking group, are justified by the cost savings and revenue benefits they will achieve.

RBS has predicted cost savings and revenue benefits of 11.8 billion – equivalent to almost three times the current pre-tax profits of the businesses it is acquiring.

'Significant pressure remains on RBS to follow through with an open, transparent and speedy integration of the businesses with the RBS franchise. [. . .] Only when delivery on those synergies begins to materialise – and preferably ahead of target – will investors refer to the multiple paid as 9x, being the post-synergy price, rather than the 32x pre-synergy level.'

But Johnny Cameron, chief executive of RBS's global banking and markets division, insists the integration of ABN Amro's businesses will open up a new group of corporate clients for RBS's debt and risk management products. Meanwhile, RBS will gain an equities business and a global payments processing platform. 'We have a whole new box of tricks to offer our clients,' he says.

© The Financial Times Ltd. 2009

Comment: The scale of achievement and the level of risk associated with the RBS acquisition of ABN Amro is evident within this article from 2007. However, less than 18 months later, RBS was 70 per cent owned by the UK government, its stock market value had fallen to £8 billion and the chairman of the company, when questioned by the government, admitted that the purchase of ABN Amro was a 'big mistake'.

7.7 Business application: horizontal growth by merger

Economic boom or bust, the attractions of horizontal merger always seem attractive to business. When the economy is growing rapidly, firms see the option to merge as a means of exploiting growth while achieving economies of scale. During a recession, in contrast, merger and economies of scale offer valuable cost-efficiencies.

The occurrence of mergers in both good and bad economic times possibly underlines the importance of economies of scale in providing firms with a competitive advantage. Size matters, costs matter. Achieving significant scale economies often costs huge sums of money and, once you merge with a rival, then that lowers the opportunities for other competitors to follow suit and achieve similar economies of scale. So, by merging, firms can achieve a competitive advantage which other competitors may find difficult to replicate. Economies of scale provide cost savings and provide the firm with the potential to dominate.

In Box 7.5, the merger of Chrysler and Fiat is discussed: two car makers struggling in a recessionary environment. Chrysler has scale and access to the US market; Fiat has efficient engines and an ability to build compact cars. Put the two together and Fiat can sell cars in the US and Chrysler can gain access to new engine technology. Negotiating with suppliers for common components may bring additional cost savings.

 ## Box 7.5 Chrysler and Fiat join forces as global slump hits smaller car manufacturers

Adapted from an article by Sarah Arnott in The Independent, *21 January 2009*

Fiat is to take 35 per cent of Chrysler as part of a deal to give both groups the scale to weather the economic storm buffeting the global motor industry. Chrysler will gain access to fuel-efficient Fiat engine and transmission technology. For Fiat, the big draw is scale. Sergio Marchionne, Fiat's chief executive, acknowledged last month that the company is too small to weather the current downturn on its own. By forming an alliance with Chrysler, the Italian group benefits from economies of scale, global reach and the infrastructure to expand out of its European market.

Marchionne said: 'The agreement will offer both companies opportunities to gain access to most relevant automotive markets with innovative and environmentally-friendly product offering, while benefiting from additional cost synergies.'

Bob Nardelli, chairman and chief executive of Chrysler, said: 'This transaction will enable Chrysler to offer a broader competitive line-up of vehicles for our dealers and customers that meet emission and fuel-efficiency standards, while adhering to conditions of the government loan.'

Fiat's European sales, which make up the vast majority of its revenue, were down by 5 per cent last year, and Chrysler's US sales halved in December alone. By joining forces, the companies hope to benefit from both the economies of scale and global reach enjoyed by larger rivals like Toyota and Volkswagen. Chrysler sold two million vehicles last year, almost all of them in the US. Fiat sold 2.5 million, the majority in its domestic market. But both are relative tiddlers compared with Toyota sales approaching 9 million.

Professor Garel Rhys, at Cardiff Business School's Centre for Automotive Industry Research, said: 'It is a high risk move . . . but if Fiat stayed on its own it would gradually wither away. If it can make a go of the Chrysler tie-up then that is a way to get scale, but it will need a number of years to do it.'

Of course, the issue with all mergers is that they look good in principle, but in reality are not always that successful. In fact, Chrysler only recently was in the same group of companies as Daimler, who make Mercedes-Benz. But after that deal failed to deliver significant returns, Chrysler was sold on.

Why mergers often fail, despite the forecast cost savings, is an interesting question. One possible explanation is over-optimistic forecasts of the benefits. It is not easy to understand how easy it will be to merge two operations. Or, in the case of Chrysler and Fiat, how effective US distribution channels will be at selling Fiats. A related point is a simple recognition that even companies in the same industry are often very different. In our first example we noted how the supermarket Morrisons owned farms, while its competitor Tesco did not. These differences are likely to affect how the companies are internally managed, how they market themselves and how they develop strategies. As such, it is extremely difficult and costly to bring two companies together that have vastly different business models.

This concern can equally be levelled at Chrysler and Fiat. The latter makes small efficient cars, the former big gas-guzzling comfort cars. The design, engineering, marketing and sales processes for each will be very different. Developing a small fuel-efficient engine into one capable of driving a bigger American car won't be easy or cheap.

© Independent News and Media Limited

So, however attractive a merger looks on paper, it is the accuracy of the vision and the vigour of the execution that are often most important in determining success.

7.8 Business application: vertical growth – moving with the value

A common feature of many business environments is *change*. Technology changes, the product on offer changes and even the tastes and preferences of consumers change. The consequence of these changes is that the value added in each stage of the vertical chain of production also changes. As costs fall, or revenues rise, then one part of the chain becomes more valuable. Similarly, as costs rise or revenues fall, then another part of the chain becomes less valuable. Predicting and understanding these trends can help enormously in developing strategies for change and ensuring greater longevity of profits.

You may, or may not, like Madonna's music. But unquestionably she is an artistic and commercial success. Madonna is an artist who is not only capable of reinventing her image and music but, as described in Box 7.6, is also very skilled at understanding business and how the market for pop stars has changed.

 Box 7.6 Madonna drops Warner Music for tour promoter

Adapted from a Reuters *article by Yinka Adegoke, 16 October 2007*

Pop star Madonna has dropped her long-term music label Warner Brothers and signed a multi-album, touring and merchandizing global partnership with Live Nation Inc. Los Angeles-based Live Nation, said the deal will see Madonna become a shareholder in the company. The deal, which has been expected for more than a week, is estimated to be worth $120 million over ten years, including a three-album commitment.

Warner Music congratulated Madonna, with whom they are parting ways after 25 years. But the world's third-largest music company also pointed out that it retains the recording and publishing rights for all of her music.

Music companies and artists have been exploring new relationships as traditional music sales drop rapidly. Fans are buying fewer CDs and are not buying enough digital music to make up for the shortfall. 'The paradigm in the music business has shifted and as an artist and a businesswoman, I have to move with that shift,' Madonna said in a recent statement.

Madonna's new deal with Live Nation also includes exploitation of her brand, fan club/websites, DVDs, music-related businesses, film projects and associated sponsorship agreements. 'For the first time in my career, the way that my music can reach fans is unlimited. . . . Who knows how my albums will be distributed in the future?' Madonna said.

According to Live Nation, Madonna's last three worldwide tours generated close to $500 million. Live Nation will recoup its payments to Madonna, including a $50 million advance, from a variety of revenue streams that will be cross-collaterized.

Until recently, the keys to the valuable parts of the pop music value chain were a competent music artist and access to music lovers through music publishing and distribution. Publishing and distribution were commonly achieved through the creation of CDs, which were then sold in music stores. Record companies were able to insist that buyers purchase all songs on an album. As such, the publishing and distribution stages of the vertical chain were extremely valuable.

As the distribution technology moved towards electronic storage and online delivery, the value of music publishing and delivery declined. Consumers were able to download music (illegally) for free and online retailers of music began to offer downloads of tracks from albums, rather than the entire album. Such moves have led to a reduction in profits for record companies and for artists such as Madonna.

It is quite clear from the discussion in Box 7.6, that Madonna and Live Nation aim to extract greater commercial value from other elements of the value chain. Concerts are an obvious target. They have already netted an estimated $500 million in six years for Madonna. Why is this? We can use our understanding of competition to understand the commercial attractions of concerts. If you wish to see Madonna in concert in your nearest capital city, then the event exists once. It happens, it's over, it's gone. You can't experience a concert as a download. You can't download parts of the concert and you can't access the concert for free. Madonna, in conjunction with Live Nation, is a monopoly provider of Madonna concerts. In contrast, Madonna and Live Nation have little control over pricing and distribution of her recorded music. The market is far more competitive and likely to generate normal profits at best.

So, understanding the sources of value and questioning where value will be derived from in the future are critical aspects of ensuring ongoing profitability.

7.9 Business application: economies of scope

Google is everywhere and offering everything. Why? The range of services now offered by Google simply reflects economies of scope – the ability to provide services jointly at a lower cost than offering each separately. But where do these economies of scope stem from?

At the core of Google's success is a search engine which is arguably unsurpassed by any competitor. The technology advantage rests on clever computer programming and a vast bank of computers – some estimate as much as a 100 000 machine server farm. Such an asset base means it becomes technically feasible and economically cheap to launch related services, such as Gmail, movie download and desktop search software. The more Google can exploit its massive technical advantage across products, the greater the economies of scope it can realize. As revenues and, ultimately, profits grow from its scope advantages, Google has more finance to pour back in to boost its technological advantage and remain dominant.

The growth of Amazon is also related to economies of scope. Amazon began by offering books for sale online. This was quickly expanded into music and movies. Currently, Amazon also sells toys, electronics, health and beauty and jewellery items. This all represents economies of scope. When Amazon built an Internet infrastructure to sell books and acquired a warehouse and distribution system for stocking and delivery, it made strong commercial sense to put more product ranges through the same pipe.

The examples of Amazon and Google illustrate what is perhaps related diversification. However, the economies of scope argument can also be used to explain some examples of unrelated diversification. As highlighted in Box 7.1, Tesco, a UK supermarket chain, developed its business from grocery into non-food electricals, and prior to this into financial services. It simply capitalized on its huge existing customer base. With details about its customers gained from loyalty cards and online shopping, Tesco can use this marketing research data to sell not only groceries but also other products such as financial services, including personal loans and insurance. Therefore, by operating as a supermarket and as a personal financial services company, Tesco is able to reduce its costs by exploiting the customer information base across multiple activities.

While grocery and financial services are very different activities, one of the core underlying assets that ensures success in both markets is an informative customer database. This database includes information on customers' ages, marital status, income levels, home address and products generally purchased within the Tesco stores. These data can be analysed and used to target particular customer groups with specific products.

Economies of scope and control

An important issue when considering economies of scope is *control*. If we extend the economies of scope condition to Tesco, then we would have:

Cost (Grocery) + Cost (Financial Services) > Cost (Grocery + Financial Services)

An obvious reason for these economies of scope is lower production costs associated with the joint use of the Tesco customer base. But, in addition, we also need to consider transaction costs. Tesco does not have to enter the financial services market in order to exploit its customer base. Rather, it could sell its customer information to a number of third parties, including existing financial services companies. The obvious problem with such an approach is that valuable information could then find its way into the hands of Tesco's rivals in the supermarket sector. Lowering the transaction costs associated with the information's additional use, therefore, protects the value of the customer base. Tesco cannot risk selling the information in the marketplace; instead, in order to exploit the asset beyond grocery, it has to enter into the financial services sector. In this particular instance, Tesco has achieved this through an exclusive arrangement with Direct Line, a leading insurance provider.

We can also use the case of Tesco to address the issue of managerial motives for merger, as discussed in Section 7.5. Managers may pursue diversification to protect their own employment, as opposed to adding value for shareholders. We even argued that, if a shareholder of Tesco was concerned about risks in the supermarket sector, they could easily diversify this risk by buying shares in a financial services company. However, we can now see that diversification will add value for shareholders if the control of the economies of scope reduces transaction costs. Tesco is a clear example of this. So too is the Virgin brand. Licensing the brand to other users would run the risk of a third party damaging the brand. (This of course does not prevent Virgin from damaging the brand via its rail operations.) However, when Virgin takes the brand into many different markets the integrity of the brand is the sole responsibility of Virgin. It retains control over the use of the brand and reduces its transaction costs.

Summary

1 Horizontal growth is the expansion of a firm's activities at the same stage of the production process.

2 Vertical growth is expansion of the firm up or down the value chain, incorporating more than one stage of production.

3 Diversified growth is an expansion of the firm's activities into related and unrelated markets.

4 Growth in its various forms can be organic, where the firm grows internally by developing ties to existing operations; alternatively, growth can occur externally, where the firm either acquires, or agrees to merge with, another firm.

5 Firms can grow for a variety of reasons, but if we accept that a firm is a profit-maximizer, then growth must be linked to long-term, profit-maximizing objectives. Growth opportunities must, therefore, offer revenue enhancements or potential cost savings.

6 Horizontal growth can promote revenue enhancements by exploiting growth in the market. As the market size grows, the firm can seek to expand its operations. Moreover, the firm can seek to grow its share of the market. Greater control of the market improves the potential to set prices. If greater market share stems from merger, or acquisition of a rival, then the elasticity of demand must fall and the potential to raise prices increases.

7 Economies of scale are important motives for horizontal growth. As a company increases its scale of operation, its average costs fall. In addition, the positive effects of learning can motivate horizontal growth. As cumulative production increases, the firm begins to learn how to produce the product more efficiently. The firm learns how to reduce its costs. However, if the size of the firm is bigger, the potential to erase cumulative output more quickly also exists.

8 Vertical growth can also be motivated by considerations of production costs. Consecutive stages of the value chain could be merged if production and transaction costs have the potential to be reduced.

9 In addition to production costs, transaction costs are also a potential reason for vertical growth.

10 Transaction costs are associated with organizing the transaction of goods and services. These include the costs associated with writing, monitoring and enforcing contractual relationships. Transactions are seen to increase when complexity and uncertainty are greater, monitoring is difficult and enforcement limited. If the transaction costs associated with buying the good or service through the market increase, then a firm will attempt to minimize its transaction costs by vertically integrating and making the good or service within the firm.

11 A specific asset is designed for one use only. Without the flexibility to deploy the asset to an alternative use, a firm can be subject to the hold-up problem. Contract prices can be renegotiated and the financial value of the specific asset can fall. In order to avoid such problems, firms will tend to vertically integrate and thereby avoid market negotiations.

12 Economies of scope exist if the production of two goods jointly is less expensive than producing the two goods separately. Diversification can sometimes be understood as a process of exploiting economies of scope, i.e. where a firm uses an asset that it has developed in its current operations to exploit opportunities in another market.

13 If diversification is pursued in an attempt to create a portfolio of activities, then the firm's overall financial risk might be reduced. However, it is questionable whether such strategies add value for shareholders who may already hold a diversified portfolio of shares in many different companies. Diversification is more likely to reduce the non-diversified employment risks faced by managers.

Learning checklist

You should now be able to:

♦ Explain the difference between horizontal, vertical and diversified growth

♦ Provide arguments for why firms may grow in a horizontal, vertical or diversified manner

♦ Explain how the learning curve links cumulative output with falling unit costs

♦ Understand and explain transaction costs

♦ Recognize the hold-up problem and explain why firms try to avoid this problem

♦ Explain economies of scope, provide examples and argue why firms might exploit scope economies

Questions connect™

1 Is a merger between rivals horizontal, vertical or conglomerate growth?

2 Horizontal growth can occur for cost and revenue reasons. Explain both of these justifications for horizontal growth.

3 Formula 1 teams are banned from in-season tests to reduce costs. The learning curve says this is a bad idea. Why?

4 What is the value chain?

5 What are transaction costs and should firms be concerned about them?

6 Your university decides to use an external catering company for the main university food outlets. What economic justifications can you provide for this decision?

7 What is the hold-up problem and how might a firm deal with this particular type of issue?

8 Explain why a range of activities can reduce risk. In order for diversification to be effective, has the correlation between activities to be high or low?

9 Why are the benefits of diversification low for shareholders?

10 What is an economy of scope and how might it lead a firm to diversify?

11 If cost advantages from cumulative production were low, would the learning curve be steep or shallow?

12 Why are horizontal mergers sometimes blocked by governments?

13 Should governments also block vertical mergers?

14 Pubs in the UK are being encouraged to take on other activities, such as those of the Post Office. On economic grounds, how would you justify such initiatives?

15 How can a firm use horizontal, vertical or diversified growth to gain a strategic advantage over its rivals?

Exercises

1 True or false?
   (a) Following a merger the price elasticity of demand should fall.
   (b) Economies of scale can be a rationale for merger.
   (c) Late delivery of supplies due to heavy traffic is an example of the hold-up problem.
   (d) An organization's total costs are production costs plus transaction costs.
   (e) Diversification reduces a firm's level of risk.
   (f) Free cash flow is cash in excess of funds required to invest in all projects with a positive net present value.

2 (a) Draw a long-run average cost curve and use it to explain the gains in scale achieved by two small firms merging.
   (b) Diversification is not about moving the firm's total cost and total revenue lines further apart; it is more concerned with reducing the volatility of earnings. Discuss.

3 Consider the following questions by referring to Box 7.3:
   (a) Explain what is meant by the term vertical integration.
   (b) How would business economists explain the location of server farms?

Chapter 8
Governing business

Chapter contents

 Learning outcomes

By the end of this chapter you should understand:

Economic Theory

LO1 Principal–agent problems

LO2 The separation of ownership from control

LO3 Alternative theories of the firm

LO4 The concept of positive and negative externalities

LO5 The notion of market failures

LO6 The use of tax and subsidies to correct market failures

LO7 The regulation of monopoly

Business Application

LO8 Why companies use stock options to reward chief executives

LO9 Why governments have introduced trading in carbon emission permits

Governing business at a glance

The issue

Actions taken by managers and workers are often not in the interests of their shareholders. Similarly, actions taken by firms, such as polluting the atmosphere, are often not in the interests of other stakeholders, such as wider society. Can these conflicts be resolved?

The understanding

Conflicts exist because of a misalignment of interests. Without government control, firms can pollute the environment without cost to themselves. The cost of pollution is instead picked up by society. By making the firm bear the responsibility and costs of pollution, both the firm's and society's interests are aligned.

   The way to achieve this is to tax the firm if it pollutes; and perhaps even provide it with subsidies if it tries to operate without pollution. More generally, one solution to the misalignment of interests is the use of financial incentives to change the behaviour of one of the parties.

The usefulness

Why do company executives receive huge bonuses via stock options? The answer is because stock options provide financial incentives for managers to act in the interests of shareholders. Can the government reduce carbon emissions by creating a market for pollution permits? We will now explore each of these issues.

8.1 Business problem: managing managers

Within all of us there is an element of Homer Simpson. The similarities at work are particularly acute, where we often have a willingness to do little but appear to be doing a great deal. Colleagues and perhaps even ourselves display a need to frequent the coffee room, the toilets or even the local pub during work hours. Such behaviour is a deviation from what our employers might consider best practice. They might consider we are employed to sit at our desks and pursue profit maximization. When such behaviour occurs, we might label it 'lazy', 'cheeky' or 'taking the Michael'. You will not be surprised to learn that economists prefer the more technical label, 'the **principal–agent** problem'.

> A **principal** is a person who hires an **agent** to undertake work on their behalf.

   Principals can suffer two confounding problems when hiring agents to work for them. First, the interests of the agent and the principal may differ. For example, the principal may value hard work, while the agent may dislike hard work. Second, principals can often find it difficult to monitor the work and effort of their agents. Given the potential difference in interests and the difficulty associated with monitoring the agent, there is little reason why the agent should expend effort on the principal's behalf.

   We can compare examples of a taxi driver and a manager to illuminate these arguments. In the case of the taxi driver, you may wish to be driven between two points using the shortest route. In contrast, the taxi driver may wish to take you via a much longer route, hoping to generate a higher fare. Hence, there is a difference in interest between you, as the principal, and the taxi driver, as the agent. However, since you are sitting in the taxi, you can monitor with ease the route taken by the driver. Therefore, if you know the area, and are not a tourist in a foreign land, the taxi driver will generally take you by the shortest route.

A manager of a company, the agent, may be tasked with improving the profitability of a company by the shareholders of that company, the principals. However, if the shareholders are buying and selling shares in many companies on the London stock market, they will find it difficult to monitor the manager on a daily basis. Unlike the passenger in a taxi, the shareholders cannot directly observe the behaviour of their manager. The manager could decide to sit in the office surfing the Internet, or practising their golf putting. When the profits of the company fail to increase, the shareholders will not be aware that the agent has been lazy. In fact, because of the lack of monitoring, the manager could blame the poor performance on external factors such as a lazy workforce, a bad sales manager or a fall in demand for the product.

> **Moral hazard** occurs when someone agrees to undertake a certain set of actions but then, once a contractual arrangement has been agreed, behaves in a different manner.

Economists describe the manager as displaying **moral hazard**-type behaviour.

The manager offers to increase the profits of the company but, once hired by the shareholders, they exploit the monitoring problems of shareholders and behave in their own best interests. In contrast, the taxi driver, actively monitored by the hiring passenger, does not display moral hazard-type behaviour because the passenger will contest the higher fare.

The costs of moral hazard-type behaviour, such as inferior performance by the agent, coupled with monitoring costs, result in what are more generally termed **agency costs**.

In the case of the taxi driver, agency costs are very low. Monitoring is easy and, therefore, moral hazard-type behaviour is unlikely. In the case of the manager, agency costs are very high, because monitoring is difficult and costly, and therefore this behaviour is likely.

> **Agency costs** reflect reductions in value to principals from using agents to undertake work on their behalf.

A natural question arises as to how principals might seek to reduce agency costs. In particular, how can shareholders motivate managers to provide higher levels of output or, as the economist would say, how can we align the interests of firms and managers so that managers act in the interest of shareholders?

The answer will be developed throughout the first part of this chapter. In the case of managers, however, modes of corporate governance are placed on the firm that provide incentives for managers to work in the interests of shareholders. At a very simple level, managers can be turned into shareholders by providing them with shares in the company. As shareholders, managers then have an interest in working hard in order to improve the performance of the company. In order to consider these ideas further, we will extend our analysis of how firms are owned and managed and examine why managers may not wish to follow the interests of shareholders. Only then can we return to the issue of how shareholders can try to motivate managers to act in their interests.

8.2 Profit maximization and the separation of ownership from control

Throughout this book we have assumed that firms are profit-maximizers. In fact, when we first introduced the idea in Chapter 5, we suggested that this was a sensible argument.

We would now like to question this assumption.

In order to maximize profits firms are required to set marginal cost, MC, equal to marginal revenue, MR. Even though professional accountants are also schooled in this central idea, many are incapable of calculating MC or MR from a company's cost and revenue data. Accountants are not fools, it is just that the task of measuring and collating data on MR and MC is extremely complex, especially when the firm makes and sells multiple products. Furthermore, the firm's costs and revenues may not be very stable. Changes in raw material prices or output prices will lead to repeated changes in MC and MR. Therefore, if anything, firms can at best only approximate profit maximization. They may seek to maximize profits, but they will never be sure what the optimal level of output and profits is.

Aside from these practical problems of trying to equate MC and MR, there are strong reasons why a firm might pursue objectives other than profit maximization. Crucially, it is often the case that the individuals who manage a firm are different from the individuals who own a firm. Table 8.1 provides data on the size of shareholdings within the telecommunications company BT. With 1.2 million shareholders, it is reasonable to say that many people and investment companies own BT. BT employed just in excess of 100 000 individuals in 2008. Therefore, with 1.2 million shareholders and only 100 000 workers, it is clear that shareholders and the people who work for BT are, in the main, different individuals. Among the largest shareholders, 204 holdings are greater than 5 million shares. Of these 204 holdings, only one relates to share options held for the benefit of employees. We can see, therefore, that the vast majority of shareholders, small and large, are not the same people who manage BT. While BT is a popular share among many individuals in the UK, the pattern of dispersed shareholdings is common among large companies and is known as the separation of ownership from control.

> **Separation of ownership from control** exists where the shareholders, who own the company, are a different set of individuals from the managers that control the business on a day-to-day basis.

> **Free riders** are individuals, or firms, who can benefit from the actions of others without contributing to the effort made by others. They gain benefits from the actions of others for free.

The **separation of ownership from control** becomes more acute when shareholders become more disperse. With 1.2 million shareholders, it is difficult for all BT shareholders to co-ordinate themselves and try to remove a poorly performing management team. Moreover, in the UK it is common for the largest shareholder to own less than 3 per cent of a company's shares. This is important because, if the largest shareholder wanted to remove a team of underperforming managers, then they would bear the full cost of this activity. This might include meetings with the managers, other large shareholders and legal advisers, and recruitment of a new management team. While bearing all these costs, the benefits of better company performance would be shared among all shareholders. Therefore, if the major shareholder has only 3 per cent, then it will only gain a 3 per cent share of the benefits of employing a new management team. All other shareholders can **free ride** on the back of the dominant shareholder.

Given the unattractive financial terms brought about by free riding and small shareholdings, even the dominant shareholder is unlikely to act against the incumbent management team.

Dispersed shareholdings, therefore, leave management teams, even bad ones, in a position where they do not have to react to shareholders' interests. So, while it might be reasonable to argue that shareholders are profit-maximizers, managers have the scope to pursue their own objectives. But what might these objectives be?

Table 8.1 Analysis of BT shareholdings 2008

Range	Number of holdings	Percentage of total	Number of shares held millions	Percentage of total
1–399	453 479	38	95	1.14
400–799	336 517	28.2	189	2.25
800–1599	235 296	19.72	263	3.13
1600–9999	161 406	13.53	471	5.6
10 000–99 999	5 233	0.44	99	1.17
100 000–999 999	736	0.06	262	3.12
1 000 000–4 999 999	328	0.03	725	8.63
5 000 000 and above	204	0.02	6297	74.96
Total	**1 193 199**	**100.00**	**8401**	**100.00**

Managerial objectives

Economists have proposed a number of alternative theories relating to the objectives that managers might pursue. The first relates to what is known as 'expense preference behaviour'. If shareholders are interested in maximizing profits, then managers are interested in maximizing their own satisfaction.

Consumption of perquisites

So, rather than work hard for the company's owners, managers would rather indulge themselves in the purchase of expensive cars, jets, lavish expense accounts that can be used to dine clients (and friends) at the most fashionable restaurants and, of course, lots of personal assistants. A clear reason for doing this is a positive recognition provided by society for success, dominance and status. In trying to meet these requirements, managers use the company's funds to finance a prestigious image make-over and lifestyle.

Managers may even spend the company's money on business projects that have little value to the shareholder but have personal value to the company's managers. Diversification, as discussed in Chapter 7, is a case in point. Companies that specialize in one product line are vulnerable to competition, or a downturn in demand. In order to protect themselves, managers may diversify and use the company's money to buy unrelated businesses. Statements of strategic change along the lines of 'yes, I know we are in waste handling, but I think we should move into leisure and purchase a cruise ship' are extreme, but sadly evident among some senior managers. However, the essential problem is that managers are using the company's and, therefore shareholders', money to diversify a risk that only managers face. If shareholders are concerned about risk in one market, they can buy shares in other companies. Hence, diversification within firms does not protect shareholders; rather, it protects managers.

Sales maximization

An alternative hypothesis recognizes that the measurement of profits can be subjective. How much will the firm decide to depreciate its assets and what provision for bad debts will it charge to the profit and loss statement this year? Given these problems, managers may prefer to maximize a more tangible measure of performance, such as sales. A common misunderstanding follows the reasoning that, if sales are increasing, then so are profits. But, as we have seen, this is not true – the law of diminishing returns and diseconomies of scale points to increases in costs as output increases. Sales maximization may, therefore, indicate that sales managers are doing a good job but, without an additional consideration of costs and ultimately profits, sales growth may not be a good indicator of overall performance.

Growth maximization

The final hypothesis is that managers will seek to maximize growth, rather than profits. It is no surprise that the pay of top directors is linked to the size of the company. The bigger the company, the greater the responsibility. What is surprising is that chief executive (the leading director of a company) pay is linked more closely to company size than it is to financial performance, such as profitability. This suggests that managers have a financial, or salary, incentive to pursue growth maximization over profit maximization. However, while seeing this rather obvious argument, there are some subtleties. If a company grows at a faster rate now, will it be in a stronger position to outperform its rivals in the future? Economies of scale can be attained more quickly, leading to a reduction in costs. In addition, as we saw in Chapters 5 and 7, increased market share brings increased power over pricing. If this is true, growth maximization now is simply a strategy for profit maximization over the long term.

Behavioural theories

Behavioural theories of the firm are based on how individuals actually behave inside firms. This is in contrast to theories such as profit maximization, which predict how individuals should behave. Important behavioural points are what goals will be set for the organization and how will the targets be set?

Goal setting

Cyert and March[1] recognized that organizations are complex environments represented by a mixture of interest groups, including shareholders, managers, workers, consumers and trade unions. Even within managers there are various sub-groups, including marketing, accounting and production. The goals of the organization, or firm, are more a reflection of these competing interests than a theoretical prediction such as profit maximization. If a marketing manager rises to the top of the organization, it is likely that marketing issues will rise to the top of the managerial decision-making agenda. Resources may flow into the marketing department and the goals of the organization may reflect marketing issues, such as the most recognized global brand or growing customer reach and market share. In contrast, if an accountant led the organization, then goals relating to sales growth, cost reduction and profitability might be set. Decision making, the development of targets and the focus of the organization are, therefore, a reflection of the coalition of interests within the organization. Whichever group has greater power, or enhanced negotiation skills, will have a greater say over the targets of the organization.

Target setting

Regardless of which goals or objectives predominate, the complexity of the environment will mean that measures and targets are difficult to set. Should sales growth be 10 per cent or 20 per cent? How do managers accommodate failure in meeting the target? In recognizing these points, Herbert Simon[2] developed the concept of **satisficing**.

> **Satisficing** is the attainment of acceptable levels of performance. Maximizing is the attainment of maximum levels of performance.

For example, 20 per cent annual growth in sales could be the maximum possible. But a 10 per cent growth in sales would be acceptable, especially if other firms or organizations were achieving similar results; 10 per cent represents a satisfactory level of performance. If managers negotiate a 10 per cent target growth rate, rather than a 20 per cent target, they are displaying satisficing rather than maximizing behaviour. Why might they do this? First, the maximum growth rate is unknown; it could be 15, 20, 25 or even 50 per cent. Second, failure to meet a target creates tension between the group setting the target and the individuals pursuing the target. Therefore, in order to avoid failure in a complex world, where the maximum is unknown, it is perhaps better to set a realistic and satisfactory target. Behavioural considerations, therefore, lead to firms and organizations setting minimum levels of performance, rather than maximum ones.

We do not have to decide which of the above alternative hypotheses are correct. Instead, we simply have to recognize that the separation of ownership from control provides managers with the incentive to pursue any of the above objectives. The problem for shareholders is the absence of direct control over managers: how might they motivate managers to behave in the interests of shareholders? The straightforward answer is to make managers shareholders. But the complex answer is to understand how difficult this might be. To understand the problem more fully, we will examine principal–agent theory.

8.3 Principal–agent theory

Agency costs between managers and shareholders

> A **principal** hires another person, the agent, to carry out work on their behalf.
>
> Shareholders are **principals** when they employ managers, the **agents**, to run their companies.

When a business is small the owner is also likely to be the manager. In this case, there is no agency relationship because the owner and the manager are the same person. Therefore, there can be no misalignment of interests. The owner-manager is likely to work very hard to ensure the success of the business. Furthermore, even if the owner-manager decides to pursue expense preference behaviour and spend the company's money on a top-of-the-range BMW, they are only robbing themself as the shareholder. An important consideration is that the value of the company to the owner does not change with the behaviour of the manager; simply, the financial benefits are being paid to the same person in different ways. For example, if the company generated £100 000 in profits, but the owner-manager decided to use £30 000 to buy the BMW and only receive a dividend of (£100 000 − £30 000) = £70 000, then the owner-manager has still received £100 000 from the company.

We can now consider what happens when the company grows and the owner wishes to sell half their stake in the company. The original owner will still manage the company, but the new shareholder will just be an owner, not a manager. Before buying the stake, any potential buyer will attempt to value the company. Crucially, the value of the company now depends upon the expense preference behaviour of the owner-manager. When the owner-manager buys a BMW with the company's money, the other shareholder is paying for half of the car, but gaining no benefit. For example, if the company again generates £100 000 in profits, then each shareholder should receive £50 000. But if the shareholder who also manages the company uses £30 000 of the profits to buy the BMW, then the remaining profits are only £70 000. Split two ways, each shareholder receives £35 000. The owner-manager has received a £30 000 car plus £35 000 in dividends = £65 000. The shareholder who does not run the company has only received £35 000 in dividends. Therefore, the value of a share in the company is not £50 000, but rather £35 000. Indeed, the more a manager displays expense preference behaviour, the lower the potential buyer will value the company.

This reduction in company value from employing an agent to manage the company is an example of an agency cost. Agency costs are not the wages associated with employing an agent; rather, they reflect reductions in value to principals from using agents to undertake work on their behalf.

The agency cost in our example is £50 000 − £35 000 = £15 000. It arises because the interests of the owner-manager are different from those of the other shareholder; and because the owner-manager is not monitored on a daily basis. It is, therefore, possible to use the company's money to fund benefits for the owner-manager at the expense of the remaining owner.

Agency costs between workers and managers

> **Piece rates** occur when a worker is paid according to the output produced. Under hourly wage rates, workers are paid for time at work.

Agency costs occur not just between owners and managers of companies. They can also occur when managers employ workers to do work for them. For example, let us consider two employment relationships. First, a supermarket employs a shelf stacker on **piece rates**. For each tray of tinned food put on the shelf, the shelf stacker receives £0.20. Second, a supermarket employs a shelf stacker on an hourly rate of £5.

If agency problems exist because principals find it difficult to monitor the effort of their agents, then piece rates will reduce agency costs. With an hourly wage rate of £5, the shelf stacker will earn £5 for one hour's work if they fill the shelf or if they sit in the staff restaurant drinking coffee and reading the paper. However, under piece rates the worker has to provide sufficient effort to place 25 trays of tinned food on the shelf in order to earn the same £5.

Under piece rates, the employer does not have to continually monitor the effort of the agent; instead, they can merely add up all the output at the end of the shift. If the agent works hard, then greater output will lead to greater pay. If they are lazy and read the newspaper, then their pay will decrease. By linking pay more directly to the effort provided, the agency costs are reduced.

We tend to see piece rates used when the output is easy to verify. For example, car salespersons are paid a commission for selling cars. It is fairly easy to verify that a car has been sold. Packers are often paid by the number of boxes that have been filled; and bricklayers are paid by the square metre of laid bricks and not by the hour.

However, when it comes to managers and many other occupations, output is more difficult to verify. How do you measure if a manager has managed? The many activities undertaken by managers, including monitoring workers, communicating and implementing business plans, reviewing operations and making investment decisions, make it difficult to measure the total output of the manager. The outputs are numerous, varied and difficult to quantify. For example, how do you measure effective communication? However, given that we have shown that company value is reduced by increased agency costs, we need to develop a means of aligning managers' interests with those of shareholders, thereby reducing agency costs and boosting company value. How might this be achieved? We need an alternative way of reducing agency costs. In the following business application, stock options will highlight how agency costs associated with employing managers might be reduced.

8.4 Business application: stock options and the reduction of agency costs

In order to reduce agency costs, principals have to develop contracts that align agents' interests with their own. Piece rates lower agency costs by forcing the agent to work hard to receive greater pay. A more complicated example is the use of **stock options** in the financial packages offered to senior managers of leading companies.

> **Stock options** provide individuals with the *option* to buy shares in the future at a price agreed in the past.

For example, assume the share price today for company X is £10. A manager at X may be offered the option to purchase 1 million shares at £10 in three years' time. Assume the manager works hard, the company makes profits and over the three years the shares rise to £12. The stock option has moved into the money. The manager can take up the option and buy at £10 and then sell instantly for £12, making £2 million profit. Stock options, therefore, link managers' and shareholders' interests via the share price. But how effective are stock options as a solution to agency problems?

An examination of the key points associated with stock options will help:

1 Stock options transfer an element of shareholder risk to the manager. Under a fixed salary contract a manager will earn perhaps £30 000 per annum. The manager will earn this salary if the company performs well or not. Under a stock option, part of the fixed contract is swapped for the stock options. The manager may now be offered a basic salary of £20 000, plus stock options. When the company performs well, the manager's stock options move into the money. The manager's pay increases whenever the stock option moves into the money and the manager executes the option, that is, uses the option to buy the shares cheaply and make a profit. But when the company underperforms, the share price drops and the stock options are worthless. Therefore, performance contracts, such as stock options, swap part of the certain salary for a chance of earning a higher overall amount. This increase in risk may not be attractive to the manager and they could decide to reject the contract or work somewhere else.

2 Stock options make a manager's pay contingent upon the share price. The share price is being used as a measure of the manager's hard work. The harder the manager works, the higher the share price climbs. But what if the share price is influenced by industry factors, such as the degree of competition, or by domestic government policy on interest rates? A manager may work very hard but, due to government policy, the share price may fall. This increases the risk being transferred to the manager. For this reason, the measure of performance should be linked closely to managerial, or worker, effort. In some cases, the measures can be very specific. Workers in telephone sales are paid a commission every time they secure a sale, while car salespersons are paid every time they sell a car. In contrast, the output measures for managers tend to be very general, based on overall profitability, or simply linked to the share price.

3 The stronger the link between worker effort and the performance measure, the stronger the incentive. This merely reflects risk again. If you work hard, but the output measure does not reflect high effort, then you receive no pay. Managers are measured by share prices and car salespersons by number of sales. We might argue that there is a stronger link between worker effort and car sales than between worker effort and share price. At a simple level, if a salesperson works hard to sell a car, then a sale may materialize. But if a manager works hard, other managers may not and, therefore, due to a lack of teamwork, the share price is unaffected. As a reflection of these arguments, what tends to be observed is that, as a percentage of their overall pay, car salespersons receive a low fixed salary component and a high performance bonus. In contrast, managers tend to receive a high fixed salary component and a lower performance bonus. Therefore, as in the case of car salespersons, when the performance measure is a more accurate measure of worker effort, the more likely it is that pay will move to performance-based, rather than fixed, salary.

4 Incentive contracts can promote a single type of behaviour. Managers with stock options face incentives to raise the company's share price. But what if shareholders are interested in more than this? Box 8.1 provides Vodafone's strategic statement.

5 Finally, a manager's behaviour and effort must be verifiable. It should not be possible for the worker or manager to influence the performance measure inappropriately. This was clearly not the case with Enron and Worldcom. With Enron, managers were able to keep liabilities off the company's balance sheet, thereby inflating its share price. Even though the company was performing badly, the managers were able to make it appear highly successful. The share price rose and stock options were cashed in. In the case of Worldcom, expenses on stationery were capitalized and moved to the balance sheet as an asset, rather than sent to the profit and loss statement as an expense. This is common practice for substantial assets such as buildings and cars, but not for stationery, which you may no longer own as you have sent it out in letters! But, again, profits were seen to rise, assets increased and the share price rose. Once again, managers cashed in on stock options.

Therefore, performance contracts can help to resolve the principal–agent problem. But only if:

◆ workers accept the contracts, receiving greater rewards for higher risks
◆ there is a link between worker effort and the performance measure
◆ the performance can be co-ordinated across a number of objectives
◆ workers cannot unduly influence the measure

We can use these points to understand some of the concerns relating to the excessive rewards provided to managers through stock options. One of the potential reasons why executive compensation has increased so markedly is to do with risk. A guaranteed payment of £100 is better than a 50:50 chance of receiving £100 or £0. But how much money would you require in order to accept the 50:50 gamble and give up the guaranteed £100? Would you require £200, £300

Box 8.1 Vodafone's strategic direction

Vodafone is uniquely positioned to succeed through our scale and scope and the customer focus of all our employees. To achieve this success, we are focused on the execution of the six strategic goals that we outlined last year; delighting our customers, leveraging our scale and scope, expanding market boundaries, building the best global team, being a responsible business and providing superior shareholder returns.

Vodafone's strategic vision is based on six approaches, of which one is shareholder returns. While each of the six approaches may seem sensible, it is difficult to envisage a performance contract which is able to reward managers for such a complexity of targets. Recently, companies have recognized this and some have moved to multiple measures of performance, splitting performance bonus between the short term and the long term. Performance is not necessarily measured by reference to the share price – it might include sales growth compared with the firm's three leading competitors, or profit growth compared to the top 25 per cent of the FTSE 100, or profitability compared with other leading global players in the sector.

Source: Vodafone website, www.vodafone.com

> Individuals can be **risk averse**, risk neutral or risk seeking.

or perhaps even £1000? If you asked for £1000, then you would be described as not liking risk, or as being **risk averse**, and, therefore, requiring a large reward for accepting the risk of the 50:50 gamble.

Assume an executive is equally risk averse. For every £100 that is taken from their guaranteed salary, a potential reward of £1000 has to be offered through the stock option. So, executives can receive large financial rewards, but they receive such rewards for (it is hoped) improving shareholder value and taking personal financial risk. We can even suggest where the executive's risk stems from. Linking a large amount of executive wealth to one company's share price does not provide the executive with a diversified portfolio of investments. The bulk of the executive's wealth is linked to one asset. We saw in Chapter 7 that diversification reduces risk. Therefore, reduced diversification must increase risk and, in order to accept greater risk, executives require a higher potential reward. As a consequence, the size of executive stock options and executive remuneration contracts increases.

The alternative view of managers using stock options to camouflage large financial rewards also has some merit. Raising the executive's salary by 100 per cent is likely to attract the wrong type of attention from shareholders and the media. By contrast, raising total financial remuneration through stock market performance provides a tangible link between pay and performance that is more palatable to the public.

However, all of our discussion has been linked to shareholders offering managers contracts that are designed to align the interests of shareholders and managers. In reality, managers propose contracts to shareholders. It is then shareholders who reject or accept the proposed financial terms for the executive(s). This is generally discussed at the company's annual general meeting. Why is this a problem?

First, managers are defining pay and performance. Admittedly, this is achieved through the company's remuneration committee that supposedly consists of independent remuneration experts and non-executive directors of the company.

Non-executive directors are directors from other companies who provide independent advice to the boards on which they are non-executives. For example, Mr X may be an executive director of company Y, his main employer. But Mr X may also be a non-executive director of company Z, providing independent advice to the board.

From our discussion of behavioural theories of the firm, we might suspect that the targets set by remuneration committees will be satisficing, not maximizing, targets. From the behavioural perspective, there is a fear that executives can negotiate the proposed financial rewards, arguing with the members of the remuneration committee what reasonable targets and performance rewards are given what is occurring in other companies. Second, due to the separation of ownership from control, once the executive(s) package is proposed, the dispersed nature of the shareholdings may lead to free riding among the shareholders, making a majority vote against the executive(s) financial terms difficult.

Performance pay and the public sector

A current trend is to introduce performance pay within the public sector. Primary care doctors in the UK are paid a fixed salary plus a performance element which is linked to certain health-care indices. These include reductions in blood pressure and cholesterol for patients at high risk of heart disease. Teachers are eligible for performance-related pay linked to pupil progression and dental professionals are paid according to the number of units of dental treatment provided to patients.

The key, as with performance contracts in the private sector, is to ensure that workers can respond to the incentives and do not divert the effort of employees away from other important value-adding activities. For example, in the dental profession, the extraction of a tooth attracts the same reward as extensive root canal work. The latter is more beneficial for the patient, but the former is quicker to deliver by the dentist. In the case of teaching, excellent teachers are increasingly allocated to teach marginal students where there is the greatest scope to improve pupil progression. Improving highly capable pupils is difficult and offers fewer financial rewards for good teachers.

The important learning point is that markets, prices and incentives direct the allocation of resources; and this is equally important in the private and public sectors.

 Box 8.2 Dentists 'pull out more teeth'

Adapted from an article on BBC News Online, 21 August 2008

Dentists are more likely to pull teeth out or fit false ones than provide fillings or crowns under an NHS deal introduced two years ago, figures show. In England, treatments that included dentures increased from 38 to 48 per cent between 2003/04 and 2007/08, and extractions from 7 to 8 per cent. But the number of crowns fell from 48 to 35 per cent and fillings from 28 to 26 per cent. Root canal work halved.

The figures also showed fewer patients being treated, despite more dentists joining the NHS after the new contract. Overall, 27 million patients were seen by an NHS dentist in England during the past two years – 1.1 million fewer than the previous two years.

The new dental contract, introduced in April 2006, was intended to allow dentists to spend more time with NHS patients in a bid to make the profession more attractive. Costs to the NHS for dental treatment increased by £56 million to £531 million in 2007/08 – an increase of 12 per cent on the previous year.

The contract between dentist and the NHS also includes a clawback, which means the NHS pays them in advance for a stated number of treatments. If they do not carry out all the work they may have to pay some of the money back. The risk is that unnecessary treatment increases and preventive check-ups fall.

Susie Sanderson, chair of the British Dental Association's Executive Board, said there were still 'significant problems'. 'Those that are able to access care are confronted with a system that discourages modern, preventive care by placing targets, rather than patients, at its heart.'

© bbc.co.uk/news

8.5 Regulation of business

We have examined the governance of managers by shareholders. We would now like to examine the governance of firms within their marketplaces. We have already seen, in Chapter 5, that monopolies are an example of marketplaces that are not in consumers' interests, with higher prices and lower output than under perfect competition. We will now also show that, in other ways, markets can act against the interest of consumers, or even the public more generally. In representing the interests of society, governments can intervene in such markets in an attempt to improve the benefits society receives from the market. We will begin by providing an overview of the issues and some further examples.

How many times have you sat at a set of traffic lights having 'to keep it real' by listening to the loud bass tunes from the car drawn up next to you? The person playing the loud music obviously likes the artist. The unfortunate problem is that everyone within earshot of the car also has to listen. The driver sets the volume of the car stereo without considering the interests of the people they may be driving past. Effectively, the interests of the driver and those of a wider group of individuals are not aligned.

Not surprisingly, the private interests of firms and wider society also differ. Polluting the environment, rather than cleaning factory emissions, is a cheap alternative for a profit-maximizing firm. Unfortunately, society as a whole has to bear the costs of a polluted environment. This is again because the interests of society and the private firm are not aligned. The firm will choose to produce more pollutants than society finds desirable.

An important but underlying issue within this book, and many other texts on economics, is that markets are an optimal means of allocating society's scarce resources. That is why we have spent so much time looking at supply, demand, perfect competition and monopoly. How do markets work and how do firms operate within markets?

> **Pareto efficient** means that no one within an economy can be made better off without making some other people worse off. Therefore, the wellbeing of society is at a maximum.

At the heart of most economists' understanding is that an economy characterized by perfectly competitive markets is **Pareto efficient**. In perfect competition firms operate at the minimum point on their long-run cost curves. Hence, they are productively efficient. Firms make the highest level of output for the lowest amount of cost. Also in perfect competition, price equals marginal cost. So, the price paid by consumers for the last unit also equals the cost of the resources used in making the last unit. Therefore, input resources are also allocated efficiently. Thus, in perfect competition the goods that consumers desire are the ones that are made and, moreover, they are made at lowest cost. Intuitively we can accept this as a good outcome, and economists go one step further and prove that it is Pareto efficient.

However, perfect competition is rarely achieved in reality and in some cases monopoly might exist. Under monopoly, products are not necessarily produced at lowest cost and they are not priced at marginal cost. So, Pareto efficiency will not hold.

> Economists use the term **market failure** to cover all circumstances in which the market equilibrium is not efficient.

Monopoly is an example of a **market failure**, with perfect competition providing a more efficient market equilibrium. But there can be other reasons for market failure. As we will discuss in detail below, so-called externalities can lead to a difference between the interests of private individuals and society and an inefficient production or consumption of goods and services from the perspective of society. For example, the production and consumption of loud music by our car driver is not an efficient (desirable) allocation of resources from the perspective of society (passers-by). We will now discuss externalities, monopoly and the problems relating to market failure. Following this, we can begin to assess various government intervention strategies for making markets potentially more Pareto efficient – that is, strategies that make people better off without making others worse off, thereby improving the wellbeing of society.

8.6 Externalities

Externalities are the effects of consumption, or production, on third parties. If production, or consumption, by one group improves the wellbeing of third parties, then a **positive externality** has occurred. If production, or consumption, by one group reduces the wellbeing of third parties, then a **negative externality** has occurred.

Marginal private cost is the cost to the individual of producing one more unit of output.

Marginal social cost is the cost to society of producing one or more unit of output.

Externalities occur when the production, or consumption, of a good or service results in costs, or benefits, being passed on to individuals not involved in the production, or consumption. **Negative externalities** occur when costs are passed on to society, or benefits are reduced. **Positive externalities** occur when costs to society are reduced or benefits are enhanced.

A number of examples will help to explain the concepts of positive and negative externalities.

The cost to the private firm of producing a particular output is the **marginal private cost**, MPC. We have previously referred to this as the marginal cost. MPC measures the costs to the firm of producing one more unit and includes those of raw materials, labour and machinery. We now wish to also include in the analysis the **marginal social cost**, MSC. This is the cost to society of producing one more unit. As the private firm or individual is a member of society, then the MSC must include the MPC. However, in addition it will also include the costs associated with using or exploiting public assets, such as the environment. So, the MSC could include costs of pollution. In such cases, the costs to society will always be bigger than the costs to the private firm. These points are summarized in Table 8.2.

MSC is greater than MPC

The consequences of this can be seen in Figure 8.1. The optimal level of output for society and the private firm will occur where marginal revenue equals marginal cost. If the firm is a price-taker, then equilibrium for the private firm occurs at point B, where MPC equals demand and, therefore, marginal revenue. The output level is 2000 units. However, for society, MSC equals demand and, therefore, marginal revenue at point A, with an output of 1000 units. Therefore, when the private firm creates negative cost externalities for the rest of society, the private firm will choose a level of output that is greater than that deemed desirable by society. In its simplest terms, the firm does not recognize the costs of pollution; society does. Therefore, society has a desire to reduce output and pollution; the firm does not.

MSC is less than MPC

If we reversed the arguments and the marginal social cost was lower than the marginal private cost, then society would find it desirable to produce more output than the private firm or individual deem optimal. For example, society might decide that it is optimal for all individuals to gain a degree. But this requires your input in terms of time, effort and tuition fees. The costs to you are greater than to society. Hence, when deciding whether to go to university, you did not take into account society's views.

Table 8.2 Marginal private and social costs

Marginal private cost	Marginal social cost
Raw materials	Raw materials
Labour costs	Labour costs
Machinery	Machinery + Environmental costs of production

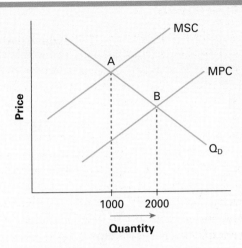

Figure 8.1 Negative cost externalities

The marginal private cost (MPC) is much lower than the marginal social cost (MSC). As a result, when choosing the optimal level of output, the private individual will choose a level of output that is higher than the socially optimal level of output. Pollution is a good example.

MPB is greater than MSB

Marginal private benefit is the benefit to the individual from consuming one more unit of output.

Marginal social benefit is the benefit to society from the consumption of one more unit of output.

The excessive car music example is a clear case of negative consumption externalities. The driver receives **marginal private benefit**, MPB, from consuming loud music. While the marginal private cost is linked to marginal cost, the marginal private benefit is linked to demand. If a consumer can place a financial value on the marginal benefit from consuming one more unit, then this value must equal the consumer's maximum willingness to pay.

The benefits for surrounding individuals are captured by the **marginal social benefit**, MSB. For simplicity, we will assume that the marginal social costs and the marginal private costs are equal. Figure 8.2 captures these points.

The optimal output of loud music for society occurs where MSC equals MSB at A, with 1000 units of output. The optimal amount of output for private individuals is where MPB equals MPC at B, with 2000 units of output. Therefore, we have 1000 too many drivers playing their music too loud. This figure would also capture the negative externalities associated with passive smoking. Private smokers gain a higher satisfaction from smoking than do non-smokers. As a result, if society is dominated by non-smokers, then smokers exhale pollutants at a level beyond what society deems desirable.

What are the business implications? If you consider advertising, the private benefits for firms are (they hope) increased sales. The benefits for consumers in society are improved information about what products are available, where they can be sourced and at what prices. If firms value higher sales more than consumers value information, firms will advertise at levels that are greater than that deemed desirable by society. If you have ever hated the adverts appearing on TV, become irritated by pop-up adverts on the Internet, or been plagued by junk (e)mail, then you now understand why you were angry.

MSB is greater than MPB

If the marginal social benefits are greater than the marginal private benefits, then society gains more than a private individual from consumption. Examples can include vaccinations and

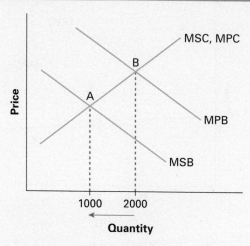

Figure 8.2 Negative benefit externalities

The marginal private benefit (MPB) is much higher than the marginal social benefit (MSB). Therefore, when choosing the optimal level of output, private individuals will consume a higher level of output than that deemed optimal by society. Loud music is an example.

education. An individual gains health benefits from being vaccinated against a disease. However, society gains more, because the individual is both likely to be more healthy and less likely to pass on the disease to other individuals. In terms of education, a university graduate may gain employment benefits from their advanced education. Society gains from the taxes paid by this educated person, as well as the advanced skills and innovative thinking that can be used within firms to generate profit, wealth, new business and new jobs.

8.7 Dealing with externalities

Clearly, if the private actions of individuals, or firms, are at variance with those of wider society, there is a case for at least asking whether anything can be done to solve the problem. We will see that some solutions are fairly straightforward to describe, but they may be difficult to implement.

Taxation and subsidy

The central problem with an externality is that the pricing mechanism does not impose the costs, or benefits, on the correct individuals. If a person smokes, or a firm pollutes the river, society bears the cost of living with a polluted environment. Therefore, a means has to be found whereby the private firm or individual internalizes, or pays all costs associated with, their behaviour. In Figure 8.3, we revisit the situation where the marginal social cost is greater than the marginal private cost, the case of river pollution by a firm. Society views 1000 units of output as efficient; the firm would rather produce 2000 units of output. The problem is that marginal private costs, MPC, are different from marginal social costs, MSC. So, the obvious solution is to make MPC and MPS equal. This is achieved by taxing the firm for polluting the river, or environment. This adds to the firm's costs and, optimally, the tax will be equal to the difference between the MPC and the MSC. The imposition of the pollution tax provides firms with an incentive to cut output and move from point B to point A, thus lowering output to the socially optimum level.

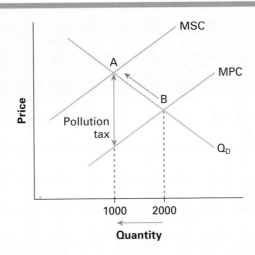

Figure 8.3 Dealing with externalities through taxation

The MPC is lower than the MSC, leading to over-production of the good from society's point of view. In order to encourage firms to produce less, the government can impose a tax. If the tax is set correctly, the MPC will become equal to the MSC, and result in private individuals choosing the same level of output as society.

Road tax for cars across a number of economies is linked to the pollution output of the car. Heavy polluters pay more road tax. This provides drivers with a clear incentive to buy cars that are more environmentally friendly. Congestion charging in London was also planned to be increased for less fuel-efficient cars. However, after reflection, it was felt that such a change may not reduce car use or pollution. A key lesson is that the use of taxes and subsidies as incentives is not always clear and obvious. See Box 8.3.

 Box 8.3 London drops £25 congestion charge for gas guzzlers

Adapted from 'Porsche victory as Boris Johnson drops £25 congestion charge' by Fiona Hamilton in The Times, *9 July 2008*

The Mayor of London has scrapped plans to make owners of gas-guzzling cars pay a £25 congestion charge. The increased charge had angered owners of so-called 'Chelsea tractors', who said they were being unfairly targeted. Conversely, the £8 charge for vehicles with the lowest emissions was due to be scrapped.

The Mayor said, 'I am delighted that we have been able to scrap the £25 charge, which would have hit families and small businesses hardest. I believe the proposal would actually have made congestion worse by allowing thousands of small cars in for free.' In addition, Porsche had also published research that it said showed that the new charge would actually increase car mileage, with drivers of high-emission cars driving to avoid the tolled areas.

Finally, there was concern that the charges would discourage people from using buses, the Tube, cycles and motorbikes by subsidizing the use of small cars.

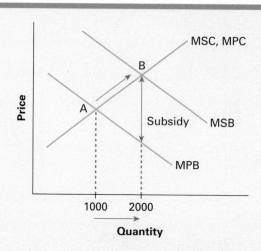

Figure 8.4 Dealing with externalities through subsidies

The MPB is lower than the MSB. As a result, private individuals under-consume the product. In order to increase the level of consumption, subsidies are offered to private individuals. This lowers the cost of consumption and individuals should consume more.

Subsidies

> A **subsidy** is a payment made to producers, by government, which leads to a reduction in the market price of the product.

An alternative to taxation is **subsidy**. Subsidies make consumption, or production, cheaper for the private individual. For example, home improvements which enhance energy efficiency, such as loft and wall cavity insulation, are often subsidized by government. Clearly, with a subsidy more energy-efficient home improvements will be purchased, since they are cheaper. So, subsidies will be used when governments fear that the private level of output will be less than the socially optimal level of output. Consider Figure 8.4. The marginal private benefit, MPB, of an energy-efficient home is associated with lower electricity bills. The marginal social benefit, MSB, also includes the wider social benefits of a cleaner environment resulting from lower electricity generation. Hence, the MSB is greater than the MPB. In order to persuade consumers to use energy-efficient home improvements at the socially optimal level, a subsidy that is equal to the difference between MPB and MSB must be offered. This effectively reduces the price of energy-efficient home improvements and consumers buy in greater quantities.

8.8 Market power and competition policy

In Chapter 5 we compared perfect competition with monopoly and argued that under monopoly the price is higher and output is lower than under perfect competition. With the introduction of Pareto efficiency, we can now move on to show how monopoly, from the perspective of society, is not necessarily a desirable form of market structure.

> **Consumer surplus** is the difference between the price a consumer is willing to pay and the price they actually pay.

In the left-hand side of Figure 8.5, we have perfect competition. The profit-maximizing level of output, Q_{pc}, is sold at a price of P_{pc}. **Consumer surplus** is the difference between the price a consumer is willing to pay and the price charged. In this case, the consumer surplus is the light blue shaded area above the market price and below the demand curve. Consumer surplus is an important measure of welfare or wellbeing. If you are willing to pay £50 for a product and you can buy it for £30, then you are £20 better off.

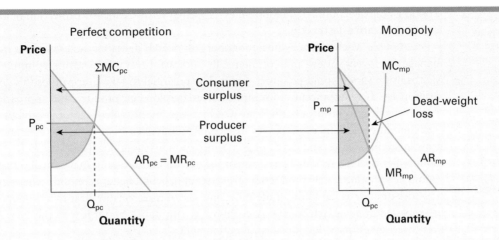

Figure 8.5 Welfare costs of monopoly

♦ The consumer surplus under perfect competition is greater than under monopoly simply because the price is lower under perfect competition.
♦ The producer surplus is greater under monopoly than under perfect competition simply because the price is higher under monopoly.
♦ However, the total of consumer and producer surplus is higher under perfect competition than under monopoly. This difference is known as the dead-weight loss of monopoly and represents a reduction in welfare to society. Since everyone can be made better off by moving to perfect competition, monopoly is not Pareto efficient.

Producer surplus is the difference between the price that a firm is willing to sell at and the price it does sell at.

Producers also have a surplus. **Producer surplus** is the difference between the price they would be willing to sell at and the price that they do sell at. Recall Chapter 5 and the discussion of profit maximization. Under the assumption of profit maximization, a firm is willing to supply one more unit of output if the price offered is greater than or equal to marginal cost. In this way, the firm at worst breaks even on the last unit supplied. So, given our definition of producer surplus and the concept of profit maximization, the firm is willing to sell at any price which is greater than marginal cost; we now only need the price that the firm sells at in order to measure producer surplus. In Figure 8.5, producer surplus is the darker blue area below the market price and above the marginal cost curve for the industry.

The case of monopoly is shown in the right-hand side of Figure 8.5. Under monopoly, the price increases and the output shrinks. Therefore, the consumer surplus must reduce. In contrast, because the monopoly sells at a higher price, producer surplus must increase. In essence, part of the consumer surplus is being transferred to the monopoly. However, and this is the important part, if we compare the total of consumer and producer surplus under perfect competition and monopoly, we can see that the total surplus is lower under monopoly. This difference is known as the **dead-weight loss** of monopoly. It is a loss of welfare to society. Under Pareto efficiency no one can be made better off without making someone else worse off. Monopoly is clearly not Pareto efficient because if we change the market into a perfectly competitive one, then the dead-weight loss will vanish. People can be made better off without making anyone else worse off. Essentially, more products are sold and sold at a lower price.

Dead-weight loss of monopoly is the loss of welfare to society resulting from the existence of the monopoly.

Dead-weight loss may not be the only detrimental aspect of monopoly. Many companies will spend resources trying to attain **monopoly status**.

Seeking out a **monopoly status** is known as undertaking 'rent-seeking activities'.

Rent-seeking activities are the allocation of resources to non-socially optimal ends and they also need to be added on to the dead-weight losses. However, following the ideas of an

> Innovation can enable a firm to overcome the entry barriers of an existing monopoly. This is **creative destruction**, with the creative innovation destroying the existing monopoly position.

economist called Schumpeter, monopolies have enjoyed the academic protection of a concept known as '**creative destruction**'.

For example, Microsoft is a global monopoly supplier of operating systems. If one innovator manages to invent a new and commercially successful way of operating computers, then Microsoft's position could be under threat. The potential to take over Microsoft's dominant position acts as a huge incentive for innovators to develop new products and approaches.

In terms of prices, output and dead-weight losses, monopolies are not good, but they do create incentives for other firms to try to become monopolies. In order to become monopolies, firms invest in research and development. Innovation brings about the destruction of existing monopolies. So, rent-seeking behaviour, or the pursuit of monopoly, may actually create innovation, new products, new production processes and, hence, better economic efficiency. While these debates can be left to the academic economist, it is reasonably clear that monopolies can be suspected of being detrimental to economic performance, and it is with this view in mind that governments have developed competition policy.

Competition policy

> The **Competition Commission** investigates whether a monopoly, or a potential monopoly, significantly affects competition.

In the UK, the Director General of Fair Trading supervises company behaviour and, where fit, can refer individual companies to the **Competition Commission** for investigation. A company can be referred for investigation if it supplies more than 25 per cent of the total market, or if a complex monopoly exists whereby a small number of big firms are seen to collude and restrict competition.

Within the definition lies the approach taken by the UK competition authorities. There is no presumption, as in economic theory, that monopolies are bad. Rather, a decision is based on each case and whether it seriously undermines competition. The Competition Commission has wide powers to make and enforce remedies.

A potential problem with the UK Competition Commission is that it simply looks at the UK market. Many mergers are now rationalized on the basis of building a company which is large enough to be an effective competitor across Europe.

If a merger is significantly large, then it can be examined by the European Commission for Competition. If the merged companies have a global turnover which exceeds €5 billion and turnover within the EU exceeds €250 million, then the EU Commission will investigate the merger. This investigation will occur even if the merging companies are not headquartered within the EU. The EU also evaluates mergers in terms of whether they will reduce competition or contestability.

8.9 Business application: carbon trading

Carbon dioxide, a greenhouse gas, is a by-product of burning fossil fuels such as oil and coal. Modern industrial economies consume vast amounts of energy on a daily basis. Energy which is provided by burning fossil fuels. Oil and coal are used to generate electricity and are used to propel cars, lorries and aircraft. As a greenhouse gas, carbon dioxide is a pollutant. Unfortunately, the creation of carbon dioxide is an example of a negative externality. The marginal private cost of producing electricity does not reflect the full marginal social cost, which also includes the effects of pollution on the environment.

Environmental and growth economists examine the rising production of greenhouse gases using an environmentally-adapted Kuznets curve.[3] The environmental Kuznets curve shows an n-shaped relationship between the production of greenhouse gases and GDP per capita. This relationship is depicted in Figure 8.6. As an economy grows and GDP per capita rises, then a

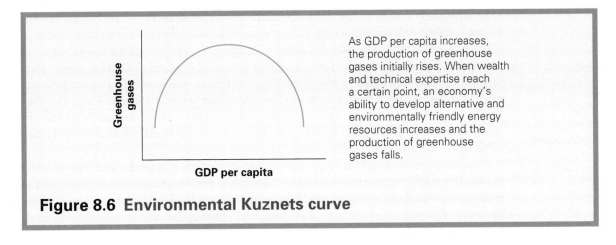

As GDP per capita increases, the production of greenhouse gases initially rises. When wealth and technical expertise reach a certain point, an economy's ability to develop alternative and environmentally friendly energy resources increases and the production of greenhouse gases falls.

Figure 8.6 Environmental Kuznets curve

greater use of fossil fuel production results in the rising production of detrimental greenhouse gases. Once an economy reaches a certain size and affluence, then there is likely to be sufficient wealth and technical expertise to address the use of fossil fuels and the generation of greenhouse gases. Financial resource and engineering expertise can be allocated to the production of hybrid fuel cars and wind turbine generation of electricity. Therefore, in advanced high GDP per capita economies the production of greenhouse gases begins to decline.

The environmental Kuznets curve provides a useful framework for examining the rise in pollution around the world. Fast-growing economies, such as China and India, have rapidly increased GDP per capita and as a consequence have significantly added to the global production of greenhouse gases. It is arguably unreasonable to ask these economies to avoid the use of fossil fuels and make greater use of environmentally friendly energy production. In particular, the developed economies of the world made ample use of fossil fuel technology throughout their own development, so why should China and India be expected to take a more expensive route to full economic development?

However, the Kuznets curve indicates that some of the additional greenhouse gases from developing economies can be balanced by a reduction in pollution from highly developed economies. Unfortunately, the statistical evidence relating to the environmental Kuznets curve suggests that even the US, the world's largest economy, has not yet reached its peak.

In order to address the rise in greenhouse gases around the world various governments have implemented schemes which aim to reduce carbon dioxide emissions. Two broad schemes are available. The first is the sale of licences to pollute, the second is permits to emit pollutants. In the former case, firms pay a fee for the right to pollute. If the fee is high enough, some firms may decide it is cheaper not to pollute. In the second system, governments issue permits which enable a given amount of pollution. This quantity-based system guarantees a direct impact on the amount of pollution, but the cost to polluters is unknown and determined by the market price for permits. Within Europe a cap-and-trade system has been adopted. This is a market for permits to emit and is a quantity-based system. The purpose of the scheme is two-fold. First, the scheme provides governments with a credible commitment to limit the number of permits. Second, the scheme provides benefits to firms that cut emissions and a penalty to those that don't. In understanding the need to credibly commit to a fixed number of permits, we will examine the **Coase conjecture**. We then move on to an examination of how the traded permit scheme provides financial incentives to limit pollution.

Ronald Coase put forward the argument that a monopoly supplier of a durable good would have no monopoly pricing power and would sell all units of output at the perfectly competitive

The **Coase conjecture** argues that a monopoly provider of a durable good will sell at the perfectly competitive price.

price. Consider a monopoly that can set prices for its durable good in two periods. In the first period, it will set a high price and sell to consumers who are desperate for the product today. In the second period, the monopoly has to set a price for all customers who decided to wait in period one. The monopoly clearly has an incentive to expand output and sell for a lower price in period two. If consumers correctly anticipate the monopoly's incentive to cut prices in period two and the good is durable, then more consumers will wait for period two. This then provides a greater incentive for the monopoly to mop up the residual demand in period two with yet more output and lower prices. In the limit, the monopoly will sell more output at the perfectly competitive price in all periods.

If a government was to sell licences to pollute, then it could be considered a monopoly provider of a durable good. The government could sell licences in period one and claim that, in order to reduce pollution, the number of licences in period two will be less. The implicit threat is that firms should buy their licences today. Unfortunately, following the Coase conjecture, this threat is not a credible commitment. Polluting firms will expect the government to take the opportunity to raise revenues by selling more licences in period two at close to the competitive price. The clear incentive for firms is to wait for the cheaper licences and expand pollution in period two.

The solution to this problem is for the government not to sell durable licences. Instead, the government should lease licences for a given period. Through leasing, the licences become non-durable. In period one, a firm buys its requirement of licences. At the end of period one, the licences become obsolete and the firm is required to buy more in period two. The government is now a monopoly supplier of consumable goods in each period. It can charge the monopoly price and so faces no incentive to expand the output of permits in each subsequent period. With a credible commitment to a fixed or falling number of permits in each future period, the government is better placed to reduce pollution.

In practice, the European system for controlling carbon emissions involves governments setting an emissions cap. Permits to pollute equal to the cap are then allocated to industries. Companies with a surplus of permits trade with those that have a surplus. In essence, there is a market in pollution permits. But importantly, the size of this market is credibly limited by the governments' decision to lease permits for one year. If a firm wishes to pollute more, then it must pay for extra permits. And paying is the crucial aspect. Through the market, paying for the right to pollute increases the marginal private cost faced by polluting firms. As such, it should reduce the equilibrium level of pollution. In essence, the requirement to pay for the right to pollute is nothing more than a tax on excessive polluters. At the same time, clean producers are in effect subsidized by being able to sell their surplus permits at a profit: concepts which we discussed in Section 8.7.

An important feature of this solution is that it generates an opportunity cost. Polluters are faced with a trade-off. They can either buy more credits to meet their level of pollution, or they can they decide to invest in new technology which is more environmentally friendly. The market for carbon permits provides firms with an alternative option and price. As permit prices rise, then it is hoped that the attractiveness of investment in cleaner technology will increase, helping to reduce long-term pollution levels. Of course, the price of permits may just as easily fall. There is a concern that too many permits were allocated during the launch phase of the carbon trading system in Europe. This resulted in a significant price fall for each permit to pollute with one ton of carbon. Governments now have this under control. Each year the supply of permits will be reduced. Our understanding of markets assures us that a reduction in supply will lead to an increase in the equilibrium price. But, of course, a recession reduces the demand for goods, which reduces the demand for energy and the demand for permits.

It should also be recognized that there are problems with a system which penalizes polluters. In a global economy there is the risk that environmental policies in Europe place heavy users of fossil fuels at a cost disadvantage relative to rivals in China, where there is no environmental tax for producing greenhouse gases. In fact, much of this risk is minimal when we consider the overall economy. Services are the major engine of economic activity and are light users of energy. Even in manufacturing, estimates indicate that energy costs represent less than 1 per cent of making cars and furniture. Heavy users of fossil fuels, such as electricity generators, do not compete internationally and so much of the cost increase from carbon permits is passed on to domestic customers. However, a big concern is the airline industry. While currently exempt from the European scheme, aviation is expected to be covered by the emission scheme from 2012. Flights within Europe will operate on a level playing field. But intercontinental flights from Europe will face a cost disadvantage in relation to flights operated by non-European companies who are not covered by the emissions system.

The remaining concerns relate to whether companies are capable of trading and making an economic gain from the system. Box 8.4 highlights that this is not entirely straightforward.

 ## Box 8.4 Lightly carbonated

Adapted from an article in The Economist, *2 August 2007*

In theory, cap-and-trade schemes allow firms to reduce their emissions at the lowest possible cost. Governments put a limit on the amount firms can pollute, and issue an equivalent number of allowances. Those companies that find they do not have enough must either cut emissions or buy spare allowances from others. But, for the system to work efficiently, firms must take advantage of all opportunities to reduce the costs of participation.

The root of the problem is that many companies view the Emission Trading System as a regulatory burden, rather than a chance to make money. They tend to put environmental experts, rather than financial whizzes, in charge of their participation in the scheme. The former, in turn, tend to concentrate on making sure that their firm has enough allowances rather than on maximizing their value. They are seldom used to trading, and are sometimes uncomfortable with the idea of 'profiteering' from a system designed to cut pollution. Governments do not help matters by handing out allowances to polluters for free, giving them little incentive to capitalize on what are actually valuable assets.

There are good reasons why some firms might be wary of emissions trading. For small firms the cost of analysing how to make money from their allowances could outweigh the benefits. Other firms are so big that the profits to be made from permits, although substantial, would not be worth managers' time.

© The Economist Newspaper Limited, London 2009

 # Summary

1 It is debatable whether firms are profit-maximizers. Measuring marginal revenue and marginal cost can be difficult in practice.

2 The owners of modern corporations are often very different from the managers. This is known as separation of ownership from control.

3 If shareholders are unable to control managers, the potential exists for managers to pursue their own objectives. Various objectives have been put forward by economists, including the consumption of perquisites, growth maximization and sales maximization.

4 Managers can be incentivized to work in the interests of shareholders by also making them shareholders. This is commonly achieved through the use of stock options.

5 Financial incentives such as stock options are only useful if four criteria are met:
   - managers are not overly risk averse
   - there is a link between manager effort and measured performance
   - performance is not focused on single activities to the detriment of other key activities or tasks
   - managers cannot falsely manipulate the performance measure, such as the share price

6 Pareto efficiency occurs when no one can be made better off without making someone else worse off.

7 Externalities exist when the costs or benefits from consumption or production are not borne entirely by the person undertaking the production or consumption.

8 The existence of externalities leads to a difference between the socially optimal level of output and the private optimal level of output.

9 The optimal level of output can be targeted by the introduction of taxes and subsidies.

10 Monopoly can result in a dead-weight loss, or lower welfare for society, when compared with perfect competition.

11 Competition policy in the UK provides a pragmatic solution to the problems presented by monopolies.

12 The Coase conjecture argues that monopoly providers of durable goods are incapable of exploiting their monopoly power.

✓ Learning checklist

You should now be able to:

- Explain the difference between a principal and an agent
- Highlight the nature of the principal–agent problem
- Explain what is meant by the separation of ownership from control
- Provide a discussion of alternative theories of profit maximization
- Explain the concepts of positive and negative externalities, and provide examples
- Explain what is meant by the term 'market failure'
- Provide an explanation and evaluation of how taxes and subsidies can be used to correct market failures
- Discuss how competition legislation functions in the UK
- Explain how stock options align the interest of managers and shareholders
- Provide an economic evaluation of carbon pollution permits

Questions connect™

1 Is profit maximization a reasonable assumption of firm behaviour?

2 Why might managers prefer to maximize sales or firm size?

3 A firm with managers and shareholders has separation of ownership from control. Why is this a potential problem for shareholders?

4 List examples where managers have been found to indulge in the consumption of perquisites.

5 What is a principal and what is an agent? Provide examples.

6 Why might performance contracts better align the interests of principals and agents? Again, provide examples.

7 Is it always possible to use performance contracts to discipline agents?

8 How do the marginal social cost and the marginal social benefit differ from marginal cost and marginal benefit?

9 List four negative externalities and four positive externalities.

10 How might taxes and subsidies be used to combat externalities?

---

11 If the marginal social cost of production exceeds the marginal private cost, then the price of production to firms is too low. Is this true and what is the solution?

12 Will a management buyout of a company increase, or decrease, agency costs?

13 Draw a diagram of MSB and MPB of train travel in rural and semi-rural areas. Illustrate how a subsidy might improve usage of train travel.

---

14 Assess the benefits of paying managers with capital rather than with income.

15 Assess the likely factors that will limit the ability of carbon trading to reduce global emissions of carbon dioxide.

Exercises

1 True or false?
   (a) Worker absence is highest on Mondays. This is an example of agency costs.
   (b) Risk-averse workers need to be compensated with higher rates of contingent pay.
   (c) Managers are said to suffer from shareholders' free riding on their hard work.
   (d) The marginal social benefit of education is likely to exceed the marginal private benefit.
   (e) A negative externality can occur when the marginal private cost is less than the marginal social cost.
   (f) Subsidizing the marginal private cost of polluters will help to reduce the amount of pollution.

2 Figure 8.7 shows the market for a good in which there is a negative production externality such that marginal social cost (MSC) is above marginal private cost (MPC). MSB represents the marginal social benefit derived from consumption of the good.

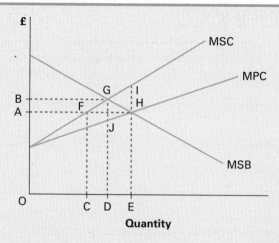

Figure 8.7 Market for a good in which there is a negative production externality

(a) If this market is unregulated, what quantity of this good will be produced?
(b) What is the socially efficient quantity?
(c) What is the amount of the dead-weight loss to society if the free market quantity is produced?
(d) What level of tax on the good would ensure that the socially efficient quantity is produced?
(e) Suggest an example of a situation in which this analysis might be relevant.

3 When considering these questions, refer to Box 8.4:
  (a) Assuming a higher demand for coal increases demand for permits, draw a demand and supply diagram which illustrates the increase in price of permits.
  (b) Draw a demand-and-supply diagram which illustrates the argument that the higher price of permits reflects a shortage of supply.
  (c) Evaluate how effective carbon trading will be in reducing carbon emissions.

Notes

1 R.M. Cyert and J.G. March, *A Behavioral Theory of the Firm*, 2nd edn. Englewood Cliffs, NJ: Prentice Hall, 1963.
2 H.A. Simon, *Models of Man: Social and Rational*. New York: Wiley, 1957.
3 Kuznets's original analysis showed an n-shaped relationship between income inequality and GDP per capita. In the early stages of economic development, income growth is seen to flow to those individuals who own capital (and so are already affluent). In later stages of development, the provision of education to everyone enables non-capital owners to share in economic growth and so income inequalities fall.

Section IV
Domestic macroeconomics

Section contents

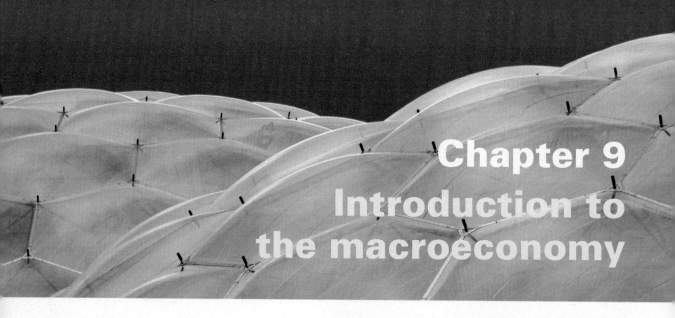

Chapter 9
Introduction to
the macroeconomy

Chapter contents

 ## Learning outcomes

By the end of this chapter you should understand:

Economic Theory

LO1 The key concepts of GDP, inflation, unemployment and the balance of payments

LO2 The concept of the business cycle

LO3 The circular flow of income

LO4 Leakages and injections

LO5 Aggregate demand and aggregate supply

LO6 How changes in aggregate demand and supply lead to changes in equilibrium GDP and inflation

Business Application

LO7 How to optimize investment decisions by understanding the business cycle

LO8 How to use income elasticities to profit during a recession

Macroeconomics at a glance

The issue

The business cycle, consisting of moderate economic activity, fast or booming economic growth and recessions, drives changes in the consumption levels of consumers and firms. Predicting the business cycle and positioning the firm for changes in economic activity are crucial for financial success.

The understanding

In simple terms, we can understand changes in macroeconomic activity as resulting from changes in overall demand and supply in the economy. In an economic boom, overall demand or supply in the economy can be rising, while in a recession, overall demand or supply can be falling. Therefore, predicting the business cycle rests on predicting economy-level demand and supply.

The usefulness

In order to survive, firms have to be financially successful in booms as well as recessions. By anticipating when the economy is likely to peak, or bottom out, firms can plan their investments in new products, new production facilities or new retail outlets. They can also change their product offerings to reflect different consumer preferences during booms and recessions.

9.1 Business problem: business cycles and economic uncertainty

Understanding the macroeconomic environment is of crucial importance to business. Just like private individuals, business also needs to take financial decisions. An individual might decide to buy a house, while a firm might decide to buy a new production facility.

Consider buying a house: two significant issues need addressing. How much should you offer for the house and how much can you afford to borrow?

When valuing the house you will need to consider whether the market price will fall in the near future, perhaps during a recession. Similarly, when thinking about how much you can borrow, you need to think about how much you will earn in the future. Will you be made unemployed during a recession? Furthermore, will an increase in interest rates make mortgage repayments impossible for you to meet?

A business deciding whether to spend many millions of pounds on a new production facility will go through the same process. What is the plant worth? How much can the business afford to borrow? Will a new facility be needed if consumer demand falls during a recession? Will changes in interest rates make the investment unprofitable?

Therefore, just like individuals, firms need to think very carefully when committing themselves to investment projects, because the **business cycle** will affect the success of the investment.

Box 9.1 highlights the collapse of the service and manufacturing sectors in many leading EU economies. Much of this collapse is a reflection of enormous cuts in consumption by households. These cuts are not only occurring in the home markets for these economies, but also across the world, leading to a marked reduction in exports. The factors driving the fall in consumption are related to levels of debt and fears of unemployment. However, these falls in

The background to the business investment decision is a recognition of the **business cycle**, where, over time, an economy can grow at a faster rate, a so-called 'economic boom', and then move into a period of slower growth, an 'economic recession.'

Box 9.1 Nowhere to hide

Adapted from an article in The Economist, *15 January 2009*

The service-led economies of America and Britain, with their underemployed estate agents, mortgage brokers and bankers, are shrinking. Yet business is no better even in countries with more manufacturing muscle than financial flab. This is an equal-opportunities crisis; the euro area's three biggest economies are in it just as deep. In Germany, industrial output fell at an annualized rate of 15.1 per cent in the three months to November. In France, it fell by 14.5 per cent and in Italy, by 19.5 per cent. Manufacturing has once again proved to be a poor refuge in uncertain times.

The crisis is global, and manufacturing is more sensitive to shifts in foreign demand than services are. America and Britain, the euro area's main export markets, are consuming less. Emerging markets are sucking in fewer capital goods from Europe. Around the world, people are buying fewer big-ticket items such as new cars and home appliances, and firms are delaying investment.

Spending at home is being squeezed too. The euro area's consumers have high savings and low debt by rich-world standards but are nervous all the same. Unemployment is rising – even in Germany and France, where the job markets have been most solid. Consumer confidence has sunk to a record low.

With consumers so skittish, service industries are not faring well either. In December, the purchasing-managers index for service industries fell to a new low. Julian Callow of Barclays Capital reckons euro-area GDP fell at an annualized rate of around 5 per cent in the fourth quarter, as bad as in America.

Consumers are pulling back fastest in Spain and Ireland. Unemployment in both countries is rocketing. Standard & Poor's downgraded Greece's credit rating from A to A–. It has also put Spain and Portugal under review, amid fears that high wage costs will prolong their recessions, as well as Ireland because of the collapse in its housing-related revenues and its state guarantees to banks.

Policy-makers are rattled. The European Central Bank cut interest rates by half a percentage point, to 2 per cent, having hinted at a pause only a month ago. Germany has beefed up its fiscal-stimulus package, as its exports sink. Too late it has realized that making things is not enough; you need to buy stuff, too.

© The Economist Newspaper Limited, London 2009

GDP, gross domestic product, is a measure of the total output produced by an economy in a given year.

Inflation is the rate of change in the average price level. Inflation of 2 per cent indicates that prices have risen by 2 per cent during the previous 12 months.

Unemployment is the number of individuals seeking work that do not currently have a job.

private sector spending might be balanced by increased government spending in Germany and cuts in interest rates making the debt repayments more affordable.

Clearly, an understanding of how the economy works and how it is likely to develop in the short, medium and long term is of crucial importance. Firms that make bad decisions will suffer financially. Firms that understand the macroeconomy and plan expansion and consolidation of the business at the right times are more likely to prosper.

In this chapter we will provide an overview of recent macroeconomic activity. In addition, we will provide a basic understanding of how the business cycle occurs, introducing the circular flow of income and then developing our application of the demand and supply framework used in the microeconomic section of this book. This will then provide the basis for an assessment of government economic policy in later chapters.

9.2 Macroeconomic issues

Key macroeconomic outputs

Macroeconomics studies the workings of the entire economy. In Figure 9.1, we have charted four key macroeconomic issues: **GDP**, **inflation**, **unemployment** and the **current account**.

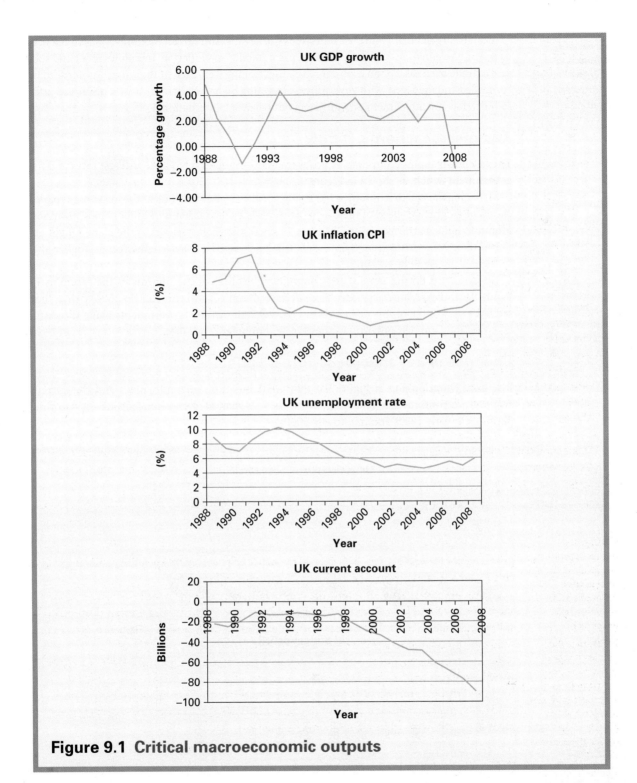

Figure 9.1 Critical macroeconomic outputs

The **current account** is the difference between exported and imported goods and services.

Interest rates are the price of money and are set by the central bank.

The **government deficit** is the difference between government spending and tax receipts. Just as students run up overdrafts, spending more than they earn, so too does the government.

It can be argued that Figure 9.1 represents the key measures of an economy: growth in GDP, or the improvement in economic activity; price stability via inflation; unemployment and success in trade overseas. For an economy to be functioning well, each of these outputs needs to be controlled and managed, with governments targeting higher economic growth, improved price stability, low unemployment and growing, but balanced, international trade.

Key macroeconomic inputs

The key policy inputs controlled by government or the central bank are **interest rates** and the **government deficit**, as shown in Figure 9.2.

Managing the macroeconomy is like flying a plane. A pilot will look at the instrument panel, check the height and speed of their own plane, perhaps take account of other planes' positions, monitor engine performance and fuel use. If any of the characteristics of the plane's flight are not to the pilot's satisfaction, then inputs will be changed – faster engine speeds, higher altitudes or a change in direction.

Governments do the same with economies. They look at the outputs of the economy in Figure 9.1 and examine the performance of the economy. If governments do not like what they see, they change the inputs described in Figure 9.2. Sometimes governments make successful take-offs and landings; other times they create monumental crashes.

Changes in key macroeconomic variables

It is clear from looking at Figure 9.1 that GDP, inflation, unemployment and the current account are continuously changing. To begin our analysis, let us concentrate on two time periods: the early 1990s and mid to late 2000s.

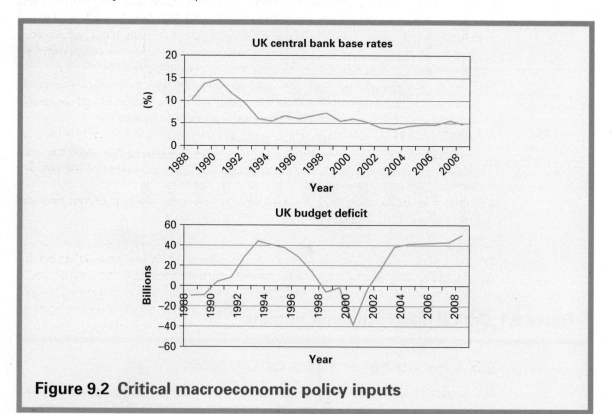

Figure 9.2 Critical macroeconomic policy inputs

In the early 1990s:

(a) inflation was high
(b) the government raised interest rates (see Figure 9.2) to try to control inflation
(c) high interest rates led to a reduction in economic activity, fewer goods and services were produced and GDP growth fell
(d) with lower production of goods and services, fewer workers were needed and unemployment increased
(e) a reduction in tax receipts, due to falling GDP, and an increase in social security payments to the unemployed led to an increase in the government deficit
(f) the high interest rate led to an increase in the value of the UK pound, exports became very expensive and the current account went into a large deficit, with imports exceeding exports.

In the mid to late 2000s:

(a) inflation was initially low and then began to rise
(b) interest rates were low because inflation was low and under control
(c) GDP growth was rising steadily in an environment of low inflation and interest rates, but then fell dramatically as the credit crunch began
(d) unemployment was low but began to rise as the economy slowed
(e) the government deficit was increasing as tax receipts fell and public spending soared
(f) the current account was still in deficit.

Observations and comments

1 The economic conditions of the mid 2000s, with rising GDP, low unemployment and inflation, were preferable to the conditions of 1990, with high inflation, falling GDP and rising unemployment. The mid 2000s were also preferable to the late 2000s and the recessionary impact of the credit crunch. Falling GDP, rising unemployment and an explosion in government borrowing are very unappealing macroeconomic features.

2 Given such problems, how does a government set and prioritize its objectives? Is low inflation more important than high GDP? Is unemployment acceptable? Should the government manage its deficit and should the current account be in surplus?

   In Chapter 10 we will return to this question and provide a review of how each key macroeconomic variable is measured, provide a review of the issues associated with each variable and, more important, the objectives generally set by government for each key macroeconomic variable.

3 Finally, why are GDP, inflation, unemployment, the current account, interest rates and government deficits all linked?

In the remainder of this chapter we will introduce the circular flow of income as a means of describing some of the linkages between the macroeconomic variables. We will then develop this analysis by adapting our supply and demand framework utilized in the microeconomic section of this book. By the end of this chapter you will be able to answer question 3. As we progress through Chapters 11, 12 and 13, you will develop your understanding of how governments can use different policies to manage the links within the macroeconomy.

9.3 The circular flow of income

In contrast to microeconomics, which examined product-specific markets such as those for pizzas or cars, macroeconomics focuses upon the workings of the whole economy. In order to

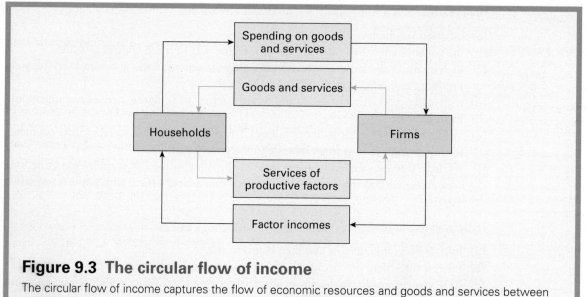

Figure 9.3 The circular flow of income

The circular flow of income captures the flow of economic resources and goods and services between households and firms. These flows of economic units are then mirrored by a flow of financial payments, which we refer to as the circular flow of income.

> The **circular flow of income** shows the flow of inputs, outputs and payments between households and firms within an economy.

begin our understanding of the macroeconomy, we will introduce the **circular flow of income** as a descriptive framework of macroeconomic activity. Figure 9.3 provides an illustration of the circular flow of income.

Within the framework of the circular flow of income, households are assumed to own the factors of production – land, labour, capital and enterprise. As producers of goods and services, firms need to use the factors of production owned by the households. Firms will clearly provide households with a financial reward for using the factors of production. In the case of labour, the financial reward is wages. Households will then use the money they have earned from firms to buy the finished goods and services, thus returning cash to the firms. A virtuous circle or, in our terminology, a circular flow of income is seen to exist.

The inner loop captures the flow of resources between the two sectors. For example, resources such as labour flow to firms from households, and then goods and services flow from firms back to households. The outer loop captures the corresponding financial flows between the two sectors. Firms pay households wages for supplying labour resources. In return, households use their income to purchase the goods and services sold by the firms.

The circular flow of income captures the essential essence of macroeconomic activity. The economy is seen as nothing more than a revolving flow of goods, production resources and financial payments. The faster the flow, the higher the level of economic output.

The level of income activity within an economy is measured as gross domestic product – GDP.

Leakages and injections

The economy described in Figure 9.3 contains only firms and households, which produce goods and spend income on goods and services. We can begin to broaden the circular flow to

A **leakage** from the circular flow is income not spent on goods and services within the economy. Leakages can be savings, taxation and imports.

An **injection** into the circular flow is additional spending on goods and services that does not come from the income earned by households in the inner loop. Injections can be investment, government spending and exports.

take account of saving by households, investment by firms, government spending and taxation, and international trade.

In order to account for these additional items we need to understand how **leakages** and **injections** fit into the circular flow of income.

Savings and investments

Rather than spend all income on goods and services, households could save a proportion of their income. Because income is being taken from the circular flow of income and saved, it represents a leakage. But an important question relates to where these savings go. If the money is placed on deposit at the bank, then the bank will try to lend the money for profit. Borrowers are likely to be firms seeking to invest in equipment, or needing to fund overdrafts. If firms invest in capital equipment, then they are buying goods and services from other firms. As a result, investment is spending in the economy that does not come from the income earned by households. As such, investments represent an injection of financial resource and spending, by firms, into the circular flow. In equilibrium, savings will equal investments. This is because banks will set an interest rate where the supply of funds from savers equals the demand for funds by investing firms.

Taxes and government spending

Government taxes the earnings of individuals and companies. Tax payments represent a leakage from the circular flow of income as they reduce the ability of households to spend on goods and services. However, the government also undertakes a number of activities that inject financial resources back into the economy. Governments buy hospitals and schools. They employ nurses and teachers. They also pay social benefits to the needy. All of which are injections.

Exports and imports

Finally, some consumption by households will be on goods made in other economies. If you buy a German car, then this represents a leakage from the UK circular flow of income, as it is income spent in another economy. However, an injection will occur if a German spends money on a British car, as this represents an export.

The various leakages and injections are illustrated in Figure 9.4, which simply extends the circular flow of income. On the left of Figure 9.4, savings, taxation and imports leak from the income households could spend on consumption. On the right of Figure 9.4, investments, government spending and exports inject spending into the circular flow of income.

Total expenditure

Total expenditure is equal to consumption, plus investment, plus government spending, plus net exports (exports minus imports).

Total expenditure is simply all the separate sources of spending within the economy. That is, consumption by households, investment by firms and public spending by government. Net exports adjust for expenditure on exports and imports by consumers, firms and government. Being able to identify the individual components of total expenditure is particularly important because it provides an understanding of which expenditures lead to an increase (or decrease) in economic activity. If consumption, investment, government spending or net exports increase, then total expenditure increases, and potentially the flow of goods and services in the inner loop also increases to match the increased demand in the economy. Similarly, if total expenditure is reduced, the flow of goods and services in the inner loop falls due to decreasing demand. We will now use these ideas to develop our understanding of changes in economic activity over time and the idea of a macroeconomic equilibrium.

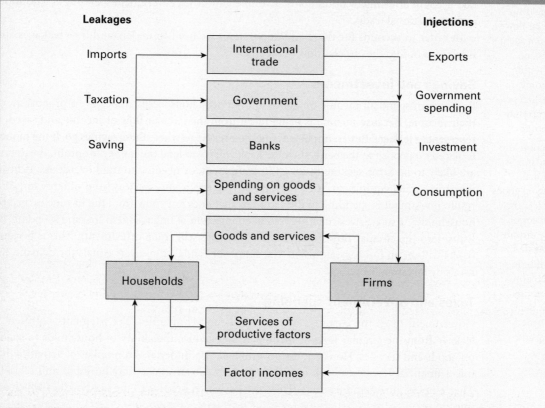

Leakages

Injections

Figure 9.4 Circular flow of income with leakages and injections

Leakages from the circular flow of income take the form of savings, taxes and imports. These are financial flows which do not head straight back into household consumption. Injections into the circular flow of income include investment spending, government spending and exports. These expenditures add to household consumption expenditure in the economy.

9.4 National income determination and business cycles

When examining individual markets in the microeconomic section of this book, we focused on the demand and supply curve for the product. Since in macroeconomics we are examining the whole economy, we need a demand and supply curve for the whole economy.

Total expenditure representing consumption, plus investment, plus government spending, plus net exports is in fact **aggregate demand**. In microeconomics, we argued that the demand for a product is negatively related to its price. As prices increase, less is demanded. We could also draw an aggregate demand curve showing a negative relationship between the average level of prices in the economy and the level of aggregate demand. However, we are going to make a subtle, but important change. We will analyse the relationship between aggregate demand and the *change* in the **price level**.

Where aggregate demand is calculated by adding up all demand changes in the economy, the price level is calculated by adding all price changes together. We will see in more detail in

> **Aggregate demand** is the total demand in an economy.

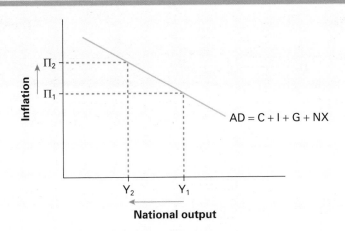

Figure 9.5 Aggregate demand and inflation

AD is aggregate demand and represents total demand in the economy. AD = C + I + G + NX, where C = consumption, I = investment, G = government spending and NX = net exports. If inflation increases from Π_1 to Π_2, then the central bank will increase interest rates in order to stem the rise in prices. The higher interest rates will lead to a reduction in aggregate demand from Y_1 to Y_2.

> **The price level is** the average change in the price of goods and services in an economy. The *change* in the average price level is a measure of inflation, where 5 per cent inflation means that prices on average have changed, i.e. increased, by 5 per cent.

Chapter 10 how governments measure overall price changes. But, in simple terms, a basket of commonly purchased goods and services is defined. In the UK, this basket exceeds 600 items and includes the cost of food, fuel and clothing items. Price changes for each item are collated on a monthly basis and from this data changes in the average price level are calculated.

The benefit of looking at the relationship between aggregate demand and inflation is that control of inflation has become a key aspect of modern macroeconomic policy. Therefore, by using inflation, rather than the level of prices, we are bringing inflation to the centre of our economic models.

Aggregate demand and inflation

Fortunately, the relationship between aggregate demand and inflation is also negative. If we assume that the central bank is tasked with keeping inflation at 2.5 per cent, as it is in the UK, then we know from experience that the higher the rate of inflation, the higher the central bank has to raise interest rates in order to stem inflation (and vice versa, if inflation falls, then the central bank has to cut interest rates in order to avoid deflation). As interest rates increase, consumers and firms are less willing to borrow in order to fund the purchase of goods and services. Therefore, aggregate demand falls. These points are picked up in Figure 9.5.

From the circular flow of income we have argued that aggregate demand is composed of consumption, investment, government spending and net exports. An increase in any of these types of expenditure will lead to an increase in aggregate demand. In Figure 9.6, we illustrate this idea by assuming that government spending has increased from G_1 to G_2. We could equally have assumed that consumption, investment or net exports had increased. The consequences of the increase in government spending are for the aggregate demand curve to shift from AD_1 to AD_2, with higher levels of economic output being demanded at all inflation levels.

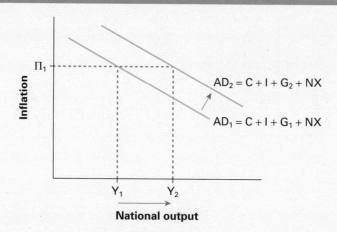

Figure 9.6 Aggregate demand, inflation and increased government spending

Aggregate demand will shift to the right if C, I, G or NX increases. As an example, we have simply assumed that government spending has increased from G_1 to G_2. Aggregate demand, therefore, shifts from AD_1 to AD_2. As this happens, the willingness to demand output at an inflation rate of Π_1 rises from Y_1 to Y_2. In Figure 9.10 (p. 215), we show how changes in aggregate demand lead to changes in equilibrium GDP and inflation.

Aggregate supply and inflation

> **Aggregate supply** is the total supply in an economy.

In Chapters 3 and 5 we saw that, as profit-maximizers, firms will supply output if the market price is equal to, or greater than, marginal cost. Therefore, an increase in the price will bring about an increase in supply from an individual firm. But, at the macro level, how will **aggregate supply** react to a change in inflation?

We need to make a distinction between **real** and **nominal** values.

> **Nominal** prices and wages are not adjusted for inflation. **Real** prices and wages are adjusted for inflation.

Assume you are earning £100 a day and inflation is 2 per cent per year. At the end of one year your *nominal* wage will still be £100 per day. But your *real* wage will only be £98. The real wage is the nominal wage adjusted for the rate of inflation. You are receiving £100 in cash, but due to inflation it can now only buy 98 per cent of what you could buy last year with £100. In order to keep your real wage constant, you need to ask for a 2 per cent pay rise because you now need £102 to buy what £100 could purchase last year.

Aggregate supply and full wage adjustment to inflation

The important issue for aggregate supply is whether or not a bout of inflation leads to nominal or real changes in relative wages and prices. For example, if inflation leads to a 3 per cent increase in prices for final products and workers also ask for a 3 per cent pay rise to compensate for the rise in prices, then the real wage and the real price of goods and services have stayed the same. Because real prices and wages are the same, the real costs and revenues faced by the firm have not changed. Aggregate supply will therefore remain unchanged as firms are faced with no reason to increase (or decrease) their willingness to supply. We can, therefore, argue that, when wages fully adjust to inflation, aggregate supply remains constant. This is illustrated in Figure 9.7 with a vertical aggregate supply curve. As inflation increases, supply stays constant.

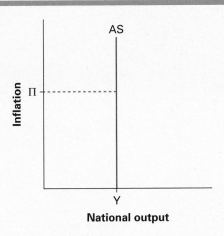

Figure 9.7 Aggregate supply and full wage adjustment to inflation

AS is aggregate supply and represents total supply in the economy. If prices and wages adjust to keep real prices and wages constant, then aggregate supply will remain constant.

Aggregate supply without full wage adjustment to price increases

We can now consider what happens if prices and wages do not adjust to keep real values constant. Assume again the price of goods and services is increasing by 3 per cent, but workers only manage to negotiate a 2 per cent increase in wages. The real cost of employing labour has now reduced by 1 per cent. Firms are experiencing a reduction in their real costs of production. If firms are profit-maximizers, then, as we saw in Chapter 5, a reduction in marginal cost leads to an increase in the profit-maximizing output of the firm (see Section 5.2). Therefore, with a reduction in the real wage rate, firms will now be willing to increase supply and overall aggregate supply increases as inflation increases. Therefore, when wages do not fully adjust to price changes, a positive relationship between inflation and aggregate supply can exist. This is shown in Figure 9.8.

At this stage, we can perhaps go one step further and suggest that Figure 9.8 represents the short run, while Figure 9.7 represents the long run. In the short run, workers may not accurately guess the inflation rate. In our example, workers agreed a 2 per cent rise in wages, when inflation turned out to be 3 per cent. In the long run, workers will try to rectify this reduction in real wages and so, over time, real wages will fully adjust to the inflation rate and real wages will remain constant. Therefore, in the short run firms might benefit from a reduction in the real wage and boost supply. But in the long run, real wages will remain constant and so will aggregate supply.

Macroeconomic equilibrium

In Figure 9.9, we have brought aggregate demand and supply together for the whole economy. We have assumed that wages do not fully adjust to inflation and, therefore, aggregate supply is not perfectly inelastic.

Equilibrium for the entire economy occurs where aggregate demand and aggregate supply intersect. From this we can then see that the economy will produce an output of Y in Figure 9.9; and the inflation rate will be Π.

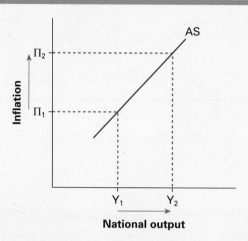

Figure 9.8 Aggregate supply without full wage adjustment to price increases

If prices increase faster than wages, then the real wage decreases. This represents a real cost reduction for firms. If firms are profit maximizers, then a reduction in the real marginal cost will motivate firms to increase output. Therefore, a reduction in the real wage leads to an increase in aggregate supply.

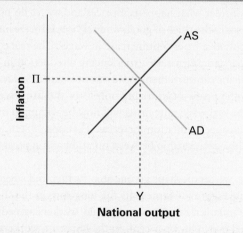

Figure 9.9 Macroeconomic equilibrium

In equilibrium, the inflation rate Π equates aggregate demand and aggregate supply at the national output level of Y.

Just as we did with product markets, we can also begin to change aggregate demand and supply and assess what happens to the equilibrium output and inflation. The following points are picked up in Figure 9.10. In the top left, if aggregate demand increases, then national output increases, or the amount of goods and services traded in the economy increases. But, in addition, inflation also increases. In the bottom left, if aggregate demand decreases, then national output reduces and inflation falls. In the top right, we can examine changes in aggregate supply. An increase in aggregate supply will lead to an increase in economic activity, but a reduction in the inflation rate. The bottom right of Figure 9.10 shows that a reduction in

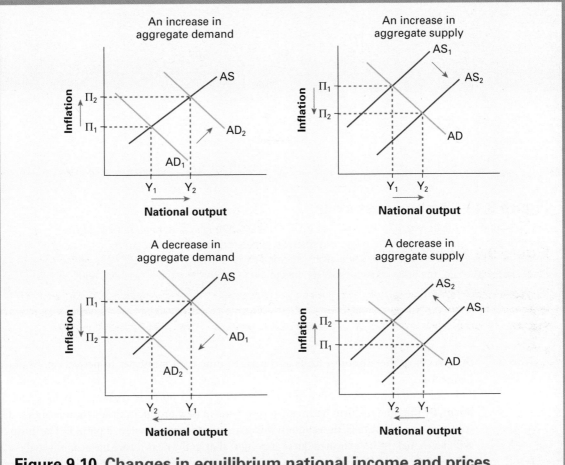

Figure 9.10 Changes in equilibrium national income and prices

Top left: an increase in aggregate demand leads to an inflationary **boom**. Bottom left: a reduction in aggregate demand leads to a deflationary **recession**. Top right: an increase in supply leads to a **deflationary** boom. Bottom right: a decrease in supply leads to an **inflationary** recession.

An increase in national output is a sign of economic growth or economic **boom**. A reduction in national output is known as a **recession**.

A decrease in the price level is **deflation**. **Inflation** is a rise in the price level.

aggregate supply will lead to a reduction in national output and an increase in the rate of inflation.

We can now say that an increase in aggregate demand leads to an **inflationary boom**. But a reduction in aggregate demand leads to a **deflationary recession**. An increase in aggregate supply leads to a deflationary boom, while a reduction in aggregate supply leads to an inflationary recession.

In Section 9.5 we use these ideas to show how a firm might try to predict the business cycle.

9.5 Business application: predicting the business cycle

While the business cycle is outside the control of individual firms, strategies for dealing with the cycle are not. An important step for firms is to predict the business cycle and this is no easy task. Even skilled economists sitting on central banks' monetary panels disagree about how fast an economy is growing and how high interest rates should be set. Alongside predicting

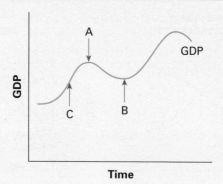

Figure 9.11 The business cycle

As the economy moves through the business cycle firms need to plan and manage their capital investments. There is little point in beginning to invest when the economy is booming, as at point A, because by the time the extra capital is in place, the economy will have moved on to B, a period of recession. Therefore, the smart businessperson has to judge when the economy is at C and likely to move to A in the future.

the growth of the economy, firms also need to time their strategies to perfection. Examine Figure 9.11.

There is no commercial value in being told that the economy is at point A, in an economic boom. By the time the firm has made investments in new products, production facilities, distribution or retail outlets, the economy will have moved into recession at point B. The business skill lies in making an educated guess at point C that in the near future the economy will be at point A. Then investments can be put in place to exploit the economic boom in a more timely fashion. Indeed, when the economy is at point A, the firm should begin to plan for the recession at point B.

In Box 9.2, the Bank of England agents around the country have been talking to businesses and asking them to score sales, investments and exports. From this survey data a summary of the conditions faced by businesses today, as well as the expected nature of conditions in the future, can be obtained.

 Box 9.2 Business outlook: demand

Adapted from the Agents' Summary of Business Conditions, Bank of England, January 2009

Consumption

For most contacts, retail sales values were down relative to the same period a year earlier (Chart 1). Sales *values* had continued to fall as many retailers had offered deep discounts in the run-up to Christmas. Demand had continued to shrink for a wide range of consumer services. Most notably, there were further reports of reduced demand for financial services and lower sales at restaurants and pubs. Consumer

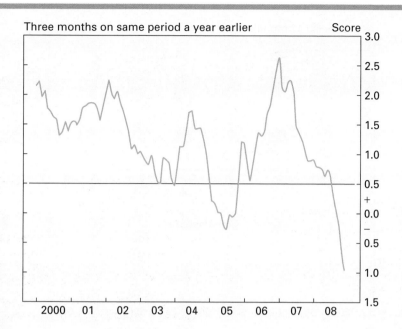

Chart 1 Retail sales values

demand for foreign travel had weakened. And despite sharp discounting, new and used car sales remained particularly low.

Looking forward, many contacts expected consumer demand to weaken further during 2009 Q1, with some anticipating a pick-up in precautionary savings in the face of mounting concerns over job security.

Business investment

Throughout 2008 Q4, there had been widespread reports of substantial reductions in investment intentions, with the Agents' scores reduced significantly (Chart 2). Cutbacks and deferrals in capital expenditure plans had become the norm for contacts visited in recent months.

Contacts' expectations of future demand had weakened materially, and the outlook for demand was cited frequently as a prime driver of reductions in investment plans. Concerns over availability of working capital and external project finance remained important factors for many firms. There were also reports that some commercial property investments had been shelved in anticipation of future falls in property values.

Overseas trade

The Agents' score for export volume of goods was reduced sharply again, following material reductions in the score earlier in the quarter (Chart 3). Indeed, the fall in scores through 2008 Q4 was, by some margin, the largest quarterly reduction since the Agents started scoring in 1997. While export demand was still seen to be stronger than domestic demand for manufactured goods, more industries were now experiencing shrinkage in exports.

Many contacts reported that the slowdown in world growth had, so far, more than offset any improvements in competitiveness arising from sterling's depreciation. In part, however, this was because some exporters had taken advantage of the depreciation to improve margins – by raising their sterling export prices.

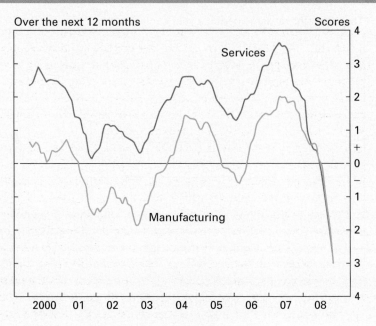

Chart 2 Business investment intentions

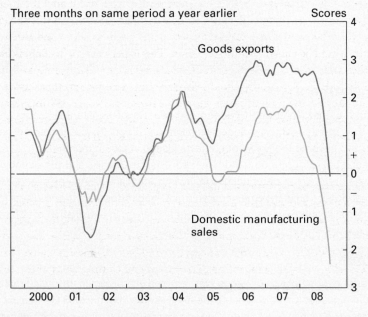

Chart 3 Manufacturing output

But how do you spot an economic boom or recession before they happen? What factors enable businesses to respond by drawing meaningful and reasonably accurate conclusions about the future state of the economy? We focus on two insights from our understanding of the economy and business experience.

Economic insights

The aggregate demand and supply framework suggests that, in order to understand the business cycle, it is useful to be able to address how much demand and supply are changing in the economy. For example, in order to understand aggregate demand it is essential to have a grasp of how fast consumption, investment, government spending and net exports are changing. In particular, it is important to know if any of these expenditures are increasing or decreasing. If aggregate demand is increasing, the economy is likely to grow; however, if aggregate demand is falling, the economy is likely to move towards recession.

Aggregate supply is, in part, influenced by the costs faced by firms. When important input prices such as oil increase, firms will be less willing to supply and aggregate supply will fall. In contrast, when new technologies become available, which lower the costs of supplying goods and services, firms will be more willing to supply and aggregate supply will increase. The Internet was seen as a technology capable of improving firms' costs and helping to develop the supply of goods and services. When aggregate supply is rising, the economy is likely to grow. However, when aggregate supply is falling, the economy is likely to move into recession.

Government agencies, statistical offices, central banks and trade bodies all provide commentary and opinion on the likely development of the economy over the short and medium term. In the main these reports are based on projections for aggregate demand and supply. However, you do not have to be a skilled economist to understand the development of the economy.

Business experience

Experience probably counts for a great deal. If you know how the market works and have experience of working in the market for a number of years, you will have seen it move through its cycles. You will have a feeling for when it is going to boom and also a feeling for when it is time to cut back and await the recession. This experience, or 'feeling', is likely to come from an assessment of the more measurable lead indicators. Markets do not generally switch from boom to bust. Rather, they gradually grow into a boom and then slowly decline into a recession. During the growth phase enquiries from customers will increase; and then these will begin to materialize into orders and sales. You may also find that customers switch to you not because of price, but because you can promise to deliver on time. This would indicate that rivals are also becoming busy. So, as sales and profit margins begin to improve, plans for expansion should follow.

Once expansion across the industry begins, you need to have an eye on when the market begins to soften, with falling prices and excess supply of goods and services. If demand in the economy either shrinks or grows at a slower rate than supply, then prices will fall and margins will shrink. So, if you think the expansion by your own company, and also that of your rivals, is too great for the likely growth rate in demand by consumers, then you need to think about re-addressing your growth options for the future. Cutting costs and reining in excess output become key in order to compete.

9.6 Business application: profiting from recession

Economies do not stop during recessions. In fact, when compared with previous years, GDP during a recession often falls by only 1–2 per cent. So, even during a recession there are still many goods and services being supplied and demanded. However, many firms do struggle during recessions and eventually either cut back on workers and generate unemployment, or close down altogether, with even greater consequences for unemployment.

The point that needs to be addressed is that, while the economy may only shrink by 1–2 per cent, this is only the net effect. For example, demand for some goods and services may have reduced by 20 per cent, while for others it could have increased by 18–19 per cent. But how can demand and profits be stabilized in a recession? To answer this question we need to recall various parts of the microeconomic components of this book.

Income elasticities

Chapter 2 covered the concept of income elasticity. For normal goods, when incomes rise, demand also rises, but when incomes fall, demand also falls. In the case of inferior goods, however, when income rises, demand falls. Similarly, when income falls, demand increases. So, during a recession demand for normal goods decreases, but demand for inferior goods increases. Therefore, the way to profit in a recession is to have product lines that are income inferior, products that customers like to buy more of when they have reduced incomes or are trying to be careful when spending money.

Consider Table 9.1, which lists the fall in sales for a number of well-known car makers. The credit crunch commenced in 2008 and resulted in a huge reduction in car sales. This fall in sales reflected both a loss of confidence among consumers and an inability to raise credit to fund a car purchase. Looking at Table 9.1, it is clear that there was an enormous difference in how the recession impacted different manufacturers. In the main, the high end luxury car makers were among the biggest fallers. This suggests that these producers are highly sensitive to changes in income.

Car makers servicing the middle to low end of the markets experienced sales cuts. But these were small in comparison to the cuts seen by high end manufacturers. Admittedly, the likes of BMW and Mercedes-Benz appear in the list of companies that experienced small falls in sales. This may be explained not by income, but by the ability of their cars to hold value. Such a characteristic is likely to be of importance to a customer buying any high ticket item in a deflationary market.

Pricing

Having products at the right price points in the market and even the ability to lower prices to gain market share are also useful tactics in a recession. Some of the big winners during the

Table 9.1 Fall in car sales during 2008 in the UK

Big fallers	%	Small fallers	%
Chrysler	−38.16	Toyota	−10.78
Jeep	−33.93	Vauxhall	−9.78
Lexus	−33.05	Volkswagen	−9.05
Porsche	−30.65	Mercedes-Benz	−9.04
Land Rover	−30.04	Ford	−7.58
		Skoda	−7.03
		BMW	−6.94
		Fiat	−6.87

Source: Society of Motor Manufacturers and Traders, www.smmt.co.uk

recession have been related to the food sector. Manufacturers of value lines for the super-markets have seen enormous growth as customers look to trade down and save on grocery expenditure.

Price discounts are also an obvious promotional tool and, if customers are price elastic, then additional revenue may be gained. However, the risk of a price war is also high and this may result in all competitors charging less and no additional customers. A means of avoiding this problem is for a company to have a side range of products that can be endlessly recycled through promotional offers, such as in ready meals, soft drinks and beer. Note how the same brands keep appearing as multi-pack offers. The niche, high quality items in these product categories cannot be promoted using special offers without risk of associating the brand with low value, low price alternatives. Reverting to high prices after the recession will then be difficult. The ultimate tactic is to combat falling sales volumes with rising prices. But, as Box 9.3 argues, this can also be difficult.

 Box 9.3 Charging ahead

Adapted from an article in The Economist, *21 August 2008*

The temptation in a downturn is to let prices slide to protect or increase market share. (eBay, an online auction site, said it would reduce the fees it charges sellers who post goods for sale on its site at a fixed price.) However, this approach can backfire if it triggers a price-cutting spiral. Moreover, managers often overestimate the extra sales that lower prices generate, so companies may be left worse off than before the cuts.

Bosses may see such price increases as a quick fix. But deciding what to charge requires careful analysis of such things as break-even points and price elasticities of demand – how buying habits change after a price rise or a discount. Real-world testing can help. McDonald's is charging more for its popular double cheeseburger (which normally costs $1) in some American restaurants than others, to gauge customers' tolerance of a permanent price rise that would help offset the higher cost of ingredients. It is also experimenting with holding the price but reducing the amount of cheese or beef in the burger.

When raising prices, firms also need to consider how rivals will react. It helps when all companies in an industry are desperate for revenue. Airlines, for instance, have followed one another by adding surcharges for fuel, baggage and other services. It also helps when a price increase is triggered by a strong industry leader. Nitto Denko, a Japanese firm that makes optical film for liquid-crystal displays, has helped defuse a price war by publicly signalling that it will focus on profitability rather than building market share.

Of course, deciding on a price increase is one thing; ensuring it happens is another. Efforts to raise sticker prices sometimes come unstuck because salespeople give discounts to favourite customers or managers make 'temporary' exceptions to the new rule. 'Once you start with the first discount, the second one is just round the corner,' warns Stephan Butscher of Simon-Kucher & Partners, a consultancy that specializes in pricing.

© The Economist Newspaper Limited, London 2009

Managing costs

A lack of fixed costs is essential for profitable performances during a recession. From Chapter 3, we know that high fixed costs require high volumes. Unfortunately, high volumes are difficult to find during a recession. It is therefore essential to have a cost base which is driven by variable costs, not fixed ones. Luxury hotels, with many frills, including swimming pools, bars, restaurants, tennis courts and concierge services, often located in expensive city centres, are nothing but a huge collection of fixed costs. Not surprisingly, luxury hotel chains do not perform well during recessions and frequent customers, such as business travellers, can often negotiate good discounts from such hotels during a lean economic period.

Retailers also have high fixed costs in terms of rent for their retail space. This has led to many such companies facing financial collapse. The other fixed cost which many companies face is debt. Financial repayments have to be kept up in good times and bad. If the company faces a fall in sales, then cash flows into the company dry up. But this does not alter its fixed cost payments, including debt commitments.

Diversification

Diversification through a portfolio of business activites was shown in Chapter 7 to reduce business risk. Car manufacturers such as Ford are renowned for this. In addition to the Ford cars, they also make Jaguars, Land Rovers, Mazdas and Aston Martins. A more extreme example is the fact that Fiat Unos are made by the same firm that makes Ferraris! The reason is that, throughout the business cycle, demand for one product in the portfolio will rise. Ferraris and Jaguars sell well during a boom, Fiat Unos and Fords sell better during a recession. Supermarkets are even more skilled at mixing the portfolio. Stores in the affluent districts of Chelsea and Mayfair will stock different products from stores located in inner-city Manchester. But during a recession and boom, each store will fine-tune its product offering. In a boom, the Manchester store will allocate more shelf space to branded items and reduce its offering of value own-label products. Then, during a recession, the store will switch back to higher value items.

Clearly, firms operating within a changing macroeconomic environment need to be able to prosper during both boom and recession. Success is critically dependent upon being able to sell products during booms and recessions and being able to read the business cycle. Then must plan ahead and be better placed than rivals to exploit the ever-changing environment.

 Summary

1 Macroeconomics is the study of economic activity at the aggregate level, examining the entire economy rather than just single markets.

2 The circular flow of income is a representation of how an economy works. Households own all factors of production and firms hire these factors to produce goods and services. Firms pay households for using input resources and households in return purchase the goods and services.

3 The level of demand for goods and services is conditioned by the level of injections into and leakages from the circular flow of income. Savings, taxation and imports all represent leakages, while investment, government spending and exports all represent injections.

4 The whole economy can be viewed as a collection of the many small markets that go into making an economy. Therefore, rather than thinking about demand we now talk about aggregate demand and similarly aggregate supply as opposed to simply supply.

5 Aggregate demand has a negative relationship with inflation. As inflation increases, the central bank increases interest rates, resulting in a reduction in aggregate demand.

6 Aggregate supply will have a positive relationship with inflation, if real wages do not adjust fully to rises in prices. However, if real wages adjust fully to inflation, then aggregate supply will be perfectly inelastic.

7   Gross domestic product, or GDP, is a measure of economic output of an economy.

8   Inflation is a measure of price changes. The quicker prices rise, the higher the rate of inflation.

9   In part, the business cycle can be explained by changes in aggregate demand and aggregate supply. As demand increases, the economy grows and inflation increases. As demand falls, the economy slows and inflation falls. If, in contrast, supply increases, then the economy grows and inflation decreases. However, if supply shrinks, the economy shrinks and inflation increases.

10 The business cycle is a description of the tendency for economies to move from economic boom into economic recession and vice versa.

11 The rate of inflation tends to change throughout the business cycle, but this is a reflection of changes in aggregate demand and supply. An increase in aggregate demand will tend to generate an inflationary boom, while an increase in aggregate supply will tend to generate a deflationary boom. Conversely, a reduction in aggregate demand will generate a deflationary recession, while a reduction in aggregate supply will generate an inflationary recession.

12 Predicting the business cycle is not an exact science. Economists and businesspeople will only ever know when an economy has hit its peak after the event, perhaps up to 12 months after. And the same is true of recessions. It is, therefore, crucial to plan and implement investment decisions in advance of any detrimental macroeconomic changes. How to achieve this is challenging. Some people use their experience – how did the economy behave in the past? What can I learn from other economies? What are the experts saying? And do I believe them?

13 An interesting question, or fallacy, surrounds the fact that GDP only falls by a small amount (1–2%) during a recession and yet many businesses suffer severe financial hardship. Why is that? In part, recessions have different impacts in different product markets. Falling consumer incomes will cut demand for normal goods, but raise demand for inferior goods. This provides an opportunity to create a mixed portfolio of products for the business cycle. Supermarkets do this through greater use of own-brand items during recessions, while many car manufacturers produce both high and low value cars.

 Learning checklist

You should now be able to:

◆ Discuss the key topics of GDP, inflation, unemployment and the balance of payments

◆ Explain what is meant by the term business cycle

◆ Provide a discussion of the circular flow of income, highlighting the various relationships between firms, households, government and international economies

◆ Explain the difference between leakages and injections

◆ Explain the determinants of aggregate demand

◆ Discuss whether or not aggregate supply will be perfectly inelastic

◆ Explain how changes in aggregate demand and supply can explain the business cycle

Questions connect

1 What are the key macroeconomic variables for an economy? How have these variables changed in your economy over the last five years?

2 What key macroeconomic variables can a government or central bank control? How have these changed for your economy during the last five years?

3 Draw a circular flow of income for an economy that has a government sector and is open to international trade.

4 Identify the leakages, injections and components of aggregate expenditure in your circular flow diagram.

5 Explain why there is a negative relationship between inflation and aggregate demand.

6 Consumer and business confidence are increasing. Illustrate the likely consequence of these changes on aggregate demand.

7 Explain why in the long run aggregate supply is perfectly inelastic, but in the short run is elastic.

8 Would an increase in aggregate demand generate an inflationary or deflationary boom? Would a reduction in aggregate supply generate an inflationary recession or a deflationary boom?

9 Explain what is meant by the term a lead indicator.

10 How does an understanding of income elasticity enable a firm to manage the consequences of the business cycle?

11 In the long run can GDP grow through an increase in aggregate demand, aggregate supply or both?

12 In an economy, if aggregate demand increases while aggregate supply stays constant, what happens to GDP and inflation?

13 An economy benefits from an influx of additional workers. Using the circular flow of income, assess how these additional workers will impact upon the output of the economy. How will the extra workers influence aggregate supply?

14 Identify the key business variables a company could monitor in order to understand whether the economy is heading towards a boom or a recession.

15 The economy has been growing for 12 months and sales are increasing, but margins, the difference between revenues and costs, are beginning to fall. Is now a good time to invest in additional production capacity?

Exercises

1 True or false?
   (a) Savings provide an injection into the circular flow of income.
   (b) Total expenditure in an economy is equal to consumption, investment, government spending and exports.
   (c) Under complete wage adjustment aggregate supply is unresponsive to a change in inflation.
   (d) Higher inflation will lead central banks to increase interest rates. This explains a negative relationship between inflation and aggregate demand.
   (e) The main injections into the circular flow of income are investment and government spending.
   (f) Diversifying macroeconomic risk through normal and inferior products is beneficial for shareholders.

2 Table 9.2 presents consumer price indices (CPIs) for the UK, USA and Spain.
   (a) Calculate the annual inflation rate for each of the countries.
   (b) Plot your three inflation series on a diagram against time.
   (c) By what percentage did prices increase in each country over the whole period – i.e. between 1999 and 2009?
   (d) Which economy has experienced most stability of the inflation rate?
   (e) Which economy saw the greatest deceleration in the rate of inflation between 2001 and 2004?

Table 9.2 Consumer prices

	United Kingdom		USA		Spain	
	Consumer price index	Inflation rate (%)	Consumer price index	Inflation rate (%)	Consumer price index	Inflation rate (%)
1999	71.7		77.6		68.2	
2000	77.3		81.4		72.9	
2001	84.6		85.7		77.7	
2002	89.6		89.4		82.4	
2003	92.9		92.1		87.2	
2004	94.4		94.8		91.2	
2005	96.7		97.3		95.5	
2006	100.0		100.0		100.0	
2007	102.4		102.9		103.6	
2008	105.7		105.3		105.6	
2009	109.3		107.0		107.5	

Table 9.3 presents some data relating to national output (real GDP) of the same three economies over a similar period, expressed as index numbers.
(f) Calculate the annual growth rate for each of the countries.
(g) Plot your three growth series on a diagram against time.
(h) By what percentage did output increase in each country over the whole period?
(i)   To what extent did growth follow a similar pattern over time in these three countries?

Table 9.3 National production

	United Kingdom		USA		Spain	
	GDP index	Growth rate (%)	GDP index	Growth rate (%)	GDP index	Growth rate (%)
1999	91.4		86.7		86.0	
2000	93.4		89.7		90.2	
2001	93.7		90.8		93.6	
2002	91.9		89.9		95.7	
2003	91.4		92.3		96.3	
2004	93.3		94.5		95.2	
2005	97.3		97.8		97.4	
2006	100.0		100.0		100.0	
2007	102.6		103.4		102.4	
2008	106.2		107.5		106.0	
2009	108.5		111.7		110.1	

3 Refer to Box 9.1 when considering the following questions:
   (a) Identify the reasons behind the collapse of the service and manufacturing sectors.
   (b) Which technical terms would economists use to describe the increase in saving and reduction in consumption?
   (c) Use an aggregate demand and supply diagram to illustrate the change in GDP.
   (d) On the same diagram used for (c), show how an increase in government spending will help to boost economic growth.

Chapter 10
Measuring macroeconomic variables and policy issues

Chapter contents

 ## Learning outcomes

By the end of this chapter you should understand:

Economic Theory

LO1 How to measure GDP using the income, expenditure and value-added approaches

LO2 How to measure inflation using index numbers

LO3 The potential causes of inflation

LO4 The costs of inflation

LO5 The reasons behind inflation targeting

LO6 Frictional, structural, demand deficient and classical as various types of unemployment

LO7 The Phillips curve

LO8 Balance of payments problems

Business Application

LO9 The importance of manufacturing competitiveness to the economy; and equally the importance of economic policy for manufacturing competitiveness

LO10 How might inflation targeting impact the business environment?

Measurement and policy issues at a glance

The issue

How are various macroeconomic variables measured? In addition, why is managing GDP, inflation, unemployment and the balance of payments important? What are the issues and trade-offs associated with targeting each aspect of the macroeconomy?

The understanding

Higher and stable GDP is associated with economic prosperity and enhanced economic growth. Higher GDP may lead to higher incomes for consumers and could facilitate investment by firms and government. High inflation may lead to economic instability and increased costs for the economy. Lower inflation might facilitate economic stability and investment planning by firms, leading to higher rates of economic growth. Unemployment reflects an underutilized resource, but labour market concerns are now switching towards productivity. The balance of payments reflects a country's trading position with the rest of the world. Just like individuals, an economy has to be concerned about running a long-term deficit. It is important to recognize that a government may not be capable of targeting all macroeconomic variables; for example, higher GDP may lead to higher inflation.

The usefulness

As businesses operate within macroeconomic environments it is essential that businesspeople are capable of deciphering the policy messages and changes instituted by governments. How will decisions regarding the management of inflation and long-term growth impact upon the economy and the firm?

10.1 Business problem: what are the macroeconomic policy issues?

Macroeconomic risks are wide ranging and vary across different parts of the global economy. Since companies operate within macroeconomic environments, managers need to be capable of understanding the key macroeconomic policy issues pursued by governments. Box 10.1 reports the views of the head of the UK central bank. During this speech, the head of the bank is trying to provide a review of the economy, highlighting the important issues and problems underlying the steps taken so far. The bank is seeking to provide stability and leadership. But for it to be successful in providing direction to the economy, it is necessary for those listening, especially in business, to understand the issues being raised and addressed by the central bank.

Read Box 10.1 and you will unfortunately recognize that these macroeconomic issues are important but difficult to grasp. The purpose of the chapter is to begin to provide you with an understanding of the important macroeconomic issues. We will then develop your understanding of policy responses in later chapters.

Interest rate policy and the Bank of England

The Bank of England has the task of keeping inflation in the UK at 2 per cent on average. In pursuing this target, the Bank of England is empowered to alter interest rates. What does this mean for business?

1 If firms borrow money to invest in capital, will interest rates be higher or lower when controlled by the central bank?
2 Will the central bank be capable of meeting the 2 per cent target?
3 Moreover, will targeting inflation have any implications for the business cycle, the growth of GDP and perhaps even the exchange rate?
4 Will central bank management of interest rates and inflation aid entry into the euro?

 Box 10.1 Inflation report

Adapted from the opening remarks by the Governor of the Bank of England, Mervyn King, 11 February 2009

The UK economy is in a deep recession. Monetary, fiscal and financial policy have all responded vigorously to that prospect. But the length and depth of the recession will depend to a significant extent on developments in the rest of the world, where a severe economic downturn has taken hold. Growth in the advanced and emerging market economies fell sharply towards the end of last year. And world trade is contracting rapidly.

The scale and synchronized nature of the downturn around the world has been driven by two factors: a further tightening of credit conditions following failures in the international banking system, which means that lending, especially to companies, is still slowing, and a collapse of confidence, or 'animal spirits' in Keynes's description, that is leading to falls in spending and production. Restoring both lending and confidence will not be easy and will take time.

To cushion the downturn in spending, policy-makers around the world have cut interest rates and loosened fiscal policy. At home, the Monetary Policy Committee has cut the Bank Rate from 5 to just 1 per cent in the space of five months. To some degree, the effect of those reductions has been blunted by the problems in the banking sector. But monetary policy is by no means ineffective and, when combined with the sharp fall in sterling of more than a quarter since the summer of 2007, the fall back in commodity prices, and the easing of fiscal policy, will provide a significant boost to demand.

10.2 GDP: measurement and policy

The aggregate demand and supply framework developed in Chapter 9 highlighted the importance of GDP and inflation. As aggregate demand or supply changed, the equilibrium level of GDP and inflation changed accordingly. We will begin by analysing GDP.

GDP

Variations in GDP over time

> The **business cycle** describes the tendency of an economy to move from economic boom to economic recession and then back into boom to repeat the cycle.

Figure 10.1 plots GDP growth for the UK over the period 1988 to 2008. GDP is an estimate of the amount of economic activity in an economy and is produced by the Office for National Statistics. Since 1988, UK GDP has grown at various rates between −1.5 per cent and 4.25 per cent per annum. Trend growth in the UK is around 2.5 per cent per annum. Whenever growth is below 2.5 per cent, the economy is experiencing slowing economic growth. Persistent slow growth can constitute a recession. Whenever GDP growth is above 2.5 per cent, the economy is heading towards economic boom. The variation between recession and boom is known as the **business cycle**. In fact, Figure 10.1 is a picture of the business cycle, where the economy moves through a series of booms and recessions.

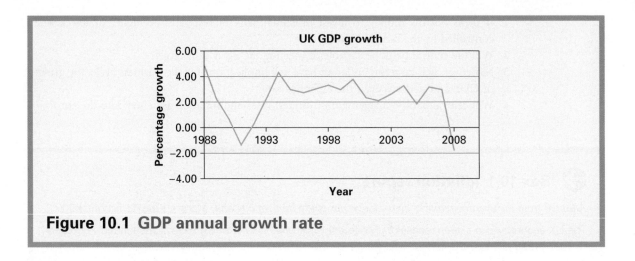

Figure 10.1 **GDP annual growth rate**

Measuring economic output

By examining the circular flow of income, in Chapter 9, we saw three potential ways of measuring output. We can measure (i) the net value of goods and services produced by firms, (ii) the value of household earnings, or (iii) the value of spending on goods and services. We are simply measuring the flow at different points; each is equally applicable and will provide a similar figure to the rest.

However, the net value of goods and services approach needs to avoid the problem of double counting.

We can examine the manufacture of a car as an example. A car contains many different parts to be assembled and then sold to a customer through a dealership. Consider paint as one component. Assume the raw materials for car paint are £100; the car paint producer mixes the materials, packages them and sends them to the car maker at a price of £200. This mixing, packaging and distribution represents £200 − £100 = £100 of value added. The car maker uses many different inputs, including paint, exhausts and engines. All the inputs cost £10 000. But the car is sold to the dealership for £12 000, so the value added from designing and assembling a car is £12 000 − £10 000 = £2000. The dealer polishes the car, shows it in a clean showroom environment, provides test drives and sells the car for £13 000. So, the value added of the dealership is £13 000 − £12 000 = £1000. If we add up all the **value added** in the economy, or we use statisticians to estimate total value added, then we have an estimate of total economic activity, or GDP.

> **Value added** is net output, after deducting goods and services used up during the production process.

Unfortunately, there are two more complications which need to be considered when measuring economic output. The first recognizes that not all factors of production are domestically owned and profits from the use of these resources will flow to another country. For example, Toyota the Japanese car manufacturer owns production facilities in Turkey and the UK. The flows of profits, interest and dividends from these assets are known as property incomes; and the balance of flows for any particular country is known as net property income. Therefore, Toyota's profits in the UK (and Turkey) will be added to the Japanese economy's gross national product (GNP). Likewise, overseas profits for large British companies, such as Vodafone, BP and Tesco, will be added to UK GNP.

The (i) output and (iii) expenditure methods will not add to the (ii) incomes measure of output without making a correction for net property income. We therefore make a distinction between GDP and GNP, which is GDP adjusted for net property income from abroad.

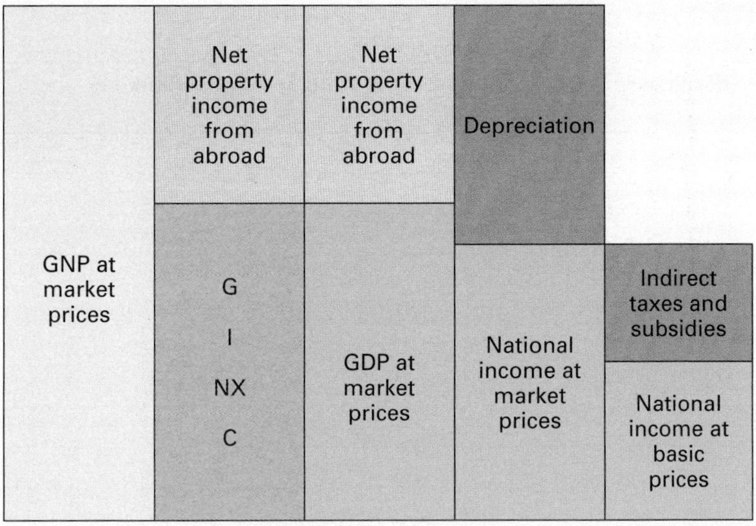

Figure 10.2 National income accounting

Measuring economic activity requires a number of considerations. The market value of what is produced in the domestic economy. Then add in the value of what is produced by operations owned in other economies. Then depreciation to recognize the cost of using capital and an adjustment for subsidies and taxes, to arrive at national income at basic prices.

The second issue is to recognize that the creation of economic output results from the use of productive capital. This is such items as plant, machinery, buildings and shops, all of which need to be maintained, repaired or replaced as they wear out. These expenditures come under the heading of depreciation. Subtracting depreciation from GDP leads to national income.

Finally, all prices are quoted as market price, which can be distorted by indirect taxes and subsidies. In order to measure economic output we would prefer price measures which are not distorted by taxes and subsidies: these are known as basic prices. Adjusting national income at market prices for the distortion of taxes and subsidies leaves us with the figure of national income at basic prices. Figure 10.2 provides an illustration of all of these adjustments.

GDP policy issues

Is higher GDP preferable? Broadly speaking, yes. Higher GDP means more goods and services are being produced. Households' economic resources are being used more fully by firms and, as a result, financial payments to households rise. The level of income within an economy is often measured as **GDP per capita**.

Table 10.1 shows the level of GDP per capita for 30 leading countries in the world. All values have been converted into US dollars. These figures suggest that average income per person in the UK is around $11 000 lower than in the US.

However, higher GDP per capita can mask a number of problematic features of an economy. One common concern is the distribution of income within an economy. Often within economies, even very developed economies within the EU, there is an unequal distribution of

> **GDP per capita** is the GDP for the economy divided by the population of the economy. GDP per capita provides a measure of average income per person.

Table 10.1 GDP per capita

Country	Rank	GDP per capita ($)	Country	Rank	GDP per capita ($)
Liechtenstein	1	118 000	Iceland	16	42 600
Qatar	2	101 000	Netherlands	17	41 300
Luxembourg	3	85 100	Switzerland	18	40 900
Bermuda	4	69 900	United Arab Emirates	19	40 400
Kuwait	5	60 800	Canada	20	40 200
Norway	6	57 500	Austria	21	39 600
Jersey	7	57 000	Sweden	22	39 600
Brunei	8	54 100	Australia	23	39 300
Singapore	9	52 900	Denmark	24	38 900
United States	10	48 000	Andorra	25	38 800
Ireland	11	47 800	British Virgin Islands	26	38 500
San Marino	12	46 100	Finland	27	38 400
Hong Kong	13	45 300	Belgium	28	38 300
Guernsey	14	44 600	Gibraltar	29	38 200
Cayman Islands	15	43 800	United Kingdom	30	37 400

Source: CIA Factbook

income. Typically those earning most see the fastest increase in future incomes. As such, the rich become richer and the poor become relatively poorer.

An additional concern is the cost incurred in generating higher levels of GDP per capita. These concerns are often focused upon damage to the environment, but it is equally possible to raise social concerns. See Figure 10.3, which highlights the different working hours typically endured by workers in a number of leading European economies. France, Denmark and Sweden have strong peaks at 36–40 hours per week. The UK has a moderate peak at this level, but then the distribution continues strongly towards 50+ hours per week. It should also be noted that the UK, when compared with the other economies, has a relatively high number of people working in the part-time range of hours. The UK works its full-time workers extremely hard and it is also very keen to have a large number of part-time workers. We describe the UK as having a very high **participation rate**. But at what cost? What else could these people be doing? Enjoying leisure, spending time with the family, staying away from stress councillors?

> **Participation rate** is the percentage of people of working age who are in employment.

Sustainable economic growth

These distributional elements aside, a broad consensus is that high levels of GDP and growth in GDP are desirable. A common reason for promoting economic growth is employment. If households are buying firms' products, then firms will be using households' labour. However,

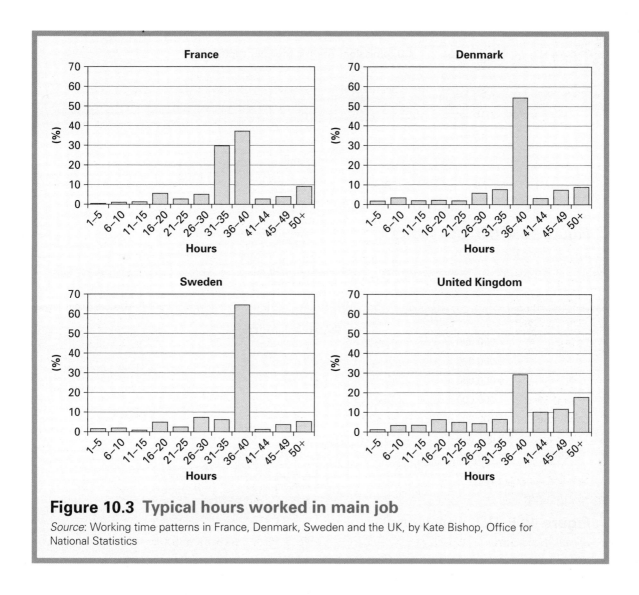

Figure 10.3 Typical hours worked in main job

Source: Working time patterns in France, Denmark, Sweden and the UK, by Kate Bishop, Office for National Statistics

when a recession occurs, households buy less, firms produce less and, as a consequence, firms employ fewer workers. As we will see later, unemployment and employment are, therefore, linked to the business cycle and economic growth.

Economies with higher levels of GDP are better able to invest in the economy's infrastructure, such as schools, hospitals and roads. This is because higher levels of GDP are likely to lead to higher incomes for workers. This in turn will result in increased taxes being paid to the government. Higher tax receipts enable the government to invest in important assets, such as schools, teachers, nurses, motorways and rail networks. Road and rail improvements help businesses to move products around, while better education and health services enable individuals to be more productive over their lifetime.

A combination of rising profits and better educational systems in a growing economy can facilitate improved levels of, and success in, research and development. Innovation can aid the development of new products that improve the lifestyle of individuals in the economy. Or innovation can bring about new and cheaper ways of making products. The Internet is a good

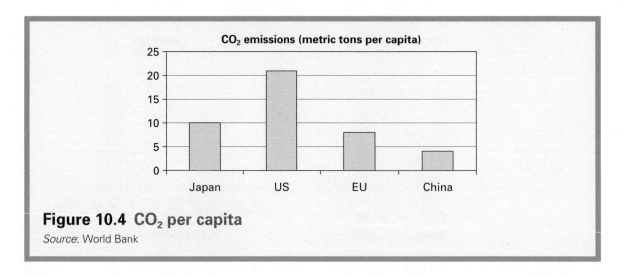

Figure 10.4 CO_2 per capita
Source: World Bank

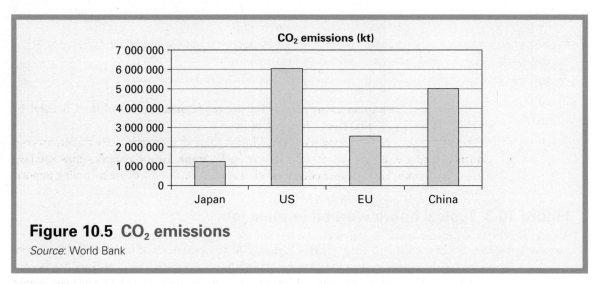

Figure 10.5 CO_2 emissions
Source: World Bank

example of both. It has changed how people can access many types of information and it has reduced the cost of providing consumers with banking and retail services.

Of course, economic growth should not be regarded as costless. We have already seen that growth can come through longer working times, leading to a reduction in leisure and family time. The other major consideration is that of the environment. As economies grow, and they grow at a faster rate, they consume more resources. Energy consumption rises with economic growth. More affluent consumers buy more cars. Increased affluence also brings greater consumption of energy-hungry appliances, such as TVs, refrigerators and air-conditioning. As a consequence, economic growth drives power consumption, which leads to higher levels of CO_2.

In Figure 10.4 data on CO_2 per capita is shown for a number of economies. The US, perhaps the most developed economy in the world, has the highest CO_2 emissions per capita. China, one of the world's fastest growing economies, has the lowest emissions per capita. But this figure is biased by China's enormous population. If we consider CO_2 emissions in Figure 10.5, we can see that China already produces almost the same amount of pollution as the US. If

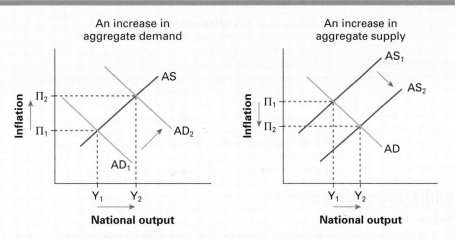

Figure 10.6 Trade-offs between GDP and inflation

Left-hand side: an increase in aggregate demand from AD_1 to AD_2 results in the equilibrium levels of GDP increasing from Y_1 to Y_2. But inflation also rises from Π_1 to Π_2.

Right-hand side: an increase in aggregate supply from AS_1 to AS_2 results in the equilibrium levels of GDP increasing from Y_1 to Y_2, while inflation falls from Π_1 to Π_2.

China's economy continues to grow, and CO_2 per capita matches that of the US, then the amount of overall pollution from China will be huge.

The implications of increasing levels of pollution from all economies have important consequences for the environment, the climate and public health. How economies grow and how energy consumption and cleaner energy creation aid economic growth are becoming important policy agendas.

Trade-off between GDP and inflation

However, a cautionary note regarding higher GDP has to be made. If higher GDP stems from an increase in aggregate demand, then higher inflation will follow. This is depicted on the left-hand side of Figure 10.6. However, if higher GDP stems from an increase in aggregate supply, then lower inflation will follow; see the right-hand side of Figure 10.6. Therefore, if economic growth is important, a crucial and basic question to ask is, how are higher levels of GDP attained and what are the implications for inflation? We will now explore these issues further by considering inflation and, more important, the targeting of inflation.

10.3 Inflation: measurement and policy

Variations in inflation over time

The **rate of inflation** is a measure of how fast prices are rising.

In Figure 10.7, we have a graph of inflation in the UK. Prices are currently rising at around 3 per cent and the government has a target rate of 2.0 per cent. Back in 1979, inflation hit 25 per cent but, more important, look at Figure 10.7 around 1990, the same years as were associated with recession in Figure 10.1. The UK experienced an inflationary recession. But in 2008 the **rate of inflation** dropped, so we then experienced a deflationary recession. Finally, note that in Figure 10.1 we pointed out the economic boom of the late 1980s; if you examine inflation around the same time, it was rising, so the UK experienced an inflationary boom.

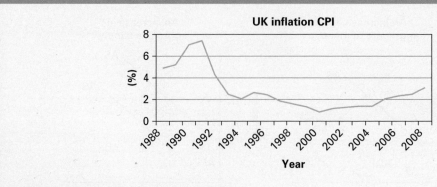

Figure 10.7 Inflation in the UK
Source: Office for National Statistics

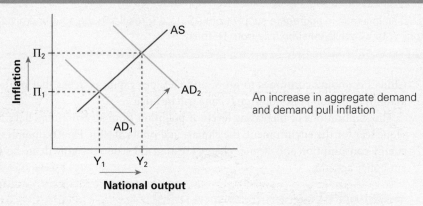

An increase in aggregate demand and demand pull inflation

Figure 10.8 Demand pull inflation
An increase in aggregate demand shifts the AD curve from AD_1 to AD_2. This results in a new equilibrium, where inflation rises to Π_2 and output to Y_2. Inflation has been pulled up by an increase in aggregate demand, while national output expands from Y_1 to Y_2.

Demand pull and cost push inflation

> **Demand pull inflation** occurs when a rise in aggregate demand leads to an increase in overall prices.
>
> **Cost push inflation** occurs when a reduction in supply leads to an increase in overall prices.

Inflation can increase if aggregate demand increases, or if aggregate supply decreases. Economists use this distinction to talk about **demand pull** and **cost push inflation**.

A rise in aggregate demand leads to many more consumers trying to buy products. But producing more products increases firms' marginal costs. This leads to firms increasing prices in order to recoup the higher costs of production. Demand pull inflation is depicted in Figure 10.8. An increase in aggregate demand moves the macroeconomic equilibrium along the aggregate supply curve, to a point where output and inflation are both higher.

In the case of cost push inflation, firms' costs of producing products increase. Wage rates might increase or, as in 2007/08, the cost of oil, wheat and other commodities increased, making fuel, plastics, distribution and food more expensive. As costs rise, firms find it difficult

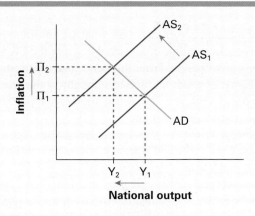

An increase in aggregate supply and cost push inflation

Figure 10.9 Cost push inflation

An increase in input prices, such as a rise in wage rates or the cost of raw materials, increases firms' costs. With higher costs, firms are less able to make a profit. Some firms exit the market and, as a result, aggregate supply is less and shifts to the left. The macroeconomic equilibrium changes, with national output falling and inflation increasing. Increasing input prices push up inflation across the economy.

to make a profit and some may even exit the market. In Figure 10.9, aggregate supply reduces and the macroeconomic equilibrium changes, with national output falling and inflation increasing.

Inflationary expectations

> **Expectations** are beliefs held by firms, workers and consumers about the future level of prices.

Expectations are also seen as an important determinant of inflationary pressures. For example, if workers think prices in general will rise by 2.0 per cent, they will ask for a 2.0 per cent pay rise in order to keep their level of earnings constant. Because they ask for 2.0 per cent, the cost of making goods goes up by 2.0 per cent, so final prices rise by 2.0 per cent. As a result, expectations become self-fulfilling prophecies. Now it should be clear why the government explicitly targets 2.0 per cent for inflation. It is trying to manage society's expectations about future price inflation. By saying inflation should be 2.0 per cent, people think it will be 2.0 per cent, so they will then demand 2.5 per cent pay rises and inflation should converge on 2.0 per cent.

Deflation

> **Deflation** is a fall in prices, usually on a yearly basis.

Deflation occurs when the general level of prices falls. On a yearly basis, the price of items such as food, housing, clothes and heating becomes cheaper when the economic environment is deflationary. The drivers of deflation are demand and cost based, just like inflation. If aggregate demand falls during a recession, then deflation can occur. If firms benefit from cost savings, then they are more willing to supply; equilibrium prices fall and deflation occurs. These arguments are the reverse of those described for inflation in Figures 10.8 and 10.9. For demand-based deflation, aggregate demand in Figure 10.8 moves from AD_2 to AD_1; and for supply-based deflation in Figure 10.9, AS_2 moves to AS_1.

The credit crunch created a significant recession and a demand-led deflationary period. The expansion of the Chinese economy and the export of manufactured items around the world increased supply and led to deflation in the price of manufactured goods.

Measuring inflation

In order to measure the rate of inflation governments use what are known as price indices. In order to do this, the government asks a sample of households across the UK to record all the products that they consume in a given period. From this data, government statisticians build what is known as a common basket of goods and services bought by the average UK household. This basket will include bread, milk, tobacco, petrol, mortgage repayments, insurance, cinema tickets, restaurant meals, train fares and so on.

Each good or service is assigned a weight. So, if mortgage repayments represent 50 per cent of individuals' monthly outgoings, then they will represent 50 per cent of the basket. If bread only represents 2 per cent of monthly outgoings, then bread will only fill 2 per cent of the basket. The prices of all these goods and services are then monitored on a monthly basis. A report of price changes within the basket is provided in Box 10.2 from the Office for National Statistics.

 ### Box 10.2 Changes to CPI and RPI shopping baskets

Adapted from the Office for National Statistics, *March 2008*

Café culture and the increasingly dominant digital technology market have had an impact on the way we spend our money. Health-conscious consumers currently favour fruit smoothies, fresh groceries and small oranges.

Fruit smoothies are included as the emerging market of healthy soft drinks continues to rise in supermarkets. Muffins are included for the first time to represent snacks such as croissants and cakes that people generally buy with a coffee in cafés around the UK.

Lager stubbies are not as popular as they were ten years ago and, although single bottles of regular-sized lager are already in the basket, the inclusion of crates (20 bottles) reflects changing spending patterns.

The way we buy music has also changed, with consumers preferring to download individual tracks rather than purchase Top 40 CD singles, which are now completely removed from the basket. Audio CDs are still represented and a new item covering the nostalgic consumption of non-chart 'classic' albums by artists such as U2, Pink Floyd and Madonna has been introduced alongside the existing Top 40 CD album.

Digital cameras and related media have been included in the basket since 2004. This year, 35mm camera film has become as redundant as the 35mm camera that fell from the basket last year.

Source: www.statistics.gov.uk

Index and base years

The **price index** can be used to deflate current prices into constant prices, where constant prices are prices expressed in the base year.

The **price index** has a base year, where the value of the index, or the basket of goods and services, is set at 100 (see Chapter 1 for a reminder). Inflation is a measure of how quickly prices are rising and it measures the difference between the price level last year and the price level this year. As such, inflation is measured as:

Inflation = (Index in current year − Index in previous year)/Index in previous year

In Table 10.2, the price index has been set at 100 for the year 2008, and it rises to 113 by the year 2012. Using the formula above, the inflation rate in 2009 was 2 per cent, while in 2011 it was 4.8 per cent.

Table 10.2 Price index and inflation

Year	Price index	Inflation	Nominal salary	Real salary
2008	100		£20 000	£20 000
2009	102	(102 − 100) × 100 = 2.0%	£20 000	£19 608
2010	105	(105 − 102) × 102 = 2.9%	£20 000	£19 048
2011	110	(110 − 105) × 105 = 4.8%	£20 000	£18 182
2012	113	(113 − 110) × 110 = 2.7%	£20 000	£17 699

 ## Box 10.3 CPI down to 3.1%, RPI down to 0.9%

Adapted from the Office for National Statistics, *January 2008*

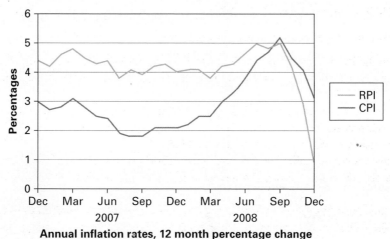

Annual inflation rates, 12 month percentage change

CPI annual inflation was 3.1 per cent in December, down from 4.1 per cent in November.

Overall, the reduction in the rate of VAT made the largest contribution to the 1.0 percentage point change in the CPI annual rate. There were also effects from a fall in the prices of petrol and diesel and from greater discounting in sales than last year. Eight of the 12 division-level categories made a large contribution to the slowdown in the CPI annual rate.

The category 'clothing and footwear' made the largest downward contribution to the change in the CPI annual rate. The reduction in the rate of VAT lowered the price of men's and women's clothing and footwear. Additionally, there was greater discounting of women's clothing and footwear than last year. Overall, the price of children's clothing fell by more than last year due to discounting in sales.

Transport costs made another large downward contribution. The largest effect came from the price of fuels and lubricants, which fell this year but rose last year. The average price of petrol fell by 6.0p per litre between November and December this year, to stand at 89.2p, compared with a rise of 1.7p last year. Diesel prices fell by 6.4p per litre this year, to stand at 102.4p, compared with a rise of 3.0p last year. There was a partially offsetting effect from transport services where air fares, and to a lesser extent coach fares, rose by more than last year.

Source: www.statistics.gov.uk

Price deflators

For example, suppose in 2008 you earned £20 000 and that by 2012 your boss had refused to give you a pay rise and you still only earned £20 000. We can calculate your real wage in each year by using the price index to convert your salary into year 2008 prices as follows:

Real salary = (Nominal salary) × (100/Price index)

So, a nominal salary of £20 000 in 2012 is a real salary of only £20 000 × (100/113) = £17 699. In other words, £20 000 has lost £2301 in value since 2008. This has wider implications: whenever prices are compared over time, whether for houses, cars, wages or wine, they need to be adjusted for inflation and converted into constant prices. Price indices provide a means of achieving this.

Costs of inflation

In recent decades governments around the world have begun to set inflation targets. This is because inflation can be costly. But this cost should not be confused with goods and services becoming more expensive.

For example: 'When I was a lad, a bag of chips cost 5p; now they cost £1.' But chips are not 20 times more expensive now than they were 25 years ago. This is because incomes have also risen by the same amount. So, we will only think inflation makes things more expensive if we suffer from **inflation illusion**. However, if we do suffer from inflation illusion, then we may cut back on consumption, believing the product to be too expensive. If enough people reduce consumption, then a recession may occur.

> People suffer **inflation illusion** if they confuse nominal and real changes.

Even without inflation illusion, inflation can still be costly. If prices are rising quickly, retailers will be constantly changing their prices. Shelf labels will have to be changed at supermarkets and price lists will have to be changed by other types of sellers. These are known as **menu costs** and the more rapidly prices rise, the more often prices have to be changed. So, inflation can create additional costs.

> **Menu costs** are associated with the activity and cost of changing prices in shops, price lists and, of course, menus.

Fiscal drag

Let us assume inflation is fully expected and full adjustment occurs. Price rises of 10 per cent are matched by wage increases of 10 per cent. There are no initial cutbacks in consumption by buyers and, therefore, no recessionary consequences. But what if the government does not adjust its tax policy?

In 2009/10, the UK government allowed individuals to earn £6475 before having to pay tax. If incomes rose by 10 per cent and the government did not lift the tax allowance by 10 per cent, then individuals would start paying more real tax. Therefore, this time, even with fully anticipated inflation, inflexibility by the government creates an inflationary cost known as **fiscal drag**.

> **Fiscal drag** occurs when tax-free income allowances grow at a slower rate than earnings. This reduces the real value of tax-free allowances, leading to high real tax receipts.

Assets and liabilities

If mortgage interest rates are 5 per cent and inflation is 2.5 per cent, then the real interest rate is 5 − 2.5 = 2.5 per cent. Viewed this way, the lender is not making 5 per cent profits out of its customers. Rather, it is gaining 2.5 per cent to cover the rise in inflation and then it is gaining 2.5 per cent as its profit. If lenders and borrowers expect 2.5 per cent inflation, then the real cost of funds is 2.5 per cent. But what happens if expectations are wrong and inflation suddenly rises to 10 per cent? The real interest rate would become 5 − 10 = −5 per cent. Lenders are now losing 5 per cent a year and borrowers are gaining 5 per cent a year. There is a transfer of wealth from lenders to borrowers.

Borrowers tend to be young people starting out in life, buying a home and raising a family. Lenders tend to be older people who have raised their family and paid off the mortgage and are now saving with banks and building societies. Therefore, a surprise rise in the inflation rate transfers wealth from old people to young people. This influences the spending patterns of old people in a negative way and young people in a positive way. An obvious cost is the need for product suppliers to react to these consumption changes and develop different product lines to meet the main spenders in the economy. Therefore, inflation can create costs through structural change.

The fear of deflation

Falling prices might sound like a good idea. Unfortunately it isn't good when the fall in prices for goods and services also impacts wages. If goods and services fall in price, then the value of labour also falls and firms will seek to pay lower wages and/or employ less workers.

You may consider that such changes leave workers no worse off. They earn less, but goods and services cost less, so they can still afford to buy the same things as last year. True, as long as some important prices or financial commitments are not fixed. Mortgages are important financial commitments which are relatively fixed. If you borrowed £100 000 last year and deflation results in a 5 per cent loss in earnings, then your mortgage increases in real terms to £105 000. Over a number of years, deflation can make your mortgage unaffordable.

If deflation also erodes asset values, let's say property prices fall, then the difference between house prices and mortgage balances deteriorates. At worst, households can be left with negative equity, where the value of the house is less than the outstanding balance of the mortgage.

Why target inflation?

The answer to this question is very simple. If aggregate supply is perfectly inelastic and aggregate demand increases, there will be no increase in output; the only impact will be higher inflation. This is illustrated in Figure 10.10. Whenever aggregate demand shifts to the right, the government, or central bank, will pursue policies to shift aggregate demand back to the left and, therefore, keep inflation constant. The economy can now only grow if the aggregate supply curve shifts to the left.

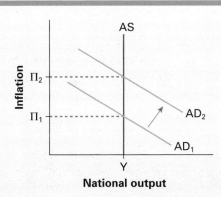

Figure 10.10 Aggregate demand and inelastic aggregate supply

AS is aggregate supply and represents total supply in the economy. As aggregate demand increases from AD_1 to AD_2, national output remains constant at Y, but inflation rises from Π_1 to Π_2.

The crucial issue is whether price stability from inflation targeting enables aggregate supply to expand and shift to the right. The belief is that inflation targeting reduces uncertainty in the economy, making investment decisions easier for firms. Volatile inflation rates lead to booms and busts within the economy, as governments try to bring inflation under control. The variations of the business cycle can make investment unprofitable. Therefore, if investment in capital increases the productive capacity of the economy and ultimately the level of aggregate supply, inflation targeting could be highly desirable. We will revisit these arguments during our discussion of fiscal, monetary and supply side policies in Chapters 11, 12 and 13.

10.4 **Unemployment**

Frictional unemployment refers to individuals who have quit one job and are currently searching for another job. As such, frictional unemployment is temporary.

Cyclical unemployment is related to the business cycle and is sometimes also referred to as demand-deficient unemployment. Cyclical unemployment reflects workers who have lost jobs due to the adversities of the business cycle.

Managing GDP and inflation have been at the fore of economic policy. As a result, unemployment was less important. This was to be expected as throughout the late 1990s and into the new millennium unemployment fell to almost negligible levels. As the credit crisis placed the brakes on the global economy, unemployment rose and governments have began to refocus on the issues and problems associated with unemployment. See Figure 10.11.

Economists identify four categories of unemployment: **frictional**, **cyclical**, **structural** and **classical**. Frictional unemployment is of little concern. The frictionally unemployed are between jobs. They have voluntarily quit one job and are searching for a new opportunity. Cyclical unemployment is a concern when an economy enters a recession. There is insufficient demand for all goods and services to keep all workers in employment. Factories and offices are reduced in size and workers are made redundant. The role of government is to help to bolster demand in the economy and reduce the impact of recession.

In the case of structural unemployment, an entire industry can go into decline. In the 1980s, Europe lost many jobs in traditional heavy industries such as ship building, steel making and the extraction of fuels, such as coal. More latterly, the financial crisis has damaged the strength of the financial system and arguably the industry will be more regulated, less diverse and less likely to be a dominant economic sector. So bankers and financiers will be in less demand in the future.

The problem faced by government is not one of trying to create additional demand, but how to transfer the skills of bankers and financiers to other sectors of the economy. This is not easy. Financial services workers (perhaps don't) understand financial matters; such individuals are

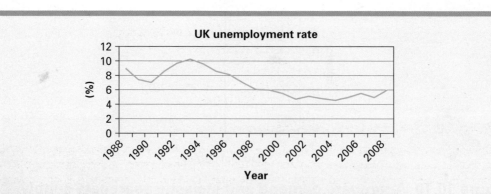

Figure 10.11 **Unemployment in the UK (claimant count)**
Source: Office for National Statistics

Structural unemployment occurs when an industry moves into decline. The structurally unemployed find it difficult to gain employment in new industries because of what is known as a mismatch of skills.

Classical unemployment refers to workers who have priced themselves out of a job.

The **claimant count** simply measures the number of people who are eligible and receiving the jobseeker's allowance.

not skilled in manufacturing, leisure services or tourism. Retraining the unemployed and bringing jobs into regions hit by structural unemployment are the difficult but key tasks.

If workers, or their unions, manage to negotiate wages that are higher than the equilibrium wage, then, as we saw in Chapter 4, demand will be less than supply. A surplus in the labour market is illustrated in Figure 10.12. When the wage rate rises above the equilibrium rate, two things happen. First, at the higher wage, more workers are willing to supply themselves for work. Second, at the higher wage, firms are less willing to demand workers. These two changes create a surplus in the market, with firms being unwilling to demand all workers who are willing to supply themselves for work. Those individuals who are willing to supply themselves for work but are not demanded by firms are unemployed.

Measuring unemployment

The government measures unemployment on a monthly basis. Over time, the measure, or definition, of unemployment has changed many times. However, the UK government has used the International Labour Organization's definition of unemployment for a number of years.

The ILO definition of unemployment is a count of jobless people who want to work, are available to work and are actively seeking employment. The ILO measure is used internationally, so a benefit of the measure is that it enables comparisons between countries to be made and it is also consistent over time.

An alternative measure used in the UK is the **claimant count**. The claimant count is generally lower than the ILO measure of unemployment because some individuals may be willing to work but are unable to register for the jobseeker's allowance.

Reflecting the separate categories of unemployment, such as frictional and structural, the measures are generally broken down into region, age and time in unemployment. This provides an assessment of where unemployment is highest, which perhaps relates to industries, thereby identifying structural unemployment. Unemployment in high age groups could reflect skill mismatch between older workers and newer industries, while time in unemployment may reflect the difference between frictional unemployment and other types of unemployment.

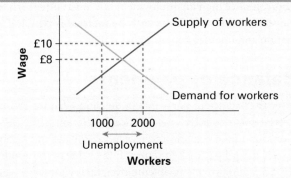

Figure 10.12 Classical unemployment

At the equilibrium wage rate of £8 per hour, the supply of workers is equal to the demand for workers. The market clears, with all workers who want to work finding employment. Unemployment is zero. If workers, or unions, are successful in raising the wage rate to £10 per hour, then the supply of workers increases as more individuals are willing to work once the wage rate increases. But, in contrast, firms are less willing to demand the more expensive workers. So, with the wage rate above the equilibrium a surplus exists, with 1000 workers unemployed.

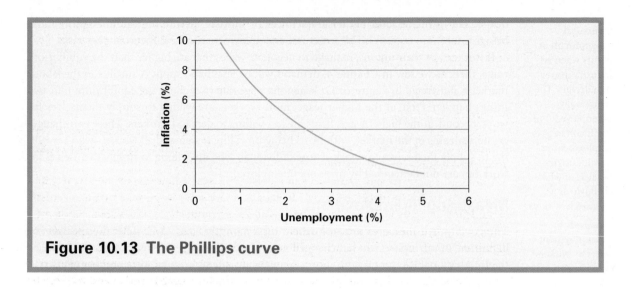

Figure 10.13 The Phillips curve

Policy issues

Should unemployment be reduced? Unemployment represents a wasted resource. Unemployed workers would like to work but cannot. If unemployed workers were employed, then GDP could increase. Furthermore, unemployment might be linked to increased stress and illness and, therefore, it places increased strains on individuals, families and the health sector. So, we can see that reducing unemployment is perhaps a good idea. However, such arguments need to be tempered by the insights offered by the **Phillips curve**.

> The **Phillips curve** shows that lower unemployment is associated with higher inflation. Simply, lower unemployment has to be traded for higher inflation.

Figure 10.13 illustrates the Phillips curve, indicating a negative relationship between inflation and unemployment. Lower unemployment is gained at the expense of higher inflation. The simple explanation behind this relationship is that unemployment can be solved by creating more demand in the economy for goods and services and ultimately this will lead to an increase in the demand for workers. However, increased demand may also lead to higher inflation. So governments can solve high unemployment but must suffer higher inflation. In Chapter 13, we will go one step further and argue that, by increasing demand, governments only generate higher inflation and unemployment remains high.

10.5 Balance of payments

We will cover the balance of payments in detail in Chapter 15 but, essentially, the balance of payments represents a country's net position in relation to the rest of the world. Consider your own position. You might provide a service to a company and receive a wage in return. You may then buy products and pay cash in return. If the value of the goods that you buy is greater than the value of work you provide to an employer, then your wage will be less than your spending. On a net basis, the cash flows into your bank account will be less than the cash flows out, and you may need an overdraft. In reverse, if you spend less than you receive as a wage, then the cash into your account will be greater than the cash out, and you will begin to save.

The balance of payments measures these flows for an economy, rather than for a person. For example, if the UK is buying, or importing, more goods and services than it is exporting to overseas, then the UK will have to transfer financial resource from the UK to overseas. In contrast, if the UK is exporting more than it is importing, then financial resource to pay for the exports will flow into the UK. Reflecting these points, the balance of payments measures the flow of goods and services between the UK and its trading partners; and the financial flows between the UK and its trading partners. The Office for National Statistics measures these flows for the government.

Policy issues

Is it bad to run a balance of payments deficit with the rest of the world?

In the short run, a one-off deficit is unlikely to be a problem, much as a temporary overdraft is unlikely to be a problem for you. At some point in the future you may expect to run a surplus by working extra hours and earning money to pay off your debts.

Similarly, a country may expect to run a deficit this year and a surplus next year. More important, why has the deficit occurred? In your case, as a student you may have an overdraft or student loan because you are investing in your future productivity as a worker. Similarly, a country may be running an external deficit with its overseas partners because it is purchasing high-productivity capital items, which will improve the country's productivity in the future.

In the long run, the real concern arises when the deficit represents a structural, as opposed to a temporary, problem. For example, you may not be a highly valuable worker and you may be earning a low wage, but you do have very expensive tastes. As a result, you will run a deficit, spending more on goods and services than you earn in income. Similarly, if a country produces low-quality output but demands high-quality and expensive products from overseas, then it will run a deficit. The way for you to solve your debt problems is either to stop spending or to improve your value as a worker and gain a higher wage. Similarly, a country has to improve the type, quality and cost of the products that it sells to the rest of the world. In essence, by becoming more internationally competitive a country may be able to generate the finances that it requires to fund its expenditure on expensive imports.

How a country improves its international competitiveness may present another trade-off for the government. Reducing aggregate demand will result in lower inflation and more internationally competitive prices. But lowering aggregate demand may also lead to a recession. Perhaps the best option is to once again return to managing aggregate supply, introducing policies that lead to an increase in aggregate supply and a reduction in the rate of inflation, coupled with an expansion of GDP.

10.6 Macroeconomic policies

The discussion has highlighted how changes in aggregate demand and aggregate supply lead to changes in GDP and inflation. Changes in these variables may ultimately lead to changes in unemployment and the balance of payments. We have also discussed the policy issues associated with GDP, inflation, unemployment and the balance of payments, arguing why governments are interested in managing each of these macroeconomic variables. Higher GDP can improve income levels across the economy, while low and stable inflation may provide a preferable investment environment for firms. The clear question is, how do governments control aggregate demand and aggregate supply and thereby manage the economy?

The answer to these questions will be discussed at length in Chapters 11, 12 and 14. However, as an introduction we can identify demand and supply side policies:

- Demand side policies influence aggregate demand.
- Fiscal policy is the use of government spending and taxation to influence the level of aggregate demand in the economy.
- Monetary policy is the use of interest rates, as well as the supply of money to the financial sector, with the aim of influencing the level of demand in the economy.

Demand side policies

In Chapter 11, we will see how the government can use fiscal policy to change the level of spending in an economy. In Chapter 12, we will develop an understanding of the banking system and explain how changes in the base rate by central banks are transmitted through the banking system to the wider economy and affect consumption and investment spending.

Supply side policies

Given that we have seen that aggregate supply can be vertical, or perfectly price inelastic, then aggregate supply defines the equilibrium level of GDP for the economy. In the long run, growth in GDP and lower inflation can only occur with an increase in aggregate supply. Therefore, sustainable economic growth, low inflation and even international competitiveness are crucially linked to developments in aggregate supply.

Supply side policies influence aggregate supply.

How aggregate supply can be managed by government and the implications of **supply side policies** for business will be discussed in Chapter 13.

10.7 Business application: international competitiveness and the macroeconomy

Achieving higher rates of economic growth, producing more highly paid jobs and generating additional exports are not all about increasing aggregate demand within an economy. The make-up of industries can be equally important. Which industries and sectors are likely to offer opportunities for growth in the future; which will decline? In contrast to many of its European counterparts the UK has seen its manufacturing base decline towards 10 per cent of GDP. At the same time, services, especially those that are in finance, accounting and legal practice, have grown enormously. London and the South East economy of the UK are heavily dependent upon these sectors. Of course, when these sectors become embroiled in a credit crisis, then companies and jobs are lost. A natural question is to ask if the UK economy needs to be more balanced in terms of the industries that prosper within its economy. Government support for other strong employers and exporters may offer ways of providing sustainability and longevity in future GDP and employment growth rates.

Manufacturing competitiveness, GDP growth and inflation

Manufacturing can be a source of economic growth. Manufacturers of products often compete in global markets. By competing overseas, manufacturers can face increased competition from international rivals. In order to compete and survive, manufacturers can face enormous incentives to improve productivity and the quality of their products.

Investing in workers' skills and new capital technology can improve productivity. Investing in product innovation can improve the quality of the product to end-users. Spillover effects into the rest of the economy may occur if high-skilled workers move to alternative employers, taking their enhanced skills with them. Moreover, workers' experience of using advanced capital equipment may enable other firms to consider purchasing such equipment. Finally, if manufacturers make machines for other companies to use, product innovation may result in improved productivity for end-users. Therefore, manufacturing competitiveness may not only drive economic growth but, through productivity gains and cost improvements, it may also enhance aggregate supply and aid the management of inflation.

Box 10.4 Services or manufacturing?

Adapted from 'Britain's lonely high-flier' in The Economist, *8 January 2009*

Rolls-Royce, the British manufacturer of commercial jet engines, is a dominant and perhaps singular example of the country's manufacturing expertise. With light-touch regulation and tax breaks that made it an uncommonly attractive place to hire foreign talent, Britain built gleaming monuments to finance. From chemists and physicists to historians, many of its brightest graduates made their way to the City of London. From the towers of Canary Wharf they looked down on the remains of what was once the world's busiest port and on a past that Britain seemed to have left far behind.

Yet with the great tides of money that once washed these shores now stilled, Derby offers a different vision of Britain's future. Over the past couple of decades or so, Rolls-Royce has transformed itself from a loss-making British firm into the world's second-biggest maker of large jet engines. Britain can do both after all. To optimists, it may even suggest a British manufacturing renaissance.

The country's manufacturing output has been growing over the years, but its share of GDP has been falling (as in other rich countries – see Chart 1). Employment in manufacturing has been in decline. Only a handful of big manufacturing firms still exist. Some, such as BAE Systems, a defence company, rely on the government. And, although industries such as car making survive, they do so almost entirely in foreign ownership. Britain remains the world's eighth-biggest exporter of goods, but its share of global markets has shrunk to a little more than 3 per cent, far behind America, China and Germany (see Chart 2). In services, it ranks second.

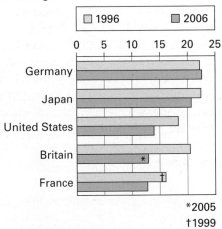

Manufacturing value added as % of total gross value added

□ 1996   ■ 2006

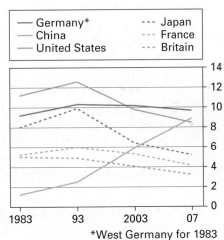

Share of world merchandise exports, %

— Germany*   --- Japan
— China   --- France
— United States --- Britain

*West Germany for 1983

Chart 1 It's all relative

Source: OECD

Chart 2 Trading places

Source: World Trade Organization

Manufacturing competitiveness and the balance of payments

The balance of payments records trading position with the rest of the world. As manufacturing declines, consumers have to import goods, which previously they would have purchased from domestic producers. Relying on imports is not a major problem. The issue is, how do we finance the purchase of imports?

In the case of the UK, the rise of the service-based economy and service-based exports, such as insurance and banking, has helped to fund the importation of goods. But since manufacturing exports are worth around five times more than exported services, the UK will have to export more services than it would have to export goods. A significant problem is that services do not export easily. Leisure centres, restaurants, cinemas, legal and accounting services and even hairdressing are not easy to export.

Manufacturing competitiveness and employment

Skills required for the manufacture of steel, cars, industrial equipment, domestic appliances, chemicals and jet fighter aircraft are fairly specific to the industry. If one of these manufacturing sectors declines, then the potential for structural unemployment is immense. Even if service sector employers were to consider locating in areas of high unemployment, the mismatch of skills between unemployed manufacturing workers and the needs of service sector providers is likely to be significant. Manufacturing competitiveness may, therefore, be important to the economy, if only to prevent costly structural change.

Not all economists would agree with the points listed above. Some may think that the points made above are valid, but that they overstate the case for manufacturing competitiveness. If manufacturing has declined, then there must be something inherently wrong about the location of manufacturing sectors in economies such as Italy or the UK. It could be that there are resources in South East Asia which are more appropriate for a manufacturing base – more abundant labour, better logistics networks, better financing options. It could be that European firms need to migrate to alternative parts of the value chain where they retain a competitive advantage. For example, Italians may have lost competitiveness in shoe manufacture, but they are still perhaps the best shoe designers. The critical success factors for the macroeconomy are adaptation, flexibility and migration to the next commercial opportunity.

Understanding policy

Regardless of how important manufacturing competitiveness is to the economy, it is clear that a case can be built for manufacturing having beneficial consequences for GDP, inflation, employment and the balance of payments or, more important, all of the macroeconomic objectives. But how will policy impact on manufacturing?

If manufacturing is a catalyst for economic growth through innovation and investment, low inflation and economic stability are essential for aiding manufacturers to invest. By keeping inflation low and stable, a government is endeavouring to create a stable environment within which firms feel the risk associated with investing are lower. With stable growth in GDP, the risk of an investment in new machinery being devalued by a recession is reduced.

In terms of aiding skill development, the government can invest heavily in higher education, channelling increasing numbers of students into undergraduate programmes, especially those linked to engineering and science. But, this does not always alleviate skills shortages. For every university graduate, the economy loses one important, but less skilled, worker, such as lorry drivers, plumbers, builders and mechanics.

10.8 Business policy: inflation targeting?

The European Central Bank and the Bank of England follow inflation-targeting policies, as do Australia, Brazil, Canada, Sweden and South Africa. In contrast, the US Federal Reserve has traditionally considered both inflation and GDP when setting interest rates. Given the importance of inflation targeting, especially within Europe, then it is useful to understand the implications for business of a policy environment characterized by inflation targeting.

What is inflation targeting?

The central bank publicizes a target goal for the inflation rate. It then steers monetary policy to try to hit the target inflation rate, raising rates to curb inflation and lowering rates to juice up growth and raise inflation. Targets differ across economies. In the UK, the inflation target is 2 per cent on average for CPI. For members of the Eurozone, the inflation target is CPI less than or equal to 2 per cent.

Figure 10.14 illustrates the level of CPI from 1990 through to 2009 in the Eurozone. European monetary union (EMU) began in 1999 and inflation targeting of CPI at 2 per cent began. It is clear from the chart that, from 1999, CPI was allowed to rise to 2 per cent and then moved close to the 2 per cent level. This was very different from the pattern in the 1990s, when inflation targeting was less important.

Of course, it should also be noted that, in 2008 and into 2009, CPI moved markedly away from target. Initially, the oil, commodity and food price spikes of early 2008 pushed up inflation; and then, following the credit crisis, inflation fell very quickly during the recession. Therefore, despite the ECB's best efforts to target 2 per cent inflation, in times of extreme economic events targeting can be very difficult.

Why conduct inflation targeting?

The central issue is macroeconomic stability. This is a more general concern than simply low inflation fanaticism. Macroeconomic stability can encompass stability in prices and in economic activity, namely GDP. Under inflation targeting, stability in pricing is seen as essential for stability in economic activity. In fact, as we develop your understanding of macroeconomic

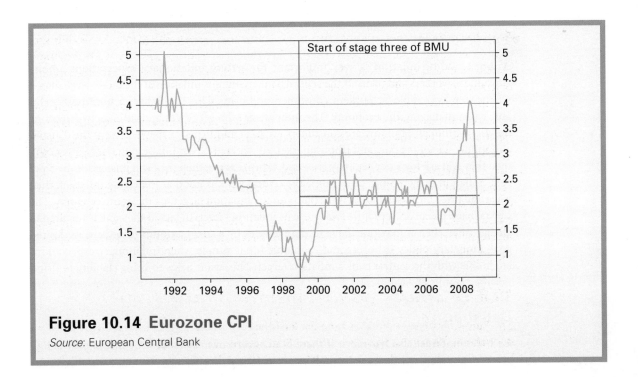

Figure 10.14 Eurozone CPI
Source: European Central Bank

policies, we will show you, in Chapter 13, that targeting inflation can be the same as targeting GDP. So, since it is easy to measure inflation quickly and accurately, but difficult to measure GDP quickly and accurately, then following an inflation target offers a reasonably sound and pragmatic policy for managing the economy. But why should inflation targeting lead to stability in GDP? The answer to this question requires an understanding of how macroeconomic events trigger behavioural changes in microeconomic actors, such as firms and consumers.

Inflation targeting: firms and consumers

The implications for business can be subtle but important. Within a regime of inflation targeting, there is little variation in the inflation rate. This improves price transparency. With stable inflation, it is easier for consumers to recognize changes in the relative prices of competing products and not confuse them for changes in all prices. e.g. inflation. Improved price transparency helps to drive competition. Stronger competition can drive down prices, promote innovation and generate economic growth.

Stable inflation also leads to small and infrequent changes in interest rates. The head of the Bank of England has suggested that his role is to be as boring as possible (indicating that, if inflation is kept under control, there will be little need for large or even unexpected changes in interest rates to bring about stability in inflation). Such boring stability will shape the decisions and behaviour of consumers and firms. Wage bargaining and investment decisions will be carried out within a context of reasonable certainty of future price levels. With reduced risk and improved decision making, a greater willingness to spend and invest should occur. As such, stability in economic activity is assured by a background of stable prices. Therefore, the implications for business are that tomorrow should be very much like today. In effect, no surprises and therefore boring. But boring has its virtues. When investing a huge sum of money in a project, which may reach fruition in three to five years' time, a lack of surprises can be very comforting. Macroeconomic stability now can lead to greater and more valuable productive capacity in the future.

Expectations

A target rate of inflation is very important for setting inflationary expectations among consumers, workers and firms. If the central bank maintains inflation at the target level, then it will be seen as credible by workers, consumers and firms. This credibility is enormously valuable when managing the economy. The individuals who set prices and ultimately determine inflation within an economy are consumers, workers and firms, as they represent the demand and supply side of product and labour markets. If workers expect inflation to rise to 5 per cent, then they will ask for 5 per cent pay rises and, if firms agree, then they will raise prices by 5 per cent. Inflation is then 5 per cent. But if the central bank is good at managing inflation, then wage and price increases should be in line with the inflation target for the entire economy. The central bank has to do very little to achieve its inflation target. In fact, if the bank is required to change rates, then it may only have to change rates by a small amount to achieve its desired goal. Monetary policy is boring and economic life is simple when inflationary expectations are in line with the central bank's inflation target. This again helps to bring stability to firms' macroeconomic environment.

Deflation

An inflation target also has merit if there is a concern over deflation. A concern over falling prices might seem a little bizarre, but it can be extremely troublesome for an economy. At one level consumers may refrain from expenditure on large ticket items if they think prices will fall in the future. But this cut in demand will lead to more price cuts and yet more waiting by consumers. A deflationary spiral can be disastrous for prices and GDP.

Deflation can also work against interest rate policies. When prices fall, profits and wages are also likely to fall. Reductions in workers' incomes and firms' earnings reduce their ability to service debt. Therefore, even if the central bank cuts interest rates, the real affordability of debt increases. Inflation targeting may help to avoid this problem by setting an expectation that the central bank is committed to inflation. If firms and workers believe this, then the horrors of deflation may be avoided. It should therefore be of no surprise that the US Federal Reserve has begun to consider the use of inflation targeting.

 ## Box 10.5 Federal Reserve considers setting inflation target, minutes reveal

Adapted from an article by Krishna Guha in The Financial Times, *7 January 2009*

The Federal Reserve is considering establishing a de facto inflation target, minutes of its groundbreaking December policy meeting revealed yesterday. The idea would be to shore up the public expectations of positive inflation and so make it less likely that a deflationary dynamic could take hold as the US recession deepens.

Policy-makers discussed the possibility of offering a 'more explicit indication of their views on what longer-run rate of inflation would best promote their goals of maximum employment and price stability.' They reasoned that the 'added clarity in that regard might help forestall the development of expectations that inflation would decline below desired levels.'

© The Financial Times Ltd. 2009

Problems with inflation targeting

Inflation targeting is not always capable of accommodating problems associated with cost push inflation. Through 2007 and into 2008, oil, commodities and food prices increased enormously. The cost of oil doubled. A cost push inflation reduces aggregate supply. This leads to falling GDP and higher inflation – a so-called inflationary contraction; recall Chapter 9 and Figure 9.10. In order to return inflation to target, the central bank would need to increase interest rates and cause GDP to fall even further. Combating cost push inflation would lead to an even greater recession.

A solution to this problem is to have some flexibility in the inflation target. In the UK, the target is for CPI to be 2 per cent *on average*. If cost push inflation is only temporary, then a rise in inflation to 4 per cent is undesirable, but can be accommodated on the presumption that in the near future inflation will move back down to trend.

The implications for business are important. Interest rates, wages, inflation and international competitiveness could all be more variable in the short run, while GDP should be more stable. On one level this policy is only beneficial to business if stability in GDP is of greater value than stability in inflation and interest rates. On another level, the acceptance of economic surprises and non-boring economic policy may represent a more realistic view of the macroeconomic environment within which a company operates.

Summary

1 GDP is a measure of economic output.

2 The circular flow of income indicates that GDP can be measured using the income, expenditure and value-added approaches.

3 To avoid double counting, the value-added approach measures the incremental amount of value added at each stage of the production process.

4 GDP is compared across economies using GDP per capita. However, such a measure may hide an unequal distribution of income among the population.

5 Higher and stable levels of GDP are desirable policy objectives. Economic stability enables firms to invest in new capital equipment, leading to improved productivity and economic growth. Higher levels of GDP can, through tax receipts, enable governments to invest in important economic infrastructure, such as education and transport. However, higher GDP might lead to higher inflation.

6 A trade-off may exist between higher GDP and higher inflation.

7 Inflation measures the rate of change of prices. Faster price rises result in higher inflation.

8 A basket of goods and services, representing commonly purchased products, is used in the measurement of inflation. A price index is developed from the basket of goods and services and changes in the price index are used to measure inflation.

9 Demand pull inflation occurs when aggregate demand increases relative to aggregate supply.

10 Cost push inflation occurs when aggregate supply increases relative to aggregate demand.

11 Inflationary expectations may also drive inflation. If workers expect prices to rise by 2 per cent, then they will ask for 2 per cent pay rises in order to maintain constant real wages. The 2 per cent pay rise may then be passed on in higher product prices and, as a result, the expectation of 2 per cent inflation becomes reality.

12 Inflation can create many costs, including the erosion of debt and increasing menu costs.

13 Inflation targeting may improve economic stability and business investment confidence. Increased investment in productive capital may improve the economy's aggregate supply, boosting GDP and reducing inflation.

14 Targeting increases in aggregate supply avoids the trade-off associated with aggregate demand, with higher demand increasing GDP and inflation.

15 Unemployment is categorized as frictional, structural, cyclical or classical.

16 The Phillips curve suggests a negative trade-off between inflation and unemployment. However, this relationship may only exist in the short run. When real wages fully adjust to inflationary changes, then unemployment will not vary with the inflation rate.

17 Following the shift towards improving aggregate supply, government policy has moved away from unemployment and more towards labour productivity.

18 A balance of payments deficit is problematic if it is persistent and reflects a country's lack of international competitiveness.

Learning checklist

You should now be able to:

◆ Explain how to measure GDP using the income, expenditure and value-added approaches

◆ Explain how inflation is measured using a basket of goods and services and index numbers

◆ Explain the main drivers of inflation

◆ Provide a discussion of the main costs of inflation and reasons behind inflation targeting

◆ List and explain the main types of unemployment

◆ Explain the potential trade-off between inflation and unemployment

◆ Explain whether a balance of payments deficit is a problem

◆ Explain the relevance of economic policy considerations for business

Questions   connect

1 Why is growth in GDP important?

2 Evaluate whether higher GDP per capita is always desirable.

3 Identify and explain the three main methods for measuring GDP.

4 What is inflation and how is it measured in your economy?

5 Explain why governments and central banks avoid high inflation and deflation.

6 What are the three main drivers of inflation?

7 As China continues to grow, demand for raw materials, food, shipping and energy will all increase. Will China's growth generate cost push or demand pull inflation in your economy?

8 Assess the key trends within unemployment data for your economy over the last five years. Use the economic unemployment categories to identify the patterns within your unemployment data.

9 During the credit crisis and global recession many bankers lost their jobs. Is this demand-deficient or structural unemployment?

10 Explain the relationship suggested by the Phillips curve. How might governments exploit this relationship?

11 If workers automatically adjusted their wage demands to keep their real wages constant, would the Phillips curve relationship still hold?

12 In Table 10.1 Liechtenstein has the highest GDP per capita in the world. Is Liechtenstein a good place to start a business?

13 The inflation forecast for next year is 3 per cent. Workers are asking for a 5 per cent pay rise. Should the firm agree to the 5 per cent rise?

14 Unemployment represents a pool of underutilized resource. Should firms relocate to areas of high unemployment?

15 Should a firm be concerned about an economy with a chronic balance of payments problem?

Exercises

1 True or false?
   (a) GDP per capita is a measure of economic prosperity.
   (b) High growth rates in GDP per capita can be accompanied by high inflation.
   (c) Nominal wages are adjusted for inflation, real wages are not.
   (d) A mismatch of skills generally results from cyclical unemployment.
   (e) The Phillips curve suggests a negative relationship between inflation and GDP.
   (f) A trade deficit is acceptable in the short run, but is troublesome in the long run.

2 Plot the data in Table 10.3, placing inflation on the Y axis and unemployment on the X axis.

Table 10.3 Inflation and unemployment rates

	Inflation rate	Unemployment rate
1997	2	8.8
1998	2.6	7.8
1999	2.5	7.1
2000	1.8	5.3
2001	1.6	4.5
2002	1.3	4.2
2003	0.8	3.7
2004	1.2	3.3
2005	1.3	3.2
2006	1.4	3.2
2007	1.3	2.9

   (a) Is there evidence in support of a Phillips curve relationship?
   (b) What is the long-run Phillips curve?
   (c) At what level of unemployment would you propose drawing the long-run Phillips curve?

3 Consider the data and figures in Section 10.2. These include Table 10.1 and Figures 10.3, 10.4 and 10.5. Evaluate whether higher GDP per capita is good or bad for society.

Chapter 11
Expenditure and fiscal policy

Chapter contents

 Learning outcomes

By the end of this chapter you should understand:

Economic Theory

LO1 The Keynesian Cross approach to modelling equilibrium output

LO2 The fiscal multiplier

LO3 The balanced budget

LO4 Problems associated with using fiscal policy

Business Application

LO5 Debt funding and crowding out

LO6 Taxation or government spending?

◉ Economic stability and demand side policies at a glance

The issue

Both the current level of economic activity and future growth in economic activity are important for business. The government has a number of policies that it can use to control current economic activity. Understanding how these policies influence the economy and business is of enormous importance to firms operating both within their domestic markets and overseas.

The understanding

Economic activity rises and falls with the business cycle. During recessions the government may try to raise economic activity, while during economic booms the government may try to reduce economic activity. Acting through the demand side of the economy, the government can influence economic activity through fiscal and monetary policy. These will be discussed at length but, essentially, by altering interest rates, government spending or taxation, the government can try to influence the level of demand in an economy – for example, raising demand during a recession and lowering demand during a boom.

The usefulness

As the government alters domestic macroeconomic policy, it is essential for business to understand how the economy will react. Some policies, if implemented incorrectly, can have a destabilizing effect on the economy. For planning purposes, it may be important to understand what type of policies will be deployed in the future. In recent times, interest rates have been very important policy tools. But, as interest rates fall to historic lows, the scope for further cuts becomes limited. Therefore, what might replace interest rate policy and how will firms need to react?

11.1 Business problem: who's spending and where?

Rising GDP should be associated with increased expenditure by consumers. More jobs and higher wages facilitate consumption. In turn, greater consumption drives sales and fuels profits. If only it were so simple. We know from the circular flow of income in Chapter 9 that consumption is only one element of total expenditure. In addition, we have spending by firms, which is classified as investment. We have government spending on education, health and public infrastructure; and we have international trade, where exports represent expenditure in the economy and imports represent expenditure in overseas economies. In Box 11.1, each of these components is changing for China. Different firms and industrial sectors will have differing exposure to consumers, investment, government spending and international trade. Therefore, the manner in which the economy grows has varying implications across industrial sectors. For example, retailers will benefit from an increase in consumption expenditure. In contrast, construction companies are more likely to benefit directly from growth in GDP, which is fuelled by firms investing in offices and factories, as well as government wishing to build hospitals and schools. Companies and economies, such as China, are heavily reliant on external demand. This means such economies are more likely to be affected by changes in consumption across other countries, with, for example, overseas consumers decreasing their demand for toys.

Box 11.1 Signs of an economic slowdown are also spreading to China

Adapted from an article by Andrew Batson and Norihiko Shirouzu in the Wall Street Journal, *12 November 2008*

Signs of a slowdown in China are spreading, with weak economic data for October illustrating why the government hurried to announce a massive stimulus plan.

Growth in China's exports continued to moderate last month, as demand for big markets like the US weakened. Merchandise exports rose 19.2 per cent in October from a year earlier, down from a 25.7 per cent rise for all of 2007. Vendors of furniture and toys who attended the Canton annual trade fair reported that orders from overseas had plunged: 174 500 buyers placed orders for $31.55 billion of goods, down 15 per cent from a year earlier. Gaoerfu Furniture last year received an order that needed 40 shipping containers. This year, the company managed only five orders, totalling six containers. In addition to the drop in exports, Chinese consumer spending on big-ticket items like cars has faded in recent months, and housing sales have plummeted.

To balance this drop in spending, China's government announced a stimulus package of $586 billion. Revitalizing the housing market and stepping up investment in infrastructure projects are central elements of the stimulus plan. The Ministry of Transport intends to increase investment by 25 per cent. The Ministry of Railways will increase investment by 20 per cent this year and will double it by next year. Railway construction is expected to create 800 000 jobs – new employment that will be crucial as layoffs in the export sector multiply.

While the drivers of aggregate demand appear to be multifaceted, they are still related. Returning to the circular flow of income: total expenditure occurs with firms, which then pay wages to workers. These wages can then fuel consumption, or leak from the circular flow of income, in savings (to meet investments), in taxes (to meet government spending) and in imports. Therefore a rise in investment can lead to a future rise in employment, wages and eventually consumption. Or an increase in investment expenditure can facilitate more investment, or more government spending. It is clear that there is a complexity of intertwined relationships at the macroeconomic level, which the firm needs to appreciate.

It is essential that businesspeople are able to disentangle the macroeconomic environment in order to understand the business opportunities and commercial threats that it poses. When will demand increase in the economy and will it impact your sector? Moreover, what factors will help to drive the various categories of expenditure? Box 11.1 alludes to the role of exports and external consumer confidence in determining economic activity. But then it can be asked, what determines consumer confidence? Employment prospects and sales might be two key drivers, which are clearly linked back to the level of economic activity, or the ever-revolving circular flow of income.

What governments have come to recognize is that stability is preferable. Volatility leads to uncertainty, and uncertainty reduces both consumer and business confidence. An increased probability of losing your job in the next 12 months will reduce your willingness to borrow and/or spend. Equally, governments have come to recognize that they can make a meaningful attempt at managing the economy. In the case of China, this involves a massive cash injection on spending into the economy by the government. Businesspeople need to be aware of how such policies feed into the circular flow of income and activate changes in consumption, investment, government spending and net exports. This chapter seeks to achieve this by developing your understanding of fiscal and monetary policy.

11.2 Consumption, investment expenditure and the business cycle

In Chapter 9, we introduced the aggregate demand and aggregate supply approach to understanding the **equilibrium** output of an economy and the price level. The approach enables a clear and insightful link to be made between micro- and macroeconomic theory.

> The **equilibrium** is generally defined as the situation where **planned aggregate expenditure** is equal to the actual output of firms.
>
> **Planned aggregate expenditure** is the total amount of spending on goods and services within the economy that is planned by purchasers.

It is unfortunate that the aggregate demand and aggregate supply approach ensures that the economy is always in equilibrium. As such, there can be no unemployment. All workers that desire a job will be employed.

This is not ideal given that we observe unemployment most of the time. We can adapt the aggregate demand and supply framework, but a useful approach is to instead introduce the Keynesian Cross as a model of equilibrium output. Under the Keynesian Cross approach, there is an assumption that prices are constant; as a result, inflation is not considered within the approach. Put simply, what firms produce is exactly equal to what consumers are planning to buy. Figure 11.1 illustrates this idea with the 45° line.

We use the 45° line because it cuts the angle 90° in half. Therefore, when we draw across a planned level of expenditure equal to 100, the actual level of output will also be 100. As a consequence, the 45° line shows all the possible equilibrium points. However, the essential question is, what will be the level of planned expenditure?

Planned expenditure

> A **closed economy** does not trade with the rest of the world. An open economy does trade with the rest of the world.

For simplicity, we will assume that we have a **closed economy** with no government sector. The only groups spending within the economy under such a scenario are consumers and firms (we have no government and no exports). Planned expenditure of aggregate demand can be expressed as:

$$PE = AD = C + I$$

where PE = planned expenditure; C = consumption; and I = investment.

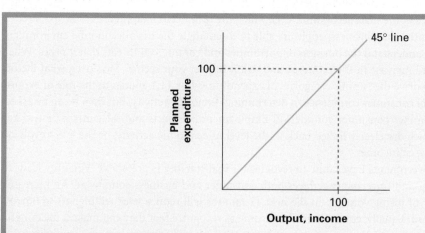

Figure 11.1 The 45° line

In equilibrium, planned expenditure is exactly equal to the output produced by all firms. So, with planned expenditure of 100, output is also 100.

Consumption

An expenditure is described as **autonomous** if it is not influenced by the level of income. Therefore, **autonomous consumption** does not change if income changes.

The **MPC (marginal propensity to consume)** is the extra consumption generated by one unit of extra income.

The **MPS (marginal propensity to save)** is simply the extra saving generated by one unit of extra income.

The level of consumption undertaken by private individuals is assumed by economists to be related to two factors: (i) a basic need to consume and (ii) the level of personal income. The basic need to consume is the level of consumption undertaken by an individual when their income is zero. It is the basic level of consumption that is required in order to survive. It is more often referred to as **autonomous consumption**, which is linked to **autonomous expenditure**.

As income increases, individuals will begin to consume more goods and services. But they may not spend all of their income on consumption. A small portion could be saved: 100 of income could result in 80 of consumption and 20 of saving. Economists link income with consumption and saving using the concepts of **marginal propensity to consume** and **marginal propensity to save**.

The marginal propensity to consume, MPC, is a measure of how much additional consumption will result from an increase in income. The MPC lies between zero and one. So, if the MPC = 0.8, then for every extra £100 of income, consumers will raise consumption by £80.

Similarly, the marginal propensity to save, MPS, is a measure of how much additional saving will result from an increase in income. Again, the MPS lies between zero and one. So, if the MPS = 0.2, then an increase in income of £100 will lead to an extra £20 of savings.

Given that individuals can either consume or save, the MPC + MPS = 1.

So, if we assume that autonomous consumption is 7 and the MPC is 0.8, then we can say that:

$$C = 7 + 0.8Y$$

where Y = personal disposable income and C = consumption.

This is nothing more than the equation of a straight line and it is drawn in Figure 11.2. Consumption has two components. A fixed amount, in this case 7, plus an amount that is determined by income, in this case $0.8 \times 100 = 80$.

When income is zero, consumption is 7. This is the intercept. The slope of the consumption line is equal to the MPC and in this case is 0.8. So, if income is 100, we can now say that consumption will be $7 + 0.8 \times 100 = 7 + 80 = 87$.

Before we move on to look at investment, it is also useful to think about what determines the marginal propensity to consume (and the marginal propensity to save). A key driver of the

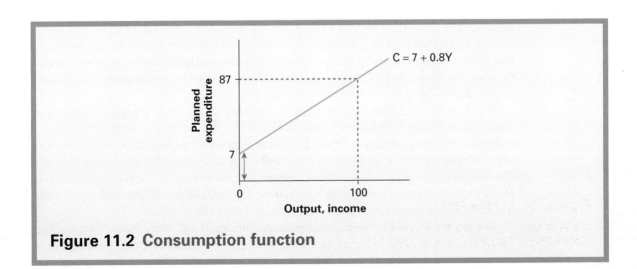

Figure 11.2 Consumption function

marginal propensity to consume is consumer confidence. As consumers become more confident about the stability of their income, they are more likely to spend. If the macroeconomic environment becomes more uncertain, or heads into a recession, then consumers may fear job losses and a reduction in income. Their confidence falls and their propensity to spend may decrease. Box 11.2 provides some measures of consumer confidence across a number of economies.

 Box 11.2 South Korea leads global fall in consumer confidence

Adapted from a Reuters *article by Susan Fenton, 6 November 2008*

Consumer confidence has dropped sharply across the globe in the past six months in the wake of the financial crisis, with consumers in South Korea, Japan and Portugal most pessimistic, a survey by the Nielsen Company shows.

Indian consumers were most optimistic, although less so than in the first half of the year. In the US – the world's biggest consumer market – confidence, which plunged in the first half of this year, was only marginally lower in the second half but slightly below the global average.

As rising concern about the economy and job security weighed on consumers, the half-yearly Nielsen Consumer Confidence Index's global average reading fell to 84, from 88 in the first half, and a peak of 99 two years ago. A reading above 100 is considered upbeat. The highest reading since the index's launch in 2005 was 137.

Investment

Investment is the demand for capital products by firms, plus changes to firms' inventories, or stocks.

We have seen how income determines the consumption decisions of private individuals. But what drives investment decisions? The answer to this question is highly debatable but, in general, and in simple terms, economists begin by assuming that investment decisions are based on instinct. How managers feel about the future is a major factor when deciding to invest money. If managers think the future looks good, they will be likely to invest. But if the future looks bad, they will cut back on investments. As such, investment decisions taken now are not influenced by the current level of income. For this reason, investment is also seen as autonomous. This means that, just like the 7 of consumption undertaken by consumers, firms set a base level of investment, say 50, but then there is no additional investment relating to increased income. The implications of this are shown in Figure 11.3, where the investment is set at 50 and remains constant at 50 for every level of income.

We can now add the consumption and investment together to arrive at aggregate demand or planned expenditure. This has been done in Figure 11.4, which, while looking complicated, is little more than an extension of Figure 11.2. From Figure 11.2 we have the consumption line, with 7 of consumption at zero levels of income and overall consumption of 87 when income is 100. We have then simply added in an additional 50 for investment. Aggregate demand, or planned expenditure, is now 7 + 50 = 57 at zero income, and overall planned expenditure, which is equal to consumption plus investment, 87 + 50 = 137.

We started with the 45° line and said that equilibrium occurs where planned expenditure equals actual output. From Figure 11.4 we now have an understanding of expenditure in an economy. We therefore only need to introduce the 45° line into Figure 11.4 and we can find

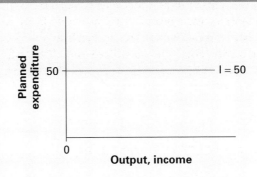

Figure 11.3 Investment

Investment has only one component, a purely fixed amount, which does not change with the level of income.

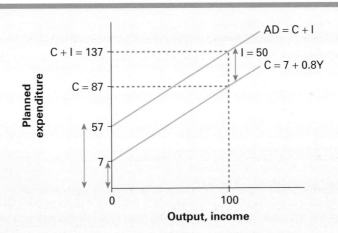

Figure 11.4 Aggregate demand: consumption plus investment

Adding investment to consumption simply increases autonomous expenditure by the increased amount of investment. In this case, investment = 50, so at all levels of income spending has increased by 50. At zero income, the level of consumption is 7; adding in investment of 50 simply means that planned expenditure = 57 when investment equals zero. Since autonomous expenditure does not change with the level of output, then, even when income = 100, the difference between consumption and investment will still be 50.

the equilibrium for the economy. Figure 11.5 shows the 45° line and the AD = C + I line together.

In our example the equilibrium level of income is 285.

Proof:

$$AD = C + I, \quad C = 7 + 0.8Y, \quad I = 50$$

$$AD = 7 + 0.8Y + 50$$
$$= 57 + 0.8Y$$

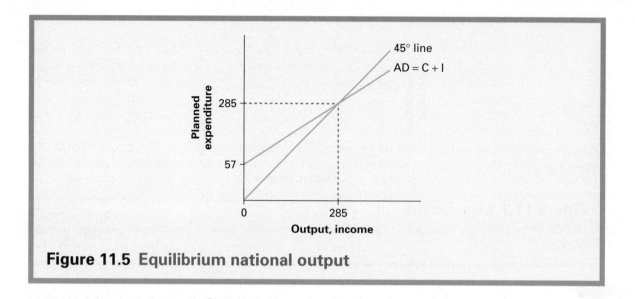

Figure 11.5 Equilibrium national output

In equilibrium national output = aggregate demand, or Y = AD (1).
Therefore Y = 57 + 0.8Y.
Rearranging,

0.2Y = 57
Y = 57/0.2 = 285

(Question 12 at the end of the chapter contains an additional example if you would like to test your ability to derive the equilibrium.)

Where the AD line crosses the 45° line must be the equilibrium, because this is where planned expenditure equals actual output.

At all output levels below 285, aggregate demand will be greater than national output. For example, if national output was only 200, then firms would not be producing enough output to meet the level of aggregate demand in the economy. Firms will have to meet the excess demand by using stocks held over from previous periods. Similarly, at all output levels above 285, national output will be greater than aggregate demand. For example, if national output is 300, aggregate demand will be less than the national output. As a result, firms will be left with excess stock.

Adjustment to the equilibrium

The economy will move to the equilibrium of 285 units by firms responding to changes in their stock levels. When output is below equilibrium, firms' stocks will reduce. Firms will interpret falling stock levels as an opportunity to expand production, because consumers are demanding more output than is currently being produced. In contrast, when output is above the equilibrium level, firms' stock levels will begin to increase. Rising stock levels will suggest to firms that current output is too high. Consumers are not demanding all that is being produced, hence the additions to stocks. Firms will, therefore, reduce output and the economy will shift towards the equilibrium.

In summary, adjustment to equilibrium occurs through firms reacting to changes in stock levels, where changing stock levels reflect differences between planned expenditure by consumers and actual output by firms.

The multiplier

Here is a simple idea. What would happen if firms decided that the economic outlook was favourable? We might expect them to increase their levels of investment from 50 to 100. But by how much would output increase? An extra 50? The answer rests on a very important insight known as the **multiplier**.

If the multiplier is 3, an increase in investment of 50 will lead to an increase in output of $3 \times 50 = 150$. But what determines the size of the multiplier?

The multiplier is directly related to the marginal propensity to save. In our example, the MPS = 0.2. Consider the following. Firms buy more computers and thereby increase investment by 50. The computer manufacturers receive the 50 and for the extra output pass this on in increased wages to their workers. The workers will use this to increase consumption by $0.8 \times 50 = 40$ and save $10 = (0.2 \times 50)$. So far, expenditure has now increased by the initial 50 increase in investment plus the 40 in consumption by the workers. If the computer workers spent the extra 40 at supermarkets, then income of supermarket workers increases by 40. They will spend $0.8 \times 40 = 32$ on consumption and save 8.

We can keep going, but even at this stage we can see that an increase of 50 in investment has led to an increase in consumption of 40 and then another 32. So, overall, the change in investment of 50 has created $50 + 40 + 32 = 122$ change in expenditure and therefore national output.

This is entirely linked to the circular flow of income introduced in Chapter 9. The 50 increase in investment is an injection into the circular flow. It moves round the cycle, 10 leaks out in savings and then 40 goes around again as consumption; 8 then leaks out in savings and then 32 goes around again. Indeed, if we did keep going we would find that the initial increase of 50 would create a total change in national output of 250, or 5×50. Why? Because the multiplier is calculated thus:

$$\text{Multiplier} = 1/\text{MPS} = 1/(1 - \text{MPC})$$

So, if the MPS = 0.2, the multiplier = 1/0.2 = 5. So, the size of the multiplier is entirely dependent upon the MPS. The higher the MPS, the faster the initial injection leaks out of the circular flow, and so less is left to go around again.

For example, if the MPS was 0.5, then 50 would go around the circular flow and 25 would leak out as savings, with only 25 going around again as consumption. Then 12.5 would leak out, leaving only 12.5 to go around again. In total, because the multiplier is now only 1/0.5 = 2, the initial injection of 50 from investment would only result in output changing by 100.

11.3 Fiscal policy

What is so exciting about the multiplier? For the economist, the multiplier means that small changes in autonomous expenditure can generate big changes in national income. In order to see the importance of this insight, we need to introduce the government sector.

If the government wishes to control the economy, such as moving it from a position of recession, then it only has to change autonomous expenditure by a small amount in order to generate a very large change in overall economic activity.

How might it do this? Asking firms to invest more is unlikely to be effective; firms invest because they want to, not because governments ask them to. But what about government spending? Could the government pump additional expenditure into the economy through its own projects such as health and education? We will answer this by examining **fiscal policy**.

We will shortly see that fiscal policy can be used to control the economy, but the implementation of effective fiscal policy may be problematic.

The **multiplier** measures the change in output following a change in autonomous expenditure (the essential or basic amount of consumption plus investment).

Fiscal policy is the government's decisions regarding taxation and spending.

Government, aggregate demand and equilibrium income

In the previous section we saw how planned expenditure, or aggregate demand, is equal to consumption plus investment, AD = C + I. In introducing the government, we are creating a third source of spending within the economy. Aggregate demand is now calculated thus: AD = C + I + G, where G = government spending. Just like investment, government spending is also autonomous. It does not vary with the level of income. Governments take political spending decisions, for example how much should be spent on education and how much on roads. In the main, the level of income does not determine government spending.

In terms of our diagrammatic approach, we simply add government spending into the analysis in much the same way as we dealt with investment. Government spending as an autonomous expenditure simply raises the aggregate demand line by the amount of government spending. In Figure 11.6, we have assumed that G = 20. With no government sector, as in Figure 11.4, we saw that, when income was zero, spending equalled 57, which consisted of autonomous consumption equal to 7 and investment equal to 50. We can now add government spending equal to 20. So, aggregate demand when income equals zero is now 77.

However, we also need to address the impact of taxation. In Figure 11.4, without tax we simply argued that consumption C = 7 + 0.8Y. But if individuals are taxed, we need to reduce their income, Y, by the amount of the tax. If the tax rate = t, then after-tax income equals $(1 - t)Y$. It is this after-tax income which individuals then use for consumption, or saving. So, if the MPC = 0.8, then consumers spend 0.8 of their after-tax income. Therefore, taking account of tax we can now say that consumption is:

$$C = 7 + 0.8 (1 - t)Y$$

and not

$$C = 7 + 0.8Y$$

The MPC determines how steep the AD line is, because it determines the link between growth in income and growth in consumption. A higher MPC will result in a steeper AD line. Tax effectively reduces the strength of the link between consumption and income, because an increase in income will be taxed before individuals can use it to increase consumption. Therefore, tax makes the AD line flatter.

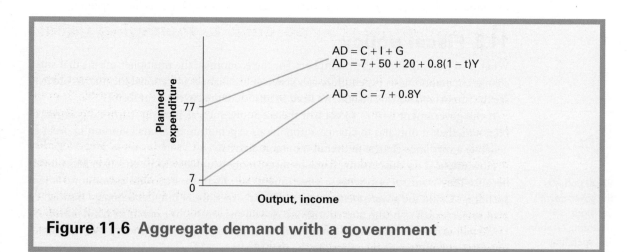

Figure 11.6 Aggregate demand with a government

Taking tax and government spending together, we can now see that the AD line with a government sector is higher because of government spending but flatter because of taxation.

What does this really tell us? The importance is in the consumption line being flatter. This means that, when taxes are applied, an increase in income has a lower impact on consumption. This is because we have opened up another avenue for leakages. By introducing the government sector, income can leak out via savings and taxes. This is significant because we have seen that the multiplier was determined by the rate of leakages and, indeed, the multiplier is now:

$$\text{Multiplier} = 1/(\text{MPS} + \text{MPT})$$

where MPS = marginal propensity to save, and MPT = marginal propensity to tax.

So, if MPS = 0.2 and the MPT = 0.22 = the UK's basic tax rate, then the multiplier = $1/(0.2 + 0.22) = 2.38$.

When we had no government sector savings the multiplier was equal to:

$$1/\text{MPS} = 1/0.2 = 5$$

Note that, introducing the government has decreased the size of the multiplier.

The balanced budget multiplier

The **balanced budget multiplier** states that an increase in government spending, plus an *equal* increase in taxes, leads to higher equilibrium output.

Reducing the size of the multiplier could mean that the government might actually make itself ineffectual. For example, the government could inject 100 into the economy and then take out 100 in higher taxes. Would the multiplier then be zero? Amazingly, the answer to this question is no.

Sounds fantastic. You can put £100 in everyone's pocket, then take it out again and make everyone richer! How does this actually work? The answer requires a close examination of aggregate demand, AD = C + I + G. An increase of 100 in government spending clearly increases AD by 100. However, the effect of increasing taxes by 100 does not reduce AD by 100. This is because of the marginal propensity to consume, MPC. As the MPC is only 0.8, an increase in taxes by 100 causes income to fall by 100; the change in consumption is therefore only $0.8 \times 100 = 80$. The net effect on aggregate demand is an increase in G of 100 and a reduction in consumption of only 80. Therefore, aggregate demand increases by 20.

The obvious question to now ask is, how do governments in practice use government spending and taxation to control the equilibrium level of output?

11.4 Government's approach to managing fiscal policy

The government's spending and taxation decisions are reflected in the government deficit. The projected expenditure and revenue sources for the government are available from the so-called Red Book. For the tax year 2009/10, the revenue and expenditure figures are shown in Figure 11.7.

The largest areas of expenditure are social security, health and education. Taken together, these three areas represent more than 60 per cent of government spending. The largest sources of revenue come from personal taxation, national insurance contributions and VAT. It is perhaps surprising that revenues from corporation taxes are only £35 billion and represent a very small fraction of total government tax revenues. Government borrowing is £175 billion (£496 billion – £671 billion), the difference between government expenditure and government revenues, and represents the government's deficit.

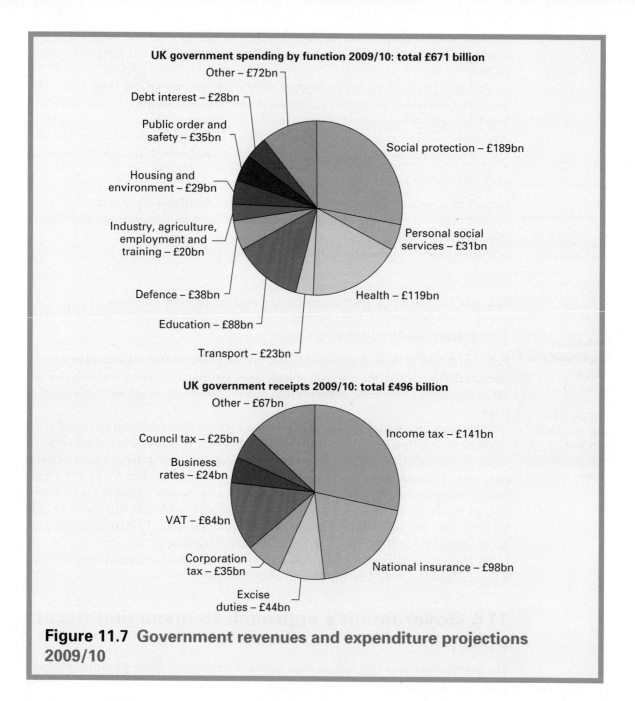

Figure 11.7 Government revenues and expenditure projections 2009/10

Deficits

The **government deficit** is the difference between government spending and taxation, or G – tY.

Government deficits as a percentage of GDP are plotted in Figure 11.8 for Germany, France, Italy and the UK. These deficits are the annual differences between government receipts and expenditures. Government deficits tend to display a cyclical pattern. As economies have fallen into recession, or slowed in growth, tax receipts have fallen behind expenditure levels and deficits have opened up. Members of the Eurozone are in normal economic times required to keep their budget deficits under 3 per cent of GDP. Because of the credit crisis and the need to

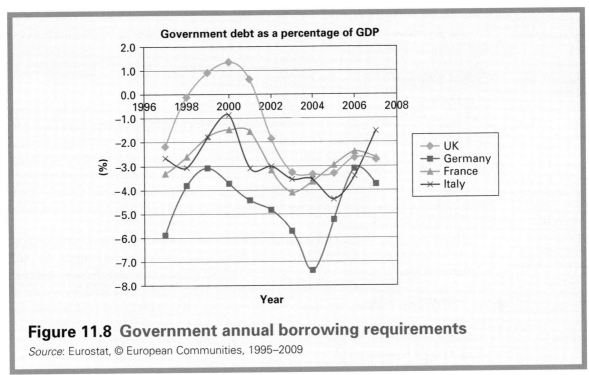

Figure 11.8 **Government annual borrowing requirements**

Source: Eurostat, © European Communities, 1995–2009

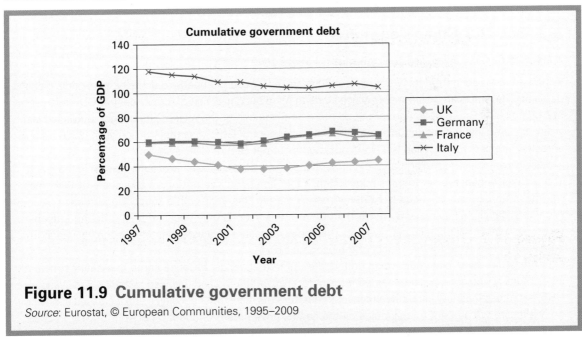

Figure 11.9 **Cumulative government debt**

Source: Eurostat, © European Communities, 1995–2009

Cumulative debt is the total outstanding government debt from borrowings over many years.

bail out banks and automobile manufacturers, the 3 per cent rule has been temporarily relaxed.

In Figure 11.9, the **cumulative debt** for France, Germany, Italy and the UK is shown. The cumulative debt is all current and outstanding debt. When governments borrow, just like firms and households, they can arrange to borrow for many years. In some instances, governments have borrowed for up to 50 years.

> The government's **fiscal stance** is the extent to which the government is using fiscal policy to increase or decrease aggregate demand in the economy.

We can see in Figure 11.9 that Italy has accumulated an enormous amount of debt compared to the size of its economy. In contrast, the UK has tried to keep government debt at less than 40 per cent of GDP.

Fiscal stance

Unfortunately, the continual link between the government deficit and the business cycle makes it difficult to appraise the government's **fiscal stance**. For example, an expansionary fiscal policy would ordinarily consist of a reduction in tax and an increase in government spending, resulting in a larger government deficit. In a recession, tax receipts will fall and create a larger deficit. It is, therefore, difficult to use the government deficit as a measure of the government's fiscal stance (see Box 11.3 for an assessment of the fiscal stance in the US and China). This is because the deficit can occur following an expansionary fiscal policy or, equally, because the economy is in recession.

> The **full employment** level of the economy is a long-run equilibrium position and the economy operates on its production possibility frontier. The economy is in neither boom nor recession.

We need, therefore, to adjust the government deficit for changes associated with the business cycle. We do this by calculating the government deficit if the economy was at its optimal, or **full employment**, level of output. We keep government spending and tax rates the same, but then assume that the equilibrium level of the economy is at its full employment level. We are, therefore, assuming the economy is not in boom or recession – it is perfectly balanced between the two extremes.

This full employment budget position is then described as the structural budget, which is adjusted for the business cycle.

 Box 11.3 China's stimulus

Adapted from 'Got a light?', in The Economist, *12 March 2009*

With the world economy in its worst crisis in 70 years, every country needs to do its bit to rekindle global demand. The American government, which plans to run a budget deficit of 12 per cent of GDP this year, has called on its Group of 20 partners to do more. Is China one of the misers? Its budget, published last week, showed that it plans to run a deficit of only 3 per cent of GDP. Was the 4 trillion yuan ($586 billion) infrastructure package unveiled last November, worth 14 per cent of GDP, a sham?

Beijing's stimulus is smaller than the number announced last year, but it is still the biggest in the world. The fact that America is set to run a budget deficit four times the size of China's as a share of GDP does not mean its demand stimulus is bigger; America started this year with a much bigger deficit. Also, America's deficit will increase by more than China's this year, largely because it is suffering a deeper recession, which will depress tax revenue. The correct measure of a fiscal stimulus is the change in the budget deficit adjusted for the impact of the economic cycle.

In China, however, even this would understate the true stimulus, because some public-infrastructure investment will be done by state-owned firms or local governments and financed by banks. Tao Wang, of UBS, estimates that new infrastructure investment, tax cuts, consumer subsidies and increased spending on healthcare will amount to a stimulus by the central government of about 3 per cent of GDP in 2009. Adding in bank-financed infrastructure spending might lift the total to 4 per cent of GDP.

Chinese investment in railways, roads and power grids is already booming. In the first two months of this year, total fixed investment was 30 per cent higher in real terms than a year earlier, and investment in railways tripled. China has been much criticized for focusing its stimulus on investment, rather than consumption, but in China in the short term this is the quickest way to boost domestic demand.

Many economies pursue a balanced budget policy, with a stated aim of ensuring a balanced budget over the medium term. This is effectively arguing that the structural budget will be zero. In boom, we might expect a budget surplus; in recession, we could see a deficit. But on balance, the budget will be just that – balanced. Structural balance still allows a contractionary, or expansionary fiscal policy. During a recession, the government can add spending into the economy through tax reductions and increases in government spending. Similarly, during an economic boom, the government can increase taxes and reduce government spending.

From the 1970s onwards, fiscal policy became less popular, reflecting the concerns of economists and politicians that an overly expansionary fiscal policy can be destabilizing for the economy. However, during the credit crisis a fiscal stimulus was an obvious means of providing a rapid expansion of spending in the economy. Governments across the world quickly realized that cuts in interest rates could be supplemented by government spending and tax cuts. Despite the immediate popularity of fiscal policy, it is still necessary to recognize the weakness which reduced its popularity from the 1970s onwards.

Fiscal policy weaknesses

Automatic stabilizers enable the economy to adjust automatically to changes in aggregate demand.

If, during a boom, income in an economy increases, tax receipts will increase, savings will increase and the government will cut back on social payments, such as unemployment benefit. This shows that the economy has automatic brakes built into the system that will help to control the rate of economic boom. Conversely, in recession, tax receipts will fall, savings will reduce and government payments will increase. This way the economy will automatically reduce the net rate of leakages and help to keep the economy moving.

Because such stabilizers work automatically, then, from a fiscal position, the economy can be placed on autopilot. There is no need for the government to overly monitor economic activity and make policy changes. It can focus its energies on other matters, such as health and education.

Fiscal policy and implementation problems

There are additional reasons for believing in the virtues of automatic stabilizers and these relate to the problems associated with actively managing fiscal policy.

Time lags

In order to actively manage fiscal policy the government needs to know when aggregate demand is falling and when it is rising. This can only be achieved with a lag. Government statisticians collect data on economic activity, but they are only able to report and, perhaps more important, confirm either a slowdown or an increase in economic activity three to six months after the event. The government then needs to consider a policy response and then introduce the response. This all takes time. Once the policy is introduced, say a cut in taxation to offset falling demand in an economy, the economy may have moved on, showing signs of economic growth. The tax stimulation is then inappropriate because it will be adding to a boom rather than assisting a recessionary problem.

Uncertainty

Assume an economy is in recession. The equilibrium level of income is £10 billion, but currently output is around £5 billion. The multiplier is 2. The economy has an output gap of £10bn − £5bn = £5bn. With a multiplier of 2, the government needs to increase aggregate demand by £2.5 billion.

Unfortunately, this example has benefited from complete certainty. We know the equilibrium level of output, the current level of output and the size of the multiplier. In practice, the government and its advisers do not know any of these values with certainty. Now let us assume that all of the factors above are estimates. We could even be generous to the government and say that it guessed the size of the multiplier and the current level of GDP accurately. But the equilibrium level of income is only £8 billion, not £10 billion. Therefore, by overestimating the optimal level of output and injecting £2.5 billion into the economy the government will push the economy straight into a boom. It simply swaps a demoralizing recession for an equally unpalatable bout of inflation.

Offsetting changes

If the government pursues an expansionary fiscal stance, it will tend to take on more debt in order to finance its spending. At some point in the future this debt has to be serviced and perhaps even repaid. In the presence of very large mountains of public debt, sensible private individuals may predict that in the future tax rates will have to rise in order to fund the current lax fiscal position of the government. In order to offset these future higher taxes, individuals might save more now. Therefore, higher government spending and reduced taxes now could generate higher levels of offsetting autonomous savings. The government's fiscal stance is effectively neutralized by the response of higher savings from the private sector.

Actively managed fiscal policy sought to manage the business cycle by adding demand during a recession and reducing demand during a boom. Due to problems of timing, uncertainty and offsetting, such policy responses have been ill-timed, misjudged and at best ineffective.

Deficits and inflation

We saw in Chapter 9 that inflation can erode the value of debt. If you borrow £100 and inflation is 10 per cent, then, in real terms, at the end of year one you will only owe £90. You, as a private individual, have very little control over the rate of inflation. But for a government the case is very different. If a government runs up a mountain of debt, the temptation to let the rate of inflation increase and erode the real value of the debt is very tempting.

This has two important implications. First, if a government is trying to manage individuals' inflationary expectations, then it needs to manage the size of the government debt. Being seen to reduce debt and fiscal deficits reduces the need to stoke up inflation. As a consequence, inflationary expectations will be lower and inflation should turn out to be lower. Second, as we see in Chapter 13, within a fixed exchange rate system such as the European single currency, harmonizing inflation across member states may aid economic convergence among those states. Therefore, as entry into the system draws nearer, the UK government needs to bring fiscal policy under control.

Crowding out

**Crowding out
occurs when
increased
government
spending reduces
private sector
spending.**

Crowding out relates back to the business problem at the beginning of this chapter. If government takes an expansionary fiscal stance, then it can achieve this by spending more public money on health, education and transport infrastructure projects. But this policy runs the risk of robbing productive resources from the private sector. For every nurse employed in a hospital, a worker is effectively removed from the private sector. This is known as crowding out, because public expenditure by government crowds out private expenditure by firms. The extent to which this occurs is debatable. When there are lots of workers without jobs, an increase in government spending will not crowd out private expenditure. Employment will rise, output will grow and income will increase. But when productive resources, such as labour, are all fully employed, then increasing public expenditure is likely to rob the private sector of its resources. Employment stays constant, at best output stays constant and so does income. An expansionary fiscal policy has no net impact on national output.

Summary

Given all of these problems, it is not surprising that economists and governments began to move away from active fiscal management of the economy. Instead, they recognized the benefits of automatic stabilizers and moved focus to monetary and supply side policies. Fiscal policy was popular from the 1930s through to the 1970s, a period during which a global depression in the 1930s meant there was no crowding out. Economic change occurred at a more sedate and predictable pace and concerns regarding inflation were less important. All this changed in the 1980s, 1990s and 2000s. With modern economies developing with great pace and complexity, inflationary aversion was everywhere and high levels of employment ensured that crowding out was a real problem. However, following the credit crisis the effectiveness of fiscal policy has returned. This is because a prolonged recession results in little crowding out. At the same time as banks, consumers and firms become insensitive to central bank base rate changes, then fiscal policy can become more attractive than monetary policy.

11.5 Foreign trade and aggregate demand

So far in our examination of aggregate demand, we have only considered economies which do not trade with the rest of the world. While we will focus on issues of exchange rates and globalization in Chapters 13 and 14, it is worth incorporating the impact of international trade on aggregate demand.

Exports are generally expressed as X and imports as Z.

Economists generally talk about net exports, or the trade balance, which is clearly X − Z. If exports are greater than imports, the economy has a trade surplus, but if imports are greater than exports, the economy has a trade deficit.

We now need to think about incorporating X and Z into our existing analysis of aggregate demand. In fairly simple terms, exports are UK products purchased by foreign consumers; Scotch whisky produced in the UK but sold in the US would be an example. So, exports add to UK aggregate demand. Imports work in the opposite direction. These are foreign products purchased by UK consumers; BMW cars made in Germany but bought in the UK would be an example. Therefore, aggregate demand can now be defined as AD = C + I + G + X − Z.

However, as with the introduction of the government sector, we need to address the factors that determine exports and imports. First, the level of UK income does not influence exports; instead, US consumers' willingness to purchase UK products is influenced by US income. As income rises in the US, consumers are willing to search out more expensive imports from overseas, such as Scotch whisky. Therefore, exports are autonomous, or independent, of the UK's level of income. In contrast, the level of UK income influences imports. As our income increases, we are willing to buy more expensive products from overseas.

We therefore have a marginal propensity to import (MPZ), which is the increase in income allocated to import products.

In terms of aggregate demand, exports are grouped with the other autonomous expenditures: autonomous consumption, investment and government spending. As such, exports represent a potential injection into the circular flow of income. Rising income levels in the US, or the European Union, are likely to result in additional UK exports to these economies. Conversely, as these economies move into recession, demand for UK products will fall.

Exports add to the complexity of planning UK domestic policy because, in order to keep aggregate demand at the equilibrium level, the government has to understand the level of domestic consumption, domestic investment and how the business cycle in other economies such as Europe and the US influence UK exports. See Box 11.4.

 ## Box 11.4 UK trade deficit narrowed to £3.9 billion in September

Adapted from the Office for National Statistics, *11 November 2008*

The UK's deficit on trade in goods and services was £3.9 billion in September, compared with the deficit of £4.4 billion in August. The surplus on trade in services was £3.6 billion, the same as in August. The deficit on trade in goods was £7.5 billion, compared with the deficit of £8.0 billion in August. Exports rose by £0.6 billion and imports rose by £0.1 billion.

There was a rise in exports of oil to the EU and and a fall in the exports of consumer goods other than cars to non-EU economies. There were increases in imports of intermediate goods, cars and chemicals from the EU and a fall in the imports of precious stones from non-EU economies.

Export prices were a half per cent lower and import prices were a half per cent higher than in August.

Source: www.statistics.gov.uk

Should we be troubled by a rising trade deficit? The answer is yes because imports represent a leakage from the circular flow of income. Leakages reduce the size of the multiplier. With imports, injections leak out of the economy more quickly and, therefore, less money is left in the circular flow to go through the next cycle. In an open economy with a government sector, the multiplier is:

Open economy multiplier with government sector $= 1/(\text{MPS} + \text{MPT} + \text{MPZ})$

Imports, therefore, increase the economy's leakages and in so doing can reduce the size of the multiplier.

In terms of fiscal policy, the open economy creates real practical problems for the government. For example, if the government increases government spending, then this represents an autonomous injection into the economy. With an open economy, however, there is a distinct possibility that this additional expenditure could leak out as imports, resulting in zero impact on the level of aggregate demand. For example, increased spending by the UK government on healthcare can now be used to pay for operations undertaken in French hospitals. The money spent on extending the UK's airport capacity could be spent by workers on foreign holidays.

Summary

Fiscal policy, in the main, relies on the power of the multiplier to provide the government with an effective tool for managing the economy. As the world's economies become more globally integrated, the scope of international leakages increases and the multiplier decreases in size and effectiveness. Moreover, fiscal policy requires timely and accurate information. The complexity of modern economies, including increasing globalization, makes these informational requirements difficult to attain.

11.6 Business application: debt funding and crowding out

Crowding out occurs when government spending absorbs economic resource that would have been used by the private sector. Increases in government spending, therefore, result in lower private sector spending. The net effect on total expenditure is zero. The government's fiscal expansion is neutralized.

Unfortunately, the problem of crowding out can be worse than this. Unless the government has enormous cash reserves, then an expansion in government spending needs to be funded by borrowings. Government debt has to increase. So who lends to governments?

The answer to this last question is varied. Lenders can include ordinary household savers, private companies, pension funds and banks. In a global financial system, lenders can also include overseas investors. So even when an economy has a very low marginal propensity to save, governments can raise huge amounts of debt by borrowing from overseas investors.

Generally, governments do not face problems when raising debt. Lenders view governments from modern developed economies as safe bets. The creditworthiness of governments is usually high. But this may not be the case when governments are seeking to increase borrowings on an unprecedented scale. In order to service debt, governments need to be capable of raising taxes. But during a recession tax receipts can fall and the ability to service enormous debts can fall. This worries individuals and companies who lend to governments. The obvious way to address these fears is to ask for a higher interest rate to cover the increased risk of lending to a heavily indebted government.

If the price of debt rises for governments, then the price of debt also rises for the private sector. This is a simple substitution effect. If the private sector is not willing to borrow at the same prices as governments are willing to pay, then lenders will simply lend to governments only. As a consequence, there is an alternative crowding out effect. Increases in government borrowings can push up the price of debt for private sector borrowers. An increase in the price of funds reduces the demand for debt by the private sector. If debt consumption falls, then so does household consumption and company investment.

 Box 11.5 Sterling sinks to 12-year low on gilts sell-off

Adapted from an article by Peter Garnham, David Oakley, Chris Giles and Jim Pickard in The Financial Times, *12 November 2008*

Sterling fell to a 12-year low against a basket of currencies yesterday amid signs that foreign investors are deserting British assets.

Since mid-September UK fixed income instruments, which consist of gilts, corporate bonds, shorter maturing bills and mortgage securities, have seen extremely heavy outflows. This has coincided with a sharp fall in sterling. The net outflows of foreign investment from UK fixed income instruments seen over the past two months wiped out about 75 per cent of the net purchases that were seen between November 2004 and mid-September 2008. During the same time periods, the Eurozone saw outflows of 25 per cent of the inflows, and for the US and Japan outflows were around 15 per cent of inflows.

The UK government is planning to increase its borrowings to £110 billion from £58.5 billion last year. Analysts said the loss of confidence in the UK could limit the government's scope to deliver a fiscal stimulus as it struggles to attract funds from overseas, potentially pushing up borrowing costs to lure investors.

This type of financial crowding out is a current concern and the fall in sterling and the sell-off of government debt instruments, such as gilts, highlight how planned increases in UK government debt may result in higher borrowing costs for the private sector. Firms and households ordinarily do not appreciate the implications of capital flows into and out of an economy but, at times of high government borrowing, such flows become crucial in determining the price of public and private sector debt.

11.7 Business application: taxation or government spending?

A fiscal stimulus can occur through increased government spending or a reduction in tax. Both approaches increase total expenditure. Government spending directly alters the amount of expenditure, while tax cuts boost disposable income, which then leads to an increase in consumption. If government spending and tax both increase total expenditure, should the form of fiscal stimulus matter to business? The answer is yes, and it matters on a number levels, including how quickly the additional expenditure hits the economy and where the expenditure is channelled.

Timing

Governments are very good at announcing huge increases in expenditure. In our terminology, this is planned expenditure. This is very different from actual expenditure. Governments are not being disingenuous. Rather, it takes time to highlight projects, design them, contract for them and begin to spend the money. Unless there are many infrastructure projects in the pipeline, then it can take many years to develop such a pipeline. Meanwhile, the economy does not receive its much needed injection of spending.

In contrast, cuts in direct taxes, such as income tax, and cuts in indirect taxes, such as those on goods and services, create an immediate change in consumers' income. Tax cuts, therefore, have the potential to provide an almost instantaneous flow of additional spending into the economy.

Channels of spending

Governments spend on projects which they find attractive. This spending tends to be focused on education, healthcare and transport. Infrastructure projects in these areas are popular: new buildings, roads, railways and airports. Huge flows of money are channelled to the construction industry. Other sectors do not receive direct spending. Of course, some industries receive subsidies, loans and capital injections. In many economies, this has involved flows of money into banks and in the US and Germany has also included cash injections into the automotive industry. But is this spending effective, efficient and valued by taxpayers?

If fiscal policy involves tax cuts, then consumers can spend money in the markets they find most desirable. If an individual does not like flying, then the value of a government-funded airport expansion is limited. But if that individuals receives a tax cut, then they can spend their additional income on a holiday within the economy.

This debate goes to the heart of market-based economies. In Chapter 1, we introduced the production possibility frontier and highlighted two approaches to the allocation of economic resources: planned economies and market-based economies. Markets are generally accepted as the most effective means of solving the problem of infinite wants and finite resources. Why, during a recession, should we sacrifice this view and suddenly believe that governments are better placed to decide where spending should occur?

One response is that consumers may not react to tax cuts. They may instead save the additional income, or run down existing debts. In addition, in an economy that has a high propensity to import, then tax cuts are unlikely to fuel an increase in domestic demand. So for these reasons the government spending may be preferable because it ensures that spending occurs and that it occurs within the economy.

Firms need to be aware of these differences between government spending and tax cuts. An understanding of the differences enables an understanding of the likely time it will take to stimulate the economy and which sectors will be winners and losers.

We term this planned expenditure through disposable income and then through consumption. Should it matter to business how the stimulus occurs?

Summary

1   The use of government spending and taxation to affect aggregate demand are examples of fiscal policy.

2   Aggregate demand is composed of consumption, investment, government spending and net exports.

3   In equilibrium, planned expenditure equals planned output. In the Keynesian Cross, the equilibrium is characterized by the 45° line.

4   Expenditure which does not change with the level of income is known as autonomous expenditure. Increases in autonomous expenditure lead to higher equilibrium levels of output.

5   The marginal propensity to consume (MPC) measures the increase in consumption from an increase in income. The marginal propensity to save (MPS) measures the increase in savings from an increase in income.

6   If a £100 million increase in autonomous expenditure leads to a £500 million increase in GDP, then the fiscal multiplier is 5. The multiplier is dependent upon the rate of leakage from the circular flow of income. In a closed economy, the multiplier is equal to 1/MPS. But in an open economy with a government sector, the multiplier is reduced by the marginal propensity to tax (MPT) and the marginal propensity to import (MPZ) and so equals 1/(MPS + MPT + MPZ).

7   Fiscal policies can act as an automatic stabilizer on the economy. Rising incomes in a booming economy will be constrained by increasing tax receipts.

8   Active fiscal policies where the government seeks to pursue an expansionary, or contractionary, fiscal policy can be problematic. Problems surrounding timing, uncertainty, offsetting behaviour, crowding out and inflation-inducing deficits can create instability in the economic system.

Learning checklist

You should now be able to:

- Use Keynesian Cross diagrams to find the macroeconomic equilibrium output
- Calculate the size of the fiscal multiplier
- Explain why the multiplier might assist fiscal policy
- Assess the government's fiscal stance
- Explain the potential problems associated with using fiscal policy

Questions connect™

1 Identify the main components of total expenditure.

2 Explain why the 45° line represents the equilibrium in a Keynesian Cross diagram.

3 What is an autonomous expenditure? Use a suitable diagram to illustrate the effect on the economy of an increase in autonomous expenditures.

4 Explain how the consumption function links consumer spending and current income. Do you think this is a reasonable explanation of consumer spending?

5 What is the fiscal multiplier? What determines the size of the multiplier? How does the multiplier differ between closed and open economies?

6 During the last five years what are the key trends in the government deficit for your own economy?

7 Explain how you would assess the size of the government deficit to determine whether the government was using fiscal policy to expand or contract the economy.

8 Explain what is meant by the term 'balanced budget multiplier'.

9 Consider the four key components of aggregate expenditure: consumption, investment government spending and net exports. Is your economy dominated by domestic private spending, domestic public spending or external demand?

10 What problems are associated with the implementation of fiscal policy?

11 Recall Chapters 9 and 10. Which key macroeconomic variable is missing from the Keynesian Cross approach? Is this a major drawback of the Keynesian Cross approach?

12 In a closed economy with no government sector consumption, C = 20 + 0.8Y, investment I = 40. What is the equilibrium level of income Y?

13 When examining fiscal policy, should business be more interested in taxation policy or government spending?

14 An economy requires a fiscal stimulus. How effective will this stimulus be if the economy has a high marginal propensity to import?

15 The marginal propensity to save in China is extremely high, in excess of 30 per cent. Google and find out why?

Exercises

1 True or false?
   (a) In equilibrium, planned expenditure will equal planned output.
   (b) The fiscal multiplier is equal to 1/MPC.
   (c) The following are autonomous expenditures: investment, government spending and net exports.
   (d) Credit offered by banks is backed by cash deposits.
   (e) Keynesians believe that inflation is a monetary problem.
   (f) If aggregate supply is perfectly inelastic, a reduction in interest rates will lead to higher inflation.

2 Table 11.1 shows some data on consumption and income (output). Planned investment is autonomous, and occurs at the rate of $60 billion per period.
   (a) Calculate savings and aggregate demand at each level of income.
   (b) For each level of output, work out the unplanned change in inventory holdings and the rate of actual investment.
   (c) If, in a particular period, income turned out to be $100 billion, how would you expect producers to react?
   (d) If, in a particular period, income turned out to be $350 billion, how would you expect producers to react?
   (e) What is the equilibrium level of income?
   (f) What is the marginal propensity to consume?
   (g) If investment increased by $15 billion, what would be the change in equilibrium income?
   (h) Use graph paper to plot the consumption function and aggregate demand schedule.
   (i) Add on the 45° line and confirm that equilibrium occurs at the same point suggested by your answer to 2(e) above.
   (j) Show the effect on equilibrium of an increase in investment of $15 billion.

Table 11.1 Income and consumption

Income (output)	Planned consumption	Planned investment	Savings	Aggregate demand	Unplanned inventory change	Actual investment
50	35					
100	70					
150	105					
200	140					
250	175					
300	210					
350	245					
400	280					

3 (a) Using a Keynesian Cross diagram, illustrate how an increase in exports would alter the equilibrium output for an economy. What evidence is there that your economy is currently benefiting from an export boom?
   (b) What evidence is there that at present consumption and investment expenditure are rising in your economy?
   (c) Explain the variety of ways through which an increase in interest rates by the central bank would impact your economy.

Chapter contents

 ## Learning outcomes

By the end of this chapter you should understand:

Economic Theory

LO1   The key features of money

LO2   The nature and economic importance of
banking

LO3   Regulation

LO4   The credit-creation process

LO5   Broad and narrow measures of money

LO6   The transaction, precautionary and speculative motives for holding money

LO7   Money market equilibrium issues

LO8   Monetary policy

Business Application

LO9   Financial stability and businesses' desire for
investment

LO10 The importance of banking to the economy

Money, banking and interest at a glance

The issue

Money is a key feature of economic activity. What are the key features of money, what is the purpose of the banking system and how is it that interest rates can be used to influence GDP and inflation?

The understanding

Money enables buyers and sellers to trade and is referred to as a medium of exchange. Banks are important because they channel liquidity from savers who have too much cash to borrowers who have a shortage of cash. The interest rate is the equilibrium price of money. By varying the interest rate, a central bank alters the cost of borrowing. Since borrowing can facilitate household consumption and firm-level investment, changing interest rates can change the level of demand in an economy.

The usefulness

Understanding how the money and banking markets work is extremely important. First, it enables an understanding of how interest rate changes are transmitted into the wider economy. This has important implications for the level of consumption and investment demand. Second, banking is such an important component of modern economies that it is essential to understand the role of banking within an economy and appreciate its ability to support economic growth and also damage economic stability when there is a banking crisis.

12.1 Business problem: understanding how the monetary environment influences the commercial environment

Such is the importance of monetary policy that interest rate changes in the US, the Eurozone and the UK are dealt with as major news events. But why is interest rate policy such a significant part of economic policy?

The answer to this question is complex and involves an understanding of money, banking and money market equilibrium.

Money is a key characteristic of most economic transactions. Goods and services are nearly always priced in monetary terms. A pizza is £5, or €7. You never see pizza priced in bottles of Coca-Cola, or any other good or service. Money is a common price and, just as importantly, money is commonly accepted as payment for goods and services and is equally accepted as payment for work. While a key feature of economic activity, money is not economic activity. The conversion of economic inputs – land, labour, capital and enterprise – into goods and services is economic activity. But money is the means of facilitating economic transactions; as such, money is the lubricant of the economic system. To understand the level of economic activity and the level of consumption and investment demand is, in part, to understand how much monetary grease is in the system.

Understanding how much money exists within the economic system is not straightforward. Notes and coins are an obvious example of money, but so too are the electronic digits of money in your bank accounts. While the Bank of England is responsible for printing additional amounts of money, the retail banks are capable of multiplying electronic credits of money. If a company pays in £1 million, then the bank may lend out £0.9 million in loans. The money supply has just increased by £0.9 million. The company thinks it has £1 million of money and the borrowers think they also have £0.9 million of money.

Expansion of the money supply by banks represents the provision of liquidity. Channelling money from savers, who have excess cash for their current transaction needs, to borrowers, who are short of cash, given their current transaction needs, is a very beneficial economic activity. But the rate at which this occurs can be problematic. Too much credit expansion, and consumption and investment demand can grow too quickly, leading to inflation. Too little credit expansion, such as during the credit crisis, and economic growth will slow.

In setting base rates for the economy, central banks attempt to set the rate of credit expansion within an economy. Base rates determine the money market rates for money. If the central bank raises the base rate, then the price of monetary funds increases. With a fixed demand for money, the central bank must reduce the money supply in order to raise the interest rate. By mopping up excess liquidity, through higher rates of interest, the central bank limits the ability of retail banks to expand credit for consumption and investment. Likewise, if the bank reduces interest rates, then money supply needs to be increased, which enables the retail banks to expand credit to borrowers.

Understanding the intricacies of the money and banking markets and the role of the central bank provides a deeper insight into how changes in the base rates can impact on the level of consumption, investment and overall economic activity. Furthermore, understanding the economic importance of banking in providing credit and liquidity also opens up an understanding of the financial risks undertaken by banks. When banks collapse or face a loss of confidence, there can be a loss of confidence and withdrawl of liquidity from the economy. Banking regulation and an understanding of the importance of banking to the economy are also key issues to understand.

We will now develop your understanding of these issues by considering the role of money, the economic importance of banking, the regulation of banking, the credit-creation process, the demand for money, money market equilibrium and monetary policies.

12.2 **What is money?**

In a **barter economy** there is no money and individuals trade by exchanging different goods and services.

Money facilitates exchange. Consider an economy with no money, generally referred to as a **barter economy**, where goods are swapped for other goods.

We are specialist economic textbook authors. That is what we produce. You might flip burgers or drive a taxi. This book could be worth 30 burgers or one taxi ride to the airport. We do not like burgers, but we do fly, so we need a taxi. But will the taxi driver want our economics textbook in return for a trip to the airport; and if the burger flipper wants our book, do we want 30 burgers in return?

You can see the problem: without money a so-called **double coincidence of wants** is required in order to exchange goods.

A **double coincidence of wants** occurs when two people trade goods and services without money. The first individual demands the good offered by the second individual, and vice versa.

As textbook authors we need to find people who want our book, and are offering goods we want in exchange. Money solves this problem. We can pay the taxi driver £30 cash and they can then use this money to buy goods which they desire, such as food, petrol or coffee; they do not have to accept the textbook.

A central role of money is that it is recognized and accepted as a medium of exchange. Workers will accept money in exchange for their labour. Shop owners will accept money in exchange for their goods and services. As a medium of exchange, money is extremely efficient because it cuts down on the need for a double coincidence of wants.

A **unit of account** is the unit in which prices are quoted.	Money also has other functions. It is generally seen to be a **unit of account**. All prices are expressed in monetary terms. A BMW is £20 000, not 100 cows. In the US the unit of account is dollars and in the Eurozone it is euros. Goods and services are expressed in a common unit, which is monetary based. This again enables efficient transactions by facilitating comparisons and transparency in pricing. A common unit of account, or price, enables buyers and sellers to understand the value of the current market price and whether or not a transaction is profitable or loss-making.

Money should also be a **store of value**. For example, milk is not a good store of value because it deteriorates quickly and goes bad. Money, as metal coins and paper banknotes, does not perish. Money earned today can be saved and used next week or next month to facilitate a future transaction. However, money is not a perfect store of value. Money as cash earns zero interest and its value is eroded by inflation. Other assets, such as houses, gold and interest-bearing accounts can all serve as stores of value.

Money is a **store of value** because it can be used to make future purchases.

However, money is the predominant medium of exchange in most economies. Today money takes the form of **fiat money**. Before fiat money, governments backed money with gold. The holder of a note could approach the central bank and demand that their note be exchanged for an equivalent value of gold. Money is no longer backed by gold, but is instead guaranteed by the government or central bank. Fiat money has a number of beneficial aspects associated with it. It is legally recognized as a medium of exchange and is culturally accepted as such. People are willing to exchange goods for money. Paper notes and coins are cheap to make (see the mass-production techniques employed by the Royal Mint in Box 12.1). A £10 note does not require £10 of resource in order to make it. In contrast, a £10 gold nugget would represent £10 of resource. Government-backed money economizes on scarce resources. But here is the problem: because a £10 note can be produced for less than £10, forgers can make a profit. Therefore, forgery has to be outlawed and the law enforced.

Fiat money is notes and coins guaranteed by the government rather than by gold deposits.

 Box 12.1 Making money: rolling in it!

The Royal Mint boasts some of the most advanced coining machinery in the world. In the foundry, strips of metal are drawn from large electric furnaces, reduced to the required thickness in a tandem rolling mill and transferred to large blanking presses where coin blanks can be punched out at the rate of 10 000 per minute. The blanks are softened and cleaned in the Annealing and Pickling Plant before the final process in the Coining Press Room. Here, the blanks are fed into coining presses where the obverse and reverse designs, as well as the milling on the edge, are stamped on to the blank simultaneously. The Royal Mint's latest presses can each strike more than 600 coins per minute, making it impossible for the human eye to separate the individual pieces as they pass through the press.

Source: Royal Mint, www.royalmint.com

A **central bank** acts as a banker to the commercial bank, taking deposits and, in extreme circumstances, making loans.

12.3 The banking system

The banking system consists of the central bank, retail banks and wholesale banks. The **central bank** issues money into the economy through the banking system and the money markets more generally. The central bank acts as banker to the retail and wholesale banks. If a retail bank has spare cash, then it can safely deposit this money at the central bank. Likewise, in extreme circumstances, if a commercial bank cannot gain funds from any other lender, then the central bank may act as the lender of last resort and provide a loan to the commercial bank.

A **retail bank** takes deposits from retail customers, borrows from other banks and the money markets and raises funds from shareholders. Taken together, all these funds are then loaned out to retail borrowers or invested in financial instruments or deposited at the central bank.

Wholesale banks take very large cash deposits and broker very large loans, both for banks and other commercial companies. Wholesale banks are sometimes referred to as investment banks. Such banks tend to locate in financial hubs such as London and New York, where they can raise money on the wholesale financial markets and bring large lenders together to lend in syndicate to large commercial borrowers.

The banking system is just one part of the broader financial system. Other major financial companies include insurance companies, building societies, hedge funds and pension funds. At root, most financial companies are involved in **financial intermediation**, which involves raising funds from individuals with excess cash, and then lending to or investing the cash in companies or individuals who are short of funds.

The balance sheet for all UK banks in Table 12.1 highlights the banking function of financial intermediation. A balance sheet is a financial statement of a company's assets and liabilities and each side must balance against the other. So, assets = liabilities.

On the liabilities side, banks raise money from shareholders. This money is referred to as capital. Banks also raise funds from depositors and by borrowing in the money markets from other banks or financial companies, such as pension funds.

On the asset side, banks make loans to households and firms. They may also place some funds in financial securities, such as government or company bonds. Or they may simply place money on deposit at the central bank.

Deposits at banks are classified as sight and time deposits. **Sight deposits** are current accounts. Customers can access their cash instantly. **Time deposits** require the customer to give the bank notice before withdrawing funds.

The central problem for most banks is that they borrow short and lend long. Money raised from depositors, especially in sight deposits, may be run down over a month as a household pays its bills. But the bank may lend to mortgage customers for 25 years. If a deposit holder requires cash quickly, then the bank cannot ask the borrower to pay quicker. This is why the bank holds some funds in securities. These funds earn a low rate of interest, but they provide the bank with instant access to cash. This is referred to as liquidity and the bank needs to trade increased liquidity against increased profits. More cash on loan means higher profits, but less liquidity. More cash in securities means higher liquidity, but lower profits.

In examining Table 12.1 further, it is important to note that the capital of UK banks is small when compared with the amount of funds generated from currency, deposits and money markets. This means that the majority of loans funded by UK banks are paid for by savers, and other lenders to the bank. Shareholders provide banks with very limited funds. This is the essence of financial intermediation, where cash from savers is channelled to borrowers. It also means that, when loans turn bad and are not repaid, banks come under enormous financial stress. Shareholders' funds can be very quickly wiped out by losses on the loan book, after which the inability to repay depositors becomes a real issue.

Such risks have resulted in governments guaranteeing deposits within banks. In addition, many governments around the world have injected billions of capital into banks to ensure their financial viability. But given that companies in other sectors are often allowed to collapse, why would a government be keen to support banking? To answer this question, we need to understand the economic importance of banking.

A **retail bank** takes deposits and makes loans to retail customers.

A **wholesale banks** takes large deposits and is involved in brokering very large loans to companies.

Financial intermediation involves channelling cash from savers to borrowers.

Sight deposits provide customers with instant access to cash.

Time deposits require the customer to give the bank notice before withdrawing cash.

Table 12.1 Balance sheet of UK banks, February 2009

Assets		Liabilities	
In foreign currency		*In foreign currency*	
Securities	984	Currency, deposits and money market instruments	4524
Loans	3725	Foreign currency capital	117
Total foreign currency assets	4709	Total foreign currency liabilities	4641
In sterling		*In sterling*	
Securities	539	Currency, deposits and money market instruments	2918
Loans	2661	Sterling capital	350
Total sterling assets	3200	Total sterling liabilities	3268
Total	7909	Total	7909

Source: Bank of England, *Bankstats*

The economic importance of banking

Banking is now central to money. While notes and coins exist, the vast majority of money is electronic and within bank accounts. In fact, bank deposits are a medium of exchange because they are accepted as payment by sellers of goods and services.

The economic importance of banking cannot be understated. Aside from being a large component of GDP and a massive source of employment within an economy, the services that banking offers are essential to a well-functioning economy. These services can be broken down into four key areas: liquidity, risk pooling, risk selection and monitoring, and risk pricing. We will consider each of these in turn.

Liquidity

Liquidity is the speed, price and ease of access to money.

A lack of liquidity between banks is known as a **credit crunch**.

Government bonds are a near-cash equivalent and therefore liquid. A government pays the holder of bonds a rate of interest in return for funding the government's debt.

The primary role of banks is to provide **liquidity** to the economy. Banks raise money from deposit holders. These account holders may be private households or companies who wish to place their money in a safe and accessible form. If you place your money in the bank, then you have a surplus of liquidity – you do not need so much cash. Similarly, there are also households and businesses who have a shortage of liquidity. This group can raise their liquidity by borrowing from the bank; that is, borrowing raises their access to cash. So, by channelling cash from savers to borrowers banks provide much needed liquidity to the economy.

However, a problem faced by banks is that they tend to borrow short and lend long. Savers and, more particularly, current account holders, tend to need quick and easy access to their cash. Borrowers, in contrast, tend to repay loans over many years. In ensuring liquidity for borrowers, banks have to carefully manage the cash flows received and repaid to savers. Banks take special care to ensure that they themselves have a mixture of assets which are almost liquid and can, therefore, be converted into cash at short notice. Gold and **government bonds** are often readily bought by other investors. So with an active market and many buyers, gold and government bonds can be easily sold and converted into cash. The problem for banks is that near-liquid assets earn low rates of interest. Banks are therefore required to trade the benefits of liquidity against lower financial returns.

In an attempt to increase the interest earned on liquid assets, banks in recent times invested some of their cash in bonds that were linked to other banks' stocks of mortgages. These bonds are called **collateralized debt obligations** (CDOs) and are paid a higher rate of interest than government bonds. However, as the sub-prime mortgage market in the US collapsed, CDOs fell in value. Other banks were unwilling to buy them or take a CDO as collateral against a loan. When banks are unwilling to trade assets with each other, then there is a restriction on liquidity in the interbank market and this has become known as the *credit crunch*. See Box 12.2 for further details.

> A **collateralized debt obligation** is a bond. The holder of the bond is paid a rate of interest in return for funding a debt.

Risk pooling

Ordinary savers could provide liquidity to borrowers. However, with limited funds, the average saver may be able to fund only one borrower or even only a small part of their need for cash. This will leave the individual saver very exposed to the risk of default by the borrower. In contrast, by pooling savers' funds, banks have access to a larger share of funds and are therefore able to fund a larger pool of risks. By choosing a varied and non-correlated set of risks, banks can use risk pooling to derive benefits from diversification. (See Chapter 7 for a reminder of diversification economies.) If one borrower defaults, then the bank is left with a bad debt. But the profitable proceeds from lending to the rest of the pool are usually sufficient to outweigh this cost. Because of the benefits to be gained from diversification, banks are able to take on greater lending risks than an individual saver. As a result, projects or transactions that would not be funded by individuals are funded by banks. Therefore, risk pooling by banks enables the economy to grow.

Risk selection and monitoring

Banks employ individuals who are experts in understanding financial risks. Bank managers are trained to assess and evaluate the merits of lending to individuals and companies. This expertise and skill enables banks to select risks more effectively than ordinary individuals with surplus savings to invest. As a result, with a well-functioning banking sector, investment options with a greater probability of financial success should be selected. If this occurs, then there should be less waste of financial resources across the economy.

Banks are also skilled at monitoring loans made to companies. Banks are able to understand when a company is in financial difficulty and when it is right to put a company into liquidation and seek repayment of the original loan. Ordinary savers are less likely to be able to understand a company's financial statement or evaluate its chances of surival in a turbulent trading environment. As a result, banks are an efficient and effective means of selecting and monitoring risk.

Risk pricing

As experts in financial risk, banks are able to provide a good assessment of risk and therefore the price for taking on such risk. The more risky the project, the higher the interest rate on the loan. Banks can also access the pool of resources held by rival banks. This enables large and risky projects to be funded, but with the financial risk shared among many banks. Finally, banks reduce the cost of borrowing. In raising financial resources from one bank, a borrower cuts down on the costs of transacting with many small savers. Therefore banks are both a cost-efficient means of distributing loans and an effective mechanism for pricing the risk associated with lending.

Box 12.2 Blocked pipes

Adapted from an article in The Economist, *2 October 2008*

The money markets are the plumbing of the economic system. Normally, they function efficiently and unseen, allowing investment institutions, companies and banks to lend and borrow trillions of dollars for up to a year at a time. They are only noticed when they go wrong. And, like plumbing, when they do get blocked they make an almighty stink.

At the moment, these markets are well and truly bunged up. In the words of Michael Hartnett, a strategist at Merrill Lynch, 'the global interbank market is effectively closed'. The equivalent of a run on banks has been taking place, without the queues of depositors. This stealthy run has been led by institutional investors and by banks themselves.

Many banks have had to be rescued by rivals or the state. Surviving banks have become ultra-cautious. The effect has been most dramatic in the overnight rate for borrowing dollars. Bank borrowing costs reached 6.88 per cent on 30 September, more than three times the level of official American rates, while some were willing to pay a remarkable 11 per cent to borrow dollars from the European Central Bank (ECB). Banks have become so risk averse that they deposited a record €44 billion ($62 billion) with the ECB on 30 September, even though they could have earned more than two extra percentage points by lending to other banks.

In the absence of private sector lenders to banks, central banks have become vital suppliers in the money markets. With the help of the ECB, the Bank of England and the Bank of Japan, the Federal Reserve agreed to lend a further $620 billion.

Liquid dynamite

It is widely assumed that central banks set the level of interest rates in their domestic markets. But the rate they announce is the one at which they will lend to the banking system. When banks borrow from anyone else (including other banks), they pay more. Every day, this rate is calculated through a poll of participating banks and published as Libor (London interbank offered rate) or Euribor (Euro interbank offered rate).

Normally, these are only a fraction of a percentage point above the official interest rates. But that has changed dramatically in recent weeks (see Chart 1). Take the cost of borrowing dollars. On 1 October

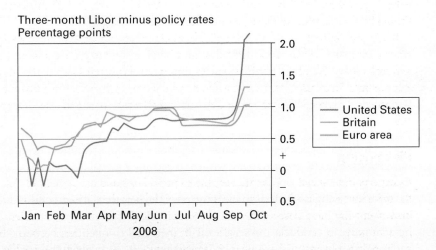

Chart 1 Plumbing under pressure

Source: Thomson Datastream

▶

banks had to pay 4.15 per cent for three-month money, more than two percentage points above the Fed funds target rate. In theory, three-month rates could be that high because markets are expecting a sharp rise in official rates. But that is hardly likely, given the depth of the crisis.

Instead, the width of the margin reflects investors' worries about the banks, not least because so many have faltered so quickly. Three months is now a long time to trust in the health of a bank. In addition, banks are anxious to conserve their own cash, in case depositors make large withdrawals or their money gets tied up in the collapse of another bank.

12.4 Regulation

Contagion occurs when the collapse of one bank leads to the collapse of more banks.

Regulation is the use of rules and laws to limit, control and monitor the activities of banks.

Banks are institutions which take financial risks with depositors' money. While traditionally banks have been seen as very safe, recent events associated with the credit crisis have shown that banks around the world are still vulnerable to collapse. In fact, banks represent an important risk known as **contagion**. Because banks can also lend to each other, if one bank collapses, then it defaults on its loans with other banks. This weakens the other banks, which can then also collapse. Contagion leads to a domino effect, with one bank toppling more banks. It should be of little surprise to know that banks are regulated. The form of regulation can vary across economies, but the main objectives of **regulation** are often to ensure financial stability and economy-wide confidence in the banking sector.

Historical review of regulation

Fixed exchange rates have a fixed rate of conversion between currencies.

The **Bretton Woods** agreement of 1944 provided a plan for managing foreign exchange rates.

The regulation of banks has changed greatly over the years. This is a reflection of changing political and economic concerns. Some of the biggest changes in financial regulation occurred during the 1980s, but were linked to events in the 1970s.

In the late 1960s, economies around the world operated **fixed exchange rate** regimes under the **Bretton Woods** agreement. We will consider such systems in more detail in Chapter 15. But, in brief, a fixed exchange rate regime fixes the rate of conversion between currencies. There is no daily movement in the exchange rate for a currency. Such systems often require controls on the movement of currency between economies. As an example, British holiday-makers in the 1960s could take no more than £50 with them out of the country.

From 1971, the fixed exchange rate systems were abandoned by leading economies. This also meant that currency controls could be abandoned. This allowed tourists and, more importantly, banks to move currency around the world. Banks could lend and invest money where it was possible to make the highest rate of return. The globalization of financial services had begun.

The challenge for economies was how to embrace the opportunities offered by free currency movements. The UK decided that it wished to become a global financial services centre and in order to compete on a global scale, deregulation was necessary.

Under the political leadership of Margaret Thatcher, the City of London financial system underwent Big Bang deregulation in 1986. This allowed financial companies to operate in a broader range of products and services. This increased competition between companies who had previously been investment banks or retail banks. It also enabled these banks to enter other markets, such as stock broking. Perhaps most importantly, foreign companies could set up operations in the UK.

A **mutual** is a financial organization that is owned by its customers. This contrasts with a bank, which is owned by shareholders.

These changes were followed by changes in the regulations placed on **mutual** deposit-taking institutions such as building societies. The UK government allowed such companies to operate more like banks, raising money in wholesale markets, and offering current accounts, personal loans and credit cards. Similarly, insurance companies were able to set up banking divisions, and banks were able to set up insurance divisions.

In 1993, the EU opened up competition further. Until that date, banks and insurance companies had to have a licence from the government of each EU country that it operated in. Following 1993, a bank or insurance company only had to be licensed in one EU country for it to be able to operate in all EU member countries. Cross-border competition began to increase.

Deregulation over the years can be argued to have achieved two simple outcomes: first, an ability for financial companies to take greater risks in a broader range of product markets; second, a need to take bigger risks because increased competition was a threat to profitability. The consequences can be seen in large part in the credit crisis and the willingness of banks to take on increased financial risk and place the stability of the entire financial system in danger.

Types of regulation

The regulation of banks and other financial institutions, including insurance companies, is often referred to as prudential regulation. Prudence is a careful and cautious approach to operating financial institutions, which aims to avoid reckless lending or investments which may undermine the stability of the regulated bank. There are various aspects to prudential regulation.

Capital adequacy

Banks in most economies are subject to capital adequacy ratios. The use of capital adequacy ratios stems from internationally agreed standards known as Basel II. A capital adequacy ratio measures the value of a bank's capital to its risk-weighted portfolio of assets. A bank's capital includes the equity invested by shareholders, retained profits and provisions for any expected losses. Assets are loans and investments. These assets are weighted according to risk. So, if loans to companies are more risky than loans to governments, then the value of the company loans will be increased by the size of the weight.

The capital adequacy ratio measures the extent to which assets within the bank are backed by shareholders' funds. If assets in the bank grow at a faster rate than shareholders' funds, then the asset growth must have come from funds provided by deposit holders and providers of debt to the bank. Therefore, capital adequacy ratios provide a guide as to who is exposed to the bank's risk of default. If governments wish to see greater protection for deposit holders, then they can insist on a greater capital adequacy ratio and shareholders have to provide greater equity to the bank. Capital adequacy is therefore a measure of bank safety. The more capital backing a bank, the bigger loss its shareholders can suffer, before losses spread to deposit holders and providers of debt. These ideas were at the heart of how the UK and other governments bailed out weak banks during the credit crunch; see Box 12.3.

Minimum reserve requirements

An alternative approach to bank regulation is the use of minimum reserve requirements. Such regulation stipulates the ratio of deposits that must be held in reserves in liquid or near-liquid form. Regulation through reserve requirements seeks to ensure that deposit holders have free and open access to funds. In contrast to capital adequacy ratios, minimum reserve requirements emphasize liquidity over safety.

Prior to the credit crunch, capital adequacy ratios were favoured over minimum reserve requirements. However, given that the credit crunch was characterized by banks' inability to access liquid funds, a move back to liquidity-based regulation could happen.

Box 12.3 State to save HBOS and RBS

Adapted from an article in The Times, *12 October 2008*

The government will launch the biggest ever rescue of Britain's high-street banks tomorrow when the UK's four biggest institutions ask for a £35 billion financial lifeline. The unprecedented move will make the government the biggest shareholder in at least two banks. Royal Bank of Scotland (RBS), which has seen its market value fall to below £12 billion, is to ask ministers to underwrite a £15 billion cash call. Halifax Bank of Scotland (HBOS), Britain's biggest provider of mortgages, is seeking up to £10 billion.

The British bank rescue could leave the government owning 70 per cent of HBOS and 50 per cent of RBS. As part of the fundraising, it is likely that banks will also have to own up to future losses from their exposure to sub-prime mortgages and other financial instruments. The Governor of the Bank of England has told the banks to ask for more than they need. This is to make sure that their capital position is strengthened sufficiently to absorb shocks and to withstand a long recession.

The Bank of England has also increased the stress test required for banks to prove that they are in a strong capital position. This is called its 'core capital ratio' and it has been boosted from six to nine.

Banking sources say the combined loss of capital of the banks as a result of the credit crisis was £150 billion but some of that has already been made up by earlier capital-raising exercises and some will not be needed because the banks will be more constrained in their future lending.

Activity-based regulation

Banking regulation can also be activity based. This can limit the services banks offer and the sectors within which they operate. Following the Wall Street Crash in 1929, banks in the US were prevented from also running insurance operations. Similar rules were also implemented in the UK and Europe. Banks often found it difficult to take over rivals and expand into new, profitable areas. However, during the last 20 years many economies have followed a policy of financial deregulation. This has enabled banks and insurance companies to move into each other's sectors. Further deregulation has enabled many banks to raise additional funds through wholesale money markets. While this raises liquidity when money markets are operating well, it also exposes banks to severe liquidity problems when the markets dry up, as in the credit crunch.

Risk-based regulation and monitoring

Banks and other financial institutions are in frequent discussions with the regulator. Monthly statutory returns provide the regulator with an ongoing picture of the institutions' financial positions and the likely risks going forward. The UK Financial Services Authority feeds this information into its risk-based regulation model. Firms are judged on risk and impact. A large bank, with low risks, still produces a high impact if it collapses and so will be monitored closely. A small company with a higher risk of collapse will be allocated less oversight, because the impact of collapse on the economy is likely to be less.

Regulators also monitor companies based on firm risk and thematic risk. Firm risks are specific to the firm, for example a firm may have a low capital adequacy ratio. In contrast, thematic risks cut across firms within the same sector. A bank may be heavily exposed to the mortgage market. Instability in this bank may then lead to a loss of confidence in other mortgage lenders. Firm and thematic risks therefore require different solutions. Firm risks require specific action within a specific firm, whereas thematic risks require co-ordinated solutions across a range of regulated companies.

When regulation fails

By the very nature of risk, it is inevitable that some financial companies will collapse at some point. However, it is the nature of the risk and the collapse that will determine the authorities' responses.

In the early 1990s, one of the UK's most venerable banks, Barings, collapsed after one of its traders ran up £800 million in losses on the Asian commodity markets. In order to protect depositors, the bank was sold to a rival for £1. (The rival also picked up the £800 million in losses!) The losses on the Asian commodity markets were a specific risk generated by a rogue trader named Nick Leeson. So the sale of the bank was a specific solution to a specific risk.

During the credit crunch many banks around the world faced collapse. In most instances, these banks have been acquired by rivals, have received enormous capital injections from their governments and have been given greater access to liquidity through credit lines offered by central banks. The credit crunch was a thematic risk, in that all banks faced limited access to liquidity and faced a loss of confidence among deposit holders and shareholders. Such risks are also referred to as **systemic risks**, or contagion, as they pose a risk to the entire financial system. If one bank collapses, then since all banks are exposed to the same thematic risk, then the fear and panic will spread to other banks, leading to further damage of the banking system.

> **Systemic risk** is a risk which can damage the entire financial system.
>
> The central bank is a **lender of last resort** if a bank cannot raise funds from any other lender.

If the risk is systemic, then banks have generally relied on the central bank to act as the **lender of last resort**. If a bank is in distress and cannot raise funds from any other lenders, then the central bank may act as the lender of last resort in order to save the distressed bank and to prevent panic from spreading to other banks.

Risks of moral hazard

> **Moral hazard** behaviour occurs when a person changes their behaviour because they are partially insulated from risk.

Moral hazard occurs when someone changes their behaviour because they are insulated from risk. For example, a car driver may become a more risky driver once they have fully comprehensive insurance.

Similarly, a central bank's acting as the lender of last resort is not without moral hazard type problems. In particular, bailing out any bank that finds itself in difficulties can provide banks with incentives to take reckless decisions. The availability of emergency funds from the central bank effectively insures banks and their shareholders against the risks they take in lending. To combat this problem, the UK government used two approaches during the credit crisis. The central bank provided liquidity as the lender of last resort. In addition, the government injected capital into the banks by becoming a shareholder. However, it became a shareholder on very favourable terms, terms which penalized those existing shareholders who had enabled the banks to take excessive risks.

12.5 Credit creation and the money supply

> **Credit creation** is the process of turning existing bank deposits into credit facilities for borrowers. The process can result in an increase in the money supply.

Importantly, banks are able to boost liquidity to borrowers by recognizing that not all depositors will withdraw their money at the same time. This enables banks to grow the amount of available money by a process known as **credit creation**.

Consider a business with which many of you will be familiar – clubbing. You go to the club and pay for drinks. In the morning, the manager of the club (being more sensible than you) awakens early and pays the previous evening's takings into the bank – let us say £1000. When your hangover subsides, around two in the afternoon, you realize that the really good night out was extremely expensive. You go to the bank and join the queue for an increase in your overdraft.

The bank is sitting on £1000 from the club and assumes that only £100 will be paid out in the near future as wages. The bank thinks it can safely lend out the remaining £900 in overdrafts. You and your fellow borrowers take the £900 and head straight back to the club for another big night out. In the morning, while you skip another lecture, the club manager returns to the bank and pays in the £900. The bank manager awaits your call for another advance on your overdraft.

The banks are playing a very clever trick: the club manager thinks he has £1000 in the bank. But then the bank also lets you and your fellow borrowers think you have an additional £900 in the bank by lending part of the club's money to you. When you spend this drinking and enjoying yourself, the club manager pays the next night's takings into the bank, and he now thinks he has £1900 in the bank. We can, therefore, see that an initial £1000 in notes and coins was converted into another £900 of money, via overdrafts. This is then paid back into the bank and the process occurs again. Just as we have a fiscal multiplier, we can now observe banks, through credit creation, developing what is known as a money multiplier.

We clearly have to make a distinction between how much *money* people think exists and how much *cash* actually exists.

> We formally refer to cash as the **monetary base,** or the stock of high-powered money, which is the quantity of notes and coins held by private individuals or held by the banking system.

The amount of money, or the money supply, is the **monetary base** plus deposits at the bank. We will see shortly that this definition can be broadened, but it clearly includes the amount of cash in circulation and the amount people think they have in the bank.

The money multiplier is, therefore, the ratio of the money supply to the monetary base.

Size of the money multiplier

The size of the money multiplier is determined by two factors: (i) the willingness of individuals to deposit money in the bank, rather than keeping it in their pockets; and (ii) the level of reserves held by the banks. For example, the credit-creation process will become greater as more individuals provide banks with cash. So, as people switch from holding money in their pockets to storing it at the bank, the more banks can create credit. Second, if banks reduce reserves from 10 per cent to 5 per cent of deposits, then more credit can be created; for example, for every £100 paid in, the banks can lend out an additional £5 by reducing reserves from 10 per cent to 5 per cent.

So, if cash deposits and reserve levels are central to the process of credit creation, what influences each of these important factors? The level of reserves is directly influenced by regulation. Governments, or central banks, may insist that banks keep a minimum level of reserves in order to meet deposit holders' cash withdrawals. This merely reflects an interest by governments to avoid bankruptcy among the banking sector. Clearly, banks also wish to avoid bankruptcy and many will use treasury management teams to build complex models capable of predicting cash flows into and out of the bank on a daily basis. The more confident the bank is that cash flows in will exceed cash flows out, the more they will be willing to lend. The less predictable these cash flows become, the more dangerous it becomes to lower reserves and lend more money.

The willingness to hold cash on deposit, rather than in your pocket, has in recent times been influenced by technological change in the financial services industry. Many firms only pay salary and wages into bank accounts. Wages are rarely paid in cash any more. Loans, mortgages and mobile phone contracts will only be offered if direct debits can be set up on your bank account. Utility suppliers – gas, electricity and water – will offer discounts if monthly direct debits are set up. Couple all these changes with the popularity of credit cards, and the overall requirement for cash in your pocket, rather than at the bank, has significantly reduced. As a consequence, more cash is in the banking sector and banks using treasury management are becoming more adept at modelling its flows and taking opportunities to create credit.

Table 12.2 Narrow and broad UK money (£bn), 2008

		£bn
	Wide monetary base M0	50
–	Banks' cash and balances at bank	–7
=	Cash in circulation	43
+	Banks' retail deposits	850
+	Building societies' deposits and shares	223
+	Wholesale deposits	683
=	Money supply M4	1799

Source: Bank of England

Measures of money

We saw above that measuring the money supply requires a distinction between cash and money on deposit. The government has used this distinction to develop a number of money measures ranging from **M0**, a narrow measure of money, to **M4**, a broad measure of money.

M0 includes all cash in circulation, all cash held within banks and all cash balances held at the central bank by commercial banks. Looking at Table 12.2, cash in circulation is £43 billion. Cash in banks and balances at (central) bank are £7 billion.

M4 extends M0 into broader measures of money and includes bank retail deposits, £850 billion, building society deposits, £223 billion, and wholesale money market deposits of £683 billion. Together these give a broad money supply of £1799 billion.

M0 is a measure of the monetary base: cash in circulation outside the banks, cash in the banks and the bank's own accounts at the Bank of England. M0 is, therefore, a narrow measure of money.

M4 takes M0 and adds easy access savings accounts at banks, time deposits at banks and deposits at building societies. M4 is, therefore, a broad measure of money.

12.6 The demand for money

The previous discussion provides an understanding of money supply. However, before we begin to consider how the government might effectively control the money supply, we also need to consider the demand for money.

Do not confuse a demand for more money with a demand for additional income. We all want more income, but may not want more money. For example, if you receive £1000 in income, the question is, how much of this £1000 will you hold in money and how much in other financial securities such as bonds or equities?

Economists identify three motives for holding money: the **transaction motive**, the **precautionary motive** and the **asset motive**.

The transaction motive

We hold money because we have to pay for goods and services at various points after we receive income payments. Consider the following scenarios: (a) you are paid on Friday and carry out all your shopping on Friday; and (b) you are paid on Friday and shop each day for food, clothes, fuel, etc. Under scenario (a), your payments and receipts of money are perfectly synchronized; under (b), they are not. Therefore, you need to hold more money in scenario (b) than in (a).

As the value of our transactions increases and as the degree of synchronization between receipts and payments deteriorates, the greater becomes the transactional motive for holding

The **transaction motive** for holding money recognizes that money payments and money receipts are not perfectly synchronized.

cash. Moreover, we need to state that demand is for real money balances, where the demand is adjusted for inflation. So, if inflation doubles, the nominal value of our receipts and payments will also double, and we will have to hold double nominal money balances, but in real terms our demand for money will remain constant.

The precautionary motive

The **precautionary motive** for holding money reflects the unpredictability of transactions and the need to hold liquid funds in order to meet these payments.

We also hold money because we are unsure when transactions will occur. For example, we might hold some money against emergencies, such as the car developing a fault and needing repairing; or we might have spare cash in order to take advantage of special offers in the shops as and when they occur.

As uncertainty increases, the precautionary motive for money will also increase. In addition, as income increases, the value of potential transactions also increases. For example, someone who owns a Ferrari needs to hold more money to fix a fault with the Ferrari than someone who owns a Mini (assuming each are equally reliable).

The asset motive

Under the **asset motive**, individuals hold money as part of a diversified asset portfolio. Some wealth is held in equities, some in bonds, a portion in property and some in money.

Individuals hold money as part of a diversified portfolio of assets. Equities are risky assets, with values going down as well as up. Bonds are financial instruments, where a firm offers to make specified repayments in the future to the bond holder. The risk is that the firm will default on the payments. Money is a low-risk asset. Aside from the exchange rate, the value of money is only affected in real terms by the inflation rate.

Clearly, the more wealth is held in cash, the more an individual is forgoing the potential higher returns from holding other financial assets such as bonds. Indeed, bonds pay a rate of return, or interest. We can argue that the higher the rate of interest on bonds, the higher the opportunity cost of holding real money balances. Therefore, as the interest rate increases, individuals will demand fewer real money balances.

We can now use these ideas to understand how the demand for money varies with prices, income, interest and risk. In Figure 12.1, individuals will hold real money balances up to the point where the marginal benefit of cash is equal to the marginal cost. The cost of holding cash is equal to the interest forgone on a bond. So the marginal cost of money is constant, and represented by the horizontal line in Figure 12.1. The marginal benefit of money is considered

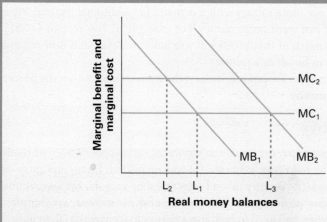

In equilibrium, individuals will desire money balances up to the amount where the marginal benefit and marginal cost of holding money are equal. If the marginal cost of holding money increases, then the desire to hold money will fall. Equally, if the marginal benefit of holding money increases, then the desire for money will increase.

Figure 12.1 Desire for real money balances

for a given level of real income. The benefits of cash are downward sloping because additional cash has greater value when we have less of it. With a high income and low cash balances, we have to be careful to match payments and receipts, we have to avoid risk and reduce our precautionary needs for cash and we have limited scope for investing our scarce cash. As our real cash balances increase, then our cash requirements are more in balance with our income level and the value of additional cash falls.

In equilibrium, our real holdings of money will be determined by the intersection of the marginal benefits and marginal costs of holding cash. In Figure 12.1, this is L_1. If interest rates increase, then the marginal cost of holding cash will increase and individuals will hold less cash, L_2. Similarly, if interest rates fall, then the opportunity cost of holding cash falls and individuals' holdings of money will increase.

If real incomes increase, then the marginal benefits of holding cash at any interest rate increase and so the marginal benefit line moves to the right and the new equilibrium level of real money balances becomes L_3 in Figure 12.1.

12.7 Money market equilibrium

Now that we understand the demand and supply of money, we can think about the money market equilibrium. Figure 12.2 shows the demand for real money balances, LL_1, and the supply of money, L_1. The demand for real money balances is negatively related to the rate of interest. This is easy to understand if we look back at Figure 12.1. If we increase the marginal cost of holding money (the interest rate), then fewer real money balances are held.

The supply of money is perfectly inelastic. As the interest rate, or price of money, increases, then the supply of money remains unchanged. This, as we will see shortly, is because the government (or central bank) adds to or reduces the money supply as it sees fit. Its decision is not influenced by the interest rate.

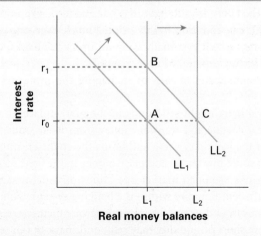

Figure 12.2 Money market equilibrium

Money demand LL is interest responsive, reflecting a trade-off between holding non-interest-bearing money and alternative interest-generating assets such as bonds. Money supply, L, is perfectly interest inelastic. In equilibrium, money demand equals money supply. An increase in money demand will lead to a higher equilibrium interest rate, while an increase in money supply will lead to a lower equilibrium interest rate.

As interest rates on bonds increase, individuals find holding money too expensive and reduce their holdings of real money balances. At the equilibrium A, the demand for real money balances is equal to the money supply at an interest rate of r_0.

We can consider a change to the demand for real money balances. If income increased, or uncertainty increased, then either the transaction motive or the precautionary motive for holding money would increase. In both instances, the demand for real money balances would shift out to the right, at LL_2. If money supply remains unchanged, the equilibrium moves to B and the interest rate rises to r_1.

If the central bank increased the money supply from L_1 to L_2, by printing more banknotes, then the supply of money would move out to the right. At the higher level of money demand, LL_2, the equilibrium moves to C and the interest rate returns to r_0. Clearly, if the central bank reduced the amount of money in the economy, then the interest rate would increase.

Controlling the money supply

We know that the money supply is composed of cash in circulation plus money on deposit at the banks. In attempting to control the money supply, it is clear that the central bank has two options open to it: (1) it could regulate the credit-creation process undertaken within banks or (2) it could control the amount of notes and coins in circulation.

Managing the credit-creation process requires regulation of the minimum reserve requirements run by banks. If a bank only holds 5 per cent of its deposits in reserve, then it can create far more credit than if it is required to hold, say, 10 per cent of its deposits on reserve. So, increasing the minimum reserve requirements of a bank can help to reduce the credit-creation process and thereby limit growth in the money supply. However, banks may not like minimum reserve requirements. Holding cash on reserve can be wasteful when the cash might be profitability loaned out to a borrower. In addition, global market banks can bypass minimum reserve requirements by using a country with the lowest reserve requirements as their base.

The second method for controlling the money supply is to print more money. Ben Bernanke, the head of the US Federal Reserve, has referred to this approach as the helicopter option. Fly above a major city and drop freshly printed notes. Everyone is then free to collect and spend the new money, which eventually will end up in the banks, whereupon the credit-creation process will further expand the money supply.

Open market operations occur when the central bank buys and sells financial assets in return for money.

A more sophisticated means of managing the monetary base is to use **open market operations**.

The central bank might sell bonds in the marketplace. If a bank bought such a bond, it would write a cheque and transfer money from its account to the central bank. This takes funds out of the banking system and limits the credit-creation process. Put into reverse, the central bank could buy bonds and place money in the bank's account.

Quantitative easing involves the central bank buying government debt, corporate debt and other financial securities. In return, cash is provided to the vendors of these assets.

Central banks use open market operations on a daily basis and the primary purpose is to ensure sufficient liquidity within the banking system. Banks that have too much liquidity may buy bonds from the central bank and increase their reserves held at the central bank; while banks that are short of liquidity may sell bonds back to the central bank in return for liquid cash.

However, in extreme cases, the central bank may wish to dramatically increase the amount of liquidity within the banking sector and it will then consider a policy of **quantitative easing**. Under quantitative easing, the central bank will purchase government debt bonds, corporate debt bonds and other financial assets, such as mortgaged-backed securities and even equities. In return, the sellers of these assets, often banks, receive cash. This then improves the banks' liquidity. Credit creation and lending can increase.

Quantitative easing was used in Japan between 2001 and 2005. During the credit crisis it was also used by central banks such as the US Federal Reserve and the UK's Bank of England.

There are problems with quantitative easing. First, if a bank sells an asset to the central bank, then it may not use the additional cash. Instead, the bank may leave the cash on reserve at the central bank. It would be likely to do this if it felt that the economic environment was so bad that to lend out the money would offer an unacceptably high level of risk.

Second, it is necessary to recognize a difference between quantitative easing and **qualitative easing**. Under quantitative easing, the quality of the central bank's balance sheet stays roughly equal. High quality bonds are swapped for cash. Under qualitative easing, the quality of the central bank's balance sheet deteriorates. Cash is swapped for poor quality assets. In this way, quantitative easing can present problems of moral hazard. Banks wishing to offload high risk, poor quality assets can swap them at the central bank for cash. These poor quality assets then appear on the central bank's balance sheet. To avoid this problem, central banks offer to buy assets at a substantial discount. This is referred to as a **haircut**.

Figure 12.3 illustrates the changing composition of the Bank of England's holdings of collateral before and after the beginning of the credit crisis. It is clear that from late 2008 onwards, the Bank of England massively expanded its provision of loans to the private sector banks and financial institutions, in return for a variety of collateral. In the main, the Bank of England was willing to take high grade government debt, gilts and treasury bonds. But there was also an increase in other sterling debt. This was principally composed of mortgage-backed securities provided by high street banks.

> Under **qualitative easing**, the central bank swaps high quality assets for poorer quality assets.
>
> A **haircut** is the discount required by the buyer of a risky asset. An asset valued at £100 and bought for £80 is said to have suffered a 20 per cent haircut. The hair cut will hopefully insure the buyer against any future losses in value of the asset.

Controlling the interest rate

The alternative to controlling the money supply is the use of interest rates. Under such a policy, interest rates are declared and, then, however much money is demanded at the official base rate

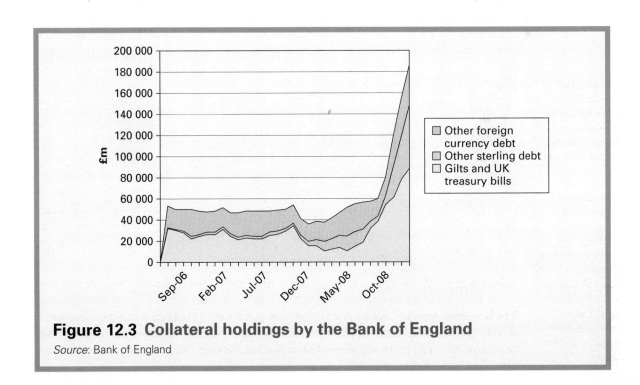

Figure 12.3 Collateral holdings by the Bank of England
Source: Bank of England

is how much money is supplied to the market. The central bank is effectively fixing the interest rate for the money market, and then managing the money supply through open market operations to ensure that the market price for money is the same as the central bank's declared rate of interest.

Control of interest rates can have additional benefits. Where demand for money is particularly unstable, it is best to set interest rates rather than money supply. For example, if the money supply is managed, then changes in money demand will lead to instability in interest rates. If the interest rate is set, however, changes in money demand simply lead to instability in money supply. If control of the economy operates more through interest rates than through money supply, it is of no surprise that policy has shifted from managing money supply to managing interest rates.

12.8 **Monetary policy**

Governments and central banks across the world attempt to use money markets and the banking sector to influence overall levels of economic activity. They seek to achieve this through the setting of interest rates. So, it is not that central banks wish to bring about equilibrium in money markets when setting interest rates; rather, they believe that changes in the interest rate can be transmitted into the real economy and thereby have implications for inflation and economic activity. How this occurs is complex and can take many months, if not years, to work.

Monetary transmission

In simplistic terms, interest rates affect consumers' willingness to consume and firms' willingness to borrow for investment. How changes in the base rate feed through into changes in economic output and inflation is referred to as the **transmission mechanism**.

The **transmission mechanism** is the channel through which monetary policy impacts economic output and prices.

Figure 12.4 provides the European Central Bank's schematic representation of the transmission mechanism. This figure links changes in the official bank base rate through to changes in the economy's price level.

The transmission mechanism is clearly complex. Changes in the central bank's base rate feed through into changes in retail bank and money market rates for loans. These changes impact the amount of credit in the economy, the price of other assets, such as shares, bonds and property, and can even alter the exchange rate. Changes in the base rate also help to manage expectations. As the central bank changes rates, it demonstrates its commitment to fighting inflation. This commitment has an impat on price and wage setting.

However, at the core of the transmission mechanism is how firms and consumers adjust their spending decisions in the light of rate changes. This drives changes in the demand for goods and services. Consumers borrow for consumption and firms borrow for investment, both of which are important components of aggregate demand. Changes in aggregate demand feed through into changes in equilibrium GDP and inflation; see Chapter 9 and Figure 9.10. In order to develop your understanding further, we will now concentrate on consumption and investment behaviour within the transmission mechanism.

Consumption

The Keynesian view of consumption, presented in Chapter 11, suggests that consumption is directly related to current income. As income increases, then, through the marginal propensity to consume, consumption will also increase. The link between interest rates and consumption must therefore act through income.

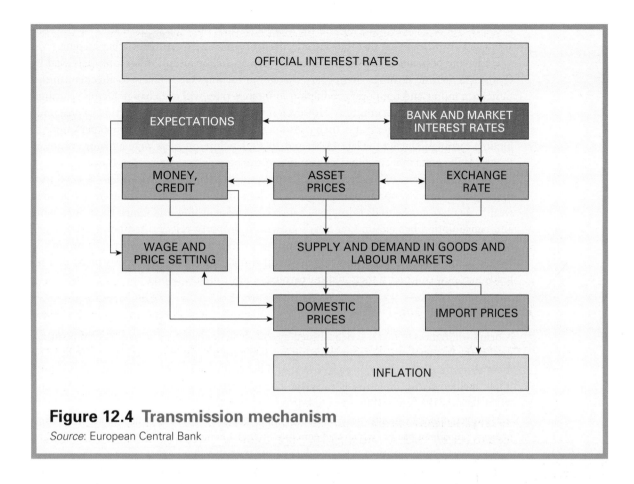

Figure 12.4 Transmission mechanism

Source: European Central Bank

A simple example from Chapter 11 is that consumers' belief in a cut in interest rates will boost investment demand. Through the multiplier, this boost in autonomous investment will then lead to higher GDP. Higher GDP will, in turn, lead to higher income for consumers and therefore higher consumption.

Interest rates can also impact directly on household consumption. Interest is the price of money. If interest rates fall, then in real terms consumers are better off. They can now purchase more credit for the same amount of expenditure (interest). So, as interest rates fall, real income rises and so does consumption.

> **Net present value** is the discounted value of a future cash flow.

Falling interest rates also raise today's value of future income. If you expect to earn £30 000 per annum in five years' time, what is it worth today? Or in economic terminology, what is the **net present value** of £30 000?

Think of the problem in reverse. If interest rates are 5 per cent, how much money must I place in the bank today in order to have £30 000 in five years' time? The answer is £23 505. So, £30 000 in five years' time is worth £23 505 today. If interest rates fall, then more has to be saved today in order to have £30 000 in the future. So falling interest rates raise the net present value of future income streams. So, if you are thinking of borrowing over the long term, falling interest rates raise your long-term income, which enables you to borrow more to spend.

> The **permanent income hypothesis** states that consumption is determined by lifetime earnings not current income.

An alternative view is the **permanent income hypothesis**, put forward by Milton Friedman. This model asserts that consumption is determined by expectations of lifetime earnings, rather than current income. So, two students working at Starbucks, earning the same wage, will only consume the same amount if they both expect to have the same lifetime earnings. In contrast, if one is expecting to be a doctor and the other a teacher, then the medical student will consume more now, knowing that they are effectively borrowing from future higher income.

Under the permanent income hypothesis, changes in consumption are only achieved by changes in lifetime earnings. Temporary changes in earnings are unlikely to affect consumption. So, a minor and temporary reduction in interest rates will not change lifetime earnings and so will not alter consumption. However, if the economy moves to a period of sustained and historically low interest rates, then consumers may come to re-adjust their expectations of lifetime earnings. During the late 1990s and 2000s, low interest rates were a major economic theme. At the same time, incomes, consumption and borrowings grew enormously.

Another key feature of the period was a rapid growth in property prices. This is asset price inflation and is picked up in Figure 12.3. Asset price inflation can increase households' lifetime wealth. Again, if households think the change is permanent they will adjust their borrowing and consumption behaviour. One year's growth in property prices is temporary. Ten years' suggests a permanent change. Coupled with low interest rates, households began to borrow heavily to fuel consumption. Following the credit crunch and the fall in property prices, households may now consider if their lifetime earnings and wealth are falling.

Investment activity

A firm's willingness to invest is determined by cost–benefit analysis. The benefits can be measured as the financial returns from investing in a new product, office or production facility. The main costs are the funds required to invest and the cost of such funds (interest). Other costs might include disruption costs. Clearly, the rate of interest is the direct cost of investing and will determine the firm's willingness to borrow and spend.

However, interest can also have an additional role to play in the appraisal of an investment project. Consider a project which will generate financial benefits for each of the next five years. A way of evaluating a project is to calculate its net present value – what value are the project's benefits (less costs) today? The method of net present value enables projects of differing lengths, say three and five years, to be compared.

If the project generates a benefit of £10 million in year five, we can work out what that value is today. We simply have to work out how much money we would need to put in the bank today in order to have £10 million in five years' time. So, if interest rates are 5 per cent, then we would need to put £7.8 million in the bank today; or, £10 million in five years' time is worth £7.8 million today. Clearly, as the interest rate increases, we can place less in the bank to achieve the £10 million in year five; or, as the interest rate increases, £10 million in year five is worth less to us today.

The discussion above indicates that interest rates affect investment decisions in two ways. First, higher rates of interest drive up the cost of borrowing and so reduce investment. Second, higher rates of interest make the value of future financial benefits smaller in today's terms; that is, higher interest rates provide a bigger discount to future cash flows and so reduce investment. Taken together, both these mechanisms result in a negative relationship between the rate of interest and the willingness to borrow and invest. See Figure 12.5.

In practice, the Bank of England's monetary committee works on the assumption that interest rate changes take one year to affect economic output and two years to affect prices. These are rules of thumb reflecting more practical considerations of economic adjustment, rather than hard precise rules predicted by economic theories.

The time lag for economic output could reflect pre-committed expenditures. You may book the family summer holiday in January. But between January and the summer, interest rates may rise. Because you are pre-committed to spending the money, the interest rate rise is

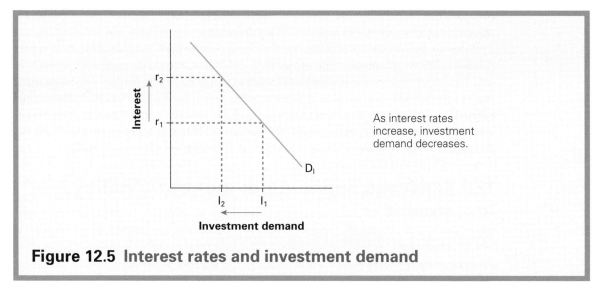

Figure 12.5 Interest rates and investment demand

unlikely to alter your expenditure, or overall aggregate demand, but it may curb the amount of expenditure you pre-commit to next year's summer holiday. The same may be true of house purchases and investment in production or retail facilities by firms, where an interest rate change takes place between the decision to spend and the actual point when the transaction takes place. The transactions will still take place because the parties are committed to the sale process. It is only in the longer term that the volume of sales and the amount of investment will reflect the new higher interest rates. In a similar manner, a fall in interest rates is unlikely to lead to an immediate increase in additional expenditure because the expenditure for the coming year has already been planned out and committed. It is only next year that you may upgrade your holiday expenditure, while within firms with strict budgetary control and annual planning cycles, additional expenditure will not occur for another 12 months.

The two-year time lag for inflation is likely to reflect the prevalence of annual wage negotiations and the evolution of inflationary expectations. For example, if interest rates are increased to fend off higher inflation, it is not clear how this policy will alter inflationary expectations. In the short term, the higher interest rate may have little impact, with consumers and firms wondering about the credibility of the monetary authorities to fight inflation. Only if rates are kept high for a period of six to 12 months will inflationary expectations change. Once these changes in expectations are made, they will not impact wages and prices until wage negotiations take place. These tend to be conducted annually. So, given that interest rates take a year to affect output, the ability to change prices and wages to the new equilibrium output level may take up to one year longer.

The problem with such long time lags is that some other problem may hit the economy in the intervening period – for example, war, terrorist attack, avian flu, stock market crash or oil price increase. All of these are very real, immediate and significant threats to economic stability.

A recent fashion: central bank independence

A final consideration is the independence of monetary policy from political motives. A fear with fiscal policy is that governments will face incentives, particularly near to elections, to alter taxation and spending for electoral gain rather than for economic stability. The same can be true for monetary policy, except it is easier to place monetary policy with a non-government agency, such as the central bank. In the US, the Federal Reserve is charged with setting interest rates to deliver stable economic growth and fight inflation. In the UK, the Bank of England is charged with using monetary policy to bring about financial stability and inflation rates of 2 per cent on average. In the Eurozone, the European Central Bank is required to sue monetary policy to achieve an inflation rate of less than 2 per cent. Providing central banks with an inflation target reduces the political incentive to change rates. In addition, as non-political bodies, central banks may be seen as more credible bodies for fighting inflation. This should help to bring inflationary expectations into line with the inflation target. However, the appointment of key monetary decision makers, at most central banks, is a government decision. So, decisions may still be taken in the light of political patronage.

12.9 Business application: monetary policy and investment

Investment and business confidence

Debt is a complementary good for firms seeking to invest. Just as car users need to buy petrol, firms when investing in new capacity often need to purchase loans. If the interest rate falls, loans become cheaper. However, the cost of the loan is not the only factor that influences a firm's decision to invest. The interest rate reflects a cost of investing, but what about the benefits? If an economy is in recession, consumption of goods and services is falling. If a firm cannot sell the output generated by new investments, the benefits of investing are very low. A recession is, therefore, likely to reduce business confidence. If businesses are not confident about being able to sell products, or make a profit because of recession, they are likely to delay investment decisions. Reductions in interest rates are unlikely to boost investment rates.

Box 12.4 highlights how consumer confidence is key to economic transaction, especially on large ticket items like housing which require loans. Uncertainty over future income growth, employment prospects and inflation all damage consumer confidence. Firms have to tune into what their suppliers are telling them, as well as their customers. Multi-million pound investments in capacity need to be timed with buoyant consumer demand. In the case of

---

 Box 12.4 Savills reports London housing activity down 40 per cent

Adapted from an article by James Rossiter in The Times, *7 May 2008*

Sales of multi-million pound London homes have fallen by 40 per cent over the past three months and the drought in housing activity looks set to continue, as Nationwide reported today that consumer confidence is at a four-year low.

Jeremy Helsby, chief executive of Savills estate agency, said: 'There is a lack of sellers and buyers lack confidence – it is all about sentiment. There is job uncertainty in the City.'

The outlook for the housing market was darkened today as Nationwide said that its monthly measure of consumer confidence in April fell to its lowest level since the survey began in May 2004. Nationwide's index fell by seven points, to 70, a fall of 22 per cent from April last year. Delivering a stark message to the Bank of England ahead of tomorrow's decision on interest rates, the Nationwide survey showed that less than one in five consumers believe the economy is in good shape. Almost half of all consumers surveyed believe the economy will worsen further in six months' time – twice as many people showing pessimism than a year ago.

property, as soon as buyers lost confidence and walked away from both the housing market and the buy-to-let market, property developers did the same. There was little point in house builders spending millions on land and buildings if consumers were not confident enough to take on loans to purchase the properties. Even a marked cut in interest rates may not entice buyers back to the market. The risk of future price falls is all that is required to raise the risks and dent consumer confidence.

Investment under low inflation and low interest rates

A more fundamental question surrounds the recent desire for low inflation and low interest rates. What are the effects of low inflation on the economy and, in particular, on business? Constantly low inflation should bring increased stability. Businesses seeking to invest millions over many years will be assured by increased price stability. Predictions regarding costs and revenues are much easier to make and firms face less uncertainty when assessing investment risks. If low inflation reduces uncertainty, active monetary policy, leading to low inflation, may boost investment because of stability issues rather than because of cheaper borrowing.

Alternatively, low inflation may reduce the need, or desire, to invest. High wage inflation increases a firm's production costs. In order to recover these cost increases, firms may seek to raise the final price for their products. In such a scenario, firms have a clear incentive to swap increasingly expensive workers for capital equipment. But in recent times price inflation has been low. Wage demands have reflected the new lower rates of inflation and, as a result, firms have potentially less need to deal with an expensive workforce by investing in machinery.

It is, therefore, very clear that monetary policy and the pursuit of low inflation have many varied implications for business. Interest rates may influence investment simply by changing the cost of borrowing. However, the impact of interest rates on economic activity, business confidence and especially consumer spending and export growth may play a greater role in investment decisions. Finally, the use of monetary policy in targeting low inflation and economic stability may influence investments in different ways. Increased stability may make firms more willing to invest simply because it is easier to assess the relative costs and revenues from investment. However, without rising inflation and a consequential rise in labour costs, the need or desire to substitute capital for workers will be diminished.

12.10 Business application: the importance of banking to the economy

Should banking be the engine of economic growth, or the lubricant of the economic system? Section 12.3 emphasized the importance of banking in providing the economy with liquidity and risk management services. As such, banking plays the role of a lubricator within the economic system. When companies or households wish to undertake economic transactions using debt, then banks channel funds from savers to borrowers. Banking, therefore, plays a facilitating role within the economy.

During the last 20 years banks have benefited from repeated rounds of deregulation. Banks in many countries around the world are now able to offer a wider range of products, including credit cards, personal unsecured loans, pensions, insurance and a variety of personal investment products. This is sometimes referred to as 'bancassurance' – a conjunction of banking and insurance.

Deregulation has also enabled banks to operate internationally, not only in the products and services that they offer, but also in sourcing financial funds from depositors, debt holders and shareholders. As an example, traditional mortgage lenders raised money from savers and then loaned this money in the form of mortgages. More latterly, companies in the US and Europe have raised funds on wholesale money markets and then loaned this money in the form of mortgages. The mortgage loans have then been bundled up and sold on to investors. The notion of a bank providing mortgages by channelling savings to borrowers was almost redundant.

Deregulation has also enabled technical innovations, both in how money is managed and in the financial instruments that are available to banks and other institutions. Banks are not simply involved in savings and loans. They are just as involved in credit derivative markets, commodity markets, interest rate swap markets and currency markets. Where there is a financial risk and where there is a need for liquidity, then deregulation has enabled banks to expand their operations and profit.

Banks and financial services in general have grown to be important, significant and perhaps the largest component of growth within modern economies. Around financial hubs, such as London, Frankfurt, New York, Hong Kong and Singapore, the wealth from financial services companies has spilled out into residential property, the growing development of nearby leisure facilities and growing traffic through nearby airports and rail stations. Financial services has driven wealth within its own sector and within the wider related economy.

As financial services has become the engine of economic growth, it has arguably required greater deregulation and a greater ability to take increased risks in order to achieve yet higher rates of return. With an almost unblemished record at achieving growth without a loss of financial stability, governments were willing to see the complexity and innovativeness of financial services continue.

When this complexity resulted in the credit crunch and the collapse of many major banks, governments were required to bail out the financial system. These bailouts came with conditions. Governments became shareholders, required increased lending to households and small business and required directors to sacrifice performance-related pay bonuses. The clear risk is that governments direct banks to meet political and social objectives; they do not necessarily direct banks to meet commercial objectives. Why should banks lend their new capital to households and small businesses? Does this offer the highest risk-adjusted rate of return. Will highly skilled managers stay at banks that cannot offer them performance-related pay? If not, will part-nationalized banking systems become less efficient, less effective, less profitable and less important to economic growth?

In the medium term, governments may take the view that owning banks is not necessary and may sell their stakes. Or they may take the view that owning banks ensures a degree of control and financial stability which is necessary for stable economic progress. If so, then governments will need to think about where they can gain new drivers of growth. This may herald a renaissance in the manufacturing sector, where companies generate jobs, accrue export earnings and in the main do not take risks with households' savings or with pension funds.

 Summary

1   Monetary policy is the use of interest rates, or money supply, to control aggregate demand.

2   Money has a number of characteristics. It has to be a store of value, a unit of account and accepted as a medium of exchange.

3   The banking system provides the economy with liquidity by channelling funds from savers to borrowers.

4 The banking system also reduces the cost of borrowing, improves monitoring and risk selection and reduces the transaction costs associated with matching savers and borrowers.

5 The objective of banking regulation is to bring financial stability to the economy.

6 Capital adequacy regulates banks by ensuring they have sufficient equity backing. This type of regulation focuses on the financial strength of the bank.

7 Minimum reserve requirements state the level of cash of near-liquid assets the bank must hold. This type of regulation focuses on the bank's liquidity.

8 Activity-based regulation limits banks' commercial activities to certain product ranges and sectors of the financial services industry.

9 The money supply is composed not only of notes and coins, but also deposits within the banking system. The narrow and broad measures of money, M0 and M4, attempt to take account of these differences.

10 Credit creation occurs when the banks create additional money supply by lending out money on deposit. This increases the money supply.

11 There are three motives for holding money: the transaction, precautionary and asset motives.

12 Increases in income lead to an increase in demand for real money balances and reflect the transaction and precautionary motives for holding money. The speculative motive reflects how changes in the interest rate lead to changes in demand for money.

13 In money market equilibrium, the demand for money equals the money supply.

14 Governments, or central banks, now seek to set the interest rate and then provide sufficient money supply in order to make the market clear.

15 It is the transmission of changes in the base rate to the economy that influences aggregate demand.

Learning checklist

You should now be able to:

- Explain the key features of money
- Understand the different types of banking and financial institutions
- Understand the structure of banks' balance sheets
- Identify the economic importance of banking
- Understand the main methods of bank regulation
- Provide an explanation of how banks create credit
- Explain why we use both broad and narrow measures of money
- Explain the three motives for holding money
- Discuss money market equilibrium using a suitable diagram
- Understand monetary policy and the transmission mechanism
- Explain how business activities are influenced by changes in interest rates
- Assess the merits of a deregulated financial services industry

Questions connect

1 Identify and explain the main features of money.

2 What are the main economic benefits to be gained from a (well run) banking system?

3 Identify the important risks that banking regulation seeks to manage.

4 Are banks regulated by liquidity or capital adequacy? Is this a problem?

5 Identify and explain the main motives for holding money.

6 If incomes increase in an economy, how would this change the demand for real money balances?

7 Using a broad definition, what are the main components of the money supply?

8 What is the money multiplier and what factors determine the size of this multiplier?

9 The central bank cuts interest rates. How will this change in interest rate alter individuals' demand for cash?

10 What is quantitative easing and how do open market operations enable a policy of quantitative easing to be implemented?

11 Explain why a consideration of net present values may be a useful aid for managers making investment expenditure decisions.

12 Identify the key stages of the monetary transmission mechanism and what factors may prevent it from working.

13 Why might central bank independence and inflation targeting go together?

14 Why is central bank control of interest rates a control on over-exuberant fiscal policy? Is such a situation beneficial for business?

15 Do you consider income or wealth to determine the level of consumption?

Exercises

1 Which of the following would lead to an increase in the transaction demand for money?
   (a) An increase in prices.
   (b) An increase in real GDP.
   (c) A period of greater economic uncertainty.
   (d) A rise in interest rates.

2 A retail bank has a policy of holding cash reserves equal to 10 per cent of deposits.
   (a) If a customer deposits £1000, how much lending can the bank create? How would this lending change if cash reserves were less than 10 per cent.
   (b) How might a recession, or a banking crisis, alter a bank's willingness to hold reserves?

3 Consider Box 12.2:
   (a) 'The money markets are the plumbing of the economic system'. Explain.
   (b) Use a demand and supply diagram to illustrate the rise in the interbank interest rate.
   (c) How is the interbank market functioning today? What policies have helped to improve the interbank market?

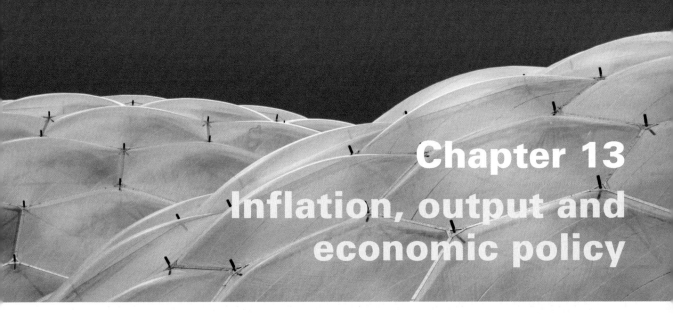

Chapter 13
Inflation, output and economic policy

Chapter contents

 Learning outcomes

By the end of this chapter you should understand:

⊚ **Economic Theory**

LO1 The short- and long-run Phillips curve

LO2 The macroeconomic demand schedule

LO3 Short- and long-run aggregate supply

LO4 The impact on macroeconomic equilibrium
     following shocks to demand and supply

LO5 Possible monetary policy responses to short-
     run equilibria

LO6 The Taylor rule

LO7 Differing views on the speed of adjustment
     to long-run equilibrium

⊚ **Business Application**

LO8 Understanding the interest rate path

LO9 Understanding the formation of inflationary
     expectations

Inflation, output and economic policy at a glance

The issue

Economic management is focused on inflation targeting and GDP. In macroeconomic equilibrium, how are inflation and GDP determined and how can government and central banks implement policies that enable inflation and GDP to be on target?

The understanding

Macroeconomic equilibrium is seen to be a reflection of equilibrium in important markets such as goods and labour. Prices and wages determine the value of employment to both workers and firms. Understanding how inflation alters real wages enables an appreciation of firms' willingness to supply output in the short term. Reactions to inflationary pressures in the longer term determine the rate of progression to long-run equilibrium.

The usefulness

Understanding the likely economic trajectory for an economy can provide businesses with a competitive edge and a greater degree of certainty. Understanding the drivers of supply and/or demand side shocks and being able to evaluate central bank changes in interest rates can provide businesses with a clearer understanding of the macroeconomic environment and provide a robust basis from which to build strategy and planning.

13.1 Business problem: why is inflation important for wage determination and debt repayment?

Economists have come to recognize that an understanding of the macroeconomic environment must be built on microeconomic foundations. After all, the macroeconomy is nothing more than a vast collection of microeconomic decisions bundled up in an enormous assortment of markets. Therefore, the equilibrium price of goods and services, and just as important the wages paid to workers and the price of debt, are likely to have a major impact on the scale of economic activity at the macroeconomic level.

In Chapter 3, when examining the productivity of firms, we focused on two factor inputs used by firms: labour and capital. These two inputs have associated costs: wages for labour and debt repayments associated with borrowed finances used for capital investment. We also know from Chapter 10, when we examined inflation in detail, that we need to consider how inflation drives a wedge between nominal and real prices. Therefore, over time, wage and debt agreements priced in nominal values will have very different real values in the future. Inflation will reduce real values; deflation will increase real values. This feature of inflation has enormous implications for businesses that are seeking to plan long-term financial cash flows and repayment schedules.

Let us begin by looking at labour. Firms employ workers for the value they can add to profits. If wage growth is less than inflation, then workers actually become cheaper to hire and their value increases. Discrepancies between inflation and wage growth provide firms with an incentive to expand economic output. In contrast, when inflation falls behind wage growth, then workers become more expensive and firms reduce employment and output. Clearly, an understanding of how inflation and wages impact on output is crucial for companies wishing to understand the future path of the economy.

Earnings growth and inflation

Figure 13.1 provides data from the UK economy on earnings growth and inflation. Throughout the period, earnings growth exceeded inflation. This would lead to rising real earnings. This can only be sustained in the long run if workers become more productive, generate more output per hour worked and so generate extra revenues to fund their higher earnings.

In the long run, prices and wages have no impact on the level of employment, economic output and therefore GDP. In the long run, the economy operates on its production possibility frontier. Every worker who desires a job is employed. This is because, in the long run, wage growth is in line with inflation. In the short run, however, unexpected changes in inflation impact the budgeted revenues and costs of firms. A worsening profit position results in output reductions, while an improving profit position results in increased outputs.

Short-run variations in output, caused by unexpected rates of inflation, are likely to be temporary. Firms and workers will form new expectations of future inflation and adjust prices and wages accordingly. New budgets will be planned and employment and output adjusted. The more rapidly and accurately prices and wages adjust to long-term levels, the more quickly the economy will return to the production possibility frontier.

Therefore, understanding the adjustment process is crucial to understanding the future path of the economy. In fact, by being closer to the adjustment process, businesses probably have a greater understanding of the correction process than economists. Factors that impede or facilitate changes in prices and wages are familiar to business. Wage negotiations with workers and unions can be difficult, contested and protracted. Similarly, the ability to change prices is constrained by competition and the actual cost of updating price lists and informing retailers. The less resistance to price and wage changes, the swifter an economy will return to equilibrium.

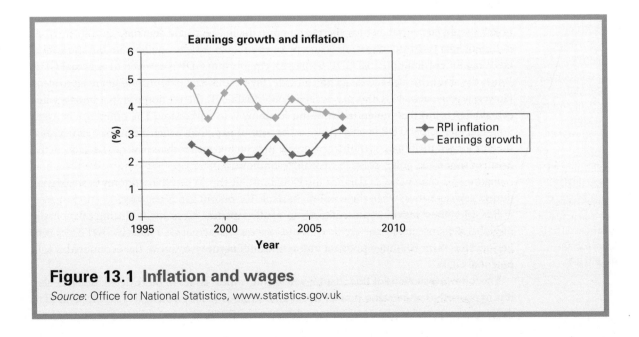

Figure 13.1 Inflation and wages

Source: Office for National Statistics, www.statistics.gov.uk

Changes in the real price of debt have similar implications for economic activity. As inflation rises, then the real value of debt falls. Firms (and consumers) who have debt repayment commitments find that the real value of debt falls (assuming incomes rise in line with inflation). Conversely, deflation raises the real value of debt. Incomes fall in line with the drop in prices for goods and services and the affordability of previously acquired debt rises.

It should therefore be clear that price, wage and debt adjustments are enormously important to the functioning of the economy, both in the short term and in enabling an economy to return to its long-run equilibrium on the production possibility frontier.

The sections within this chapter will provide you with an understanding of the relationship between inflation and employment in the short and long run. This will be developed into an understanding of the macroeconomic equilibrium in the short and long run. This will provide a clear link between the microeconomics goods and labour market and the broader macro-economy. The analysis will then be extended to provide you with an understanding of how the economy reacts to demand and supply side shocks. A consideration of monetary policy and inflation targeting will then be offered, followed by a review of different economists' perceptions of how quickly the economy will adjust to long-run equilibrium.

13.2 Short- and long-run macroeconomic equilibrium

In Chapters 11 and 12, we presented the economic ideas behind fiscal and monetary policy. These previous chapters showed *how* demand side policies work. The aim of this chapter is to show more clearly the circumstances *when* these policies will be used by policy-makers.

If an economy is in long-run equilibrium, then the level of GDP is that associated with a point on the economy's production possibility frontier (recall the discussion in Chapter 1). All land, labour, capital and enterprise that are willing to be supplied are employed within firms in the pursuit of profit. The economy is said to be at its **full employment level**. At the full employment level, an economy is producing at its **potential GDP**. Therefore, if an economy is in long-run equilibrium, there is little need to correct a recession by providing a boost to spending. Similarly, there is little need to slow the economy by increasing taxes or interest rates. In simple and clear terms, because long-run equilibrium results in full employment, fiscal and monetary policy should be neutral, neither increasing nor reducing aggregate demand.

In the short run, by contrast, an economy can be shown to be in equilibrium but the level of GDP can differ from potential GDP. Short-run equilibrium GDP is referred to as **actual GDP**. When the short run and the long run coincide, then actual and potential GDP are equivalent. However, when actual GDP is greater than potential GDP, the economy is in a boom; when actual GDP is less than potential GDP, the economy is in a recession. The difference between potential and actual GDP is referred to as the **output gap**. Only when an output gap exists is there any need for fiscal, or monetary, policy to be active rather than neutral. As such, active fiscal, or monetary, policy seeks to close the economy's output gap.

Figure 13.2 charts OECD data on the global output gap. When the economy is strong, the output gap is positive; when the economy is weak, the output gap is negative.

Box 13.1 discusses the rapid contraction of the Japanese economy following the collapse of global demand during the credit crisis. In this case, as actual GDP falls by over 3 per cent per quarter, there is a huge political and economic incentive to move the economy back to potential GDP.

The following sections of this chapter will examine these issues in more detail. In particular, it is important to understand how differences in short- and long-run aggregate supply lead to different short- and long-run equilibrium levels of GDP. To develop this understanding, it is

---

In **full employment**, all factors of production that wish to be employed are employed.

Any point on the production possibility frontier represents **potential GDP**.

Short-run equilibrium GDP is **actual GDP**.

The difference between actual and potential GDP is known as the **output gap**.

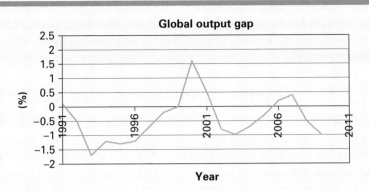

Figure 13.2 Output gap

Output gap is measured as actual GDP less estimated potential GDP, expressed as a percentage of estimated potential GDP.

Source: OECD

 Box 13.1 Japan's economy shrinks by 3.3 per cent

Adapted from an article by Mure Dickie in The Financial Times, *16 February 2009, and from 'Japan's economy shrinks most since 1974', adapted from* Blomberg, *16 February 2009*

Japan's economy contracted 3.3 per cent in the three months to December compared with the previous quarter, as a slowdown in exports led to the worst performance in 35 years.

On an annualized basis, gross domestic product declined at a rate of 12.7 per cent, underlining the depth and severity of a slump that has dispelled early hopes that the world's second largest economy might be able to shrug off the effects of the global financial crisis. The contraction was three times as bad as that of the US in the same quarter.

Evidence of Japan's slowdown can be found across the economy. On Monday, the country's electric utilities industry association said that power generation had fallen by 6.4 per cent in January as the industrial sector gears down. This was the sixth straight monthly decline and the steepest fall since a 6.9 per cent drop recorded in July 2005.

Exports plunged by an unprecedented 13.9 per cent from the third quarter, as demand for Corolla cars and Bravia televisions collapsed. Toyota Motor Corporation, Sony Corporation and Hitachi Ltd – all of which forecast losses – are firing thousands of workers, heightening the risk that a decline in household spending will prolong the recession.

'The economy is in terrible shape and the scary part is that we're likely to see a similar drop this quarter,' said Seiji Adachi, a senior economist at Deutsche Securities Inc. in Tokyo. 'All we can do is wait for overseas demand to pick up.'

'There's no doubt that the economy is in its worst state in the postwar period,' Economic and Fiscal Policy Minister, Kaoru Yosano, said in Tokyo. 'The Japanese economy, which is heavily dependent on exports of autos, electronics and capital goods, has been severely hit by the global slowdown.'

necessary to understand the short- and long-run equilibrium markets for labour. Moreover, in order to understand the adjustment from actual to potential levels of GDP, it is necessary to form an opinion about the rate of adjustment following the implementation of active fiscal, or monetary, policy. As will become evident, some economic schools of thought believe fiscal policy is more effective than monetary policy in closing the output gap. Each of these areas of concern will be discussed in turn, but we will start with the labour market and show how long-run equilibrium in the market for jobs leads to an understanding of long-run aggregate supply and potential GDP.

13.3 Employment, inflation and output

> The **Phillips curve** shows that lower unemployment is associated with higher inflation. Simply, lower unemployment has to be traded for higher inflation.

The **Phillips curve** was developed by Professor Phillips from the London School of Economics in 1958 after observing inflation and unemployment in the UK. 'Observe' is the crucial word, because the initial theoretical reasons for a Phillips curve relationship between unemployment and inflation were weak.

The Phillips curve, as illustrated in Figure 13.3, seemed very attractive. This was because it showed a clear trade-off between unemployment and inflation. The government merely had to decide which, of inflation and unemployment, it disliked more. If the government disliked unemployment, then it had to suffer higher inflation. The problem of the Phillips curve being simply an observation became a serious concern in the 1970s when the relationship broke down. As unemployment increased, so did inflation. Governments no longer witnessed a trade-off between inflation and unemployment.

If a trade-off between inflation and unemployment ever existed, then it did so in the short run. This is because, in the long run, the economy operates on its production possibility frontier at the full employment level. Therefore, in the long run, GDP, and as a consequence unemployment, are fixed. Whatever the level of inflation, there can be no trade-off with un-employment in the long run.

Consider Figure 13.4, which includes both a short- and long-run Phillips curve. The short-run Phillips curve depicts the trade-off between inflation and unemployment, while the long-run Phillips curve shows the fixed level of unemployment.

In Figure 13.4, long-run equilibrium unemployment is fixed at 3.0 per cent. It does not matter what the rate of inflation is, unemployment is constant in the long run. In addition, in long-run equilibrium, the economy is also positioned on its short-run Phillips curve, SPC_1, where it intersects the long-run Phillips curve. Therefore, unemployment is 3.0 per cent and

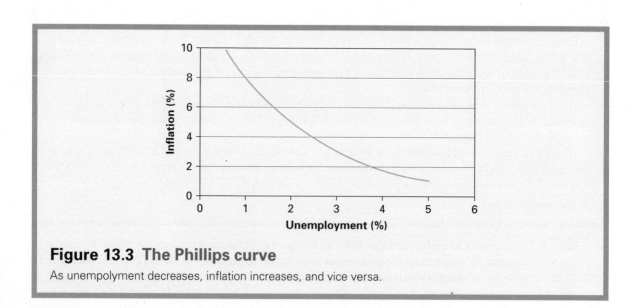

Figure 13.3 The Phillips curve
As unempolyment decreases, inflation increases, and vice versa.

inflation is 2.0 per cent in the long run. This is consistent with a central bank inflation target of 2.0 per cent.

Now consider a positive shock to the level of demand in the economy. This increase in demand will raise GDP and therefore cut unemployment. The economy moves along SPC_1 to A. As unemployment is cut, inflation rises above the target rate, to 4 per cent. The central bank now increases interest rates to bring inflation back to target. The level of economic activity slows and the economy moves back along the SPC_1 into long-run equilibrium, where unemployment is constant and inflation is 2 per cent.

A reduction in demand would move the economy along SPC_1 to point B, with higher unemployment and lower inflation. The central bank would now cut interest rates, enabling the economy to grow. As jobs are created, the economy moves along SPC_1 back into long-run equilibrium.

In the long run, unemployment is constant because the **real wage** is constant. The real wage is equal to the **nominal wage** divided by inflation, often written as W/P. So, a wage rise of 2 per cent when inflation is also 2 per cent results in a constant real wage. If the real wage remains constant, then the cost incentive to hire or fire workers is zero. However, if an unexpected increase in aggregate demand moves the economy to point A, then inflation rises. With a given nominal wage level, firms will hire more workers when prices rise. This is because faster rising prices result in a lower real wage. So a temporary increase in inflation can lead to a temporary reduction in unemployment. However, once the central bank raises interest rates, it reinforces long-run inflationary expectations of the target rate (2 per cent). Firms and workers negotiate pay and price increases of 2 per cent. Therefore, constant real wages, constant unemployment rates and target long-run inflation rates resume and the economy moves back to its long-run equilibrium.

In Box 13.2, the story of workers at JCB who took a pay cut to save jobs is reported. This is similar to being at point B in Figure 13.4. Due to a collapse in aggregate demand, the inflation rate is less than expected. Real wages rise and firms cut back on employment. JCB workers recognized that their real wages were now too high given the amount of demand for JCB's products. So they cut their nominal wages. This saved jobs and moved them back into long-run equilibrium.

> **Real wages** are earnings adjusted for inflation.
>
> **Nominal wages** are earnings unadjusted for inflation. If a worker earns £30 000 per year, this is their nominal wage. If inflation is 5 per cent per year, then at the end of the year, the real wage is £30 000/1.05 = £28 571.

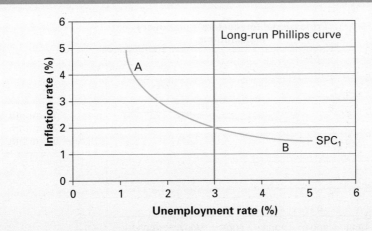

Figure 13.4 Long-run Phillips curve

In the long run, there is no trade-off between inflation and unemployment. In the short run, differences between expected and actual inflation can lead to a trade-off between inflation and unemployment.

Box 13.2 JCB workers take pay cut to avoid layoffs

Adapted from an article by Sam Jones in The Guardian, *23 October 2008*

Thousands of workers at the manufacturing firm JCB have voted to accept a pay cut of £50 a week to prevent the loss of 350 jobs. The GMB union said around 2500 of its members at seven JCB plants in England and Wales had agreed to work a four-day week for the next 13 weeks to help the company weather the economic downturn.

The company has been badly hit by the downturn in property and construction. In July this year, it warned of a 'rapid decline' in demand.

The union said the move – believed to be the first of its kind in the current economic slump – showed the recession was getting worse and called on the government to instigate a major public works programme to ease its impact.

'I am delighted that we have been able to save 350 jobs,' said GMB officer, Keith Hodgkinson. 'The short time is part of a worsening recession and these GMB members expect the government and the Bank of England to take the necessary steps to begin large-scale public works to at least slow the recession down and prevent it getting too deep.'

© Guardian News and Media Ltd 2008

Inflationary expectations are always changing as new economic events occur. Expectations will also depend upon the time horizon. Figure 13.5 shows the average forecast of inflation (inflationary expectations) held by professional economic forecasters in the Eurozone. Over a five-year horizon most forecasters expect inflation to be around 2 per cent, which is the European Central Bank's target rate of inflation. But in the near term, professional forecasters are expecting some deviation from 2 per cent.

These short-run variations in inflationary expectations away from the long-run values can be incorporated into our model by considering a movement in the short-run Phillips curve.

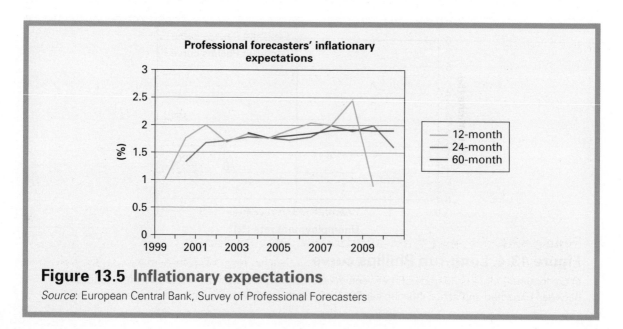

Figure 13.5 Inflationary expectations
Source: European Central Bank, Survey of Professional Forecasters

A central bank could change its inflation target to, say, 3 per cent, or firms and workers could believe that the central bank will be incapable of maintaining a 2 per cent inflation target even in the long run. In either case, inflationary expectations will rise and the short-run Phillips curve will move up, as in Figure 13.6. However, the long-run equilibrium level of unemployment and GDP will remain constant. Only long-run inflation will rise to 3 per cent. Why? The answer is simple: because inflationary expectations have risen to 3 per cent, firms and workers will now negotiate nominal wage increases of 3 per cent. As a result, real wages will remain constant and, therefore, so will unemployment and GDP. So even with a change in inflationary expectations, unemployment and GDP still remain at their constant long-run values.

The same is true in a period of deflation, where a fall in inflationary expectations would result in the short-run Phillips curve moving down from SPC_1 to SPC_3. Long-run equilibrium unemployment will remain constant, but inflation will be lower.

The key point to understand is that, in the long run, there is no trade-off between inflation and unemployment.

Insights from the Phillips curve

The Phillips curve analysis provides two important insights, which we can develop further. First, the analysis has shown that we need to consider the short and the long run. Importantly, because labour and wages are a main input and cost for a firm, then any variation in wages results in a change in a firm's willingness to supply. Therefore, the Phillips curve analysis highlights the need to understand both short- and long-run aggregate supply within the economy.

Second, we need to be concerned about the speed of adjustment from the short to the long run. If a reduction in demand moves an economy to point B in Figure 13.4, then unemployment increases and inflation falls. If firms and workers are able to cut prices and wages quickly, then the economy will rapidly return to its long-run equilibrium. Cutting prices is possible, but cutting wages is rarely seen as acceptable by workers. An increase in demand moves the economy to A, so firms and workers need to increase prices and wages in order to ensure that

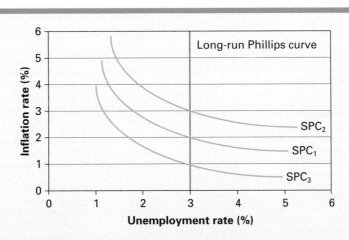

Figure 13.6 **Expectations-augmented Phillips curve**

If inflationary expectations increase to 3 per cent, then the short-run Phillips curve moves up. The new long-run equilibrium is 3 per cent unemployment and 3 per cent inflation. In reverse, a fall in inflationary expectations would see the short-run Phillips curve move down from SPC_1 to SPC_3.

real wages remain constant. Raising wages makes workers happy, but funding a pay rise by raising prices is not seen as that attractive by consumers or competitive by firms. In addition, prices and wages are often negotiated and set for 12 months. Therefore, for a variety of reasons, sluggish wage and price adjustments limit the scope for rapid adjustment to the long-run macroeconomic equilibrium.

Rapid adjustment in prices and wages suggests that an economy needs little active fiscal or monetary policy, while sluggish adjustments provide the possibility for fiscal or monetary intervention to move the economy more swiftly towards its equilibrium.

In order to develop your understanding of these issues, we will develop the short- and long-run Phillips curve ideas into short- and long-run aggregate supply schedules. From this, we can then examine macroeconomic equilibrium using aggregate demand and supply frameworks and consider likely responses to demand and supply side shocks to the economy. We can then consider the competing views on the need and scale of intervention, which relate to perceived views on the economy's speed of adjustment.

13.4 Inflation, aggregate demand and supply

Macroeconomic demand schedule

Aggregate demand is total demand in the economy. Aggregate demand is equal to the sum of consumption, investment, government spending and net exports. There is a negative relationship between inflation and aggregate demand. As inflation rises, less is demanded; as inflation falls, more is demanded. This relationship is illustrated in Figure 13.7. Movements along the macroeconomic demand schedule show how changes in inflation alter the interest rate set by central banks, which impacts aggregate demand, and therefore GDP.

As inflation rises above the central bank's target rate, then interest rates are increased. Through the transmission mechanism, explained in Chapter 12, higher interest rates lead to a reduction in consumption and investment. This fall in demand leads to a reduction in GDP. Conversely, if inflation falls below the central bank's target rate, then interest rates will be cut, leading to an increase in consumption and investment, and rising levels of GDP.

A shift in the macroeconomic demand schedule results from changes in aggregate demand, which are not a result of changes in the real interest rate set by the central bank. So, a reduction tax and/or imports would lead to an increase in aggregate demand and a shift in the macroeconomic demand schedule to the right.

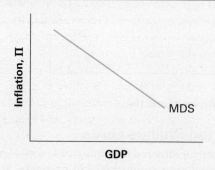

If the central bank targets inflation, then an increase in the inflation rate above target will be countered by an increase in interest rates. This increase in the price of debt will lower consumption and investment. This explains the negative relationship between inflation and the macroeconomic demand schedule.

Figure 13.7 Macroeconomic demand schedule

The press release from the Bank of England in Box 13.3 highlights the relationship between inflation, interest rates and macroeconomic demand. As demand in the global and UK economy plummeted, the Bank of England was greatly concerned about undershooting the inflation target of CPI = 2 per cent. It has therefore slashed interest rates, down this time to 1 per cent.

 Box 13.3 Bank of England reduces bank rate by 0.5 percentage points, to 1.0 per cent

Adapted from the Bank of England's press release, 5 February 2009

The Bank of England's Monetary Policy Committee today voted to reduce the official Bank Rate paid on commercial bank reserves by 0.5 percentage points, to 1.0 per cent.

The global economy is in the throes of a severe and synchronized downturn. In the UK, output dropped sharply in the fourth quarter of 2008 and business surveys point to a similar rate of decline in the early part of this year. The underlying picture for consumer spending appears weak. Businesses have responded to the worsening outlook by running down inventories, cutting production, scaling back investment plans and shedding labour.

At its February meeting, the Committee noted that, although the transmission mechanism of monetary policy was impaired, the past cuts of 4 per cent in Bank Rate would in due course nevertheless have a significant impact. Together with the recent easing in fiscal policy, the substantial fall in sterling and past falls in commodity prices, the cut would provide a considerable stimulus to activity as the year progressed. Nevertheless, the Committee judged that there remained a substantial risk of undershooting the 2 per cent CPI inflation target in the medium term at the existing Bank Rate level. Accordingly, the Committee concluded that a further reduction in Bank Rate of 0.5 percentage points to 1.0 per cent was warranted this month.

Long-run aggregate supply

The long-run Phillips curve shows that unemployment is constant in the long run and, therefore, the economy operates at full potential. As such, GDP is constant and any changes in inflation do not alter employment, or GDP. This is because, in the long run, real wages are held constant through nominal wage increases being kept in line with inflation. Long-run aggregate supply is therefore vertical, or inflation inelastic, as illustrated in Figure 13.8.

In simple terms, if wages and prices double, firms are not inclined to hire more workers, and similarly workers are not motivated to provide more labour. The financial benefits of economic activity have remained constant and so the level of economic activity remains constant. All changes in inflation are fully compensated in changes in prices and wages. Output is therefore independent of inflation and aggregate supply is vertical.

This is not to say that the full employment level of GDP is fixed. It is possible for an economy to attract more economic resources. A rising birth rate, an inflow of migrant workers or the discovery of oil and gas are all examples of increased economic endowments, which would result in the long-run aggregate supply schedule moving to AS_2 in Figure 13.8. Equally, if a new technology reduced the costs of economic transactions, such as Google's ability to provide low-cost information, especially on prices, then less time/resource is needed for shopping and more time is available for labour. With more labour time, the economy can grow to GDP_2. Finally, a rise in productivity, such as that brought about by more workers engaging in university education, can also lead to an increase in the full employment level of the economy.

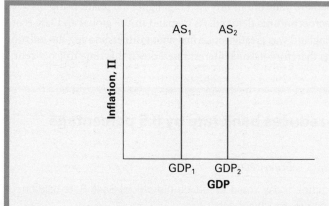

Long-run aggregate supply is constant and represents the full employment level of the economy. Any change in long-run supply must reflect real changes in economic factor inputs, technology or productivity.

Figure 13.8 Long-run aggregate supply

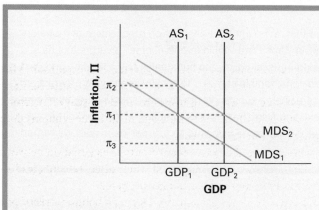

At a target inflation rate of π_2, an increase in demand must be offset by a rise in interest rates. An increase in long-run supply can be accommodated on the demand side by a reduction in interest rates.

Figure 13.9 Long-run equilibrium

Long-run equilibrium

In Figure 13.9, we have drawn long-run aggregate supply and the macroeconomic demand schedule together. The central bank has an inflation target of π_1 and the economy is currently in equilibrium at this rate of inflation. A positive shock to demand, such as an increase in government spending, results in the macroeconomic schedule moving to the right, to MDS_2, and inflation rises to π_2. In order to achieve the target rate of inflation, the central bank must now increase interest rates, which cuts private sector consumption and investment and returns the macroeconomic demand schedule to MDS_1. Inflation is restored to the target rate of π_1.

If the economy benefits from a supply shock, then long-run aggregate supply moves to the right and the rate of inflation falls to π_3. The central bank can accommodate this shock by relaxing interest rates and allowing demand to increase until the target rate of π_1 is achieved. Until the arrival of the credit crisis, many central banks took the view that cheap imports from China and the supply of migrant labour from Eastern Europe represented a beneficial supply shock. These events enabled many economies to enjoy lower interest rates (which may well have fuelled the credit crisis).

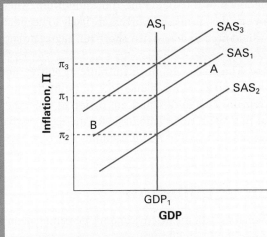

The economy is in long-run equilibrium, with an inflation rate of π_1 and output of GDP_1. On SAS_1, nominal wage growth is agreed to be π_1. Inflation higher than π_1 reduces real wages and enables firms to raise output. The economy moves to A. Inflation less than π_1 raises real wages and forces firms to reduce output. The economy moves to B. If π_2 becomes the expected rate of inflation and the agreed rate of nominal wage increases, then the economy will move to SAS_2 and return to long-run equilibrium. Points A and B correspond with points A and B in Figure 13.4.

Figure 13.10 Short-run aggregate supply

13.5 Short-run aggregate supply

In the short run, there is no presumption that real wages remain constant. A simple look at the real world will show you that constant real wages cannot be assumed. This is because, for most jobs, nominal wages are fixed in advance for anything from one to three years. Therefore, nominal wage adjustment is not instantaneously linked to inflation. As such, the economy does not have to be at the full employment level in the short run.

Wage bargaining is extremely expensive and involves many hours of negotiation between managers, unions and workers. These costs can be magnified when disagreements lead to strikes. Therefore, companies prefer to limit negotiations to once per year.

Workers may even benefit from inflexible wage agreements. During a boom, workers' pay may not rise quickly. But this can be compensated in a recession by pay not falling. Workers are therefore willing to sacrifice short-term constant real wages for short-term nominal wage guarantees.

For these reasons, it is necessary to examine the short-run equilibrium of the economy, where real wages are not held constant. If nominal wages are held constant and the rate of inflation rises, then real wages fall and employment increases. Recall Figure 13.4 and the movement along SPC_1 to A. We now have to incorporate these ideas into an understanding of short-run aggregate supply. Figure 13.10 helps to develop this understanding.

Figure 13.10 illustrates a long-run aggregate supply line, AS_1, and two short-run aggregate supply lines, SAS_1 and SAS_2. Each short-run aggregate supply line is drawn for a given rate of nominal wage growth. So, if workers and firms have agreed a wage increase of 5 per cent, then we might assume that the economy is on SAS_1. If they have agreed a nominal wage increase of 2 per cent, then they can assume the economy is on SAS_2.

The economy begins in long-run equilibrium, with output at GDP_1 and inflation at π_1. Workers and firms have agreed nominal wage growth of π_1, which therefore places them on SAS_1. If inflation turns out to be π_1, then real wages are held constant and the economy remains in long-run equilibrium. If inflation turns out to be higher than π_1, say π_3, then real wages will fall and the price of goods and services rises faster than expected. This provides firms with an incentive to hire more workers and raise short-run output. The economy moves along SAS_1 to point A. Inflation and GDP rise.

If inflation falls back to π_1, then the economy moves back to long-run equilibrium, where SAS_1 intersects AS_1. If inflation remains above π_1, then firms and workers are likely to negotiate higher nominal wage growth of π_3 and we would need to draw a new short-run aggregate supply line, SAS_3, which is higher than SAS_1.

If inflation is less than π_1, real wages rise. This makes employment more expensive, and firms reduce employment and output. The economy moves along SAS_1 to point B, where inflation and output fall. If the economy remains at B for a significant period of time, then firms and workers may come to expect that the long-term inflation rate for the economy has fallen to π_2. If they then agree nominal wage rate increases of π_2, the economy moves to SAS_2, and back into long-run equilibrium.

13.6 Short- and long-run equilibrium

We can now integrate our short-run supply analysis with the macroeconomic demand schedule and examine the short- and long-run macroeconomic equilibrium.

Consider Figure 13.11; the economy is in both short- and long-run equilibrium, with an output of GDP_1 and an inflation rate of π_1. Then follows a drop in consumer and business confidence. Consumption and investment fall and the macroeconomic demand schedule moves from mds_1 to mds_2. SAS_1 is drawn for an assumed nominal wage growth of π_1. The fall in demand moves the economy to a new short-run equilibrium, where inflation is π_2 and output is GDP_2. The fall in inflation has raised real wages and firms have reacted by cutting output.

As firms and workers adjust to the new macroeconomic environment, they revise their expectations of inflation and agree lower nominal wage growth. This moves the economy to short-run aggregate supply at SAS_2. Inflation falls further to π_3 and output begins to rise to GDP_3. Only when nominal wage growth falls even further and the economy moves onto SAS_3 does GDP return to the full employment and long-run equilibrium level.

Deflation and the credit crisis

The credit crisis led to a fall in consumption and investment. However, at the time inflation was above target in many economies, so the fall in demand helped economies move back

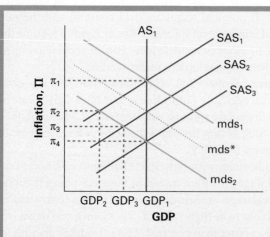

A fall in demand moves the economy away from its initial long-run equilibrium. Progressive changes in inflationary expectations then alter nominal wage growth agreements, leading to shifts in short-run aggregate supply. The initial shift in demand creates a recession. The progressive changes in short-run supply eventually return the economy to its long-run equilibrium level of output.

mds* represents a rapid fiscal and monetary expansion, designed to swiftly move the economy back to long-run equilibrium, thus avoiding a prolonged recession.

Figure 13.11 Short- and long-run equilibrium

towards their target inflation rate. If the target rate of inflation was π_2, then a drop to π_4 was not necessary. Governments and central banks welcomed the reduction in inflation, but were concerned about a long-run adjustment which also included a significant recession at GDP_2, and deflation with price levels falling all the way to π_4.

The swift reductions of interest rates and the planned increases in government expenditure were combined monetary and fiscal expansions designed to rapidly increase macroeconomic demand, thus enabling the economy to return to long-run equilibrium quickly and not go through a prolonged adjustment of prices, wages, supply and output. The blue dotted mds* in Figure 13.11 illustrates this point.

Why avoid deflation if adjustment to full employment can be reached in the long run? The first issue is time to adjust. If full employment at π_4 takes many years, then unemployment will be high for a prolonged period of time. It is then better to act quickly with monetary and fiscal packages.

The second issue relates to the impact of deflation on consumption. If consumers postpone consumption of high ticket items in the expectation of cheaper prices in the future, then consumption today falls further. In Figure 13.11, the macroeconomic demand schedule moves further to the left. This generates a bigger recession, more unemployment and more deflation. The risk, then, is that further deflation motivates households to withhold yet more consumption, which simply repeats the cycle and exacerbates the overall macroeconomic problem.

Third, deflation raises the real value of debt. If prices fall, then the value of labour falls and wage growth should fall and perhaps even become negative. This makes previously incurred debts less affordable. Households transfer earnings from consumption to debt repayment. The macroeconomic demand schedule shifts to the left and we observe more deflation, a larger fall in GDP and greater unemployment.

The simple lesson is that falling prices are not necessarily a good thing.

Adjustment to permanent supply shocks

Improvements in supply, such as greater availability of cheap manufactured items from China and migrant labour from Eastern Europe, improve the long-run equilibrium output of the economy. Long-run aggregate supply, short-run aggregate supply and potential GDP move to the right in Figure 13.12. With a target inflation rate of π_1, the central bank needs to respond to the permanent supply shock by cutting interest rates and enabling macroeconomic demand to catch up with supply.

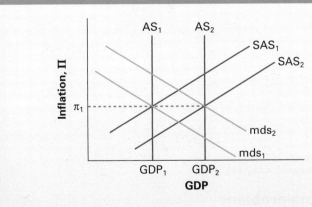

A permanent supply shock results in long-run potential GDP increasing. With an inflation target of π_1, the central bank accommodates this improvement in supply by cutting interest rates and enabling demand to expand.

Figure 13.12 Adjustment to a permanent supply shock

In reality, the transmission mechanism may be slow and households and firms may take time to react to the lower interest rates. Therefore, the short-run equilibrium for the economy may not make full use of the new higher potential GDP and inflation will go below target. This is what occurred across most of Europe during the late 1990s and early 2000s. The Bank of England referred to this as the NICE – non-inflationary, constantly expanding – decade.

Adjustment to a temporary supply shock

Under a temporary supply shock, potential output is unaffected – because the shock is temporary. Therefore, long-run aggregate supply is unaltered. For a temporary supply shock, short-run aggregate supply changes. In the summer of 2008, oil prices rose to a record US$135 a barrel. Since oil and its derivatives represent a significant input cost for many firms, this increase in costs represented a temporary supply shock (oil soon fell off record highs and by October 2008 was trading at US$60). Box 13.4 provides more information on how this shock affected emerging economies.

 ## Box 13.4 Inflation in emerging economies

Adapted from 'An old enemy rears its head' in The Economist, *22 May 2008*

China's official rate of consumer-price inflation is at a 12-year high of 8.5 per cent, up from 3 per cent a year ago (see Chart 1). Russia's has leapt from 8 to over 14 per cent. Most Gulf oil producers also have double-digit rates. India's wholesale-price inflation rate (the Reserve Bank's preferred measure) is 7.8 per cent, a four-year high.

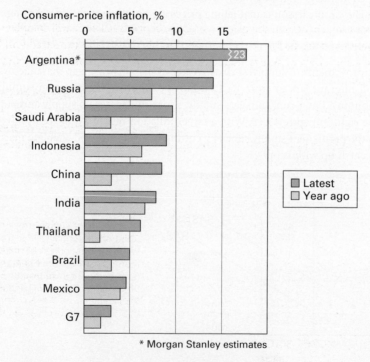

Chart 1 An emerging problem

Source: National statistics

The recent jump has been caused mainly by surging oil and food prices. For example, in China food prices have risen by 22 per cent in the past year, whereas non-food prices have gone up by only 1.8 per cent.

Some central banks, including those in Brazil, Indonesia and Russia, have nudged up interest rates this year. But they have not kept pace with inflation, so real rates have fallen and are now negative in most countries. Many policy-makers in emerging economies argue that serious monetary tightening is not warranted: higher inflation, they say, is due solely to spikes in food and energy prices, caused by temporary supply shocks and speculation. Higher interest rates cannot call forth more pigs or grain. They expect inflation to ease later this year as higher prices prompt an increase in supply (food prices have started to edge down over the past month) and as sharp rises in commodity prices drop out of year-on-year comparisons.

© The Economist Newspaper Limited, London 2009

Figure 13.13 illustrates the effect of a temporary supply shock and the options available to policy-makers. The economy begins in long-run equilibrium at the target rate of inflation. The increase in oil prices moves the short-run aggregate supply schedule to SAS_2. The short-run macroeconomic equilibrium now consists of higher inflation and lower GDP. The central bank now needs to decide whether it wishes to prioritize inflation or GDP. In the UK and Europe, the priority was clearly inflation and so the central banks were willing to see slowing economic growth and wait for oil prices to fall and see short-run aggregate supply return to SAS_1. In contrast, the US Federal Reserve took the view that, along with the credit crunch, the substantial risk to GDP was the greater concern and so cut interest rates – the consequences of which were to provide a stimulus to GDP, through higher demand, and a further rise in inflation.

Shocks to demand

Assessing changes in the macroeconomic demand schedule will complete our analysis. Shocks to demand are fairly simple to understand because there is no trade-off between output and inflation. Any attempt to stabilize inflation will also stabilize output, and vice versa. Consider Figure 13.14.

The economy is in long-run equilibrium, with output at GDP_1 and inflation at π_1. The target rate of inflation is also π_1. Macroeconomic demand increases to mds_2. Inflation and output rise. The central bank responds by increasing interest rates, which leads to a reduction in demand. Inflation and GDP both return to their long-run equilibrium target levels. If demand

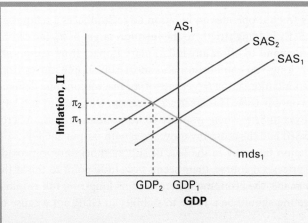

A temporary supply shock reduces short-run supply to SAS_2. This moves the economy away from its long-run equilibrium of GDP_1 and π_1. Inflation rises to π_2 and GDP falls to GDP_2. The central bank can accommodate this shock and boost demand and GDP, but will suffer even higher inflation.

Figure 13.13 A temporary supply shock

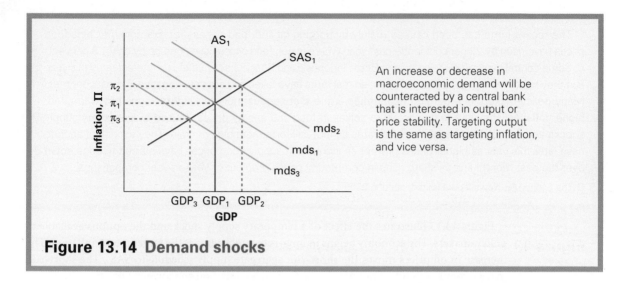

Figure 13.14 Demand shocks

had fallen to mds_3, then the central bank would have reacted to falling inflation and GDP by cutting interest rates. This would have raised consumption and investment spending, and returned the economy to its long-run equilibrium of π_1 and GDP_1.

13.7 Monetary policy rules

If all shocks were demand based, then it would be relatively simple to set monetary policy rules for central banks. In theory, targeting inflation is equivalent to targeting GDP. The only practical difficulty is having full knowledge of potential GDP. Since this is difficult to measure, and since in a growing economy it is always increasing, inflation targeting seems more appropriate. This of course presumes that measures of inflation are reliable and that important economic agents, such as firms and workers, base their decisions on central banks' measures of inflation.

A slight concern in the UK is that the central bank targets consumer price inflation, while firms and workers negotiate wages based on retail price inflation. The latter places more emphasis on housing costs. However, as long as consumer and retail price inflation are reasonably correlated in the long run, then the central bank's target measure should be inconsequential.

The worry for a central bank is when it operates an inflation target and faces a temporary supply side shock; see Figure 13.15. By holding strictly to the inflation target of π_1, the central bank must alter macroeconomic demand to offset any inflationary impact from temporary supply side shocks. If we begin in long-run equilibrium and short-run supply moves from SAS_1 to SAS_2, then in order to keep inflation at the target rate of π_1, macroeconomic demand has to be reduced and move the economy to A. This creates a recession, with output at GDP_2. If short-run aggregate supply moves to SAS_3, then, in order to keep inflation at π_1, macroeconomic demand has to be increased and the economy moves to B with output at GDP_3.

The clear consequences of inflation targeting in the face of supply shocks are to provide volatility in GDP and stability in prices. Of course, there seems very little point to this if the purpose of monetary policy is to enable the economy to return to its long-run, full employment level of GDP. Inflation targeting should be a route to stability in GDP, not a cause of instability.

An additional problem faced by central banks is to understand the source of the macroeconomic shock. Is it demand or supply based? Data only become available over time and so

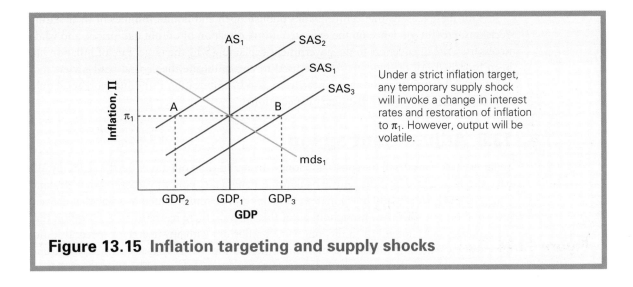

Figure 13.15 Inflation targeting and supply shocks

the correct diagnosis and policy response is difficult, especially if demand and supply shocks occur together or overlap in a particular time period.

Reflecting these difficulties, central banks are pragmatic in their approach to managing the economy and tend to follow what is known as a **Taylor rule**.

> A **Taylor rule** links interest rate changes to short-term deviations in both inflation and output from long-term equilibrium values.

The Taylor rule can be represented by the following equation:

$$i = \pi + i^* + a(\pi - \pi^*) + b(GDP - GDP^*)$$

π is the rate of inflation, π^* is the target rate of inflation, GDP is actual GDP, GDP^* is potential GDP and i^* is the real interest rate; a and $b > 0$. The more the central bank is concerned about inflation deviating from the target rate, the larger a, and the more interest rates will change. Similarly, the higher the value for b, the more concerned the central bank is with variations in GDP and the more rates will change to bring about long-run equilibrium and potential GDP.

Inflation targeting in practice

The Bank of England and the European Central Bank both operate flexible inflation targets. In the UK, inflation is targeted at 2 per cent on average, while in the Eurozone inflation of 2 per cent or less is targeted. In both instances, the inflation target is not a specific value. In the UK, inflation can be above 2 per cent in some periods and below in others, so long as the average rate converges on 2 per cent.

In the autumn of 2008, driven by high oil, fuel and food prices, UK inflation hit 5 per cent, a huge deviation from target. The central bank could have immediately corrected this problem by implementing a huge increase in interest rates. However, we now understand that such a decision would have had dire consequences for economic output. Forcing an economy into a recession is neither economically nor politically sound.

Importantly, the inflation target is sufficiently flexible to enable the central bank to balance concerns over inflation against concerns over output. By making the inflation target one based on an average, the central bank is effectively enabled to manage inflation and output.

The central bank still faces a balancing act because it needs to recognize the impact of high inflation on future inflationary expectations. By not correcting high inflation immediately, firms and workers may come to expect higher inflation in the future. This will lead to higher nominal wage growth and higher inflation in the future.

It is for these reasons that central banks publish open and honest minutes of their setting decisions, provide guidance on the expected future direction of output and prices, and when necessary write open letters to the government explaining why the target rate of inflation has been breached. All of these actions are used to communicate the central bank's view that inflation will return to trend in the near term, and by implication firms and workers should not adjust their long-term inflationary expectations.

13.8 Adjustment speed

So far we have considered the short- and long-run equilibrium outcomes for the economy. We have also highlighted how the central bank can use monetary policy to accommodate demand and supply side shocks and how inflation targeting can be implemented in a way that delivers price and output stability. Throughout all of this analysis, there has been an assumption that the economy does not adjust to the long-run equilibrium with any degree of speed. If it did, there would be no need for fiscal or monetary intervention. With rapid adjustment, wages and prices would instantly change and short-run aggregate supply would adjust immediately, bringing the economy back to its long-run equilibrium.

Clearly, the economy does not appear to adjust instantaneously, but the speed with which it does adjust is debated within economics. Moreover, the most suitable policy responses are also contested. Beliefs regarding adjustment speeds and policy responses highlight differing philosophical traditions within economics. While it is not our intention to train you as economists, a businessperson can benefit from some understanding of the competing macroeconomic perspectives.

New Classical

At one extreme, are the New Classical economists. This group of economists hold the belief that markets adjust instantly, leading to a clearing equilibrium. This full and rapid flexibility in prices and output ensures that, following any demand or supply shock, the economy quickly, if not instantly, returns to its long-run, full employment level of output. A clear consequence of this belief is that there is no need for fiscal or monetary policy interventions. Instead, this group of economists focus on long-run aggregate supply as the economy's output constraint. If growth is desirable, then policy-makers need to focus on policies which enable long-run supply to expand in a stable and consistent manner. Such growth policies will be considered in Chapter 14.

Gradual Monetarist

The next group of economists are the Gradual Monetarists, who believe that markets adjust quickly but not instantaneously. For Gradual Monetarists, the long-run equilibrium can be attained in a relatively short time period, such as a year or two. Competitive product markets lead to flexibility in pricing. While free and open labour markets ensure a quick transition to new nominal wage growth rates. Firms and workers quickly, but not perfectly, arrive at new expectations of future price levels and so the adjustment of short aggregate supply is reasonably quick. Over a period of one to two years, the economy returns to potential GDP. Since the economy returns quickly to potential GDP, Gradual Monetarists also accept that supply side policies are important for long-term growth.

Active fiscal and monetary policy are frowned upon by Gradual Monetarists. If the economy can correct itself within an acceptable timeframe, there is no need for intervention. In fact, any policy stimulus is likely to lead to an over-correction of the economy. As the economy itself adjusts, the policy response will simply multiply the effects. This could drive the economy into a deeper recession, or lead to higher inflation.

The best monetary response stems from the quantity theory of money, which states that $MV = PY$, where M is the money supply, V is the velocity of circulation, P is the price level and Y is real GDP. If PY is nominal GDP and is equal to £10 billion, and M = £1 billion, then the velocity of circulation is 10, i.e. cash must go through everybody's pockets ten times in order to facilitate £10 billion of economic transactions. Gradual Monetarists believe that Y is constant, as depicted by a vertical long-run aggregate supply schedule. They also believe that V is a constant. This means that there is a direct relationship between M and P: inflation is driven by growth in the money supply. If you wish to control inflation, then adopt a *gradual* change in the money supply.

Moderate Keynesian

Moderate Keynesians take the view that the economy will eventually return to its long-run equilibrium, but the adjustment will not necessarily be quick. Moderate Keynesians believe that prices, wages and inflationary expectations are slow to adjust. Without flexibility in prices and wages, short-run aggregate supply will not adjust quickly either. Due to this slow adjustment, there is significant benefit to be gained from active fiscal and monetary policies. These demand side policies quickly alter macroeconomic demand and enable the economy to return to potential GDP. Once in long-run equilibrium, Moderate Keynesians accept that potential GDP places a constraint on the economy and supply side policies are key to improved long-term growth.

Extreme Keynesian

Finally, we turn to Extreme Keynesians, who take the opposite view to that held by New Classical economists. Extreme Keynesians are extremely concerned that prices and wages are sticky. For a variety of reasons, including the cost of changing prices and the effect of unions on controlling wage rates, adjustment of short-run aggregate supply is sluggish. The attainment of potential GDP may not be achieved for many years. Economies can move into recession and then remain there, turning the economic episode into a depression. Governments therefore have an enormous duty to push spending into the economy. Extreme Keynesians believe that fiscal policy is better able to do this than monetary policy. Extreme Keynesians do not accept the quantity theory of money and question whether V and Y are constant, therefore any expansion of the money supply is unlikely to be inflationary. For Extreme Keynesians, the core concern is output.

None of these competing views of thought are incorrect. Neither are they correct. This is because the speed of adjustment to potential GDP is not constant. Rather, adjustment speeds vary according to the nature and scale of shocks which impact the economy. For example, when change is small and gradual, the monetarists are more likely to be correct. This is because, when change is small and gradual, firms and workers can easily change their expectations regarding prices. It is easy for these important economic actors to understand what is happening and adjust their behaviour accordingly. Expectations are broadly correct and short-run aggregate supply moves quickly, leading to a rapid restoration of potential GDP.

Now consider the credit crisis, an event described by leading economists as 'unprecedented'; apparently, 'it is difficult to exaggerate the scale of events witnessed in financial markets'. Such is the extreme nature of the credit crisis that not even economists can begin to understand what has occurred and what the impact will be on prices and output. There can be little doubt that consumers and firms will struggle to adapt their expectations rapidly and accurately.

Hence the risk to output in the near term is huge. The Keynesians can claim to have a more accurate view of the world at this point in history. Not surprisingly, governments provided economies with enormous fiscal injections, while at the same time central banks cut interest rates.

However, the debate still continues. See Box 13.5.

 Box 13.5 Putting the air back in

Adapted from an article in The Economist, *30 October 2008*

The standard response to a demand shock is to use monetary policy: cut interest rates and increase the money supply. Lower interest rates spur spending by making saving less rewarding. The trouble is deep cuts in interest rates have not reduced the cost of bank credit for firms and households.

Central banks have provided huge amounts of liquidity to the money markets. Traditionally, this would be seen to fuel inflation. But with banks using this additional liquidity to refinance their own debt, rather than grow lending, the money supply is stagnating. The link between money supply and inflation is broken.

If scared banks, firms and households cling more tightly to cash rather than lend it or spend it, the downturn will deepen. At the extreme, the demand for cash is so strong than not even interest rates at zero can get the economy moving. When standard monetary-policy responses reach their limit, fiscal options, such as cutting taxes and increasing public spending, come into play.

The use of fiscal policy to fine-tune the business cycle went out of fashion around 30 years ago. But when skittish banks and investors are turning away from funding private spending, there is a strong case for a more active fiscal policy to prop up demand. However, fiscal policy has its limits. A run of big budget deficits increases the risk that a government will default or repay its debts only by forcing its central banks to print money, thus creating inflation. If public debt spirals upwards as the economy stagnates, investors will worry that future taxpayers will be unable to shoulder the burden.

13.9 Business application: understanding the interest rate path

For businesses, it is crucial to understand the future path of interest rates. This is because businesses borrow to fund investment and so changes in the interest rate alter the cost of investing.

Companies also use debt to leverage their financial returns. Leverage is a very important financial concept. The use of debt by companies enables higher returns to shareholders. Consider the following. A company has £1 million of shareholders' cash to invest. A project is offering a 10 per cent rate of return, so after one year, the shareholders' funds will have grown to £1.1 million. Alternatively, the company could approach a bank and use its £1 million of equity to raise £9 million of debt. The company now has £10 million to invest. After one year and a 10 per cent rate of return, the investment is worth £11 million. So shareholder equity is now £2 million (£11 million less £9 million of debt). Not surprisingly, managers and shareholders like to use debt to enable companies to grow faster. Leverage is also known as gearing because, like a car, the more debt, the higher the gear, the faster the car and company run.

Debt is, therefore, a very attractive complement to equity financing. Of course, it comes at a cost – the rate of interest – and we should factor this into our calculations. The £2 million of equity at the end of year two should be reduced by the amount of interest that is paid. In fact, because the benefits of leverage come with high levels of debt to equity, the cash flow needed to fund interest repayments can be considerable. Therefore, interest rates matter to companies, not only because of investments but also because of the financial engineering that leverage brings to a company's finances. Understanding the future track for interest rates is crucial for appraising investment decisions and managing cash flows.

The Taylor rule enables business managers to achieve a broad understanding of where interest rates are likely to go in the future. A greater divergence between actual inflation and target inflation will lead to a change in rates. Equally, a departure of actual GDP from potential GDP will lead to an interest rate response. Data published by central banks can be used to assess the difference between actual and target values for GDP and inflation.

In Figure 13.6, fan charts for inflation and GDP from the Bank of England are presented. The darker lines within the fan charts represent the Bank's view of the most probable path for inflation and GDP. The fainter lines, which fan out over time, are less likely possibilities. The UK inflation target is 2 per cent and potential GDP has been growing at around 2.5 per cent per annum. The inflation fan chart suggests that the Bank will cut interest rates in order to avoid deflation and bring inflation back towards target. A consideration of the GDP fan charts indicates that the Bank thinks GDP will fall below target for most of 2008 through to 2010. This output gap will direct the Bank to also cut rates in order to enable the economy to return to potential GDP.

Further out, the Bank's forecast becomes less accurate, or certain. However, two trends are discernible from the fan charts. Inflation is expected to fall below target even by 2012 and GDP is expected to rise after 2010. So, we can expect loose monetary policy until 2010. If inflation then returns to target and the economy grows, we may see a rise in interest rates to return monetary policy to a more long-term neutral position. If inflation remains below target, lax monetary policy may continue.

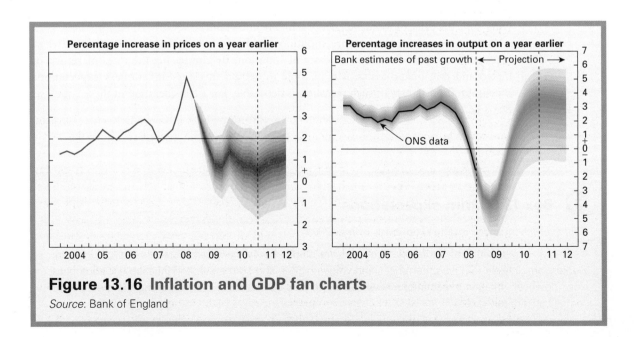

Figure 13.16 Inflation and GDP fan charts

Source: Bank of England

13.10 Business application: understanding the formation of inflationary expectations

If growth in wages and prices is fundamental to the macroeconomic equilibrium, then it must be important for business to understand and respond to changing inflationary expectations. If, for example, workers believe that inflation will rise faster in the future, then they will seek to achieve higher pay awards. Firms need to form their own inflationary expectations. Do they share the same expectations as their workers and do they believe they have the potential to pass on higher wages to customers, through higher prices. Without the ability to generate additional revenue, then the real cost of labour climbs and firms become less willing to supply.

So, how are inflationary expectations formed? The answer to this question is not precise, but requires a number of factors to be recognized.

First, central banks have come to recognize that inflation targets are a powerful tool for controlling inflationary expectations, but only if the central bank is credible in achieving the inflation target. If, on average, the central bank brings inflation to the target level, then workers and firms can confidently form expectations of future price stability. In addition, repeated requests from government for workers, especially in the public sector, to undertake pay restraint and accept pay rises in line with inflation also help. Costs rise in line with inflation and inflationary expectations remain subdued.

However, workers and, more generally, households are exposed to a variety of markets, and over time track price changes. Over the last ten years, an influx of cheap imports from China and South East Asia has helped to form low inflationary expectations. The cost of computers, mobile phones, TVs and cars has fallen in real terms. However, in more recent times, the prices of food and energy have risen enormously. Households have recognized these significant shifts and duly increased their inflationary expectations.

An important consideration is the accuracy of households' beliefs regarding future inflation based on today's price changes. Households appear to use today's prices to form three- to five-year inflationary expectations. These are questionable when inflation is being driven by volatile commodity prices. Today's prices may be high, tomorrow they could be lower. But in three years' time the price of food and energy is highly uncertain.

Alternative measures of future inflation can be found in the money markets, where investors buy bonds linked to the rate of inflation. By comparing the rates of return on linked and non-linked assets, it is possible to extract investors' inflationary expectations. But, again, the accuracy of such measures is debatable. For a consideration of these issues, see Box 13.6.

 ### Box 13.6 Grim expectations

Adapted from an article in The Economist, *26 June 2008*

As long as expectations of future price changes are stable, policy-makers can breathe easily. Firms and workers are unlikely to push other prices and wages higher, and so the surge in inflation will soon pass. Now, however, inflation expectations have started to pick up sharply, which is putting the credibility of central bankers to the test.

There are two main ways of divining expected inflation, each with its own flaws. The first is to ask people what they think the inflation rate will be. Recent replies are worrying. A survey by the University of Michigan shows that inflation is expected to be over 5 per cent in the next year, the strongest reading since 1982. In Britain, expectations have risen to their highest level since the central bank's survey began in 1999. A poll of the euro area, carried out by the European Commission, also shows a rise in the balance of consumers expecting higher inflation (see left-hand chart, below).

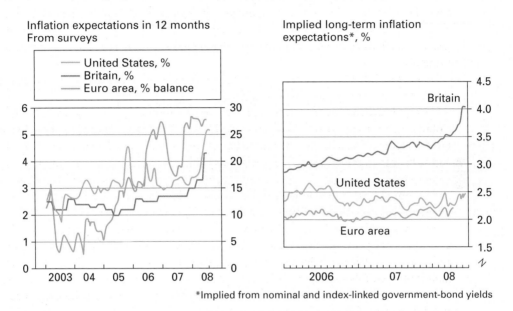

*Implied from nominal and index-linked government-bond yields

Chart 1 Expecting the worst

Sources: Bank of England; European Commission; University of Michigan; Barclays Capital; Reuters; Thomson Datastream

One reason to question these shifts is that consumers' perceptions often differ from reality. Consumers may be overly sensitive to changes in the price of frequent purchases, such as food and fuel, while they overlook the stability of other prices. As the effect of the commodity shock fades, expectations are likely to follow recorded inflation back down again. Another frequent complaint is that expectations are usually measured one year ahead when, arguably, what matters are people's beliefs about medium-term inflation. Measures derived from financial markets may be less volatile, but have shortcomings of their own.

An established gauge is the yield gap between conventional and index-linked bonds. Inflation expectations are implied by the extra return investors demand to forgo protection against future price increases. On this basis, they are increasingly nervous about the inflation outlook in the euro area and especially in Britain (see right-hand chart, above). One problem with such gauges is that they are based on nominal bond yields, which include a risk premium for inflation's volatility. Also, pension funds are eager buyers of index-linked assets because the rules require them to buy securities to match their commitments to protect some pensioners against inflation. That pushes down real yields and pushes up implied inflation expectations.

However imprecise the measures of inflation expectations, central banks in America, the euro area and Britain have all said it is important to keep them anchored. But how inflation psychology works is little understood.

Summary

1 In long-run equilibrium, the economy operates at its full employment level.

2 The full employment level of an economy is the same as potential GDP.

3 In the short run, economic output is actual GDP.

4 The difference between actual and potential GDP is known as the output gap.

5 The Phillips curve shows a negative statistical relationship between the rate of inflation and the rate of unemployment.

6 In the long run, equilibrium unemployment is fixed. Therefore, there can be no relationship between unemployment and inflation. The long-run Phillips curve is vertical.

7 Any movement along the short-run Phillips curve represents a temporary change in real wage rates. In the long run, real wages are held constant.

8 If inflationary expectations change, then the short-run Phillips curve will move. Expectations of higher inflation will result in the short-run Phillips curve moving up.

9 The speed of adjustment from the short to the long run is determined by the flexibility of wages and prices.

10 The macroeconomic demand schedule shows a negative relationship between inflation and the demand for output.

11 Long-run aggregate supply is fixed at potential GDP.

12 Short-run aggregate supply is determined by nominal wage growth.

13 If inflation differs from nominal wage growth, then real wages change and in the short run firms move along their short-run aggregate supply line.

14 In the short-run equilibrium, actual GDP can differ from potential GDP. But as workers and firms adjust wages to the new level of inflation, the economy adjusts to the long-run equilibrium of potential GDP.

15 Permanent supply side shocks can be accommodated by a reduction in the long-run interest rate.

16 Temporary supply side shocks may reduce GDP, but if they are offset with additional demand, then inflation is likely to rise.

17 The management of demand shocks brings stability to prices and output.

18 A Taylor rule suggests that a central bank sets interest rates according to the departure of inflation rates from target and also GDP from target.

19 Different groups of economists hold differing views about the flexibility of prices and wages, and the speed with which the economy will return to long-run equilibrium.

20 New Classical economists think adjustment is instantaneous. Extreme Keynesians believe adjustment is very slow. Gradual Monetarists think adjustment takes a couple of years and think monetary policy should enable a gradual expansion of the money supply. Moderate Keynesian economists think the economy will eventually return to long-run equilibrium, but a strong dose of fiscal and monetary policy will help in the short run.

Learning checklist

You should now be able to:

◆ Explain the relationship described by the Phillips curve

◆ Understand the key differences between the short- and long-run Phillips curve

◆ Link the short- and long-run Phillips curve and short- and long-run aggregate supply

◆ Identify the short- and long-run macroeconomic equilibrium

◆ Explain the adjustment to long-run equilibrium

◆ Assess monetary policy responses to demand and supply shocks in the economy

◆ Understand the different views among economists regarding the speed of adjustment to long-run equilibrium

Questions   connect™

1   Explain why, when unemployment increases, inflation may decrease. Use a suitable diagram to illustrate this relationship.

2   Use numerical examples to explain the difference between nominal and real wages. How have nominal and real wages developed in your economy over the last five years?

3   If real wages are held constant, what is the relationship between unemployment and inflation in the long run?

4   If real wages are constant in the long run, is it still possible to observe a negative relationship between inflation and unemployment?

5   The central bank has an inflation target. Inflation rises above the target. What will happen next to interest rates and aggregate demand?

6   Explain why aggregate supply is inelastic in the long run and elastic in the short run.

7   The central bank follows an inflation target and the economy benefits from an improvement in productivity. What will happen to interest rates?

8   Can a central bank with an inflation target fight cost-push inflation?

9   Using a suitable diagram, illustrate why central banks are keen to avoid the potential black hole of a deflationary spiral.

10   What is the Taylor rule? How might business use the Taylor rule to forecast future interest rates?

11   Assume that you are a New Classical economist. What are your recommendations for monetary policy? How do these differ from an Extreme Keynesian's? Are these two views relevant to modern economies?

12   Use a diagram to illustrate how a monetary response to a loss of consumer confidence stabilizes inflation and GDP.

13   If nominal wages increase faster than the rate of inflation, under what circumstances can employment remain constant?

14 What do you consider to be the key benefits of inflation targeting?

15 Access data from your national statistical office on the rate of unemployment and the inflation rate. Plot the data, using a package such as Excel, and establish whether you can see a short-run Phillips curve relationship.

Exercises

1 Which of the following has caused the move from SPC_1 to SPC_2 in Figure 13.17?
(a) A rise in the full employment rate.
(b) An increase in nominal wages.
(c) An increased expectation of higher unemployment.
(d) An increased expectation of higher inflation.

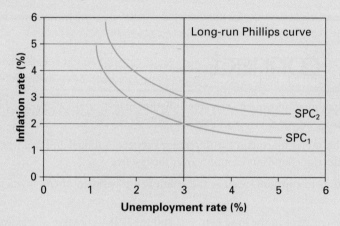

Figure 13.17

2 This exercise examines monetary and fiscal policy using the MDS and the aggregate supply schedule. Figure 13.18 shows two macroeconomic demand schedules (MDS_a and MDS_b) and the aggregate supply schedule (AS). First, we consider the effects of monetary policy in the classical model – specifically, an increase in nominal money supply.

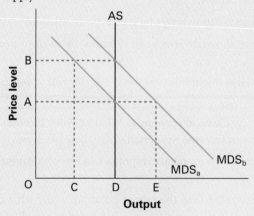

Figure 13.18 Macroeconomic equilibrium

(a) Identify the 'before' and 'after' MDS.

(b) What was the original equilibrium price and output?

(c) What is equilibrium price and output after the policy is implemented?

Next, consider fiscal policy – again in the classical model. Suppose there is a reduction in government expenditure:

(d) Identify the 'before' and 'after' MDS.

(e) What was the original equilibrium price and output?

(f) What is the equilibrium price and output after the policy is implemented? The Keynesian model is characterized by sluggish adjustment. Consider the period *after* the policy but *before* adjustment begins.

(g) Identify price and output.

(h) The MDS represents points at which goods and money markets are in equilibrium. In the position you have identified in (g), adjustment has still to take place – so, in what sense is the goods market in 'equilibrium'?

---

3 Consider Box 13.5:

(a) Why is an understanding of inflationary expectations important for the economy and business?

(b) How are inflationary expectations likely to differ between students, households with young children and the retired?

(c) Will higher inflationary expectations always feed into future higher inflation?

Chapter 14
Supply side policies and economic growth

Chapter contents

 ## Learning outcomes

By the end of this chapter you should understand:

Economic Theory

LO1 How economic growth is linked to growth in long-run aggregate supply

LO2 The neoclassical model of economic growth

LO3 The convergence hypothesis

LO4 The endogenous growth model

LO5 The types of policies used to develop economic growth

Business Application

LO6 Should firms produce or consume innovation?

LO7 BRIC economies and the opportunities for business growth

Supply side policies and economic growth at a glance

The issues

Different economies grow at different rates. How do economies grow and how can governments involve business in developing economic growth?

The understanding

Economic growth can be linked to the development of long-run aggregate supply. The output potential of an economy is fixed if aggregate supply is perfectly inelastic. Changes in aggregate demand only alter the inflation rate. Therefore, in order to make the economy grow, it is essential to increase the level of aggregate supply. At a simplistic level, improving aggregate supply can be achieved by either increasing the availability of factor inputs, such as labour, or by increasing the productivity of factor inputs, so that more output can be produced with more input. However, a more interesting question relates to how fast an economy can grow. Neoclassical theory argues that growth will converge across economies to a common rate. Endogenous growth theory counters this view, suggesting that governments can develop policies which will enable the economy to grow at faster rates.

The usefulness

The growth rate of an economy has important implications for business. First, sales and revenue growth will, in part, be related to economic growth. Second, government policies designed to improve productivity within an economy may aid a firm to reduce its costs.

Economic growth is measured as the percentage change in GDP per year.

14.1 Business problem: assessing economic growth

The growth rates for various EU economies and the United States are presented in Figure 14.1. Growth rates have varied by economy and over time. All economies slowed between 2001 and 2002, reflecting the impact of the terrorist events of 9/11 on the global economy. After 2002, most economies grew until the arrival of the credit crisis in late 2008. Then, all major economies slowed and headed for recession. Over the period and across economies, average growth seems to have been around 2 per cent per annum.

The importance of growth rates becomes more apparent over time. For example, assume that we have an economy and the level of GDP is 100. The economy now grows at four hypothetical growth rates, 1, 2.5, 4 and 10 per cent. The amount of GDP in each year, for each growth rate, is tabulated in Table 14.1.

The amount of GDP in year 10 is vastly different depending upon the growth rate of the economy, varying from 110 under a growth rate of 1 per cent, to 259 under a growth rate of 10 per cent. Therefore, over time the growth rate of an economy has enormous implications for the generation of individuals' incomes and the potential for companies to grow. As a consequence, governments, workers and firms are extremely interested in the projected growth rates for an economy.

For example, through a simple examination of the circular flow of income, economic growth is associated with growth in the flow of income between households and firms. More products

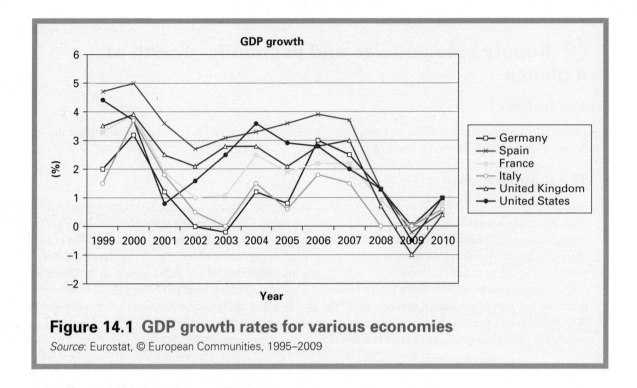

Figure 14.1 GDP growth rates for various economies

Source: Eurostat, © European Communities, 1995–2009

Table 14.1 Impact of different growth rates

Year	Growth rate			
	1%	2.5%	4%	10%
0	100	100	100	100
1	101	103	104	110
2	102	105	108	121
3	103	108	112	133
4	104	110	117	146
5	105	113	122	161
6	106	116	127	177
7	107	119	132	195
8	108	122	137	214
9	109	125	142	236
10	110	128	148	259

are produced, more income is paid to workers/households and more products are sold. As a result, the faster an economy grows, the faster incomes rise and sales increase. While this makes economic growth an attractive opportunity for business, an additional consideration also has to be examined.

In the main, governments try to make the economy grow through developments in aggregate supply, providing firms with the ability, or incentive, to supply more output. Firms will supply more if the marginal costs of production fall. Policies designed to reduce companies' costs and, moreover, boost productivity are central to developing aggregate supply and economic growth. This means that economic growth and the development of sales is not the only benefit for firms. Policies designed to aid economic growth may also aid the cost structures faced by firms. Companies that understand why economic growth is important and how growth might be achieved are better placed to understand government policy and exploit the opportunities offered by economic growth. This chapter will provide you with an overview of supply side theories and economic growth.

14.2 Growth and aggregate supply

We saw in Chapter 13 that demand side policies (fiscal and/or monetary interventions) are only capable of moving the economy back to full employment. Such policies reduce the difference between actual and potential GDP and so only close the output gap. Real expansion of the economy involves an increase in potential GDP. Therefore, we can only envisage real economic growth occurring if aggregate supply increases. In Figure 14.2, with perfectly inelastic long-run aggregate supply, aggregate demand begins at AD_1. The equilibrium level of output is GDP_1 and the rate of inflation is Π_0. Following a fiscal or monetary stimulus, aggregate demand increases to AD_2. At the new equilibrium of B, GDP remains unchanged at GDP_1, but inflation has increased to Π_1. We can say that, when aggregate supply is perfectly inelastic, increases in aggregate demand will be entirely inflationary. In contrast, if aggregate supply increases to AS_2, then the economy moves to equilibrium, C, potential GDP increases to GDP_2 and inflation falls to Π_2. Therefore, growth through improvements in aggregate supply seems preferable.

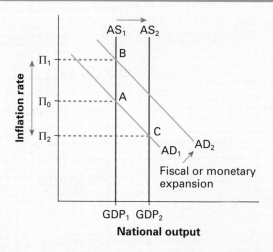

Figure 14.2 Inelastic aggregate supply and changes in aggregate demand

With perfectly inelastic long-run aggregate supply, a fiscal or monetary stimulus leading to an increase in aggregate demand will be purely inflationary. At equilibria A and B, GDP is constant at GDP_1. While at A inflation is Π_0, but at B, following the increase in aggregate demand, inflation has increased to Π_1.

In contrast, an increase in aggregate supply from AS_1 to AS_2 moves the equilibrium from A to C. GDP increases to GDP_2 and inflation falls to Π_2.

Clearly, if economic growth is desirable, then moving aggregate supply, or increasing the potential productive output of the economy, is key. Increasing productive potential is not easy, but there are generally three avenues for economic growth: more factor inputs, greater productivity and innovation. We will examine each in turn.

More factor inputs

In Chapter 1, we introduced the production possibility frontier and showed how the level of output for an economy is constrained by the level of factor inputs (land, labour, capital and enterprise). As the economy gains more economic factor inputs, then its productive potential increases. This is the same as the long-run aggregate supply moving to the right and potential GDP increasing.

For a number of economies, economic growth has occurred through an increase in factor inputs. In the case of China, recent economic growth has been enabled by a transfer of workers within the economy. Individuals who were previously involved in self-subsistence agriculture (growing food for themselves and their family) have migrated to the industrialized cities and taken employment in factories. If the output per hour worked in a factory is greater in volume and, more importantly, value than the output per hour worked as a farmer, then GDP increases. The problem for China, as discussed in Box 14.1, is whether the flow of additional workers will continue.

 Box 14.1 Reserve army of underemployed

Adapted from an article in The Economist, *4 September 2008*

China has by far the world's biggest labour force, of around 800 million – almost twice that of America, the European Union and Japan combined. Thus recent claims that it is running short of cheap labour would, if true, have huge consequences not just for China but also for the rest of the world.

The great fall

China's working-age population

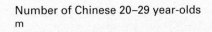

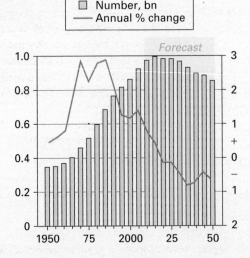

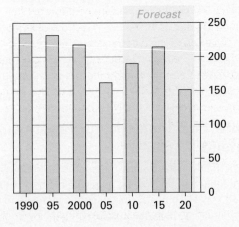

Sources: UN Population Division; Standard Chartered

A seemingly unlimited supply of cheap workers has been one of the main forces behind China's rapid economic growth. But, over the past couple of years, factory owners have complained of labour shortages and wages have risen more rapidly, leading some to conclude that China's 'surplus' labour has been used up. The country's one-child policy, introduced in 1979, has caused the growth in its labour supply to slow sharply (see chart). After rising by 1.3 per cent a year during the decade to 2005, the population of working age is expected to increase at an annual rate of 0.7 per cent until 2015, and then shrink by 0.1 per cent a year until 2025. At the same time, the shift of workers from agriculture to industry, which has been an important source of productivity gains, will also slow. Jonathan Anderson, an economist at UBS, reckons that these two trends will reduce China's sustainable growth rate from 9–9.5 per cent today to 7–7.5 per cent by 2025.

© The Economist Newspaper Limited, London 2009

Similar access to resource problems also exist for other fast-growing economies. The United Arab Emirates and Dubai especially have experienced double-digit economic growth for over a decade. But while a massive expansion of infrastructure projects, including accommodation, hotels, man-made islands, shopping malls and metro rail systems, all increase the employed capital within the economy, the need for additional power means that even their own reserves of gas and oil are insufficient to meet the needs of a rapidly growing economy. See Box 14.2.

 Box 14.2 Gulf states may soon need coal imports to keep the lights on

Adapted from an article by Carl Mortished in The Times, *19 May 2008*

They are countries so rich in oil and gas that they would never want for fuel to drive their booming economies and the lavish lifestyles of their rulers. Now, however, in a role reversal that makes selling sand to Saudi Arabia look like a sensible business transaction, the oil-rich Gulf states are planning to import coal. An acute shortage of natural gas has led to the city states of the United Arab Emirates seeking alternative fuels to keep the air cool, the lights on and the water running.

Abu Dhabi is working with Suez, the French utility company, on a nuclear power project but coal is emerging as the best quick fix to avert blackouts as the world's biggest hydrocarbon exporters struggle to cope with infrastructure weakness and a development boom. Some of the world's biggest oil exporters may soon find themselves reliant on imported fuel from a leading coal exporter, such as South Africa.

A sudden gas shortage has caught the Gulf states by surprise at a time when demand for power and water desalination is increasing annually at double-digit percentage rates. Investment in infrastructure has lagged behind the region's population expansion and construction boom. Anecdotes abound of apartment complexes left empty because there is not enough capacity in the local electricity grid.

According to Wood Mackenzie, the energy consultancy, the UAE's demand for gas will double within a decade if power consumption continues to grow. Dubai's peak power consumption rose by 15 per cent last year, according to DEWA's statistics.

© 2009 Times Newspapers Ltd.

Greater productivity

If it is not possible to gain more factor inputs, then economic growth can be achieved by producing more output with the same level of factor inputs. In simple terms, economic factors such as labour must produce more output per day, and thereby become more productive.

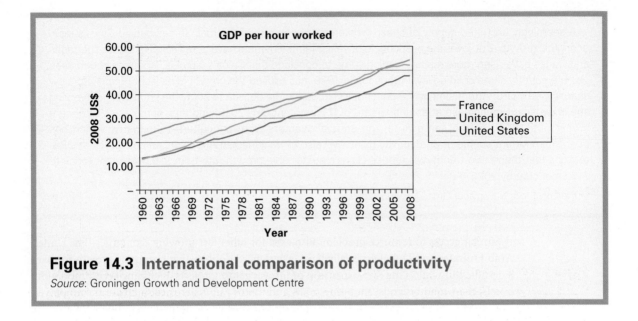

Figure 14.3 International comparison of productivity

Source: Groningen Growth and Development Centre

This avenue of growth is very important for many developed economies. Unlike economies such as India and China, many EU economies are already fully developed. The transition and transfer of workers from agriculture to manufacturing and services occurred two centuries ago. The main avenue for growth is therefore through productivity improvements.

A key measure of productivity is GDP per hour worked. This is a useful measure of productivity because, by working in standard units of GDP and time, it enables a comparison across economies. In addition, and perhaps more importantly, from Chapter 9 we know that GDP is a measure of value added – in the hour worked, how much more value does the worker add to the final output? This enables a comparison across economies which produce very different goods and services. It also focuses upon income generation per hour.

Over the last 50 years, there has been a fairly consistent productivity gap between the UK and the US. In comparison, France has managed to close its gap with the US. See Figure 14.3. If the UK could close the productivity gap, then either GDP and economic prosperity would rise or the UK workforce could earn the current level of income for fewer hours worked. Productivity growth is therefore very appealing.

We argued in Chapter 3, when examining the cost curves of individual firms, that the marginal cost curve (above average variable cost) is the firm's supply curve. Therefore, at the macroeconomic level, aggregate supply must be the sum of all firms' marginal cost curves (above average variable cost).

The firm is only willing to supply more output at any given price if its marginal costs decrease. Figure 14.4 provides details of the UK's GDP per capita gap with other developed economies and then breaks this gap into two sources, labour utilization and productivity. For example, the gap between UK and French GDP per capita is very small. But the means of producing this level of GDP per capita are very different. The utilization rate of French labour is 25 per cent less than in the UK, but this is offset by French workers being 30 per cent more productive than their UK rivals. If the UK could raise its labour productivity, then at the same utilization rate, GDP per capita would accelerate beyond that of France and perhaps some of the other countries in the table.

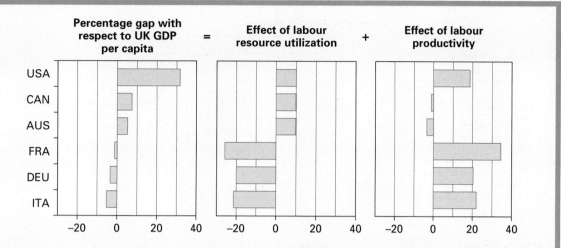

Figure 14.4 The UK productivity gap and sources of income difference

The US has higher GDP per capita than the UK because it utilizes more of its working age population in employment and on average each worker is more productive. France is similar to the UK in terms of GDP per capita and it achieves this by using fewer workers, but these workers are more productive than those used in the UK.

Source: OECD 2005

Innovation

If we look back in history, we can identify a number of important inventions which have had an enormous impact on economic activity. Examples include the invention of the steam engine, the development of the railways, the introduction of electricity and telecommunications, the creation of the motor car, the growth of commercial aviation and more latterly the beginning of the Internet.

Improvements in travel, such as the railway, aviation and container ships, aid the movement of goods and services around the globe. This improves access to resources, lowers costs and boosts economic activity. The same arguments can be applied to telecommunications and the Internet. Products which were previously sold in shops are now sold online from massive distribution warehouses. This frees up retail units and labour, which can be employed in other parts of the economy, leading to more economic growth.

Clearly, a key driver of technological change is research and development (R&D). As new ideas, new knowledge and new techniques are discovered in science, engineering and medicine, innovation and technological change may result. However, again across economies there are marked differences in how research and development are funded, as well as who the main providers of R&D activities are. If we examine Figure 14.5, it can be seen that, when compared with France and the UK, the US takes a much larger share of its R&D funds from industry. In addition, universities and government undertake much less R&D activity in the US. Taken together, the two charts indicate that R&D in the US is far more concentrated in the industrial sector of the economy.

The question to ask is, does a concentration of R&D activities in the industrial sector have any implications for economic growth? A strong suspicion has to be that, when knowledge and new ideas are created in the industrial sector, then the resulting innovations have a far greater prospect of being commercialized. Therefore, R&D which is industrial and commercial in conception and creation may lead to far greater impacts on long-term economic growth.

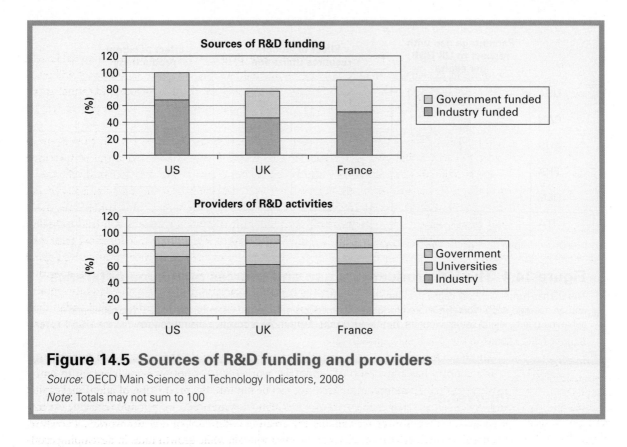

Figure 14.5 Sources of R&D funding and providers

Source: OECD Main Science and Technology Indicators, 2008

Note: Totals may not sum to 100

In order to understand how we can model growth, we will next consider economic models of growth.

14.3 Neoclassical growth theory

Assume we have a simple model where the economy's output is determined by three things: (i) technical progress, (ii) capital and (iii) labour. There are simple but appealing features of this approach. If we allow the number of workers to increase (our population grows) but keep capital constant, then, from Chapter 3, we know that the economy will run up against the law of diminishing returns. Extra workers will not continue to improve the rate of productivity. Indeed, marginal productivity might become negative, driving down total productivity. This problem was first recognized by Thomas Malthus in 1798, who predicted that, with a fixed supply of land, adding additional workers to the land would result in slower growth of food output than growth rates in population. Essentially, diminishing returns would ensure that at some point the population would outgrow its supply of food and begin to starve. (Reflecting this point, economics is still known as the dismal science, which for professional members of the subject is less worrying than the term 'Armageddon'.)

Clearly, in the developed world we have not starved. So, the law of diminishing returns has been held back. This has been achieved by either (a) improving technical progress in agriculture or (b) the employment of more capital. We can see evidence of each. Technical progress has developed with improved knowledge of fertilizers, insecticides and herbicides, improved irrigation systems and, more controversially, genetic modifications. Capital in the form of tractors and combine harvesters has also helped to improve the productivity of land and workers.

How long can growth keep improving?

Robert Solow developed a model of economic growth in the 1950s and the fundamental insight from his approach was that economic growth would not increase for ever. Rather, it will reach a steady state. In growth rate equilibrium, or the steady state output, labour and capital are all assumed to be growing at the same rate. Hence, capital per worker and output per worker are constant.

If the labour force is growing at 10 per cent, then capital also has to grow at 10 per cent in order to keep capital per worker constant. Increases in capital are funded out of increased investment. Banks provide loans for investment from savings. For a 10 per cent increase in investment funds, income or output must grow at 10 per cent in order to guarantee a 10 per cent increase in savings. Essentially, labour growth rates set the tempo for capital investment and economic growth. Indeed, a common fallacy is that higher savings will lead to higher investment, higher capital per worker and higher growth. This is only true for short-term economic growth rates. In the short term, providing all workers with more productive capital improves productivity and raises economic growth; but a blank cheque has also been written for the future, in that all the extra capital has to be maintained. Increased maintenance requires a greater proportion of economic output to go into the renewal of existing capital, rather than the development of new additional capital. As a result, economic growth slows and reverts back to the steady state growth rate.

The **convergence** hypothesis states that poor countries grow more quickly than average, but rich countries grow more slowly than average.

This has a fundamental and particularly troublesome conclusion: growth rate **convergence**.

If a country has a low ratio of capital per worker, it does not take much output to renew existing capital. Therefore, more resource can be put into the production of additional capital per worker. However, if capital per worker is high, then more effort is put into renewing existing capital and less resource is available for creating additional capital per worker. Therefore, economic growth rates in modern economies will fall, while growth rates in developing economies will grow. We, however, see little evidence of either. On average, the world's richest and most developed economies exhibit persistent and comparable growth rates to the world's poorest developing economies. However, emerging economies in East Asia and the Pacific have managed to consistently grow at a pace which exceeds that of the developed economies. See Figure 14.6.

14.4 Endogenous growth theory

The neoclassical model is problematic: convergence is not observed and growth is determined either by labour force growth or, at best, by developments in technology. However, neoclassical economists see even developments in technology as being exogenous, or determined outside the model.

For neoclassical economists, growth is determined by technological development, but technological development is not affected by economic growth.

For example, technological development occurs with mad professors staggering out of their labs, the air filled with fumes and the word 'eureka' being proclaimed. These dotty individuals who stumble across new insights of economic importance, such as plastic, computers, nuclear power and the Internet, find such knowledge by chance. None of these discoveries are based within economics. Clearly nuclear physics, biology and chemistry are different subjects, but surely within an economy, government and the economic system can provide structures, incentives and institutions that foster and promote technological development. Leaving such a beneficial activity to chance, in the hands of dotty individuals, is not good policy.

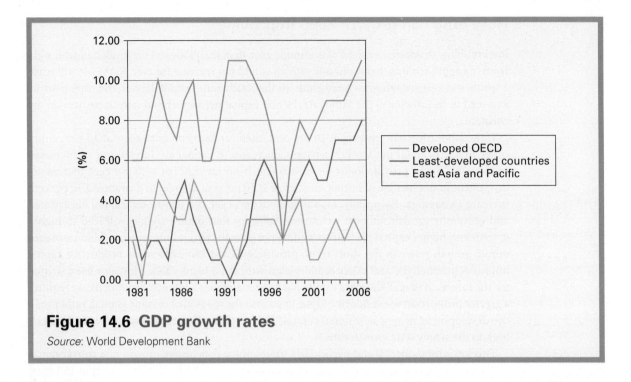

Figure 14.6 GDP growth rates

Source: World Development Bank

However, **endogenous growth theory** has to make a brave assumption: that of constant returns to capital (or something similar), such as knowledge. The Solow model does not allow increasing growth rates from increased capital accumulation because of diminishing returns. Nor does it allow increasing returns; if it did, growth rates would explode exponentially and that is not observed in reality. But how might we envisage a situation of constant returns to capital? Investment by individual firms in capital will still exhibit diminishing returns. But if investments by one firm have positive externalities, then constant returns to capital are possible. For example, if one firm invests heavily in broadband infrastructure for the Internet, then all other firms who wish to use the Internet to deliver media, online shopping and even teaching materials, will also receive a positive boost to their online investments. This way, an increase in investment from one firm leads to increases in productivity across many firms. The economic growth rate can now increase over time through positive externalities.

The more fundamental point is that governments now have a role in developing how the economy grows over time. Under the neoclassical model, growth was determined by labour force growth and chance inventions. In the endogenous world, governments have the potential to increase technological developments and direct economic decision makers to investment activities with positive externalities. For business, this is important because industrial planning, initiatives for training and tax breaks for R&D become critical components of government's desire to increase potential output and, therefore, aggregate supply.

14.5 Supply side policies

Education markets and long-term growth

Governments around the world are keen to widen participation in higher education. Universities have been tasked with taking in students from poor and deprived areas. Such a policy is political and economic. Bringing a broader and larger number of individuals into

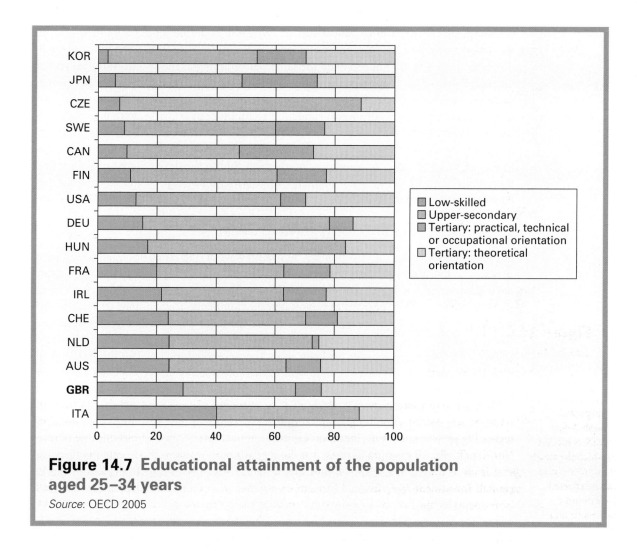

Figure 14.7 **Educational attainment of the population aged 25–34 years**
Source: OECD 2005

higher education widens the skill base of the workforce. This has positive externalities. With higher cognitive skills among the workforce, more advanced productive capital can be employed by firms. This is not about employing more machines per worker, it is about utilizing more productively advanced machines per worker. In addition, a university education enables people to learn for themselves and think critically. If people can learn for themselves, then they might react better to change. So, when new ways of operating come along, firms adapt quicker and exploit new ideas more readily. Also, by thinking critically, managers can develop new means of operation more rapidly. In this way, education is at the core of technological improvement. The higher the income level of the economy, the greater scope the economy has for funding educational improvements. More education, the greater the rate of technological development, both within university labs and in the workplace.

An important point is to establish the optimal mix of skills for an economy. It is perhaps not desirable to allocate resources to the provision of a university education for all workers. Figure 14.7 provides a comparison of skill levels for many developed economies.

The UK (GBR)'s problem is not in the provision of university education. If anything, the UK has one of the workforces with the highest percentage of graduates. Rather, the UK's problem is its large percentage of low-skilled workers. Where it would be more desirable to transfer these workers to the upper secondary and tertiary level of skills, those UK individuals who do not enter university are not receiving the same skills training as they do in countries such as Germany and France. It appears, therefore, that the UK has many educated managers, but an underskilled set of workers. This can be very problematic. If managers wish to pursue innovative products or employ advanced production techniques, then workers are ill-equipped to respond. They simply do not have the skill base to exploit advanced technologies. The argument may be a generalization, but the points for government are simple. Higher education in the UK is doing well. Attention now needs to be paid to the development of skills within those individuals who choose not to attend university. Moreover, these individuals and their employers need to be provided with incentives to engage in skills development.

Labour markets and long-term growth

For managers to be capable of exploiting innovative ways of operating, or taking advantage of new capital machinery, labour markets have to be accommodating. The existence of strong trade unions and legislation that either limits redundancies or raises redundancy payments will constrain the ability of firms to exploit new developments. Trade unions will seek to protect their members' interests and perhaps block changes that result in redundancies. Therefore, throughout the 1980s there was a strong impetus from government to reduce the power of trade unions and make it easier for firms to make workers redundant. Two things have happened. First, trade unions have begun to work with, rather than against, companies, developing greater collaborative relationships seeking, for example, to help businesses improve productivity by raising workers' awareness of inefficient practices and perhaps even supporting the development of skills and education within the current workforce. Second, the rise of the stakeholder perspective argues that firms are a collection of interest groups, including consumers, workers, managers, shareholders and government and each needs to work with and recognize the needs of others. Therefore, cultural change and regulatory change in the labour market free up the rapid redeployment of economic resource and can improve labour efficiency and economic growth.

Research, development and innovation

Government can play a role in providing incentives to undertake research in new productive processes, or even encourage the exploitation of existing knowledge. Tax breaks for R&D expenditure can be a useful incentive to undertake research. More recently, the government announced tax breaks on directors' remuneration packages for high-technology industries, the idea being that in order to attract the most able individuals from around the world, very attractive pay packages had to be offered. Highly valued skills are attracted into the economy and it is hoped, over time, local workers will observe, learn and develop similar skills. If such skills are based in high-technology industries, which will flourish in the future, then the UK is attracting the right type of economic expertise in order to survive in the future.

Industrial networks are also seen as an important means of developing positive externalities and economic growth. Local regions are beginning to specialize in particular industries: Yorkshire in food production, Cambridgeshire in technological development, London in finance, Oxfordshire in motor racing and Manchester in higher education. Again, for these industries to sustain the engine of economic growth, they need support industries and it is better to plan for these than hope that they appear. Managers need training and financial resources need to be put in place to aid investment, and the government can help to deliver these through regional development agencies.

Financial services

A common discussion of growth theories relates to savings and investment, with higher savings leading to higher investments. This misses a number of points. High levels of savings in an economy could be lent to firms overseas. Further, the financial services industry, as an intermediary between savers and borrowers, may enhance growth. For example, by being experts in investment appraisal, financial services firms can more effectively screen out poor investment opportunities. Therefore, development in the financial services sector can lead to better investments within the economy. With higher, rather than lower, quality investments being undertaken, the capital stock can become more productive and economic growth should improve. Moreover, the existence of insurance can protect firms from the financial consequences of risks, such as fire, earthquake, etc. Therefore, insurance can be seen as necessary for expensive capital accumulation. Without it firms would be less willing to invest, leading to a reduction in growth rates.

Much of this thinking drove large-scale deregulation of the financial services industry, especially in economies such as the US and UK. In order to play a strong role in supporting broader industries, financial services needs to be free to grow into new markets, invent new products and spread liquidity throughout the economy. So-called light touch regulation was put in place, which monitored the industry but rarely became involved in questioning the commercial or strategic decisions taken by many financial institutions. In the wake of the credit crisis, it has become clear that financial instituions are indeed enormously important to the functioning of the wider economy and that the need to protect the financial industry from collapse is crucial. How governments in the future manage to promote this crucial sector for growth within a tighter regulatory framework will be a formidable challenge.

Other policies

Tax cuts

In the 1980s, the UK and US governments reduced personal taxation rates, arguing that such policies provided incentives for individuals to work longer and raise productive output. However, most evidence tends to suggest that many individuals recognized that, with the tax cut, they could actually reduce the hours they worked and still earn the same amount of income as they did under the higher tax rates. A possible explanation for this behaviour is that individuals valued leisure time more than they did income. Therefore, following the tax cuts, individuals decided that, rather than seek higher income levels, they would retain the current income level and instead opt for more time spent with family and friends enjoying various leisure activities.

Privatization

Privatization was also popular in the 1980s and 1990s. Previously, water, telephone, gas, electricity, rail and airlines were all supplied by government companies. Most nationalized industries acted as monopolies and were deemed to be inefficient through lack of competition. Furthermore, any increase in investment by nationalized industries had to be funded by the taxpayer. Such a system limited funds because the government had competing projects such as health and education to invest in. It was also not clear how financial performance would be ensured. Privatized companies can access the world's major finance markets and raise significant sums of money. Furthermore, unlike the government, private investors would be keen to ensure that the privatized industries operated at a profit and similarly only invested in profitable and productive assets. Therefore, as the privatized industries were and are important components of the national infrastructure, it is easy to see how increased investment and improvements in operational efficiency could have positive externalities for the rest of the economy – particularly if productivity improvements occurred in communications and transport. Reflecting these arguments, the governments privatized these nationalized industries and enabled new companies to compete in these markets.

The growth of competition has been slow to develop. In the case of telecommunications, economies of scale created an effective entry barrier. However, as technology changed and mobile communications became more popular, new companies found it easier to enter the market. In terms of utilities, we can now buy gas from electricity producers and vice versa. The market appears far more competitive, at least for those customers who wish to shop around. Therefore, if competition is increasing in these markets, then prices should be falling and firms will be seeking new and innovative ways of operating. In the long term, important factor inputs for other companies, such as communication, energy and transport, all become cheaper and overall supply in the economy improves.

Private finance initiatives

In seeking to develop the opportunities for the private sector to be involved in public sector activities, numerous governments have turned to **private finance initiatives** (PFIs). Generally, PFIs involve the national or local government contracting with a private sector supplier for a public infrastructure project. Examples include buildings, hospitals, schools, roads, bridges and railways. The private sector raises funds, builds the asset and ultimately owns the asset. The government then pays an annual leasing fee for the asset. In the UK, the average cost of a PFI project to the public purse is just under £100 million and lasts for around 25 years.

> **Private finance initiatives** involve the private sector in financing, building and owning infrastructure projects in return for an annual leasing fee from the government.

There are a number of benefits associated with PFIs. First, the private sector is seen to be better at costing and delivering infrastructure projects. Project and budget over-runs should be minimized. Commercial organizations are better at understanding and managing financial risk. They also have a clear means of selling their assets and leases in an open and private market. In contrast, it can be argued that the only benefit to government when building infrastructure projects is the ability to raise funds at a lower rate than the private sector. Governments are experts at raising money and spending. They are not experts at design, construction and running infrastructure.

While PFIs have become popular, they are not without criticism. A number of projects have experienced over-runs. Some private providers have become insolvent, leaving the government to finish the project and pick up the final bill. Furthermore, while private firms may be very cost effective when building infrastructure projects, the initial transaction costs (see Chapter 7) can be extremely high. Many projects take up to 36 months to agree a contract between the private firm and the government. Lawyers' bills are extremely expensive, as is the time of senior managers and senior civil servants.

Summary

There are clearly many possible policy prescriptions for economic growth but, broadly speaking, governments seek to develop labour productivity, capital productivity or technological progress. More fundamentally, governments are beginning to return to the idea that they can *design* an economy, which will outperform in terms of growth. The neoclassical model advises governments to sit back and wait for the economy to develop. The endogenous growth theory directs governments to think about how businesses relate to the educational system, how financial services relate to the development of business and how the labour market reacts to the needs of business. Economic policy has moved to an understanding of how to enhance the whole economic system by thinking about how the individual parts work together and in particular how positive externalities can be generated throughout the economic system.

14.6 Business application: how does innovation promote business?

A common perception is that research and development can provide firms with a competitive advantage and we are not going to argue with this view. In fact, in Chapter 5 when we considered monopoly, we put forward the idea of creative destruction. By way of a quick reminder – through innovation, firms can overcome the entry barriers of an incumbent monopoly. As such, innovation can offer firms a competitive advantage and enable the generation of profits.

In our discussion of how innovation drives economic growth in Section 14.2, we also highlighted how innovation is predominately funded and carried out by commercial enterprises in the US, suggesting a strong link between industrial R&D and overall growth in GDP. Such views also help to underpin a policy prescription for more engineering and science graduates. The future strength of an economy is seen to be dependent upon the continual creation of new ideas and technology.

Such views also drive concerns about brain drain and infringements of intellectual property rights. Government, industry and universities in developed economies invest billions in building up R&D capabilities, only to see companies in emerging economies either attract scientific talent or copy designs and technology for little cost.

Recent thinking and evidence within economics is beginning to question the significance of these concerns. Yes, innovation can provide firms with a competitive advantage, but only if consumers are also willing to be innovative and take advantage of the new technology. It is, therefore, the market-based transaction of technology which is important for firms and economic growth more generally.

At the retail level, innovation requires consumers to be adventurous in their consumption. This may require good access to credit facilities and retail environments which enable consumers to experience and sample new innovative products.

We should also recognize that firms are also consumers and buy inputs and support services from other companies. With the growing importance of outsourcing, the adoption of new technologies by firms in areas such as information technology from support services is generally seen as important for productivity growth and higher GDP.

If the purchase and adoption of new technology is the driver of economic growth, then an economy is as dependent on venturesome consumers and business managers as it is on scientists and engineers. Box 14.3 picks up these issues in more detail.

 Box 14.3 Venturesome consumption

Adapted from an article in The Economist, *27 July 2006*

For a growing number of economists and policy-makers, the greatest fear of all – not least because its long-term consequences may be so deep – is that America is losing its global lead in technology. In the battle to invent and innovate, China and India, in particular, with their gazillion-strong cohorts of engineering and science graduates, will soon overwhelm the dullards and liberal arts students churned out by America's education system. Nor is this a uniquely American worry. You hear similar worries in Europe too, although there the fear is less of losing the lead than of falling even further behind.

▶

Innovative thinking

In a marvellously contrarian new paper, Amar Bhidé, of Columbia University's business school, argues that there is a misconception of how innovation works and of how it contributes to economic growth.[1] Mr Bhidé finds plenty of nice things to say about many of the things that most trouble critics of the American economy: consumption as opposed to thrift; a plentiful supply of consumer credit; Wal-Mart; even the marketing arms of drug companies. He thinks that good managers may be at least as valuable as science and engineering. But he has nothing nice to say about the prophets of technological doom.

Mr Bhidé says that the doomsayers are guilty of 'techno-fetishism and techno-nationalism'. This consists, first, of paying too much attention to the upstream development of new inventions and technologies by scientists and engineers, and too little to the downstream process of turning these inventions into products that tempt people to part with their money and, second, of the belief that national leadership in upstream activities is the same thing as leadership in generating economic value from innovation.

The least internationally mobile innovation is the downstream sort, where big ideas are made suitable for a local market. This downstream innovation, which is far more complex and customized than the original upstream invention, is the most valuable kind and what America is best at. Moreover, perhaps most important is that most of the value of innovations accrues to their users not their creators.

The most important part of innovation may be the willingness of consumers, whether individuals or firms, to try new products and services. In his view, it is America's venturesome consumers that drive the country's leadership in innovation. Particularly important has been the venturesome consumption of new innovations by American firms. One reason why American firms are able to be so venturesome is that they have the managers capable of adapting their organizations to embrace innovation. America's downstream firms are arguably the world's leaders in finding ways to encourage consumers to try new things, not least through their enormous marketing arms and by ensuring that there is a lavish supply of credit.

© The Economist Newspaper Limited, London 2009

14.7 Business application: the BRIC economies

The BRIC economies are those of Brazil, Russia, India and China. These are seen as important economies in the future; they are growing fast and they are enormous. Other economies are also growing fast, but since they are smaller in size and population, their impact on the world economy is likely to be much less than the BRIC economies.

Growth in the BRIC economies has been impressive. For example, the growth of the Chinese economy has been one of the major economic miracles of the past 25 years. Compound growth rates approaching 10 per cent per annum over such a time period are almost unmatched by any other economy.

China's strength is built on technological expertise and an abundance of labour. Much the same can be said of India. Russia, while also technologically capable, is also reaping the benefits of vast energy resources. In a similar manner, Brazil too has access to important forestry and energy resources. With massive populations, vast natural resources and reasonable educational expertise, the BRIC economies can be expected to grow for many years to come. They can achieve this because they have yet to run up against the production possibility frontier. Or perhaps more accurately, the frontier and aggregate supply are constantly expanding in the BRIC economies.

When aggregate demand increases in the BRIC economies, it is met with additional aggregate supply, the economy grows and GDP rises. We are clearly considering an increase in AD_1,

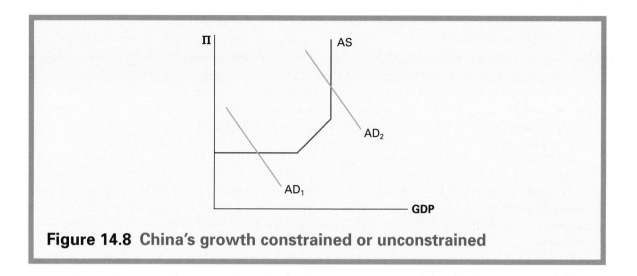

Figure 14.8 China's growth constrained or unconstrained

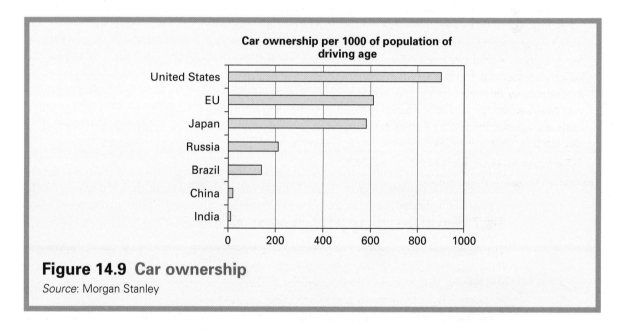

Figure 14.9 Car ownership
Source: Morgan Stanley

where aggregate supply is elastic, as in Figure 14.8. Rapid growth and low inflation go together. Only when an economy is fully developed does aggregate supply become inelastic and growth slow.

The implications of such rapid growth in the BRIC economies are enormous for business. As economies grow, the potential for growth in incomes and household consumption also increases. As incomes grow, then new consumption possibilities become a reality for the increasingly affluent households. Consider Figure 14.9, which describes car ownership in a number of economies. In the US, 900 in every 1000 people of driving age own a car; or, put another way, nearly every person who can drive a car, owns a car. In China, only 20 in every 1000 people of driving age own a car. The scope for car consumption to expand in China and other BRIC economies is enormous. These rapidly expanding economies are very attractive when compared with the slow-growing economies of the EU and North America.

In addition, the growth of car consumption is not the only industry which may seek out a future in the growth of the BRIC economies. Banking, insurance, consumer electronics, computing, TVs and tourism all currently form small shares of household consumption in BRICs. Foreign companies are queuing up to cash in on the potential for economic and consumption growth to explode in the BRIC economies.

However, there should be a note of caution. The BRIC economies are still at a very different stage of economic development from other western economies. It is not simply the case that BMW can arrive in India or China and sell thousands of 5 series cars. While consumption is expanding in the auto market, the product has to be right for the level of income. This explains why domestic producers in the BRICS have sought to buy old technology for small cars from western auto companies. This enables domestic companies to build small, cheap, attractive cars at minimal cost; vehicles which the average household in a BRIC economy would feel proud to own but which have become less preferable in the developed economies of the world. So, the product has to suit the needs of the market.

A final and important concern for foreign companies seeking to gain from the growth of the BRICs is the share of GDP enjoyed by households. It is very interesting and exciting to see GDP increase by 10 per cent per annum. But where is this additional growth in GDP going? We know that the key units within an economy are households, firms, government and foreign consumers. Are these all growing at 10 per cent, or is a large slice of growth flowing to particular sectors of the economy? In the case of China, much of the growth has been driven by exports to the rest of the world. However, with an abundance of labour, wage rates have been kept relatively low. This has meant that the gains from export growth have flowed to firms rather than workers. This will clearly limit the expansion of consumption growth. Firms seeking to profit on the growth in China need to recognize this feature and factor it into any decision to enter the Chinese economy.

As business economists, we can now understand the majority of these issues and considerations. We are merely combining an understanding of economic growth and the circular flow of income. As you become more confident with the material of this book, then you too need to be capable of identifying the various aspects of economics which can be combined to provide you with a deeper understanding of your business environment.

 Summary

1 Supply side economics is concerned with improving the potential output of the economy.

2 Economic growth can be driven by increased factor inputs, enhanced productivity and improvements in technology.

3 If it is assumed that aggregate supply is perfectly inelastic in the long run, then increasing aggregate supply is the only way of generating additional economic output without raising inflation.

4 Neoclassical growth theory asserts that diminishing returns will lead to a natural growth rate for an economy. Any increase in the natural growth rate can only stem from technological progress or an increase in the number of workers.

5 Neoclassical growth theory leads to the conclusion that all economies will converge on a common growth rate. Empirical evidence does not support this idea.

6 In response to neoclassical growth theory, endogenous growth theory asserts that diminishing returns to capital in one firm, or industry, might generate constant returns to scale across the entire economy.

In essence, investments in capital by one firm, or industry, have positive externalities for the rest of the economy. Economies can now grow at different rates, rather than converge, depending upon the generation of productivity-enhancing positive externalities.

7 Under endogenous growth theory, the government has a role in facilitating growth. Developments in education, financial services, levels of R&D and freer labour markets should all lead to higher future growth rates.

Learning checklist

You should now be able to:

◆ Explain how economic growth is linked to growth in long-run aggregate supply

◆ Identify the main sources of economic growth

◆ Provide a review of the neoclassical model of economic growth

◆ Explain and evaluate the convergence hypothesis

◆ Explain the endogenous growth model and highlight how and why it is different from the neoclassical growth model

◆ Explain and evaluate the various types of policy used to develop economic growth

◆ Explain how and why business can be central to economic growth

Questions connect

1 Identify and explain the main sources of economic growth. What are the main sources of growth in your economy?

2 Economic growth through a higher utilization of current economic resources comes with what problems or opportunity costs?

3 Which are equivalent, the production possibility frontier and aggregate demand, or the production possibility frontier and aggregate supply?

4 Explain why GDP per hour worked is a useful measure of productivity.

5 What distinguishes the UK from France and the US in terms of R&D funding and the provision of R&D activities?

6 The Solow model of growth predicts long-run steady state growth rates. What justification can be provided for this prediction?

7 Explain the convergence hypothesis. Does the convergence hypothesis hold in reality?

8 What does the endogenous growth model assume about returns to scale? Is this assumption reasonable?

9 How do the Solow and endogenous models of growth differ in their prescriptions for the role of government in economic growth?

10 What are supply side policies? Provide examples of current supply side policies and assess how you would measure the success of such policies on promoting economic growth.

11 Is R&D important for economic growth, or is it the willingness of consumers to be innovative in their consumption that is important for economic growth?

12 Consider whether there is a simple link between more R&D and higher economic growth.

13 Does neoclassical growth theory provide an adequate understanding of economic growth? Is endogenous growth theory any better than the neoclassical approach?

---

14 Does it matter if growth occurs through increased utilization of resources or higher productivity of resources?

15 What are the key benefits associated with privatization and private finance initiatives?

Exercises

1 True or false?
   (a) An annual growth rate of 2 per cent per annum leads to a seven-fold increase in real output in less than a century.
   (b) Sustained growth cannot occur if production relies on a factor whose supply is largely fixed.
   (c) In the neoclassical growth theory, output, capital and labour all grow at the same rate.
   (d) Higher savings enable a higher long-run rate of growth.
   (e) Given the convergence hypothesis, we can expect all poor countries to catch up with the richer countries.
   (f) Growth may be stimulated by capital externalities: that is, higher capital in one firm increases capital productivity in other firms.

2 Which of the following policy suggestions are appropriate for improving economic growth in an economy?
   (a) The encouragement of R&D.
   (b) A reduction in marginal tax rates to increase labour supply.
   (c) Investment grants.
   (d) The establishment of training and education schemes to improve human capital.
   (e) An expansion of aggregate demand to increase the level of employment.
   (f) The encouragement of dissemination of new knowledge and techniques.

3 Refer to Box 14.3 when considering the following questions:
   (a) What is the difference between product innovation and consumer innovation?
   (b) For a modern economy to grow, which consumers need to be innovative, retail or wholesale?
   (c) For an economy to prosper, the supply and demand of innovation have to be in balance. Discuss.

Note

1 Amar Bhidé, *The Venturesome Economy: How Innovation Sustains Prosperity in a More Connected World*. Princeton, NJ: Princeton University Press, 2008.

Section V
Global economics

Section contents

Chapter 15
Exchange rates and the balance of payments

Chapter contents

Learning outcomes

By the end of this chapter you should understand:

Economic Theory

LO1 Fixed exchange rates

LO2 Floating exchange rates

LO3 The performance differences between fixed and floating exchange rates

LO4 The balance of payments

LO5 How to evaluate fiscal and monetary policy under different exchange rate regimes

LO6 Optimal currency zones

LO7 Issues relating to European monetary union

Business Application

LO8 Is there is a gain to business from not being in the euro?

LO9 How hedging can be used to reduce exchange rate risk and create speculative investments

Exchange rates at a glance

The issues

There are many currencies in the world. The US dollar, UK sterling and the euro are all examples of important currencies. Over time, the strength of the US dollar against UK sterling or the euro varies. When the dollar is strong, it can be exchanged for more euros than when it is weak. This generates issues for business and government. What price will businesses receive for their goods and services when they are exported overseas? Also, why is it beneficial for a number of economies to share a currency, such as the euro?

The understanding

In order to understand exchange rate movements and the potential benefits from being a member of the euro, it is necessary to understand the balance of payments, as well as floating, versus fixed, exchange rate regimes. Once this knowledge is in place, it is possible to address the effectiveness of domestic fiscal and monetary policy under the euro.

The usefulness

In part, trading overseas is determined by how internationally competitive an economy is. The euro, by fixing the exchange rate across all member economies, requires greater price flexibility within member economies. Firms need to understand these issues. Furthermore, by understanding hedging, firms can understand how exchange rate volatility can be managed.

15.1 Business problem: should the UK be a member of the euro?

There are numerous issues associated with whether or not the UK should adopt the euro, but not all of them have business implications. For example, many individuals see the pound as a symbol of 'Britishness'. The pound as a currency and the picture of the sovereign on notes and coins are seen by many as key aspects of their nationality. Indeed, this deep cultural affinity with the national currency is not a uniquely British view. Upon adopting the euro, the French held a day of national celebration and mourning as a sign of respect for the French franc.

For business the euro is not a cultural identity problem because, as many businesspeople will tell you, 'business is no place for sentiment'. Rather, the euro has simple operational implications and profound macroeconomic consequences. Changing prices from pounds to euros and cutting back on the need for currency conversions are simple operational implications. The macroeconomic implications are far greater. Consider the following by way of a brief introduction to the issues.

Imagine boats in a harbour bobbing up and down. Each boat represents an economy: the UK, France, Germany, Spain, Italy and so on. The waves are the business cycles. When each economy had its own currency, the boats were connected together with ropes. So, as the wave hits the first boat it is able to rise up and then fall. The next boat then moves up and down, and so on. Each boat, or each economy, has some flexibility in dealing with the business cycle. Under the common currency of the euro, Germany, France, Spain and Italy and all other members have swapped the ropes for an iron bar welded across the front of all their boats. In the face of the business cycle, the Eurozone members now move together. The flexibility of the ropes has been swapped for the size and stability of a huge integrated Eurozone economy. The question for the UK is whether it wishes to swap its flexible rope for a stable but relatively inflexible weld to the rest of Europe.

The answer to this problem rests on two broad areas: (i) an understanding of the trade-off between flexibility and stability; and (ii) an understanding of how strong the welds are between the different boats. This chapter will investigate these issues, highlighting how the international environment, through exchange rates and intranational economic policies, affects business.

15.2 Forex markets and exchange rate regimes

> **Forex markets** are where different currencies are traded.

Whenever you travel abroad you convert pounds sterling into euros, US dollars, etc. Since we are talking about a **forex market**, the item being traded must have a price. The price of currency is simply the rate at which it can be converted. In Table 15.1 various exchange rates for the euro are listed. For example, €1 will buy £0.8951 or 114.5150 yen.

If these are the prices from the forex market, then the obvious question is, how does this market work? Who is demanding and selling currency?

The answer is fairly simple: individuals and firms buy and sell currencies whenever they undertake transactions with other economies. For example, whenever an import into the UK occurs, pounds have to be exchanged for another currency. Similarly, whenever an export out of the UK occurs, the foreign purchaser needs to sell their own currency in exchange for pounds. We can, therefore, think of imports as generating the supply of pounds in the market and exports as generating the demand for pounds in the market. In Figure 15.1, we have a traditional demand and supply curve for pounds.

> Under a **fixed exchange rate regime**, the government fixes the exchange rate between the domestic currency and another strong world currency, such as the US dollar.

If we begin in equilibrium with Q_S equal to Q_D, then the exchange rate is e_0, or £1 can be converted to €1.0. If exports from the UK to Europe rise, then European consumers will need to demand more UK pounds. The demand curve for pounds shifts from Q_D to Q_{D1}. The exchange rate for pounds appreciates, with £1 being converted into €1.2. If exports fall, demand shifts from Q_D to Q_{D2} and the value of the currency depreciates, with £1 being converted into only €0.8. Similarly, if UK consumers import more goods into the country, they will have to supply more pounds in exchange for euros. We could also envisage a change in supply. If the supply of pounds shifted to the right, the pound would fall in value. But if supply shifted to the left, the pound would rise in value.

Exchange rate regimes

The exchange rate market can be characterized as operating under two extreme regimes. In a **fixed exchange rate regime**, the government sets an exchange rate and then uses the central

Table 15.1 Forex rates for the euro

Currency	Rate
UK – pound	0.8951
Japan – yen	114.5150
USA – dollar	1.2860
Hong Kong – dollar	9.9809

Source: Financial Times, February 2009

Under a **floating exchange rate regime**, the exchange rate is set purely by market forces.

A **dirty float** occurs when the government claims that the exchange rate floats, but it is in fact managed by the government or central bank.

bank to buy and sell currency to keep the market rate fixed. Under a **floating exchange rate regime**, the exchange rate is set by market forces, with holders of foreign currency demanding and selling various currencies.

A third system is known as a **dirty float**. The government claims that the currency floats but in fact, through the central bank, the currency is secretly bought and sold to achieve a target exchange rate.

We will examine the fixed and floating exchange rate regimes and then provide an analysis of their relative strengths and weaknesses.

Fixed exchange rate

In Figure 15.2, we adapt our previous figure and illustrate how a fixed exchange rate works. For simplicity, assume the government sets the exchange rate at e_0. If demand and supply meet at this rate, then the market is in equilibrium and there is no need for any market intervention. However, if, in accordance with an export boom, there is an increase in the demand for pounds, the demand curve will shift to Q_{D1}. The market would like to be in equilibrium at B, with an exchange rate of £1 equals €1.2. But the government is fixing the price at £1 equals €1.0. The government is effectively pricing below the equilibrium price and, as we saw in Chapter 4, this leads to market disequilibrium. At the fixed rate of £1 equals €1.0, the willingness to supply pounds is A, but the willingness to demand pounds is C. Therefore, in the market there is an excess demand for pounds equal to the distance A to C. The government, or the central bank, has to meet this excess demand by supplying an additional AC pounds to the market. The extra pounds are effectively swapped for US dollars, euros, etc. and are added to the central bank's foreign currency reserves.

In Figure 15.3, we can consider what happens if the demand for pounds falls to Q_{D2}. Now there will be an excess supply of pounds equal to AE. The central bank now needs to buy the excess supply of pounds. In order to buy pounds, it has to offer something other than pounds in return. When the central bank was selling pounds it will have received euros and other currencies in return. These were added to the bank's currency reserves. It now uses these reserves to buy back the pounds.

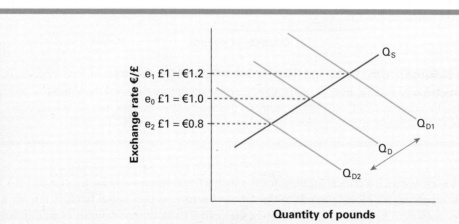

Figure 15.1 The forex market

As the demand for pounds increases, the exchange rate appreciates. When the demand for pounds falls, the exchange rate depreciates.

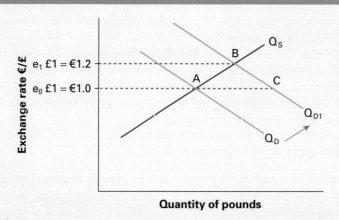

Figure 15.2 Increased demand under fixed exchange rates

As the demand for pounds increases, the market would like to move from A to B. But the government has fixed the price at £1 equals 11.0. It, therefore, has to supply the additional AC pounds in order to keep the price at £1 equals 11.0.

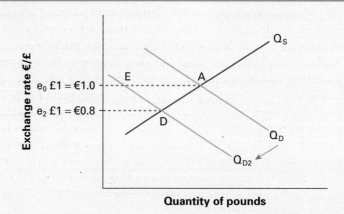

Figure 15.3 Reduced demand under fixed exchange rates

As the demand for pounds decreases, then at the fixed exchange rate of £1 equals 11.0, supply is greater than demand by the amount AE. In order to maintain the fixed exchange rate, the government has to purchase the excess supply of pounds using its foreign currency reserves.

However, there is a critical problem for the central bank. It is feasible for the central bank to keep supplying additional pounds to the market because, as the central bank, it can ask for more pounds to be printed. Unfortunately, the central bank cannot commit to an indefinite purchase of the pound because, in order to do this, it has to have an infinite supply of foreign currency, such as US dollars and euros. Since the US Federal Reserve controls the supply of dollars and the European central bank controls the supply of euros, the Bank of England will soon run out of foreign currencies with which to buy the pound.

Devaluation

If the currency is being continually supported by the central bank, it is probably the case that the fixed exchange rate has become vastly different from the long-term market rate for the currency. The correct policy response is not to keep buying the currency. Instead, the currency should be allowed to devalue. In our example, the fixed exchange rate of £1 equals €1.0 is abandoned and the government seeks to manage the exchange rate at the new equilibrium of £1 equals €0.8.

This potential for devaluation creates a fundamental weakness within fixed exchange rates: they are open to **speculative attack**.

> A **speculative attack** is a massive capital outflow from an economy with a fixed exchange rate.

If the government has fixed the exchange rate at £1 equals €1.0, but you think it will soon have to devalue to £1 equals €0.8, then the best thing to do is take pounds and convert them into euros: £1 million will buy you €1.0 million. If many people do this, massive capital outflows will be observed. Note that people are cutting demand for pounds and instead demanding euros. This means the government has to offer more support to the pound at £1 equals €1.0. It will soon give up and, when it devalues to £1 equals €0.8, you can take your €1.0 million and convert it back into €1.0m/0.8m = £1.25m. So, by changing your money into euros and then waiting for a devaluation you have made £0.25 million, or a 25 per cent return on your investment.

Floating exchange rates

As demand and supply for a currency change, the equilibrium price adjusts accordingly. As demand rises, so does the value of the currency, and as demand falls, the currency depreciates in value. Under a **floating exchange rate** system there is no impact on the central bank's foreign currency reserves as there is no intervention in the marketplace.

> Under a **floating exchange rate** system there is no market intervention by the government or the central bank.

In the long run, floating exchange rates *should* obey **purchasing power parity**.

Consider the following example. Assume the exchange rate is £1 equals €1.5. We will also assume that a pair of designer jeans cost £50 in London and €75 in Paris. With the current exchange rate, the price of the jeans is identical in London and Paris (£50 × 1.5 = €75).

Now assume that inflation in Paris is zero, but inflation in London is 10 per cent. At the end of the year, the jeans in London have increased in price by 10 per cent and so now cost £55. The jeans in Paris have stayed the same, €75. If the exchange rate is still £1 equals €1.5, then we can save £5 by buying the jeans in Paris and importing them into the UK. Clearly £5 is not much of a saving, but if we were in business and set about buying 1000 pairs of jeans, then it might be worthwhile importing from Paris.

> **Purchasing power parity** requires the nominal exchange rate to adjust in order to keep the real exchange rate constant.

However, as we begin to import jeans we have to sell pounds and demand euros. As we (and everyone else) do this, the value of the euro will rise. In fact, it will rise to £1 equals €1.36. Why? Well, if we now convert the price of the jeans in Paris back to pounds, we have €75/1.36 = £55. All that happens is that the nominal exchange rate adjusts so that the price of jeans in Paris is identical to the price of jeans in London. The real exchange rate is constant and, as a result, we have purchasing power parity – it costs the same to buy goods in London as it does in Paris.

Clearly, this is an extreme illustrative example. Consumers need to be aware of the price differences between Paris and London. The price difference has to be big enough to make consumers interested in exploiting the price differential. Finally, the cost of moving the goods from Paris to London has to be lower than the price difference.

The Economist magazine has for a number of years used the price of a Big Mac to assess purchasing power parity. Details of this are provided in Box 15.1. While the limitations of this approach are discussed, it should be noted that the Big Mac index has been surprisingly accurate in predicting future exchange rate movements.

Box 15.1 The Big Mac index: McCurrencies

From The Economist, *25 May 2006*

The Economist's Big Mac index is based on the theory of purchasing power parity (PPP). If purchasing power parity holds, then using the current exchange rate, the price of a Big Mac in the US should be equal to the price of a Big Mac in China, the UK, the EU, etc. *The Economist's* Big Mac index from January 2009, shown in Table 15.2, suggests that a number of currencies are overvalued compared with the US dollar and a number are also undervalued. The Chinese yuan would have to rise by 46 per cent in order for Big Macs to cost the same in China and the US, while the euro would have to fall by 24 per cent in order to make the Big Mac in Europe the same price as in the US.

The index was never intended to be a precise predictor of currency movements, simply a take-away guide to whether currencies are at their 'correct' long-run level. Curiously, however, burgernomics has an impressive record in predicting exchange rates: currencies that show up as overvalued often tend to weaken in later years. But you must always remember the Big Mac's limitations. Burgers cannot sensibly be traded across borders and prices are distorted by differences in taxes. In addition, it is also likely that income levels, wages and the cost of non-tradable inputs, such as rents. in different economies are likely to affect the domestic price level.

Table 15.2 The Big Mac index

	Under(−)/over(+) valuation against the dollar (%)
US	
Australia	−38
Brazil	−32
China	−46
Euro area	+24
Russia	−44
Switzerland	+62
UK	−5

Source: The Economist, January 2009

© The Economist Newspaper Limited, London 2009

Exchange rates in practice

As indicated at the beginning of this section, fixed and floating exchange rate regimes are extremes. The Chinese yuan is fixed in the short term against a basket of currencies, including the US dollar, the euro, the Japanese yen and the UK pound. The euro floats against all other currencies, as does the US dollar. The UK pound is also seen as a floating currency. But the central bank and government saw the rapid depreciation of the pound in late 2008 as a way of supporting UK exports during the economic recession. While not directly entering the forex market to buy and sell pounds, comments in press interviews were clearly designed to manage the currency downwards.

A concern with the Chinese currency is that the Chinese government is seeking to undervalue the yuan. In so doing, a cheaper yuan will drive more exports and protect Chinese jobs. However, the degree to which the yuan is undervalued is debatable; see Box 15.2.

Box 15.2 How undervalued is the Chinese yuan?

Adapted from 'Burger-thy-neighbour policies' in The Economist, *5 February 2009*

China has been accused of 'manipulating' its currency by Tim Geithner, America's new treasury secretary, and this week Dominique Strauss-Kahn, the managing director of the IMF, said that it was 'common knowledge' that the yuan was undervalued.

Of course, China manipulates its exchange rate – in the sense that the level of the yuan is not set by the market but is influenced by foreign exchange intervention. The real issue is whether Beijing is deliberately keeping the yuan cheap to give exporters an unfair advantage. From July 2005, when it abandoned its fixed peg to the dollar, Beijing allowed the yuan to rise steadily, but since last July it has again been virtually pegged to the greenback. And there are concerns that China may allow the yuan to depreciate to help its exporters – with worrying echoes of the beggar-thy-neighbour policies that exacerbated the Depression. But American politicians are wrong to focus only on the yuan's dollar exchange rate. Since July, the yuan has gained 10 per cent in trade-weighted terms. It is up 23 per cent against the euro, and 30 per cent or more against the currencies of many other emerging economies.

In early 2005, two American senators brought a bill to Congress that threatened a tariff of 27.5 per cent on all Chinese imports unless the yuan was revalued by that amount. This curiously precise figure was the midpoint of a range of estimates (15–40 per cent) of the yuan's undervaluation. The bill was dropped, but the yuan has since risen by that magic amount in real trade-weighted terms.

Those who argue that the yuan is still too cheap point to three factors: China's foreign exchange reserves have surged; it has a huge current account surplus; and prices are much cheaper in China than in America. Start with official reserves. If China had not bought lots of dollars over the past few years, the yuan's exchange rate would have risen by more.

Now consider the current account. Some economists say it is wrong to define the yuan's fair value by the revaluation required to eliminate the current account surplus. Trade does not have to be perfectly balanced to be fair. And China's surplus partly reflects its high saving rate. A stronger yuan will help to shift growth away from exports towards domestic consumption. Therefore, policies to boost domestic spending will be more important than its exchange rate.

Finally, consider Chinese prices. An alternative way of defining the 'fair' value of a currency is purchasing power parity (PPP): the idea that, in the long run, exchange rates should equalize prices across countries. A Big Mac cost 48 per cent less in China than in America, which might suggest that the yuan is 48 per cent undervalued against the dollar. Using a simple model, which adjusts the Big Mac price differences in countries' GDP per head and relative labour costs, gives the result that the yuan is now less than 5 per cent undervalued.

15.3 **Fixed versus floating exchange rates**

> **Volatility** is a measure of variability. In the case of exchange rates, a concern over volatility is a concern over how much the exchange rate changes.

Given that both fixed and floating exchange rates are used by different governments, it should be expected that each system must have benefits and drawbacks. These are generally related to exchange rate **volatility, robustness** and **financial discipline.**

Volatility

Clearly, under a fixed exchange rate there is no volatility in the short term. The government fixes the exchange rate. In contrast, floating exchange rates are volatile. The value of the

Robustness is a concern with flexibility, or the ability to accommodate change.

Financial discipline is the degree to which a government pursues stringent monetary policy and targets low inflation.

exchange rate changes on a daily and even hourly basis. A sense of the volatility is shown in Figure 15.4, illustrating the changing exchange rate between the euro and the pound sterling.

Accommodation of economic shocks

However, we also need to consider long-term volatility. In Figure 15.3, we could begin at equilibrium A under a floating exchange rate. The demand for the currency begins to shift to Q_{D2}. Over time, there is a gradual adjustment to the new equilibrium at D. The exchange rate slowly moves down and firms and consumers wishing to exchange money slowly adjust to the changing exchange price. In contrast, under a fixed exchange rate the government is committed to supporting the equilibrium at A. If under pressure from a speculative attack and the government decides to stop supporting the currency and allows it to devalue to the equilibrium at D, then there is a sudden and dramatic change in the exchange price. Such changes can be more dangerous than gradual adjustment. Indeed, currency devaluations often lead to volatility in the rest of the financial markets, such as stock markets.

So, from the perspective of business, floating exchange rates create short-term uncertainty due to their volatility, but they provide gradual adjustment in the long run, which may be preferable to dramatic one-off changes offered by fixed exchange rates.

Consider our example of the boats in the harbour. The boats connected by ropes are the economies with floating exchange rates. They are flexible and able to accommodate environmental changes. In the case of the boat, this was the rise and fall of the waves. We witnessed above, when examining purchasing power parity, that environmental change might exist in the form of inflationary differences between economies. If the UK inflation rate is 3 per cent and the euro rate is 2 per cent, then it becomes attractive for UK consumers to buy euro products rather than UK products. As they do this, they sell pounds and demand euros. The value of the pound will fall, reflecting the inflationary differences between the UK and the Eurozone. When full adjustment has occurred, euro products cost the same as UK products.

Under fixed exchange rates there is no scope for exchange rate adjustment; purchasing power parity may not hold. Instead, UK companies become increasingly uncompetitive against euro companies. Imports increase, demand for domestic UK-produced goods falls, and the UK moves into recession. The recession will be expected to reduce inflation within the UK.

Therefore, under a fixed exchange rate, purchasing power parity is gained through changes in domestic prices rather than exchange rate changes.

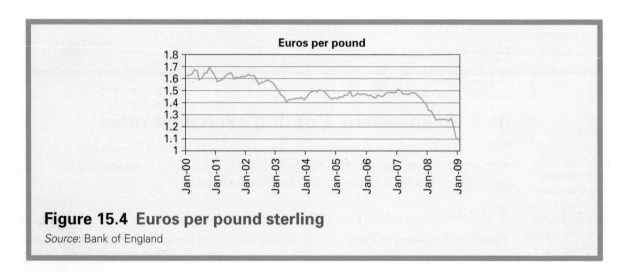

Figure 15.4 Euros per pound sterling
Source: Bank of England

Financial discipline

As we have seen above, floating exchange rates can accommodate inflationary differences between economies. This has led to some individuals taking the view that floating exchange rates do not provide monetary discipline. Therefore, governments under floating exchange rates have little incentive to control inflation. In contrast, fixed exchange rates, by their inherent inflexibility, struggle to accommodate inflationary differences. Therefore, fixed exchange rates force governments to take financial discipline seriously.

There is some truth in this. The UK entered the European exchange rate mechanism in the early 1990s in an attempt to control inflation. But there is also the view that governments can and do target inflation even under floating exchange rates. The pound, US dollar and even the euro all float, but each central bank is tasked with keeping inflation under control.

We now need to explain the balance of payments and the relationship with exchange rates and macroeconomic policy.

15.4 The balance of payments

As a record of all transactions made with the rest of the world, the **balance of payments** has three accounts: (i) the **current account**, (ii) the **capital account**, and (iii) the **financial account**.

Current account

The current account measures imports and exports and can be further divided into visible and invisible trade. Visible trade is the export and import of tangible or visible goods. Exporting a car is clearly an example of visible trade. Invisible trade captures intangible services. A London-based business consultant working for a German client is an example of an invisible export. Added together, visible and invisible trade make the trade account. After adjusting for net transfer payments, such as interest and profits on foreign assets, we get to the current account. Figure 15.5 illustrates the trade account for the UK. It is clearly evident that the UK imports more goods than it exports. But this is partially offset by the net export of services to the rest of

> The **balance of payments** records all transactions between a country and the rest of the world.
>
> The **current account** is a record of all goods and services traded with the rest of the world.
>
> The **capital account** records, among other things, net contributions made to the EU.
>
> The **financial account** records net purchases and sales of foreign assets. (This was previously known as the capital account.)

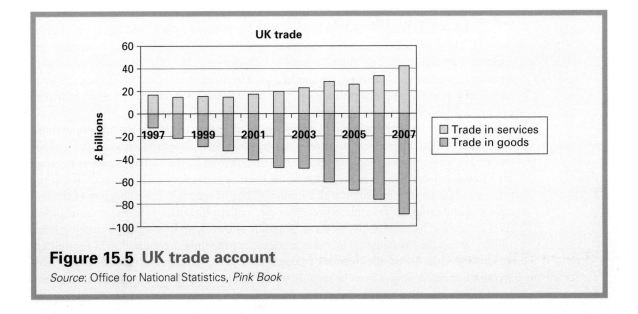

Figure 15.5 UK trade account
Source: Office for National Statistics, *Pink Book*

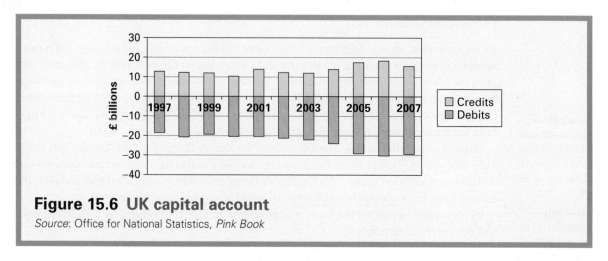

Figure 15.6 UK capital account
Source: Office for National Statistics, *Pink Book*

the world. This pattern reflects the decline of manufacturing over the last 20 years in the UK and the growth of sectors such as financial services in London, as well as travel services and telecommunications services.

Capital account

Payments by the UK towards the Common Agricultural Policy and other EU contributions are collated under the capital account, as are payments from the EU to the UK for social and infrastructure development projects. Figure 15.6 shows that, throughout the last decade, the UK has been a net payer, with debits exceeding credits.

Financial account

The financial account captures all investments into an economy by foreign individuals and companies. It also captures all investments made outside an economy by its companies and private individuals. There are three broad types of investment activity. The first is direct investment, where for example a foreign company may buy a rival within another country; equally, the foreign company may build its own offices or factory inside another economy. The second is termed portfolio investment, which involves the purchase of shares and bonds in another country. Third are other investments, including loans between banks which operate internationally. In Figure 15.7, the three types of investment into the UK (the credits) are shown. Direct and portfolio investments have been dwarfed by other investments for the last five years of the data series. This reflects the massive flows of cash into UK banks from foreign providers of capital. This is likely to decline markedly following the credit crunch.

In summary, the current, capital and financial accounts seek to record all transactions, whether they be goods, services or purely finance, which take place between a country and the rest of the world. Indeed, we will see shortly that as long as the exchange rate is floating, the three accounts will sum to zero; that is, the balance of payments will be zero. Clearly, the three accounts are only measured with a limited degree of accuracy. The smuggling of alcohol, cigarettes and drugs, for example, represents aspects of international trade that go unrecorded. As a result, the balance of payments is generally shown with a so-called balancing item, which corrects for any statistical mistakes in measuring the three accounts. But, in Figure 15.8, we show the balance on the financial account (credits less debits). For the data period, this account has nearly always been in surplus, which it must be if the debits on the current and capital accounts are to be balanced.

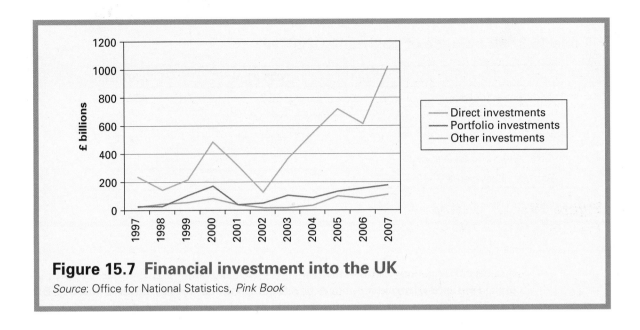

Figure 15.7 Financial investment into the UK

Source: Office for National Statistics, *Pink Book*

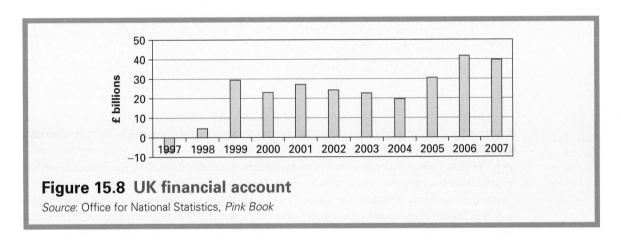

Figure 15.8 UK financial account

Source: Office for National Statistics, *Pink Book*

Balance of payments and floating exchange rates

Under a floating exchange rate, the balance of payments must equal zero. This stems from equilibrium in the forex market. In equilibrium, the demand for UK pounds must equal the supply of UK pounds. In the current account, we have individuals demanding and supplying pounds as they import and export goods and services. In the financial account, we have individuals supplying and demanding pounds as they buy and sell international assets. Therefore, if the forex market is in equilibrium, then the demand and supply of pounds from the current and financial account must also be equal.

Balance of payments and fixed exchange rates

Under a fixed exchange rate, the situation is vastly different. We saw that point C in Figure 15.2 and E in Figure 15.3 were points of disequilibria in the forex market. At point C in Figure 15.2,

Table 15.3 UK balance of payments, 2006–07

	2006 (£bn)	2007 (£bn)
1 Current account	−45.0	−52.6
2 Capital account	0.9	2.7
3 Financial account	41.9	39.8
4 Net errors and omissions	2.2	10.1
Balance of payments (1 + 2 + 3 + 4)	0	0

Source: Office for National Statistics

the demand for pounds is greater than the supply of pounds at the exchange rate of e_0. We can explain this excess demand for pounds by reference to the current and financial accounts. For example, if UK exports are greater than imports, foreign consumers demanding pounds to pay for the exports will outweigh UK consumers supplying pounds to pay for imports. If UK investors do not wish to buy foreign assets at the existing exchange rate, then the supply of pounds will be less than the demand. In contrast, if we consider point E in Figure 15.3, the supply of pounds at the fixed exchange rate of e_0 led to an excess supply of pounds. We can, again, explain this excess supply of pounds by reference to the current and financial accounts. For example, if UK imports are greater than exports, then the supply of pounds will increase. But if foreign investors are not willing to buy British assets at the exchange rate of e_1, then the demand for pounds will be less than the supply.

Therefore, under a fixed exchange rate, the balance of payments will not necessarily be zero.

In order to make the balance of payments zero, we have to incorporate the concept of **official financing**.

> **Official financing** is the extent of government intervention in the forex markets.

We know that, in order to keep the exchange rate at its fixed level, the government must buy up the excess supply of pounds. This is called official financing and is added into the balance of payments as the final balancing item. It represents the extent to which the government has changed its foreign currency reserves by either buying up the excess supply of pounds or, alternatively, adding to its reserves by selling pounds in the forex market.

If we examine Table 15.3, we can see the actual values for each of the three accounts during 2006 and 2007. It is clear that the balancing item, or net errors and omissions, for 2007 is very large. It might be worth checking the figure in the future to see if the government revises its estimates of the three accounts. Information on the trade of goods and services or assets might have been recorded slowly, with correct figures not becoming known for some time. As a result, the figures provided by the government are only an initial estimate.

15.5 Exchange rates and government policy

We can now begin to consider the effectiveness of fiscal and monetary policy under fixed and floating exchange rate regimes. While this is theoretically interesting, it also has practical implications. The UK currently operates a floating exchange rate regime. If it were to enter the euro, then the exchange rate with all euro members would be fixed for ever. Before we consider fiscal and monetary effectiveness, we need to understand two further points: (a) the real exchange rate and (b) perfect capital mobility.

Real exchange rate

International competitiveness depends upon the real and not the nominal exchange rate.

> The **real exchange rate** is the relative price of domestic and foreign goods measured in a common currency.

The **real exchange rate** = (€/£ exchange rate) × (£ price of UK goods/€ price of Eurozone goods)

If the nominal exchange rate appreciated, then UK goods would become more expensive than European goods. European consumers would have to change more euros into pounds in order to buy UK goods. If the price of European goods rose quicker than the price of UK goods, because inflation was higher in Europe than in the UK, then the UK would become more competitive. So, even if the nominal exchange rate stays constant, but inflation is 10 per cent in Europe and only 5 per cent in the UK, the real exchange rate will appreciate by 5 per cent.

In summary, international competitiveness is influenced by the nominal exchange rate and the relative price level between the two countries.

Perfect capital mobility

> Under **perfect capital mobility**, expected returns on all assets around the world will be zero. If interest rates are 5 per cent higher in New York than in London, then, in order to compensate, the exchange rate will rise by 5 per cent, making dollars more expensive to buy. Therefore, the expected rates of return in London and New York are then identical. Or, in economic terminology, interest parity holds.

If you had £1000 to invest in a savings account, you might visit a finance site on the Internet and ask for a ranking of savings rates offered by leading banks and building societies. If you are not concerned about when you get access to the money, you might sensibly choose the bank offering the highest rate.

Now we will assume that you are richer and have £1 million to invest. It is now worth thinking beyond the UK: what interest rates are being offered by banks in the UK, the US, Germany or Japan? If the rates in New York are 10 per cent, but only 5 per cent in all other countries, then you can double your interest by moving your money to New York.

Or can you? A slight problem exists. In order to invest in the US you need to sell your pounds and demand dollars. As more dollars are demanded, the price or exchange rate must appreciate. At the extreme, if financial capital is free to move around the world, then interest parity must hold and there is no incentive to move your money.

Fiscal and monetary policy under fixed exchange rates

Monetary policy

If interest parity holds, then movement in the exchange rate will offset any differential in interest rates between countries. However, this all assumes that exchange rates are floating. What happens when the exchange rate is fixed? Any difference in the interest rate between the two countries will now represent a guaranteed profit. As a result, financial capital will flow to the country with the highest interest rate.

The only way to stop capital flows putting pressure on the exchange rate is to set a single interest rate for both countries. This is a loss of monetary independence for at least one of the countries.

Fiscal policy

If we begin by backtracking to Chapter 11, in a closed economy, if the government increases aggregate demand through a fiscal stimulus, then a central bank with an inflation target will increase interest rates and cut aggregate demand in order to keep inflation under control. But under a fixed exchange rate, there is a loss of monetary independence. The central bank seeks interest parity and so cannot change the interest rate from that set by its international trading partners. Therefore, any increase in fiscal policy will not be constrained by a tightening of monetary policy.

Fiscal policy is, therefore, seen as being more powerful under fixed exchange rates.

We can even go one step further and examine what would happen if the central bank tries to increase interest rates. Because interest parity does not hold, financial capital will flow into the economy. There will be an excess demand for the currency in the forex market. The central bank is committed to printing more money in order to meet the excess demand. But an increase in the supply of money leads to a reduction in the equilibrium price of money. The price of money is the interest rate. So, an initial increase in the interest rate leads to a future reduction in the interest rate. Monetary policy is ineffective.

Why enter into a fixed exchange rate?

Aside from the stability offered by a fixed exchange rate, a very powerful benefit can be found in the real exchange rate, which is a measure of international competitiveness. The government is only fixing the nominal exchange rate. International competitiveness can be achieved by improving the real exchange rate. This is achieved by keeping the inflation rate in the economy at, or below, the inflation rates of its key trading partners. If inflation in the UK averages 2.5 per cent but its international competitors are suffering 5 per cent inflation, then each year the UK becomes 2.5 per cent cheaper.

As such, fixed exchange rates can have a strong disciplinary effect on domestic inflation. This disciplinary effect can exist in a number of forms. First, individuals under the economic consequences of a fixed exchange rate have lower inflationary expectations.

Second, if inflation rises at a faster rate in the UK, then UK goods become less competitive. Exports fall, aggregate demand falls and employment falls. Wages and prices in the UK fall, inflation is reduced and UK goods become competitive again.

Fiscal and monetary policy under floating exchange rates

Monetary policy

We will now see that monetary policy is more powerful under floating exchange rates and fiscal policy is less effective. If we begin with monetary policy, a reduction of interest rates will boost internal demand. Individuals will consume more and companies will raise investment levels. Furthermore, if interest parity holds, then a reduction in the interest rate must be offset by a reduction in the exchange rate. This reduction in the exchange rate leads to an improvement in the level of international competitiveness. Products are now cheaper for foreign consumers and so exports will rise.

Monetary policy under floating exchange rates is reinforced. A reduction in interest rates stimulates domestic and international demand for domestic goods and services.

Fiscal policy

If the government introduces a fiscal stimulus, then aggregate demand will increase and so will inflation. In order to control the inflation, the central bank will raise interest rates. In order to ensure interest parity, the exchange rate must also rise. Goods and services now cost more abroad. The rising exchange rate has reduced the international competitiveness of the economy. Exports fall and the initial fiscal stimulus provided by the government is offset by falling external demand.

Under floating exchange rates, fiscal policy is neutralized by rising interest rates, a rising currency and falling exports.

We can use the ideas developed within this section to examine European monetary union.

15.6 **European monetary union**

Monetary union is the permanent fixing of exchange rates between member countries.

In the case of European **monetary union**, conversion rates for French francs into euros, German marks into euros, Italian lire into euros, etc. were agreed and then carried out.

On 1 January 2002, everyone in the Eurozone only had euros to spend. At the same time, management of national currencies by national central banks stopped and the European Central Bank began managing the euro and setting one interest rate for the whole of the Eurozone. We can understand this because we know that fixed exchange rates lead to a loss of monetary independence. But what are the major implications of euro membership for the UK and for businesses generally across the EU?

Starting with the simple, but less than obvious, the nominal exchange rate between each of the member states is fixed at 1 euro for 1 euro. The more serious issue is the real exchange rate and international competitiveness. Remember the real interest rate is the nominal exchange rate adjusted for the relative price level between countries. So, even though everyone in the Eurozone has fixed the nominal exchange rate, differences in inflation rates will lead to changes in the real exchange rate and international competitiveness. We can examine Figure 15.9. Over the period 2002 to 2008, Spain consistently had a higher level of inflation than many other EU economies. It may be that Spain had a lower overall price level to start with and so Spain's prices have been catching up with the rest of Europe. Regardless, the price competitiveness of Spain has fallen.

If we now start to think through the points, we can begin to see a fundamental issue for the euro. A single interest rate is set by the ECB for the entire Eurozone. So, the ECB could not help Spain by raising interest rates without penalizing Germany, which had low inflation. Fiscal policy is more powerful under a fixed exchange rate, so the Spanish government could decide to create a recession in Spain in order to reduce inflationary pressures and improve international competitiveness. But if Spain is pushed into a recession, when the rest of the Eurozone is growing, Spain's business cycle will no longer be synchronized with all other members and the one-size-fits-all interest rate policy from the ECB will not help Spain.

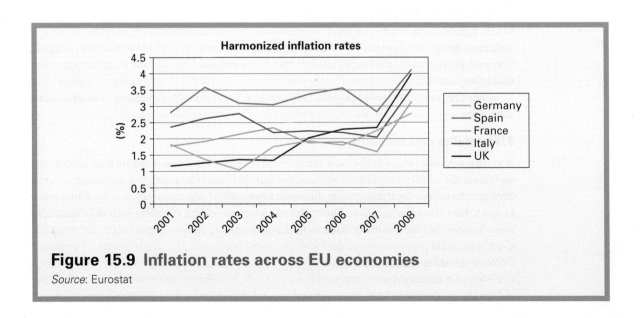

Figure 15.9 Inflation rates across EU economies

Source: Eurostat

Maastricht criteria and the stability pact

It is, therefore, of no surprise that strict conditions were placed on potential members of the euro, through the so-called Maastricht criteria. These conditions have now been imposed as continuing conditions as part of the stability pact. In summary, the criteria seek to create macro-economic harmonization between the member states and ensure continuing harmonization.

Before entry, potential adopters of the euro had to have low inflation and low interest rates. In the previous two years, no devaluation of the national currency was allowed. This prevented countries from seeking any early real exchange rate advantage. Furthermore, on the fiscal side, government budget deficits were to be around 3 per cent of GDP and overall debt to GDP ratio should be 60 per cent. These rules were also imposed in an attempt to control fiscal stances and prevent a build-up of inflationary pressures within member countries. The stability pact of 1997 was a further agreement that the Maastricht criteria would continue to operate even after entry.

Optimal currency zones

The Maastricht criteria and the stability pact were and are attempts to keep all member economies moving together. But a more theoretical set of conditions for the success of a currency zone, such as the euro, were put forward by Robert Mundell in the 1960s.

Mundell began to think about the factors that would lead to an **optimal currency zone**.

Three criteria were put forward as important for the success of a currency zone.

> An **optimal currency zone** is a group of countries better off with a common currency than keeping separate currencies.

1. Trade integration

The first is the degree of trade between member countries of the currency zone. Trade integrates economies. However, perhaps more importantly, highly integrated economies have the most to gain from a temporary devaluation of their currency against their partners' currency. A single currency is basically a credible commitment to co-operate, rather than starting an international price war through exchange rate adjustments.

2. Similarities in industrial sectors

The second criterion concerns how the economies will deal with macroeconomic shocks. The more similar the industrial structure across all the member countries, the more likely they are to stay synchronized. For example, if all members have similar industries, an external shock, such as a rise in the oil price, or in the case of Europe, a recession in the US leading to a reduction in export growth, will lead to similar effects in all economies. No one country will suffer more than another. In contrast, if only one member country was very reliant on oil, or the US, then that economy would go into recession, while all the other countries would remain unaffected.

3. Flexibility and mobility

If all else fails, then there is the final safety net criterion. Factor resources such as labour and capital should display mobility and price flexibility. If an economy suffers a specific shock and goes into recession, then the quicker domestic prices adjust, the more rapid is the adjustment to international competitiveness. Furthermore, the more willing resource, such as labour, is to move throughout the currency zone to find employment, the less important is the need for specific national governments to deal with domestic problems. The single monetary policy of the central bank will suffice.

Clearly, if a country is not integrated through trade, industry or factor resource transfers, the greater the need for it to keep its own currency and its own monetary independence.

Is Europe an optimal currency zone?

In terms of Europe, the evidence tends to suggest that the Eurozone is integrated to a degree, and so could represent a successful currency zone. But perhaps the more important issue is one of continuing integration and stability brought about by the euro. The longer the euro succeeds as a common currency, the more closely integrated the member economies will become. The euro promotes price transparency – goods priced in Germany, for example, can be compared directly with goods priced anywhere else in the Eurozone. First, this promotes trade, which is the first criterion for an optimal currency zone. Second, currency stability and transparency make cross-border investments more certain. In the absence of currency exchange rate risks, companies will be more willing to operate in other member states. The structural or industrial mix of each economy will, therefore, merge; this is the second criterion. Third, price transparency promotes competition and, therefore, an increased need or willingness for workers, employers and producers to keep prices under control and pursue international competitiveness; this is the third criterion.

UK entry into the euro

The UK government has set five tests that must be met before the UK can enter into the euro. These are listed and explained in Box 15.3. Following our discussion of the stability pact and the key factors supporting an optimal currency zone, it is easy to see why the government has chosen tests of economic convergence and flexibility. These are the key factors that would facilitate the UK's entry into the euro. If the UK economy converges with the other euro economies, then the interest rate, set for Europe by the ECB, will be similar to the interest rate that would have been set by the Bank of England for the UK. If the UK manages to diverge from other euro economies, then flexibility in product and labour markets will enable internal adjustment. Finally, the tests of investment, financial services, employment and growth relate to the economic benefits from being a member of the euro; without benefits, there would be little reason for entering.

In assessing whether the UK should join the euro, we can return to our analogy of the boats in the harbour. The question rests on whether or not the UK wishes to retain a floating exchange rate between the pound and the euro, and in effect keep a flexible rope between itself and Europe. Or will the UK economy move close enough to the rest of Europe, in terms of its economic cycle, price levels and productivity rates, to make a solid weld between the UK and the euro area? Making a decision based on these questions would provide a structured approach to entry and is clearly how the government would like to proceed.

However, it is also possible that delaying the decision to enter the euro until all five tests have been passed could be damaging to the UK economy.

1. Lost trade

The euro, as a shared currency among member states, facilitates cross-border trade by making pricing easier and reducing the need for currency transactions. Evidence suggests that the euro has raised cross-border trade between Eurozone members by as much as 30 per cent.

2. Lower foreign investment

Companies wishing to operate in the EU are more likely to invest in the Eurozone than in the UK because, without the euro, the UK is a more costly option, particularly in terms of exchange rate volatility. Lower investment will lead to reduced employment and perhaps even lower wages as UK labour endeavours to become more internationally competitive.

Box 15.3 Should the UK join the euro?

The UK Treasury has five economic tests that will define whether a clear and unambiguous case can be made. So far, the UK has not passed all five tests. These are:

1 sustainable *convergence* between Britain and the economies of a single currency
2 whether there is sufficient *flexibility* to cope with economic change
3 the effect on *investment*
4 the impact on our *financial services* industry
5 whether it is good for *employment*

Convergence in the past has been limited; interest rates have been higher in the UK than in the euro area. Business cycles are more volatile in the UK, reflecting the greater importance of oil, the housing market and company finances.

Flexibility is important for both labour and product markets. Firms need to be flexible in pricing, reacting to increased competition and the greater needs of consumers. Wages need to increase in line with productivity growth and workers need wide-ranging skills to accommodate potential changes in the job market.

Lower levels of inflation, enabling firms to plan and invest in confidence, should improve investment. Furthermore, investment should be capable of responding to companies' increased needs for funds in the face of increased investment opportunities.

Financial services will be profoundly affected by the euro. With financial services representing around 8 per cent of GDP, the acceptance of the euro needs to be beneficial for London's financial centre.

The euro needs to improve employment and economic growth. However, this clearly depends upon the flexibility of the UK economy and the convergence of the UK with the rest of the Eurozone.

Source: UK Treasury

3. Weaker financial markets

As a powerful world currency, financial services companies will be keen to locate their operations in the Eurozone, rather than in the UK. This will reduce employment in the UK and damage London's position as a leading financial centre.

4. Reduced competitiveness

The euro is perhaps already improving competitiveness in the Eurozone. With greater price transparency, price dispersions for the same product across the Eurozone have fallen since its inception, particularly for large consumer items such as electrical goods.

5. Convergence

It is not clear that the UK will converge with the Eurozone. In fact, the members of the Eurozone are more likely to converge and become increasingly integrated as a result of the euro. In terms of convergence, the UK may end up chasing a moving target.

6. Euro policy and politics

To debate reform of euro fiscal and monetary policy, you have to be a member. As an outsider, the UK cannot direct the future of the euro.

All of these points relate back to our boats in the harbour. As the UK bobs up and down with a rope connecting it to the Eurozone, trade and investment are more difficult with Europe. Being located on the stable platform that is the Eurozone, with boats all welded together, makes trade more possible. The Eurozone is bigger and financial services will view its large economy as more attractive than the smaller UK economy. Finally, if you are sitting in a small boat bobbing up and down in the harbour, you only have yourself to talk to. On the large platform that is the Eurozone, you can engage in many important debates relating to the euro.

15.7 Business application: monetary sovereignty, exchange rate depreciation and export growth

We began this chapter by raising the issue of whether or not the UK should become a member of the Eurozone. We can now return to that question and begin a stronger assessment of the effects on business of staying out of the euro.

There are some simple advantages to UK businesses of adopting the euro. Trade with other member states is less complex. Price transparency is assured by common pricing and financial risks associated with currency movements are reduced. These potential benefits are undoubtedly important and some business and policy leaders would prefer to see the UK enter the Eurozone for these reasons.

The counter-argument is one that considers the impact of adopting the euro on the UK's macroeconomic environment, a consideration which is now brought to the fore by the recessionary impact of the credit crisis.

Adopting the euro would require significant changes to the way the UK economy is managed. The UK, like the EU, seeks to follow a fairly strict fiscal policy rule, where, in normal economic conditions (not a severe credit crisis), government deficits must not exceed 3 per cent of GDP. So adopting the euro would not change this policy. However, the UK would have to abandon its monetary sovereignty. Interest rate decisions would instead be passed to the European Central Bank, which sets rates for the benefit of the entire Eurozone.

We are back to our example of boats in the harbour. The economic shock and subsequent recession caused by the credit crisis can be dealt with by the Bank of England in a manner which is of greatest benefit to the UK economy. In effect, by retaining monetary sovereignty and setting its own monetary policy, the UK can rise and fall in the turbulent waves independent of its main trading partners.

The main potential benefit of an independent monetary policy for the UK is the ability for the pound to fall in value against the economy's main trading partners. As interest rates are cut, the pound falls and UK exports become cheaper. If foreign consumers are enticed by cheaper prices, then aggregate demand in the UK can increase through higher international demand.

The retention of monetary policy provides UK policy-makers with flexibility and it is this that we are trading against the known benefits of price transparency and minimal exchange rate risk associated with being a member of the euro. These points are discussed in more detail in Box 15.4.

Many of these arguments do require some reflection before it is possible to recognize if the retention of monetary sovereignty is good for UK business.

First, will a fall in the value of the pound drive export growth? As we have seen in this chapter, the UK is not a major exporter of goods. Instead, its strength lies in services, especially financial services, where there is less demand following the credit crisis. Moreover how price sensitive are consumers of UK exports? If their demand is inelastic, then even a major fall in

Box 15.4 Pound's fall may herald recovery not doom

Adapted from an article by Anatole Kaletsky in The Times, *17 November 2008*

The UK economy, which had previously looked more vulnerable to the global recession than any other G7 country, is now likely to suffer less than the rest of Europe, as a result of unprecedented policy stimulus from the lowest interest rates in history and a super-competitive currency following record falls in the value of the pound.

The last observation links directly to the new economic story that suddenly broke out in Britain this weekend – the fear of a 'run on the pound'. This sudden anxiety is a weirdly distorted echo of the great policy debate that raged in Britain throughout the postwar era until it was settled by the collapse of John Major's economic policy in 1992 and six years later by Gordon Brown's decision to keep Britain out of the euro. Since Black Wednesday, almost no British politician or economist has been silly enough to use the 'weakness' or 'strength' of sterling as a proxy for the state of the British economy, never mind to suggest that a fall in the exchange rate is a portent of economic doom. That said, a few remaining euro-enthusiasts still believe that Britain should have joined the single currency and, failing that, should now behave like a shadow member, trying to stabilize its currency and not to deviate too much from Eurozone monetary and fiscal policies.

The upshot is that, far from being feared as a 'punishment' for Britain's monetary independence or long-term fiscal profligacy, the present fall in the pound should be seen as part of the solution to Britain's economic problems. As Mervyn King noted at his press conference last week, the UK needs to revive economic activity and avert deflation, but also to restructure its economy to reduce dependence on consumer spending and housing. It would also be helpful to reduce the country's reliance on foreign capital inflows. What all these requirements mean, as a matter of simple arithmetic, is that the structure of Britain's trade must shift substantially, to the point where exports either exceed imports or the remaining trade deficit is matched by inflows of capital from foreigners investing in UK property, businesses and other assets, in the expectation of better returns than they can earn elsewhere, either from higher return on capital or a future rise in sterling.

The textbook way to achieve such a shift in foreign trade and capital inflows is to combine bold cuts in interest rates, which lead to a sharp, though usually temporary, currency devaluation, with a squeeze on consumer demand. An obvious conclusion is that the present currency weakness, far from reopening a debate in Britain about joining the euro, should be seen as a vindication of the decision to keep an independent monetary policy and a floating currency.

the value of the pound will not significantly alter the level of UK exports. A related concern is that many of the UK's main trading partners are major economies in the EU and so they are also in recession. An ability to cut the value of the pound will not have much effect on export growth if, due to an income effect, many buyers of exports cut back.

The other consideration is to note that monetary sovereignty focuses upon the benefits to be gained from having independent control over the nominal exchange rate. While adjusting the real exchange rate through lower rates of inflation is not easy, it is still a policy option open to economies within the Eurozone seeking to gain international competitiveness.

15.8 Business application: hedging

The value of currencies changes every minute. Over a month, or indeed a year, the value of a currency can change enormously. This represents an exchange rate risk to exporters and importers and, as discussed in Box 15.5, can have important implications for a company's profits. To provide a numerical example, a UK company might agree to buy steel from a French company over the next year. The price of the steel is agreed and fixed at the beginning of the contract in euros, say €1000 per ton. If, at the beginning of the contract, €1 is worth £0.66, the company is paying £666 per ton. However, if over the year the euro becomes stronger and is worth £0.80, then the price of the steel increases to £800 per ton. The euro price of the steel has

---

 ## Box 15.5 US company earnings hit by FX turbulence

Adapted from an article by Anuj Gangahar in The Financial Times, *4 February 2009*

US companies increasingly cite currency fluctuations among the reasons for slumping sales and profits as volatile foreign exchange markets hit corporate America with fourth-quarter earnings season in full swing.

In recent years, US businesses have become steadily more exposed to foreign exchange risk as they draw more business from beyond America. Standard & Poor's estimates that companies in the benchmark S&P 500 index made almost 50 per cent of their sales outside the US by the end of 2007, up from 30 per cent in 2001.

The list of companies that have reported the pinch of currency risk in recent weeks is long and distinguished:

◆ **Procter & Gamble**, often thought of as a recession-resistant company, cut its full-year profit forecast last week as unfavourable foreign exchange movements reduced net sales by 5 per cent and the dollar appreciated versus the euro, sterling and Canadian dollar.
◆ **Mattel**'s fourth-quarter net sales were down by 11 per cent from last year and included an unfavourable impact from changes in currency exchange rates of 5 percentage points.
◆ **Starbucks**' international total net revenues fell by 8 per cent compared with the same period last year, primarily as a result of the stronger dollar relative to sterling and the Canadian dollar.
◆ **McDonald's**, **Kimberly-Clark** and **Wal-Mart** also lowered earnings guidance in December because of currency fluctuations.

As a result of this greater impact of currency swings, companies are starting to put greater emphasis on trying to hedge their foreign exchange exposure, according to a recent survey from JPMorgan. US companies estimated that 42 per cent of their forecast foreign income was hedged in December, up from less than 7 per cent in April, the survey of clients found. A variety of instruments, including simple forward contracts, are used to hedge currency risk. Other instruments are futures, options and collars – a protective options strategy. The JPMorgan survey also estimated that G7 currencies would fluctuate by an annualized 20 per cent this quarter, double the average since 2000, emphasizing the growing need to hedge against potentially adverse currency movements.

However, even those that have actively hedged in the past may have been caught out recently. 'There have always been active hedgers and most companies have at least had an awareness of this,' said George Nunn, head of foreign exchange and rates structuring for the Americas at BNP Paribas. 'In terms of risk management, the typical process is for companies to estimate future revenues and decide on the basis of that estimate how much they will hedge.' Because the recession meant that, in most cases, revenues had been overestimated, Mr Nunn said, many companies found that they were overhedged 'and so are being forced to unwind trades'.

The process of corporate deleveraging was still not over, he said, and unwinding some of the overhedging was part of that process. 'Company earnings are clearly going to get hurt as a result of this, alongside other factors,' Mr Nunn added.

Table 15.4 Spot and forward exchange rates for pound sterling

Currency	Spot price	One month	One year	% change
US dollar	1.4637	1.4543	1.4546	0.62

Source: Bank of England, February 2009

> **Hedging** is the transfer of a risky asset for a non-risky asset.

not changed, but the change in the exchange rate makes the steel more expensive in pounds. So how do you protect yourself against such risks? The answer is you **hedge**.

In the forex market there is ample opportunity to hedge. In Table 15.4, we have the various forward exchange rates for the pound against the US dollar. The exchange rate is known as the spot price. This is the exchange rate now, i.e. the exchange rate that you might get 'on the spot'. The next set of columns list the forward prices. These are the exchange rates at which people are willing to sell a currency at one month, three months or one year into the future. The spot price is $1.4637 per £1; but the one-year forward price is $1.4546 per £1, or 0.62 per cent less. This difference reflects expectations about how the currency will move over the next year and a reward for taking the risk of agreeing to sell at an agreed price in the future.

Our steel importer can now hedge its exchange rate risk. Rather than face the risk of the pound falling against the euro, it can agree in the financial markets a rate for the next month, the month after, and even for one year into the future. Its future payments then become less risky; it has hedged the currency risk.

Speculation

We have argued that businesses might seek to reduce risk by hedging exchange rate movements. It is also the business of some individuals and companies to make money out of hedging. They do this by speculating that the forward price is wrong. For example, if the one-month forward price for converting pounds into US dollars is £1 = $1.5, but you think that in one month the spot price will fall to £1 = $1, then you can potentially make a very large profit.

Consider the following scenarios. A company goes to the bank and borrows £1 million. It then converts this into US dollars at the spot price of £1 = $1.5. The company now has $1.5 million. Assume that the one-month forward price for converting pounds into dollars is also £1 = $1.5 and the company also buys the forward rate.

What happens if the forward rate is correct?

If the forward rate is correct, then the spot price at the end of the month is also £1 = $1.5. The company can enter into the following (and profitless exercise): change its $1.5 million into £1 million and use the forward contract to change its £1 million into $1.5 million. It is no better off.

What happens if the forward rate is wrong?

If, after one month, the spot price has fallen to £1 = $1, then the company can take its $1.5 million and convert it into £1.5 million. It can then pay off its £1 million loan and it still has £0.5 million left. It then uses the forward contract to further increase its investment returns by converting the remaining £0.5 million into $0.75 million. It started owing £1 million and ended up with $0.75 million cash in the bank! Before you go out and borrow lots of money and try this strategy for yourself, remember it is high risk. The spot price could just as easily move in the other direction and then you would end up owing more than you initially borrowed.

Summary

1 The foreign exchange market is where currencies are traded.

2 In a floating exchange rate, the value of the currency reflects changes in the supply and demand of the currency. When demand increases, the currency appreciates in value; when demand falls, the currency falls in value.

3 Under purchasing power parity, the price of goods in one economy is the same as the price of goods in another economy when converted into the same currency.

4 In the long run, a floating exchange rate will adjust to ensure purchasing power parity holds.

5 Under a fixed exchange rate regime, the government commits to managing the value of a currency at a set price. If the market shows signs of wishing to move above the fixed price, the government supplies more currency to the market. In contrast, if the market shows signs of wishing to move below the set price, the government supports the currency by increasing demand for the currency.

6 Fixed exchange rates do not ensure purchasing power parity and in the long run the prospect of devaluation can lead to speculative attack.

7 Most major currencies – such as the pound, the US dollar and the euro – float. Some minor economies fix their exchange rate to the dollar; Argentina is an example.

8 When considering the virtues of fixed and floating exchange rates, it is sensible to consider volatility, robustness and financial discipline.

9 Floating exchange rates are more volatile than fixed exchange rates. But the prospect of speculative attacks and devaluations can make fixed rates a source of wider economic uncertainty and volatility.

10 Floating exchange rates allow economies to adapt to external changes such as inflationary differences. Fixed exchange rates require economies to be highly integrated as they cannot accommodate change within the fixed rate.

11 Because fixed exchange rates are inflexible, they are seen as promoting financial discipline and the pursuit of low inflation.

12 The balance of payments records the transactions undertaken by a country with the rest of the world. It has three main accounts: the current account, the capital account and the financial account. The current account measures the trade of goods and services. The capital account measures the flow of transfer payments, such as UK government payments to the EU Commission. The financial account measures the investment flows.

13 Under a floating exchange rate, the balance of payments balances. The equilibrium market price of the currency means that the demand and supply of the currency that stems from the transactions recorded in the current, capital and financial accounts must balance. Under a fixed exchange rate, equilibrium in the forex market is only achieved by the government intervening. Therefore, for the balance of payments to balance, the level of intervention has to be included. This is called official financing, and it simply measures the use of the foreign currency reserves.

14 Monetary policy is more powerful than fiscal policy under a floating exchange rate system. Fiscal policy is more powerful than monetary policy under a fixed exchange rate system.

15 European monetary union is a fixed exchange rate system between all member countries: 1 euro in Germany is worth 1 euro in Italy. However, the euro floats against all other national currencies, such as the pound and the US dollar.

16 The success of the euro depends upon whether its member economies represent an optimal currency zone. For such a zone to exist, trade between members has to be high, the economies need to respond to external economic shocks in a similar way, and price flexibility or factor mobility has to be high. In essence, economies have to be either highly integrated and synchronized or capable of quickly adapting to differences through price changes.

17 The Eurozone is reasonably integrated and as the system progresses it is likely to become more synchronized. The use of a single interest rate policy from the European Central Bank and the control of fiscal expenditure through the criteria set down in the stability pact should force economies to cut internal levels of inflation and synchronize their business cycles.

18 By fixing the nominal exchange rate between member economies of the euro, international competitiveness is strongly linked to the cost and productivity of factor inputs. Eurozone economies with low labour costs and high productivity growth rates should attract increased attention from businesses seeking to enhance their cost-effectiveness.

19 Currency markets and the volatility within them represent business opportunities for speculators. Firms that do not like risk will try to hedge currency risk by purchasing forward rates, which guarantee the exchange rate in one month, three months or one year. Speculators, in contrast, will seek to buy forward when they expect the forward and spot rates to be different.

Learning checklist

You should now be able to:

- Explain how fixed exchange rates work
- Evaluate fixed versus floating exchange rates
- Explain the power of fiscal and monetary policy under fixed and floating exchange rate regimes
- Explain the features of an optimal currency zone
- Understand the importance of China's saving rate in the development of macroeconomic conditions around the world
- Explain hedging and how firms might use hedging within forex markets

Questions   connect™

1 What are fixed and floating exchange rate systems?

2 Use a diagram to illustrate how a fixed exchange rate can be maintained when the foreign exchange market price is moving above and also below the fixed priced.

3 What is a devaluation, and why might a speculative attack foretell a devaluation?

4 The price of computers in countries A and B is identical in year one. Throughout year two, inflation is higher in country B. What do you expect to happen to the exchange rate between countries A and B throughout year two?

5   What is the real exchange rate and why is it better than the nominal exchange rate at measuring international competitiveness?

6   Explain the concept of perfect capital mobility.

7   How does perfect capital mobility limit monetary policy under a fixed exchange rate regime?

8   What is an optimal currency zone? Do you consider the EU to be one?

9   Identify and explain the main accounts within the balance of payments.

10   If a country is running a trade deficit with the rest of the world, which account is in deficit?

11   Assess whether it is a problem to run a trade deficit or a trade surplus.

12   Explain how a company can manage the financial risk associated with exchange rate volatility.

13   A country has a current account surplus of £6 billion, but a financial account deficit of £4 billion:
   (a) Is the exchange rate system fixed or floating?
   (b) Is its balance of payments in deficit or surplus?
   (c) Are its foreign exchange reserves rising or falling?
   (d) Is the central bank buying or selling domestic currency?
   Explain.

14   Under fixed and floating exchange rates, which type of policy is most effective, fiscal or monetary? Why does the Eurozone have one interest rate, set by the European Central Bank?

15   Should the UK be a member of the euro?

Exercises

1   True or false?
   (a) The US dollar is a floating currency.
   (b) The Chinese yuan is a managed float.
   (c) A rise in the real exchange rate reduces the competitiveness of the domestic economy.
   (d) After converting into euros, the price of Chanel perfume in Singapore is the same as in Schiphol airport; this is an example of purchasing power parity.
   (e) If the current account is in surplus and the balance of payments is not zero, then a floating exchange rate regime is in existence.
   (f) Monetary policy is more effective under a floating exchange rate.

2   Figure 15.10 shows the position in the foreign exchange market: DD is the demand schedule for sterling and SS the supply schedule. Assume a two-country world (the UK and the Eurozone):
   (a) Explain briefly how the two schedules arise.
   (b) Identify the exchange rate that would prevail under a clean float. What would be the state of the overall balance of payments at this exchange rate?
   (c) Suppose the exchange rate were set at OA under a fixed exchange rate regime. What intervention would be required by the central bank? What would be the state of the balance of payments?
   (d) Suppose the exchange rate was set at OC. Identify the situation of the balance of payments and the necessary central bank intervention.

(e) If the authorities wished to maintain the exchange rate at OC in the long run, what sorts of measures would be required?

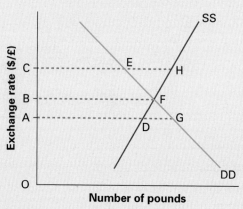

Figure 15.10 The foreign exchange market

3 Refer to Box 15.5 when considering the following questions:
   (a) What is hedging and how might firms benefit from it?
   (b) Explain what is meant by 'over-hedging'.
   (c) If Mattell buys in Chinese yuan and sells in US dollars, what currency risks has it faced recently?

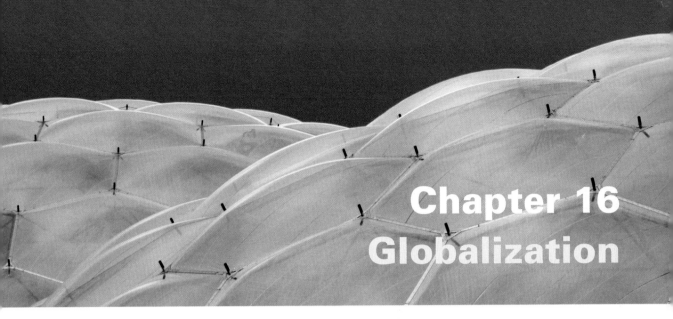

Chapter 16
Globalization

Chapter contents

 Learning outcomes

By the end of this chapter you should understand:

Economic Theory

LO1 The cultural, political and economic drivers of globalization

LO2 The concept of comparative advantage

LO3 The use of tariffs and quotas

LO4 How to assess the rise in international trade

LO5 The reasons behind the rise and fall in foreign direct investment

Business Application

LO6 Understanding the impediments to an exploitation of comparative advantage

LO7 Understanding the sources of international competitiveness in the IT sector

Globalization at a glance

The issues

The world economy is becoming increasingly integrated, with more and more products being sold across national boundaries and firms operating in more than one economy. The issues for business are numerous, but include: why is globalization happening; what opportunities does it present; and what threats might develop from globalization?

The understanding

The increase in cross-border trade and the number of firms operating in more than one country can be related to a number of issues. In recent times, barriers to international trade, such as tariffs, have fallen. The World Trade Organization has played an important role, but so has the development of trade blocs, such as the EU. Falling transportation costs and developments in communications technology have also made international trade and international operations more feasible. But this only explains why trade is easier. Why trade occurs is related to an important economic concept known as 'comparative advantage'.

The usefulness

In understanding why globalization is occurring and where it is occurring, business can begin to understand where opportunities in the global economy exist for the enhancement of costs and revenues. Similarly, as globalization is a double-edged sword, an understanding of the implications of globalization will help to highlight where threats of increased competition are likely to come from in a global economy.

16.1 Business problem: how do we take advantage of the global economy?

The world has changed. As little as 20 years ago, taking a holiday in Spain was common, but taking a holiday in the Caribbean, the Far East or even Australia was something very different. Now backpacking around the world by students, and the retired, is reasonably common. Given this trend in travel, it is of no surprise that one airline alliance decided to call itself 'One World'. Perhaps part of the mystique associated with international travel was the inaccessibility of the traveller. Communications back home generally took the form of a postcard, which invariably arrived home after the traveller. In recent years, improvements in the integration of telecommunications networks has allowed mobile phones to work almost anywhere. Text messages, video messages and voice calls mean that someone on holiday in Thailand is just as accessible as someone on the other side of town.

World travellers and international telecommunications are not the only changing features of the world. Once you are abroad, there are now many commonalities. For example, have you ever been abroad and failed to find a McDonald's or a Starbucks? This relentless march of global brands has its benefits. You can walk into a McDonald's anywhere and know what you are going to receive. The brand provides comfort and certainty in its continued deliverance of a Big Mac and fries. But the power of the global brand can be felt just as much at home as it can overseas. Take a quick look at yourself. Is there a Nokia phone in your pocket, a pair of Nike trainers on your feet and a pair of Levis on your bum? There is a reasonable chance that you have one of these, or at least something similar.

What does all this mean for business? Globalization provides opportunities and threats for business. The willingness of consumers in faraway markets to consume international products, such as Big Macs, provides opportunities for McDonald's to grow. But at the same time, by operating overseas, McDonald's gains potential access to cheaper labour, raw materials and finance. In contrast, noodle shops in Hong Kong and fish and chip shops in the UK now face international competition from the likes of McDonald's. The fast-food market is a clear and tangible example of globalization and increased competition. But the influences of globalization are far-reaching. Speak to almost any businessperson and they will recognize the importance of globalization. Read any business paper or magazine and you will find an article on globalization. Businesses are actively seeking out cost advantages by using the global market to source labour, finance or raw materials. They are then using these advantages to increase the presence of their brands around the world.

In this chapter we will examine the economic rationale behind globalization and highlight some of its main drivers in recent times. An examination of global products and operations, and global labour and financial markets, will provide an understanding of this important trend in the modern business environment.

16.2 Why is the global economy developing?

There are many potential drivers of globalization, ranging from the economic, through the political to the cultural. In this section, we will examine each in turn in an attempt to provide a working knowledge of globalization and the future developments for business.

Culture

The process of globalization must to some extent be facilitated by a convergence of cultures. For example, St Patrick's Day is a celebration of the patron saint of Ireland. Yet the day itself is now celebrated by many other nationalities the world over. Admittedly, many of the Irish have at some point emigrated to other parts of the world, but this does not explain the extent to which other cultures are willing to assume the St Patrick's Day celebrations.

Anthony Giddens, a leading sociological writer on globalization, has argued that globalization is the cultural suspension of space and time. If space is a cultural reference point for geography and national identity, the willingness of many other cultures to celebrate St Patrick's Day surely reflects a suspension of cultural space. Individuals from the UK, Australia and the US, in celebrating the Irish patron saint's day, are suspending, in part, their cultural attachment to their own national culture.

If national cultural identity was important in the past, what is leading to a suspension of time and space under globalization? Some of the answers to this question lack any firm empirical support, but they do seem plausible.

Travel

Increased international travel promotes an acceptance of other cultures. Travel facilitates experimentation with different types of food, language and customs. The old adage of 'when in Rome act like a Roman' can be an enlightening and enjoyable experience for many travellers. When they then return home, they periodically like to consume products from these distant places.

Film and media

Hollywood and the American entertainment industry are successful industries. They produce films, TV sit-coms and a variety of music that are enjoyed not only by Americans but also by many people around the world. The portrayal of American lifestyles, the types of cars driven, the use of coffee shops, the consumption of burgers, pizzas, doughnuts and soft drinks, and the belief that opportunity exists for everyone, can all be viewed and absorbed while watching such movies or TV programmes. So, if viewers around the world enjoy watching American culture, then perhaps they will also enjoy partaking in, or consuming, American culture? If this is true, then American media are an important facilitator for US companies selling their brands around the globe.

Technology and communications

The ability to communicate with anyone, at any time, anywhere in the world increases the perception of a global village, as opposed to a large fragmented global system. Financial centres in Tokyo, London and New York probably helped to develop the first impressions of a continuous, integrated global financial system. In recent times, global news providers, such as the BBC, Sky and CNN, have developed formats built around the 24-hour clock, with the news rooms moving between continents as the sun and daylight move around the world. This, in the terminology of Giddens, enables individuals to suspend time and space. A suspension of space is evident by the view that the global economy is everywhere, not somewhere. Similarly, time is a human concept, which slices up the day. But time is continuous; it has no beginning and no end. The continuous, ever-rolling nature of 24-hour news, financial centres and global business provides the opportunity for individuals, wherever they are in the world, to suspend time. It does not matter if it is midnight here, somewhere in the world it is 10.00am and, therefore, someone is making news and someone is making a profit. The global person and the global business are not constrained by time or space.

While telecommunications and the media have made the world feel smaller, transport technologies have made the movement of people and products more affordable. Jumbo jets make the transport of individuals between continents cheap, fast and reliable. Similarly, the invention of the container vessel in the 1960s, carrying many steel box containers with various cargoes, meant that one ship could exploit economies of scale, whereas previously a single exporter with a small cargo would have had to hire a small ship to transport their product around the world. Furthermore, the development of land-based infrastructure such as deep-sea ports, motorways and rail networks has helped to make the movement of goods around the world and overland much more feasible and affordable. Such have been the improvements, that estimates by the World Bank suggest that transport costs are now 80 per cent less than a century ago.

Culture and politics are facilitators of globalization. They enable firms and consumers to buy, sell and even produce on a global basis. But there has to be a motive for firms and consumers to act globally. Why do they wish to take advantage of a political freedom to act internationally and satisfy the global appetite of consumers?

Economic rationales

The **law of comparative advantage** states that economies should specialize in the good that they are *comparatively* better at making.

The economic answer begins with an analysis of what is known as the **law of comparative advantage**.

The key word is *comparative*. We can highlight its importance with the following example. In Table 16.1, we have the required hours to produce one car or one TV. In the EU, it takes 30 hours to make a car and five hours to make a TV. The EU is more productive than the UK in the case of cars and TVs. If we had said that each economy should specialize in what it is good at, the UK would make nothing and the EU would make everything. This is not a good idea because the UK could make something and add to world output. This is why we employed the word 'comparative'.

Table 16.1 Output and opportunity costs

		Hours to make one unit	Opportunity cost
EU	Cars	30	6 TVs
	TVs	5	1/6 car
UK	Cars	60	10 TVs
	TVs	6	1/10 car

In the last column of Table 16.1, we have the opportunity cost. In this case, the opportunity cost is how many cars (TVs) have to be given up in order to produce one more TV (car). In the case of the EU, if workers were transferred from TVs to cars, then the cost of making one more car is the loss of six extra TVs.

We can now compare the relative cost of providing cars and TVs in the EU and the UK. The EU can produce cars more cheaply than the UK. The EU only sacrifices six TVs for each extra car; the UK has to sacrifice ten TVs. In the case of TVs, the EU has to sacrifice one-sixth of a car for each extra TV, but the UK only has to sacrifice one-tenth of a car for each extra TV. The UK can produce TVs more cheaply than the EU. We can now say that the EU has a comparative advantage in car production and the UK has a comparative advantage in TV production. Therefore, if the EU specializes in cars and the UK in TVs, total output will be greater than if both were to try to produce cars and TVs for themselves. For example, if the UK gives up six cars and produces 60 extra TVs, the EU can make the extra six cars by giving up only 36 TVs, providing a net addition of 24 TVs. Similarly, if the EU makes ten more cars and gives up 60 TVs, the UK makes these extra TVs for the loss of only six cars, thus providing the world with four extra cars.

Terms of trade ✓

While trade between the EU and the UK will lead to higher output, it needs to be profitable for trade to actually occur. Since the EU is comparatively better at producing cars, it will be an exporter of cars, or it will provide an international supply of cars. This is illustrated in Figure 16.1 with the upward-sloping supply curve. If the EU did not trade with the rest of the world, the price of cars (in TVs) would be 6. Once the international price of cars begins to rise above 6, the EU is willing to supply an additional amount of cars, or effectively increase its export of cars.

In contrast, the UK has a comparative disadvantage in the production of cars. If it did not trade with the rest of the world, the price of a car in the UK would be 10 (TVs). However, if the international price for cars is less than 10, the UK would increase its willingness to demand cars. In effect, the UK would be importing cars. Since the EU is willing to export at prices above 6 TVs and the UK is willing to demand at prices below 10 TVs, there must be an equilibrium international price for cars, which in Figure 16.1 is P_{car}. The actual value for P_{car} will depend upon the elasticities of supply and demand for cars in the international market.

We could draw a similar figure for TVs, but this time the UK would be exporting and the EU importing. Again, the equilibrium price for TVs would lie between the opportunity cost of TVs in the UK and the EU, at a price of P_{TV}.

A country's terms of trade measure the price ratio of exports to imports; in this case, the UK's terms of trade would be the ratio P_{TV}/P_{car}. More generally, it is a weighted average of a country's export prices to its import prices, $P_{exports}/P_{imports}$.

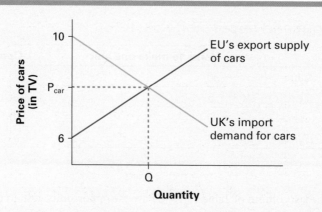

Figure 16.1 **International trade of cars expressed as the opportunity cost of making TVs**

If a country's terms of trade improve, then the price of its exports is rising relative to the price of its imports. It has to export less in order to fund its imports. This can happen if either the exchange rate changes or the equilibrium price for exports or imports changes.

In the case of the UK, the terms of trade are illustrated in Figure 16.2 Over the period 1980 through to 2007, the terms of trade have been improving, with a steady rise in the ratio of export to import prices. This has very important economic implications for an open economy, such as the UK, where imports and exports are equal to 60 per cent of GDP. As the terms of trade improve, then the purchasing power of UK GDP increases. Exports earn a greater income for the UK and imports cost the UK economy relatively less. Therefore, an improvement in the terms of trade leads to an improvement in the value of GDP. Economists measure this using **command GDP**.

The fundamental importance of comparative advantage ✓

Comparative advantage and the gains from trade are very powerful arguments and have provided many governments with a rationale for freer international trade. However, it must be remembered that comparative advantage is not simply an international matter. The decision-making and behaviour of many ordinary individuals conforms to comparative advantage. Families increasingly take their children to daycare centres rather than one parent leaving paid employment. Why? Because the daycare centre, when looking after many children, can exploit economies of scale which the single family cannot. The daycare centre has a comparative advantage in the care of children. With cheaper daycare, the opportunity cost of going to work is now less than the opportunity cost of staying at home and looking after the children. Similarly, why do some people specialize as decorators, doctors, academics or bank managers? Because they have a comparative advantage in their chosen vocation. Painting a wall is fairly straightforward, but in taking the time to do this, an academic, doctor or bank manager has to give up some possibly very lucrative fee-paying work or a large amount of free time. It is, therefore, more efficient to employ a decorator who is a specialist and can do the job much more quickly.

The overriding message is that comparative advantage applies to all of us. The notion of comparative advantage and international trade is nothing more than an extension of these

Gross domestic product (GDP) measures the volume of goods and services produced by a nation. By adjusting this measure to reflect movements in the terms of trade, **command GDP** describes the purchasing power of a nation's output.

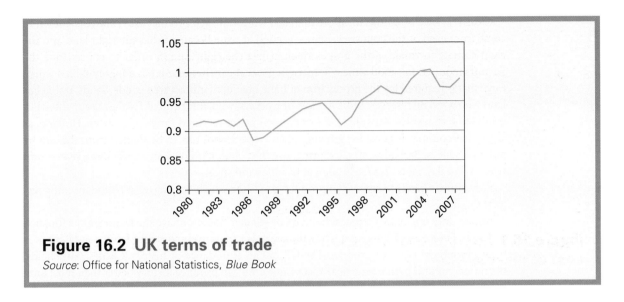

Figure 16.2 UK terms of trade

Source: Office for National Statistics, *Blue Book*

ideas, but crucially it is being argued that factor inputs, such as labour and capital, should be employed where they have a comparative advantage. As such, we should not look at the individual, as in the case of a decorator or doctor; nor should we look at an individual economy, such as the UK. Rather, we should be looking at the global economy and seeking ways to enable resources to be allocated to their most productive ends across the globe. In this way, globalization is a natural consequence of comparative advantage. Economies do not seek to produce all the products that they need. Instead, they produce what they are comparatively good at and then trade it for products in the global economy that they are not good at making. In this way, globalization is simply like the doctor hiring a decorator to paint their house; and a decorator hiring a doctor to cure their illness. But what are the sources of comparative advantage?

Factor abundance ✓

Think of a country and then consider what products it is famous for. Table 16.2 contains some obvious examples.

Table 16.2 Countries and their exports

Country	Product
France	Wine
Germany	Cars
Saudi Arabia	Oil
Canada	Wheat
India	Textiles
Holland	Plants
Australia	Sheep
Barbados	Holidays

Clearly, France is famous for more than just wine, but each product listed above is known to come from each of the countries. France is good at wine because it has the right land and the right climate for making the grapes ripen at just the right rate in order to concentrate the flavours required for good wine. Germany is good at cars because it has a highly skilled work-force that is required for the production of high-quality manufactured goods. Saudi Arabia has land with good oil reserves. India has lots of workers, who are required for the labour-intensive production of textiles. Australia has lots of open places required for grazing sheep. Holland, as a very flat country, is good for growing plants that do not like to be shaded from the sun by hills and valleys. Barbados, situated just above the equator, is excellent at providing year-round tropical holidays; it is also fairly good at bananas and sugar.

Economies, therefore, appear to produce goods for which they have an abundance of a key factor input.

Britain does not export tropical holidays or wine. It does not have the factor inputs for such products. France and Barbados do. It is, therefore, comparatively cheap for France and Barbados to produce these types of product. The UK has an abundance of history. Castles, battlefields, the monarchy and parliament all attract visitors. We can produce history better than most and, in exchange, France provides us with wine, India with textiles, Australia with sheep and Barbados with tropical holidays.

Comparative advantage is clearly linked to the endowment of resources within an economy.

Two-way trade

There is a key flaw with the argument that international trade is based on comparative advantage and factor abundance. Many countries trade the same product. For example, the UK sells cars to Germany in the form of Jaguars, Minis and Toyotas. Germany exports cars to the UK in the form of BMWs, VWs and Mercedes. The UK also exports more cheese than it imports. We refer to this as *intra-industry trade*.

It took economists many years to formally model and explain intra-industry trade. But finally, in 1979, the Nobel Laureate Paul Krugman developed a model of trade which recognized the importance of consumer tastes and economies of scale. Krugman's first observation was that consumers appreciate diversity. The availability of choices matters to customers with tastes for differentiated products. In such a world, markets are characterized by segments and niches. Producing exclusively for the domestic market may not enable a firm to achieve economies of scale. But if a firm has the option to trade internationally, then it can access more consumers who share a taste and preference for its particular brand. International trade, then, enables larger volumes and the attainment of minimum efficient scale. So, importantly, international trade can lead to lower cost production and increased variety.

Trade restrictions

Despite the accepted benefits of comparative advantage, international trade has in the past been impeded by various governments around the world.

A problem with comparative advantage is that it raises economic output for the world. But this does not mean it improves economic prosperity for all individuals.

For example, in trading with the EU, if the UK decided to abandon car production and specialize in TV production, workers in the car industry would become unemployed and there is no reason to suggest that they will be happy making TVs. So, in this case, UK car-makers do not find comparative advantage particularly attractive.

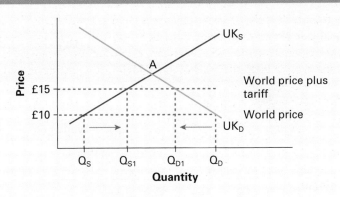

Figure 16.3 Imposition of a tariff

A tariff makes imports more expensive. Domestic supply increases and the demand for imports ($Q_{D1} - Q_{S1}$) decreases.

However, uncompetitive industries do not have to simply roll over and die. If the industry has political influence, perhaps stemming from the number of voters that they potentially employ, then the government can be asked to provide so-called **protectionist measures**.

Tariffs are examples of trade protection. A tariff is a tax on imports and, therefore, raises the price of imports.

> **Protectionist measures** seek to lower the competitiveness of international rivals.

For a more in-depth example of tariffs, we can examine Figure 16.3. Without imports for this good, UK supply and UK demand would form an equilibrium at A. However, the world price for this product is much lower, at £10. UK supply at £10 is only Q_S and UK demand is much greater at Q_D. This excess of UK demand over UK supply is met by imports. If the government imposes an import tariff of £5, then the world price effectively rises to £16. UK firms now raise supply from Q_S to Q_{S1}. But because the product now costs more, UK demand falls from Q_D to Q_{D1}. The level of excess demand is now much less and as a consequence the level of imports falls.

In the face of tariffs, imports fall and domestic supply increases. When tariffs are removed, international competition leads to a reduction in domestic supply and an increase in imports.

The case for tariffs is limited. They are a form of government intervention that simply supports inefficient domestic producers. Furthermore, tariffs in the main support domestic producers, and not domestic consumers. UK consumers under a tariff have to pay more for the good, via a tax to government, than they would if no tariff existed.

An alternative form of support for domestic producers could take the form of a *subsidy*. This is illustrated in Figure 16.4. A subsidy makes production cheaper for the domestic industry. The industry is more willing to supply and the supply curve shifts to the right. The domestic consumer pays the international price for the product, but a reduction in imports is brought about by the increase in domestic supply.

However, there is a question regarding how the government will fund the subsidy. Governments finance themselves principally through taxation. So increased domestic subsidies must lead to higher taxes. However, while a tariff is a tax paid by the consumer buying the product, a subsidy can be funded by taxing everyone. Funding a subsidy via increased taxation spreads the burden of supporting the domestic industry. But why should some people support an industry that they perhaps do not buy products from?

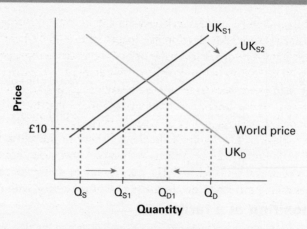

Figure 16.4 The effect of a subsidy

A subsidy makes domestic production cheaper. Domestic producers are willing to supply more and the supply curve shifts to the right from UK_{S1} to UK_{S2}. Domestic supply at the world price of £10 then increases from Q_S to Q_{S1}; imports $(Q_D - Q_{S1})$ shrink by the same amount.

Non-tariff barriers ✓

Governments can restrict trade in other ways.

A **quota** restricts trade by limiting the amount of a product that can be imported into a country. For example, a steel quota might limit the importation of steel to 200 million tons a year. Since quotas restrict international supply, then the price in the domestic market must increase.

> A **quota** has the same effect as a tariff. It makes goods more expensive for consumers and it raises the profits of inefficient domestic firms.

Those foreign firms that also manage to gain part of the quota can also sell inside the UK at the higher price. Under a tariff, domestic consumers pay a tax to government. Under a quota, some of the price increase leaks out of the economy to foreign firms.

Other methods include the application of standards. The EU is infamous for asserting that a banana must show a certain curve to its overall shape. The cynical view is that bananas from certain parts of the world are not 'curvy' enough. The EU can then proudly claim to reduce trade barriers on bananas. Those that are not curvy enough are not bananas, so the trade barrier still exists. Red tape required for import licences, driving on the left-hand side of the road, and an outright ban on British beef even after the BSE scare vanished – all can be viewed as means of restricting international trade.

Reasons for protecting trade

While the protection of domestic industries from international competition appears to be very contentious, a number of arguments are still put forward for creating barriers to trade.

Defence or national interest

Governments may wish to support an industry that has strategic value. Steel is very important to the UK economy and the government would not wish to see the economy dependent upon another economy for steel, the fear being that at some point in the future we manage to fall out with the steel supplier and our access to steel is terminated. But why not provide incentives for the steel producers to become more efficient, rather than pricing international competition out of the domestic market with tariffs?

Infant industry

Sometimes an industry might seek government protection. During the period of protection, the industry is expected to develop its capabilities to a level where it is able to compete internationally. But if a company is capable of making profits at some point in the future, then why does the capital market fail to provide it with funds? Is it the case, perhaps, that the industry is incapable of ever becoming internationally competitive? Domestic wages, the price of raw materials or the level of technology may mean that the industry will never catch up. Furthermore, during the five years that it might take to develop the industry, what are the international competitors going to be doing? They are unlikely to be doing nothing. Instead, they will be looking to develop their competitive advantage, through improvements in production and operating efficiency. The case for infant industries can become continual, with industries asking for extensions to the period of protection with no real hope of protection ever being withdrawn.

Way of life

The UK and perhaps even France place an economic value on the attractiveness of the countryside. If French and UK farmers are internationally uncompetitive, then, over time, they will stop farming. This *could* lead to a reduction in the management of the countryside. If true, then it might be desirable to think about protecting farmers from international competition. In so doing, trade protection also protects society from the loss of a positive externality, a well-managed countryside. This argument is sometimes used in support of the Common Agricultural Policy.

Politics

A main driver of globalization has been the merging of political and economic views on international trade. We have seen that economists are keen to promote the idea of international trade based on comparative advantage. Economists also find it hard to support trade restrictions: first, because trade restrictions prevent comparative advantage and, second, because tariffs and quotas support inefficient domestic producers at the expense of consumers, or taxpayers. Politicians have now also recognized the economic arguments against trade restrictions.

International institutions

This recognition of the importance of international trade can be traced back to the end of the Second World War, when political leaders of the time decided that stability in the world would be enhanced by greater political and economic integration. As a result, a number of supranational institutions were set up, for example the United Nations, the World Bank and the World Trade Organization (WTO, formerly known as the General Agreement on Tariffs and Trade – GATT).

GATT, formed in 1947, was an international institution that brought countries together to negotiate reductions in tariffs. Various rounds of negotiation were held and each round lasted many years. The Tokyo Round began in 1973 and ended in 1979, with an average tariff reduction of 33 per cent. The Uruguay Round began in 1986 and ended in 1993. While this again reduced tariffs, the round also agreed the creation of the World Trade Organization. While GATT was a place for countries to come together and discuss trade barriers and disputes, the WTO is an organization with power. Countries can now ask the WTO to rule on trade disputes and even impose fines on countries that fail to uphold international trade.

Trade blocs ✓

> A **trade bloc** is a region or group of countries that have agreed to remove all trade barriers among themselves.

In 1965, the Treaty of Rome led to the development of what is now known as the European Union. As an area of free trade between member nations, it can be described as a **trade bloc**.

Aside from the EU, there is also, for example, the North American Free Trade Area (NAFTA), a trade bloc promoting trade between the US, Canada and Mexico; while in South East Asia there is ASEAN, the Association of South East Asian Nations.

The importance of political institutions, such as the UN, and trade blocs, such as the EU, is that politicians increasingly recognize the economic importance of international trade and economic integration. Without international competition, domestic producers might not seek to innovate, drive down costs and keep prices low. Without access to international markets, domestic companies might not gain access to the cheapest, or most productive, factor inputs. These arguments are extremely persuasive, as evidenced by the continued success of the EU and the eagerness of other countries to join it. However, the balance of power between regional trade blocs and true internationally free trade engendered by the WTO is beginning to shift. Box 16.1 highlights how economies could retreat from globalization into regionalization unless the Doha round is successful.

 Box 16.1 Doha round hopes dashed by acrimony

Adapted from an article by Chris Giles in The Financial Times, *2 February 2009*

The completion of the Doha trade round, started in 2001, appeared as far away as ever at the weekend, when a gathering of trade ministers at the World Economic Forum in Davos descended into acrimony. Normally, the closing session of the forum displays ritualistic expectation that the trade round will be completed in the coming year, but there was little such optimism in 2009.

Pascal Lamy, director-general of the World Trade Organization, insisted that countries were 80 per cent of the way to completing the deal, but would only say that the economic crisis 'made it both easier and more difficult to conclude the round': easier because the crisis underlined the importance of the round, but more difficult for countries to make concessions that might harm parts of their electorates.

Speaking earlier in Davos, Kamal Nath, the Indian trade minister, blamed the US election for stymieing negotiations last year and highlighted the difficulties he faced in sensitive areas such as rice. For India, he said, lives were at stake, while for the US the only issue was commerce.

All the trade ministers in Davos warned of a growing threat of protectionism. Celso Amorim, Brazil's foreign minister, said it was not just in isolated examples but also in measures around the world 'that fall within the form of ideology of economic nationalism'.

There was particular anger aimed at the US House of Representatives' decision to insert 'buy American' provisions into the fiscal stimulus package it passed. Mr Amorim thought these provisions infringed WTO rules, a position that was supported, although less vehemently, by Baroness Ashton, European trade commissioner and Doris Leuthard, Swiss trade minister.

This criticism led Howard Dean, former chairman of the Democratic National Committee, to warn from the floor: 'It will be very difficult to proceed in Doha unless we make progress on labour and environmental standards.'

His remarks provoked uproar from the trade ministers of developing countries, who insisted that trying to put labour and environmental standards back into the Doha round would re-open all the acrimony that led to the near-collapse of the negotiations in Cancún in 2003.

'If the US wanted to do something positive for the environment, eliminate tariffs on ethanol,' Mr Amorim said angrily, as Brazil has long campaigned against US restrictions on imports of Brazilian ethanol.

16.3 A closer look at the EU

The EU has its origins in the European Community which was established among six economies in 1957. These were West Germany, France, Italy, the Netherlands, Belgium and Luxembourg. By the 1990s, membership had expanded and included most of the economies of Western Europe. Finally, in 2004, EU enlargement added a further ten Eastern European economies, including the likes of Poland and the Slovak Republic. The EU now comprises 27 member countries.

Table 16.3 shows that the EU in terms of GDP and population is now comparable to the US. While China has a bigger population, economic growth has not yet caught up with the EU, US and Japan, but with three times as many individuals the potential to close the gap exists.

An important feature of the EU is the limited presence of internal trade barriers. Tariffs and quotas between member states have been abolished, leading to an increased movement of internal free trade. The creation of the euro facilitated further the ease with which trade could occur by removing the difficulty of price comparisons and the need to convert competing currencies.

Regulatory harmonization in labour markets, tax regimes and patent systems has eased the administrative burden faced by firms wishing to operate beyond their national boundary. Furthermore, financial deregulation, principally in banking and insurance, has ensured that companies licensed to operate in one member economy are free to operate throughout the EU. The intention is to reduce domestic oligopolies and increase cross-border competition. Many of these initiatives were associated with the creation of the single European market in 1992, where the EU market was envisaged to be free of national regulations, taxes or informal practices.

Benefits of the EU

The strength of the EU economy is arguably greater and deeper than the sum of its parts. This is because the size, scope and diversity of the member states leads to increased competition, the realization of economies of scale and the improved attainment of comparative advantage.

We have already argued that increased trade enables economies to specialize in the production of goods and services in which they have a comparative advantage. This allocation of scarce resources to the production of goods with the lowest opportunity cost raises the combined output of trading partners. With 27 member economies, the opportunities for pursuing comparative advantage are enormous, especially when such economies are geographically disperse, have differing factor endowments and are at differing stages of economic development.

Furthermore, a producer who is restricted to their domestic market may face an overall market size which is smaller than the minimum efficient scale in production. Access to larger international markets, in contrast, facilitates the attainment of scale economies, leading to reduced production costs and perhaps improved pricing for consumers.

Table 16.3 Comparing the EU, 2004

	EU	US	Japan	China
GDP (US$ billions)	11 560	13 890	4813	3121
Population (millions)	319	301	127	1320

Source: World Bank

Table 16.4 Consumption gains from the single market

Range of estimates (% of GDP)	Countries
2–3	France, Germany, Italy, UK
2–5	Denmark
3–4	The Netherlands, Spain
4–5	Belgium, Luxembourg
4–10	Ireland
5–16	Greece
19–20	Portugal

Source: C. Allen et al. (1998) The competition effects of the single market in Europe, *Economic Policy*, 27: 441–486

While natural scale economies may lead to the development of oligopolies in national economies, the removal of trade barriers leads to increased cross-border competition and a reduction in natural entry barriers. All of these can lead to increased levels of competition. This competition may generate lower prices, innovation in the pursuit of cost efficiencies and the development of new products. These are factors which can improve the economic performance of the EU economy.

There is evidence to support these economic arguments, at least in terms of increased consumption. Table 16.4 reports estimated gains for a number of member countries. The results indicate that smaller economies gained more than larger ones, and also that the largest gains came where the most protected industries were opened up to competition. The results reflected the consumption gains following a one-off permanent shift in aggregate supply. However, they fail to reflect any ongoing endogenous growth effect, where, for example, increased competition drives further innovation and economic growth.

A consequence of increased trade and competition has been the emerging corporate strategy of being a pan-European company. One simple manifestation of this is the swapping of Internet country designations such as www. . . . co.uk, co.fr and co.de, for the more regional designation of www. . . . eu. Coupled with this geographic rebranding exercise has been the growth of cross-border mergers, especially the fragmented industries of telecommunications, banking and energy, which until recently have been fairly immune from the effects of the single European market. Spain's Telefonica acquired the UK telecommunication company O2, creating the largest telecommunications company in the Western world, while Santander, a Spanish bank, has acquired a number of British banks.

Within the EU economy, super-large companies which can exploit economies of scale are likely to be the most competitive. As such, consolidation and horizontal merger is likely. The single market therefore brings with it benefits and risks. Trade, competition and consolidation bring cost reduction, but may place national economies at the mercy of super-regional companies. The perceived balance of these risks and benefits, coupled with national pride, is likely to dominate the development of corporate mergers and takeovers for some time to come.

Issues facing the EU

The Common Agricultural Policy (CAP) was until 2003 a system of subsidies which provided price support for agricultural produce. It has now been modified to become a system of direct income payments to farmers, thereby enabling farming to survive, but not creating a direct price distortion in the market for produce. The CAP represents €40 billion of expenditure, or 40 per cent of the EU's budget. France is the biggest recipient, receiving almost €9 billion, followed by Spain with €7 billion, Germany with €6 billion and the UK with €4 billion.

The CAP is strongly defended by the French, who view the French farming sector as a key aspect of their national identity. In particular, the reputation of French gastronomy rests on its ability to grow and create fine cheese, meat, vegetables and wine. In addition, the beauty of the French countryside is arguably protected by the continued presence of farmers.

There is strong opposition to the French. In particular, the UK has questioned the wisdom of the CAP. With agriculture representing less than 2 per cent of EU GDP, why does 40 per cent of the EU budget go to support this sector? Would it be more sensible to allocate a significant portion of the EU budget to education and science, thereby building knowledge capital and generating opportunities for further economic growth?

Outside the EU, world trade negotiations have stalled on the unwillingness of the EU to remove the CAP and its agricultural trade barriers to non-member countries. However, within this situation a subtlety exists. According to the World Bank, it would be more beneficial for world trade if the EU reduced external tariffs rather than dismantled the CAP. The reason is that the CAP reduces the price of agricultural products in the EU and beyond. Removing the CAP would make it more expensive for countries in Africa, the Middle East and elsewhere to import EU agriculture. However, removing trade tariffs would make it easier for such countries to export to the EU.

The issues surrounding the CAP are unlikely to be resolved in the near future, since in 2002 the EU agreed that no further changes to the CAP would occur before 2013, and the French appear keen to hold everyone to that agreement.

EU enlargement

The addition of ten new members in 2004 was the single biggest expansion of the EU. Bulgaria and Romania joined in 2007, while Croatia is awaiting final approval. Turkey is still signalling its eagerness to join. Enlarged membership brings benefits as well as problems. Each new country opens up yet more markets for member countries to compete in with no trade barriers. In the case of the new accession countries, enlargement also presents an ample supply of cheap yet reasonably skilled workers, offering manufacturing companies the opportunity to relocate and exploit cost savings. This has been illustrated most obviously by the automobile industry, with the likes of Volkswagen and Ford moving European production to the new member states.

The problems brought by these new member nations reflect their transition economy status, moving from communist state planning to free market economics. Privatization programmes, poor legal infrastructure, weak bank finances, plus a need to invest heavily in transport and communications infrastructure, education and health, mean that many of these new economies face a constraint on their growth. Longstanding EU members from Western Europe have recognized the need to divert development spending into the new member states. But change will take time and will also come at the expense of development expenditure in the economies of Germany, France, the Netherlands and the UK.

Undoubtedly, the EU is a successful trade bloc and a model for others such as NAFTA and ASEAN. Its ongoing problems are small when compared with the size of its economy, the amount of cross-border trade and the degree of corporate competition. While national politicians may disagree on the way to deal with the issues presented by the EU, few would wish to sacrifice the economic power and benefits derived from being a member.

16.4 To what extent are markets becoming global?

Globalization occurs at many levels. Firms can export overseas or even operate overseas. They can exploit cheaper labour, capital or finance overseas. An examination of globalization requires an analysis of numerous issues.

Global product markets

In considering global product markets, we will concentrate on trading internationally, as opposed to operating internationally. Trading internationally is the export and import of goods and services from domestic locations to international markets – for example, BMW selling cars to other countries. McDonald's in Hong Kong is operating internationally. We will consider this later.

Indices for world merchandized exports and world GDP are plotted in Figure 16.5. The values for world exports and GDP were set to equal 100 in 1950. This does not mean that world GDP and world exports were equal in 1950. Instead, by setting GDP in 1950 = 100, we can examine the growth in GDP over time and, similarly, the growth in world exports. For example, the index value for world GDP in 2000 was around 300. Therefore, between 1950 and 2007 world GDP grew by $(300 - 100)/100 = 200$ per cent. In contrast, the index for world exports was over 600 by 2005. As a result, we can say that between 1950 and 2007 world exports grew by $(600 - 100)/100 = 500$ per cent.

Looking at Figure 16.5, the growth of world GDP has been fairly constant throughout the period 1950–2005. The GDP line increases at a fairly steady rate throughout the period. In contrast, world exports initially grew at the same rate as world GDP and then, in the late 1970s, the slope of world exports becomes much steeper and the acceleration in world exports becomes evident.

Since exports are a component of aggregate demand and, therefore, GDP, we can now say that from the early 1980s a growing proportion of world GDP was being exported.

This is clear evidence that the development of GATT, the WTO and the various trade blocs, such as the EU, have been extremely successful in promoting international trade. But we still need to ask whether product markets are becoming increasingly global.

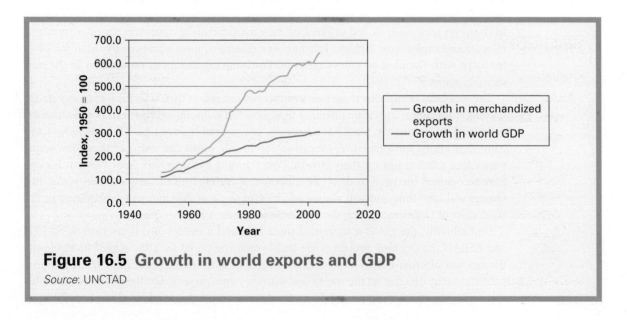

Figure 16.5 **Growth in world exports and GDP**

Source: UNCTAD

Table 16.5 Leading exporters and importers, 2007

Rank	Exporters	Value	Share	Annual percentage change	Rank	Importers	Value	Share	Annual percentage change
1	Germany	912.3	10.0	21	1	US	1625.5	16.1	17
2	US	818.8	8.9	13	2	Germany	716.9	7.6	19
3	China	593.3	6.5	35	3	China	561.2	5.9	36
4	Japan	565.8	6.2	20	4	France	465.5	4.9	17
5	France	448.7	4.9	16	5	UK	463.5	4.9	18
6	Netherlands	358.2	3.9	21	6	Japan	454.5	4.8	19
7	Italy	349.2	3.8	17	7	Italy	351.0	3.7	18
8	UK	346.9	3.8	13	8	Netherlands	319.3	3.4	21
9	Canada	316.5	3.5	16	9	Belgium	285.5	3.0	22
10	Belgium	306.5	3.3	20	10	Canada	279.8	2.9	16

Source: UNCTAD

In Table 16.5, we have the world's ten biggest exporters and importers. They are the same countries. This should not be a surprise. A country that is a significant importer needs to finance its consumption and it can achieve this by also exporting a great deal. A more productive approach is to assess where each country is trading. In Tables 16.6 and 16.7, the exports and imports of the US and the EU with various regions are shown.

It is very clear that the vast bulk of trade occurs between developed countries or regions of the world. Little, if any, trade from the US is with the Middle East or Africa. The EU displays a similar pattern, but it also conducts little trade with Asia. Therefore, it is reasonable to argue

Table 16.6 US trade with various regions, 2007

Region	Exports (%)	Region (%)	Imports (%)
World	100.0	World	100.0
North America	36.7	Asia	36.6
Asia	26.5	North America	27.4
Europe	23.1	Europe	20.8
South and Central America	7.4	South and Central America	6.9
Middle East	2.9	Middle East	3.6
Africa	1.6	Africa	3.2
CIS	0.6	CIS	1.0

Source: UNCTAD

Table 16.7 EU trade with various regions, 2007

Region	Exports	Region	Imports
World	100.0	World	100.0
Europe	74.0	Europe	71.8
North America	9.0	Asia	11.9
Asia	7.4	North America	5.9
Middle East	2.5	CIS	3.0
Africa	2.5	Africa	2.7
CIS	2.2	South and Central America	1.8
South and Central America	1.3	Middle East	1.6

Source: UNCTAD

that, while world trade has increased, it is not global. Rather, trade has increased between the developed economies of the world. It has not included the less-developed economies of the world.

Global operations

Exports are the sale of domestic production to overseas markets. Globalization is more than this. Many leading firms around the world have operations in more than one country.

Multinational enterprises are usually large companies with production and/or sales operations in more than one country.

The United Nations Conference for Trade and Development has developed an **index of transnationality** that seeks to measure a firm's exposure to non-domestic markets.

Selected companies are shown in Figure 16.6. Many of us probably find it very easy to understand why Nestlé, a Swiss chocolate confectioner, is the most globally integrated company in the world.

When multinational enterprises operate overseas, they have to invest in foreign markets. This might be represented by the purchase, or building, of a production facility; alternatively, the company may decide to acquire an existing company in the foreign market and use it as the foundation for international expansion.

As we saw with international trade, **foreign direct investment** (FDI) has exhibited rapid growth in the last 25 years. The amounts of global FDI for various years are shown in Figure 16.7. There was acceleration of FDI from the late 1980s, which peaked around 2000. Terrorist events and a collapse of the stock market in the early years of the millennium led to lack of financing for FDI. But as the global economy stabilized and grew, so did FDI. The data do not record the impact of the credit crisis. But with lack of finance and slow global growth after 2008, FDI is likely to have fallen.

The distribution of FDI around the world is also very interesting. In Tables 16.8 and 16.9, we have the ten largest recipients of FDI, split by developed and developing economies. The US

> The **transnationality index** is an average of three ratios: foreign assets/total assets, foreign workers/total workers and foreign sales/total sales for the firm.

> The purchase of foreign assets is commonly known as **foreign direct investment (FDI)**.

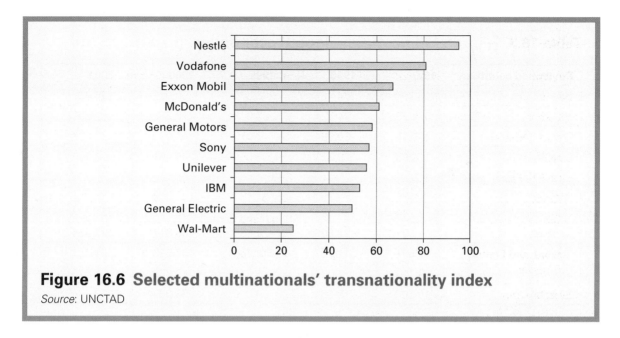

Figure 16.6 **Selected multinationals' transnationality index**
Source: UNCTAD

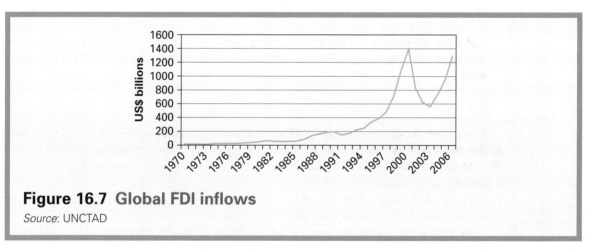

Figure 16.7 **Global FDI inflows**
Source: UNCTAD

and Europe are much bigger recipients of FDI than the rest of the world. In developing economies, China is the largest recipient of FDI. But in 2004, with only US$47 billion of FDI, China was only sixth overall, behind the Netherlands. So, as with international trade, FDI also appears to be large, but not entirely global. Most FDI appears to be attracted to a small number of economies, many of which are developed as opposed to developing.

Why do firms become global?

There are a variety of reasons why firms become global, but essentially these reasons relate to costs and revenues.

Revenue growth

A company's growth is constrained by the size and growth of its domestic market. If we take a company like Wal-Mart, which already dominates the US grocery market, its opportunities for

Table 16.8 Top ten FDI host (developed) economies in 2001 (US$m)

Developed countries	1997	1998	1999	2000	2001
US	103 398	174 434	283 376	300 912	124 435
UK	33 229	74 324	87 973	116 552	53 799
France	23 174	30 984	47 070	42 930	52 623
Belgium and Luxembourg	11 998	22 691	133 059	245 561	50 996
Netherlands	11 132	36 964	41 289	52 453	50 471
Germany	12 244	24 593	54 754	195 122	31 833
Canada	11 527	22 809	24 435	66 617	27 465
Spain	7 697	11 797	16 758	37 523	21 781
Italy	3 700	2 635	6 911	13 377	14 873
Sweden	10 968	19 564	60 850	23 367	12 734

Source: UNCTAD

Table 16.9 Top ten FDI host (developing) economies in 2001 (US$m)

Developed countries	1997	1998	1999	2000	2001
China	44 237	43 751	40 319	40 772	46 846
Mexico	14 044	11 933	12 534	14 706	24 731
Hong Kong, China	11 368	14 770	24 596	61 938	22 834
Brazil	18 993	28 856	28 578	32 779	22 457
Bermuda	2 928	5 399	9 470	10 980	9 859
Poland	4 908	6 365	7 270	9 342	8 830
Singapore	10 746	6 389	11 803	5 407	8 609
South Africa	3 817	561	1 602	888	6 653
Chile	5 219	4 638	9 221	3 674	5 508
Czech Republic	1 300	3 718	6 324	4 986	4 916

Source: UNCTAD

growth are limited by the size of the US market. But if it operates overseas, as it does in the UK through the Asda chain, then its sales can increase. Sales growth in overseas markets may also be cheaper. Consider the adverts of many leading global companies, particularly mobile phone operators and car makers. The advert often has no voice-over. The advert usually involves images and music, so that if it is made for the UK market, it can then also be screened in other markets too. Different economies can offer different growth rates, especially if sales are income elastic. For example, in highly developed economies, such as the US and Western Europe, the demand for insurance products is income inelastic; a 10 per cent rise in income will generate a less than 10 per cent rise in demand for insurance. However, in the Far East insurance is income elastic; a 10 per cent rise in income will lead to a bigger than 10 per cent rise in the demand for insurance. Therefore, in the developed world insurance is set to become a smaller proportion of national income, while in the Far East it is set to become an increasing proportion of national income. As a consequence, large insurance companies have rushed to set up operations in the Far East.

Costs

Firms may operate overseas because they have an international cost advantage and can compete effectively in foreign markets. Alternatively, firms may be seeking international expansion in order to gain a cost advantage.

Sources of international competitiveness

Sources of international competitiveness can be categorized as national, industrial or firm-specific. Most obviously, comparative advantage resulting from the factor endowments of the economy (such as labour, raw materials or capital) can provide firms with an international competitive advantage. Operating overseas enables a firm to exploit these advantages.

> National **sources of international competitiveness** are likely to stem from the characteristics of the national economy.

Additional sources of national competitiveness may stem from macroeconomic conditions. Inflation may be falling, making prices internationally competitive. Supply side policies, such as increased levels of education and training and improved communications infrastructure, plus better functioning capital markets, may provide firms with an improved ability to operate internationally by creating the workers and capital needed to manage overseas operations, with capital markets providing the necessary finances in order to fund such investments.

Industrial sources of international competitiveness stem from the competitive structure of the domestic market.

In Chapters 5 and 6, we introduced perfect competition, monopoly and oligopoly as different types of market structure. The characteristics of these structures may aid international competitiveness. For example, a monopoly in the domestic market may provide a firm with the necessary financial resources to invest in an overseas operation. Similarly, if economies of scale are an important cost advantage in the domestic market, such scale economies may provide the firm with the competitive advantage to move into the international markets. For example, the US, being a very large market, enables many of its domestic suppliers to operate at the minimum efficient scale. With low costs, many of these producers can consider developing operations overseas.

> **Firm-specific** sources of international competitiveness stem from the characteristics of the firm's routines, knowledge and/or assets.

Firms may have knowledge, or expertise, in any aspect of their operations, for example design, production, distribution or marketing. With a lack of national- or industrial-based advantages, **firm-specific** competences may provide a firm with an advantage over its rivals. For example, Tesco and Sainsbury's both operate in the same UK supermarket business. They have access to the same factor inputs and benefit from the same industrial structure, so why has Tesco outperformed Sainsbury's? Tesco must have some firm-specific advantage over Sainsbury's. The advantage could stem from a brand name, management know-how, logistics technology or even being able to build stores quicker and more cheaply than rival operators. Clearly, since the advantage lies within the firm, it is firm-specific. The asset may not be tangible, but it is an advantage that is specific to the firm.

Economies of scope, specific assets and internationalization

This specific nature of the asset is essential for an understanding of internationalization by a firm. If, as discussed in Chapter 7 when analysing growth strategies, the firm's specific advantage generates economies of scope, internationalization provides a way of exploiting scope economies. Investment in a brand for the domestic market may present an economy of scope if the brand can also be used to enter an international market, thereby saving on the cost of developing a new brand. Research and development associated with a new product, such as a microprocessor, a drug or a plasma TV, could represent an economy of scope if the product can be launched in more than one market. But should a firm exploit its own brand or new product development itself? Or, instead, sell rights to use its brand name or product development to an operator in the international market? This is the make or buy decision also discussed in Chapter 7. If the asset is specific, then the transaction costs of selling access to the brand or product knowledge to a third party may be very high. A hold-up problem could occur where the third party threatens to damage the brand or provide competitors with access to the product knowledge. In order to reduce the transaction costs, it is better for the firm to exploit firm-specific assets internationally within its own operations, rather than to sell access rights to other firms.

In summary, if a firm has a specific asset such as knowledge or branding which provides it with a competitive advantage, the best way to exploit that asset is to retain control. Expanding the firm's operations into international markets enables the firm-specific competitive advantage to be exploited. Transferring the asset to a third party is likely to increase transaction costs.

Accessing international competitiveness

Companies can operate overseas to exploit cheaper factor inputs, such as cheaper labour, lower raw material cost and better capital equipment. But cheap labour may not be productive labour, or it may be labour with a poor level of skills. So, the quality of labour also needs to be considered. Operating in international markets also cuts down on transportation costs. Products need not be transported around the world. Instead, they can be produced and sold in the local market.

A common concern regarding multinational enterprises has been the exploitation of workers. Wages in developing economies tend to be less than in developed economies. Firms are tempted to move overseas in order to reduce labour costs. If developing economies are also associated with more relaxed employment laws, then the use of child labour, long working hours and limited holidays may also make such places look attractive to large multinational enterprises. However, if multinational enterprises do exploit workers, then, referring back to Tables 16.8 and 16.9, it is worth considering why FDI is more prevalent in the developed world than the developing world.

A basic observation and answer to this question would be that FDI measures investment in capital not labour. For example, a Japanese company investing in a plasma TV manufacturing plant in Wales is investing in high-technology capital equipment to produce products for the developed world. A UK clothing retailer hiring workers in South East Asia to make clothes is unlikely to invest very much in capital. FDI may, therefore, not be a good measure of the extent of global operations.

16.5 Business application: globalization – exploiting comparative advantage

Nothing is ever as easy as it sounds. The reduction in trade barriers around the world has arguably freed up world business and enabled the most competitive firms to flourish. However, a number of problems still exist. These include problems of communication and control, legal matters, access to inputs and a brand which has a global reach.

Communication and co-ordination

First, there is the matter of communication and co-ordination among suppliers, workers and customers. Language is an obvious barrier to good communication. Ordering raw material supplies for your production facility in a foreign language is fairly easy to master, especially with the aid of an interpreter. Explaining complex technical processes, however, or trying to justify recruitment procedures, marketing plans, operational procedures or financial control through budgeting will require an understanding of local culture, traditional business practice and perhaps even an awareness of local law. Therefore, communication and co-ordination of the international operation requires a great deal of specialist expertise.

Legal issues

Second, local laws may differ substantially from those of the home base. Employment law could be different, resulting in higher redundancy payments and longer periods of notice before employment can be terminated. There might be stronger trade union representation, leading to more industrial disputes. Environmental controls could be harsher, leading to cleaner but more costly production. Contract law could differ and the legal system could be ineffective at enforcing contracts. Even import restrictions might apply. For example, companies operating in the EU, but from non-EU countries, are required to source more than 70 per cent of their production inputs from within the EU.

Quality of inputs

Third, input factors can have varying quality across countries. Labour is an obvious example, with basic skills such as literacy and numeracy varying across developed and developing economies. Such skills are essential for training, developing and managing staff. Furthermore, such skills are essential for staff that are required to use machinery in the production process, particularly machinery that is computer-controlled and might require adjustments to be made to it. If the supply of staff with the appropriate level of skills is limited, then development of the local workforce may well be necessary. While enhancing skills might be seen in a favourable light by the local community, no one will be more grateful than other local firms, which in the fullness of time will be seeking to poach the international company's highly productive workers.

Image and brand

Finally, we must return to one of the key ideas laid down by Nobel Laureate Paul Krugman. Global trade needs to be understood in terms of the needs of customers. Global brands become successful because they meet the tastes and preferences of a global audience. While the products and services required by global consumers may change over time, the key services, vision and experience appear constant. See Box 16.2 for more details.

Box 16.2 Ten-year trends: rise of machines and mobile technology

Adapted from an article by Peter Walshe in The Financial Times, *21 April 2008*

Top 10 most powerful global brands			
Rank	Brand	Brand value ($m)	Brand value change (%)
1	Google	86 057	30
2	GE	71 379	15
3	Microsoft	70 887	29
4	Coca-Cola	58 208	17
5	China Mobile	57 225	39
6	IBM	55 335	65
7	Apple	55 206	123
8	McDonald's	49 499	49
9	Nokia	43 975	39
10	Marlboro	37 324	–5

Source: Financial Times, Global Brands 2008

The level of loyalty or 'bonding' (the key metric that helps determine the brand contribution) of the current top 100 most powerful brands is more than twice that of the average brand. The brand with the highest bonding this year is also the most valuable – **Google**, with 45 per cent. In 1998, this honour went to **Gillette** (48 per cent), which still has one of the highest bonding scores, showing the power and endurance of a strong, well-managed relationship with consumers. But it also illustrates the shift from grocery and personal care brands to technology.

The number of technology brands has more than doubled, including the shift of telecommunications brands to wireless. In 1998, mobile phone penetration rates in many Western countries were less than 50 per cent and computers were still a significant investment for a family. Ten years ago most consumers had not even heard of Google, today's number one.

Top brands' success comes from four key areas:

◆ Most of the brands in the rankings have strong business basics, usually backed by a strong corporate culture, for example **GE**, **IBM** and **McDonald's**.
◆ The second crucial element is that the brand stands for something. The most successful brands are very clear about what they offer the consumer. **Gillette** is 'the best a man can get'; **L'Oreal** is 'because you're worth it' and 'for everything else there's **Mastercard**'.
◆ The third criterion is whether a brand acts like a leader in its category. A brand needs to demonstrate leadership in a relevant way. Perhaps there is something in the innovation or product style or how the brand interfaces with the customer that sets it apart and drives perceptions. **Nokia**, **Porsche** and, of course, **Google** have this quality in spades.
◆ Finally, a strong brand needs to deliver on its promise through a consistently good experience – preferably a great one. **BMW**'s driving experience, **BlackBerry**'s ubiquitous convenience for mobile professionals and **Zara**'s delivery of tailored fashion at affordable prices all get users talking.

'It is no coincidence that virtually all of the Brandz Top 20 most valuable brands invest heavily in providing consistently superior product, service and retail brand design as the most tangible and compelling expression of a positive brand experience.'

© The Financial Times Ltd. 2009

16.6 Business application: sources of international competitiveness

It is important for businesspeople the world over to understand the crucial difference between competitive advantage and a sustainable competitive advantage. A competitive advantage may provide you with some short-term strength over your rivals. But if your advantage can be mimicked, then you do not have a sustainable competitive advantage. India, as a location, has a competitive advantage in outsourcing IT, data processing and call centre services. Much of this advantage stems from a reasonable IT and telecommunications infrastructure, and reasonably skilled staff who speak English and who are willing to work for much less than similar staff in the US and Europe.

Unfortunately, India does not necessarily possess a sustainable advantage. Now that it is known that large corporations are willing to outsource business services, many locations

 Box 16.3 The empire strikes back

Adapted from an article in The Economist, *13 September 2008*

IBM's thinking about emerging markets, and indeed about what it means to be a truly global company, has changed radically in the past few years. In 2006, Sam Palmisano, the company's chief executive, gave a speech at INSEAD, a business school in France, describing his vision for the 'globally integrated enterprise'. The modern multinational company, he said, had passed through three phases. First came the nineteenth-century 'international model', with firms based in their home country and selling goods through overseas sales offices. This was followed by the classic multinational firm, in which the parent company created smaller versions of itself in countries around the world. IBM worked liked that when he joined it in 1973.

The IBM he is now building aims to replace that model with a single integrated global entity in which the firm moves people and jobs anywhere in the world, 'based on the right cost, the right skills and the right business environment. And it integrates those operations horizontally and globally.' This way, 'work flows to the places where it will be done best.' The forces behind this had become irresistible, said Mr Palmisano.

This ambitious strategy was a response to fierce competition from the emerging markets. In the end, selling the personal-computer business to Chinese computer company Lenovo was relatively painless: the business had become commoditized. But the assault on its services business led by a trio of Indian outsourcing upstarts, Tata Consulting Services, Infosys and Wipro, threatened to do serious damage to what Mr Palmisano expected to be one of his main sources of growth. So, in 2004, IBM bought Daksh, an Indian firm that was a smaller version of the big three, and built it into a large business able to compete on cost and quality with its Indian rivals. Indeed, IBM believes that, all in all, it now has a significant edge over its Indian competitors.

Being willing to match India's low-cost model was essential, but Mr Cannon-Brookes, head of strategy for IBM Growth Markets, insists that IBM's enthusiasm for emerging markets is no longer mainly about cheap labour. Perhaps a bigger attraction now, according to IBM, is the highly skilled people it can find in emerging markets. 'Ten years, even five years ago, we saw emerging markets as pools of low-priced, low-value labour. Now we see them as high-skills, high-value,' says Mr Cannon-Brookes. As for every big multinational, winning the 'war for talent' is one of the most pressing issues, especially as hot labour markets in emerging markets are causing extremely high turnover rates. In Bangalore, for example, even the biggest firms may lose 25 per cent of their staff each year. IBM reckons that its global reach gives it an edge in recruitment and retention over local rivals.

around the world will seek to copy India's low-cost strategy. In fact, even some regions in the EU which are in need of economic regeneration could place themselves in direct competition with India. The clear problem for India is that its strategy can be copied. Therefore, it is substitutable and that means it faces elastic, or price-sensitive, consumers. However, as incomes rise, wages rise, so it will become ever more difficult to remain internationally competitive.

So how do you continue to reap the benefits from globalization? You must find a strategy which is sustainable; one which other locations or companies find very difficult to copy. In the absence of imitators, firms face fewer rivals and less-intense price competition. While the availability of cheap labour within a location can be copied, industrial and/or firm-level characteristics are much more differentiated. Silicon Valley has been a success for a variety of reasons, but none that relate to cheap labour.

Silicon Valley benefits from economic clustering – the co-location of supportive and competitive firms. Competition between rivals spurs innovation, while the co-location of supportive industries enables innovation. Silicon Valley may provide industry-level sources of international competitiveness by the concentration of similar companies in one area. Skilled technical and scientific workers are attracted to the area and can move between projects and companies without having to move home. Moreover, important support services such as banking and venture capital are likely to locate in the area and develop expertise in financing specialist IT innovation companies. As firms within Silicon Valley develop, firm-specific routines around developing innovation strategies and commercializing knowledge creation begin to emerge. These industrial and firm-level characteristics are much more difficult to copy and as such lead to the development of higher value-added services, where the advantage is unlikely to be competed away on price.

The challenge for India is not that difficult. It has entrepreneurial spirit, it has cash resources to invest in innovation and it has the engineering and technical skills to develop a sustainable competitive advantage. Moreover, the lessons from India are appropriate for many national economies and companies faced with global competition. The very existence of competition suggests a lack of entry barriers, substitutability and low prices. Profits, wages and economic wealth will never be generated in such industries. It is therefore important to move to less competitive positions within the value chain. We are already beginning to observe automotive companies, such as Volkswagen, locating their assembly lines in Eastern Europe where wages are lower but productivity is comparable with Western Europe. In contrast, design, engineering, product development and marketing have remained within the home economy. These are much more involved, complex tasks which are difficult to copy by low-wage economies, leading to lower competition and a higher rate of return to this section of the value chain.

After the credit crisis, the UK faces the acute problem that the economy is overly dependent on the banking and financial sector. Banking and finance generated significant wealth from activities within the UK and overseas. The UK could rebalance its economy by focusing on and developing other industries in which it excels. Hi-tech aeronautical engineering, fashion, music and media are prominent examples. But if these sectors fail to fill any void left by the collapse of banking, then the long-term real exchange rate for the UK pound will have to fall in order to retain some of the UK's international competitiveness. When your economic output is less valued around the world, then the price you charge and the income you earn have to fall.

So, globalization offers opportunities and threats. Working out how to maximize the opportunities and tame the threats is the art of business management, but through an understanding of micro and macro business economics you should now be prepared to meet the challenge.

Summary

1 The reasons for increasing globalization are numerous but include the cultural, technological, economic and political.

2 Comparative advantage is an important economic reason behind the rise of globalization. Comparative advantage states that countries should specialize in the goods and services which they are comparatively better at producing.

3 Comparative advantages are most likely to arise from an abundance of a particular factor resource. France is good at wine because it has an abundance of productive land and the right climate. Germany is good at producing high-quality cars because it has an abundance of highly skilled labour and high-quality capital equipment.

4 Two-way trade in the same product between countries may still exist even in the face of comparative advantage. Cars are an example. The UK and Germany may trade cars with each other, but the types of car will be different. This simply reflects differences in taste and preference among German and UK car drivers and not comparative advantage in production.

5 In the past, countries have tried to protect industries from international competition by imposing trade barriers. Tariffs and quotas are common examples. Unless the industry is of strategic or defensive importance to the economy, then economists generally agree that trade restrictions are against the public interest.

6 The leading political reasons for globalization have been the acceptance of the economic importance of comparative advantage and a willingness to reduce trade barriers. The formation of trade blocs such as the EU and the work of GATT and the WTO have been important in the process of reducing trade restrictions.

7 Following the successes of GATT and the WTO, the trade of goods and services across national boundaries has grown faster than world GDP. This would suggest that the provision of goods and services is more globally integrated than ever before.

8 However, when examining the pattern of international trade flows, it is apparent that the vast majority of international trade occurs between a small number of developed economies. So, while trade has increased, it is questionable to what extent trade is actually global.

9 Companies operating in more than one country are known as multinational enterprises.

10 Foreign direct investment (FDI) occurs when a company invests outside its domestic base. Throughout the 1990s, FDI grew rapidly. But in recent years it has shown a marked decline.

11 Firms may begin to operate overseas for two basic reasons: (i) to increase sales and (ii) to reduce costs.

12 However, international operations incur specific problems, such as language problems, legal issues, co-ordination problems and possible damage to the global brand. As a consequence, some multinational enterprises are beginning to reappraise their global activities, as evidenced by the falling levels of FDI.

Learning checklist

You should now be able to:

♦ List and explain the main drivers of globalization

♦ Explain comparative advantage and identify potential sources of comparative advantage

♦ Explain the impact of tariffs and quotas on domestic prices, firms and consumers

♦ Explain the reasons why trade restrictions have fallen

♦ Assess whether the rise in international trade is global

♦ Provide reasons for the growth in FDI

Questions connect™

1　Identify the various factors that have promoted the globalization of business.

2　How does comparative advantage explain international trade?

3　If the terms of trade improve for a country, then how has the price of exports changed relative to the price of imports?

4　Economies of scale and product differentiation are important for explaining what feature of international trade?

5　Identify the main types of protectionist policy.

6　If international trade has benefits for the global economy, explain why some countries still find advantages in protectionist policies.

7　What is the World Trade Organization and how important is this body for international trade?

8　What is foreign direct investment and what types of company undertake it?

9　What are the key benefits for business and consumers from membership of trade blocs such as the EU?

10　Evaluate whether the EU should remove the Common Agricultural Policy.

11　What problems do global businesses face when exploiting international business opportunities?

12　Use a diagram to explain the impact of a tariff and a quota on the domestic price of a good or service.

13　Is cheap labour a source of sustainable comparative advantage?

14　Is globalization a threat or an opportunity for business?

15　What problems might a firm face when managing global operations?

Exercises

1 True or false?
   (a) Comparative advantage reflects international differences in the opportunity costs of producing different goods.
   (b) The need to protect infant industries is a powerful argument in favour of protectionist measures.
   (c) The imposition of a tariff stimulates domestic demand.
   (d) The purchase of a share in Microsoft by someone who is not a citizen of the US is an example of foreign direct investment.
   (e) Comparative advantage could stem from an abundance of factor endowments.
   (f) The increase in world merchandise trade has not been entirely global.

2 This exercise examines the gains from trade in a two-country, two-good model. To simplify matters for the time being, we assume that the two countries share a common currency; this allows us to ignore the exchange rate. The two countries are called Anywaria and Someland; the two goods are bicycles and boots. The unit labour requirements of the two goods in each country are shown in Table 16.10; we assume constant returns to scale.
   (a) Which of the countries has an absolute advantage in the production of the two commodities?
   (b) Calculate the opportunity cost of bicycles in terms of boots and of boots in terms of bicycles for each of the countries.
   (c) Which country has a comparative advantage in the production of bicycles?

Table 16.10 Production techniques

	Unit labour requirements (hours per unit output)	
	Anywaria	Someland
Bicycles	60	120
Boots	30	40

Suppose there is no trade. Each of the two economies has 300 workers, who work 40 hours per week. Initially, each country devotes half of its resources to producing each of the two commodities.
   (d) Complete Table 16.11.

Table 16.11 Production of bicycles and boots, no trade case

	Anywaria	Someland	'World' output
Bicycles			
Boots			

Trade now takes place under the following conditions: the country with a comparative advantage in boot production produces only boots. The other country produces sufficient bicycles to maintain the world 'no-trade' output, devoting the remaining resources to boot production.

(e) Complete Table 16.12 and comment on the gains from trade.

Table 16.12 Production of bicycles and boots

	Anywaria	Someland	'World' output
Bicycles			
Boots			

(f) On a single diagram, plot the production possibility frontier for each country. What aspect of your diagram is indicative of potential gains from trade?

3 Refer to Box 16.3 when considering the following questions:
(a) Identify the competitive strengths and weaknesses of India as a centre for off-shore business services.
(b) A common complaint is that 'India is stealing all our jobs'. Is this a real business and economic problem?

Allocative efficiency This occurs when price equals marginal cost, or P = MC.

Average fixed cost This is calculated as total fixed costs divided by the number of units produced.

Average revenue This is the average price charged by the firm and is equal to total revenue/quantity demanded: (PQ)/Q.

Average total cost This is calculated as total cost divided by the number of units produced.

Average variable cost This is calculated as total variable cost divided by the number of units produced.

Barriers to entry These make entry into a market by new competitors difficult.

Barter economy In this system there is no money and individuals trade by exchanging different goods and services.

Bretton Woods A 1944 agreement which provided a plan for managing foreign exchange rates.

Central bank This acts as a banker to the commercial bank, taking deposits and, in extreme circumstances, making loans.

Ceteris paribus This means all other things being equal.

Circular flow of income This shows the flow of inputs, outputs and payments between households and firms within an economy.

Collateralized debt obligation A bond for which the holder is paid a rate of interest in return for funding a debt.

Command GDP The purchasing power of a nation's output.

Common values These occur in an auction where the value of the item is identical for all bidders, but each bidder may form a different assessment of the item's worth.

Competition Commission This investigates whether a monopoly, or a potential monopoly, acts against the public interest.

Complete contract Under a complete contract, all aspects of the contractual arrangement are fully specified.

Consumer surplus The difference between the price you are charged for a product and the maximum price that you would have been willing to pay.

Contagion This occurs when the collapse of one bank leads to the collapse of more banks.

Contestable market A market where firms can enter and exit the market freely.

Credible commitment A credible commitment or threat has to be one that is optimal to carry out.

Credit creation The process of turning existing bank deposits into credit facilities for borrowers. The process can result in an increase in the money supply.

Cross-price elasticity This measures the responsiveness of demand to a change in the price of a substitute or complement.

Cross-sectional data The measurements of one variable at the same point in time across different individuals.

Demand curve This illustrates the relationship between price and quantity demanded of a particular product.

Dirty float This occurs when the government claims that the exchange rate floats, but it is in fact managed by the government.

Disequilibria In situations of disequilibria, at the current price the willingness to demand will differ from the willingness to supply.

Diversification The growth of the business in a related or an unrelated market.

Diversified portfolio A diversified portfolio of activities contains a mix of uncorrelated business operations.

Economic growth This is measured as the percentage change in GDP per year.

Economies of scale Long-run average costs fall as output increases.

Economies of scope These are said to exist if the cost of producing two or more outputs jointly is less than the cost of producing the outputs separately.

Elasticity A measure of the responsiveness of demand to a change in price.

Endogenized If costs are endogenized, then the firms inside the industry have strategically influenced the level and nature of costs.

Exit barriers These make exit from a market by existing competitors difficult.

Exogenous costs Exogenous means external, outside. The exogenous costs of the firm are outside its control.

Expectations Beliefs held by firms, workers and consumers about the future level of prices.

Externalities The effects of consumption, or production, on third parties. If production, or consumption, by one group improves the wellbeing of third parties, then a **positive externality** has occurred. If production, or consumption, by one group reduces the wellbeing of third parties, then a **negative externality** has occurred.

Factors of production Resources needed to make goods and services: land, labour, capital and enterprise.

Fiat money Notes and coins guaranteed by the government rather than by gold deposits.

Financial intermediation This involves channelling cash from savers to borrowers.

Finite resources The limited amount of resources that enable the production and purchase of goods and services.

Fiscal policy The government's decisions regarding taxation and spending.

Fixed costs These are constant. They remain the same whatever the level of output.

Fixed exchange rate A fixed rate of conversion between currencies.

Fixed exchange rate regime The government fixes the exchange rate between the domestic currency and another strong world currency, usually the US dollar.

Forex markets These are where different currencies are traded.

Full employment This occurs within an economy when all markets are in equilibrium.

Full employment rate This is when the economy is in a long-run equilibrium position and the economy operates on its production possibility frontier. The economy is in neither boom nor recession.

Game theory This seeks to understand whether strategic interaction will lead to competition or co-operation between rivals.

Government bonds A near-cash equivalent and therefore liquid. A government pays the holder of bonds a rate of interest in return for funding the government's debt.

Gresham's Law This states that an increasing supply of bad products will drive out good products from the market.

Haircut The discount required by the buyer of a risky asset.

Hedging The transfer of a risky asset for a non-risky asset.

Hold-up problem This involves renegotiation of contracts and is linked to asset specificity.

Horizontal growth This occurs when a company develops or grows its activities at the same stage of the production process.

Imperfect competition A highly competitive market where firms may use product differentiation.

Income elasticity This measures the responsiveness of demand to a change in income.

Index numbers These are used to transform a data series into a series with a base value of 100.

Indivisibilities Assets that cannot be divided into smaller units.

Infinite wants The limitless desire to consume goods and services.

Input markets These are where factor inputs, such as land, labour, capital or enterprise, are traded.

Kinked demand curve The idea behind the kinked demand curve is that price rises will not be matched by rivals, but price reductions will be matched.

Law of demand This states that, *ceteris paribus*, as the price of a product falls, more will be demanded.

Learning curve This suggests that, as cumulative output increases, average costs fall.

Lender of last resort This is the central bank if a bank cannot raise funds from any other lender.

Liquidity This means the ease with which an asset can be converted into cash.

Macroeconomics The study of how the entire economy works.

Marginal cost The cost of creating one more unit.

Marginal private benefit The benefit to the individual from consuming one more unit of output.

Marginal private cost The cost to the individual of producing one more unit of output.

Marginal product The addition to total product after employing one more unit of factor input.

Marginal profit The profit made on the last unit; it is equal to the marginal revenue minus the marginal cost.

Marginal revenue The revenue received by selling one more unit of output.

Marginal social benefit The benefit to society from the consumption of one more unit of output.

Marginal social cost The cost to society of producing one or more unit of output.

Market economy In a market economy, the government plays no role in allocating resources. Instead, markets allocate resources to the production of various products.

Market equilibrium The market equilibrium occurs at the price where consumers' willingness to demand is exactly equal to firms' willingness to supply.

Market structure The economist's general title for the major competitive structures of a particular marketplace.

Menu costs These are associated with the activity and cost of changing prices in shops, price lists and, of course, menus.

Microeconomics The study of how individuals make economic decisions within an economy.

Minimum efficient scale (MES) The output level at which long-run costs are at a minimum.

Mixed economy In a mixed economy, the government and the private sector jointly solve economic problems.

Models or **theories** These are frameworks for organizing how we think about an economic problem.

Monetary base The quantity of notes or coins held by private individuals or the banking system.

Monetary union The permanent fixing of exchange rates between member countries.

Monopoly A marketplace supplied by only one competitor, so no competition exists.

Moral hazard This occurs when someone agrees to undertake a certain set of actions but then, once a contractual arrangement has been agreed, behaves in a different manner.

Mutual A financial organization that is owned by its customers, in contrast to a bank which is owned by shareholders.

Negative relationship This exists between two variables if the values for one variable increase (decrease) as the value of the other variable decreases (increases).

Net present value The discounted value of a future cash flow.

Nominal wages Earnings unadjusted for inflation.

Normal economic profits These are equal to the average rate of return which can be gained in the economy.

Normative economics This offers recommendations based on personal value judgements.

Official financing The extent of government intervention in the forex markets.

Oligopoly A market that consists of a small number of large players.

Opportunity costs The benefits forgone from the next best alternative.

Output gap The difference between actual and potential GDP.

Panel data This combines cross-sectional and time series data.

Percentage This measures the change in a variable as a fraction of 100.

Perfect competition Briefly, perfect competition is a highly competitive marketplace.

Perfect information This assumes that every buyer and every seller knows everything. No one has an informational advantage.

Permanent income hypothesis This states that consumption is determined by lifetime earnings not current income.

Phillips curve This shows that higher unemployment is associated with lower inflation.

Piece rates These occur when a worker is paid according to the output produced. Under hourly wage rates, workers are paid for time at work.

Planned economy In a planned economy, the government decides how resources are allocated to the production of particular products.

Pooling equilibrium A market where demand and supply for good and poor products pools into one demand and one supply.

Positive economics This studies objective or scientific explanations of how the economy works.

Positive relationship This exists between two variables if the values for both variables increase and decrease together.

Price expectations Beliefs about how prices in the future will differ from prices today.

Price taker If a firm accepts the market price, it is a price taker.

Private finance initiative (PFI) This involves the private sector financing, building and owning infrastructure projects in return for an annual leasing fee from the government.

Private values In an auction, these occur where each bidder has a private subjective value of an item's worth.

Production possibility frontier This shows the maximum amount of products that can be produced by an economy with a given amount of resources.

Productive efficiency This means that the firm is operating at the minimum point on its long-run average cost curve.

Protectionist measures These seek to lower the competitiveness of international rivals.

Qualitative easing The central bank swaps high quality assets for poorer quality assets.

Quantitative easing This involues the central bank buying government debt, corporate debt and other financial securities; in return, cash is provided to the vendors of these assets.

Rationalization This is associated with cutbacks in excess resources in the pursuit of increased operational efficiencies.

Real wages Earnings adjusted for inflation.

Regulation The use of rules and laws to limit, control and monitor the activities of banks.

Retail bank This takes deposits and makes loans to retail customers.

Revenue equivalence theorem This states that under private values each auction format will generate the same level of revenue for the seller.

Satisficing The attainment of acceptable levels of performance. Maximizing is the attainment of maximum levels of performance.

Separating equilibrium This is where a market splits into two clearly identifiable sub-markets with separate supply and demand.

Short run A period of time where one factor of production is fixed. We tend to assume that capital is fixed and labour is variable.

Sight deposits These provide customers with instant access to cash.

Single-period game In a single-period game, the game is only played once. In a repeated game, the game is played a number of rounds.

Specific asset A specific asset has a specific use; a general asset has many uses.

Speculative attack A massive capital outflow from an economy with a fixed exchange rate.

Store of value Money is a store of value because it can be used to make future purchases.

Strategic interdependence Firms within an oligopoly are seen to be strategically interdependent. The actions of one firm will have implications for its rivals.

Subsidy A payment made to producers, by government, which leads to a reduction in the market price of the product.

Substitutes These are rival products; for example, a BMW car is a substitute for a Mercedes, or a bottle of wine from France is a substitute for a bottle from Australia.

Sunk cost An expenditure that cannot be regained when exiting the market.

Supernormal profits These exist if the return to investors or shareholders is in excess of normal economic profits.

Supply curve This depicts a positive relationship between the price of a product and firms' willingness to supply the product.

Switching costs The costs of moving between products.

Systemic risk A risk which can damage the entire financial system.

Tangency equilibrium This occurs when the firm's average revenue line just touches the firm's average total cost line.

Taylor rule This links interest rate changes to short-term deviations in both inflation and output from long-term equilibrium values.

Time deposits These require the customer to give the bank notice before withdrawing cash.

Time series data The measurements of one variable at different points in time.

Total costs These are simply fixed costs plus variable costs.

Total product The total output produced by a firm's workers.

Total revenue Price multiplied by number of units sold.

Trade bloc A region or group of countries that have agreed to remove all trade barriers between themselves.

Transaction costs The costs associated with organizing the transaction of goods or services.

Unit of account The unit in which prices are quoted.

Variable costs These change or vary with the amount of production.

Vertical chain of production This encapsulates the various stages of production from the extraction of a raw material input, through the production of the product or service, to the final retailing of the product.

Vertically integrated A company is said to be vertically integrated if it owns consecutive stages of the vertical chain.

Wholesale bank This takes large deposits and is involved in brokering very large loans to companies.

Winner's curse This is where a winning bid exceeds the true value of the sale item.